The

CORNEL WEST

Reader

Prophesy Deliverance! An Afro-American Revolutionary Christianity (1982)
Theology in the Americas: Detroit II (1982)
(Co-Editor)
Post-Analytic Philosophy (1985)
(Edited with John Rajchman)
Prophetic Fragments (1988)
The American Evasion of Philosophy (1989)
Out There: Marginalization and Contemporary Cultures (1990)
(Co-Editor)
The Ethical Dimensions of Marxist Thought (1991)
Breaking Bread (1991)
(with bell hooks)
Prophetic Thought in Postmodern Times (1993)
Prophetic Reflections (1993)
Race Matters (1993)
Keeping Faith: Philosophy and Race in America (1993)
James Snead, White Screens, Black Images (1994)
(Edited with Colin McCabe)
Jews & Blacks : Let the Healing Begin (1995)
(with Michael Lerner)
The Future of the Race (1996)
(with Henry Louis Gates, Jr.)
Struggles in the Promised Land (1997)
(Edited with Jack Salzman)
Restoring Hope (1997)
The War Against Parents (1998)
(with Sylvia Ann Hewlett)
The Future of American Progressivism (1998)
(with Roberto Mangabeira Unger)
The Courage to Hope: From Black Suffering to Human Redemption (1999)
(Edited with Quinton Hosford Dixie)

The
CORNEL WEST
Reader

Cornel West

BASIC
CIVITAS
BOOKS

A MEMBER OF THE PERSEUS BOOKS GROUP

Published by Basic *Civitas* Books,

A Member of the Perseus Books Group

Book design by Victoria Kuskowski

A CIP catalog record for for this book is available from

the Library of Congress

ISBN 0-465-09109-1 (cloth); ISBN 0-465-09110-5 (pbk.)

01 02 / 10 9 8 7 6 5 4

. . . Write about this young man squeezing drop by drop the slave out of himself and waking one fine morning feeling that real human blood, not a slave's, is flowing in his veins.

—*Anton Chekhov*

To be a musician is really something. It goes very, very deep. My music is the spiritual expression of what I am—my faith, my knowledge, my being. . . . When you begin to see the possibilities of music, you desire to do something really good for people, to help humanity free itself from its hang-ups.

—*John Coltrane*

To the memory and legacy of
my modern artistic soul mates

John Coltrane
Federico García Lorca
Franz Kafka
Paul Celan
Tennessee Williams
Giacomo Leopardi
Samuel Beckett
Sarah Vaughan
Muriel Rukeyser
Thomas Hardy
Nikos Kazantzakis
Toni Morrison

And above all
Anton Chekhov

CONTENTS

PREFACE

THE PRIMARY AIM OF this reader is to lay bare the basic structure of my intellectual work and life. This reader takes the form of a variety of voices and an array of interests that focus on two fundamental themes: the art of living and the expansion of democracy.

My painful quest for wisdom is an endless journey that tries to delve into the darkness of my soul to create a more mature and compassionate person. My political project of deepening democracy in the world is a perennial process of highlighting the plight of the wretched of the earth and broadening the scope of human dignity.

This volume not only represents the progression of my thought but also consists of my reflections on it. I chose these pieces rather than others from my corpus because they best represent the crucial moments of an evolving whole. This whole—fraught with tensions and contradictions—reflects my attempt to shatter my own parochial limits and provincial shortcomings. My efforts to understand myself are inseparable from understanding what it means to be human, modern, American, black, male and straight in global and local contexts. And since this text was put together at a unique moment in my life—when Eros erupted and life quickened—it marks a turning point in many ways.

This volume will, I hope, keep these ideas alive in the mind of the reader so that they may be debated and refined. In my travels as a speaker, I continue to be struck by the persistence of certain themes and concerns of my audiences. These include, of course, race but, more generally, focus on questions of the good and how one might lead a meaningful life—a life in dialogue with history, connected to community—without falling into despair. This reader should serve as a reproach to easy despair and an inspiration to those who wish to travel with me on this quest.

I would like to thank my agent, Gloria Loomis, for her extraordinary care and support of my work. I would like to acknowledge the visionary and superb editorial work of my friend and brother Tim Bartlett. This book exists, in part, because of him. And I would like to thank my friends and sisters Vanessa Mobley and Libby Garland for their excellent editorial assistance. It was sheer fun to work with them. Finally, I would like to congratulate my dear mother upon receiving a well-deserved recognition as an exemplary teacher and principal in the form of the new Irene B. West Elementary School in Sacramento, California.

INTRODUCTION

To Be Human, Modern and American

AS WE APPROACH THE deathbed of this ghastly century, an uncanny sense of terror and hope should haunt us. As at the sad funeral of a loved one, we remember the cruel circumstances and heroic energies of those who are now the culinary delight of terrestrial worms. My own work and life have always unfolded under the dark shadows of death, dread and despair in search of love, dialogue and democracy. I am first and foremost a blues man in the world of ideas—a jazz man in the life of the mind—committed to keeping alive the flickering candles of intellectual humility, personal compassion and social hope while living in our barbaric century. I am primarily a dramatist of philosophic notions and historical narratives that partake of blood-drenched battles on a tear-soaked terrain in which our lives and deaths are at stake.

My work is a feeble attempt to understand and respond to the guttural cry that erupts from the depths of the soul of each of us. The existential quest for meaning and the political struggle for freedom sit at the center of my thought. My writings focus on the specific and contemporaneous ways in which we grapple with concrete and universal issues of life and death, oppression and resistance, joy and sorrow.

I am a Chekhovian Christian with deep democratic commitments. By this I mean that I am obsessed with confronting the pervasive evil of unjustified suffering and unnecessary social misery in our world. And I am determined to explore the intellectual sources and existential resources that feed our courage to be, courage to love and courage to fight for democracy. Three related and fundamental questions motivate my writings: What does it mean to be *human*? What does it mean to be *modern*? What does it mean to be *American*?

My perennial wrestling with these overwhelming queries, which suffuses the essays in this volume, is rooted in my terrifying experience and constant awareness of the radical contingency and fragility of life. I find the incomparable works of Anton Chekhov—the best singular body by a modern artist—to be the wisest and deepest interpretations of what human beings confront in their daily struggles. His salutary yet sad portraits of the nearly eight thousand characters in his stories and plays—comparable only to Shakespeare's variety of personages—provide the necessary ground, the background noise, of any acceptable view of what it means to be human. His magisterial depiction of the cold Cosmos, indifferent Nature, crushing Fate and the cruel histories that circumscribe desperate, bored, confused and anxiety-ridden yet love-hungry people, who try to endure against all odds, rings true for me. Furthermore, I find inspiration in his refusal to escape from the pain and misery of life by indulging in dogmas, doctrines or dreams as well as abstract systems, philosophic theodicies or political utopias.

In short, Chekhov provides exemplary tragicomic dramas, subject to multiple interpretations, for serious thinking and wise living. His art yields the most intelligent reflection and depiction of the limits of critical intelligence in confronting our worldly existence. Yet his acute sense of the incongruity in our lives is grounded in a magnificent compassion for each of us. Chekhov understands what drives the cynic without himself succumbing to cynicism. He appreciates the childlike fantasies of the sentimentalist without yielding to the childishness of sentimentalism. Like the best blues and jazz artists, he enacts *melancholic* yet *melioristic* indictments of misery without concealing the wounds inflicted or promising permanent victory. He stays in touch with the everyday realities of ordinary people and highlights our peculiar wrestlings with appearance and reality, opinion and knowledge, illusion and truth—of beauty, love and the collective struggle for a decent society. Like his literary ancestors Sophocles and Shakespeare and his twentieth-century progeny Kafka and Beckett, Chekhov leads us through our contemporary inferno with love and sorrow, but no cheap pity or promise of ultimate happiness.

I remain a Christian—despite Chekhov's agnosticism—primarily because the concrete example of the love and compassion of Jesus rendered in the biblical Gospel narratives constitutes the most absurd and alluring mode of being in the tragicomic world. In this way, I stand in the skeptical Christian tradition of Montaigne, Pascal and Kierkegaard—figures in touch with (and often tortured by) an inescapable demon of doubt inscribed within their humble faith. This tradition enables me feebly to love my way through the absurdity of life and the darkness of history. Their bold intellectual thought and courageous existential witness have little to do with much or most of institutional Christianity or any organized religion. In fact, Erasmus is one of the few towering Christian figures who could exemplify this thought and witness and remain in the established church of his day.

My Chekhovian Christian conception of what it means to be human puts a premium on death and courage. To be human is to suffer, shudder and struggle courageously in the face of inevitable death. To think deeply and live wisely as a human being is to meditate on and prepare for death. The quest for human wisdom requires us to learn how to die—penultimately in the daily death of bad habits and cruel viewpoints and ultimately in the demise of our earthly and temporal bodies. To be human, at the most profound level, is to encounter honestly the inescapable circumstances that constrain us, yet muster the courage to struggle compassionately for our own unique individualities and for more democratic and free societies. This courage contains the seeds of lived history—of memory, maturity and melioration—in the face of no guaranteed harvest. Hence, my view of what it means to be human is preeminently existential—a focus on particular, singular, flesh-and-blood persons grappling with dire issues of death, dread, despair, disease and disappointment. Yet I am not an existentialist like the early Sartre, who had a systematic grasp of human existence. Instead, I am a Chekhovian Christian who banks his all on radical—not rational—choice and on the courage to love enacted by a particular Palestinian Jew named Jesus, who was crucified by the powers that be, betrayed by cowardly comrades and misconstrued by corrupt churches that persist, and yet is remembered by those of us terrified and mesmerized by the impossible possibility of his love.

My Chekhovian Christian viewpoint is idiosyncratic and iconoclastic. My sense of the absurdity and incongruity of the world is closer to the Gnosticism of Valentinus, Luria or Monoimos than that of historic religious orthodoxies—yet, unlike them, it retains a deep sense of history. My intellectual lineage goes more through Schopenhauer, Tolstoy, Rilke, Melville, Lorca, Kafka, Celan, Beckett, Soyinka, O'Neill, Kazantzakis, Morrison and, above all, Chekhov (all great dramatic poets of death, courage and compassion) than most theologians and philosophers. And, I should add, it reaches its highest expression in music—as in Brahms's *Requiem* and Coltrane's *A Love Supreme*. Music at its best achieves this summit because it is the grand archaeology into and transfiguration of our guttural cry, the great human effort to grasp in time (with the most temporal of the arts) our deepest passions and yearnings as prisoners of time. Profound music leads us—beyond language—to the dark roots of our scream and the celestial heights of our silence.

To be modern is to have the courage to use one's critical intelligence to question and challenge the prevailing authorities, powers and hierarchies of the world. Despite my Chekhovian Christian conception of what it means to be human—a view that invokes premodern biblical narratives—I am a quintessentially modern thinker in that I weave disparate narratives in ways that result in novel forms of self-exploration and self-experimentation. To be modern is to live dangerously and courageously in the face of relentless self-criticism and inescapable fallibilism; it is to give up the all-too-human quest for certainty and indubitability owing to the historicity of our claims. Yet to give in to sophomoric relativism ("Anything goes" or "All views are equally valid") is a failure of nerve, and to succumb to wholesale skepticism ("There is no truth") is a weakness of the will and imagination. Instead, the distinctive mark of modernity is to pursue the treacherous trek of dialogue, to wager on the fecund yet potentially poisonous fruits of fallible inquiry, which require communicative action, risk-ridden conversation, even intimate relation.

My conception of what it means to be modern is shot through with a sense of the dialogical—the free encounter of mind, soul and body that relates to others in order to be unsettled, unnerved and unhoused. This experience of dialogue–the I-Thou relation with the uncontrolled other–may result in a dizziness, vertigo or shudder that unhinges us from our moorings or yanks us from our anchors. This thoroughly modern lightness of being–produced, in part, from the innovations of modern science and technology or improvisations of modern music and the arts– is both frightening and energizing. This loss of our footing and gain of our free- dom compel us to acknowledge that the very meaning of being modern may be the lack of any meaning, that our quest for such meaning may be the very mean- ing itself–without ever arriving at any fixed meaning. In short, the hermeneutical circle in which we find ourselves, as historical beings in search of meaning for our- selves, is virtuous, not vicious, because we never transcend or complete the circle. Like Sisyphus, we go endlessly up and down with noble aims and aspirations, but no ultimate harmony or achieved wholeness.

My Chekhovian Christian conception of what it means to be modern focuses on the night side of modernity, the underside of our contemporary predicament. Therefore I highlight the forms of self-making and self-creating of those whose suffering is often rendered invisible by the Enlightenment discourse on the light of natural reason and the Romantic preoccupation with imaginative transforma- tion. Of course, to be deeply modern is to be critical of the blindness of certain forms of critical intelligence and to imagine forms of transformation far beyond Romantic versions of imaginative transformation. Therefore my critiques of modernity extend, refine and expand modern consciousness and practice. Yet my Chekhovian Christian perspective of what it means to be modern cuts even deeper. It gives up on the very possibility of arriving at a definitive, definite–or dogmatic–end point of modernity. Instead, it stresses the very means by which and procedures through which we pursue our aims. In short, it highlights the di- alogical process and democratic practices through which we pursue the very ends we cherish.

To be American is to be part of a dialogical and democratic operation that grap- ples with the challenge of being human in an open-ended and experimental man- ner. Although America is a romantic project in which a paradise, a land of dreams, is fanned and fueled with a religion of vast possibility, it is, more funda- mentally, a fragile experiment–precious yet precarious–of dialogical and demo- cratic human endeavor that yields forms of modern self-making and self-creating unprecedented in human history. From Thomas Jefferson to Elijah Muhammad, Geronimo to Dorothy Day, Jane Addams to Nathanael West, it holds out the pos- sibility of self-transformation and self-reliance to New World dwellers willing to start anew and recast themselves for the purpose of deliverance and betterment. This purpose requires only a restlessness, energy and boldness that galvanizes people to organize and mobilize themselves in a way that makes new opportuni- ties and possibilities credible and worth the effort.

To be American is to give ethical significance to the future by viewing the present as terrain capable of transcending any past and thereby arriving at a new identity and community. From the revolutionary hopes of European settlers on Amerindian land and bodies to millennial hopes of Mormons and Baptists against Old World Protestant establishments, Americans give weight and gravity to the possibility that future prospects can trump present troubles. From Emerson's Yes to tomorrow against the defeat of today through Whitman's song of the open road given the weight of the fixed form and ancient verse to James's and Dewey's obsession with fruits, consequences and effects against Descartes's stress on origins, beginnings and starting points, American culture accentuates what is to come, what is not yet as opposed to what is and what has been. Of course, such a futuristic orientation often degenerates into an infantile, sentimental or melodramatic propensity toward happy endings, so that dreams of betterment downplay the dark realities of suffering in our midst. In this way, American discourses on innocence, deliverance or freedom overlook the atrocities of violence, subjugation or slavery in our past or present. To be American is to downplay history in the name of hope, to ignore memory in the cause of possibility. Our great truthtellers—mainly artists—remind us that history will haunt us and memory should keep us honest. Melville, Hawthorne, Twain, Faulkner, Fitzgerald, O'Neill, Tennessee Williams, Theodore Dreiser, Toni Morrison, Thomas Pynchon, Lorraine Hansberry and others spin out candid narratives and painful truths about our all-too-human complicity with evil and evasion of dark realities, which no country or social experiment can ignore without danger. My Chekhovian Christian perspective tries to remain true to the heart-wrenching tales and truths of such American artists. They remind us of the all-too-human forms of mendacity and hypocrisy pervasive in American life.

To be American is to raise perennially the frightening democratic question: What does the public interest have to do with the most vulnerable and disadvantaged in our society? This query of democratic import goes back to Cleisthenes of 508 B.C. in Athens. Shouldn't democracy be a form of plebodicy—not theodicy—that focuses our attention on the unjustified suffering and unnecessary social misery of ordinary human beings here and abroad? And yet isn't American democracy one in which arbitrary power is not fully curtailed and, hence, the political, corporate and financial elites—unregulated by substantive public accountability—wield forms of power that cause pain and grief for fellow citizens that need not be? Are not democratic practices historically transgressive and even subversive actions of heroic citizens that transform inherited forms such that their decency and dignity are recognized by elites? Is not the grand paradox of American democracy at its inception that the people are distrusted and contained, their power dispersed and diluted so that elites may prosper at the expense of workers' power, women's power and especially black, brown, yellow and red power? Can

America ever really be truly America without a full-fledged multiracial and multi-gendered democracy—a democracy that flourishes in the political, economic, cultural and even existential spheres? Can the dignity of everyday people thrive in an oligarchic and plutocratic economy? Can American democracy be true to its ideals without a nonracist and nonsexist culture and society? Does not pervasive homophobia require a nonheterosexist social arrangement? These are the challenging questions of Whitman, Dewey, Addams, Baldwin, Lorde and Martin Luther King, Jr.

Can America, the last grand empire of the twentieth century, meet such a challenge? Is a multiracial and multisexual *political* democracy the best we—or humankind—can do? Is economic democracy in a global economy a pipe dream? Is the globalization of democracy a fantasy in the face of unaccountable multinational corporate power? Is the vision of existential democracy—of Maurice Maeterlinck, Walt Whitman and Anton Chekhov—a mirage? Is it possible that democracy can be a way of being in the world, not just a mode of governance circumscribed by corporate power and monied interests? These are the great questions of the twenty-first century, the grand challenges of the next wave of democratic possibility. Have we reached the limits of the American religion of possibility? Do class, race and gender hierarchy have the last word on how far democracy can go in our time? My Chekhovian Christian viewpoint says No! No! No! But maybe. Indeed, surely, if we fail to speak our fallible truths about the social misery in our midst here and abroad, if we fail to expose the vicious lies about our past and present and if we fail to bear our imperfect yet courageous witness of love and democracy at the birth of our new century! Let it be said of us centuries from now that we were bold and visionary in our efforts to live with courage and compassion in the face of death, to pursue dialogue over and against the overwhelming odds of misunderstanding and violence and to fight for old and new forms of democracy at the beginning of a century that may well produce novel forms of barbarism and bestiality if we fail to respond to the tests of our time.

The Chekhovian Christian perspective put forward in this reader is my testament of hope for the twenty-first century. The words, sentences and paragraphs are but linguistic marks that track my journey of blood, sweat and tears, which tries to achieve and enact the best of what it means to be human, modern and American. These marks often fall far short of the high mark—and pale in the face of good music—yet they point toward a certain kind of musical life that painfully pursues a compassionate individuality and courageously struggles for a more free and democratic world. This reader is my attempt to transfigure our guttural cry into a call to care—for causes bigger and grander than our own precious cry.

PART ONE

I have great suspicion of autobiographical writing. So much of it reeks of self-indulgence and self-absorption, yet any serious engagement with the world includes a questioning of one's self. Whenever I write about the struggle to be human under modern circumstances in an American setting, I am writing, in part, about myself. My brief autobiographical excursions focus on persons, institutions, movements and books that sustained or paralyzed me in light of my cry for help. I plan to write a full-length intellectual autobiography in the near future.

One

THE MAKING OF AN AMERICAN RADICAL DEMOCRAT OF AFRICAN DESCENT

My close friends and comrades Paul Sweezy and Harry Magdoff—the long-distance runners of the American Left—convinced me to publish a version of my philosophy dissertation in 1991. My diligent and supportive editor, Susan Lowes, suggested that I write an autobiographical introduction. I have yet to write a more probing and revealing piece about my personal and intellectual development in order to situate myself and my work after the fall of Soviet communism and the Velvet revolutions in Eastern Europe.

A WHOLESALE CRITICAL INVENTORY of ourselves and our communities of struggle is neither self-indulgent autobiography nor self-righteous reminiscence. Rather, it is a historical situating and locating of our choices, sufferings, anxieties and efforts in light of the circumscribed options and alternatives available to us. We all are born into and build on circumstances, traditions and situations not of our own choosing, yet we do make certain choices that constitute who we are and how we live in light of these fluid circumstances, traditions and situations.

The most significant stage-setting for my own life pilgrimage has been neither academic life nor political organizations, but rather my closely knit family and overlapping communities of church and friends. These pillars of civil society—my loving parents, siblings, and communities—transmitted to me ideals and images of dignity, integrity, majesty and humility. These ideals and images—couched within Christian narratives, symbols, rituals and, most importantly, concrete moral examples—provided existential and ethical equipment with which to confront the crises, terrors and horrors of life. The three major components of this equipment were a Christian ethic of love-informed service to others, ego-deflating humility about oneself owing to the precious yet fallible humanity of others, and politically engaged struggle for social betterment. This Christian outlook, as exemplified in our time by Martin Luther King, Jr., serves as the basis for my life vocation.

As a youth, I resonated with the sincere black militancy of Malcolm X, the defiant rage of the Black Panther Party, and the livid black theology of James Cone. Yet I did not fully agree with them. I always felt that they lacked the self-critical moment of humility I discerned in the grand example of Martin Luther King, Jr.

Such humility has always been a benchmark of genuine love for, and gratitude to, ordinary people whose lives one is seeking to enhance. I witnessed this same kind of integrity and dignity in the humble attitude to black folk of my early heroes: the Godfather of Soul, James Brown; the legendary baseball player Willie Mays; my pastor, Rev. Willie P. Cooke (of Shiloh Baptist Church in Sacramento, California); my grandfather, Rev. C. L. West, of Metropolitan Baptist Church in Tulsa, Oklahoma; and my older brother, Clifton L. West III, to me an exemplary human being. In this way, Martin Luther King, Jr., has always been not so much a model to imitate, but *the* touchstone for personal inspiration, moral wisdom and existential insight. I heard him speak in person only once, when I was ten years old (1963), and I remember not his words, but his humble spirit and sense of urgency.

My first noteworthy political action—besides marching with my family in a civil rights demonstration in Sacramento—was the coordination of a citywide strike of students demanding courses in black studies. At the time there were four black student body presidents in Sacramento high schools (including myself). My good friend Glenn Jordan and I decided to launch this effort during the 1969–1970 school year, and we had good results.

My critical self-inventory highlights the fact that I was born eight years after the end of the Age of Europe (1492–1945). Much of who and what we are has to do with where and with what our immediate ancestors confronted the advent of modernity during the Age of Europe. And for most of us there is no escape from the effects of European modernity in that, by the early twentieth century, the handful of states located between the Atlantic Ocean and the Ural mountains (in addition to the former British colony, the United States) controlled more than two-thirds of the land and peoples on the globe. My perspective on the achievements and deficiencies of this Age of Europe is shaped and colored by being a descendant of seven generations of Africans in the Western Hemisphere, enslaved and exploited, devalued and despised by Euro-Americans; and three generations of African-Americans, subordinated and terrorized by legal racist practices in the South. Both of my parents were born in Jim (and Jane) Crow Louisiana in the late 1920s and early 1930s. With the post-World War II decentering of Europe, the dwarfing of European populations, the demystifying of European cultural hegemony, the deconstruction of European philosophical systems and, most important, the decolonization of the Third World, I came of age during the eclipse of one epoch and the emergence of another.

My early formative years were spent during what Henry Luce called the "American century"—a period of unprecedented economic boom in the United States, the creation of a large middle class, i.e., a prosperous working class with a bourgeois identity, and a mass culture primarily based on African-American cultural products (music, style, etc.). I arrived on the scene just when black, and some white, blood, sweat and tears broke the back of an apartheid-like rule of law in the South and overturned discriminatory laws (though not *de facto* practices) in employment, housing and education. In 1970, when I entered Harvard College, I became part of the first generation of young black people to attend prestigious lily-white institutions of higher learning in significant numbers—institutions still coping with the new wave of Jewish faculty and students who had confronted an earlier tribal civility, snobbish gentility, and institutional loyalty of primarily well-to-do white Anglo-Saxon Protestants. Owing to my family, church, and the black social movements of the 1960s, I arrived at Harvard unashamed of my African, Christian, and militant decolonized outlooks. More pointedly, I acknowledged and accented the empowerment of my black styles, mannerisms, and viewpoints, my Christian values of service, love, humility and struggle, and my anticolonial sense of self-determination for oppressed people and nations around the world. But I soon discovered that this positive black identity, these persuasive Christian values, and this deep commitment to struggles for freedom were not enough. Given my privileged position (as a student—only about 18 percent of black young people were enrolled in college at the time) and grand opportunities, I needed a more profound understanding of history, a deeper grasp of the complex, conflict-ridden dynamics of societies and cultures and a more flexible perspective on human life.

My passionate interest in philosophy was—and remains—primarily motivated by the radical historical *conditionedness* of human existence and the ways in which possibilities and potentialities are created, seized and missed by individuals and communities within this ever changing conditionedness, including our in escapable death, illness and disappointment. This attention to the historical character of all thought and action has led me to be suspicious of intellectual quests for truth unwilling to be truthful about themselves, including my own. So though I find delight in the life of the mind—inseparable from, yet not identical with, struggles for freedom—I do not put primary value on intelligence or book knowledge. Rather, I believe we have a moral obligation—for the quality of human life and protection of the environment—to be wise, especially about the pitfalls and shortcomings of mere intelligence and book knowledge.

My three decisive years at Harvard College empowered me in a variety of ways. Although I first majored in philosophy and then changed to Near Eastern languages and literature (especially biblical Hebrew and Aramaic) in order to graduate a year early, my major focus was on history and social thought. I learned much of the former from Samuel Beer, H. Stuart Hughes and Martin Kilson; of the latter from Talcott Parsons, Hilary Putnam, Preston Williams, Terry Irwin and John Rawls. My political involvement consisted of daily work (beginning at 6:00 A.M.) in the breakfast program in Jamaica Plain with left black friends like Steven Pitts, weekly trips to Norfolk State Prison with fellow supporters like

Valerie Hepburn, and campus activism led by the Black Student Organization. The major action of this student group was the legendary 1972 takeover of Massachusetts Hall (including the president's office) to oppose Harvard's investments in Gulf Oil and to support the anti-imperialist forces in Angola. Randall Robinson, founder of TransAfrica but at that time a Harvard law student, played a crucial and courageous leadership role, as did the chief undergraduate spokesman, Harvard Stephens. I could not go into the building with my comrades because of trumped-up charges brought by the Cambridge Police Department and two Hebrew tests I had to take in order to catch up with my class. Instead, I joined the support work outside, which culminated in a march of 5,000 people on the first weekend of the takeover.

In the early 1970s, varieties of black nationalism were predominant at Harvard. Imamu Amiri Baraka's Congress of African People (CAP), Ron Karenga's early writings, the politics of the Republic of New Africa (RNA) and, to some extent, the Nation of Islam were attractive to black student activists. As a product of the black church I have always acknowledged some of the tenets of black nationalism, namely, black intelligence, beauty, character and capacity, and their subjection to vicious attack by white-supremacist practices. The fundamental issue of black identity—the affirmation of African humanity and ability—is a precondition for any black progressive politics. Yet my Christian universalist moral vision and my progressive international political perspective—derived from my readings of Frantz Fanon, Kwame Nkrumah and Karl Marx (promoted by the Black Panther Party over what Huey Newton called "porkchop nationalism")—made me deeply suspicious of the politics of black nationalists. I worked with them on antiracist issues—and we discussed, laughed and partied together weekly—but I always staked out my Christian version of democratic socialist values and politics.

My conversations with Trotskyists—especially the provocative lectures given by Peter Camejo—reinforced an anti-Stalinist stance I had already adopted, exposed me to a Leninist view I remained unpersuaded of and promoted an appreciation of black nationalist insights within a larger multiracial organization. I learned much from readings of Trotskyist intellectuals like Leon Trotsky himself, C. L. R. James, Perry Anderson and others, but I was not convinced. At this time, my major intellectual influences on political matters were the early Reinhold Niebuhr (of *Moral Man and Immoral Society*), R. H. Tawney (especially *The Acquisitive Society* and *Equality*), Julius K. Nyerere (*Essays on Socialism*), the early Leszek Kolakowski (*Towards a Marxist Humanism*) and the dissenting Marxist humanists Marković and Stojanović I was most excited by the powerful essays by Harold Cruse in *Rebellion or Revolution,* a book I much preferred over his classic *The Crisis of the Negro Intellectual.* Yet I remained critical of Cruse's cultural nationalist followers at Harvard, most of whom were my close friends. At that time, Martin Luther King, Jr., was a grand example of integrity and sacrifice but, in sharp contrast to Malcolm X, not a distinct voice with a credible politics in our Harvard conversations. Malcolm X's voice was as fresh as ever. We were all convinced that Malcolm X would hold *our* position and have *our* politics if he were alive. We rarely if ever asked this question of King in those days, even Christians like myself, principally owing to our blindness to his affirmation of democratic socialist politics and our downplaying of (read: ignorance of) his anti-imperialist (not just anti-Vietnam war) stance. King was for us the Great Man who died for us—but not yet the voice we had to listen to, question, learn from and build on. This would change in the next decade.

When I arrived at Princeton's philosophy department—by far the best in the country at the time—I anticipated three basic intellectual challenges: the undermining of my Christian faith by the powerful tools of analytical philosophy; the way in which the works of Ludwig Wittgenstein—my philosophic hero at the time—were interpreted by Princeton's philosophy department; and how the department's social philosophers might regard the Hegelian Marxist tradition, i.e., Georg Lukács and the Frankfurt School, whom I had recently been seduced by. I quickly discovered the first issue was an irrelevant one for my teachers and peers. Nobody cared about religious faith—though Walter Kaufmann and Richard Rorty regarded the issue with historic curiosity. So I kept my Pascal, Kierkegaard, Montaigne, Thurman and Unamuno close to my heart and read Frege, Carnap, Quine and Kuhn.

My eye-opening and horizon-broadening encounter with Richard Rorty made me an even stronger Wittgensteinian, although with gestures toward Dewey. Rorty's historicist turn was like music to my ears—nearly as sweet as the Dramatics, the Spinners, or the Main Ingredient, whom I then listened to daily for sanity. My allegiance to the Hegelian Marxist tradition was deepened by Sheldon Wolin—the major influence, along with Rorty and C. P. Macpherson—on my thought at the time. It was during the two short years at Princeton that I became convinced that the values of individuality—the sanctity and dignity of all individuals shaped in and by communities—and of democracy, as a way of life and mode of being-in-the-world, not just a form of governance, were most precious to me. This is why, when I returned to Harvard as a Du Bois Fellow to write my dissertation, I turned first to T. H. Green, the British neo-Hegelian of the late nineteenth century, and then to the ethical dimensions of Marxist thought. Marx's own debts to the Romantics' preoccupation with many-sided personality and full-fledged individuality (as in Friedrich Schiller's *Letters on Aesthetic Education*) and to the early socialists' focus on universal suffrage, women's rights, abolitionism and workplace democracy intrigued me. I became convinced that Marx's own intellectual development should be understood in terms of this fascinating tension between the moral conviction of the flowering of individuality under wholesale democratic socioeconomic and political conditions and the theoretical concern of

explaining scientifically the dynamics and tendencies of profit-driven capitalist societies that foster a narrow individualism and a truncated political democracy.

This book, *The Ethical Dimensions of Marxist Thought,* written over a decade ago
when I was in my mid-twenties, was my attempt to understand Marxist thought
as one grand stream, among others, of the larger modern articulation of historical
consciousness, an articulation fanned by Romantic quests for harmony and
wholeness and fueled by concrete revolutionary and reformist movements for
freedom, equality and democracy. Such quests and movements may result in
aborted authoritarian arrangements or be crushed by powerful capitalist powers.
Yet the precious values of individuality and democracy that can guide and regulate such quests and movements sit at the center of Marx's own thought. Hence I
take the reader, step by step and text by text, through Marx's own intellectual development in order to show how he incorporated modern historical consciousness
(as he constructed and understood it) in relation to his ethical values of individuality and democracy, and how these values clashed with what he viewed as the
pernicious and vicious effects of the fundamental class-ridden capitalist processes
of capital accumulation and the commodification of labor. My brief examinations
of subsequent Marxists, like Friedrich Engels, Karl Kautsky and Georg Lukács,
try to show that their diverse conceptions of modern historical consciousness in
relation to ethical issues differ greatly from that of Marx.

The scope of this essay is limited, yet its focus on Marxist ethical reflection regarding methodology and substance is timely. There is not only a paucity of
highly detailed interpretations of Marx's intellectual development, but also a need
for more investigation of the kind of turn toward history and social theory Marx
made and how it contrasts with that of subsequent noteworthy disciples and followers. And though I wrote *The American Evasion of Philosophy: A Genealogy of Pragmatism* six years after my dissertation, there is no doubt that my interpretation of
Marxist thought is influenced by the works of John Dewey, the early Sidney
Hook and Richard Rorty. My basic claim is that Marx's turn toward history resembles the antifoundationalist arguments of the American pragmatists, yet Marx
wants to retain a warranted-assertability status for social explanatory claims in
order to understand and change the world.

Marx wisely shuns any epistemic skepticism (as promoted by the deconstructive critics of our day) and explanatory agnosticism or nihilism (as intimated by
those descriptivist anthropologists and historians bitten by the bug of epistemic
skepticism). Instead, Marx refuses to conflate epistemic and methodological issues, philosophic and social theoretical ones, matters of justification for the certain
or absolute grounds for knowledge–claims and matters of explanation that provide persuasive yet provisional (or revisable) accounts of social and historical
phenomena. Like so many critics today, Marx's immediate followers often made
a "category mistake" of collapsing epistemological concerns of justification in phi-

losophy into methodological concerns of explanation in social theory. This unwarranted collapse is the basic reason why antifoundationalists in epistemology became full-fledged skeptics and why descriptivists in the social sciences shun subtle explanations of change and conflict in society and culture. Needless to say, the complex relation of epistemic skepticism and explanatory nihilism to the sense of political impotence and historical cynicism among such critics—even as they monotonously invoke slogans that knowledge is culturally constructed, historically constituted and politically laden—cries out for explanation. One major reason is that they are reacting against narrow conceptions of social theory, especially positivistic, economistic and reductionist versions of Marxism. This book shows that, despite the deep tensions in Marx's thought, there are other and better versions of Marxism put forward by Marx himself in his best moments. My point here is not that Marx's social theory fully accounts for all social and historical phenomena; rather, it is that social theory wedded in a nuanced manner to concrete historical analyses must be defended in our present moment of epistemic skepticism, explanatory agnosticism, political impotence (among progressives) and historical cynicism.

So it is necessary to discredit the fashionable trashing of Marxist thought in the liberal academy. Besides predictable caricatures of Marxist thought by conservatives, this trashing principally proceeds from ironic skeptics and aesthetic historicists. The former shun any theory that promotes political action with purpose; for them, any social project of transformation reeks of authoritarian aims. The latter highlight wholesale contingency and indeterminacy, with little concern for how and why change and conflict take place. So we have disciples of Jacques Derrida and Michel Foucault who talk about the subtle relations of rhetoric, knowledge and power, yet remain silent about concrete ways in which people are empowered to resist and what can be gained by such resistance. In addition, we have the so-called new historicists, preoccupied with "thick descriptions" of the relativity of cultural products, including those formerly neglected by traditional bourgeois male critics—while thoroughly distrustful of social *explanatory* accounts of cultural practices.

Needless to say, crude Marxist perspectives warrant scrutiny and rejection. Yet in these days of Marxist bashing, it is often assumed that vulgar Marxist thought exhausts the Marxist tradition—as if monocausal accounts of history, essentialist conceptions of society or reductionist readings of culture are all Marxist thought has to offer. One wonders whether any such critics have read Marx's *Eighteenth Brumaire, Class Struggles in France* or the *Grundrisse*.

Faddish ironic skepticism and aesthetic historicism are contemporary assaults on the twin pillars of Marxist social theory: historically specific accounts of structures such as modes of production, state apparatuses and bureaucracies and socially detailed analyses of how such structures shape and are shaped by cultural

agents. These pillars require that one's understanding of history, society and culture highlight latent and manifest multifarious human struggles for identity,
power, status and resources. More pointedly, it demands that one bite the explanatory bullet and give analytical priority to specific forms of struggle over others. For sophisticated Marxists, this does not mean that class explains every major
event in the past or present or that economic struggles supersede all others. It simply suggests that in capitalist societies, the dynamic processes of capital accumulation and the commodification of labor condition social and cultural practices in
an *inescapable* manner. How such practices are played out in various countries and
regions for different races, classes and genders in light of the fundamental capitalist processes will be determined in an experimental and empirical manner. Like
other refined forms of historical sociology, Marxist theory proceeds within the
boundaries of warranted-assertable claims and rationally acceptable conclusions.
Its assertions can be wrong in part because they are believed to be right.

The high intellectual moments of Marxist theory—Marx's own historical and
economic analyses, Georg Lukács's theory of reification and Antonio Gramsci's
conceptions of hegemony—are those that bring together explanatory power, analytical flexibility and a passion for social freedom. Yet certain crucial phenomena
of the modern world—nationalism, racism, gender oppression, homophobia, ecological devastation—have not been adequately understood by Marxist theorists.
My rejoinder simply is that these complex phenomena cannot be grasped, or
changed, without the insights of Marxist theory, although we do need other theories to account for them fully.

Efforts to link the fundamental capitalist processes of capital accumulation and
the commodification of labor to progressive traditions of ordinary people are not
a call to revive old debates about base and superstructure. Similar to the best
work of Raymond Williams, W. E. B. Du Bois, Eugene Genovese and Simone de
Beauvoir, I am suggesting that we focus on the oppositional cultures of oppressed
peoples that extend far beyond their workplaces. In other words, we need a serious Simmelian moment (as in Georg Simmel's *The Philosophy of Money*) in Marxist
theory that probes into the lived experiences of people in light of fundamental
capitalist processes. The aim here is not to reduce cultural efforts to ideological
battles, but rather to discern and determine the distinctive elements of the structures of feeling, structures of meaning, ways of life and struggle under dynamic
circumstances not of people's own choosing. In this way, Marxist theory can give
social substance and political content to postmodern themes of otherness, difference and marginality. And limited epistemological debates about foundationalism
and skepticism, realism and pragmatism can give way to more fruitful exchanges
about clashing methodological, theoretical and political conceptions of how to understand and change contemporary cultures and societies.

When I arrived as Assistant Professor of Philosophy of Religion at Union Theological Seminary in New York City in 1977, one of my concerns was precisely this issue: defending sophisticated Marxist theory as an indispensable—though by itself inadequate—intellectual weapon in the struggle for individuality and democracy. I decided to teach at Union Seminary for three reasons: It was (and still is) the center of liberation theology in the country; it was one of the best places for black theological education in the country; and it allowed me to teach and read widely in philosophy, social theory, history, literary criticism and cultural thought. Union was the perfect place to become a broadly engaged cultural critic with a strong grounding in the history of philosophy and criticism. In fact, I received another education at Union from my supportive colleagues—especially my closest friend, James Washington, Professor of Church History. My faith was tested and deepened, my mind was stretched and refined, my soul was refreshed and readied for battle.

After serious intellectual exchanges with James Cone, Beverly Harrison, Dorothea Sölle, Tom Driver, James Forbes, Jr., David Lotz, Milton Gatch and Donald Shriver—and trips to Brazil, Jamaica, Costa Rica, Mexico, Europe and later South Africa—the incarnation of progressive thought in concrete struggles for freedom was no mere dream. Despite a relative quietism on the U.S. Left, I witnessed and participated in an intellectual and political ferment in these places reminiscent of our 1960s. At home, the Theology in the Americas movement—the major national progressive multiracial and religious activity in the country in the 1970s—culminated in a historic gathering in Detroit. The results were published in 1982 by Orbis Press in a volume entitled *Theology in the Americas: Detroit II*, coedited by Caridàd Guidote (a professor and Filipina nun), Margaret Coakley (a white American nun) and myself. The same year I published *Prophesy Deliverance! An Afro-American Revolutionary Christianity* (Westminster Press), based in part on lectures I gave at Rev. Herbert Daughtry's House of the Lord Pentecostal Church in Brooklyn, New York. Rev. Daughtry was the founder and then head of the National Black United Front—one of the few progressive organized responses to the conservative Reaganite policies of the early 1980s.

Two crucial encounters shaped the kind of democratic socialism I would promote: the intense intellectual exchanges with Stanley Aronowitz and my membership in Michael Harrington's new organization, Democratic Socialists of America (DSA). In addition to James Washington and to my younger colleagues—Mark Ridley-Thomas, Anders Stephanson, Farah Griffin, Jerry Watts, Anthony Cook and Michael Dyson—I have never had a more enhancing intellectual interlocutor than Stanley Aronowitz. We read voraciously and talked incessantly about the impasse of the Left and the crisis of Marxism—he was then writing his important work *The Crisis in Historical Materialism*. His leadership of *Social Text*—the major journal in which Marxism encountered cultural politics in the 1980s and 1990s—pushed me toward a serious engagement with the works and lives of Fredric Jameson, Antonio Gramsci, Raymond Williams, Cedric Robinson, Anders Stephanson, Edward Said, Bertell Ollman, Barbara Fields, Stuart Hall, Ellen Willis, Audre Lorde, Eric Foner, bell hooks, Rick Wolff, Sohnya Sayres and Michel Foucault. This engagement still sets the framework for how I relate Marxist thought to the cultural politics of difference, i.e., race, gender, sexual orientation, age. This framework is an integral part of my work with the editorial collective of *Boundary 2: An International Journal of Literature and Culture*—Paul Bové, Jonathan Arac, William Spanos, Michael Hayes, Daniel O'Hara, Donald Pease, Joseph Buttigieg, Margaret Ferguson and Nancy Fraser.

Michael Harrington's DSA in 1982 was the first multiracial socialist organization close enough to my kind of politics that I could join. I was then, and remain, a sharp critic and staunch defender of DSA. After seven years on the national political committee—and many protracted ideological struggles—I now serve as an honorary chairperson. My own Gramscian democratic socialism is not in the mainstream of DSA, but it is an acceptable and legitimate perspective within the organization, and one that is sharpened and refined by defenders of other versions of democratic socialism.

I put forward my own critiques of the late Michael Harrington's conception of democratic socialism in my book *Prophetic Fragments* (Africa World Press, 1988) and in my review of his last book, *Socialism: Past and Future,* in the *Nation* (6–13 January 1990). Michael Harrington meant much to me as a person and I learned tangible and intangible lessons from him as we interacted in meetings and on trips together. We shared three fundamental points: the necessity of rethinking and reinterpreting the insights of the Marxist tradition in the light of new circumstances; the need for a national multiracial democratic socialist organization that puts a premium on intellectual exchange and political relevance; and the necessity of articulating a distinctive U.S. road to greater freedom, justice and equality. Harrington was, despite some political faults and intellectual flaws, a masterful organic intellectual who held these three points together in creative tension better than anyone else of his generation.

My friendships with Harry Magdoff and Paul Sweezy began just as I was moving from Union to Yale Divinity School in 1984. In our work together on a special issue on religion and the Left for *Monthly Review* (July–August 1984), we realized that our versions of Marxist theory overlapped in significant ways. Their critical allegiance to historical materialist analyses that are magnanimously global in character yet meticulously specific in content fit well with my Gramscian accounts that link the rule of capital—the powers of transnational corporations, banks and political elites—to the race- and gender-skewed ill-fed, ill-housed and ill-clad. As the caretakers of one of the oldest Marxist journals in the United States, they have defended and updated Marxist theory while opening its pages to non-Marxist socialists like myself who share their concern about the significance of Marxist theory as an indispensable intellectual weapon for freedom fighters in the present.

I am a non-Marxist socialist in that, as a Christian, I recognize certain irreconcilable differences between Marxists of whatever sort and Christians of whatever sort. Since my conception of Christian faith is deeply, though not absolutely, historical, this disagreement is not primarily a metaphysical issue; rather, it is a basic existential difference in the weight I put on certain biblical narratives, symbols and rituals that generate sanity and meaning for me. My Christian perspective—mediated by the rich traditions of the black church that produced and sustains me—embraces depths of despair, layers of dread, encounters with the sheer absurdity of the human condition and ungrounded leaps of faith alien to the Marxist tradition. Like so much of black music, Christian insights speak on existential and visceral levels neglected by the Marxist tradition. This is not so because the Marxist tradition is Eurocentric—for there are traditions and figures in Europe that do speak to existential issues, e.g., Samuel Beckett, T. S. Eliot, Martin Buber, Susanne Langer. Rather, the Marxist tradition is silent about the existential meaning of death, suffering, love and friendship owing to its preoccupation with improving the social circumstances under which people pursue love, revel in friendship and confront death. I share this concern.

Yet like both Russian novelists and blues singers, I also stress the concrete lived experience of despair and tragedy and the cultural equipment requisite for coping with the absurdities, anxieties and frustrations as well as the joys, laughter and gaiety of life. In this deep sense, Marxism is not and cannot serve as a religion. And if it is cast as a religion, it is a shallow secular ideology of social change that fails to speak to us about the ultimate facts of human existence. To put it charitably, Marxist thought does not purport to be existential wisdom—of how to live one's life day by day. Rather, it claims to be a social theory of histories, societies and cultures. Social theory is not the same as existential wisdom. Those theories that try to take the place of wisdom disempower people on existential matters, just as those wisdoms that try to shun theory usually subordinate people to the political powers that be.

My writings constitute a perennial struggle between my African and American identities, my democratic socialist convictions and my Christian sense of the profound tragedy and possible triumph in life and history. I am a prophetic Christian freedom fighter principally because of distinctive Christian conceptions of what it is to be human, how we should act toward one another and what we should hope for. These conceptions—put forward in a variety of diverse streams and strains of the Christian tradition stretching back over centuries—have to do with the indispensable yet never adequate capacities of human beings to create error-proof or problem-free situations, theories or traditions—hence the strong antidogmatic or fallible character of prophetic Christian thought and practice, which encourage relentless critical consciousness; the moral claim to view each and every individual as having equal status, as warranting dignity, respect and love, especially those who are denied such dignity, respect and love by individuals, families, groups, social structures, economic systems or political regimes—hence the prophetic Christian identification and solidarity with the downtrodden and disinherited, the degraded and dispossessed; and lastly, the good news of Jesus Christ, which lures and links human struggles to the coming of the kingdom—hence the warding off of disempowering responses to despair, dread, disappointment and death.

Prophetic Christianity has a distinctive, though not exclusive, capacity to highlight critical, historical and universal consciousness that yields a vigilant disposition toward prevailing forms of individual and institutional evil, an unceasing suspicion of ossified and petrified forms of dogmatism and a strong propensity to resist various types of cynicism and nihilism.

Prophetic Christian conceptions of what it is to be human, how we should act and what we should hope for are neither rationally demonstrable nor empirically verifiable in a necessary and universal manner. Rather, they are embedded and enacted in a form of life—a dynamic set of communities that constitute a diverse tradition—that mediates how I interpret my experiences, sufferings, joys and undertakings. There are indeed good reasons to accept prophetic Christian claims, yet they are good not because they result from logical necessity or conform to transcendental criteria. Rather, these reasons are good (persuasive to some, nonsense to others) because they are rationally acceptable and existentially enabling for many self-critical finite and fallible creatures who are condemned to choose traditions under circumstances not of their own choosing. To choose a tradition (a version of it) is more than to be convinced by a set of arguments; it is also to decide to live alongside the slippery edge of life's abyss with the support of the dynamic stories, symbols, interpretations and insights bequeathed by communities that came before.

I have always shunned the role of theologian because I have little interest in systematizing the dogmas and doctrines, insights and intuitions of the Christian tradition. Nor do I think that they can be rendered coherent and consistent. The theological task is a noteworthy endeavor—especially for the life of the church—yet my vocation uses Christian resources, among others, to speak to the multilayered crises of contemporary society and culture. So I am more a cultural critic with philosophic training who works out of the Christian tradition than a theologian who focuses on the systematic coherency or epistemic validity of Christian claims.

This vocation puts social theory, historiography, cultural criticism and political engagement at the center of my prophetic Christian outlook. I do not believe that there are such things as Christian social theory, Christian historiography, Christian cultural criticism or Christian politics—just as there are no such things as Christian mathematics, Christian physics or Christian economics. Rather, there is prophetic Christian thought and practice informed by the best of these disciplines that highlights and enhances the plight of the loveless, luckless, landless and other victims of social structural arrangements. In this way, my prophetic vocation overlaps in significant ways with those of such Marxists as Harry Magdoff and Paul Sweezy. In the present methodological debate against ironic skeptics, aesthetic historicists, political cynics and explanatory agnostics, we stand together in defense of Marxist theory and socialist politics—even as we may disagree on how we conceive of Marxist theory or the kind of socialism we promote.

My move to Yale Divinity School in 1984 afforded me the opportunity to reflect on the crisis in American philosophy—as in *Post-Analytic Philosophy* (1985), edited by my good friend John Rajchman and myself, and in my book *The American Evasion of Philosophy* (1989). This coincided with an intense campus drive for clerical unionism at Yale (one of the few labor victories of the 1980s) and against Yale's investments in South African companies. Again, my arrest and jail resulted. This action served as a fine example for my wonderful son, Clifton, quickly approaching adolescence—an example he has followed as a progressive student body president of his predominantly black middle school in Atlanta.

Partly owing to this action, my request for leave was denied and I was forced to teach a full program at Yale (two courses) and the University of Paris VIII (three courses) in the spring of 1987. I commuted every five to seven days from New Haven to Paris from February to April. To be on the same faculty with Gilles Deleuze (who retired that spring) and Jean-François Lyotard was an honor. Yet I was amazed at the French students' ignorance of U.S. philosophy and the hunger for Afro-American history and culture. In my graduate seminar on John Dewey, Hilary Putnam, Stanley Cavell and Richard Rorty, brilliant students had never heard of Dewey—in fact, one wanted to study with him (unaware he had died in 1952)! My Afro-American intellectual history course was scheduled for twenty, but over a hundred students (many from African and Arab countries) enrolled. Student activism regarding educational reform was increasing at the time, and I participated in many lively discussions and actions.

When I returned from Paris, I decided to leave Yale—for personal reasons linked with my lovely African wife-to-be, Elleni Gebre Amlak—and went back to Union. But after a short year I decided to go to Princeton University, to teach in the religion department and direct the Afro-American studies program. My major motivation was to constitute a critical mass of black scholars—with the great Toni Morrison at the center—although I also was eager to learn from other superb scholars there.

At present, besides completing *Breaking Bread,* a book written with bell hooks on the black crisis (including black male/female relations), a collection of essays *(Prophetic Criticism)* and a work on David Hume (seven years in the making), my focus is twofold: the battle in the arts, popular culture and the academy over Eurocentrism and multiculturalism, and the crisis in black and progressive leadership. In 1990, I coedited (with Russell Ferguson, Martha Gever and Trinh T. Minhha) *Out There: Marginalization and Contemporary Cultures* (MIT Press) for the New Museum of Contemporary Art. This landmark text may set the framework for the debate between conservatives like Allan Bloom, Africanist thinkers such as Leonard Jeffries, feminist theorists countering patriarchal canons like Elaine Showalter, and democratic socialists of African descent like myself. This battle will continue to rage well into the twenty-first century. My major aim is to rescue the ambiguous legacy of the European age from conservatives, to accent the racist, patriarchal and homophobic currents that still run through American intellectual and cultural life while criticizing any separatist politics or parochial outlook and linking the new cultural politics of difference to a democratic socialist perspective. My critical appreciation of the hip-hop culture of American youth, especially black youth, reflects this dialectical reading of our present moment. I applaud the spirit of resistance against racism, yet condemn its misogynist and homophobic elements.

The crisis of leadership in black and progressive communities is symptomatic of the paucity of credible strategies and tactics for social change in the United States. It also reflects the relative inability of the Left to mobilize and organize over time and space. Needless to say, there is no easy way out of this impasse.

The effort is more difficult due to the pervasive disarray of the progressive movement in the United States. Never before in our history has the U.S. Left been so bereft of courageous leaders of vision, intelligence and integrity. We simply do not have formidable figures that the public identifies with progressive causes. Aside from those preoccupied with electoral politics and admirable local activists with little national attention, there are no major leaders who articulate in bold and defiant terms—with genuine passion and analytical clarity—the moral imperative to address the maldistribution of resources, wealth and power, the escalating xenophobia, ecological devastation, national decline and spiritual impoverishment we are facing. This crisis of leadership adds to the balkanization of U.S. progressive politics—its fragmentation, isolation and insularity. Given the power of big business and cultural conservatism, the U.S. Left has potency primarily when strong leadership—rooted in extraparliamentary organizational activity—energizes and galvanizes demoralized progressives and liberals across racial, class, regional, age and gender lines. This usually does not last long—so the propitious moment must be seized.

We find it hard to seize this moment not only because of the establishment's strategies of repression and incorporation, but also owing to the consumer culture—with its addictive seductions and pacifying pastimes—which often saps and disperses our energies for collective struggle. Market morality engulfs us in such a way that it is difficult to arrange our lives so that communal activity supersedes personal pursuits. Market mentality makes it hard for us to believe our sacrificial progressive efforts will make a real difference in our busy and short lives. And since there can be no substantive progressive politics without oppositional sub-cultures, institutions and networks, the predominant "market way of life" presents a—maybe *the*—major challenge for progressive politics.

At the moment, the most explosive issues in U.S. society revolve around black bodies and women's wombs—race and abortion. And, in a fundamental sense, the starting points—through not landing grounds—for progressive politics in the 1990s may be enhancement of the poor, especially those of color, and protection of women's rights. Yet reform measures such as progressive taxation and appoint-ment of liberal judges fall far short of what is required. We also need a progres-sive cultural renaissance that reshapes our values, restructures how we live and puts struggle and sacrifice closer to the center of what we think and do. Only then will our fight to turn back a market-driven, conservative United States—already far down the road to social chaos and self-destruction—be not only desirable, but also credible. The defense of the relevance of Marxist thought, including its ethi-cal dimensions, after the Cold War is an indispensable weapon in this fight.

At the forefront of this fight stands Jesse Jackson. His historic presidential cam-paigns were the major progressive responses to Reagan's conservative policies. His 1988 bid was the first time since the last days of Martin Luther King, Jr.'s Poor People's Campaign—with the grand exception of Mayor Harold Washing-ton's election in Chicago—that the nearly *de facto* segregation in U.S. progressive politics was confronted and partly surmounted.

Yet Jackson's courageous leadership is problematic. His televisual style—a style too preoccupied with TV cameras—relies on personal charisma at the expense of grassroots organizing. His brilliance and energy sustain his public visibility at the expense of programmatic follow-through. This style downplays people's partici-patory possibilities—at the level of followership and leadership. More pointedly, it shuns democratic accountability. Pure democracy must never be a fetish for pro-gressives. Work must get done; decisions must be made. But criticism and demo-cratic practices are the lifeblood of any progressive organization worthy of the name. Jackson's televisual style not only mitigates against this; it tends to pre-clude it. So despite his salutary social democratic politics, Jackson's televisual style may be reaching the point at which it undermines his crucial message.

This televisual style must give way to a collective model of progressive leader-ship that puts a premium on grassroots organizing, criticism and democratic ac-countability. The future of U.S. progressive politics lies with those engaged local activists who have made a difference, yet who also have little interest in being in the national limelight. They engage in protracted organizing in principled coalitions that bring power and pressure to bear on specific issues—especially issues of jobs, housing, health and child care, education and ecological protection. Without such activists there can be no progressive politics. Yet state, regional and national networks are also necessary for an effective progressive politics. This is why locally based collective (and especially multiracial and multigender) models of leadership are needed. These models must shun the idea of one national progressive leader; they must highlight critical dialogue and democratic accountability within and across organizations. These models of collective leadership will more than likely not be part of the lethargic electoral system riddled with decreasing revenues (i.e., debt), loss of public confidence, self-perpetuating mediocrity and pervasive corruption. Rather, the future of U.S. progressive politics lies in the capacity of a collective leadership to energize, mobilize and organize working and poor people. Democratic socialists can play a crucial role in projecting an all-embracing moral vision of freedom, justice and equality and making social analyses that connect and link activists together. In this way we can be a socialist leaven in a larger progressive loaf. Yet this loaf will never get baked if we remain separate, isolated, insular and fragmented. America's massive social breakdown requires that we come together—for the sake of our lives, our children and our sacred honor.

Source: "Introduction: The Making of an American Democratic Socialist of African Descent," *The Ethical Dimensions of Marxist Thought* (New York: Monthly Review Press, 1991), pp. xv–xxxiv.

Two

ON MY INTELLECTUAL VOCATION

Although I was trained as a professional philosopher, I have never held a position in a philosophy department. I have turned down a number of offers from philosophy departments, because I cherish my intellectual freedom to teach and write about a vast array of subjects. I have never aspired to be a professional academic or scholar. Instead, I have tried to be a man of letters in love with ideas in order to be a wiser and more loving person, hoping to leave the world just a little better than I found it. I take great delight in the free play of the mind, and I believe intellectual work is indispensable for social change. Yet, in the end, I place compassion far above smartness and wisdom light-years ahead of cleverness. The quest for wisdom is rooted in an erotic relation to the world—a deep desire to love and passion to know before one dies. So I speak of my intellectual work and life as a calling, not a career; a vocation, not a profession.

George Yancy is an American philosopher of African descent who interviewed black philosophers for his celebrated book African-American Philosophers: 17 Conversations. *The book is a real treat.*

George Yancy: When and where were you born?

Cornel West: In Tulsa, Oklahoma, June 2, 1953.

Yancy: Given that your father was a civilian air force administrator, your family moved around quite a bit. How did eventually growing up in a segregated part of Sacramento, California, shape your early consciousness?

West: Well, in one sense, of course, it was inescapable because it was segregated, Jim Crowed in its own unique Californian way, but in another sense it meant that from early on whiteness was really not a point of reference for me because the world was all black. So much of my life was spent where I didn't interact with white brothers and sisters at all. And I think, in the end, that was a very positive thing, because it gave me a chance to really revel in black humanity, and when it became time to interact with white brothers and sisters, I could really see them just as humans. I didn't have to either deify them or demonize them; I didn't have to put them on a pedestal or put them in the gutter. I could just view them as human beings, and I think that was quite a contribution of my own context.

Yancy: I see. So what was it specifically about your experience of the absurd, at the age of thirteen or fourteen, that made the work of Søren Kierkegaard so attractive to you at such an early age?

West: I think early on I was just in some sense seized by a certain kind of terror that struck me as being at the heart of things human and a profound sadness and sorrow that struck me as being at the core of the human condition. And so in reading Kierkegaard from the Bookmobile, and here was someone who was seriously and substantively wrestling with a certain level of melancholia, I was struck by his very honest and candid—I want to stress honest and candid—encounter with what he understood to be this terror, this suffering and this sadness and sorrow. It resonated deeply with me. Prosser Hall Frye used the wonderful phrase "the tragic qualm" to describe this encounter. It is a kind of vertigo, a dizziness, a sense of being staggered by the darkness that one sees in the human condition, the human predicament.

Yancy: And how did reading Kierkegaard at such an early age impact your later philosophical development?

West: I think that it was decisive. It gave me a profoundly Kierkegaardian sensibility that required then that philosophizing be linked to existentially concrete situations, wrestling with decision, commitment, actualized possibility and realized potential. And so I tended then to have a deep suspicion of what Arthur Schopenhauer calls "university philosophy" or "academic philosophy," which tended to be so much concerned with abstract concepts and forms of universalizing and always in track or pursuit of necessity as opposed to the concrete, the particular, the existential, the suffering beings and the loving beings that we are and can be. You have to realize that I was coming out of the church, and so there was always Job sitting there, Daniel sitting there, and even Christ, especially the Christ between Good Friday and Easter, the Christ during that very dark Saturday, which struck me as highly illuminating of what it meant to be human. How do you really struggle against the suffering in a loving way, to leave a legacy in which people would be able to accent their own loving possibility in the midst of so much evil? So in that sense I think that the black church and its profound stress on the concrete and the particular—wrestling with limit situations, with death, dread, despair, disappointment, disease, and so on—has been influential on my Kierkegaardian outlook.

Yancy: How influential were your parents in terms of your early intellectual development?

West: Fundamental. They gave the greatest gift I could receive—unconditional love. They also exemplified such love in their dealings with others. They also encouraged my intellectual curiosity and energy, yet always put it in a Christian perspective—understanding and changing the world is but sounding brass and tinkling cymbal without genuine love and compassion.

Yancy: I've had the opportunity to see you teach at both Princeton and Harvard and there is often this preacherly, although critical, style that you use. How has African American homiletics shaped your pedagogical approach within the walls of academia?

West: Well, I've always wanted to be myself, and, of course, that is a perennial process. I did not in any way want only an image of Union or Yale or Princeton or Harvard to shape me. I wanted to shape my own image in those contexts, and to be myself meant to be involved, engaged, passionate and so forth. I do think, though, that we have to make a very important distinction between passionate rhetoric that tries to communicate and the sermonic or the preacherly, because passionate rhetoric is simply a way of exemplifying a certain level of self-involvement and self-investment in what one is talking about, and I think the sermonic or the homiletic or the preacherly has no monopoly on that kind of self-involvement and self-investment. It's true that the black homiletical tradition in certain forms (and there are homiletical forms, of course, that are not passionate), particularly those forms coming out of Baptist and Pentecostal churches, tends to be self-involved and self-invested. I am no doubt influenced by a number of those styles, but, for me, it's much more just a question of acknowledging anytime you're engaged in serious philosophical reflection that so much is at stake, your whole life, the structures of meaning that you try to create, the structures of value that you hold, your mode of being in the world. So, in questioning yourself at such a deep level and at such a fragile and delicate level, I can't but help, at least in my case, overflow with passion.

Yancy: Although you switched to Near Eastern languages and literature at Harvard University, talk about what led you to pursue philosophy proper.

West: Well, as I've said, I read Kierkegaard, but I also read Will Durant's *The Story of Philosophy* about five times, and I had read some other popular histories. For example, I was reading in and out of Bertrand Russell's *The History of Western Philosophy* early on. When I went to Harvard, I talked with Bob Nozick, who was my tutor and was actually quite wonderful, and I told him what I was reading and he said, "Well, that's wonderful, Cornel, but we are going to introduce you to some high-powered philosophy so you'll be able to build on what you've read." But it was clear to me, I think, because I did have Sartre with me at the time, that I was being introduced to analytical philosophy at Harvard. Analytical philosophy was very interesting. It always struck me as being very interesting and full of tremendous intellectual curiosities. It is wonderful to see the mind at work in such an intense manner, but, for me, it was still too far removed from my own issues. There were such issues as the problem of evil, suffering, misery and how to engage in struggle, how to talk about courage, how to talk about joy, etc. For me, such issues were much more at the center of things. So even as an undergraduate, I was taking biblical Hebrew, Aramaic, and Koine Greek, classical Greek, as a way of being able to read some of the religious literary texts that were of interest to me. In that sense it was a kind of antidote to a lot of the analytical philosophy.

Yancy: Who were some of the high-powered philosophers Nozick had in mind?

West: Oh, I would think beginning with Gottlob Frege, Bertrand Russell, Rudolf Carnap, Willard Quine and then probably on to Burton Dreben and himself. There were some wonderful folk at Harvard at the time. Harvard was experiencing a kind of golden age in philosophy. I was really lucky to be there.

Yancy: Do you see yourself as a professional philosopher?

West: No, not at all. I think that my concern has always been just trying to make sense of the world and trying to leave the world a little better than I found it. I think that if I were to call myself anything it would be a man of letters who's deeply immersed in philosophical texts, in literary texts, deeply concerned also with scientific texts, but science much more as one element in the quest for wisdom rather than science as a way of gaining knowledge in order to dominate nature. So, in that sense, I have an intellectual curiosity that is quite broad, but I've never viewed myself as an academic or professional philosopher in a narrow sense.

Yancy: Would you say that departments of philosophy are just too limiting for your rather variegated and broad intellectual project?

West: Well, not necessarily. You have to find someplace to gain a foothold. I could be in a philosophy department and still do what I want to do. You know, my aim was always to teach at Union Seminary, which I was able to do in '77. That was quite a breakthrough because Union Seminary, for me, was the real institutional site that brought together all of my interests. It was a Christian seminary, it was deeply shaped by progressive politics, Marxism, feminism, antihomophobic thought and black liberation theology. It was in New York and it was where the great Paul

Tillich and Reinhold Niebuhr, who were two of my heroes early on, had spent so much of their careers.

Yancy: If you had to trace your philosophical identity, provide a short list of names and texts.

West: That's a very good question. Well, with respect to the modern period, I would begin with Pascal's *Pensées,* and from there I would go to Hume's "Skepticism with Regard to the Senses" and "Skepticism with Regard to Reason," those two chapters in book one of his *Treatise on Human Nature.* I would then go on to Kant's 1791 piece called *On the Failure of All Modern Philosophical Theodicies.* It's an essay that is really pivotal. Now this essay goes hand in hand with Schelling's 1809 treatise on the essence of freedom. Schelling lived another forty-five years, but he never published anything else, which is quite interesting. I would then go to Schopenhauer and Kierkegaard, two fundamental figures. From there, I would then go to Nietzsche's *The Genealogy of Morals.* I would then go to literary figures, both novelists and playwrights, like Ibsen, Strindberg and Chekhov, Thomas Hardy, Tolstoy, and then Kafka, Eugene O'Neill, *The Iceman Cometh,* Tennessee Williams's *A Streetcar Named Desire* and then to Toni Morrison's *Beloved.* I think that there you would capture at least a crucial part of my own intellectual lineage, as it were.

Yancy: Why is Kant's theodicy piece so pivotal?

West: Well, because it showed that the problem of evil could not be theoretically resolved at all. It was a question of coping, he argued, with artistic wisdom and negative wisdom. It was through the wrestling of a Kant, whom we associate with a kind of obsession with rationality and autonomy, that I was able to see his other side, which is his artistic wisdom, his negative wisdom, and his reading of the book of Job in that essay, which I think is quite fascinating, is rarely talked about by scholars of Kant. The profound book of Job, of course, becomes linked to the great tradition of modern drama that one sees in an O'Neill.

Yancy: Is there a black musical motif that shapes your writing? I'm thinking specifically of your short story entitled "Sing a Song."

West: That short story was published in *Prophetic Fragments.* I had worked on novels and short stories early on, over twenty years ago, but I've only published one short story. But it's true that black music, especially the blues, is one fundamental source or creative lens through which I view the world. There is no doubt about that. It's a profoundly tragic-comic, neither sentimental nor cynical, stress on struggle. Keep keeping on, trying to hold the blues at arm's length by means of singing the blues or enacting the blues. And most importantly, I think, always viewing oneself as embedded and embodied and also indebted to those who came before. So there is that sense of radical conditionedness on the one hand and, on the other, a sense of freedom, but still within that context of radical conditionedness, especially to oneself. There is the sense of trying to muster the courage to be oneself, the courage to wrestle with the truth about oneself, the truth about America, the truth about the world and the courage to fight for justice. Those notions of freedom, courage and joy would probably be the three fundamental motifs in my work, and I think that they are probably best enacted in the best of the black musical tradition.

Yancy: What shapes your synoptic style of writing?

West: Part of it, for me, has to do with a sense of history, which is very important. Anytime you have a sense of history, then you are always talking about the very complex relations of the present to the past and ways in which futures are embedded in the present. And anytime you talk about history, it usually takes some narrative form, there is some story likeness, and that tends to be easier to follow oftentimes. I think that is probably one factor that shapes my synoptic style of writing. Also, there is a certain kind of openness about one's own self such that people can see that you're being self-critical and they can see how you are complicitous with some of the very things that you talk about. In other words, it's not a matter of simply pointing fingers or calling names, but really showing that you are in the very mess that you are trying to grasp. Moreover, this tends to open people up a little bit. If you're willing to take a risk and become vulnerable, then it tends to open others to take a risk and become vulnerable with regard to listening to what you're saying.

Yancy: Is there anything that can be called "African American philosophy"?

West: So much would hinge upon what we mean by "philosophy." If we understand philosophy as a type of autonomous discourse that somehow transcends history, I would say no, because I don't think that there is such a thing in general. If, however, we understand it as a certain cultural response to the world and trying to come up with holistic views, synoptic visions and synthetic images of how things hang together, then certainly there is an Afro-American philosophical tradition, I believe, most definitely. But also I tend to be rather Jamesian in my understanding of philosophy. I think that philosophy is in one sense connected to certain temperaments and that we see those temperaments through images of the world. In this case, the notion of an image has to do with philosophical articulation, a *Weltanschauung,* a worldview and so forth. Art, for example, can be viewed as an image of the world through which we see a certain temperament of the artist. But I also believe that philosophy and art are really intimately interlinked, because they have to do with the nature of our articulation. The last line of Federico García Lorca's play entitled *Blood Wedding* is significant. That last line, "the dark root of the scream," is so very important, for it is a question of how we take that scream, that guttural cry we make and transform and transfigure that scream, that cry, into linguistic articulation, into a way of understanding the world, a way of trying to make the world in some sense intelligible. I never want to lose sight of that scream and that cry, because I think that really sits at the center of any serious philosophy that's grappling with life.

Yancy: Why is there such a paucity of African American professional philosophers?

West: Well, we haven't reached a point where we've convinced enough young black brothers and sisters that to engage in philosophical discourse in academic spaces is desirable, attractive, appealing or just hip or cool. There is a great deal of philosophical reflection going on in black America, no doubt about that, from barbershops to hip-hop music, to mainstream rhythm and blues and so on. The singer Babyface has his own philosophical sensibility with his conceptions of life and so on. Stevie Wonder certainly does. In academic philosophy we simply haven't made it attractive enough. But it also has much to do with the image of a philosopher, which is primarily dominated by the analytical philosopher, who is clever, sharp and good at drawing distinctions, but who doesn't really relate it to history, struggle, engagement with suffering, how we cope with suffering, how we overcome social misery, etc.

Yancy: So, one way of making philosophy attractive to African Americans is to link it to these larger historical processes.

West: Absolutely right.

Yancy: What does the "black experience" have to offer American philosophy that is of philosophical value?

West: A profound sense of the tragic and the comic rooted in heroic efforts to preserve human dignity on the night side, the underside of modernity. In short, a deep blues sensibility that highlights concrete existence, history, struggle, lived experience and joy.

Yancy: Do you think that African American philosophers have failed to fulfill the role of organic intellectual?

West: I don't think that all of them should. I think we've got to have a variety of different paradigms of philosophizing. For example, some might be linked to a community that would involve overcoming the "gown-town" distinction and some would not. So, I don't think that there has been a failure per se. I would like to see more, but I think we have to have a division of labor, and we have to have a certain tolerance for plurality and diversity of roles and functions among black philosophers.

Yancy: Talk about the specific impact of Richard Rorty's thought on your own philosophical reflections.

West: It's on two levels. On the one hand, he is just a very good personal friend and colleague, and as a young person it's so nice to have a figure to take interest in your work and your mind, to be such a fascinating and challenging interlocutor and conversational partner. But that's a very personal thing and that is what I encountered at Princeton in 1973, six years before he wrote *Philosophy and the Mirror of Nature* and became famous. He remains a very, very good friend and colleague. On the other hand, intellectually, I think that Rorty was tremendously liberating for me, because from my readings of Kierkegaard, Nietzsche, Gadamer, Heidegger and the later Wittgenstein, which I had read before I went to Princeton, I was already predisposed toward the kind of antifoundationalism, contextualism and deep thoroughgoing historicism he was putting forward. Now he couched it within a certain self-styled pragmatism, and I had already actually been predisposed to pragmatism, having studied pragmatism under Israel Scheffler at Harvard. But he was able to couch it in such a grand worldview that he could really show how things hang together, and that is what I think I was able to acquire from him more than anything else. It was this deep historicist sensibility of always trying to show how things hang together, along with antifoundationalism and contextualism that he was putting forward. So in that regard, his work was pivotal. There is no doubt about it, even given my disagreements, Rorty is pivotal, both at the personal as well as the intellectual level.

Yancy: In a *Transition* essay, Rorty argues that you are "still enamored of the idea that your own academic discipline, namely, philosophy, is somehow more closely linked to prophetic vision than are, say, anthropology, literary criticism, or economics, or art history."

West: No, I don't think that is true. I think that brother Rorty makes such a claim because of my own influences coming out of the Marxist tradition, where the role of social theory is highlighted. I really do believe that we've got to be able to give some fallible yet persuasive explanations of wealth, power and the state as weapons in our institutional and individual struggles to overcome forms of social misery. But I don't think that philosophy is any closer. If I were to go out on a limb, I would probably make a case for art, but I'm not sure that I want to go that far. I think that Schelling and Schopenhauer make the strongest cases in the modern Western philosophical tradition as to why art illuminates more than other forms of cultural production. Actually, I think that there is something to that. I think that when you look at a Chekhov, a Coltrane, a Tolstoy or a Toni Morrison, you actually see deep, deep, existentially deep, sea diving taking place. That is not the case in most texts in anthropology, most texts in sociology and so on. But, on the other hand, it is also true that there are some sociologists, like my own favorite, Georg Simmel, who get very deep. They tend to be those who are highly suspicious of their profession, but they are using certain insights of professional sociologists as springboards to engage in deep-sea diving. Very much so.

Yancy: Again, in the same *Transition* piece, Rorty argues that "it will be easier to encourage such protest [where we're talking about social protest] if we toss aside the last remnants of Marxist thought and in particular the desire for a general theory of oppression."

West: Well, I disagree with the first part and agree with the second part. I think that the Marxist intellectual tradition remains indispensable in order to keep track of certain forms of social misery, especially these days in terms of the oligopolies and monopolies that take the form of transnational corporations with a disproportionate amount of wealth and power, not just in America but around the world. You need some Marxist theoretical insights in order to keep track of that. At the same time, I am against general theories of oppression, and therefore, for me, my particular stand within the Marxist tradition is linked primarily to that of Gramsci, which always places stress on historical specificity, on concrete circumstances and situations. This does not require a general theory of oppression per se. And in that regard I think one can talk about a Gramscian strand in the Marxist tradition that is suspicious of general theory, which resonates with Rorty's suspicion of general theory, but it's still not a question of eliminating the remnants of Marxism per se. Not at all. I don't see how, in fact, we can understand the market forces around the world and the fundamental role of transnational corporations, the subordination of working people, the tremendous class conflicts going on around the world at the marketplace between management and labor without understanding some of the insights of the Marxist tradition.

Yancy: In his controversial essay in the *New Republic,* Leon Wieseltier claims that you maintain that the abolition of transcendence is necessary for religion and that you don't realize the dire contradiction that you've created. What's your response?

West: I never knew what Leon was talking about. I've never rejected transcendence per se. There are many, many different varieties and versions of transcendence. You can reject certain forms of transcendence while you defend others. But I certainly would never want to reject transcendence per se. Paul Ricoeur has taught us that you have to have some distanciation, some critical distance from an object of investigation in order even to engage in reflection, and that is a certain kind of transcendence right there. And certainly anybody like myself who talks about struggle, who comes out of a Christian tradition, which includes some kind of overcoming—to use the Hegelian term, *Aufhebung,* which is a kind of transcendence—would never really want to call into question transcendence per se. Also keep in mind that there are many Hegelian forms of transcendence, but they're always involved in an interplay between transcendence and immanence, with some verticality and some horizontality.

Yancy: Staying with the concept of transcendence, what does a "Westian," as it were, conception of God look like?

West: Well, I don't think that we have such a thing as a "Westian" anything, really. There are certain lenses through which I look at the world, but, for me, any God-talk is so inextricably linked to talk about so many other things that it would have to do with the nature of the stories and narratives where God is invoked as an agent in order to provide illuminations about what it means to be human. And so I tend to side with those in the Christian tradition who put a high premium on Christ. So I'm a kind of Christocentric thinker in that regard and therefore, following Karl Barth, the greatest Christocentric thinker of the twentieth century, I think that our concrete images of God are best rendered in the various narratives told about Christ as loving, struggling, sacrificing, suffering and overcoming. And so in that regard, I probably would want to send somebody to certain Barthian texts or make certain links to James Cone, who, of course, was a very close student of Karl Barth.

Yancy: In terms of your Christocentric perspective, what value do you place on a priori and a posteriori arguments for the existence of God?

West: I don't believe that any arguments for or against the existence of God have much weight one way or the other. Not at all. I think that particular way of couching the question is already impoverished, and it reflects a certain kind of ahistorical way of understanding God-talk of which I am highly suspicious. I think it's interesting that there have been these fascinating attempts—St. Augustine, St. Anselm and a whole host of others—though often misunderstood by we moderns. But that strikes me as just a kind of cultural practice that is relatively impoverished in terms of engaging in a form of God-talk that has played a certain role in philosophical reflection. But I can't think that way at all. It is not my way of being oriented to understanding what it means to be human in relationship to a religious tradition, or the Christian tradition in this case.

Yancy: Do you believe that there is a "salvific" role for you to play vis-à-vis blacks here in the United States?

West: No. I never use the word "salvific" in that sense. I don't think that salvation is anything that we humans have anything to do with. Certainly, I would use the language of betterment, amelioration, breakthrough, progress, trying to overcome and trying to alleviate and attenuate the hell that we are catching. I certainly want to play some role, but I think one plays one's role whether one is a philosopher, carpenter, musician, mother, father or uncle. That's just a human endeavor. It's really a question of trying to serve, and that is something that each and every human being can do. For me, it's linked to my coming out of the Christian tradition, you know, "Knowest ye the greatest among you will be your servant." In that regard, it is not salvific at all, but it's certainly one of rendering service, which to me is the finest, the highest, honor that one can have in relationship not just to black people, but human beings as a whole.

Yancy: Speaking of rendering service, Du Bois seems to add a gendered spin on this activity of rendering service in terms of his belief that the Negro race, as he put it then, would be saved by its exceptional *men.*

West: I think that we have to weaken the claim and say that to those to whom much is given, much is required if they are willing to serve. And so those who have had a certain kind of privilege, those who have been able to benefit from the struggles of so many other people, have some obligation and duty to serve others, to make some contribution to a cause much bigger than that of themselves or their own personal careers. I agree with that weaker version. Unfortunately, Du Bois's claim was deeply ensconced within a profoundly elitist conception of culture. He was actually following Matthew Arnold in so many ways. And one has to separate the elitism from the honest acknowledgment that some people have more opportunities than others, some people have more privileges than others. And the question becomes how you use, deploy, those privileges, and how you use your privilege in such a way that it is in some way enhancing and empowering for those who are less privileged than you. Du Bois would agree with the weaker claim and there, I think, we would both be on common ground.

Yancy: Do you see the category of race as the dominating discourse in the United States?

West: Oh, absolutely. Whenever you have a civilization that is shaped by 244 years of chattel slavery, enslavement of African people, and 81 years of Jim Crow, minstrels as the first national pastime, jazz as its highest art form, you can't claim that race has not been a fundamental construct that has shaped how we've gone about making sense of the world. And as constructed as the concept of race is, its effects and consequences through culture have been immense and will continue to be immense far into the twenty-first century.

Yancy: And, of course, you're also pushing for an emphasis on class, yes?

West: You can't talk about the vicious legacy of white supremacy without talking about the legacies of economic inequality, class inequality and also the pernicious practices of male supremacy and heterosexism, homophobia, ecological abuse, losing sight of the humanity of disabled people and so forth. All of these have to be part and parcel of the various evils in American civilization and ultimately, of course, evils in human civilization across the board in modern times.

Yancy: Continuing with this issue of racism, as a postmodernist and historicist you are skeptical of epistemological foundations. Therefore, how do you convince, let's say, a KKK member that his or her respective racist ideology is *false,* that he or she has actually *gotten the world wrong?*

West: I think that your question is a good one, but I'm not sure that I am a postmodernist. I've never really described myself that way. For me, Kierkegaard is about as antifoundationalist as they come, and I would never call him a postmodernist. I would talk about John Dewey in the same way. He is about as antifoundationalist as they come, but I would not call him a postmodernist. I mean, we've got the most thoroughgoing antifoundationalists around and yet they would not be considered postmodernists. And so I'm not so sure that I would want to accept that adjective, though I do recognize that postmodernists do highlight antifoundationalism.

Yancy: But you do embrace a contextualist and revisionist thesis.

West: Absolutely! And I think that this is both Christian, coming out of Pascal and Kierkegaard, and modern, coming out of Dewey and later Wittgenstein. However, I think your question is still a good one. In terms of your question, it would have to do with context, it would have to do with the language of the Ku Klux Klan member to whom I was speaking. When you want to constitute a dialogue with the KKK or whomever, you have got to be able to communicate with them. First, what sort of narratives are they using? Second, how do you engage in immanent critiques of their narratives to get them to see that they're actually involved in a deep contradiction or a major blindness by downplaying certain elements of those narratives and highlighting other elements of those narratives?

Now if the KKK is, as more than likely, Christian, then you've got to wrestle over their understandings, renderings or interpretations of certain Christian narratives and how in fact they become tied to a white-supremacist perspective. We know that modern Christianity is thoroughly shot through with white supremacy like every other institution in modernity early on: science, journalism, right across the board, churches, including mosques, synagogues and so on. White supremacy cuts through, saturates and permeates every institutional nook and cranny of modernity. Hence, how then do you muster resources based on the tradition out of which they come, that serves as the basis for criticizing the white supremacy to which they are captive? It's a question of how you weave narratives and how you reweave them in such a way that a person would be open to a critique of white supremacy.

Now that's just the intellectual level. Then you've got the matter of certain interests. For example, why is it that they're so invested in white supremacy? What are the wages of whiteness that they accrue, given the investment? And that becomes psychocultural and psychosexual and all of these different dimensions: the intellectual, the argument in relation to self-interest, the psychocultural and psychosexual anxieties associated with black bodies or brown bodies or red bodies. All of these elements must go into the conversation if you're trying to convince and persuade a person that he or she is wrong. And at that point I don't think that it's at all a question of epistemic skepticism or epistemic foundationalism. That is just an impoverished way of posing the question, which, unfortunately, tends to be rather typical of many courses in morality. They don't have that thicker historical context as part and parcel of the understanding of moral discourse and ethical exchange. But even after all of this, of course, one may still be unsuccessful.

Yancy: You commented that you would not describe yourself as a postmodernist. Would you elaborate on this?

West: I am first and foremost a modern Christian person of African descent in America trying to love my way through the darkness of an advanced capitalist global system and the thunder of postmodern market-driven culture. The complex interplay of skepticism and hope, doubt and faith—in Pascal, Montaigne, Kierkegaard and Coltrane—is shot through my work. Yet the centrality of compassion and love in my view locks me into premodern figures (like Jesus) and modern writers (like Chekhov and Hardy). *Postmodern* is an adjective that highlights certain features of our culture—it is not a school of thought or descriptive term for a philosophical position. In fact, Pyrrho's skepticism is much more radical than Derrida's—at the existential level, which is where late moderns like me begin and, if possible, linger.

Yancy: Was the New York Society of Black Philosophers instrumental in terms of helping to create a critical mass of African American philosophers?

West: Well, for me, it was crucial. It was monumental in terms of facilitating a context in which persons concerned with philosophical reflections of the black experience, all of whom were not black, though large numbers were, could meet regularly at Al Prettyman's place there in New York. Howard McGary, Lucius Outlaw and many others—I guess it must have been about ten or twelve of us who met there all the time. Actually, David Dinkins [New York City's former mayor] used to stop in every once in a while. He was a friend of Blumsberg's. There was also Frank Kirkland, who came later on, and a host of other people. We gave papers, encouraged reflection, gave each other encouragement and, most importantly, we took each other seriously, which meant giving each and every one of us the benefit of being wrong. That, to me, is probably the most enabling and ennobling form of support one can give another human being, whether an intellectual or not. That's what we were able to do. We really constituted an intellectual neighborhood, a real community of inquirers wrestling with the construct of race to philosophical traditions. And though it is still active, I haven't been part of it for years. However, I can't imagine myself without it.

At the same time, I was part of the *Social Text* collective, Fredric Jameson, Stanley Aronowitz, Rick Wolff, Steve Resnick and others. I was also part of the *Boundary 2* collective, Paul Bové, William Spanos, Joseph Buttigieg, Jonathan Arac, Donald Pease, Margaret Ferguson and others. I was actually lucky to be part of a number of different high-powered, highly engaging, highly challenging subcultures, really, that were far removed from the academy, but were as intellectually challenging as anything in the academy.

Yancy: Out of all of the African American philosophers, you're the most visible.

West: That's true. Well, you know, part of it has to do with the fact that for twenty years I've been lecturing almost 150 times a year. And so I get a chance to meet a lot of people, and a lot of people get to hear me in so many different contexts. One becomes thoroughly multicontextual in terms of one's language, in terms of how one communicates with people. And, of course, there is television, which is another context that really projected my image. I've oftentimes been misunderstood, but that's often the case with television. But I think that the multicontextualism, the traveling, the engagement in so many different milieus more than anything else accounts for my visibility.

Yancy: Before we conclude, briefly talk about how your opinion of Minister Louis Farrakhan has changed since your audience with him.

West: Before I met him, of course, all I knew him by was his own deep commitment to black freedom and his deep love for black people, both of which are expressed within his own very limited vision of how you achieve black freedom. And I never had a chance to sit down with him and break bread. After sitting down and breaking bread and exchanging over time this rather intense dialogue, it was clear to me that he, like any other human being, is open to being convinced, persuaded, and had his own views, arguments, perspectives, etc. And so from the beginning, I approached him as I approach anybody, which is first an act of charity, to see in fact what openness, what positive elements are part of his view where I can resonate with him, and then of course to highlight the negative and highly objectionable ones. But, over time, I've definitely seen a change in him, no doubt about it.

Yancy: What is your overall philosophical project?

West: It's hard to say. I think that fundamentally it has to do with wrestling with the problem of evil in modernity, especially as it relates to people of African descent in particular. And all human beings catch hell in general, but it has very much to do with the dark side, the underside of the human predicament. That's why it cuts across, I think, so many disciplines. How do you preserve some compassion in the face of the absurd, some sense of joy in the face of the nullity and nothingness that characterizes so much of our human endeavors?

Yancy: As an African American intellectual, who is Cornel West?

West: I think that I'm just a brother who comes out of the black church on the block, trying to make sense of the world, and making a blow for freedom in the short time that I'm here, and having fun in the meantime. I would also say that I'm one-half of the person my brother is and one-third of the person my father was, and then hope that I can actually resonate and keep alive in some sense the depths of my mother, and the determination of my sisters!

SOURCE: From *African American Philosophers: 17 Conversations,* edited by George Yancy, pp. 32–48.
Copyright © 1998. Reproduced by permission of Routledge, Inc.

Three

SING A SONG

I returned to Harvard in fall 1975 after finishing my graduate course work and oral exams at Princeton. My former Harvard mentors Martin Kilson and Preston Williams made it possible for me to join the first class of fellows at the W. E. B. Du Bois Institute. I put my dissertation aside and immersed myself in literature. I founded a literary group that read primarily Russian and black classics, and attended courses on American poetry. Later that year, after aborted novels and short stories, I finally wrote and submitted this autobiographical short story. I had hit on the motif of my work to come—to sing in spoken word and written texts like Duke Ellington played and Sarah Vaughan sang, to swing, to create an intellectual performance that had a blues sensibility and jazzlike openness, to have the courage to be myself and find my voice in the world of ideas and in the life of the academy.

For they who fashion songs must live too close to pain,
Acquaint themselves too well with grief and tears;
Must make the slow, deep, throbbing pulse of years
And their own heartbeats one; watch the slow train
Of passing autumns paint their scarlet stain
Upon the hills, and learn that beauty sears,
The whole world's woe and heartbreak must be theirs,
And theirs each vision smashed, each new dream slain.

But sing again, oh you who have heart,
Sweet songs as fragile as a passing breath.
Although your broken heartstrings make your lyre,
And each pure strain must rend the soul apart;
For it was ever thus: to sing is death;
And in your spirit flames your body's pyre.

—FRANK YERBY

I

I love music. I don't think it's in my genes, so it must have something to do with my upbringing.

As a youth, I went to nightclubs every weekend. I never understood the real significance of this weekly routine until I left Harlem.

We moved from our place on Lenox Avenue not long ago. We lived across the street from Harlem Hospital. Over the past months, my hearing has begun to fail me. My wife convinced me that the almost constant sirens of the ambulances weren't helping matters. So we moved out to Queens, nowhere near a hospital. It's a neighborhood without gang fights, shoot-outs, or loud sirens. Better for my eardrums, but the quiet annoys me.

II

One night, while I slept, my hearing failed me for almost thirty minutes. I was furious—and frightened. One whole episode in my dream was like a silent movie. No sound, just body movements.

The next morning, Saturday morning, I made my biweekly trip back to Harlem to Johnny's barbershop. I could see Jackson, Hook and Brother Will through the large front window.

Jackson was an old high-school classmate of mine. Now he has a good job with the city. He drives a garbage truck—and makes almost twice as much money as my wife, who is a nurse.

Hook is a bona fide hustler. He makes money any way he can. And somehow he seems to have a lot of it. I first met Hook two years ago at his brother's service station. His brother was sick at the time, so Hook was managing the station. During the Arab boycott, just when all the other gas stations were raising their prices, Hook started a gas war. His challenge lasted two days. He made a mint during the challenge, though his middlemen cut off his gas supplies after the first day. The next day Hook filled at least forty cars with a mixture of gas, water, Kool-Aid, and any other fluid he could find. My car was one of those forty.

But it worked out well for me. When my car stalled on St. Nicholas Avenue, it was demolished by another car—luckily, I was out of it. So my insurance and I bought a new car. And believe me, the assistance was heaven-sent.

I really do like Hook, even aside from this selfish reason. I like him because of his independence. He listens only to himself. The length of his jail record is the best testimony for that. Hook believes in autonomy. Nobody tells him what to do, be it the police, his wife or his best friend. He's unemployed right now—but living comfortably.

Brother Will is the pastor of Guiding Light Apostolic Church of God in Christ.

My wife tells me that he can drive the devil out of Satan himself by the sheer volume of his voice. I've known Brother Will for over twenty years and still have no desire to hear him preach. I guess I've seen too many of his sermons to take his oral ones seriously. But he's basically a good man, with a quick mind and a quicker eye.

As I entered Johnny's, Brother Will, sitting in the high chair, said loudly, "Ah, look who the wind blew in! That educated sinner, Zek!"

I must explain here that my real name is Ezckiel. Ezekiel Clifton Satterfield. My father gave me this burden-bearing name. I never did like it; sounds too important. So I tell folks to call me Zek. Just Zek.

Johnny exclaimed, "My man Zek, haven't seen ya' in a while! How's life on the island been treatin' ya'?"

"Not too bad, Johnny," I replied, "Cain't complain at all."

Jackson and Hook exchanged similar greetings with me as I took my seat.

I grabbed the *Amsterdam News* and glanced at the headline. It read:

THE DUKE OF MUSIC IS GONE

I yelled, "Duke Ellington, the Duke, died? My Jesus!"

Hook interjected, "Yeah, Zek. The Duke is gone, man. It's a shame."

Johnny mumbled, "Old Duke was the King. Our King. Cool, suave, and always down-to-earth. We seem to be losing all our kings these days."

"Yeh, but is he really the King these days, Johnny?" asked Jackson.

"What'chu mean, man, 'Is he really the King these days'? You know damn well he's the King!" hollered Hook.

"Naw, I ain't sayin' he *ain't* the King. I'm sayin' that young folks today might not think he's the King like we do," retorted Jackson.

"Well, shit. Oh, 'scuse me, Reb. Forget young folks, they ain't got no taste. Their James Brown or Barry White cain't touch the Duke. Damn, don't let me get ta talkin' 'bout the greatness of the Duke 'cause I'll be here all night!" shouted Hook.

"Please watch your tongue," Brother Will remarked. "I cain't stand the truth to be put in such unclean language."

"Glad ya' agree with me, Reb," said Hook, with a smile.

Brother Will continued, "Ya' know, that's what's wrong wit' the church today. The young folk don't 'preciate the music of the past. They always want ta jazz up the spirituals and gospels, like they in some nightclub. I don't mind the guitars, but I cain't stand that fast, funky beat of those boys who play the drums for that youth choir of ours. I truly believe that's the main reason why the Holy Ghost don't come to Guidin' Light as much as it use' ta."

I remained silent. The death of the Duke had shaken me. My head sunk in sadness. My idol had succumbed to Nature. His music from now on would be the spiritual extension of a man now but dust. It frightened me. I was scared of losing my hearing. I realized then the power of music, its sustaining and redeeming power. I wondered whether silence was a kind of death.

Jackson was still defensive. "Just like we think the Duke is King, so my kids think that James Brown or Barry White is King. Who are we to say who's really the King or not? Times change. We got to realize that."

Hook shouted back, "If change means goin' from the Duke to what young folks like, I ain't gon' change! Change ain't just change, Jackson. There's change from bad to good and from good to bad. Ya' gotta take your pick!"

Johnny added in support, "That's right Jackson. Ya' know that the Duke is King. Why make his crown less worthy by lettin' anybody who young folks like wear it?"

"A-m-a-n!" said Brother Will. "That's like lettin' any man be Christ just 'cause some folks say he is the Christ. Ya' see, there's true prophets and false prophets. And ya' know the false ones when ya' see 'em! Just like I know that the true Christians love those old spirituals and gospels and the false ones love that jazzed-up stuff."

"Settle down, Reb, or ya' ain't gon' have no sideburns left. I cain't shape 'em when ya' get excited like that!" cautioned Johnny.

Hook sat back in his chair and said, "Ya' need to stop bendin' the Holy Book your way, Reb. 'Cause singin' or listenin' to the spirituals or gospels ain't never made nobody no true Christian. Christ in the flesh ain't never even heard 'em. I like 'em and I don't even believe in Christ outside the flesh, wit' my hell-bound self. Respectin' good music ain't got nothin' to do wit' no religion. It all comes down to a matter of 'preciation. Young folks don't 'preciate nothin', the spirituals, the Duke, nothin'! They been spoiled rotten. I was down at City College the other day messin' around. I asked this young brotha' what he was studyin' to be. He told me he wasn't even interested in studyin.' He said he was just playin' along with the game. Then I asked him why in the hell he was in college. He said, 'That's your problem, old brotha', you still believe games are played only on these petty streets in Harlem. Well, let me clue you in, these streets have only low-level games, with everything to lose and hardly nothin' to gain. The real games are played on different streets, like Wall Street and Pennsylvania Avenue.' Then I told him, 'Well, since ya' ain't studyin' nothin', it looks like ya' gon' be stayin' here wit' me playin' these low-level games on these petty streets!'"

Hook went on, "I was about to go upside the little bastard's head, but it looked too hard to knock some sense into! Ya' know, he really got me warm! Like I don't know that them big corporations and the government are bloodsuckers. Shit, he ain't never even paid no taxes yet!"

Hook seemed delighted as usual to speak his mind on the young folks issue. His usual diatribe against the young was one form of enjoyment for him. Since his last four-month stint in jail, he frequently would air his hostility toward young folks, especially men under thirty. He complained that they were soft. They had no courage. They succumbed to the wishes of their friends and submitted to the rule of pseudoleaders.

As Brother Will stepped down from the high chair, Johnny said, "Come on, Hook! It's your turn to get your beard trimmed and thank God it didn't rain yesterday on your conk, 'cause I ain't in no mood to cook no hair today!"

When Hook was seated in the high chair, he turned to me and said, "Why ya' so quiet this mornin', Zek? With your educated mind, I'm sure you got somethin' to say 'bout these issues."

I looked at Hook with a friendly frown. I had been following the conversation closely; I also had glanced farther down in the newspaper article and observed that James Brown, Barry White and many others publicly mourned the loss of the "late, great Duke of music."

So I said to Hook, "It's true that young folk don't 'preciate things like we do. I see it in my own Bessie Mae. But there's no clear-cut reason for it. Jackson, you try to understand young folks, but you lose your own views in the process. You act as if their ways are automatically worth endorsin'. As if the mere march of time is the march of truth. Hook, you want everybody to be as independent as you, but don't realize that most folks, young and old, just ain't like that. To be independent is not only to be free, but also lonely. Most folks cain't stand loneliness. Only a select few have the courage to endure such pain. To be independent is to be an outsider. Such persons possibly enrich the lives of others, but they usually live self-destructive lives themselves. To be truly free is to clearly see the true depths of life. This demands that you step to the edge of a slippery cliff. Few avoid fallin' over and the bottom down below has no cushion. I personally—"

"Wait a cotton-pickin' minute, brotha' Zek!" Hook said, politely interrupting me. "I know you're educated and all that. And I respect ya' more for it 'cause you're a self-learnet' man. But at the moment I only wantcha' to answer the questions on the table, Is the Duke really the King for all, young and old? And are young folks soft?"

I continued, "Oh, yeh. Duke is definitely the King. Young folks simply have no one who can compare with him. Just as there is no one today who can compare with Ellison in writin' or Du Bois in learnin'. Ya' see, the young folks today lack discipline—and ain't nothin' worthwhile been produced without discipline. But discipline is based on authority, and what authority is worthy of their loyalty? Corrupt governments, status-ridden churches, the suspicious media, adulterous parents, manipulative peers? To whom or toward what can they turn? Solely to music. So they have turned to music. Music has become the air they breathe, the very sunlight they absorb. They imitate its rhythms in their walk, their talk. Yet they are soft, for they have never really suffered. That's why so much of their music lacks depth."

I stopped and was quiet. I could hear Jackson snoring a bit. He had begun to doze sometime after I separated the march of time from the march of truth. Aside from Jackson, the only noise in the barbershop was the clicking of Johnny's scissors on Hook's mustache. As usual, no one replied. It is assumed, for some odd reason, that I have the last word. I never knew whether this custom arose out of deference or indifference to me. I did know in regard to Jackson, though.

When the time came for me to take my seat in the high chair, Brother Will, Jackson and Hook had left. Two young men entered just as they walked out the door. After my haircut, I paid Johnny and said good-bye. As I was leaving, Johnny scratched his head and said, "I tend to think ya' spoke words of wisdom this mornin', Zek. But if what ya' said is true, then what happens to young folks who can't hear no music? Ya' know, my sister Essie got a pretty little girl who can't hear a word. She's deaf." Johnny looked perplexed and continued, "Well, I guess she probably just reads, writes, or does somethin' else, but don't mind me, Zek. Take it slow, and tell Phyllis I send my hello."

III

Whenever Phyllis stands with her hands on her hips on the front porch looking down the street for my car, I know she's mad. Whenever she decides to attend the Saturday night meeting of the church missionary society, I *know* she's upset.

She greeted me with a medium holler, "Ezekiel, I don't know why we have to go through this every time you go to Johnny's. With all the things that need to be done 'round this house, you go and spend the whole day there! I know all y'all doin' is talkin' trash!"

She became even madder when I didn't get mad.

"Well, I'm goin' to Motha' Hinton's for a missionary society meetin'. Tell Bessie Mae to warm up that chicken in the oven," she said. "And there's some salad in the icebox," she added, in a low and reluctant soft voice.

I knew she was mad, so I just let her release her steam, a technique that has worked well for eighteen married years now. But as she left, I momentarily wondered why she was so upset.

I was really quite hungry, though I hadn't realized it until Phyllis mentioned that chicken in the oven. When I entered the house, Bessie Mae shouted, "Is that you, Dad? I know you must be starvin'. The food will be ready in a minute."

I must explain here that Phyllis and I had a little girl eighteen years ago. I named her Bessie, after my favorite blues singer. Phyllis named her Mary, after her Savior's mother. So we compromised and that's how Bessie Mae got her name.

Bessie Mae's voice was always like music to my ears. Not any particular words, but the soft sweet tone of their sound. The legato style of her expression. The enchanting rhythm of her delivery.

I walked into the kitchen mentally waltzing to syncopated thoughts.

Bessie Mae gave me a big hug and a kiss on the cheek.

I said jokingly, "Since when do I get all this good sugar! You must've broken up with Raymond again, so that now I get all that surplus affection!"

She blushed. "Come on now, Dad, don't play like that. You know I've always been and always will be your Bessie."

Though I could hardly hear her words, I chuckled in reply, "I'm just not used to that much sugar from such a sweet young pretty girl!"

"By the way," she said, "Raymond will be over in a few minutes. He told me this morning he wanted to talk to you about his job."

I would not have heard her remarks about Raymond had she not repeated them when I returned to the kitchen with my high-powered hearing aid.

We sat silently, ate, and watched *The Jeffersons*. In the middle of the program, Bessie turned to me and asked, "Dad, why do you think black folks talk so loud? Not only on TV, but also in real life. We always seem to shout or holler when we speak to one another. Why?"

"It's tension, honey. Nerves. We got a lot of tension to release."

The doorbell rang, and Raymond joined us in the kitchen. After the program, Raymond and I retired to the den. He seemed a bit shy and began to speak in a low tone of voice.

"Mr. Satterfield, I've been wantin' to talk to you for a long time. I told Bessie it had to do with my job, but it's really more than just that."

I interrupted, "You gotta talk a little louder, Raymond. My hearing's been fading on me lately."

"Oh, Okay," replied Raymond. "What I really want to talk about is you. Your life. Ya' see, I ain't never had no man around the house, only women. You're kinda the first man I really respect and look up to. Plus I'm thinkin' 'bout quittin' my job and maybe goin' back to school. And I know you're a man of a lotta education. So first, how'd ya' ever get interested in learnin'?"

"I'm honored that ya' think so highly of me, really 'preciate it, son. To tell ya' the truth, I never got interested in learnin', I just always was interested as far back as I can remember. It's like tryin' to remember your first memory. Ya' see, my father was a Baptist preacher down South for a while, so I had all kinds of religious books around. Since my mother died in childbirth, havin' me that is, it was only me and Pops. After he quit preachin', he came on up to the city and got a job at Penn Station downtown. When he came home from work, he taught me everything he knew. And believe me, that was a lot. We read and talked 'bout every-thing. Oh, how he loved that story about Gilgamesh! Ya' know, his dream was to start a bookstore on 125th Street and Seventh Avenue."

"I guess it never came true," said Raymond, with sympathy.

"Yeah, it was just a fantasy and he knew it. He knew wigs would be more pop-ular than books in Harlem for years to come. He used to always say, with a grin, 'I may be educated, but I ain't no fool!'"

"Why did he quit preachin'?"

"He quit 'cause he thought there was enough preachers around talkin'. He be-lieved God had sent him here to write. Pops thought that some preachers were called by God to speak and others to write. In his last days, he became a kind of self-styled atheist. He said he couldn't believe in a God that only called black preachers to speak and none to write. He came to believe that he could be saved only by leaving volumes of books behind 'im. He longed for immortality, but only in the form of the written word."

A beam of puzzling dismay flashed across Raymond's face. He asked, "What did he write?"

"Nothin'," I softly replied. "Not a word. He died an alcoholic, distressed over his failure to gain his salvation. Ya' know, Pops could really speak, he was an ab-solute master of the spoken word. But for some odd reason he hated his gift. He thought God had called him for another mission, a mission for which he had no gift."

"Do you have this gift, Mr. Satterfield?"

"I'm not really sure. But let's not call it a gift. It's really a capacity. Ya' see, that's where I think Pops was wrong. He had a gift for speaking, it came natural. It flowed like water from a faucet. But writin' ain't no gift, it's a capacity. It takes time and long, lonely hours to develop this capacity. Pops couldn't accept this, and that's what killed him in a sense. He hated solitude and silence, but that's what you need to develop the capacity of writin'."

"Did you ever preach?" Raymond asked.

"Naw, naw. I'm not a religious person, though I value what religious folks are searchin' for. What they and Pops try to find in religion, I find in music."

"Oh, so you're a musician or composer?"

"Yeah, I guess you can say that. But I've become one only within the past few weeks. That's when I began to write. Ya' see, I believe writin' is a kind of music composed for those who no longer hear the sweet music of persons, for those who live in silence. I write in order to sing for those who live in this silence."

We heard a loud door slam in the next room.

"Bessie Mae, Ezekiel, where are you two?" called out Phyllis, as she entered the house out of breath.

"Dad is talkin' to Raymond in the den. I'm here in the kitchen watchin' TV,

Momma," Bessie called back.

"Ya' know, Raymond," I said, "I don't know how we got on this tangent 'bout Pops, but let's drop it and talk for a moment 'bout your future plans. Ya' say ya' might go back to school?"

"I'm really not sure, Mr. Satterfield. But I am sure that I want to be respected in the community as an educated man, somethin' like yourself. Everybody wants to be respected for somethin'. Folks in Harlem are respected for havin' fine women and cars, for bein' a good musician or athlete. I'd like to be respected for my learnin'."

"Oh, I see. Ya' really want praise and fame. Ain't nothin' wrong with praise and fame if ya' can find what ya' really need to enjoy 'em. And what ya' really need to enjoy 'em is peace of mind. Without peace of mind, ain't nothin' worth nothin'! Ya' have peace of mind when ya' have what ya' really need to enjoy what ya' really want, even if ya' never get what'chu really want. And peace of mind ain't nothin' but being in harmony with yourself and others, like harmonious notes in a melody."

Phyllis knocked on the door and whispered softly, "Ezekiel, it's almost ten o'clock."

"Thanks, darlin'. I 'preciate your concern—for your daughter," I replied, saying the last phrase under my breath.

"I really should be goin', Mr. Satterfield. I enjoyed it, believe me," said Raymond, humbly and with appreciation.

He and I went into the kitchen. Bessie and Phyllis were watching TV. Phyllis still seemed a bit upset, though no longer mad. So I planted a juicy kiss on her big brown check. Just as I began to relay to her Johnny's hello, the phone rang.

IV

"Brotha' Zek," said Hook, "they're havin' a special tribute to the Duke tonight down at Sam's club. Some of the best jazz and blues singers in the country gon' jam there tonight. Like Count Basie, Lionel Hampton, Billy Eckstine, Sarah Vaughan, Nancy Wilson. All the stars, man. Why don't ya' meet me down there and we can pay our respects to the King together."

"Um . . . it does sound like it's gon' be quite a tribute. All those big folk gon' be at Sam's?"

"Yeh, man. It's a special Harlem tribute to the Duke. It's a private community tribute before the press and media make their big splash at Carnegie Hall on Monday."

"All right, I'll meet'cha there, Hook."

"Where ya' goin' this time of night, Ezekiel?" asked Phyllis.

"Darlin', there's a special tribute to Duke Ellington tonight down at Sam's. You know how I idolized the Duke and all. So I thought I'd go pay my respects."

"'Pay your respects'? At a nightclub? How can you pay your respects in a worldly nightclub to someone whose soul is now being judged? I tell ya', I've been married to ya' for eighteen long years and I don't understand your ways any more now than I did when we first got married!" she exclaimed.

"I should be back around three or so. There's quite a slate of performers, like Eckstine, Vaughan, Basie. . . ."

"Ezekiel, you watch yourself now," she said, with a worried voice. "I've been feelin' funny 'bout 'cha since last night when ya' kept singin' that verse of Bessie Mae's record over and over in your sleep.

> *Wake up ev'ybody, 'no more sleepin' in bed*
> *No more backward thinkin', time for thinkin' ahead*

You must have said those lines at least ten times last night. You seemed either to be dream singin' or just unable to hear your own voice. I told ya' to hush three times but ya' totally ignored me. I figured somethin' was wrong and I've been prayin' hard ever since."

"Don't worry, darlin'. That episode last night was a fluke. But I sure love ya' for lovin' me so much. I could never do without your love and prayers."

I bent down and gave her a sentimental kiss. I then walked slowly into the bedroom. I was frightened at her revelation, but I knew my false lack of concern would calm her down.

I had trouble choosing the appropriate clothes to wear to Sam's club. I hadn't gone to a nightclub since my youth. My slacks were all cuffed. I was pretty sure the fashion had changed from cuffed to uncuffed to bell-bottom cuffed. Well, at least I would be a little in style with my cuffs. My shirts were all right. But my ties were ridiculous. They were all as thin as licorice and as wrinkled as leprous skin. Even an iron was useless. So I threw on my old navy-blue sports coat over a purple turtleneck, slipped into my black pimp socks, the only stylish part of my outfit, tied my brown side-winding shoes and put on my dark hat. I was sharp! Or at least felt so. And isn't feeling so what it's really all about?

V

I jumped into my car and headed toward the Harlem River. I love to drive along the Harlem River, down Harlem River Drive, just to see the calmness of the water. As I approached the river, I could see the glistening ripples of the strong current. Suddenly I realized I was still wearing my high-powered hearing aid. For a moment, I decided to stop and take it off. But I changed my mind. Since I wasn't going to the club to impress some beautiful young lady with my sexy ear and since I wanted to hear the music of the great stars, I decided to keep it on. I took one last look at the river, then went directly to the club.

I parked on 138th Street across from Harlem Hospital and a few blocks down from Sam's club. After locking the car, I pulled out the only relic of my youthful nightclub days, my old mauve-colored shades. I must have looked like a clown walking down the street with those shades and my outdated clothes. I did hear a few brothers and sisters giggle as I passed. But it was a giggle of acceptance and accommodation.

As I drew closer to the club, I could hear the syncopated beat of the drums and the up-tempo of the guitar from the music inside. At the door of the club, the collective chant of the dancers inside resounded in my ears.

> *It ain't what'cha know,*
> *It's how ya' feel!*
> *Don't worry 'bout being right,*
> *Just be fa' real!*

Before entering, I noticed a sign on the door. It read:

> *For those who want to groove*
> *We got the music that moves and soothes!*

At the door I was told the entertainment tonight was downstairs. On the way down the steep stairs leading to the dance floor, I wondered whether the tribute was over, or if it just had not yet begun.

The stairway was lined with curvaceous females, consciously and unconsciously soliciting lustful male glances. Young men, sporting the latest fashions and conked hair, posed as if for portraits, their Kools dangling from their mouths. They stood staidly, partly blocking the stairway.

As I worked my way past the line of women, I overheard a cute swarthy young lady whisper to her friend, "Look at this old dude—he's as cool as he wants to be, with his old-time rags and purple shades!"

Her friend giggled.

But from behind, I heard a familiar voice exclaim, "This brotha' is sho'nuff sharp tonight! Good to see ya' made it, Brotha' Zek!"

It was Hook. We greeted each other with a rhythmic handshake.

"Come on, Zek. Let's push our way through this crowd and pay our respects to the Duke!"

As we forged ahead, Hook looked around and said, "I bet we're the only ones here who can really 'preciate the Duke like he should be 'preciated."

By the time we reached the lower level, I had begun to believe him. There were no pictures of the Duke, no signs of the tribute, and definitely no jazz band or blues singers providing the music. It was undeniably a disco party.

I asked the bouncer whether there was to be a tribute for Duke Ellington. He replied indeed there was. Tomorrow night. I turned and stared at Hook.

"That damn Jackson told me it was tonight!"

I said to myself, "Where the hell is Jackson? I see he's not around." I thought of turning back, but the ensuing uphill battle discouraged me. I figured it would be easier to pay, have a quick drink, and exit through one of the doors from the lower-level room. So I paid and went in. Hook followed, but I sensed that our companionship for the night was over. He went his way and I went mine.

The murky room was jam-packed. The music was loud yet overshadowed by vociferous outcries and visceral shouts. Many of the dancers blew whistles which sounded like small sirens. The clamorous crowd began to dance around in a ring and chant in cadence with the offbeat,

> *Shit!*
> *Got-damn!*
> *Get off your ass and jam!*

The chant was ironic; there was no room to sit anywhere.

People of all sizes and shades of the Negroid spectrum filled the misty, sweltering room. Flashing fluorescent multicolored lights shone just bright enough to see who was wearing what and who was with whom. The floor was filled with banana-skin females dancing with jet black men and chocolate-colored women dancing with paperbag-brown males.

The weekly routine of my youth had really not changed for these young people—or Hook, for that matter. The Party still revolved exclusively around music. It was still a release of tension, of nerves. A kind of cathartic ritual, the Party still served as a comforting place of retreat, a precious secular sanctuary in which to lay one's burdens down. It remained a kind of homecoming for people chasing after the carnal grail.

Watching the vivacious dancers, I could see my former Self. There I was, finger-popping and ass-twitching. But I also could see me now through my former Self. There I was, wall-flowering and analyzing.

But just then the cute swarthy young lady asked me to dance. I was delighted. I did the "Popcorn," a dance Bessie had taught me a few years ago. The young lady did something else. But my backwardness was unimportant. We were both having great fun. I felt so good and even racially proud as I watched this young lady move. You should have seen her! She was so enchanting, so masterful in her movements, so graceful in her steps, so sexy with her hands.

Gradually I began to notice smoke coming from the room above. The disc jockey turned the music up full blast to combat loud sirens outside and the small sirens inside. But the dancers seemed to take little notice of the smoke.

They began to stomp on the floor and shout,

> *We gonna turn this motha' out!*
> *We gonna turn this motha' out!*

The collective chant must have sounded like voices singing out of empty cisterns and exhausted wells. I'll never know. I could no longer listen.

The louder they shouted, the less I heard. The less I heard, the more pain I felt. And the deeper the pain, the more I could see. Clearly see.

VI

I saw a dark, somber light in the midst of the fire-covered Party. Live corpses fell to the ground and stretched their hands toward the dark light.

I said to the corpses, though I did not hear it, "Why persecutest thou thyselves so?"

They could not feel the grief in my heart or see the tears in my eyes. My words made them tremble.

When I looked closer, I could see female apparitions resembling fading petals on a fiery bough of darkness, gasping for breath in time with the fast, funky beat of male drummers. The drummers were blind. They could not see the ghastly dancers or their gasps of exhaustion. They beat the drums with dry human bones, as the sultry faces of the women ghosts became covered with perspiration of blood. Yet the ghosts continued to dance and pointed to a crude poster hanging over the drummers. It read:

> *Party! We don't need no music!*
> *Party! We got soul!*

The apparitions had visible shadows of luscious female bodies. The few yolk-colored bodies stood out clearest under the dark, somber light. My mauve-colored shades allowed me to detect this. I also noticed that the shadows of the male drummers had no necks. There was no link between their bodies and their heads.

VII

Hook never did attend the special tribute for the Duke at Sam's. Nor did Sam's ever hold the special tribute for the Duke. Most of the club burned down that April night. Hook was one of the many fatalities. It must have been one of Phyllis's prayers that spared me a similar fate.

But I am in Harlem Hospital, partially burned and permanently deaf. I no longer can hear loud sirens, or Bessie's pleasant voice, or Duke's melodies. Yet I love music more than ever. In fact, now I sing.

SOURCE: "Epilogue: Sing a Song," *Prophetic Fragments* (Grand Rapids, Mich.: Wm. B. Eerdmans Publishing Co., 1988), pp. 281–294. Originally appeared in the black student journal of Williams College in 1982.

PART TWO

MODERNITY AND ITS DISCONTENTS

My work is shaped by an obsession with modernity and the problem of evil. In fact, the major blindness in my writings may well be my relative neglect of premodern contexts. Yet since historical consciousness is a preoccupation of modern thinkers, I do give some attention to premodern realities that help illuminate the human doings and sufferings in modernity. In stark contrast to my Afrocentric friends (whose focus on Africa's grand achievements warrants serious attention), I have remained committed to exploring the legacies of Athens and Jerusalem, the two fundamental pillars of modernity. Classical antiquity—Homeric epics, Socratic elenchus, Platonic dialogues, Aristotelian exegesis and above all the tragedians and comic artists—has disproportionately shaped our modern sensibilities. The heritages of Judaism, Christianity and Islam provide the other foundational background for modernity.

Four

THE IGNOBLE PARADOX OF MODERNITY

This brief piece served as the foreword for the Spirits of the Passage exhibition of the earliest slave ship ever recovered, the Henrietta Marie. *Sponsored by the Mel Fisher Maritime Heritage Society, this exhibition brought to national consciousness the international slave trade. We rarely view modernity through the lens of the enslaved and their descendants—yet we fail to do so at our peril.*

THE SPIRITUAL STRIVINGS OF New World Africans began on the treacherous voyages of the transatlantic slave trade. These Dantesque journeys were the ignoble origins of Western modernity and the criminal foundations of American democracy. They constituted the *night* side of the Age of Enlightenment, the reality left unlit by the torch of natural reason. African slavery sits at the center of the grand epoch of equality, liberty and fraternity, a center often concealed by modern myths of progress and liberation. And black doings and sufferings remain burdened by the unspeakable memories of the Middle Passage—the chamber of horrors enacted on slave ships like the *Henrietta Marie*.

Like other indescribable evils of the recent past, the centuries-long slave trade forces us to wrestle with levels of unjustified anguish and unmerited pain that are difficult to fathom. Most of us would prefer to turn our heads and hearts from this ghastly past and dream of a better future. Yet the pernicious effects and insidious consequences of New World slavery still linger in our perceptions and inform our sensibilities in regard to black people. The vicious legacy of institutionalized hatred of Africans is still with us (even if its raw forms are a bit out of fashion at the moment).

Slavery is nearly as old as human civilization itself, but when the *Henrietta Marie* first landed in Barbados on July 9, 1698, with 250 Africans aboard, the construct of "race" was hardly formulated. The African slave trade was sustained by profit-hungry elites of all kinds: Christian, Muslim, Jewish, European, Arab, African and American. Yet the distinctive feature of New World slavery was its "racial" character. After a few decades of transracial slavery—in which whites, blacks and reds were owned by whites—this ancient form of subjugation became an exclusively black and white affair. This racialization of American slavery was rooted in economic calculations and psychocultural anxieties that targeted black bodies.

Thus, the profitable sugar, tobacco and cotton plantations of the New World were housed and husbanded by African labor, with the result that African men, women and children defined the boundaries of European culture and civilization.

In fact, the human family was carved into modern "racial" pigeonholes—white, black, red, brown, yellow—in order to control, confine, discipline and dishonor Africans. Racialized persons and racist practices were systematized and canonized principally owing to the financial interests and psychic needs that sustained the slave trade and New World slavery. The fundamental meaning of this white-supremacist ideology is this: New World Africans enter European modernity cast as disposable pieces of property, as commodifiable bits of chattel slavery subject to arbitrary acts of violent punishment and vicious put-down. In short, legalized terror and institutionalized hatred, in the name of white supremacy and Western progress, rendered black peoples economically exploited, politically oppressed and culturally degraded.

As Orlando Patterson noted in his magisterial work *Slavery and Social Death,* enslaved Africans experienced social annihilation. With no legal status, social standing or public worth—indeed, no foothold in the human family—black people were natally alienated; that is, they had no claim to any of the rights that signified equality, liberty or fraternity in European modernity. This meant, in part, that the glorious revolutions of 1776 in North America and 1789 in France were rooted in and based on the economic profits and psychic wages extracted from enslaved Africans. White supremacy is an integral component of European progress, with the evil of African slavery a precondition of progressive breakthroughs in the modern world.

The great paradox of Western modernity is that democracy flourished for Europeans, especially men of property, alongside the flowering of the transatlantic slave trade and New World slavery. Global capitalism and nascent nationalisms were predicated initially on terrors and horrors visited on enslaved Africans on the way to, or in, the New World. This tragic springboard of modernity, in which good and evil are inextricably interlocked, still plagues us. The repercussions and ramifications of this paradox still confine and circumscribe us—in our fantasies and dreams, our perceptions and practices—in these catastrophic times.

Yet the "natural" state of American society is to deny this paradox and downplay the grave consequences of its past and present reality. Instead, race is reduced to specks on our cultural lens to be cleansed in order to be "color-blind" (after more than three centuries of African slavery and seventy years of Jim Crow). Or it is recast as ethnicity, so that we all become immigrants who rejoiced upon landing in America (even if black people's right to vote was delayed for nearly two hundred years after 1776). In other words, America's historical amnesia about black humiliation and black suffering is seen as a basic prerequisite for a better

American future of racial harmony. Yet history—the past as history and the present as history—will not let us off so easily. The lofty claims of American exceptionalism that hold this country to be somehow outside the iron laws of history ring now more hollow than ever. No civilization fails to reap what it sows. No nation escapes the poison of its ignoble paradox.

The first death knell was heard in the barbaric Civil War, in which over 600,000 human beings died by murder or disease. In this instance, the poison returned with a vengeance. And although the Abraham Lincoln–led Union won the war, the white-supremacist South won the peace—after a grand but brief interlude of multiracial democratic experimentation. The second death knell was sounded in the turbulent 1960s, during which over 330 uprisings in 257 cities shook the foundations of American society. And although the Martin Luther King–led black freedom movement won precious civil and voting rights, conservative elites triumphed in the economic sphere. Hence joblessness and job ceilings still constrained most black Americans. Presently, the racially coded discourses about welfare reform, affirmative action, public schools, public health care, prisons, criminal punishment, suburbanization and immigration still bespeak the weight of the paradox.

The great irony of black striving in America is that the ignoble paradox of modernity has yielded deep black allegiance to the promises of American democracy. The primeval screams and silent tears of enslaved Africans, the victims of American democracy, have been transfigured into the complex art of jazz, the most democratic of art forms. The terrors and horrors of black life have been fought against in the name of a fairer and freer American democracy. The best of the black freedom struggle—men and women like Ida B. Wells-Barnett, A. Philip Randolph, Fannie Lou Hamer and Martin Luther King, Jr.—has been America at its best. And yet the promises of American democracy, under the gravity of its underlying paradox, remain unfulfilled for most black people in America.

In this sense, the horrible realities and unbearable memories evoked by the *Henrietta Marie* still haunt us. The American government—the mouthpiece of the American people—has not yet even acknowledged the impact of slavery on the present. It has erected no monuments, admitted no memory, made no reparations, accepted no responsibility for the lives lost, wasted and stunted by the ugly legacy symbolized by the *Henrietta Marie*. The dominant American tradition of myopic denial, evasion and avoidance of its root paradox still encourages us to turn our backs on the spirits of the Africans who suffered, unacknowledged, during and after the Middle Passage—and on the spirits of their descendants.

Thomas Jefferson trembled when he reflected on the price America may pay for its denial. Herman Melville wrote with heartfelt fear about the consequences in *Benito Cereno*. And Toni Morrison laid bare the human costs—for all of us—in

Beloved. Can we, as a people and as individuals, muster the vision and courage to grapple honestly with this ignoble paradox of American democracy before we become as shipwrecked as the *Henrietta Marie,* overcome by lashing winds and rain in the deadly Florida straits, caught between the Dry Tortugas and the Marquesas Keys?

SOURCE: "The Ignoble Paradox of Western Modernity," Foreword from *Spirits of the Passage: The Transatlantic Slave Trade in the Seventeenth Century,* by Madeleine Burnside, edited by Rosemarie Robotham (New York: Simon & Schuster, 1997), pp. 8–10.

Five

RACE AND MODERNITY

Of all my books, Prophesy Deliverance! *remains my favorite. Written in my twenties, the work of a young writer trying to catch a vast array of fish with a variety of conceptual nets, it is wide-ranging, political and outrageously ambitious. I could not have written it anywhere but at Union Theological Seminary in New York City. The influence of my late friend and brother Professor James Melvin Washington is pervasive. My debts to the theology of Professor James Cone, the ethics of Professor Beverly Harrison and the wisdom of Professor James Forbes, Jr., are deep. The impact of Foucault in light of dialogue with my brothers Professors Edward Said and Paul Bové at Columbia and especially Professor Stanley Aronowitz (then) at Columbia is immense. The intellectual ferment in New York in those days is worth a memoir! How wonderfully intense it was!*

AMERICAN AFRICANS IN CONFLICT: ALIENATION IN AN INSECURE CULTURE

MODERNITY, COLONIAL PROVINCIALITY, LOCALISM

The Age of Enlightenment, from 1688 to 1789—roughly from the Glorious Revolution in England to the tumultuous French Revolution—constitutes the emergence of European modernity.[1] This occurred within an embryonic capitalist global economy that supported absolutist monarchies. It throve, mostly because of black slavery in the Western Hemisphere and the exploitation of working men, women and children in the rural household industry of western Europe. The most populous European country, France, was the chief industrial center. Holland, especially the vivacious city of Amsterdam, maintained its two-century dominance in commerce and shipping as the major financial center in Europe.

The basic features of early modern European culture were the increasing acceptance of the authority of science, the appearance of a new kind of pagan neoclassicism and the subjectivist turn in philosophy. The intellectual defense and institutional support of the practices of scientists became more and more persuasive to the literate population. These practices were guided by an adherence to a new paradigm of knowledge, an experimental method that attempted to test hypotheses and yield objective conclusions by appealing to evidence and observation. The increasing acceptance of the authority of science resulted in assaults on the authority of the church and on its theology and religious practices.

This Enlightenment revolt against the prestige of the church was part of a search for models of uncensored criticism. It led to a recovery of classical antiquity and especially a deep appreciation and appropriation of the artistic and cultural heritage of ancient Greece. This classical revival—or neoclassical movement in eighteenth-century Europe—was partly the result of a four-hundred-year European love affair with Greece and Rome. This affair began in the Early Renaissance (1300–1500), intensified in the High Renaissance (1500–1530), cooled in the Mannerist era (1530–1600) and appeared again in full force during the Baroque period (1600–1750). In short, early modern European culture promoted a new, modern type of paganism.

The emergence of European modernity also witnessed a subjectivist turn in philosophy. This quest, initiated by Descartes, gave first place to concepts of the subject, the ego or the self and preeminence to the notion of representative knowledge. The subject, ego or self constituted the starting point for philosophical inquiry, and mental representations by the subject, ego or self supplied the principal means for subjects to make contact with objects, ideas to copy things or concepts to correspond to the external world. Philosophy became the queen of the emerging scientific disciplines within this new paradigm as a metadiscipline that provided objective and valid grounds for knowledge claims put forward in the newer disciplines, especially physics. This turn in philosophy granted science a monopoly on truth in the marketplace of ideas, to the dismay of both artists and theologians. As Hans-Georg Gadamer has noted in our own time, this monopoly on truth entails a prejudice against prejudice, a supposed transcendence of prejudice through objectivity.

Immanuel Kant deepened Descartes's subjectivism by erecting new formal foundations upon a transcendental subject, which constitutes an objective world by means of a universal conceptual scheme. In one grand stroke, he thus legitimated Newtonian science, vindicated Protestant morality and set art in a realm of its own. The ultimate consequence of this architectonic endeavor was to isolate early modern European culture into separate spheres of goodness, truth and beauty—and morality, science and art—reinforcing meanwhile the role of philosophy as a tribunal of pure reason for the claims of culture.

Between 1776 and 1782 texts appeared and events occurred that were representative of this early modern period. These included Adam Smith's *The Wealth of Nations* (1776), Edward Gibbon's *The History of the Decline and Fall of the Roman Empire* (1776), the American Revolution (1776), David Hume's *Dialogues Concerning Natural Religion* (1779), Gotthold Lessing's *Nathan the Wise* (1779), Immanuel Kant's *Critique of Pure Reason* (1781) and the first part of Jean Jacques Rousseau's *Confes-*

sions (1781). In these are the intellectual agenda of the period: the rise of the bourgeois capitalist order, the struggle between Christianity and neoclassical paganism, the widening gaps between philosophy, ethics and art and the increasing alienation of the individual.

The end of this period was marked by the birth of the United States, the first new nation, through a colonial, not a social revolution. After a century and a half of the reconciling of self-imposed exile with a well-developed European social and political consciousness, the problem of provinciality had become central in the development of American culture.[2] It resulted primarily from the geographical displacement of European peoples from that European civilization whose superiority they openly acknowledged. Adding to this, an antagonism to the indigenous American peoples and an unwillingness to mingle with unchristian African slaves created an alienated, intensely self-conscious and deeply anxiety-ridden society.

The first stage of American culture was thus saturated with colonial provinciality. The first Americans looked to their parent civilization for intellectual and cultural resources, applying these to very un-European conditions principally by means of crude imitation. The most provocative commentators on the problematic of provinciality in American culture have been Alexis de Tocqueville, George Santayana and Van Wyck Brooks.[3] In de Tocqueville's view, American culture smothered intellectual life in pursuit of democracy and equality, thereby vitiating the aristocratic requisites for cultural vitality. To Santayana, the agonized conscience of Calvinism and the metaphysical comfort of transcendentalism weighted like a genteel incubus upon the American mind, partly explaining the odd American juxtaposition of intellectual conservatism with technological inventiveness. For Van Wyck Brooks, American vacillation between Puritan purity and vulgar materialism, echoing William James's "angelic impulses" and "predatory lusts," fragmented the intellectual tradition and generated an unrestrained quest for wealth.[4]

Colonial provinciality reached its zenith in the first major figure of the Genteel tradition, Jonathan Edwards. The most profound of European-American thinkers, he constructed his defense of Calvinism from a sophisticated blend of the empiricism of Locke, the determinism of Newton and the idealism of Plato.

Edwards's valorizing of Newton bespoke his attitude toward the authority of science, an attitude close to that of his own lesser contemporary and rival, Cadwallader Colden.[5] Yet Edwards distinguished the domain of science from the special arena of religious knowledge, the intuitive realm where the sixth sense, that of the heart, reserved for the elect, reigns. His fierce struggle against the voluntaristic Arminians likewise defended complex versions of original sin and predestination familiar from European Calvinism.

The Enlightenment left a comparable European stamp on the area of political thought. Jefferson's doctrine of natural rights and theory of moral sentiments revealed his debts both to classical antiquity and to Locke, Shaftesbury and Frances Hutchinson.[6] The anticlericalism of Thomas Paine, and its concomitant defense of the freedom of conscience and speech, further exemplified the critical spirit of the European Enlightenment in America. Lastly, the radical environmentalism of Benjamin Rush and his humanitarian advocacy of the abolition of slavery and the rehabilitation of criminals revealed an Enlightenment belief in the unlimited possibilities of individuals in society when guided by reason.

American culture during the provincial period culminated in the Calvinist pietism, Enlightenment rationalism and liberal republicanism of William Ellery Channing.[7] The vernal American Schleiermacher, Channing is the pivotal figure of the Genteel tradition in its transition from Calvinism to transcendentalism, at the turning point between the colonial provinciality and the postcolonial provinciality in American culture. His revolutionary humanitarianism, bordering on utopian socialism, condemned slavery, bigotry and pagan worldliness. He proposed to overcome these through Christian pietism, moral use of scientific knowledge and the perfection of human nature through self-realization in democratic communities.

Channing's humanitarianism unfortunately did not serve either as guide or as norm for American practice toward Africans during the provincial period. The non-Christianity and black skin color of the dark pagan peoples threatened the self-identity of Puritan colonists inextricably bound to Christianity.[8] Since the absence of or even novel interpretation of Christian beliefs could often bring about mistreatment or banishment, the growing idea of white supremacy legitimated still harsher treatment for Africans.

In *The Souls of Black Folk* (1903), W. E. B. Du Bois eloquently described a double consciousness in black Americans, a dual lens through which they saw themselves.[9] For Du Bois, the dialectic of black self-recognition oscillated between being *in* America but not *of* it, from being black natives to black aliens. Yet Du Bois overlooked the broader dialectic of being American yet feeling European, of being provincial but yearning for British cosmopolitanism, of being at once incompletely civilized and materially prosperous, a genteel Brahmin amid uncouth conditions. Black Americans labored rather under the burden of a triple crisis of self-recognition. Their cultural predicament was composed of African appearance and unconscious cultural mores, involuntary displacement to America without American status, and American alienation from the European ethos complicated through domination by incompletely European Americans.

This predicament was qualitatively different from that of other Africans in the diaspora, in the Caribbean, Canada and Central and South America. Africans in the United States confronted a dominant Protestant European population whose own self-identity suffered from an anxiety-ridden provinciality. The black American struggle for self-identity has always contributed constructively to the American struggle for self-identity, though the latter has only exacerbated and complicated it in return.

During the colonial provincial stage of American culture, Africans were worse than slaves; they were also denuded proto-Americans in search of identity, systematically stripped of their African heritage and effectively and intentionally excluded from American culture and its roots in European modernity. Their search for identity focused principally on indigenous African practices, rituals, religions and worldviews they had somehow retained.[10]

The process of cultural syncretism that combined indigenous African practices and provincial American culture generated a unique variant of American life, one far removed from, yet still tied to, European modernity. Added ingredients in this were the distinctly antimodern values and sensibilities of the southern United States, the geographic cradle of black America.

The first stage of African practice in America was neither barbarian nor provincial. Africans valued human life and sustained in their alien environment a religious cosmology that gave meaning to human existence. And it was not provincial, because it worshiped neither at the altar of British nor at the altar of American cultural superiority. Black people were relatively uninformed about British culture and not yet fully American. More pointedly, they had not yet arrived at a synthetic Afro-American identity.

THE HEYDAY OF MODERNITY, POSTCOLONIAL PROVINCIALITY, CHRISTIAN PRACTICES

The heyday of modernity, the golden age of the modern period, fell roughly between 1789 and 1871—that is, from the French Revolution to the unification of the German empire. During it, early modern European culture took root and flowered in the authority of science, in modern paganism and in the historicizing of philosophical subjectivism. The industrializing capitalist world order consolidated at this time, and nation-states emerged, both phenomena enjoying the confidence of the new bourgeoisie. The dominated classes—factory workers and the rural labor force—began to grumble, but since they had limited organization and vision, this yielded minimal results.

This was, above all, the German Age, and the year 1807 alone witnessed the completion of Hegel's *The Phenomenology of Spirit,* Goethe's *Faust,* Part I, and Beethoven's Fifth Symphony.

Yet despite the romantic reply to the bland universality, glib generality and monotonous uniformity of the Enlightenment, the authority of science emerged with flying colors. Romanticism attacked scientific arrogance and pretense, yet the brunt of its assault fell not on science per se, but rather on the crudely mechanistic model of Newton's popular imitators. The conceptions of the mind and the world characteristic of this model repelled the Romantics. Disgusted with superficial distinctions, they relegated the dissective power of the mind to the understanding *(Verstand)* and its integrative activities to reason *(Vernunft),* replacing mechanistic models with organic ones.[11]

The Romantics venerated a reason very different from that of the Enlightenment, which appealed ultimately to the experimental method and aimed to keep the imagination at bay. Romantic reason, on the other hand, is the epitome of a free creative imagination transcending the limits of the world of sense.

The Romantic movement, the golden age of European modernity, conveyed a sense of novelty.[12] The French Revolution, which in one stroke replaced feudal institutions with bourgeois capitalism, embodied the possibilities of social reconstruction and revolutionary transformation. The European exploration of other cultures and societies likewise buttressed curiosity about the unknown and brought to light distinctive features of its own emerging constituent national cultures. Lastly, widespread technological innovation and the increase of wealth in the early stages of the Industrial Revolution reinforced belief in the capacity of humankind to master nature and enjoy its fruits.

With Napoleon, the Romantic dream of transforming the social order mellowed to temperate efforts at self-realization.[13] The fascination with exotic and primitive peoples illustrated by the popular myth of the noble savage persisted, yet it soon revealed the repressive imperialist regimes that often evolve in interaction with foreigners. The tremendous energies generated by the early Industrial Revolution continued, but alienations and the formation of new class antagonisms revealed unforeseen instabilities in bourgeois capitalism.

Hegel's historicizing of subjectivism cast would-be academic philosophers into the social, political and cultural struggles of the period. His grand project took, in some sense, however, the form of a Christian Christology gone mad. In place of Kant's presupposed subject of knowledge, Hegel put a transindividual subject that externalized itself in the world and progressively evolved within it in a dialectical fashion. This development can be discerned, of course, only by the most adroit philosopher, namely, Hegel himself. This development is simultaneously the freedom march of humankind and the progressive self-consciousness of that transindividual subject, what Hegel called the *Weltgeist,* or World Spirit.

The year 1859 was momentous for cultural works that portrayed the central themes and concerns of the golden age: Darwin's *The Origin of the Species,* Mill's *On Liberty,* Marx's *Critique of Political Economy,* Wagner's *Tristan und Isolde,* George Eliot's *Adam Bede,* Dickens's *A Tale of Two Cities,* Meredith's *The Ordeal of Richard Feverel,* Tennyson's *The Idylls of the King,* FitzGerald's *Rubaiyat of Omar Khayyam* and Turgenev's *A Nest of Gentlefolk.* The dominant themes and concerns in these are the historical and evolutionary character of human existence, the scope of freedom and democracy in the prevailing order and the emerging sentiments of European nationalism and of racism and sexism.

European hegemony over the life of the mind proved to be a major preoccupation of American culture during its provincial period. American artists and writers strove consciously to establish an autonomous national culture no longer dependent on that of Europe. American ought to sing its own songs, write its own poems, novels and philosophy. America must look deep down within itself without using the lens of the parent civilization to do so.

The most important product of this self-absorptive mood in America was Ralph Waldo Emerson. In his famous lecture of 1837, "The American Scholar," Emerson portrayed Europe as the symbol of the dead past. The present task of American thinkers was to liberate themselves from slavish dependence on Europe. His message of self-reliance was not merely a reflection of a democratic and intuitive philosophy or a Jeffersonian vision of the self-sufficient yeoman farmer, but an attack on the prevailing provincialism of America in his day. Of course, without the idealism of Plato, the natural-law theory of the Stoics and the romanticism of Coleridge and Carlyle, there was little of intellectual substance left to "the sage of Concord," save his energetic spirit, charismatic style and piercing wit. The postcolonial agenda of American culture called for homespun originality and indigenous inventiveness, despite the eclecticism and pretense this might entail.

Eclecticism and pretentiousness mark the most significant literary products of the American renaissance, as seen in the major works of Edgar Allan Poe, James Fenimore Cooper, Walt Whitman, Nathaniel Hawthorne, Herman Melville, Emily Dickinson and Henry David Thoreau.[14] It is not that the works are artistic failures, but rather that they are products of a culture under the grip of provincialism, of a culture proud yet not solidified, boastful but not self-confident, eager to flex its muscles but without agile flexibility.

Edgar Allan Poe, for example, with his English childhood and Parisian sensibilities, cared neither to imitate English literary models nor to write an authentic American tale. Instead, he created fantasies in which European aristocracy roamed about in bone-chilling German castles. James Fenimore Cooper's mythology loomed too large and his debt to the Scottish Sir Walter Scott was too pronounced. Walt Whitman, the effervescent American Goethe, was penetrating and provocative but hardly profound, a master of rhythmic and colorful language never able to attain a natural or comfortable idiom of expression. Though Whitman was, without a doubt, the most influential American poet of the period, his songs of himself and his democratic vistas of America seem too fabricated—or simply fail to ring true at all.

Postcolonial American culture's preoccupation with breaking away from Europe was far removed from the situation among Africans in the United States at the time. The initial tenacity with which Africans held on to their indigenous practices and the reluctance of many Southern white slaveholders to teach Christianity to the slaves limited the Christianizing process in the early period. Even the Great Awakening of the 1740s, which swept the country like a hurricane, failed to reach the masses of slaves. Only with the Great Western Revival at the turn of the nineteenth century did the Christianizing process gain a significant foothold among black people.[15]

The central questions at this juncture are: Why did large numbers of American black people become Christians? What features of Protestant Christianity persuaded them to become Christians?

The Baptist separatists and the Methodists, religious dissenters in American religious culture, gained the attention of the majority of slaves in the Christianizing process. The evangelical outlook of these denominations stressed individual experience, equality before God and institutional autonomy. Baptism by immersion, practiced by the Baptists, may indeed have reminded slaves from Nigeria and Dahomey of African river cults, but this fails fully to explain the success of the Christianizing process among Africans.[16]

Black people became Christians for intellectual, existential and political reasons. Christianity is, as Friedrich Nietzsche has taught us and liberation theologians remind us, a religion especially fitted to the oppressed. It looks at the world from the perspective of those below. The African slaves' search for identity could find historical purpose in the exodus of Israel out of slavery and personal meaning in the bold identification of Jesus Christ with the lowly and downtrodden. Christianity also is first and foremost a theodicy, a triumphant account of good over evil. The intellectual life of the African slaves in the United States—like that of all oppressed peoples—consisted primarily of reckoning with the dominant form of evil in their lives. The Christian emphasis on against-the-evidence hope for triumph over evil struck deep among many of them.

The existential appeal of Christianity to black people was the stress of Protestant evangelicalism on individual experience, and especially the conversion experience. The "holy dance" of Protestant evangelical conversion experiences closely resembled the "ring shout" of West African novitiate rites: Both are religious forms of ecstatic bodily behavior in which everyday time is infused with meaning and value through unrestrained rejoicing.[17]

The conversion experience played a central role in the Christianizing process. It not only created deep bonds of fellowship and a reference point for self-assurance during times of doubt and distress; it also democratized and equalized the status of all before God. The conversion experience initiated a profoundly personal relationship with God, which gave slaves a special self-identity and self-esteem in stark contrast with the roles imposed upon them by American society.

The primary political appeal of the Methodists and especially of the Baptists for

black people was their church polity and organizational form, free from hierarchical control, open and easy access to leadership roles and relatively loose, un-
complicated requirements for membership. The adoption of the Baptist polity by
a majority of Christian slaves marked a turning point in the Afro-American experience.

On the one hand, the major organization among black Americans, the Christian churches, followed a polity farthest removed from modern bureaucratic and
hierarchical forms of organization.[18] In this sense, the organizational form of most
Afro-American churches, charismatic and often autocratic in leadership, neither
promoted nor encouraged widespread respect for and acquisition of bureaucratic
skills requisite for accountable leadership and institutional longevity. In short, the
Christian churches' organizational form imposed considerable constraints on the
administrative capabilities and institutional capacities of black people.

On the other hand, this organizational form ensured autonomous control over
the central institution in the Afro-American community, which set blacks in the
United States apart from other Africans in the diaspora. Independent control over
their churches promoted the proliferation of African styles and manners within
the black Christian tradition and liturgy. It also produced community-minded political leaders, polished orators and activist journalists and scholars. In fact, the
unique variant of American life that we call Afro-American culture germinated in
the bosom of this Afro-Christianity, in the Afro-Christian church congregations.

THE DECLINE OF MODERNITY, INDUSTRIAL PROVINCIALITY, INCLUSIONARY PRACTICES

The decline of European modernity between 1871 and 1950—from the unification
of the German empire to the emergence of the United States as the unquestioned
supreme world power—occurred within the political and socioeconomic contours
of an increasingly crisis-ridden monopoly-capitalist world economy. This yielded
devastating world wars, holocaust-producing fascist regimes and sharp reaction
against repressive Communist governments. The dominated classes in industrial
nations—including victims of racist and sexist oppression—flexed their political
muscles more in this period and embarked on various courses toward inclusion in
and ineffective opposition to the liberal capitalist order. The proliferation of mass
culture, especially luxury consumer goods, effected a prolonged entrée of significant segments of the dominated classes into the bourgeois world of educational
and occupational opportunities, middlebrow culture and comfortable living.

In this modernist period, it seemed as if, for the West, "things fell apart; the center could not hold," to revise William Butler Yeats, the greatest English-language
poet of the period. For science, a crisis set in. János Bolyai, N. I. Lobachevski, Karl
F. Gauss and Bernhard Riemann had already called into question the omnipres-

ence of Euclidean geometry by discovering three-dimensional space and thereby making possible new, non-Euclidean geometries. Einstein's theory of special relativity undermined the prevailing Newtonian physics. Niels Bohr and Werner Heisenberg promoted the indeterministic character of quantum phenomena, which subsequently threatened classical laws of logic such as the law of distribution. Kurt Gödel demonstrated the incompleteness of mathematics, and L. E. J. Brouwer rejected two-value logic and the law of excluded middle, hence paving the way for intuitionist mathematics.

For modern paganism, despair also set in. This revealed itself most clearly in 1922. That year, the modernist year *par excellence,* witnessed within twelve months the appearance of some of the most profound and probing works in the history of the modern West. These included T. S. Eliot's *The Wasteland,* James Joyce's *Ulysses,* Hermann Hesse's *Siddharta,* Osip Mandelstam's *Tristia,* Eugene O'Neill's *Anna Christie,* Bertolt Brecht's *Baal,* e. e. cummings's *The Enormous Room,* Sinclair Lewis's *Babbitt,* Jean Toomer's "Song of the Sun," Wallace Stevens's "The Comedian as the Letter C," Max Weber's *Economy and Society,* I. A. Richards's *Foundations of Aesthetics* (with C. K. Ogden and James Wood) and Sigmund Freud's essay on jealousy, paranoia and homosexuality. These were published in the same year that Mussolini's Blackshirts marched on Rome, and less than a year after Lenin and Trotsky's suppression of the Kronstadt rebellion, a suppression that soured the hopes of many sympathizers of the Russian Revolution.

In philosophy during the modernist period, major attacks were also made upon the primacy of the subject. Despite Hegel's historicizing of the subjectivist turn in philosophy, academic philosophers managed to overthrow Hegelianism and replace it either with analytical realism in Britain, neo-Kantianism in Germany or phenomenology in France, themselves later attacked by structuralism, existentialism and analytical behaviorism.

During the decline of European modernity the most precious ideals of science, politics, philosophy and the arts were radically called into question. This period was thus well disposed toward apocalyptic, crisis-centered views of history, which stressed shock, the violation of expected continuities and a deep sense of futility. Lionel Trilling—with his Arnoldian outlook and tactful candor—suggests that the modernist element signifies nihilism, "a bitter line of hostility to civilization," "a disenchantment with culture itself."[19]

This modernist temper projects the sense of an abrupt break with all tradition, a radical disruption from the past, which implies not so much a revolution, but rather a devolution or dissolution. Virginia Woolf reflected this modernist temper when she wrote, "On or about December 1910 human character changed."[20]

The industrial provincial stage of American culture neither escaped nor engulfed the modernist temper.[21] New attempts appeared to extend the Genteel tradition—or provide metaphysical comfort for agonized consciences—in the form of highly sophisticated idealist philosophical systems, as in the works of Borden Parker Bowne, James Edwin Creighton and, above all, Josiah Royce. The monumental literary achievement of the expatriate Henry James subjected the Genteel tradition to close scrutiny and detailed analysis, appraising it as a mere interesting habit of mind among a host of others. The Genteel tradition no longer survived as a holistic worldview, but rather as a subterranean sensibility upon which to build anew.[22]

During the modernist period, industrial provincial American culture presented clear-cut alternatives to its artists: either indigenize or become European. This dilemma was illustrated most graphically by the two exemplary American literary artists of the era, the seminal Mark Twain and the supercilious T. S. Eliot. For Twain, the aim was neither to resort to the eclectic strategies of Whitman or Melville nor to imitate the models and manners of Europe. Rather, it was to create the first genuine American idiom in literature. Similar to his colleague and fellow critic Ezra Pound, Eliot did not imitate Europeans, but rather became one. Although he expatriated to London, he had Paris on his mind and wrote his mature poetry under the influence of French symbolists and the classical European tradition of Homer, Ovid, Virgil and Dante. In this sense, Eliot was no longer from St. Louis and Pound no longer from Idaho. Both rested outside the gravity of industrial provincial American culture, not simply because they removed themselves from it, but rather because they discarded it.

On the philosophical front, this either-or dilemma took the form of a choice between warmed-over idealism and indigenous pragmatism, between updating the Genteel tradition and promoting a new reformist orientation.[23] Just as a dialogue between the Twain and Eliot streams never materialized, so a debate between Royce and Dewey never occurred. Both streams avoided each other, partly because of the divergent roads they chose and possibly because of their fundamental incompatibility.

The either-or dilemma of industrial provincial American culture is found only in the trained and talented artists and intellectuals of the rising Afro-American petite bourgeoisie, such as Alexander Crummell, W. E. B. Du Bois, Jean Toomer, Henry Ossawa Tanner, Alain Locke, Richard Wright, Laura Wheeler Waring, and others. The almost exclusive priority of African practices in the United States in this period was to gain inclusion within the rapidly expanding American capitalist order. With the increase of xenophobic sentiments and movements, the escalation of crypto-fascist terror in the southern part of the United States, and the vast immigration of eastern and southern European laborers to urban centers in the northern section of the United States, achieving Afro-American inclusion within the mainstream of American society proved difficult.

Public discourse within the Afro-American community concerning this inclusion was shaped by the debate that took place between the early W. E. B. Du Bois and Booker T. Washington—the two major spokesmen of the Afro-American petite bourgeoisie.[24] There were, of course, other interlocutors in the debate, including William Monroe Trotter of the Niagara Movement, Ida B. Wells-Barnett of Chicago, Rev. James Bowen of the Methodist Episcopal clergy, and Rev. George Washington Woodbey of the Socialist Party, but the privileged positions and voices of Du Bois and Washington drowned them out.

For both Du Bois and Washington, the pressing issues were neither impractical ones such as the redistribution of wealth, a more humane mode of production or opposition to American imperialism (in Puerto Rico and the Philippines) nor impertinent ones such as the undesirability of miscegenation or the removal of the Christian taint on Afro-American culture. Rather, these two petit bourgeois leaders directed their attention to the form and content of Afro-American inclusion in American society.

Both agreed on the form: nonviolent reform within the legal, political and economic channels of American life. They differed on the content: Washington favored self-help initiatives in the economic sphere and promoted a slow agrarian proletarianization process tied to increased Afro-American property holdings and wealth acquisition, whereas Du Bois opted for upward mobility in the social and political spheres and supported a protest movement that would achieve equal legal, social and political status for Afro-Americans in American society. They violently clashed, not simply because of their divergent viewpoints but, more important, because their limited access to resources and talent forced them to struggle for power on overlapping terrain.

The Du Bois–Washington debate set the framework for inclusionary African practices in the United States in this century. The numerous black ideological battles between integrationism and nationalism, accommodationism and separatism are but versions and variations of the Du Bois–Washington debate.[25] For example, Marcus Garvey, the great Jamaican leader of the first mass movement among Africans in the United States, simply gave Washington's self-help orientation a nationalist slant and back-to-Africa twist; his personal admiration of Washington is indisputable.

The first minor attempt to burst out of the framework of the Du Bois–Washington debate was the socialist viewpoint set forth in the pages of *The Messenger,* edited by the Young Turks Chandler Owen and A. Phillip Randolph.[26] This perspective, which echoed George Washington Woodbey's position more than a decade earlier, not only called into question the procapitalist assumption circumscribing the Du Bois–Washington debate, but also linked the enhancement of Afro-Americans to the radical elements of the labor movement. This valuable addition proved to be premature at the time, especially given the racist character of the labor movement. But in decades to come, this perspective proved to be portentous. Randolph's long and distinguished yet flawed career bears out the depths of his foresight. In short, he was the pioneer on the frontier of Afro-American labor relations.

A second minor attempt to step outside the confines of the Du Bois–Washington debate consisted of the African Blood Brotherhood's amalgam of revolutionary black nationalism and scientific socialism.[27] Its principal figures—Cyril Briggs, Richard B. Moore, W. A. Domingo, Harry Haywood—were the first African Communists in the United States. Their major contribution was that they put imperialist issues on the agenda of the Afro-American liberation movement. Yet such issues—along with untimely revolutionary rhetoric—remained on the back burner for petit bourgeois intellectuals and entrepreneurs, proletarian preachers and parishioners in urban centers and sharecroppers, tenant farmers and day laborers in rural areas throughout Afro-America.

The major vehicles by which black progress occurred in this period were patronage relationships with white elites and bosses in city machines, organized protest and boycott efforts (usually church-based) against discrimination, labor shortages during the two world wars, participation in the progressive labor movement (especially in the unionization of industrial workers) and achievements in athletics and entertainment. These diverse means of Afro-American upward social mobility constituted ad hoc measures that presupposed political oppression, economic exploitation and social degradation as the prevailing realities and posited inclusion within the American liberal capitalist order as the desirable goal. Such inclusionary measures signified the Afro-American encounter with the modern world on a significant scale for the first time; they revealed the difficulties presented by racist American society, the desperation of a bastard people in hostile circumstances and the determination of Africans in the United States, despite limited organization and vision, to be free.

THE END OF MODERNITY, POSTINDUSTRIAL COSMOPOLITANISM, DISPERSIVE PRACTICES

We live now three decades after the end of European modernity. The very term *postmodernism* reflects fear of the future; it is a backward-looking term. We witness the nuclear and ideological standoff between the capitalist (not necessarily free) United States and the Communist (definitely unfree) Soviet Union, both imperialist powers suffering immense internal decay. The dominated classes in industrial and postindustrial nations have accelerated the speed of their inclusion within the liberal capitalist regimes, accompanied by widespread tranquilizing and depoliticizing by mass culture. Poor, developing nations have launched successful political, anticolonial revolutions, yet often lapse into a neocolonial dependence on developed capitalist countries. A few developing nations even have had successful social revolutions, though they usually fall into the neocolonial Soviet orbit.

The recent stirrings of postmodernism can be illustrated in the following ways:

First, the crisis in science that emerged in European modernism is now becoming a more wide-spread crisis in the authority of science, in many ways similar to the crisis in the authority of the church in the Age of Enlightenment. This rudimentary state of demythologizing science relegates scientific descriptions and theories of the self, world and God alongside rather than above religious, artistic and moral descriptions and theories of the self, world and God. This demythologizing process is promoted (usually unintentionally) by major figures in the philosophy of science, such as N. R. Hanson, Michael Polanyi, Thomas Kuhn, Imre Lakatos and, above all, Paul Feyerabend.[28] This process signifies a deep authority crisis in knowledge, a kind of demonopolizing of science on truth and reality in the marketplace of ideas. It raises the prospect of a possible plurality of epistemic authorities on truth and reality as well as a frightening full-blown relativism or laissez-faire policy regarding access to truth and reality.

Second, the despair of modern paganism during the European modernist period has degenerated into various forms of cynicism, fatalism, hedonism and narcissism in the lowbrow, middlebrow and highbrow cultures of postmodernism. These attitudes and sensibilities—recently studied by Ihab Hassan, Raymond Olderman, Christopher Lasch, Heinz Kohut, Jerome Klinkowitz, and others—can be glimpsed in mass-consumer culture, in popular movies, in television programs and through disco records.[29] Postmodernist sentiments also can be found in such literary works as Jorge Borges's *Labyrinths* (1964), William Burroughs's *Naked Lunch* (1962), Donald Barthelme's *Snow White* (1967), Ishmael Reed's *The Free-Lance Pallbearers* (1967), John Barth's *Lost in the Funhouse* (1968), Ronald Sukenick's *The Death of the Novel* (1969), Kurt Vonnegut, Jr.'s *Slaughterhouse-Five* (1969), Raymond Federman's *Double or Nothing* (1972), Thomas Pynchon's *Gravity's Rainbow* (1973) and Philip K. Dick's *A Scanner Darkly* (1977). This degeneration—in mass culture and sophisticated literary texts—reveals, to a certain extent, the dead end to which modern paganism has come: impotent irony, barren skepticism and paralyzing self-parody.

Third, philosophical attacks on the primacy of the subject are deepened and extended in postmodernism. In short, postmodernism is an accentuation and acceleration of the major developments and processes in European modernism. It is a deepening of the decline of modernity, with little sense of what is to follow, if anything at all. It bears the birth pains of slow epoch transition, the ironic excesses of prolonged historical suspension and the ecstatic anticipations of a new, though not necessarily better, era.

The postindustrial cosmopolitan stage of American culture—the prevailing situation with its avant-garde domesticated by absorption into the marketable mainstream, its artists as professors, academic critics as artists and philosophers as technicians—witnesses the emergence of the United States as the cultural vanguard in postmodernism. For the first time, European audiences look to the

United States for artistic and cultural leadership. This leadership is not simply a result of the hegemony of U.S. world power or its supreme nuclear capacity. More important is the fact that it is an effect of a nation that has steadily gained cultural self-confidence while other leading European countries flounder in either self-pity (Germany), self-defeat (England) or self-obsession (France).

The point is not so much that the United States has come of age, but rather that the United States has seized Western cultural leadership in a declining and decadent age.[30] Of course, the United States has no Jean-Paul Sartre or Martin Heidegger, no Samuel Beckett or even Gabriel García Márquez. Yet cultural leadership in the West no longer requires such stellar figures; productive academic figures now suffice.

In postindustrial cosmopolitan American culture, the either-or dilemma of the previous period evaporates. Taking their cues from William Faulkner—without the size of his canvas, the complexity of his vision and the depths of his talent—postmodern American artists are able to learn from Europe without a feeling of inferiority, digging deep into American life without a sense of provinciality. In philosophy, the choice is no longer between the last of the Genteel tradition and the reformist orientation—idealism or pragmatism, Royce or Dewey—or even between the reformist orientation and the new realism. The very framework of such a choice has been eclipsed by the linguistic turn in philosophy, with its analytical rigor and technical argumentation.[31] Philosophy in the United States is no longer an arena in which comprehensive worldviews are adopted and intellectual attitudes cultivated, but rather a professional field of study where intricate puzzlelike problems are solved, resolved or dissolved.

The professionalization and specialization at work in postindustrial cosmopolitan American culture find their counterparts in the process of differentiation currently proceeding in the Afro-American experience. This differentiation generates dispersive practices among Afro-Americans; heretofore untouched intellectual territories, secular outlooks, business ventures, occupational positions, geographic locations and even sexual experimentations are now being discovered and enacted by Afro-Americans. This differentiation—though an index of progress—has rendered the collective enhancement of Afro-Americans even more problematic.

The paradox of Afro-American history is that Afro-Americans fully enter the modern world precisely when the postmodern period commences; that Afro-Americans gain a foothold in the industrial order just as the postindustrial order begins; and that Afro-Americans procure skills, values and mores efficacious for survival and sustenance in modernity as the decline of modernity sets in, deepens and yearns to give birth to a new era and epoch. The members of the Afro-American petite bourgeoisie make significant gains in such circumstances, but even they have a fragile economic position and vulnerable political status, and they experience cultural atrophy. At the same time, the Afro-

American underclass and the poor working class exhibit the indelible traces of their oppression in modernity and their dispensability in postmodernity: relative political powerlessness and perennial socioeconomic depression, cultural deterioration reinforced by devastated families and prefabricated mass culture, and subversive subcultures dominated by drugs and handguns, which surface as civil terrorism in black ghettos and American cities.

A GENEALOGY OF MODERN RACISM

The notion that black people are human beings is a relatively new discovery in the modern West. The idea of black equality in beauty, culture and intellectual capacity remains problematic and controversial within prestigious halls of learning and sophisticated intellectual circles. The Afro-American encounter with the modern world has been shaped first and foremost by the doctrine of white supremacy, which is embodied in institutional practices and enacted in everyday folkways under varying circumstances and evolving conditions.[32]

My aim in this section is to give a brief account of the way in which the idea of white supremacy was constituted as an object of modern discourse in the West, without simply appealing to the objective demands of the prevailing mode of production, the political interests of the slaveholding class or the psychological needs of the dominant white racial group. Despite the indispensable role these factors would play in a full-blown explanatory model to account for the emergence and sustenance of modern racism in the West, I try to hold these factors constant and focus solely on a neglected variable in past explanatory models—namely, the way in which the very structure of modern discourse *at its inception* produced forms of rationality, scientificity and objectivity as well as aesthetic and cultural ideals that require the constitution of the idea of white supremacy.

This requirement follows from a logic endemic to the very structure of modern discourse. This logic is manifest in the way in which the controlling metaphors, notions and categories of modern discourse produce and prohibit, develop and delimit specific conceptions of truth and knowledge, beauty and character, so that certain ideas are rendered incomprehensible and unintelligible. I suggest that one such idea that cannot be brought within the epistemological field of the initial modern discourse is that of black equality in beauty, culture and intellectual capacity. This act of discursive exclusion, of relegating this idea to silence, does not simply correspond to (or is not only reflective of) the relative powerlessness of black people at the time. It also reveals the evolving internal dynamics of the structure of modern discourse in the late seventeenth and eighteenth centuries in western Europe—or during the Enlightenment. The concrete effects of this exclusion and the intellectual traces of this silence continue to haunt the modern West: on the nondiscursive level, in ghetto streets, and on the discursive level, in methodological assumptions in the disciplines of the humanities.

I shall argue that the initial structure of modern discourse in the West "secretes" the idea of white supremacy. I call this "secretion"—the underside of modern discourse—a particular logical consequence of the quest for truth and knowledge in the modern West. To put it crudely, my argument is that the authority of science, undergirded by a modern philosophical discourse guided by Greek ocular metaphors and Cartesian notions, promotes and encourages the activities of observing, comparing, measuring and ordering the physical characteristics of human bodies. Given the renewed appreciation and appropriation of classical antiquity, these activities are regulated by classical aesthetic and cultural norms. The creative fusion of scientific investigation, Cartesian epistemology and classical ideals produced forms of rationality, scientificity and objectivity that, though efficacious in the quest for truth and knowledge, prohibited the intelligibility and legitimacy of the idea of black equality in beauty, culture and intellectual capacity. In fact, to "think" such an idea was to be deemed irrational, barbaric or mad.

THEORETICAL CONSIDERATIONS: THE GENEALOGICAL APPROACH

I call this inquiry a "genealogy" because, following the works of Friedrich Nietzsche and Michel Foucault, I am interested in the emergence *(Entstehung),* or the "moment of arising," of the idea of white supremacy within the modern discourse in the West.[33] This genealogy tries to address the following questions: What are the discursive conditions for the possibility of the intelligibility and legitimacy of the idea of white supremacy in modern discourse? How is this idea constituted within the epistemological field of modern discourse? What is the complex configuration of metaphors, notions, categories and norms that produces and promotes such an object of modern discourse?

My genealogical approach subscribes to a conception of power that is based neither simply on individual subjects, e.g., heroes or great personages as in traditional historiography, nor on collective subjects, e.g., groups, elites or classes as in revisionist and vulgar Marxist historiography. Therefore I do not believe that the emergence of the idea of white supremacy in the modern West can be fully accounted for in terms of the psychological needs of white individuals and groups or the political and economic interests of a ruling class. I will try to show that the idea of white supremacy emerges partly because of the powers within the structure of modern discourse—powers to produce and prohibit, develop and delimit forms of rationality, scientificity and objectivity that set perimeters and draw boundaries for the intelligibility, availability and legitimacy of certain ideas.

These powers are subjectless—that is, they are the indirect products of the praxis of human subjects. They have a life and logic of their own, not in a transhistorical realm but within history alongside, yet not reducible to, demands of an economic system, interests of a class or needs of a group. What I am suggesting is not a history without a subject propagated by the structuralist Marxist Louis Althusser, but rather a history made by the praxis of human subjects, which often results in complex structures of discourses that have relative autonomy from (or are not fully accountable in terms of) the intentions, aims, needs, interests and objectives of human subjects.[34]

I am further suggesting that there is no direct correspondence between nondiscursive structures, such as a system of production (or, in Marxist terms, an economic base), and discursive structures, such as theoretical formations (or, in Marxist terms, an ideological superstructure). Rather, there are powers immanent in nondiscursive structures and discursive structures.[35] Traditional, revisionist and vulgar Marxist types of historiography focus primarily on powers within nondiscursive structures, e.g., powers of kings, presidents, elites or classes, and reduce the powers within discursive structures to mere means for achieving the intentions, aims, needs, interests and objectives of subjects in nondiscursive structures. This reductionism is not wrong; it is simply inadequate. It rightly acknowledges noteworthy concrete effects generated by the relationship between powers in discursive structures and those in nondiscursive structures, but it wrongly denies the relative autonomy of the powers in discursive structures and hence reduces the complexity of cultural phenomena.

The primary motivation behind such reductionism (such as personalistic analyses of race prejudice or orthodox Marxist accounts of racism) is to ensure an easy resolution of a highly complex problem, without calling into question certain fundamental assumptions that inform such resolutions. These fundamental assumptions, such as the subject-based conception of power, and easy resolutions, such as the elimination of race prejudice by knowledge or the abolition of racism under socialism, preclude theoretical alternatives and strategic options. In this way, these fundamental assumptions and hypothetical resolutions illustrate the effects of the powers immanent in certain liberal and Marxist discourses.

THE STRUCTURE OF MODERN DISCOURSE

I understand "the structure of modern discourse" to be the controlling metaphors, notions, categories and norms that shape the predominant conceptions of truth and knowledge in the modern West. These metaphors, notions, categories and norms are circumscribed and determined by three major historical processes: the scientific revolution, the Cartesian transformation of philosophy and the classical revival.[36]

The scientific revolution is usually associated with the pioneering breakthroughs of Copernicus and Kepler in astronomy, Galileo and Newton in physics, and Descartes and Leibniz in mathematics. These breakthroughs were pre-Enlightenment, most of them occurring during the seventeenth century, the so-called Age of Genius. The scientific revolution is noteworthy (to say the least) primarily because it signified the authority of science. This authority justified new modes of knowledge and new conceptions of truth and reality; it set the framework for the advent of modernity.

The originating figures of the scientific revolution went beyond the Renaissance problematic—of finding a compromise formula that reconciled Christian and classical modes of thinking and living—yet stopped short of drawing thoroughly secular conclusions from their breakthroughs, that is, of waging intellectual war on natural religion and dogmatic theology. Galileo's Platonism and Newton's Socinianism illustrate this peculiar protomodern worldview of making peace between science and religion.[37]

For our purposes, the scientific revolution is significant because it highlights two fundamental ideas: *observation* and *evidence*. These two ideas have played, in an isolated manner, a role in previous paradigms of knowledge in the West (since the times of Aristotle and Aristarchus). But the scientific revolution brought these ideas together in such a way that they have become the two foci around which much of modern discourse evolves. The modern concepts of hypothesis, fact, inference, validation, confirmation and verification cluster around the ideas of observation and evidence.

The major proponents of the scientific revolution, or, more specifically, of the authority of science, were two philosophers, Frances Bacon and René Descartes. Bacon is noteworthy primarily because of his metaphilosophical honesty. For him, the aim of philosophy was to give humankind mastery over nature by means of scientific discoveries and inventions. He then promoted the philosophical importance of the inductive method as a means of arriving at general laws to facilitate this human mastery. Despite Bacon's acceptance of orthodox religion, his rejection of Copernican theory, and his lack of acquaintance with some of the major scientific discoveries of his time—e.g., the work of Andreas Vesalius on modern anatomy, William Gilbert on magnetism or William Harvey (Bacon's own medical attendant) on the circulation of blood—Bacon's writings, especially *The Advancement of Learning,* did much to promote the authority of science.[38]

Descartes is highly significant because his thought provided the controlling notions of modern discourse: *the primacy of the subject and the preeminence of representation.* Descartes is widely regarded as the founder of modern philosophy not simply because his philosophical outlook was profoundly affected by the scientific revolution, but, more important, because he associated the scientific aim of predicting and explaining the world with the philosophical aim of picturing and representing the world. In this view, the fruits of scientific research do not merely provide more useful ways for human beings to *cope* with reality; such research also yields a true *copy* of reality. Descartes's conception of philosophy as a tortuous move from the subject to objects, from the veil of ideas to the external world, from immediate awareness to extended substances, from self-consciousness to things in space and ultimately from doubt to certainty was motivated primarily by an attempt to provide a theoretical basis for the legitimacy of modern science. Martin Heidegger made this crucial connection between Cartesian philosophy and modern science in his famous essay "The Age of the World View":

> We are reflecting on the nature of modern science in order to find its metaphysical basis. What conception of the existent and what concept of truth cause science to become research?
>
> Understanding as research holds the existent to account on the question of how and how far it can be put at the disposal of available "representation." Research has the existent at its disposal if it can either calculate it in advance, in its future course, or calculate it afterwards as past. Nature and history become the object of expository representation. . . .
>
> This objectification of the existent takes place in a re-presentation which aims at presenting whatever exists to itself in such a way that the calculating person can be secure, that is, certain of the existent. Science as research is produced when and only when truth has been transformed into such certainty of representation. In the metaphysics of Descartes the existent was defined for the first time as objectivity of representation, and truth as certainty of representation.[39]

Bacon and Descartes had basic differences: Bacon held the inductive orientation and Descartes the deductive viewpoint, Bacon the empiricist outlook and Descartes the rationalist (mathematical) perspective. Despite these differences, both of these propagandists of modern science agreed that scientific method provides a new paradigm of knowledge and that observation and evidence are at the center of scientific method. In *The New Organon,* Bacon likened his ideal natural philosopher to the bee, which collects "its material from the flowers of the garden and of the field" and digests it "by a power of its own." In his *Discourse on Method,* Descartes set forth as a rule that "observations" become "the more necessary the further we advance in knowledge." And, as D'Alembert acknowledged in *The Encyclopedia,* both Bacon and Descartes "introduced the spirit of experimental science."[40]

The last major historical process that circumscribed and determined the metaphors, notions, categories and norms of modern discourse was the classical revival. This classical revival–in response to medieval mediocrity and religious dogmatism–was initiated in the Early Renaissance (1300–1500), principally with humanist studies in Roman art and Latin literature, such as Giotto in painting, Petrarch in letters and Dufay in music. This revival intensified during the High Renaissance (1500–1530), with Da Vinci, Raphael, Bramante and the early Michelangelo in the arts; Ariosto, Rabelais and Erasmus in literature; and Josquin and Lassus in music. The revival mellowed in the Mannerist era (1530–1600), as illustrated by El Greco, Tintoretto and the later Michelangelo in the arts; Montaigne, Cervantes and Shakespeare in literature; and Marenzio, Gabrieli and Frescobaldi in music. The revival was strengthened in the Baroque period (1600–1750), as seen in the works of Velasquez and Rembrandt in the arts; Racine, Milton and Vondel in literature; and Bach and Handel in music. The classical revival culminated in the neoclassical movement in the middle of the eighteenth century, with the paintings of David and Ingres, the lyrics of Hölderlin, the tragedies of Alfieri, the verse and prose of Landor and the music of Haydn and Mozart. The Enlightenment revolt against the authority of the church and the search for models of unrestrained criticism led to a highly charged recovery of classical antiquity, and especially to a new appreciation and appropriation of the artistic and cultural heritage of ancient Greece.

For our purposes, the classical revival is important because it infuses Greek ocular metaphors and classical ideals of beauty, proportion and moderation into the beginnings of modern discourse. Greek ocular metaphors—Eye of the Mind, Mind as Mirror of Nature, Mind as Inner Arena with its Inner Observer—dominate modern discourse in the West.[41] Coupled with the Cartesian notion of knowledge as inner representation, modern philosophical inquiry is saddled with the epistemological model of intellect (formerly Plato's and Aristotle's Nous, now Descartes's Inner Eye) inspecting entities modeled on retinal images, with the Eye of the Mind viewing representations in order to find some characteristic that would testify to their fidelity.

The creative fusion of scientific investigation, Cartesian philosophy, Greek ocular metaphors and classical aesthetic and cultural ideals constitutes the essential elements of modern discourse in the West. In short, modern discourse rests upon a conception of truth and knowledge governed by an ideal value-free subject engaged in observing, comparing, ordering and measuring in order to arrive at evidence sufficient to make valid inferences, confirm speculative hypotheses, deduce error-proof conclusions and verify true representations of reality.

THE EMERGENCE OF MODERN RACISM: THE FIRST STAGE

The recovery of classical antiquity in the modern West produced what I shall call a "normative gaze," namely, an ideal from which to order and compare observations. This ideal was drawn primarily from classical aesthetic values of beauty, proportion and human form and classical cultural standards of moderation, self-control and harmony.[42] The role of classical aesthetic and cultural norms in the emergence of the idea of white supremacy as an object of modern discourse cannot be underestimated.

These norms were consciously projected and promoted by many influential Enlightenment writers, artists and scholars, of whom the most famous was J. J. Winckelmann. In his widely read book, *History of Ancient Art,* Winckelmann portrayed ancient Greece as a world of beautiful bodies. He laid down rules—in art and aesthetics—that should govern the size of eyes and eyebrows, of collarbones, hands, feet and especially noses. He defined beauty as noble simplicity and quiet grandeur. In a celebrated passage he wrote:

> As the depth of the ocean always remains calm however much the surface may be agitated, so does the expression in the figures of the Greeks reveal a great and composed soul in the midst of passions.[43]

Although Winckelmann was murdered in middle life, never set foot in Greece and saw almost no original Greek art (only one exhibition of Greek art in Munich), he viewed Greek beauty and culture as the ideal or standard against which to measure other peoples and cultures.

Winthrop Jordan and Thomas Gossett have shown that there are noteworthy premodern racist viewpoints aimed directly and indirectly at nonwhite, especially black, people.[44] For example, in 1520 Paracelsus held that black and primitive peoples had a separate origin from Europeans. In 1591, Giordano Bruno made a similar claim, but had in mind principally Jews and Ethiopians. And Lucilio Vanini posited that Ethiopians had apes for ancestors and had once walked on all fours. Since theories of the separate origin of races were in disagreement with the Roman Catholic church, Bruno and Vanini underwent similar punishment: Both were burned at the stake. Of course, biblically based accounts of racial inferiority flourished, but the authority of the church prohibited the proliferation of nonreligious, that is, protomodern, accounts of racial inferiority.

What is distinctive about the role of classical aesthetic and cultural norms at the advent of modernity is that they provided an acceptable authority for the idea of white supremacy, an acceptable authority that was closely linked with the major authority on truth and knowledge in the modern world, namely, the institution of science. In order to see how this linkage took place, let us examine the categories and aims of the major discipline that promoted this authority, that is, those of natural history.

The principal aim of natural history is to observe, compare, measure and order animals and human bodies (or classes of animals and human bodies) *based on visible, especially physical, characteristics.* These characteristics permit one to discern identity and difference, equality and inequality, beauty and ugliness among animals and human bodies.

The governing categories of natural history are preeminently *classificatory* categories—that is, they consist of various taxonomies in the form of tables, catalogs, indexes and inventories which impose some degree of order or representational schema on a broad field of visible characteristics. *Observation* and *differentness* are the essential guiding notions in natural history. Foucault wrote:

> Natural history has as a condition of its possibility the common affinity of things and language with representation; but it exists as a task only in so far as things and language happen to be separate. It must therefore reduce this distance between them so as to bring language as close as possible to the observing gaze, and the things observed as close as possible to words. Natural history is nothing more than the nomination of the visible. . . .
>
> Natural history . . . covers a series of complex operations that introduce the possibility of a constant order into a totality of representations. It constitutes a whole domain of empiricity as at the same time describable and orderable.[45]

The initial basis for the idea of white supremacy is to be found in the classificatory categories and the descriptive, representational, order-imposing aims of natural history. The captivity of natural history to what I have called the "normative gaze" signifies the first stage of the emergence of the idea of white supremacy as an object of modern discourse. More specifically (and as Ashley Montagu has tirelessly argued), the genealogy of racism in the modern West is inseparable from the appearance of the classificatory category of race in natural history.

The category of race—denoting primarily skin color—was first employed as a means of classifying human bodies by François Bernier, a French physician, in 1684. He divided humankind into basically four races: Europeans, Africans, Orientals, and Lapps.[46] The first authoritative racial division of humankind is found in the influential *Natural System* (1735) of the most preeminent naturalist of the eighteenth century, Carolus Linnaeus. For Linnaeus, species were fixed in number and kind; they were immutable prototypes. Varieties, however, were members of a species that might change in appearance. The members of a species produced fertile offspring; interfertility was the test for the division of species. There were variations of kind within a species; the races were a prime example. For Linnaeus, there were four races: Homo Europaeus, Homo Asiaticus, Homo Afer, and Homo Americanus.

Winthrop Jordan has argued that Linnaeus did not subscribe to a hierarchical ranking of races, but rather to "one chain of universal being." Jordan states:

> It was one thing to classify all living creation and altogether another to arrange it in a single great hierarchy; and when Linnaeus undertook the first of these tasks he was not thereby forced to attempt the latter. In the many editions of the

Systema Naturae he duly catalogued the various kinds of men, yet never in a hierarchic manner.[47]

Yet it is quite apparent that Linnaeus implicitly evaluated the observable characteristics of the racial classes of people, especially those pertaining to character and disposition. For example, compare Linnaeus's description of the European with the African:

> European. White, Sanguine, Brawny. Hair abundantly flowing. Eyes blue. Gentle, acute, inventive. Covered with close vestments. Governed by customs.
> African. Black, Phlegmatic, Relaxed. Hair black, frizzled. Skin silky. Nose flat. Lips tumid. Women's bosom a matter of modesty. Breasts give milk abundantly. Crafty, indolent. Negligent. Anoints himself with grease. Governed by caprice.[48]

Linnaeus's use of evaluative terms revealed, at the least, an implicit hierarchy by means of personal preference. It also is important to note that he included some remarks about the African woman, but that he said nothing about the European woman (nor the American and Asiatic woman). It also is significant that in the 1750s when he first acknowledged that hybridization of species occurs, he chose black people and apes as the probable candidates, while restricting such unions to black women and male apes.

Georges Louis Leclerc de Buffon accepted hybridization without question in his famous *Natural History of Man* (1778). Although Buffon, like Linnaeus, viewed races as mere chance variations, he held that white was "the real and natural color of man." Black people and other races were variations of this natural color, yet somehow not members of a different species. He remained uncertain about the objective reality of species. Buffon believed that black skin was caused by hot climate and would change if the climate became colder. Although he was a fervent antislavery advocate, he claimed that black people had "little genius" and then added, "The unfortunate negroes are endowed with excellent hearts, and possess the seeds of every human virtue."[49]

THE EMERGENCE OF MODERN RACISM: THE SECOND STAGE

In the works of Johann Friedrich Blumenbach, one of the founders of modern anthropology, the aesthetic criteria and cultural ideals of Greece began to come to the forefront. Like Linnaeus and Buffon, Blumenbach held that all human beings belonged to the same species and that races were merely varieties. Yet contrary to the claims by Winthrop Jordan, Ashley Montagu, and Thomas Gossett concern-

ing Blumenbach's opposition to hierarchic racial ranking or irritation at those
who use aesthetic standards for such ranking, Blumenbach praised the symmetri-
cal face as the most beautiful of human faces precisely because it approximated
the "divine" works of Greek art, and specifically the proper anatomical proportions found in Greek sculpture.[50] Applying the classical ideal of moderation, he
claimed that the more moderate the climate, the more beautiful the face. The net
result was that since black people were farthest from the Greek ideal and located
in extremely hot climates, they were, by implication, inferior in beauty to Europeans.

The second stage of the emergence of the idea of white supremacy as an object
of modern discourse primarily occurred in the rise of phrenology (the reading of
skulls) and physiognomy (the reading of faces). These new disciplines—closely
connected with anthropology—served as an open platform for the propagation of
the idea of white supremacy not principally because they were pseudosciences,
but, more important, because these disciplines acknowledged the European value-
laden character of their observations. This European value-laden character was
based on classical aesthetic and cultural ideals.

Pieter Camper, the Dutch anatomist, made aesthetic criteria the pillar of his
chief discovery: the famous "facial angle." Camper claimed that the "facial
angle"—a measure of prognathism—permitted a comparison of heads of human
bodies by way of cranial and facial measurements. For Camper, the ideal "facial
angle" was a 100-degree angle which was achieved only by the ancient Greeks.
He openly admitted that this ideal conformed to Winckelmann's classical ideal of
beauty. Following Winckelmann, Camper held that Greek proportions and
stature exemplified beauty and embodied perfection. Camper further held that a
beautiful face, beautiful body, beautiful nature, beautiful character and beautiful
soul were inseparable. He tried to show that the "facial angle" of Europeans mea-
sured about 97 degrees and those of black people between 60 and 70 degrees,
closer to the measurements of apes and dogs than to human beings.

Although many anthropologists readily accepted the "facial angle" as a scientific notion,[51] Camper made it clear that his aim was not simply to contribute to
the new discipline of anthropology, but also to promote the love of classical antiquity to young artists and sculptors. As George Mosse has noted, historians of
race theories often overlook the fact that Camper and many subsequent theoreti-
cians of race and racism were trained as artists and writers. Camper was a painter
by training and, in fact, won the gold medal of the Amsterdam School of Art two
years before he published his work on the "facial angle."[52]

Johann Kaspar Lavater, the father of physiognomy, explicitly acknowledged
that the art of painting was the mother of his new discipline. Moreau, an early editor of Lavater's work, clearly noted that the true language of physiognomy was

painting, because it spoke through images, equally to the eye and to the spirit.[53] This new discipline linked particular visible characteristics of human bodies, especially those of the face, to the character and capacities of human beings. This discipline openly articulated what many of the early naturalists and anthropologists tacitly assumed: *The classical ideals of beauty, proportion and moderation regulated the classifying and ranking of groups of human bodies.* In short, physiognomy brought the "normative gaze" into daylight.

Lavater believed that the Greek statues were the models of beauty. His description of the desirable specimen—blue eyes, horizontal forehead, bent back, round chin and short brown hair—resembled the beautiful person preferred by Camper. The common Greek ideals of beauty, though slightly distorted (to say the least), were the principal source of this "normative gaze." Lavater's new discipline was highly influential among scientists—for example, Jean Baptiste Porta and Christian Meiners—and artists. His close friend, the famous Goethe, aided him in editing and publishing his physiognomic formulations and findings, and Sir Walter Scott, among others, popularized them in his novels.

Lavater's promotion of what I call the "normative gaze" consisted no longer of detailed measurements, as was the case with the naturalists, but rather of the visual glance. He wrote: "Trust your first quick impression, for it is worth more than what is usually called observation."[54] Therefore it is not surprising that Lavater put forth an elaborate theory of noses, the most striking member of the face. Neither is it surprising that subsequent classifications of noses, based on Lavater's formulations, associate Roman and Greek noses with conquerors and persons of refinement and taste.

The next and last step we shall consider in this genealogy of racism in late-seventeenth- and eighteenth-century Europe is the advent of phrenology, the new discipline holding that human character could be read through the shape of the human head. Franz Joseph Gall, a highly regarded German physician, argued in 1796 that the inner workings of the brain could be determined by the shape of the skull. For example, he associated an arched forehead with a penchant for metaphysical speculation, a skull arched at the rear with love of fame and a skull large at the base with a criminal disposition. In the nineteenth century, when racist ideology was systematized, this new discipline took on a life of its own with Johann Kaspar Spurzheim, Anders Retzius, Carl Gustav Carus and others; it also aided in allying modern racism with nationalism and repressed sexuality in bourgeois morality.

THEORETICAL CONSEQUENCES: RESTRICTIVE POWERS IN MODERN DISCOURSE

A major example of the way in which the restrictive powers of modern discourse delimit theoretical alternatives and strategic options in regard to the idea of white supremacy is seen in writings of radical environmentalists of the period—those one would expect to be open to the idea of black equality in beauty, culture and intellectual capacity. Yet even these progressive antislavery advocates remain captive to the "normative gaze."

The major opponent of predominant forms of a hierarchic ranking of races and the outspoken proponent of intermarriage in the United States during this era, Samuel Stanhope Smith, illustrates this captivity. In his day Smith stood at the pinnacle of American academia. He was president of Princeton University and an honorary member of the American Philosophical Society. He was awarded honorary degrees from Harvard and Yale. In his well-known *Essays* of 1787 (and revised in 1810) Smith argued that humankind constituted one species and that human variations could be accounted for in reference to three natural causes: "climate," "state of society" and "habits of living." He believed "that colour may be justly considered as an universal freckle."[55]

The "normative gaze" operative in Smith's viewpoint is located, as in Buffon, in the assumption that physical, especially racial, variations are always degenerate ones from an ideal state. For Smith, this ideal state consisted of highly civilized white people. As Winthrop Jordan notes, "Smith treated the complexion and physiognomy of the white man not merely as indication of superiority but as the hallmark of civilization."[56] Smith justified this ideal standard and legitimized his "normative gaze" by appealing to the classical ideals of beauty. In a patriotic footnote he wrote:

> It may perhaps gratify my countrymen to reflect that the United States occupy those latitudes that have ever been most favourable to the beauty of the human form. When time shall have accommodated the constitution of its new state, and cultivation shall have meliorated the climate, the beauties of Greece and Circasia may be renewed in America; as there are not a few already who rival those of any quarter of the globe.[57]

Smith's radical environmentalism (along with his adherence to Greek aesthetic ideals) led him to adopt the most progressive and sympathetic alternative for promoting the welfare of black people permissible within the structure of modern discourse: integration, which *uplifts* black people, assimilation, which *civilizes* black people and intermarriage, which *ensures less Negroid features* in the next generation. For example, Smith wrote:

> The great difference between the domestic and field slaves gives reason to believe that, if they were perfectly free, enjoyed property, and were admitted to a liberal participation of the society rank and privileges of their masters, they would change their African peculiarities much faster.[58]

This theoretical alternative was taken to its logical consequence by the distinguished American antislavery advocate, publicizer of talented black writers, and eminent physician Benjamin Rush. This logical consequence was the elimination of the skin color of black people. In a paper entitled "Observations Intended to Favour a Supposition that the Black Color (As it is called) of the Negroes is Derived From the Leprosy," Rush denounced the idea of white supremacy, then stated: "Is the color of Negroes a disease? Then let science and humanity combine their efforts and endeavor to discover a remedy for it."[59] In one bold stroke, Rush provided grounds for promoting abolitionism, opposing intermarriage (who wants to marry diseased persons!) and supporting the Christian unity of humankind. In his opinion, his viewpoint also maximized the happiness of black and white people:

> To encourage attempts to cure this disease of the skin in Negroes, let us recollect that by succeeding in them, we shall produce a large portion of happiness in the world. . . .
>
> Secondly, we shall add greatly to their happiness, for however well they appear to be satisfied with their color, there are many proofs of their preferring that of the white people.[60]

RACISM IN THE ENLIGHTENMENT

The intellectual legitimacy of the idea of white supremacy, though grounded in what we now consider marginal disciplines (especially in its second stage), was pervasive. This legitimacy can be illustrated by the extent to which racism permeated the writings of the major figures of the Enlightenment. It is important to note that the idea of white supremacy not only was accepted by these figures, but, more important, it was accepted by them *without their having to put forward their own arguments to justify it*. Montesquieu and Voltaire of the French Enlightenment, Hume and Jefferson of the Scotch and the American Enlightenment, and Kant of the German Enlightenment not merely held racist views; they also uncritically—during this age of criticism—believed that the *authority* for these views rested in the domain of naturalists, anthropologists, physiognomists and phrenologists.

Montesquieu's satirical remarks in *Spirit of the Laws* about black people (and his many revisions of these remarks) may seem to suggest an equivocal disposition toward the idea of white supremacy. Yet his conclusion leaned toward support of the idea:

> It is impossible for us to suppose that these beings should be men; because if we supposed them to be men, one would begin to believe we ourselves were not Christians.[61]

Voltaire's endorsement of the idea of white supremacy was unequivocal. In his essay "The People of America," he claimed that black people (and Indians) were distinct species from Europeans:

The Negro race is a species of men as different from ours as the breed of spaniels is from that of greyhounds. The mucous membrane, or network, which nature has spread between the muscles and the skin, is white in us and black or copper-colored in them. . . .

If their understanding is not of a different nature from ours, it is at least greatly inferior. They are not capable of any great application or association of ideas, and seemed formed neither for the advantages nor the abuses of philosophy.[62]

Hume's racism was notorious; it served as a major source of proslavery arguments and antiblack education propaganda. In his famous footnote to his essay "Of National Characters," he stated:

I am apt to suspect the negroes, and in general all the other species of men (for there are four or five different kinds) to be naturally inferior to the whites. There never was a civilized nation of any other complexion than white, nor even any individual eminent either in action or speculation. No ingenious manufactures amongst them, no arts, no sciences. . . .

In Jamaica indeed they talk of one negroe as a man of learning; but 'tis likely he is admired for very slender accomplishments, like a parrot, who speaks a few words plainly.[63]

Jefferson arrived at mildly similar conclusions in his *Notes on Virginia*. Regarding the intellectual capacities of black people, he wrote:

Comparing them by their faculties of memory, reason, and imagination, it appears to me, that in memory they are equal to the whites; in reason much inferior . . . and that in imagination they are dull, tasteless and anomalous. . . . Never yet could I find that a black had uttered a thought above the level of plain narration; never see even an elementary trait of painting or sculpture.[64]

Finally, Kant, whose views were based heavily on Hume's claims, held that "the negroes of Africa have by nature no feeling that rises above the trifling." In his *Observations on the Feeling of the Beautiful and Sublime,* Kant noted:

Mr. Hume challenges anyone to cite a simple example in which a negro has shown talents, and asserts that among the hundreds of thousands of blacks who are transported elsewhere from their countries, although many of them have even been set free, still not a single one was ever found who presented anything great in art or science or any other praiseworthy quality, even though among the whites some continually rise aloft from the lowest rabble, and through superior gifts earn respect in the world. So fundamental is the difference between the two races of man, and it appears to be as great in regard to mental capacities as in color.[65]

Kant further revealed his racist views when, in reply to advice that a black person gave to Father Labat, he wrote,

And it might be that there was something in this which perhaps deserved to be considered; but in short, this fellow was quite black from head to foot, a clear proof that what he said was stupid.[66]

THE EMERGENCE OF MODERN RACISM: INEVITABLE OR CONTINGENT?

The emergence of the idea of white supremacy as an object of modern discourse seems inevitable in that, besides the practical need to justify nonwhite domination (especially in the early nineteenth century), the only available theoretical alternative for the unhampered search for truth and knowledge in the modern West consisted of detailed observation, measurement, comparison and ordering of the natural and human kingdom by autonomous subjects in the light of the aesthetic and cultural ideals of classical antiquity. Given the Enlightenment obsession with criticism, especially criticism of the church and religion, the past was divided into four major epochs:

[T]he great river civilizations of the Near East; Ancient Greece and Rome; the Christian millennium; and modern times, beginning with the "revival of letters." These four epochs were rhythmically related to each other: the first and third were paired off as ages of myth, belief and superstition, while the second and fourth were ages of rationality, science and Enlightenment.[67]

The implications of Frank Snowden's thesis in his book *Blacks in Antiquity: Ethiopians in the Greco-Roman Experience* call into question the notion that the Enlightenment recovery of classical antiquity—its aesthetic and cultural ideals—inevitably required, on the discursive level, the emergence of the idea of white supremacy as an object of modern discourse. Snowden's thesis is that racial prejudice did not exist in classical antiquity. He claims that in the first major encounter in European records of black people in a predominantly white society the idea of black equality in beauty, culture and intellectual capacity was seriously entertained. In regard to ideals of beauty, he notes that Herodotus called Ethiopians the most handsome people on earth; Philostratus spoke of charming Ethiopians with their strange color; Pseudo-Callisthenes held the black Queen of Meroë (visited by Alexander the Great) to be of wondrous beauty; and the poet Martial, though pursued by a woman whiter than snow, sought a "super-black" woman.[68] Snowden goes as far as to state: "On the whole . . . the number of expressed preferences for blackness and whiteness in classical literature is approximately equal."[69]

If Snowden's viewpoint is correct, two noteworthy issues arise. First, it permits us to accent the crucial role that the advent of modern science played in *highlighting the physical appearances of people in relation to what it is to be human, beautiful, cultured and intelligent*. In this regard, the primacy of observation—the "gaze" character of scientific knowledge—may be as important as the classical ideals latent in such observations at the inception of modern discourse. Second, Snowden's claims require that I provide an account of why the Enlightenment revival of classical antiquity ignored or excluded black statues and the proportions and measurements of black figures as part of classical aesthetic ideals.

Snowden's thesis is highly plausible and extremely provocative, but I find it neither persuasive nor convincing. His claims are too exorbitant, but they do contain kernels of truth. Race indeed mattered much less in classical antiquity than it does in modern times. But race did matter in classical antiquity, as can be seen from the evidence meticulously gathered by Snowden, Sikes, Westermann and others.[70] The crucial difference seems to be that racial differences were justified on cultural grounds in classical antiquity, whereas at the inception of modern discourse, racial differences are often grounded in nature, that is, ontology and later biology.

And even if race prejudice did not exist in classical antiquity, the minority status of black people in Greece and Rome still rendered black statues, proportions and measurements marginal to cultural life. Hence, the black presence, though tolerated and at times venerated, was never an integral part of the classical ideals of beauty.

The emergence of the idea of white supremacy as an object of modern discourse seems contingent, in that there was no iron necessity at work in the complex configuration of metaphors, notions, categories and norms that produce and promote this idea. There is an accidental character to the discursive emergence of modern racism, a kind of free play of discursive powers that produce and prohibit, develop and delimit the legitimacy and intelligibility of certain ideas within a discursive space circumscribed by the attractiveness of classical antiquity.

Yet even such claims about the contingency of the emergence of the idea of white supremacy in the modern West warrant suspicion. This is so because, as we noted earlier, this genealogical approach *does not purport to be an explanation of the rise of modern racism, but rather a theoretical inquiry into a particular neglected variable, i.e., the discursive factor, within a larger explanatory model.* This variable is significant because it not only precludes reductionist treatments of modern racism; it also highlights the cultural and aesthetic impact of the idea of white supremacy on black people. This inquiry accents the fact that the everyday life of black people is shaped not simply by the exploitative (oligopolistic) capitalist system of production, but also by cultural attitudes and sensibilities, including alienating ideals of beauty.

The idea of white supremacy is a major bowel unleashed by the structure of modern discourse, a significant secretion generated from the creative fusion of scientific investigation, Cartesian philosophy and classical aesthetic and cultural norms. Needless to say, the odor of this bowel and the fumes of this secretion continue to pollute the air of our postmodern times.

Source: "American Africans in Conflict: Alienation in an Insecure Culture" and "A Genealogy of Modern Racism," from *Prophesy Deliverance: An Afro-American Revolutionary Christianity*, pp. 27–65, 154–162. Copyright © 1982 by Cornel West. Used by permission of Westminster John Knox Press.

Six

BLACK STRIVINGS IN A TWILIGHT CIVILIZATION

If all of my writings but one had to disappear, this essay is the one piece I hope would survive. Its fundamental point of the basic full-fledged humanity of black people continuous with that of others and Du Bois's lifelong effort to convince the West of this basic truth are at the core of my work and life. Needless to say, this essay is my first and only sustained encounter with the greatest of all black intellectuals—Du Bois. Yet he and I are birds of very different feathers. My freestyle, California spirit stands in stark contrast to his austere, New England soul. My Chekhovian Christian sensibilities rooted in gut-bucket blues and jazz dispositions violently clash with his Enlightenment and Victorian sentiments based on his Fisk, Harvard, Berlin, Atlanta and New York experiences. To put it bluntly, I am much closer (and proudly so) to the funk of a James Brown or George Clinton, the soul of a Curtis Mayfield, Richard Pryor or Aretha Franklin than he. Yet we remain soul mates in our struggle for oppressed peoples, especially black humanity. I thank my close friend and brother Skip Gates for suggesting I write this essay on Du Bois and modernity.

In memory of my beloved father, Clifton L. West (1928–1994)

> *How shall Integrity face Oppression? What shall Honesty do in the face of Deception, Decency in the face of Insult, Self-Defense before Blows? How shall Desert and Accomplishment meet Despising, Detraction and Lies? What shall Virtue do to meet Brute Force?*

> —W. E. B. Du Bois

> *The hatred and contempt of the oppressed masses are increasing, and the physical and moral forces of the wealthy are weakening; the deception on which everything depends is wearing out, and the wealthy classes have nothing to console themselves with in this mortal danger. To return to the old ways is not possible; only one thing is left for those who do not wish to change their way of life, and that is to hope that "things will last my time"—after that let happen what may. That is*

what the blind crowd of the rich are doing, but the danger is ever
growing and the terrible catastrophe draws near.

–LEO TOLSTOY

What we need are books that hit us like a most painful misfortune,
like the death of someone we loved more than we love ourselves, that
make us feel as though we had been banished to the woods, far from
any human presence, like a suicide. A book must be the ax for the
frozen sea within us.

–FRANZ KAFKA

Speak–
But keep yes and no unsplit.
And give your say this meaning:
Give it the shade.

–PAUL CELAN

W. E. B. DU BOIS IS the towering black scholar of the twentieth century. The scope of his interests, the depth of his insights and the sheer majesty of his prolific writings bespeak a level of genius unequaled among modern black intellectuals. Yet, like all of us, Du Bois was a child of his age. He was shaped by the prevailing presuppositions and prejudices of modern Euro-American civilization. And despite his lifelong struggle—marked by great courage and sacrifice—against white supremacy and for the advancement of Africans around the world, he was, in style and substance, a proud black man of letters primarily influenced by nineteenth-century Euro-American traditions.

For those of us interested in the relation of white supremacy to modernity (African slavery in the New World and European imperial domination of most of the rest of the world) or the consequences of the construct of "race" during the Age of Europe (1492–1945), the scholarly and literary works of Du Bois are indispensable. For those of us obsessed with alleviating black social misery, the political texts of Du Bois are insightful and inspiring. In this sense, Du Bois is the brook of fire through which we all must pass in order to gain access to the intellectual and political weaponry needed to sustain the radical democratic tradition in our time.

Yet even this great titan of black emancipation falls short of the mark. This is not to deny the remarkable subtlety of his mind or the undeniable sincerity of his heart. The grand example of Du Bois remains problematic principally owing to his inadequate interpretation of the human condition and his inability to immerse himself fully in the rich cultural currents of black everyday life. His famous notion of the Talented Tenth—including his revised version—reveals this philosophic inadequacy and personal inability.

What does it mean to claim that Du Bois put forward an inadequate interpretation of the human condition or that he failed to immerse himself fully in the cultural depths of black everyday life? Are these simply rhetorical claims devoid of content—too abstract to yield conclusions and too general to evaluate? Are some interpretations of the human condition and cultural ways of life really better than others? If so, why? These crucial questions sit at the center of my critique of Du Bois, because they take us to the heart of black life in the profoundly decadent American civilization at the end of the twentieth century—a ghastly century whose levels of barbarity, bestiality and brutality are unparalleled in human history.

My assessment of Du Bois primarily concerns his response to the problem of evil—to undeserved harm, unjustified suffering and unmerited pain. Do his evolving worldview, social analysis and moral vision enable us to understand and endure this "first century of world wars" (Muriel Rukeyser's apt phrase),[1] in which nearly 200 million fellow human beings have been murdered in the name of some pernicious ideology? Does his work contain the necessary intellectual and existential resources enabling us to confront the indescribable agony and unnameable anguish likely to be unleashed in the twenty-first century—the first century involving a systemic gangsterization of everyday life, shot through with revitalized tribalisms—under the aegis of an uncontested, fast-paced global capitalism? As with any great figure, to grapple with Du Bois is to wrestle with who we are, why we are what we are and what we are to do about it.

Du Bois was first and foremost a black New England Victorian seduced by the Enlightenment ethos and enchanted with the American Dream. His interpretation of the human condition—that is, in part, his idea of who he was and could be—was based on his experiences and, most importantly, on his understanding of those experiences through the medium of *an Enlightenment worldview* that promoted *Victorian strategies* in order to realize an *American optimism;* throughout this essay, I shall probe these three basic foundations of his perspective. Like many of the brilliant and ambitious young men of his time, he breathed the intoxicating fumes of "advanced" intellectual and political culture. Yet in the face of entrenched evil and demonic power, Du Bois often found himself either shipwrecked in the depths of his soul or barely afloat with less and less wind in his existential sails.

My fundamental problem with Du Bois is his inadequate grasp of the tragicomic sense of life—a refusal candidly to confront the sheer absurdity of the human condition. This tragicomic sense—tragicomic rather than simply "tragic," because even ultimate purpose and objective order are called into question—propels us toward suicide or madness unless we are buffered by ritual, cushioned by community or sustained by art. Du Bois's inability to immerse himself in black everyday life precluded his access to the distinctive black tragicomic sense and black encounter with the absurd. He certainly saw, analyzed and empathized with black sadness, sorrow and suffering. But he didn't feel it in his bones deeply enough, nor was he intellectually open enough to position himself alongside the sorrowful, suffering, yet striving ordinary black folk.[2] Instead, his own personal and intellectual distance lifted him above them even as he addressed their plight in his progressive writings. Du Bois was never alienated by black people—he lived in black communities where he received great respect and admiration. But there seemed to be something in him that alienated ordinary black people. In short, he was reluctant to learn fundamental lessons about life—and about himself—from them. Such lessons would have required that he—at least momentarily—believe that they were or might be as wise, insightful and "advanced" as he; and this he could not do.

Du Bois's Enlightenment worldview—his first foundation—prohibited this kind of understanding. Instead, he adopted a mild elitism that underestimated the capacity of everyday people to "know" about life. In "The Talented Tenth," he claims, "knowledge of life and its wider meaning, has been the point of the Negro's deepest ignorance."[3] In his classic book *The Souls of Black Folk,* there are eighteen references to "black, backward, and ungraceful" folk, including a statement of his intent "to scatter civilization among a people whose ignorance was not simply of letters, but of life itself."[4]

My aim is not to romanticize those whom Sly Stone calls "everyday people" or to cast them as the sole source of wisdom. The myths of the noble savage and the wise commoner are simply the flip sides of the Enlightenment attempts to degrade and devalue everyday people. Yet Du Bois—owing to his Puritan New England origins and Enlightenment values—found it difficult not to view common black folk as some degraded "other" or "alien"—no matter how hard he resisted. His honest response to a church service in the backwoods of Tennessee at a "Southern Negro Revival" bears this out:

A sort of suppressed terror hung in the air and seemed to seize us,—a pythian madness, a demoniac possession, that lent terrible reality to song and word. The black and massive form of the preacher swayed and quivered as the words crowded to his lips and flew at us in singular eloquence. The people moaned and fluttered, and then the gaunt-cheeked brown woman beside me suddenly leaped straight into the air and shrieked like a lost soul, while round about came wail and groan and outcry, and a scene of human passion such as I had never conceived before.

Those who have not thus witnessed the frenzy of a Negro revival in the untouched backwoods of the South can but dimly realize the religious feeling of the slave; as described, such scenes appear grotesque and funny, but as seen they are awful.[5]

Du Bois's intriguing description reminds one of an anthropologist visiting some strange and exotic people whose rituals suggest not only the sublime, but also the satanic.[6] The "awfulness" of this black church service, similar to that of my own black Baptist tradition, signifies for him both dread and fear, anxiety and disgust. In short, a black ritualistic explosion of energy frightened this black rationalist. It did so not simply because the folk seem so coarse and uncouth, but also because they are out of control, overpowered by something bigger than themselves. This clearly posed a threat to him.

Like a good Enlightenment *philosophe,* Du Bois pits autonomy against authority, self-mastery against tradition. Autonomy and self-mastery connote self-consciousness and self-criticism; authority and tradition suggest blind deference and subordination. Self-consciousness and self-criticism yield cosmopolitanism and highbrow culture. Authority and tradition reinforce provincialism and low-brow culture. The educated and chattering class—the Talented Tenth—are the agents of sophistication and mastery, while the uneducated and moaning class—the backward masses—remain locked in tradition; the basic role of the Talented Tenth is to civilize and refine, uplift and elevate the benighted masses.[7]

For Du Bois, education was the key. Ignorance was the major obstacle—black ignorance and white ignorance. If the black masses were educated—in order to acquire skills and culture—black America would thrive. If white elites and masses were enlightened, they would not hate and fear black folk. Hence America—black and white—could be true to its democratic ideals. "The Negro Problem was in my mind a matter of systematic investigation and intelligent understanding. The world was thinking wrong about race, because it did not know. The ultimate evil was stupidity. The cure for it was knowledge based on scientific investigation."[8]

This Enlightenment naïveté—not only in regard to white supremacy, but with respect to any form of personal and institutional evil—was momentarily shaken by a particular case involving that most peculiar American institution—lynching.

> At the very time when my studies were most successful, there cut across this plan which I had as a scientist, a red ray which could not be ignored. I remember when it first, as it were, startled me to my feet: a poor Negro in central Georgia, Sam Hose, had killed his landlord's wife. I wrote out a careful and reasoned statement concerning the evident facts and started down to the Atlanta Constitution office. . . . I did not get there. On the way news met me: Sam Hose had been lynched, and they said that his knuckles were on exhibition at a grocery store farther down on Mitchell Street, along which I was walking. I turned back to the university. I began to turn aside from my work. . . .

Two considerations thereafter broke in upon my work and eventually disrupted it: first, one could not be a calm, cool, and detached scientist while Negroes were lynched, murdered and starved; and secondly, there was no such definite demand for scientific work of the sort that I was doing. . . .[9]

Then, in the very next month, Du Bois lost his eighteen-month-old son, Burghardt, to diphtheria.[10] If ever Du Bois was forced to confront the tragedy of life and the absurdity of existence, it was in the aftermath of this loss, which he describes in his most moving piece of writing, "Of the Passing of the First-Born," in *The Souls of Black Folk*. In this powerful elegiac essay, Du Bois not only mourns his son, but speaks directly to death itself—as Prometheus to Zeus or Jesus to his Heavenly Father.[11]

But hearken, O Death! Is not this my life hard enough,—is not that dull land that stretches its sneering web about me cold enough,—is not all the world beyond these four little walls pitiless enough, but that thou must needs enter here,—thou, O Death? About my head the thundering storm beat like a heartless voice, and the crazy forest pulsed with the curses of the weak; but what cared I, within my home beside my wife and baby boy? Wast thou so jealous of one little coign of happiness that thou must needs enter there,—thou, O Death?[12]

This existential gall to go face-to-face and toe-to-toe with death in order to muster some hope against hope is echoed in his most tragic characterization of the black sojourn in white-supremacist America:

Within the Veil was he born, said I; and there within shall he live,—a Negro and a Negro's son. Holding in that little head—ah, bitterly!—the unbowed pride of a hunted race, clinging with that tiny dimpled hand—ah, wearily!—to a hope not hopeless but unhopeful, and seeing with those bright wondering eyes that peer into my soul a land whose freedom is to us a mockery and whose liberty a lie.[13]

What is most revealing in this most poignant of moments is Du Bois's refusal to linger with the sheer tragedy of his son's death (a natural, not a social, evil)—without casting his son as an emblem of the race or a symbol of a black deliverance to come.[14] Despite the deep sadness in this beautiful piece of writing, Du Bois sidesteps Dostoyevsky's challenge to wrestle in a sustained way with the irrevocable fact of an innocent child's death. Du Bois's rationalism prevents him from wading in such frightening existential waters. Instead, Du Bois rushes to glib theodicy, weak allegory and superficial symbolism. In other words, his Enlightenment worldview falters in the face of death—the deaths of Sam Hose and

Burghardt. The deep despair that lurks around the corner is held at arm's length by rational attempts to boost his flagging spirit.

Du Bois's principal intellectual response to the limits of his Enlightenment worldview was to incorporate certain insights of Marx and Freud. Yet Marx's powerful critique of the unequal relations of power between capitalists and the proletariat in the workplace and Freud's penetrating attempt to exercise rational control over the irrational forces at work in self and society only deepened Du Bois's commitment to the Enlightenment ethos. And though particular features of this ethos are essential to any kind of intellectual integrity and democratic vision—features such as self-criticism and self-development, suspicion of illegitimate authority and suffocating tradition—the Enlightenment worldview held by Du Bois is ultimately inadequate, and in many ways antiquated, for our time. The tragic plight and absurd predicament of Africans here and abroad requires a more profound interpretation of the human condition—one that goes far beyond the false dichotomies of expert knowledge versus mass ignorance, individual autonomy versus dogmatic authority and self-mastery versus intolerant tradition. Our tragicomic times require more democratic concepts of knowledge and leadership that highlight human fallibility and mutual accountability, notions of individuality and contested authority that stress dynamic traditions and ideals of self-realization within participatory communities.

The second fundamental pillar of Du Bois's intellectual project is his Victorian strategies—namely, the ways in which his Enlightenment worldview can be translated into action. They rest upon three basic assumptions. First, that the self-appointed agents of Enlightenment constitute a sacrificial cultural elite engaged in service on behalf of the impulsive and irrational masses. Second, that this service consists of shaping and molding the values and viewpoints of the masses by managing educational and political bureaucracies (e.g., schools and political parties). Third, that the effective management of these bureaucracies by the educated few for the benefit of the pathetic many promotes material and spiritual progress. These assumptions form the terrain upon which the Talented Tenth are to operate.

In fact, Du Bois's notion of the Talented Tenth is a descendant of those cultural and political elites conceived by the major Victorian critics during the heyday of the British empire in its industrial phase.[15] S. T. Coleridge's secular clerisy, Thomas Carlyle's strong heroes and Matthew Arnold's disinterested aliens all shun the superficial vulgarity of materialism and the cheap thrills of hedonism in order to preserve and promote highbrow culture and to civilize and contain the lowbrow masses. The resounding first and last sentences of Du Bois's essay "The Talented Tenth" not only echo the "truths" of Victorian social criticism, they also bestow upon the educated few a salvific role. "The Negro race, like all races, is going to be saved by its exceptional men."[16] This bold statement is descriptive, prescriptive and predictive. It assumes that the exceptional men of other races have saved their "race" (Gladstone in Britain, Menelik in Ethiopia, Bismarck in Germany, Napoleon in France, Peter in Russia?). Here Du Bois claims that exceptional black men ought to save their "race" and asserts that if any "race"—especially black people—is to be saved, exceptional men will do it. The patriarchal sensibilities speak for themselves.[17] They are unargued for, hence unacceptable.

Like a good Victorian critic, Du Bois argues on rational grounds for the legitimacy of his cultural elite. They are worthy of leadership because they are educated and trained, refined and civilized, disciplined and determined. Most important, they have "honesty of heart" and "purity of motive." Contrast Matthew Arnold's disinterested aliens, "who are mainly led, not by their class spirit, but by a general *humane* spirit, by the love of human perfection," in *Culture and Anarchy* (1869) with Du Bois's Talented Tenth:

> The men of culture are the true apostles of equality. The great men of culture are those who have had a passion for diffusing, for making prevail, for carrying from one end of society to the other, the best knowledge, the best ideas of their time, who have laboured to divest knowledge of all that was harsh, uncouth, difficult, abstract, professional, exclusive; to humanize it, to make it efficient outside the clique of the cultivated and learned, yet still remaining the *best* knowledge and thought of the time, and a true source, therefore, of sweetness and light.[18]

> Who are to-day guiding the work of the Negro people? The "exceptions" of course. . . . A saving remnant continually survives and persists, continually aspires, continually shows itself in thrift and ability and character. . . .
>
> Can the masses of the Negro people be in any possible way more quickly raised than by the effort and example of this aristocracy of talent and character? Was there ever a nation on God's fair earth civilized from the bottom upward? Never; it is, ever was and ever will be from the top downward that culture filters. The Talented Tenth rises and pulls all that are worth the saving up to their vantage ground. This is the history of human progress; and the two historic mistakes which have hindered that progress were the thinking first that no more could ever rise save the few already risen; or second, that it would better the unrisen to pull the risen down.[19]

Just as Arnold seeks to carve out discursive space and a political mission for the educated elite in the British empire somewhere between the arrogance and complacency of the aristocracy and the vulgarity and anarchy of the working classes, Du Bois wants to create a new vocabulary and social vocation for the black educated elite in America somewhere between the hatred and scorn of the white-supremacist majority and the crudity and illiteracy of the black agrarian masses. Yet his gallant efforts suffer from intellectual defects and historical misconceptions.

Let us begin with the latter. Is it true that in 1903 the educated elite were guiding the work of the Negro people? Yes and no. Certainly the most visible national black leaders tended to be educated black men, such as the ubiquitous Booker T. Washington and, of course, Du Bois himself. Yet the two most effective political forms of organizing and mobilizing among black people were the black women's club movement led by Ida B. Wells-Barnett and the migration movement guided by Benjamin "Pap" Singleton, A. A. Bradley and Richard H. Cain.[20] Both movements were based in black civil society—that is, black civic associations like churches, lodges, fraternal orders and sororities. Their fundamental goals were neither civil rights nor social equality, but rather respect and dignity, land and self-determination. How astonishing—and limiting—that Du Bois fails to mention and analyze these movements that will result in the great Mary McLeod Bethune's educational crusade and the inimitable Marcus Garvey's Back-to-Africa movement in a decade or so!

Regarding the intellectual defects of Du Bois's noble endeavor: First, he assumes that highbrow culture is inherently humanizing, and that exposure to and immersion in great works produce good people. Yet we have little reason to believe that people who delight in the works of geniuses like Mozart and Beethoven or Goethe and Wordsworth are any more or less humane than those who dance in the barnyards to the banjo plucking of nameless rural folk in Tennessee. Certainly those fervent white supremacists who worship the Greek and Roman classics and revel in the plays of the incomparable Shakespeare weaken his case.[21] Second, Du Bois holds that the educated elite can more easily transcend their individual and class interests and more readily act on behalf of the common good than the uneducated masses. But is this so? Are they not just as prone to corruption and graft, envy and jealousy, self-destructive passion and ruthless ambition as everyone else? Were not Carlyle's great heroes, Cromwell and Napoleon, tyrants? Was it not Arnold's disinterested aliens who promoted and implemented the inhumane policies of the imperial British bureaucracies in India and Africa? Was not Du Bois himself both villain and victim in petty political games as well as in the all-too-familiar social exclusions of the educated elite?

Du Bois wisely acknowledges this problem in his 1948 revision of "The Talented Tenth":

> When I came out of college into the world of work, I realized that it was quite possible that my plan of training a talented tenth might put in control and power, a group of selfish, self-indulgent, well-to-do men, whose basic interest in solving the Negro Problem was personal; personal freedom and unhampered enjoyment

and use of the world, without any real care, or certainly no arousing care, as to what became of the mass of American Negroes, or of the mass of any people. My Talented Tenth, I could see, might result in a sort of interracial free-for-all, with the devil taking the hindmost and the foremost taking anything they could lay hands on.[22]

He then notes the influence of Marx on his thinking and adds that the Talented Tenth must not only be talented, but have "expert knowledge" of modern economics, be willing to sacrifice and plan effectively to institute socialist measures. Yet there is still no emphatic call for accountability from below, or any grappling with the evil that lurks in the hearts of all of us. He recognizes human selfishness as a problem without putting forward adequate philosophical responses to it or institutional mechanisms to alleviate it. In the end, he throws up his hands and gives us a grand either/or option. "But we must have honest men or we die. We must have unselfish, far-seeing leadership or we fail."[23]

Victorian social criticism contains elements indispensable to future critical thought about freedom and democracy in the twenty-first century. Most important, it elevates the role of public intellectuals who put forward overarching visions and broad analyses based on a keen sense of history and a subtle grasp of the way the world is going in the present. The rich tradition of Victorian critics—Thomas Carlyle, John Ruskin, Matthew Arnold, John Morley, William Morris, and, in our own century, L. T. Hobhouse, J. A. Hobson, C. F. G. Masterman, R. H. Tawney, Raymond Williams, E. P. Thompson, and others—stands shoulders above the parochial professionalism of much of the academy today. In our era, scholarship is often divorced from public engagement, and shoddy journalism often settles for the sensational and superficial aspects of prevailing crises.[24] As the distinguished European man of letters George Steiner notes in regard to the academy:

> Specialization has reached moronic vehemence. Learned lives are expended on reiterative minutiae. Academic rewards go to the narrow scholiast, to the blinkered. Men and women in the learned professions proclaim themselves experts on one author, in one brief historical period, in one aesthetic medium. They look with contempt (and dank worry) on the "Generalist." . . . It may be that cows have fields. The geography of consciousness should be that of unfenced *errance,* Montaigne's comely word.[25]

Yet the Victorian strategies of Du Bois require not piecemeal revision, but wholesale reconstruction. A fuller understanding of the human condition should lead us far beyond any notions of free-floating elites, suspicious of the tainted masses—elites who worship at the altar of highbrow culture while ignoring the barbarity and bestiality in their own ranks. The fundamental role of the public intellectual—distinct from, yet building on, the indispensable work of academics, experts, analysts and pundits—is to create and sustain high-quality public discourse addressing urgent public problems that enlightens and energizes fellow citizens, prompting them to take public action. This role requires a deep commitment to the life of the mind—a perennial attempt to clear our minds of cant (to use Samuel Johnson's famous formulation)—which serves to shape the public destiny of a people. Intellectual and political leadership should be neither elitist, nor populist; rather it ought to be democratic, in that each of us stands in public space, without humiliation, to put forward our best visions and views for the sake of the public interest. And these arguments are presented in an atmosphere of mutual respect and civic trust.

The last pillar of Du Bois's project is his American optimism. Like most intellectuals of the New World, he was preoccupied with progress. And given his genuine commitment to black advancement, this preoccupation is understandable. Yet, writing as he was in the early stages of the consolidation of the American empire (some eight million people of color had been incorporated after the Spanish-American War), when the United States itself was undergoing geographical and economic expansion and millions of "new" Americans were being admitted from eastern Europe, Du Bois tended to assume that U.S. expansionism was a sign of probable American progress. In this sense, in his early and middle years, he was not only a progressivist, but also a kind of American exceptionalist.[26] It must be said, to be sure, that unlike most American exceptionalists of his day, he considered the color line the major litmus test for the country. Yet he remained optimistic about a multiracial democratic America.

Du Bois never fully grasped the deeply pessimistic view of American democracy behind the Garvey movement.[27] In fact, he never fully understood or appreciated the strong—though not central—black nationalist strain in the black freedom movement. As much as he hated white supremacy in America, he could never bring himself to identify intimately with the harsh words of the great performing artist Josephine Baker, who noted in response to the East St. Louis riot of July 1917, which left over two hundred black people dead and over six thousand homeless, "The very idea of America makes me shake and tremble and gives me nightmares." Baker lived most of her life in exile in France. Even when Du Bois left for Africa in 1961—as a member of a moribund Communist Party—his attitude toward America was not that of an Elijah Muhammad or a Malcolm X. He was still, in a significant sense, disappointed with America, and there is no disappointment without some dream deferred. Elijah Muhammad and Malcolm X were not disappointed with America. As bona fide black nationalists, they had no expectations of a white-supremacist civilization; they adhered neither to American optimism nor to exceptionalism.

Black nationalism is a complex tradition of thought and action, a tradition best expressed in the numerous insightful texts of black public intellectuals like Maulana Karenga, Imamu Amiri Baraka, Haki R. Madhubuti, Marimba Ani, and Molefi Asante. Black nationalists usually call upon black people to close ranks, to distrust most whites (since the reliable whites are few and relatively powerless in the face of white supremacy) and to promote forms of black self-love, self-defense and self-determination. It views white supremacy as the definitive systemic constraint on black cultural, political and economic development. More pointedly, black nationalists claim that American democracy is a modern form of tyranny on the part of the white majority over the black minority. For them, black sanity and freedom require that America not serve as the major framework in which to understand the future of black people. Instead, American civilization—like all civilizations—rises and falls, ebbs and flows. And owing to its deep-seated racism, this society does not warrant black allegiance or loyalty. White supremacy dictates the limits of the operation of American democracy—with black folk the indispensable sacrificial lamb vital to its sustenance. Hence black subordination constitutes the necessary condition for the flourishing of American democracy, the tragic prerequisite for America itself. This is, in part, what Richard Wright meant when he noted, "The Negro is America's metaphor."

The most courageous and consistent of twentieth-century black nationalists—Marcus Garvey and Elijah Muhammad—adamantly rejected any form of American optimism or exceptionalism. Du Bois feared that if they were right, he would be left in a state of paralyzing despair, a kind of despair that results not only when all credible options for black freedom in America are closed, but also when the very framework needed to understand and cope with that despair is shattered. The black nationalist challenge to Du Bois cuts much deeper than the rational and political possibilities for change—it resides at the visceral and existential levels of what to do about "what is" or when "what ought to be done" seems undoable. This frightening sense of foreboding pervades much of black America today—a sense that fans and fuels black nationalism.

Du Bois's American optimism screened him from this dark night of the soul. His American exceptionalism guarded him from that gray twilight between "nothing to be done" and "I can't go on like this"—a Beckett-like dilemma in which the wait and search for Godot, or for freedom, seem endless. This militant despair about the black condition is expressed in that most arresting of black nationalist speeches by Rev. Henry Highland Garnet in 1843: "If we must bleed, let it come all at once—rather die freemen than live to be slaves. It is impossible like the children of Israel, to make a grand Exodus from the land of bondage. The pharaoh's on both sides of the blood-red waters!"[28]

Du Bois's response to such despair is to say "we surely must do something"— for such rebellion is suicidal and the notion of a separate black nation quixotic.

So, he seems to say, let us continue to wait and search for Godot in America—even if it seems, with our luck, that all we get is "Pozzo" (new forms of disrespect, disregard, degradation and defamation).

American optimism couched within the ideals of the American experiment contains crucial components for any desirable form of black self-determination or modern nationhood: precious standards of constitutional democracy, the rule of law, individual liberties and the dignity of common folk. Yet American optimism—in the ugly face of American white-supremacist practices—warrants, if not outright rejection, at least vast attenuation. The twenty-first century will almost certainly not be a time in which American exceptionalism will flower in the world or American optimism will flourish among people of African descent.

If there are any historical parallels between black Americans at the end of the twentieth century and other peoples in earlier times, two candidates loom large: Tolstoy's Russia and Kafka's Prague—soul-starved Russians a generation after the emancipation of the serfs in 1861 and anxiety-ridden central European Jews a generation before the European Holocaust in the 1940s. Indeed, my major intellectual disappointment with the great Du Bois lies in the fact that there are hardly any traces in his work of any serious grappling with the profound thinkers and spiritual wrestlers in the modern West from these two groups—major figures obsessed with the problem of evil in their time.

We see in Du Bois no engagement with Leo Tolstoy, Fyodor Dostoyevsky, Ivan Turgenev, Alexander Herzen, Lev Shestov and Anton Chekhov or Franz Kafka, Max Brod, Kurt Tucholsky, Hermann Broch, Hugo Bergmann and Karl Kraus. These omissions are glaring because the towering figures in both groups were struggling with political and existential issues similar to those facing black people in America. For example, the Russian situation involved the humanity of degraded impoverished peasants, the fragile stability of an identity-seeking empire and the alienation of superfluous intellectuals; the central European Jewish circumstance, the humanity of devalued middle-class Jews, the imminent collapse of a decadent empire and the militant despair of self-hating intellectuals. The intellectual response on the part of the Russian authors was what Hegel would call "world-historical"—they wrote many of the world's greatest novels, short stories, essays and plays. The writers I cite put forward profound interpretations of the human condition that rejected any Enlightenment worldview, Victorian strategy or worldly optimism. And although the central European Jewish authors are often overlooked by contemporary intellectuals—owing to a tendency to focus on western Europe—their intellectual response was monumental. They composed many of this century's most probing and penetrating novels, short stories, autobiographies and letters.

Both Russian and central European Jewish writers share deep elective affinities that underlie their distinctive voices: the "wind of the wing of madness" (to use

Baudelaire's phrase) beats incessantly on their souls. The fear of impending social doom and dread of inevitable death haunt them, and they search for a precious individuality in the face of a terror-ridden society and a seductive (yet doubtful) nationalist option.[29] In short, fruitful comparisons may be made between the Russian sense of the tragic and the central European Jewish sense of the absurd and the black intellectual response to the African American predicament. Tolstoy's *War and Peace* (1869), *The Death of Ivan Ilych* (1886) and "How Much Land Does a Man Need?" (1886) and Chekhov's *Three Sisters* (1901)—the greatest novel, short story, brief tale and play in modern Europe—and Kafka's "The Judgment" (1913), "The Metamorphosis" (1915), "In the Penal Colony" (1919) and "The Burrow" (1923)—some of the grandest fictive portraits of twentieth-century Europe—constitute the highest moments and most ominous murmurings in Europe before it entered the ugly and fiery inferno of totalitarianism. Similarly, the intellectual response of highbrow black artists—most of whom are musicians and often of plebeian origins—probe the depths of a black sense of the tragic and absurd which yields a subversive joy and sublime melancholia unknown to most in the New World. The form and content of Louis Armstrong's "West End Blues," Duke Ellington's "Mood Indigo," John Coltrane's "Alabama" and Sarah Vaughan's "Send in the Clowns" are a few of the peaks of the black cultural iceberg—towering examples of soul-making and spiritual wrestling that crystallize the most powerful interpretations of the human condition in black life. This is why the best of the black musical tradition in the twentieth century is the most profound and poignant body of artistic works in our time.

Like their Russian and central European Jewish counterparts, the black artists grapple with madness and melancholia, doom and death, terror and horror, individuality and identity. Unlike them, the black artists do so against the background of an African heritage that puts a premium on voice and body, sound and silence, and the foreground is occupied by an American tradition that highlights mobility and novelty, individuality and democracy. The explosive products of this multilayered cultural hybridity—with its new diasporic notions of time and space, place and face—take us far beyond Du Bois's enlightened optimism. Instead, the profound black cultural efforts to express the truth of modern tragic existence and build on the ruins of modern absurd experiences at the core of American culture take us to the end of this dreadful century. These black artistic endeavors prefigure and pose the most fundamental and formidable challenges to a twilight civilization—an American empire adrift on turbulent seas in a dark fog. William Faulkner, Mark Twain, Thomas Pynchon and, above all, the incomparable Herman Melville—the only great Euro-American novelists to be spoken of in the same breath as Tolstoy and Kafka, Armstrong and Coltrane—grasp crucial aspects of this black condition, just as Richard Wright, Ralph Ellison, James Baldwin and, preeminently, Toni Morrison guide us through the tragedies and absurdities within the Veil (or behind the color curtain) to disclose on the page what is best revealed in black song, speech, sermon, bodily performance and the eloquence of black silence. Yet despite his shortcomings, the great Du Bois remains the springboard for any examination of black strivings in American civilization.

On Black Strivings

Black strivings are the creative and complex products of the terrifying African encounter with the absurd *in* America—and the absurd *as* America. Like any other group of human beings, black people forged ways of life and ways of struggle under circumstances not of their own choosing. They constructed structures of meaning and structures of feeling in the face of the fundamental facts of human existence—death, dread, despair, disease and disappointment. Yet the specificity of black culture—namely, those features that distinguish black culture from other cultures—lies in both the *African* and *American* character of black people's attempts to sustain their mental sanity and spiritual health, social life and political struggle in the midst of a slaveholding, white-supremacist civilization that viewed itself as the most enlightened, free, tolerant and democratic experiment in human history.

Any serious examination of black culture should begin with what W. E. B. Du Bois dubbed, in Faustian terms, the "spiritual strivings" of black people—the dogged determination to survive and subsist, the tenacious will to persevere, persist and maybe even prevail.[30] These "strivings" occur within the whirlwind of white supremacy—that is, as responses to the vicious attacks on black beauty, black intelligence, black moral character, black capability and black possibility. To put it bluntly, every major institution in American society—churches, universities, courts, academies of science, governments, economies, newspapers, magazines, television, film and others—attempted to exclude black people from the human family in the name of white-supremacist ideology. This unrelenting assault on black humanity produced the fundamental condition of black culture—that of *black invisibility and namelessness*.

This basic predicament exists on at least four levels—existential, social, political and economic. The existential level is the most relevant here because it has to do with what it means to be a person and live a life under the horrifying realities of racist assault. To be a black human being under circumstances in which one's humanity is questioned is not only to face a difficult challenge, but also to exercise a demanding discipline.

The sheer absurdity of being a black human being whose black body is viewed as an abomination, whose black thoughts and ideas are perceived as debased and whose black pain and grief are rendered invisible on the human and moral scale is the New World context in which black culture emerged. Black people are first and foremost an African people, in that the cultural baggage they brought with

them to the New World was grounded in their earlier responses to African conditions. Yet the rich African traditions—including the kinetic orality, passionate
physicality, improvisational intellectuality and combative spirituality—would undergo creative transformation when brought into contact with European languages and rituals in the context of the New World. For example, there would be
no jazz without New World Africans with European languages and instruments.

On the crucial existential level relating to black invisibility and namelessness,
the first difficult challenge and demanding discipline is to ward off madness and
discredit suicide as a desirable option. A central preoccupation of black culture is
that of confronting candidly the ontological wounds, psychic scars and existential bruises of black people while fending off insanity and self-annihilation. Black
culture consists of black modes of being-in-the-world obsessed with black sadness and sorrow, black agony and anguish, black heartache and heartbreak without fully succumbing to the numbing effects of such misery—to never allow such
misery to have the last word. This is why the "*ur*-text" of black culture is neither
a word nor a book, not an architectural monument or a legal brief. Instead, it is
a guttural cry and a wrenching moan—a cry not so much for help as for home, a
moan less out of complaint than for recognition. The most profound black cultural products—John Coltrane's saxophone solos, James Cleveland's gut gospels,
Billie Holiday's vocal leaps, Rev. Gardner Taylor's rhapsodic sermons, James
Baldwin's poignant essays, Alvin Ailey's graceful dances, Toni Morrison's disso-
nant novels—transform and transfigure in artistic form this cry and moan. The
deep black meaning of this cry and moan goes back to the indescribable cries of
Africans on the slave ships during the cruel transatlantic voyages to America and
the indecipherable moans of enslaved Afro-Americans on Wednesday nights or
Sunday mornings near godforsaken creeks or on wooden benches at prayer
meetings in makeshift black churches. This fragile existential arsenal—rooted in
silent tears and weary lament—supports black endurance against madness and
suicide. The primal black cries and moans lay bare the profoundly tragicomic
character of black life. Ironically, they also embody the life-preserving content of
black styles—creative ways of fashioning power and strength through the body
and language which yield black joy and ecstasy.

Du Bois captures one such primal scene of black culture at the beginning of *The
Souls of Black Folk* (1903), in chapter 1, "Of Our Spiritual Strivings." He starts with
thirteen lines from the poem "The Crying of Water" by Arthur Symons, the English symbolist critic and decadent poet who went mad a few years after writing
the poem. The hearts of human beings in a heartless slave trade cry out like the
sea: "All life long crying without avail, / As the water all night long is crying to
me."[31]

This metaphorical association of black hearts, black people and black culture
with water (the sea or a river) runs deep in black artistic expression—as in

Langston Hughes's recurring refrain, "My soul has grown deep like the rivers," in "The Negro Speaks of Rivers." Black striving resides primarily in movement and motion, resilience and resistance against the paralysis of madness and the stillness of death. As it is for Jim in Mark Twain's *The Adventures of Huckleberry Finn* (1885), the river—a road that moves—is the means by which black people can flee from a menacing racist society.

Du Bois continues with the musical bars of the Negro spiritual "Nobody Knows the Trouble I've Seen." This spiritual is known not simply for its plaintive melody, but also for its inexplicable lyrical reversal:

> *Nobody knows the trouble I've seen*
> *Nobody knows but Jesus*
> *Nobody knows the trouble I've seen*
> *Glory hallelujah!*[32]

This exemplary shift from a mournful brooding to a joyful praising is the product of courageous efforts to look life's abyss in the face and keep "keepin' on." This struggle is sustained primarily by the integrity of style, song and spirituality in a beloved community (e.g., Jesus' proclamation of the Kingdom). It is rather like Ishmael's tragicomic "free and easy sort of genial, desperado philosophy" in *Moby-Dick,* but it is intensified by the fiery art of Aretha Franklin's majestic shouts for joy.

The first of Du Bois's own words in the text completes the primal scene of black culture:

> Between me and the other world there is ever an unasked question: unasked by some through feelings of delicacy; by others through the difficulty of rightly framing it. All, nevertheless, flutter round it. They approach me in a half-hesitant sort of way, eye me curiously or compassionately, and then, instead of saying directly, How does it feel to be a problem? they say, I know an excellent colored man in my town; or, I fought at Mechanicsville; or, Do not these Southern outrages make your blood boil? At these I smile, or am interested, or reduce the boiling to a simmer, as the occasion may require. To the real question, How does it feel to be a problem? I answer seldom a word.
>
> And yet, being a problem is a strange experience,—peculiar even for one who has never been anything else, save perhaps in babyhood. . . .[33]

This seminal passage spells out the basic components of black invisibility and namelessness: *black people as a problem people rather than people with problems; black people as abstractions and objects rather than individuals and persons; black and white worlds divided by a thick wall (or a "Veil") that requires role-playing and mask-wearing rather than*

genuine humane interaction; black rage, anger and fury concealed in order to assuage white fear
and anxiety; and black people rootless and homeless on a perennial journey to discover who they
are in a society content to see blacks remain the permanent underdog.

To view black people as a "problem people" is to view them as an undifferenti-
ated blob, a homogeneous bloc or a monolithic conglomerate. Each black person
is interchangeable, indistinguishable or substitutable, since all black people are believed to have the same views and values, sentiments and sensibilities. Hence one
set of negative stereotypes holds for all of them, no matter how high certain
blacks may ascend in the white world (e.g., "savages in a suit or suite"). And the
mere presence of black bodies in a white context generates white unease and discomfort, even among whites of goodwill.

This problematizing of black humanity deprives black people of individuality,
diversity and heterogeneity. It reduces black folk to abstractions and objects born
of white fantasies and insecurities—as exotic or transgressive entities, as hypersex-
ual or criminal animals.[34] The celebrated opening passage of Ralph Ellison's classic novel, *Invisible Man* (1952), highlights this reduction:

> I am an invisible man. No, I am not a spook like those who haunted Edgar Allan
> Poe; nor am I one of your Hollywood-movie ectoplasms. I am a man of sub-
> stance, of flesh and bone, fiber and liquids—and I might even be said to possess
> a mind. I am invisible, understand, simply because people refuse to see me. Like
> the bodiless heads you see sometimes in circus sideshows, it is as though I have
> been surrounded by mirrors of hard, distorting glass. When they approach me
> they see only my surroundings, themselves, or figments of their imagination—in-
> deed, everything and anything except me.[35]

This distorted perception—the failure to see the humanity and individuality of
black people—has its source in the historic "Veil" (slavery, Jim Crow, and segregation) that separates the black and white worlds. Ironically, this refusal to see a people whose epidermis is most visible exists alongside a need to keep tight surveillance over these people. This Veil not only precludes honest communication
between blacks and whites; it also forces blacks to live in two worlds in order to
survive. Whites need not understand or live in the black world in order to thrive.
But blacks must grapple with the painful "double-consciousness" that may result
in "an almost morbid sense of personality and a moral hesitancy which is fatal to
self-confidence."[36] Du Bois notes:

> The worlds within and without the Veil of Color are changing, and changing
> rapidly, but not at the same rate, not in the same way; and this must produce a
> peculiar wrenching of the soul, a peculiar sense of doubt and bewilderment. Such
> a double life, with double thoughts, double duties, and double social classes,

must give rise to double words and double ideals, and tempt the mind to pretence or to revolt, to hypocrisy or to radicalism.[37]

Echoing Paul Laurence Dunbar's famous poem "We Wear the Mask," Du Bois proclaims that "the price of culture is a Lie."[38] Why? Because black people will not succeed in American society if they are fully and freely themselves. Instead, they must "endure petty insults with a smile, shut [their] eyes to wrong."[39] They must not be too frank and outspoken and must never fail to flatter and be pleasant in order to lessen white unease and discomfort. Needless to say, this is not the raw stuff for healthy relations between black and white people.

Yet this suppression of black rage—the reducing "the boiling to a simmer"—backfires in the end. It reinforces a black obsession with the psychic scars, ontological wounds and existential bruises that tend to reduce the tragic to the pathetic. Instead of exercising agency or engaging in action against the odds, one may wallow in self-pity, acknowledging the sheer absurdity of it all. After playing the role and wearing the mask in the white world, one may accept the white world's view of one's self. As Du Bois writes: "It is a peculiar sensation, this double-consciousness, this sense of always looking at one's self through the eyes of others, of measuring one's soul by the tape of a world that looks on in amused contempt and pity."[40]

Toni Morrison explores this dilemma of black culture through her moving portrayal of the character of Sweet Home—a place that functions like a person (echoes of Thomas Hardy's Heath) in her profound novel *Beloved* (1987), similar to Jean Toomer's Karintha and Fern in his marvelous and magical text *Cane* (1923): "For the sadness was at her center, the desolated center where the self that was no self made its home."[41]

This theme of black rootlessness and homelessness is inseparable from black namelessness. When James Baldwin writes about these issues in *Nobody Knows My Name* (1961) and *No Name in the Street* (1972), he is trying to explore effective ways to resist the white-supremacist imposition of subordinate roles, stations and identities on blacks. He is attempting to devise some set of existential strategies against the overwhelming onslaught of white dehumanization, devaluation and degradation. The search for black space (home), black place (roots) and black face (name) is a flight from the visceral effects of white supremacy. Toni Morrison characterizes these efforts as products of a process of "dirtying you": "That anybody white could take your whole self for anything that came to mind. Not just work, kill, or maim you, but dirty you. Dirty you so bad you couldn't like yourself anymore. Dirty you so bad you forgot who you were and couldn't think it up."[42]

Toni Morrison's monumental novel holds a privileged place in black culture and modernity precisely because she takes this dilemma to its logical conclusion—that black flight from white supremacy (a chamber of horrors for black people) may lead to the murder of those loved ones who are candidates for the "dirtying" process. The black mother, Sethe, kills her daughter, Beloved, because she loved her so, "to outhurt the hurter," as an act of resistance against the "dirtying" process.

> And though she and others lived through and got over it, she could never let it happen to her own. The best thing she was, was her children. Whites might dirty *her* all right, but not her best thing, her beautiful, magical best thing—the part of her that was clean. No undreamable dreams about whether the headless, feetless torso hanging in the tree with a sign on it was her husband or Paul A; whether the bubbling-hot girls in the colored-school fire set by patriots included her daughter; whether a gang of whites invaded her daughter's private parts, soiled her daughter's thighs and threw her daughter out of the wagon. *She* might have to work the slaughterhouse yard, but not her daughter.
>
> And no one, nobody on this earth, would list her daughter's characteristics on the animal side of the paper. No. Oh no. . . . Sethe had refused—and refused still. . . .
>
> What she had done was right because it came from true love.[43]

Is death the only black space (home), place (roots) and face (name) safe from a pervasive white supremacy? Toni Morrison's Sethe echoes Du Bois's own voice upon the painful passing of his firstborn. For Sethe, as for Tolstoy's Ivan, Chekhov's Bishop Pyotr, Kafka's Josephine, Hawthorne's Goodman Brown, Hardy's Jude, Büchner's Woyzeck, Dreiser's Hurstwood and Shakespeare's Lear, death is the great liberator from suffering and evil.

> But Love sat beside his cradle, and in his ear Wisdom waited to speak. Perhaps now he knows the All-love, and needs not to be wise. Sleep, then, child,—sleep till I sleep and waken to a baby voice and the ceaseless patter of little feet—above the Veil.[44]

The most effective and enduring black responses to invisibility and namelessness are those forms of individual and collective black resistance predicated on a deep and abiding black *love*. These responses take the shape of prophetic thought and action: bold, fearless, courageous attempts to tell the truth about and bear witness to black suffering and to keep faith with a vision of black redemption. Like the "*ur*-texts" of the guttural cry and wrenching moan—enacted in Charlie Parker's bebop sound, Dinah Washington's cool voice, Richard Pryor's comic performances and James Brown's inimitable funk—the prophetic utterance that focuses on black suffering and sustains a hope-against-hope for black freedom constitutes the heights of black culture. The spiritual depths (the how and what) of Martin Luther King's visionary orations, Nat King Cole's silky soul, August Wilson's probing plays, Martin Puryear's unique sculpture, Harold and Fayard Nicholas's existential acrobatics, Jacob Lawrence's powerful paintings, Marvin Gaye's risky falsettos, Fannie Lou Hamer's fighting songs and, above all, John Coltrane's *A Love Supreme* exemplify such heights. Two of the greatest moments in black literature also enact such high-quality performances. First, James Baldwin's great self-descriptive visionary passage in *Go Tell It on the Mountain* (1953):

> Yes, their parts were all cut off, they were dishonored, their very names were nothing more than dust blown disdainfully across the field of time—to fall where, to blossom where, bringing forth what fruit hereafter, where?—their very names were not their own. Behind them was the darkness, nothing but the darkness, and all around them destruction, and before them nothing but the fire—a bastard people, far from God, singing and crying in the wilderness!
>
> Yet, most strangely, and from deeps not before discovered, his faith looked up; before the wickedness that he saw, the wickedness from which he fled, he yet beheld, like a flaming standard in the middle of the air, that power of redemption to which he must, till death, bear witness; which, though it crush him utterly, he could not deny; though none among the living might ever behold it, *he* had beheld it, and must keep the faith.[45]

For Baldwin, the seemingly impossible flight from white supremacy takes the form of a Chekhovian effort to endure lovingly and compassionately, guided by a vision of freedom and empowered by a tradition of black love and faith.[46] To be a bastard people—wrenched from Africa and in, but never fully of, America—is to be a people of highly limited options, if any at all. To bear witness is to make and remake, invent and reinvent oneself as a person and people by keeping faith with the best of such earlier efforts, yet also to acknowledge that the very new selves and peoples to emerge will never fully find a space, place or face in American society—or Africa. This perennial process of self-making and self-inventing is propelled by a self-loving and self-trusting made possible by overcoming a colonized mind, body and soul.

This is precisely what Toni Morrison describes in the great litany of black love in Baby Suggs's prayer and sermon of laughter, dance, tears and silence in "a wide-open place cut deep in the woods nobody knew for what at the end of a path known only to deer and whoever cleared the land in the first place." On those hot Saturday afternoons, Baby Suggs "offered up to them her great big heart."

> She told them that the only grace they could have was the grace they could imagine. That if they could not see it, they would not have it.
>
> "Here," she said, "in this here place, we flesh; flesh that weeps, laughs; flesh that dances on bare feet in grass. Love it. Love it hard. Yonder they do not love

your flesh. They despise it. They don't love your eyes; they'd just as soon pick em out. No more do they love the skin on your back. Yonder they flay it. And O my people they do not love your hands. Those they only use, tie, bind, chop off and leave empty. Love your hands! Love them. Raise them up and kiss them. Touch others with them, pat them together, stroke them on your face 'cause they don't love that either. *You* got to love it, *you!* And no, they ain't in love with your mouth. Yonder, out there, they will see it broken and break it again. What you say out of it they will not heed. What you scream from it they do not hear. What you put into it to nourish your body they will snatch away and give you leavins instead. No, they don't love your mouth. *You* got to love it. This is flesh I'm talking about here. Flesh that needs to be loved. Feet that need to rest and to dance; backs that need support; shoulders that need arms, strong arms I'm telling you. And O my people, out yonder, hear me, they do not love your neck unnoosed and straight. So love your neck; put a hand on it, grace it, stroke it and hold it up. And all your inside parts that they'd just as soon slop for hogs, you got to love them. The dark, dark liver—love it, love it, and the beat and beating heart, love that too. More than eyes or feet. More than lungs that have yet to draw free air. More than your life-holding womb and your life-giving private parts, hear me now, love your heart. For this is the prize." Saying no more, she stood up then and danced with her twisted hip the rest of what her heart had to say while the others opened their mouths and gave her the music. Long notes held until the four-part harmony was perfect enough for their deeply loved flesh.[47]

In this powerful passage, Toni Morrison depicts in a concrete and graphic way the enactment and expression of black love, black joy, black community and black faith that bears witness to black suffering and keeps alive a vision of black hope. Black bonds of affection, black networks of support, black ties of empathy and black harmonies of spiritual camaraderie provide the grounds for the fragile existential weaponry with which to combat black invisibility and namelessness.

Yet these forceful strategies in black culture still have not successfully come to terms with the problem. The black collective quest for a name that designates black people in the United States continues—from colored, Negro, black, Afro-American, Abyssinian, Ethiopian, Nubian, Bilalian, American African, American, African to African American. The black individual quest for names goes on, with unique new ones for children—e.g., Signithia, Tarsell, Jewayne—designed to set them apart from all others for the purpose of accenting their individuality and offsetting their invisibility. And most important, black rage proliferates—sometimes unabated.

Of all the hidden injuries of blackness in American civilization, black rage is the most deadly, the most lethal. Although black culture is in no way reducible to or identical with black rage, it is inseparable from black rage. Du Bois's renowned eulogy for Alexander Crummell, the greatest nineteenth-century black intellectual, is one of the most penetrating analyses of black rage. Du Bois begins his treatment with a virtually generic description of black childhood—a description that would hold for Arthur Ashe or Ice Cube, Kathleen Battle or Queen Latifah:

> This is the history of a human heart,—the tale of a black boy who many long years ago began to struggle with life that he might know the world and know himself. Three temptations he met on those dark dunes that lay gray and dismal before the wonder-eyes of the child: the Temptation of Hate, that stood out against the red dawn; the Temptation of Despair, that darkened noonday; and the Temptation of Doubt, that ever steals along with twilight. Above all, you must hear of the vales he crossed,—the Valley of Humiliation and the Valley of the Shadow of Death.[48]

Black self-hatred and hatred of others parallels that of all human beings, who must gain some sense of themselves and the world. But the tremendous weight of white supremacy makes this human struggle for mature black selfhood even more difficult. As black children come to view themselves more and more as the degraded other, the temptation of hate grows, "gliding stealthily into [their] laughter, fading into [their] play, and seizing [their] dreams by day and night with rough, rude turbulence. So [they ask] of sky and sun and flower the never-answered Why? and love, as [they grow], neither the world nor the world's rough ways."[49]

The two major choices in black culture (or any culture) facing those who succumb to the temptation of hate are a self-hatred that leads to self-destruction or a hatred of others—degraded others—that leads to vengeance of some sort. These options often represent two sides of the same coin. The case of Bigger Thomas, portrayed by Richard Wright in his great novel *Native Son* (1940), is exemplary in this regard:

> Bigger's face was metallically black in the strong sunlight. There was in his eyes a pensive, brooding amusement, as of a man who had been long confronted and tantalized by a riddle whose answer seemed always just on the verge of escaping him, but prodding him irresistibly on to seek its solution. The silence irked Bigger; he was anxious to do something to evade looking so squarely at this problem.[50]

The riddle Bigger seeks an answer to is the riddle of his black existence in America—and he evades it in part because the pain, fear, silence and hatred cut so deep. Like the "huge black rat" that appears at the beginning of the novel, Bigger reacts to his circumstances instinctually. Yet his instinct to survive is intertwined with his cognitive perception that white supremacy is out to get him like the evil that targets Job in the Hebrew Bible. To make himself and invent himself as a black person in America is to strike out against white supremacy—out of pain, fear, silence and hatred. The result is psychic terror and physical violence—committed against black Bessie and white Mary.

> Bigger rose and went to the window. His hands caught the cold steel bars in a hard grip. He knew as he stood there that he could never tell why he had killed. It was not that he did not really want to tell, but the telling of it would have involved an explanation of his entire life. The actual killing of Mary and Bessie was not what concerned him most; it was knowing and feeling that he could never make anybody know what had driven him to it. His crimes were known, but what he had felt before he committed them would never be known. He would have gladly admitted his guilt if he had thought that in doing so he could have also given in the same breath a sense of the deep, choking hate that had been his life, a hate that he had not wanted to have, but could not help having. How could he do that? The impulsion to try to tell was as deep as had been the urge to kill.[51]

The temptation to hate is a double-edged sword. Bigger's own self-hatred not only leads him to hate other blacks, but also to deny the humanity of whites. Yet he can overcome this self-hatred only when he views himself as a self-determining agent who is willing to take responsibility for his actions and acknowledge his connection with others. Although Wright has often been criticized for casting Bigger as a pitiful victim, subhuman monster and isolated individualist—as in James Baldwin's "Everybody's Protest Novel" and "Many Thousands Gone" in *Notes of a Native Son* (1955)—Wright presents brief moments in which Bigger sees the need for transcending his victim status and rapacious individualism. When his family visits him in jail, Bigger responds to their tears and anger:

> Bigger wanted to comfort them in the presence of the white folks, but did not know how. Desperately, he cast about for something to say. Hate and shame boiled in him against the people behind his back; he tried to think of words that would defy them, words that would let them know that he had a world and life of his own in spite of them.[52]

Wright does not disclose the internal dynamics of this black world of Bigger's own, but Bigger does acknowledge that he is part of this world. For example, his actions had dire consequences for his sister, Vera.

> "Bigger," his mother sobbed, trying to talk through her tears. "Bigger, honey, she

won't go to school no more. She says the other girls look at her and make her 'shamed. . . ."

He had lived and acted on the assumption that he was alone, and now he saw that he had not been. What he had done made others suffer. No matter how much he would long for them to forget him, they would not be able to. His family was a part of him, not only in blood, but in spirit. He sat on the cot and his mother knelt at his feet. Her face was lifted to his; her eyes were empty, eyes that looked upward when the last hope of earth had failed.[53]

Yet even this family connection fails to undercut the layers of hate Bigger feels for himself and them. It is only when Bigger receives unconditional support and affirmation across racial lines that his self-hatred and hatred of others subsides—for a moment, from white Jan, the boyfriend of the slain Mary.

He looked at Jan and saw a white face, but an honest face. This white man believed in him, and the moment he felt that belief he felt guilty again; but in a different sense now. Suddenly, this white man had come up to him, flung aside the curtain and walked into the room of his life. Jan had spoken a declaration of friendship that would make other white men hate him: a particle of white rock had detached itself from that looming mountain of white hate and had rolled down the slope, stopping still at his feet. The word had become flesh. For the first time in his life a white man became a human being to him; and the reality of Jan's humanity came in a stab of remorse: he had killed what this man loved and had hurt him. He saw Jan as though someone had performed an operation upon his eyes, or as though someone had snatched a deforming mask from Jan's face.[54]

In both instances, Bigger lurches slightly beyond the temptation of hate when he perceives himself as an agent and subject accountable for the consequences of his actions—such as the victimization of his own black sister and a white person. Yet the depths of his self-hatred—his deep-seated colonized mind—permit only a glimpse of self-transformation when the friendship of a white fellow victim is offered to him.

Similar to Bigger Thomas, Alexander Crummell was inspired by a white significant other—Beriah Green. This sort of sympathetic connection makes the temptation of hate grow "fainter and less sinister. It did not wholly fade away, but diffused itself and lingered thick at the edges."[55] Through both Bigger Thomas and Alexander Crummell we see the tremendous pull of the white world and the tragic need for white recognition and affirmation among so many black people.

The temptation of despair is the second element of black rage in Du Bois's analysis. This temptation looms large when black folk conclude that "the way of

the world is closed to me." This conclusion yields two options—nihilism and hedonism. Again, two sides of the same coin. This sense of feeling imprisoned,
bound, constrained and circumscribed is a dominant motif in black cultural expressions.[56] Again, Wright captures this predicament well with Bigger Thomas:

"Goddammit!"

"What's the matter?"

"They don't let us do *nothing*."

"Who?"

"The *white* folks."

"You talk like you just now finding that out," Gus said.

"Naw. But I just can't get used to it," Bigger said. "I swear to God I can't. I
know I oughtn't think about it, but I can't help it. Every time I think about it I
feel like somebody's poking a red-hot iron down my throat. Goddammit, look!
We live here and they live there. We black and they white. They got things and
we ain't. They do things and we can't. It's just like living in jail. Half the time I
feel like I'm on the outside of the world peeping in through a knot-hole in the
fence."[57]

The temptation of despair is predicated on a world with no room for black space,
place or face. It feeds on a black futurelessness and black hopelessness—a situation
in which visions and dreams of possibility have dried up like raisins in the sun.
This nihilism leads to lives of drift, lives in which any pleasure, especially instant
gratification, is the primary means of feeling alive. Anger and aggression usually
surface in such lives. Bigger says: "I hurt folks 'cause I felt I had to; that's all.
They was crowding me too close; they wouldn't give me no room. . . . I thought
they was hard and I acted hard. . . . I'll be feeling and thinking that they didn't see
me and I didn't see them."[58]

The major black cultural response to the temptation of despair has been the
black Christian tradition—a tradition dominated by music in song, prayer and sermon. The unique role of this tradition is often noted. Du Bois writes: "That the
Negro church antedates the Negro home, leads to an explanation of much that is
paradoxical in this communistic institution and in the morals of its members. But
especially it leads us to regard this institution as peculiarly the expression of the
inner ethical life of a people in a sense seldom true elsewhere."[59]

Even Bigger Thomas—the most cynical and secular of rebels in the black literary tradition—is captivated by the power of black church music, the major caress-
ing artistic flow in the black *Sittlichkeit* (ethical life).

The singing from the church vibrated through him, suffusing him with a mood
of sensitive sorrow. He tried not to listen, but it seeped into his feelings, whis-

pering of another way of life and death. . . . The singing filled his ears; it was complete, self-contained, and it mocked his fear and loneliness, his deep yearning for a sense of wholeness. Its fulness contrasted so sharply with his hunger, its richness with his emptiness, that he recoiled from it while answering it.[60]

The black church tradition—along with the rich musical tradition it spawned—generates a sense of movement, motion and momentum that keeps despair at bay. As with any collective project or performance that puts a premium on change, transformation, conversion and future possibility, the temptation of despair is not eliminated, but attenuated. In this sense, the black church tradition has made ritual art and communal bonds out of black invisibility and namelessness. Ralph Ellison updates and secularizes this endeavor when he writes,

> Perhaps I like Louis Armstrong because he's made poetry out of being invisible. I think it must be because he's unaware that he *is* invisible. And my own grasp of invisibility aids me to understand his music. . . . Invisibility, let me explain, gives one a slightly different sense of time, you're never quite on the beat. Sometimes you're ahead and sometimes behind. Instead of the swift and imperceptible flowing of time, you are aware of its nodes, those points where time stands still or from which it leaps ahead. And you slip into the breaks and look around. That's what you hear vaguely in Louis' music.[61]

The temptation of doubt is the most persistent of the three temptations. White supremacy drums deeply into the hearts, minds and souls of black people, causing them to expect little of one another and themselves. This black insecurity and self doubt produce a debilitating black jealousy in the face of black "success"—a black jealousy that often takes the form of what Eldridge Cleaver called "nigger rituals"—namely, a vicious trashing of black "success" or a black "battle royal" for white spectators. Understandably, under conditions of invisibility and namelessness, most of those blacks with "visibility" and a "name" in the white world are often the object of black scorn and contempt. Such sad, self-fulfilling prophecies of black cowardice make the temptation of doubt especially seductive—one that fans and fuels the flames of black rage. Du Bois states:

> Of all the three temptations, this one struck the deepest. Hate? He had outgrown so childish a thing. Despair? He had steeled his right arm against it, and fought it with the vigor of determination. But to doubt the worth of his life-work,—to doubt the destiny and capability of the race his soul loved because it was his; to find listless squalor instead of eager endeavor; to hear his own lips whispering, "They do not care; they cannot know; they are dumb driven cattle,—why cast your pearls before swine?"—this, this seemed more than man could bear; and he

closed the door, and sank upon the steps of the chancel, and cast his robe upon the floor and writhed.[62]

The two principal options for action after one yields to the temptation of doubt in black culture are: authoritarian subordination of the "ignorant" masses or individual escape from these masses into the white mainstream. These two options are not two sides of the same coin—though they often flow from a common source: an elitist vision that shuns democratic accountability. And although this elitist vision that of the Exceptional Negro and Talented Tenth who are "better than those other blacks"—is found more readily among the black educated and middle class, some of the black working poor and very poor subscribe to it too. Even Bigger Thomas.

As he rode, looking at the black people on the sidewalks, he felt that one way to end fear and shame was to make all those black people act together, rule them, tell them what to do, and make them do it. . . . But he felt that such would never happen to him and his black people, and he hated them and wanted to wave his hand and blot them out. Yet, he still hoped, vaguely. Of late he had liked to hear tell of men who could rule others, for in actions such as these he felt that there was a way to escape from this tight morass of fear and shame that sapped at the base of his life. He liked to hear of how Japan was conquering China; of how Hitler was running Jews to the ground; of how Mussolini was invading Spain. He was not concerned with whether these acts were right or wrong; they simply appealed to him as possible avenues of escape. He felt that some day there would be a black man who would whip the black people into a tight band and together they would act and end fear and shame. He never thought of this in precise mental images; he felt it; he would feel it for a while and then forget. But hope was always waiting somewhere deep down in him.[63]

This hope for black unity and action was based on a profound doubt concerning the ability of black people to think for themselves and act on principles they had examined, scrutinized and deliberately chosen. Ironically, this same elitist logic is at work among those who uncritically enter the white mainstream and accuse black people of lacking discipline and determination. Alexander Crummell overcame the difficult challenge of self-doubt and the doubt of other black folk by moving to Africa and later returning to America to fight for and "among his own, the low, the grasping, and the wicked, with that unbending righteousness which is the sword of the just."[64]

In the end, for Du Bois, Alexander Crummell triumphed over hate, despair and doubt owing to "that full power within, that mighty inspiration"[65] within the Veil. He was able to direct his black rage through moral channels sustained primarily by black bonds of affection, black networks of support and black ties of empathy. Yet few today know his name and work, principally due to the thick Veil of color then and now. "His name today, in this broad land, means little, and comes to fifty million ears laden with no incense of memory or emulation. And herein lies the tragedy of the age: not that men are poor,—all men know something of poverty; not that men are wicked,—who is good? not that men are ignorant,—what is Truth? Nay, but that men know so little of men."[66]

For Du Bois, "the problem of the twentieth century is the problem of the color-line"[67] largely because of the relative lack of communication across the Veil of color. For Du Bois, the vicious legacy of white supremacy contributes to the arrested development of democracy. And since communication is the lifeblood of a democracy—the very measure of the vitality of its public life—we either come to terms with race and hang together, or ignore it and hang separately. This is why every examination of black strivings is an important part of understanding the prevailing crisis in American society.

A TWILIGHT CIVILIZATION

In our time—at the end of the twentieth century—the crisis of race in America is still raging. The problem of black invisibility and namelessness, however, remains marginal to the dominant accounts of our past and present and is relatively absent from our pictures of the future. In this age of globalization, with its impressive scientific and technological innovations in information, communication and applied biology, a focus on the lingering effects of racism seems outdated and antiquated. The global cultural bazaar of entertainment and enjoyment, the global shopping mall of advertising and marketing, the global workplace of blue-collar and white collar employment and the global financial network of computerized transactions and megacorporate mergers appear to render any talk about race irrelevant.[68]

Yet with the collapse of the Soviet empire, the end of the Cold War and the rise of Japan, corrupt and top-heavy nation-states are being eclipsed by imperial corporations as public life deteriorates due to class polarization, racial balkanization and especially a predatory market culture.[69] With the vast erosion of civic networks that nurture and care for citizens—such as families, neighborhoods and schools—and with what might be called the gangsterization of everyday life, characterized by the escalating fear of violent attack, vicious assault or cruel insult, we are witnessing a pervasive cultural decay in American civilization. Even public discourse has degenerated into petty name-calling and finger-pointing—with little room for mutual respect and empathetic exchange. Increasing suicides and homicides, alcoholism and drug addiction, distrust and disloyalty, coldheartedness and mean-spiritedness, isolation and loneliness, cheap sexual thrills and cowardly patriarchal violence are still other symptoms of this decay. Yet race—in the coded language of welfare reform, immigration policy, criminal punishment, affirmative action and suburban privatization—remains a central signifier in the political debate.

As in late nineteenth-century Russia and early twentieth-century central Europe, the ruling political Right and center hide and conceal the privilege and wealth of the few (the 1 percent who own 48 percent of the net financial wealth, the top 10 percent who own 86 percent, the top 20 percent who have 94 percent!) and pits the downwardly mobile middlers against the downtrodden poor.[70] This age-old strategy of scapegoating the most vulnerable, frightening the most insecure and supporting the most comfortable constitutes a kind of iron law signaling the decline of modern civilizations, as in Tolstoy's Russia and Kafka's central Europe: chaotic and inchoate rebellion from below, withdrawal and retreat from public life from above and a desperate search for authoritarian law and order, at any cost, from the middle. In America, this suggests not so much a European style of fascism, but rather a homespun brand of authoritarian democracy—the systemic stigmatizing, regulating and policing of the degraded "others"—women, gays, lesbians, Latinos, Jews, Asians, American Indians and especially black people. As Sinclair Lewis warned over a half century ago, fascism, American-style, can happen here.

Welfare reform means, on the ground, poor people (disproportionately black) with no means of support. Criminal punishment means hundreds of thousands of black men in crowded prisons—many in there forever. And suburban privatization means black urban poor citizens locked into decrepit public schools, dilapidated housing, inadequate health care and unavailable child care. Furthermore, the lowest priorities on the global corporate agenda of the political Right—the low quantity of jobs with a living wage and the low quality of life for children—have the gravest consequences for the survival of any civilization. Instead, we have generational layers of unemployed and underemployed people (often uncounted in our national statistics) and increasing numbers of hedonistic and nihilistic young people (of all classes, races, genders and regions) with little interest in public life and with little sense of moral purpose.

This is the classic portrait of a twilight civilization whose dangerous rumblings—now intermittent in much of America, but rampant in most of black urban America—will more than likely explode in the twenty-first century if we stay on the present conservative course. In such a bleak scenario—given the dominant tendencies of our day—Du Bois's heralded Talented Tenth will by and large procure a stronger foothold in the well-paid professional managerial sectors of the global economy and more and more will become intoxicated with the felicities of a parvenu bourgeois existence. The heroic few will attempt to tell unpleasant truths about our plight and bear prophetic witness to our predicament as well as try to organize and mobilize (and be organized and mobilized by) the economically devastated, culturally degraded and politically marginalized black working poor and very poor. Since a multiracial alliance of progressive middlers, liberal slices of the corporate elite and subversive energy from below is the only vehicle by which some form of radical democratic accountability can redistribute resources and wealth and restructure the economy and government so that all benefit, the significant secondary efforts of the black Talented Tenth alone in the twenty-first century will be woefully inadequate and thoroughly frustrating. Yet even progressive social change—though desirable and necessary—may not turn back the deeper and deadly processes of cultural decay in late twentieth-century America.

As this Talented Tenth comes to be viewed more and more with disdain and disgust by the black working poor and very poor, not only class envy, but class hatred in black America will escalate—in the midst of a more isolated and insulated black America. This will deepen the identity crisis of the black Talented Tenth—a crisis of survivor's guilt and cultural rootlessness. As the glass ceilings (limited promotions) and golden cuffs (big position and good pay with little or no power) remain in place for most, though not all, blacks in corporate America, we will see anguish and hedonism intensify among much of the Talented Tenth. The conservative wing of black elites will climb on the bandwagon of the political Right—some for sincere reasons, most for opportunistic ones—as the black working poor and very poor try to cope with the realities of death, disease and destruction. The progressive wing of the black elite will split into a vociferous (primarily male-led) black nationalist camp that opts for self-help at the lower and middle levels of the entrepreneurial sectors of the global economy and a visionary (disproportionately woman-led) radical democratic camp that works assiduously to keep alive a hope—maybe the last hope—for a twilight civilization that once saw itself as the "last best hope of earth."

After ninety-three years of the most courageous and unflagging devotion to black freedom witnessed in the twentieth century, W. E. B. Du Bois not only left America for Africa, but concluded: "I just cannot take any more of this country's treatment. We leave for Ghana October 5th and I set no date for return. . . . Chin up, and fight on, but realize that American Negroes can't win."[71]

In the end, Du Bois's Enlightenment worldview, Victorian strategies and American optimism failed him. He left America in militant despair—the very despair he had avoided earlier—and mistakenly hoped for the rise of a strong postcolonial and united Africa. Echoing Tolstoy's claim that "It's intolerable to live in Russia. . . . I've decided to emigrate to England forever"[72] (though he never followed through) and Kafka's dream to leave Prague and live in Palestine (though he died before he could do so),[73] Du Bois concluded that black strivings in a twilight civilization were unbearable for him, yet still imperative for others—even if he could not envision black freedom in America as realizable.

For those of us who stand on his broad shoulders, let us begin where he ended—with his militant despair; let us look candidly at the tragicomic and absurd character of black life in America in the spirit of John Coltrane and Toni Morrison; let us continue to strive with genuine compassion, personal integrity and human decency to fight for radical democracy in the face of the frightening abyss—or terrifying inferno—of the twenty-first century, clinging to "a hope not hopeless but unhopeful."

SOURCE: From *The Future of the Race,* by Henry Louis Gates and Cornel West (New York: Alfred A. Knopf, 1996), pp. 53–112, 180–196.

Seven

THE NEW CULTURAL POLITICS OF DIFFERENCE

This synthetic and synoptic essay was written as the theoretical lead piece for a volume entitled Out There *(1991), for the New Museum of Contemporary Art. I coedited this work with a marvelous group of artists and critics—Russell Ferguson, Martha Gever and Trinh T. Minh-ha. We met regularly over eighteen months choosing essays, revising frameworks and discussing contemporary art. It is one of the few signature pieces I have written.*

IN THESE LAST FEW years of the twentieth century, there is emerging a significant shift in the sensibilities and outlooks of critics and artists. In fact, I would go so far as to claim that a new kind of cultural worker is in the making, associated with a new politics of difference. These new forms of intellectual consciousness advance reconceptions of the vocation of critic and artist, attempting to undermine the prevailing disciplinary divisions of labor in the academy, museum, mass media and gallery networks, while preserving modes of critique within the ubiquitous commodification of culture in the global village. Distinctive features of the new cultural politics of difference are to trash the monolithic and homogeneous in the name of diversity, multiplicity and heterogeneity; to reject the abstract, general and universal in light of the concrete, specific and particular; and to historicize, contextualize and pluralize by highlighting the contingent, provisional, variable, tentative, shifting and changing.

Needless to say, these gestures are not new in the history of criticism or art, yet what makes them novel—along with the cultural politics they produce—is how and what constitutes difference, the weight and gravity it is given in representation and the way in which highlighting issues like exterminism, empire, class, race, gender, sexual orientation, age, nation, nature and region at this historical moment acknowledges some discontinuity and disruption from previous forms of cultural critique. To put it bluntly, the new cultural politics of difference consists of creative responses to the precise circumstances of our present moment—especially those of marginalized First World agents who shun degraded self-representations, articulating instead their sense of the flow of history in light of the contemporary terrors, anxieties and fears of highly commercialized North

Atlantic capitalist cultures (with their escalating xenophobias against people of color, Jews, women, gays, lesbians and the elderly). The thawing, yet still rigid, Second World ex-Communist cultures (with increasing nationalist revolts against the legacy of hegemonic party henchmen) and the diverse cultures of the majority of inhabitants on the globe smothered by international communication cartels and repressive postcolonial elites (sometimes in the name of communism, as was the case in Ethiopia) or starved by austere World Bank and IMF politics that subordinate them to the North (as in free-market capitalism in Chile) also locate vital areas of analysis in this new cultural terrain.

The new cultural politics of difference is neither simply oppositional in contesting the mainstream (or *malestream*) for inclusion, nor transgressive in the avant-gardist sense of shocking conventional bourgeois audiences. It embraces the distinct articulations of talented (and usually privileged) contributors to culture who desire to align themselves with demoralized, demobilized, depoliticized and disorganized people in order to empower and enable social action and, if possible, to enlist collective insurgency for the expansion of freedom, democracy and individuality. This perspective impels these cultural critics and artists to reveal, as an integral component of their production, the very operations of power within their immediate work contexts (academy, museum, gallery, mass media). This strategy, however, also puts them in an inescapable double bind—while linking their activities to the fundamental, structural overhaul of these institutions, they often remain financially dependent on them (so much for "independent" creation). For these critics of culture, theirs is a gesture that is simultaneously progressive and co-opted. Yet without social movement or political pressure from outside these institutions (extraparliamentary and extracurricular actions like the social movements of the recent past), transformation degenerates into mere accommodation or sheer stagnation, and the role of the "co-opted progressive"—no matter how fervent one's subversive rhetoric—is rendered more difficult. There can be no artistic breakthrough or social progress without some form of crisis in civilization—a crisis usually generated by organizations or collectivities that convince ordinary people to put their bodies and lives on the line. There is, of course, no guarantee that such pressure will yield the result one wants, but there is a guarantee that the status quo will remain or regress if no pressure is applied at all.

The new cultural politics of difference faces three basic challenges—intellectual, existential and political. The intellectual challenge—usually cast as methodological debate in these days in which academicist forms of expression have a monopoly on intellectual life—is how to think about representational practices in terms of history, culture and society. How does one understand, analyze and enact such practices today? An adequate answer to this question can be attempted only after one comes to terms with the insights and blindnesses of earlier attempts to grapple with the question in light of the evolving crisis in different histories, cultures and societies. I shall sketch a brief genealogy—a history that highlights the contingent origins and often ignoble outcomes—of exemplary critical responses to the question. This genealogy sets forth a historical framework that characterizes the rich yet deeply flawed Eurocentric traditions that the new cultural politics of difference builds upon yet goes beyond.

The Intellectual Challenge

An appropriate starting point is the ambiguous legacy of the Age of Europe. Between 1492 and 1945, European breakthroughs in oceanic transportation, agricultural production, state consolidation, bureaucratization, industrialization, urbanization and imperial dominion shaped the makings of the modern world. Precious ideals like the dignity of persons (individuality) or the popular accountability of institutions (democracy) were unleashed around the world. Powerful critiques of illegitimate authorities—of the Protestant Reformation against the Roman Catholic church, the Enlightenment against state churches, liberal movements against absolutist states and feudal guild constraints, workers against managerial subordination, women against sexist practices, people of color and Jews against white and gentile supremacist decrees, gays and lesbians against homophobic sanctions—were fanned and fueled by these precious ideals refined within the crucible of the Age of Europe. Yet the discrepancy between sterling rhetoric and lived reality, glowing principles and actual practices, loomed large.

By the last European century—the last epoch in which European domination of most of the globe was uncontested and unchallenged in a substantive way—a new world seemed to be stirring. At the height of England's reign as the major imperial European power, its exemplary cultural critic, Matthew Arnold, painfully observed in his "Stanzas from the Grand Chartreuse" that he felt some sense of "wandering between two worlds, one dead / the other powerless to be born." Following his Burkean sensibilities of cautious reform and fear of anarchy, Arnold acknowledged that the old glue—religion—that had tenuously and often unsuccessfully held together the ailing European regimes could not do so in the mid-nineteenth century. Like Alexis de Tocqueville in France, Arnold saw that the democratic temper was the wave of the future. So he proposed a new conception of culture—a secular, humanistic one—that could play an integrative role in cementing and stabilizing an emerging bourgeois civil society and imperial state. His famous castigation of the immobilizing materialism of the declining aristocracy, the vulgar philistinism of the emerging middle classes and the latent explosiveness of the working-class majority was motivated by a desire to create new forms of cultural legitimacy, authority and order in a rapidly changing moment in nineteenth-century Europe.

For Arnold (in *Culture and Anarchy,* 1869), this new conception of culture seeks to do away with classes; to make the best that has been thought and known in the world current everywhere; to make all men live in an atmosphere of sweetness and light. . . .

This is the *social idea* and the men of culture are the true apostles of equality. The great men of culture are those who have had a passion for diffusing, for making prevail, for carrying from one end of society to the other, the best knowledge, the best ideas of their time, who have laboured to divest knowledge of all that was harsh, uncouth, difficult, abstract, professional, exclusive; to humanize it, to make it efficient outside the clique of the cultivated and learned, yet still remaining the best knowledge and thought of the time, and a true source, therefore, of sweetness and light.

As an organic intellectual of an emergent middle class—as the inspector of schools in an expanding educational bureaucracy, Professor of Poetry at Oxford (the first noncleric and the first to lecture in English, rather than Latin) and an active participant in a thriving magazine network—Arnold defined and defended a new secular culture of critical discourse. For him, this discursive strategy would be lodged in the educational and periodical apparatuses of modern societies as they contained and incorporated the frightening threats of an arrogant aristocracy and especially of an "anarchic" working-class majority. His ideals of disinterested, dispassionate and objective inquiry would regulate this new secular cultural production, and his justifications for the use of state power to quell any threats to the survival and security of this culture were widely accepted. He aptly noted, "Through culture seems to lie our way, not only to perfection, but even to safety."

This sentence is revealing in two ways. First, it refers to "our way" without explicitly acknowledging who constitutes the "we." This move is symptomatic among many bourgeois, male, Eurocentric critics whose universalizing gestures exclude (by guarding a silence around) or explicitly degrade women and people of color. Second, the sentence links culture to safety—presumably the safety of the "we" against the barbaric threats of the "them," that is, those viewed as different in some debased manner. Needless to say, Arnold's negative attitudes toward British working-class people, women and especially Indians and Jamaicans in the empire clarify why he conceives of culture as, in part, a weapon for bourgeois, male, European "safety."

For Arnold, the best of the Age of Europe—modeled on a mythological mélange of Periclean Athens, late Republican/early Imperial Rome and Elizabethan England—could be promoted only if there was an interlocking affiliation among the emerging middle classes, a homogenizing of cultural discourse in the educational and university networks and a state advanced enough in its policing techniques to safeguard it. The candidates for participation and legitimation in this grand endeavor of cultural renewal and revision would be detached intellectuals willing to shed their parochialism, provincialism and class-bound identities for Arnold's middle-class-skewed project: "Aliens, if we may so call them—persons who are mainly led, not by their class spirit, but by a general *humane* spirit, by the love of human perfection." Needless to say, this Arnoldian perspective still informs much of the academic practices and secular cultural attitudes today—dominant views about the canon, admission procedures and collective self-definitions of intellectuals. Yet Arnold's project was disrupted by the collapse of nineteenth-century Europe—World War I. This unprecedented war brought to the surface the crucial role and violent potential not of the masses Arnold feared, but of the state he heralded. Upon the ashes of this wasteland of human carnage—some of it the civilian European population—T. S. Eliot emerged as the grand cultural spokesman.

Eliot's project of reconstituting and reconceiving European highbrow culture—and thereby regulating critical and artistic practices—after the internal collapse of imperial Europe can be viewed as a response to the probing question posed by Paul Valéry in "The Crisis of the Spirit" after World War I: "This Europe, will it become *what it is in reality,* i.e., a little cape of the Asiatic continent? or will this Europe remain rather what it seems, i.e., the priceless part of the whole earth, the pearl of the globe, the brain of a vast body?"

Eliot's image of Europe as a wasteland, a culture of fragments with no cementing center, predominated in postwar Europe. And though his early poetic practices were more radical, open and international than his Eurocentric criticism, Eliot posed a return to and revision of tradition as the only way of regaining European cultural order and political stability. For Eliot, contemporary history had become, as James Joyce's Stephen declared in *Ulysses* (1922), "a nightmare from which I am trying to awake"—"an immense panorama of futility and anarchy" as Eliot put it in his renowned review of Joyce's modernist masterpiece. In his influential essay "Tradition and the Individual Talent" (1919) Eliot stated:

> Yet if the only form of tradition, of handing down, consisted in following the ways of the immediate generation before us in a blind or timid adherence to its successes, "tradition" should positively be discouraged. We have seen many such simple currents soon lost in the sand; and novelty is better than repetition. Tradition is a matter of much wider significance. It cannot be inherited, and if you want it you must attain it by great labour.

Eliot's fecund notion of tradition is significant in that it promotes a historicist sensibility in artistic practice and cultural reflection. This historicist sensibility—regulated in Eliot's case by a reactionary politics—produced a powerful assault on existing literary canons (in which, for example, Romantic poets were displaced by the Metaphysical and Symbolist ones) and unrelenting attacks on modern Western civilization (such as the liberal ideas of democracy, equality and freedom).

Like Arnold's notion of culture, Eliot's idea of tradition was part of his intellectual arsenal, to be used in the battles raging in European cultures and societies.

Eliot found this tradition in the Church of England, to which he converted in 1927. Here was a tradition that left room for his Catholic cast of mind, Calvinistic heritage, puritanical temperament and ebullient patriotism for the old American South (the place of his upbringing). Like Arnold, Eliot was obsessed with the idea of civilization and the horror of barbarism (echoes of Joseph Conrad's Kurtz in *Heart of Darkness*) or more pointedly the notion of the decline and decay of European civilization. With the advent of World War II, Eliot's obsession became a reality. Again unprecedented human carnage (fifty million dead)—including an undescribable genocidal attack on Jewish people—throughout Europe as well as around the globe put the last nail in the coffin of the Age of Europe. After 1945, Europe consisted of a devastated and divided continent, crippled by a humiliating dependency on and deference to the United States and the Soviet Union.

The second historical coordinate of my genealogy is the emergence of the United States as *the* world power. The United States was unprepared for world-power status. However, with the recovery of Stalin's Russia (after losing twenty million lives), the United States felt compelled to make its presence felt around the globe. Then with the Marshall Plan to strengthen Europe against Russian influence (and provide new markets for U.S. products), the 1948 Russian takeover of Czechoslovakia, the 1948 Berlin blockade, the 1950 beginning of the Korean War and the 1952 establishment of NATO forces in Europe, it seemed clear that there was no escape from world-power obligations.

The post–World War II era in the United States, or the first decades of what Henry Luce envisioned as "The American Century," was not only a period of incredible economic expansion, but one of active cultural ferment. In the classical Fordist formula, mass production required mass consumption. With unchallenged hegemony in the capitalist world, the United States took economic growth for granted. Next to exercising its crude, anticommunist, McCarthyist obsessions, buying commodities became the primary act of civic virtue for many American citizens at this time. The creation of a mass middle class—a prosperous working class with a bourgeois identity—was countered by the first major emergence of subcultures of American non-WASP intellectuals: the so-called New York intellectuals in criticism, the Abstract Expressionists in painting and the bebop artists in jazz music. This emergence signaled a vital challenge to an American, male, WASP elite loyal to an older and eroding European culture.

The first significant blow was dealt when assimilated Jewish Americans entered the higher echelons of the cultural apparatus (academy, museums, galleries, mass media). Lionel Trilling is an emblematic figure. This Jewish entrée into the anti-Semitic and patriarchal critical discourse of the exclusivistic institutions of American culture initiated the slow but sure undoing of the male WASP cultural hegemony and homogeneity. Lionel Trilling's project was to appropriate Matthew Arnold for his own political and cultural purposes—thereby unraveling the old male WASP consensus, while erecting a new post–World War II liberal academic consensus around Cold War, anticommunist renditions of the values of complexity, difficulty, variousness and modulation. In addition, the postwar boom laid the basis for intense professionalization and specialization in expanding institutions of higher education—especially in the natural sciences, which were compelled to respond somehow to Russia's successful ventures in space. Humanistic scholars found themselves searching for new methodologies that could buttress self-images of rigor and scientific seriousness. For example, the close reading techniques of New Criticism (severed from their conservative, organicist, anti-industrialist ideological roots), the logical precision of reasoning in analytic philosophy, and the jargon of Parsonian structural-functionalism in sociology helped create such self-images. Yet towering cultural critics like C. Wright Mills, W. E. B. Du Bois, Richard Hofstadter, Margaret Mead and Dwight Macdonald bucked the tide. This suspicion of the academicization of knowledge is expressed in Trilling's well-known essay "On the Teaching of Modern Literature":

> Can we not say that, when modern literature is brought into the classroom, the subject being taught is betrayed by the pedagogy of the subject? We have to ask ourselves whether in our day too much does not come within the purview of the academy. More and more, as the universities liberalize themselves, turn their beneficent imperialistic gaze upon what is called life itself, the feeling grows among our educated classes that little can be experienced unless it is validated by some established intellectual discipline.

Trilling laments the fact that university instruction often quiets and domesticates radical and subversive works of art, turning them into objects "of merely habitual regard." This process of "the socialization of the anti-social, or the acculturation of the anti-cultural, or the legitimization of the subversive" leads Trilling to "question whether in our culture the study of literature is any longer a suitable means for developing and refining the intelligence." Trilling asks this question not in the spirit of denigrating and devaluing the academy, but rather in the spirit of highlighting the possible failure of an Arnoldian conception of culture to contain what he perceives as the philistine and anarchic alternatives becoming more and more available to students of the 1960s—namely, mass culture and radical politics.

This threat is partly associated with the third historical coordinate of my genealogy—the decolonization of the Third World. It is crucial to recognize the importance of this world-historical process if one wants to grasp the significance of the end of the Age of Europe and the emergence of the United States as a world power. With the first defeat of a Western nation by a non-Western nation—in

Japan's victory over Russia (1905)—and with revolutions in Persia (1905), Turkey (1908), China (1912) and Mexico (1911–1912), and much later the independence of India (1947) and China (1949) and the triumph of Ghana (1957), the actuality of a decolonized globe loomed large. Born of violent struggle, consciousness-raising and the reconstruction of identities, decolonization simultaneously brings with it new perspectives on that long-festering underside of the Age of Europe (of which colonial domination represents the *costs* of "progress," "order" and "culture"), as well as requiring new readings of the economic boom in the United States (wherein the black, brown, yellow, red, female, elderly, gay, lesbian, and white working class live the same *costs* as cheap labor at home in addition to U.S.-dominated Latin American and Pacific Rim markets).

The impetuous ferocity and moral outrage that motors the decolonization process is best captured by Frantz Fanon in *The Wretched of the Earth* (1961):

> Decolonization, which sets out to change the order of the world, is obviously a program of complete disorder. . . . Decolonization is the meeting of two forces, opposed to each other by their very nature, which in fact owe their originality to that sort of substantification which results from and is nourished by the situation in the colonies. Their first encounter was marked by violence and their existence together—that is to say the exploitation of the native by the settler—was carried on by dint of a great array of bayonets and cannons. . . .
>
> In decolonization, there is therefore the need of a complete calling in question of the colonial situation. If we wish to describe it precisely, we might find it in the well-known words: "The last shall be first and the first last." Decolonization is the putting into practice of this sentence.
>
> The naked truth of decolonization evokes for us the searing bullets and bloodstained knives which emanate from it. For if the last shall be first, this will only come to pass after a murderous and decisive struggle between the two protagonists.

Fanon's strong words, though excessively Manichaean, still describe the feelings and thoughts between the occupying British army and colonized Irish in Northern Ireland, the occupying Israeli army and subjugated Palestinians on the West Bank and Gaza Strip, the South African army and oppressed black South Africans in the townships, the Japanese police and Koreans living in Japan. His words also partly invoke the sense many black Americans have toward police departments in urban centers. In other words, Fanon is articulating century-long heartfelt human responses to being degraded and despised, hated and haunted, oppressed and exploited, marginalized and dehumanized at the hands of powerful, xenophobic, European, American, Russian and Japanese imperial countries.

During the late 1950s, 1960s and early 1970s in the United States, these decolonized sensibilities fanned and fueled the civil rights and black power movements, as well as the student antiwar, feminist, gray, brown, gay and lesbian movements. In this period we witnessed the shattering of male, WASP cultural homogeneity and the collapse of the short-lived liberal consensus. The inclusion of African Americans, Latino/a Americans, Asian Americans, Native Americans and American women into the culture of critical discourse yielded intense intellectual polemics and inescapable ideological polarization that focused principally on the exclusions, silences and blindnesses of male, WASP cultural homogeneity and its concomitant Arnoldian notions of the canon.

In addition, these critiques promoted three crucial processes that affected intellectual life in the country. First is the appropriation of the theories of postwar Europe—especially the work of the Frankfurt school (Marcuse, Adorno, Horkheimer), French/Italian Marxisms (Sartre, Althusser, Lefebvre, Gramsci), structuralisms (Lévi-Strauss, Todorov) and poststructuralisms (Deleuze, Derrida, Foucault). These diverse and disparate theories—all preoccupied with keeping alive radical projects after the end of the Age of Europe—tend to fuse versions of transgressive European modernisms with Marxist or post-Marxist left politics and unanimously shun the term "postmodernism." Second, there is the recovery and revisioning of American history in light of the struggles of white male workers, women, African Americans, Native Americans, Latino/a Americans, gays and lesbians. Third is the impact of forms of popular culture, such as television, film, music videos and even sports, on highbrow literate culture. The black-based hiphop culture of youth around the world is one grand example.

After 1973, with the crisis in the international world economy, America's slump in productivity, the challenge of OPEC nations to the North Atlantic monopoly of oil production, the increasing competition in hi-tech sectors of the economy from Japan and West Germany and the growing fragility of the international debt structure, the United States entered a period of waning self-confidence (compounded by Watergate) and a nearly contracting economy. As the standards of living for the middle classes declined, owing to runaway inflation, and the quality of living fell for most, due to escalating unemployment, underemployment and crime, religious and secular neoconservatism emerged with power and potency. This fusion of fervent neonationalism, traditional cultural values and "free market" policies served as the groundwork for the Reagan-Bush era.

The ambiguous legacies of the European Age, American preeminence and decolonization continue to haunt our postmodern moment as we come to terms with both the European, American, Japanese, Soviet and Third World *crimes against* and *contributions to* humanity. The plight of Africans in the New World can be instructive in this regard.

By 1914 European maritime empires had dominion over more than half of the land and a third of the peoples in the world—almost 72 million square kilometers of territory and more than 560 million people under colonial rule. Needless to say, this European control included brutal enslavement, institutional terrorism and cultural degradation of black diasporan people. The death of countless millions of Africans during the centuries-long transatlantic slave trade is but one reminder, among others, of the assault on black humanity. The black diasporan condition of New World servitude—in which blacks were viewed as mere commodities with production value, who had no proper legal status, social standing or public worth—can be characterized as, following Orlando Patterson, natal alienation. This state of perpetual and inheritable domination that diasporan Africans had at birth produced the *modern black diasporan problematic of invisibility and namelessness*. White-supremacist practices—enacted under the auspices of the prestigious cultural authorities of the churches, printed media and scientific academics—promoted black inferiority and constituted the European background against which black diasporan struggles for identity, dignity (self-confidence, self-respect, self-esteem) and material resources took place.

An inescapable aspect of this struggle was that the black diasporan peoples' quest for validation and recognition occurred on the ideological, social and cultural terrains of other nonblack peoples. White-supremacist assaults on black intelligence, ability, beauty and character required persistent black efforts to hold self-doubt, self-contempt and even self-hatred at bay. Selective appropriation, incorporation and rearticulation of European ideologies, cultures and institutions alongside an African heritage—a heritage more or less confined to linguistic innovation in rhetorical practices, stylizations of the body in forms of occupying an alien social space (hairstyles, ways of walking, standing, hand expressions, talking) and means of constituting and sustaining camaraderie and community (e.g., antiphonal, call-and-response styles, rhythmic repetition, risk-ridden syncopation in spectacular modes in musical and rhetorical expressions)—were some of the strategies employed.

The modern black diasporan problematic of invisibility and namelessness can be understood as the condition of *blacks' relative lack of power to represent themselves to themselves and others as complex human beings, and thereby to contest the bombardment of negative, degrading stereotypes put forward by white-supremacist ideologies*. The initial black response to being caught in this whirlwind of Europeanization was to resist the misrepresentation and caricature of the terms set by uncontested nonblack norms and models, and to fight for self-representation and recognition. Every modern black person, especially cultural disseminators, encounters this problematic of invisibility and namelessness. The initial black diasporan response was a mode of resistance that was *moralistic in content* and *communal in character*. That is, the fight for representation and recognition highlighted moral judgments regarding black "positive" images over and against white-supremacist stereotypes. These images "re-presented" monolithic and homogeneous black communities, in a way that could displace past misrepresentations of these communities. Stuart Hall has talked about these responses as attempts to change "the relations of representation."

These courageous yet limited black efforts to combat racist cultural practices uncritically accepted nonblack conventions and standards in two ways. First, they proceeded in an *assimilationist manner* that set out to show that black people were really like white people—thereby eliding differences (in history, culture) between whites and blacks. Black specificity and particularity was thus banished in order to gain white acceptance and approval. Second, these black responses rested upon a *homogenizing impulse* that assumed that all black people were really alike—hence obliterating differences (class, gender, region, sexual orientation) between black peoples. I submit that there are elements of truth in both claims, yet the conclusions are unwarranted owing to the basic fact that nonblack paradigms set the terms of the replies.

The insight in the first claim is that blacks and whites are in some important sense alike—that is, in their positive capacities for human sympathy, moral sacrifice, service to others, intelligence and beauty, or negatively, in their capacity for cruelty. Yet the common humanity they share is jettisoned when the claim is cast in an assimilationist manner that subordinates black particularity to a false universalism, that is, nonblack rubrics or prototypes. Similarly, the insight in the second claim is that all blacks are in some significant sense "in the same boat"—that is, subject to white-supremacist abuse. Yet this common condition is stretched too far when viewed in a *homogenizing* way that overlooks how racist treatment vastly differs owing to class, gender, sexual orientation, nation, region, hue and age.

The moralistic and communal aspects of the initial black diasporan responses to social and psychic erasure were not simply cast into simplistic binary oppositions of positive-negative, good-bad images that privileged the first term in light of a white norm so that black efforts remained inscribed within the very logic that dehumanized them. They were further complicated by the fact that these responses were also advanced principally by anxiety-ridden, middle-class black intellectuals (predominantly male and heterosexual), grappling with their sense of double-consciousness—namely their own crisis of identity, agency and audience—caught between a quest for white approval and acceptance and an endeavor to overcome the internalized association of blackness with inferiority. And I suggest that these complex anxieties of modern black diasporan intellectuals partly motivate the two major arguments that ground the assimilationist moralism and homogeneous communalism just outlined.

Kobena Mercer has talked about these two arguments as the *reflectionist* and the *social engineering* arguments. The reflectionist argument holds that the fight for black representation and recognition must reflect or mirror the real black community, not simply the negative and depressing representations of it. The social engineering argument claims that since any form of representation is constructed—that is, selective in light of broader aims—black representation (especially given the difficulty of blacks gaining access to positions of power to produce any black imagery) should offer positive images of themselves in order to inspire achievement among young black people, thereby countering racist stereotypes. The hidden assumption of both arguments is that we have unmediated access to what the "real black community" is and what "positive images" are. In short, these arguments presuppose the very phenomena to be interrogated, and thereby foreclose the very issues that should serve as the subject matter to be investigated.

Any notions of the "real black community" and "positive images" are value-laden, socially loaded and ideologically charged. To pursue this discussion is to call into question the possibility of such an uncontested consensus regarding them. Stuart Hall has rightly called this encounter "the end of innocence or the end of the innocent notion of the essential Black subject . . . the recognition that 'Black' is essentially a politically and culturally *constructed* category." This recognition—more and more pervasive among the postmodern black diasporan intelligentsia—is facilitated in part by the slow but sure dissolution of the European Age's maritime empires, and the unleashing of new political possibilities and cultural articulations among formerly colonialized peoples across the globe.

One crucial lesson of this decolonization process remains the manner in which most Third World, authoritarian, bureaucratic elites deploy essentialist rhetorics about "homogeneous national communities" and "positive images" in order to repress and regiment their diverse and heterogeneous populations. Yet in the diaspora, especially among First World countries, this critique has emerged not so much from the black male component of the Left as from the black women's movement. The decisive push of postmodern black intellectuals toward a new cultural politics of difference has been made by the powerful critiques and constructive explorations of black diasporan women (for instance, Toni Morrison). The coffin used to bury the innocent notion of the essential black subject was nailed shut with the termination of the black male monopoly on the construction of the black subject. In this regard, the black diasporan womanist critique has had a greater impact than the critiques that highlight exclusively class, empire, age, sexual orientation or nature.

This decisive push toward the end of black innocence—though prefigured in various degrees in the best moments of W. E. B. Du Bois, Anna Cooper, C. L. R. James, James Baldwin, Claudia Jones, the later Malcolm X, Frantz Fanon, Amiri Baraka and others—forces black diasporan cultural workers to encounter what Hall has called the "politics of representation." The main aim now is not simply access to representation in order to produce positive images of homogeneous communities—though broader access remains a practical and political problem. Nor is the primary goal here that of contesting stereotypes—though contestation remains a significant though limited venture. Following the model of the black diasporan traditions of music, athletics and rhetoric, black cultural workers must constitute and sustain discursive and institutional networks that deconstruct earlier modern black strategies for identity formation, demystify power relations that incorporate class, patriarchal and homophobic biases and construct more multivalent and multidimensional responses that articulate the complexity and diversity of black practices in the modern and postmodern world.

Furthermore, black cultural workers must investigate and interrogate the Other of blackness-whiteness. One cannot deconstruct the binary oppositional logic of images of blackness without extending it to the contrary condition of blackness-whiteness itself. However, a mere dismantling will not do—for the very notion of a deconstructive social theory is oxymoronic. Yet social theory is what is needed to examine and *explain* the historically specific ways in which "whiteness" is a politically constructed category parasitic on "blackness," and thereby to conceive of the profoundly hybrid character of what we mean by "race," "ethnicity" and "nationality." For instance, European immigrants arrived on American shores perceiving themselves as "Irish," "Sicilian," "Lithuanian" and so on. They had to learn that they were "white" principally by adopting an American discourse of positively valued whiteness and negatively charged blackness. This process by which people define themselves physically, socially, sexually and even politically in terms of whiteness or blackness has much bearing not only on constructed notions of race and ethnicity, but also on how we understand the changing character of U.S. nationalities. And given the Americanization of the world, especially in the sphere of mass culture, such inquiries—encouraged by the new cultural politics of difference—raise critical issues of "hybridity," "exilic status" and "identity" on an international scale. Needless to say, these inquiries must traverse those of "male-female," "colonizer-colonized," "heterosexual-homosexual" and others as well.

In light of this brief sketch of the emergence of our present crisis—and the turn toward history and difference in cultural work—four major historicist forms of theoretical activity provide resources for how we understand, analyze and enact our representational practices: Heideggerian *destruction* of the Western metaphysical tradition, Derridean *deconstruction* of the Western philosophical tradition, Rortian *demythologization* of the Western intellectual tradition and Marxist, Foucaultian, feminist, antiracist or antihomophobic *demystification* of Western cultural and artistic conventions.

Despite his abominable association with the Nazis, Martin Heidegger's project is useful in that it discloses the suppression of temporality and historicity in the dominant metaphysical systems of the West from Plato to Rudolf Carnap. This is noteworthy in that it forces one to understand philosophy's representational discourses as thoroughly historical phenomena. Hence, they should be viewed with skepticism, as they are often flights from the specific, concrete, practical and particular. The major problem with Heidegger's project—as noted by his neo-Marxist student Herbert Marcuse—is that he views history in terms of fate, heritage and destiny. He dramatizes the past and present as if it were a Greek tragedy with no tools of social analysis to relate cultural work to institutions and structures or antecedent forms and styles.

Jacques Derrida's version of deconstruction is one of the most influential schools of thought among young academic critics. It is salutary in that it focuses on the political power of rhetorical operations—of tropes and metaphors in binary oppositions like white/black, good/bad, male/female, machine/nature, ruler/ruled, reality/appearance—showing how these operations sustain hierarchical worldviews by devaluing the second terms as something subsumed under the first. Most of the controversy about Derrida's project revolves around this austere epistemic doubt that both unsettles binary oppositions while it undermines any determinate meaning of a text, that is, book, art object, performance, building. Yet, his views about skepticism are no more alarming than those of David Hume, Ludwig Wittgenstein or Stanley Cavell. He simply revels in it for transgressive purposes, whereas others provide us with ways to dissolve, sidestep or cope with skepticism. None, however, slide down the slippery, crypto-Nietzschean slope of sophomoric relativism as alleged by old-style humanists, be they Platonists, Kantians or Arnoldians.

The major shortcoming of Derrida's deconstructive project is that it puts a premium on a sophisticated ironic consciousness that tends to preclude and foreclose analyses that guide action with purpose. And given Derrida's own status as an Algerian-born, Jewish leftist marginalized by a hostile French academic establishment (quite different from his reception by the youth in the American academic establishment), the sense of political impotence and hesitation regarding the efficacy of moral action is understandable—but not justifiable. His works and those of his followers too often become rather monotonous, Johnny-one-note rhetorical readings that disassemble texts with little attention to the effects and consequences these dismantlings have in relation to the operations of military, economic and social powers.

Richard Rorty's neopragmatic project of demythologization is insightful in that it provides descriptive mappings of the transient metaphors—especially the ocular and specular ones—that regulate some of the fundamental dynamics in the construction of self-descriptions dominant in highbrow European and American philosophy. His perspective is instructive because it discloses the crucial role of narrative as the background for rational exchange and critical conversation. To put it crudely, Rorty shows why we should speak not of History, but histories, not of

Reason, but historically constituted forms of rationality, not of Criticism or Art, but of socially constructed notions of criticism and art—all linked, but not reducible to political purposes, material interests and cultural prejudices.

Rorty's project nonetheless leaves one wanting, owing to its distrust of social-analytical explanation. Similar to the dazzling new historicism of Stephen Greenblatt, Louis Montrose and Catherine Gallagher—inspired by the subtle symbolic-cum-textual anthropology of Clifford Geertz and the powerful discursive materialism of Michel Foucault—Rorty's work gives us mappings and descriptions with no explanatory accounts for change and conflict. In this way, it gives us an aestheticized version of historicism in which the provisional and variable are celebrated at the expense of highlighting who gains, loses or bears what costs.

Demystification is the most illuminating mode of theoretical inquiry for those who promote the new cultural politics of difference. Social structural analyses of empire, exterminism, class, race, gender, nature, age, sexual orientation, nation and region are the springboards—though not landing grounds—for the most desirable forms of critical practice that take history (and herstory) seriously. Demystification tries to keep track of the complex dynamics of institutional and other related power structures in order to disclose options and alternatives for transformative praxis; it also attempts to grasp the way in which representational strategies are creative responses to novel circumstances and conditions. In this way, the central role of human agency (always enacted under circumstances not of one's choosing)—be it in the critic, artist or constituency and audience—is accented.

I call demystificatory criticism "prophetic criticism"—the approach appropriate for the new cultural politics of difference—because although it begins with social structural analyses, it also makes explicit its moral and political aims. It is partisan, partial, engaged and crisis-centered, yet always keeps open a skeptical eye to avoid dogmatic traps, premature closures, formulaic formulations or rigid conclusions. In addition to social structural analyses, moral and political judgments and sheer critical consciousness, there indeed is evaluation. Yet the aim of this evaluation is neither to pit art objects against one another like racehorses nor to create eternal canons that dull, discourage or even dwarf contemporary achievements. We listen to Ludwig van Beethoven, Charlie Parker, Luciano Pavarotti, Laurie Anderson, Sarah Vaughn, Stevie Wonder or Kathleen Battle, read William Shakespeare, Anton Chekhov, Ralph Ellison, Doris Lessing, Thomas Pynchon, Toni Morrison or Gabriel García Márquez, see works of Pablo Picasso, Ingmar Bergman, Le Corbusier, Martin Puryear, Barbara Kruger, Spike Lee, Frank Gehry or Howardena Pindell—not in order to undergird bureaucratic assents or enliven cocktail party conversations, but rather to be summoned by the styles they deploy for their profound insight, pleasures and challenges. Yet all evaluation—including a delight in Eliot's poetry despite his reactionary politics or a love

of Zora Neale Hurston's novels despite her Republican party affiliations—is inseparable from, though not identical or reducible to, social structural analyses, moral
and political judgments and the workings of a curious critical consciousness.

The deadly traps of demystification—and any form of prophetic criticism—are
those of reductionism, be it of the sociological, psychological or historical sort. By
reductionism I mean either one-factor analyses (that is, crude Marxisms, feminisms, racialisms, etc.) that yield a one-dimensional functionalism, or a hypersub-
tle analytical perspective that loses touch with the specificity of an artwork's form
and the context of its reception. Few cultural workers of whatever stripe can walk
the tightrope between the Scylla of reductionism and the Charybdis of aestheticism—yet demystificatory (or prophetic) critics must.

THE EXISTENTIAL CHALLENGE

The existential challenge to the new cultural politics of difference can be stated
simply: How does one acquire the resources to survive and the cultural capital to
thrive as a critic or artist? By cultural capital (Pierre Bourdieu's term), I mean not
only the high-quality skills required to engage in critical practices but, more important, the self-confidence, discipline and perseverance necessary for success
without an undue reliance on the mainstream for approval and acceptance. This
challenge holds for all prophetic critics, yet it is especially difficult for those of
color. The widespread, modern, European denial of the intelligence, ability,
beauty and character of people of color puts a tremendous burden on critics and
artists of color to "prove" themselves in light of norms and models set by white
elites whose own heritage devalued and dehumanized them. In short, in the court
of criticism and art—or any matters regarding the life of the mind—people of color
are guilty, that is, not expected to meet standards of intellectual achievement, until
"proven" innocent, that is, acceptable to "us."

This is more a structural dilemma than a matter of personal attitudes. The profoundly racist and sexist heritage of the European Age has bequeathed to us a set
of deeply ingrained perceptions about people of color, including, of course, the
self-perceptions that people of color bring. It is not surprising that most intellectuals of color in the past exerted much of their energies and efforts to gain acceptance from and approval by "white normative gazes." The new cultural politics of
difference advises critics and artists of color to put aside this mode of mental
bondage, thereby freeing themselves to both interrogate the ways in which they
are bound by certain conventions and to learn from and build on these very
norms and models. One hallmark of wisdom in the context of any struggle is to
avoid knee-jerk rejection and uncritical acceptance.

Self-confidence, discipline and perseverance are not ends in themselves. Rather
they are the necessary stuff of which enabling criticism and self-criticism are

made. Notwithstanding inescapable jealousies, insecurities and anxieties, one telling characteristic of critics and artists of color linked to the new prophetic criticism should be their capacity for and promotion of relentless criticism and self-criticism—be it the normative paradigms of their white colleagues that tend to leave out considerations of empire, race, gender and sexual orientation, or the damaging dogmas about the homogeneous character of communities of color.

There are four basic options for people of color interested in representation—if they are to survive and thrive as serious practitioners of their craft. First, there is the Booker T. Temptation, namely, the individual preoccupation with the mainstream and its legitimizing power. Most critics and artists of color try to bite this bait. It is nearly unavoidable, yet few succeed in a substantive manner. It is no accident that the most creative and profound among them—especially those with staying power beyond mere flashes in the pan to satisfy faddish tokenism—are usually marginal to the mainstream. Even the pervasive professionalization of cultural practitioners of color in the past few decades has not produced towering figures who reside within the established white patronage system, which bestows the rewards and prestige for chosen contributions to American society.

It certainly helps to have some trustworthy allies within this system, yet most of those who enter and remain tend to lose much of their creativity, diffuse their prophetic energy and dilute their critiques. Still, it is unrealistic for creative people of color to think they can sidestep the white patronage system. And though there are indeed some white allies conscious of the tremendous need to rethink politics, it's naive to think that being comfortably nested within this very same system—even if one can be a patron to others—does not affect one's work, one's outlook and, most important, one's soul.

The second option is the Talented Tenth Seduction, namely, a move toward arrogant group insularity. This alternative has a limited function—to preserve one's sanity and sense of self as one copes with the mainstream. Yet it is, at best, a transitional and transient activity. If it becomes a permanent option, it is self-defeating in that it usually reinforces the very inferiority complexes promoted by the subtly racist mainstream. Hence it tends to revel in a parochialism and encourage a narrow racialist and chauvinistic outlook.

The third strategy is the Go It Alone Option. This is an extreme rejectionist perspective that shuns the mainstream and group insularity. Almost every critic and artist of color contemplates or enacts this option at some time in their pilgrimage. It is healthy in that it reflects the presence of independent, critical and skeptical sensibilities toward perceived constraints on one's creativity. Yet it is, in the end, difficult if not impossible to sustain if one is to grow, develop and mature intellectually, as some semblance of dialogue with a community is necessary for almost any creative practice.

The most desirable option for people of color who promote the new cultural politics of difference is to be a Critical Organic Catalyst. By this I mean a person who stays attuned to the best of what the mainstream has to offer—its paradigms, viewpoints and methods—yet maintains a grounding in affirming and enabling subcultures of criticism. Prophetic critics and artists of color should be exemplars of what it means to be intellectual freedom fighters, that is, cultural workers who simultaneously position themselves within (or alongside) the mainstream while clearly aligned with groups who vow to keep alive potent traditions of critique and resistance. In this regard, one can take clues from the great musicians or preachers of color who are open to the best of what other traditions offer, yet are rooted in nourishing subcultures that build on the grand achievements of a vital heritage. Openness to others—including the mainstream—does not entail whole-sale co-optation, and group autonomy is not group insularity. Louis Armstrong, W. E. B. Du Bois, Ella Baker, José Carlos Mariátegui, M. M. Thomas, Wynton Marsalis, Martin Luther King, Jr., and Ronald Takaki have understood this well.

The new cultural politics of difference can thrive only if there are communities, groups, organizations, institutions, subcultures and networks of people of color who cultivate critical sensibilities and personal accountability—without inhibiting individual expressions, curiosities and idiosyncrasies. This is especially needed given the escalating racial hostility, violence and polarization in the United States. Yet this critical coming together must not be a narrow closing ranks. Rather, it is a strengthening and nurturing endeavor that can forge more solid alliances and coalitions. In this way, prophetic criticism—with its stress on historical specificity and artistic complexity—directly addresses the intellectual challenge. The cultural capital of people of color—with its emphasis on self-confidence, discipline, perse-verance and subcultures of criticism—also tries to meet the existential require-ment. Both are mutually reinforcing. Both are motivated by a deep commitment to individuality and democracy—the moral and political ideals that guide the cre-ative response to the political challenge.

THE POLITICAL CHALLENGE

Adequate rejoinders to intellectual and existential challenges equip the practition-ers of the new cultural politics of difference to meet the political ones. This chal-lenge principally consists of forging solid and reliable alliances of people of color and white progressives guided by a moral and political vision of greater democ-racy and individual freedom in communities, states and transnational enterprises, for instance, corporations and information and communications conglomerates.

Jesse Jackson's Rainbow Coalition is a gallant yet flawed effort in this regard—gallant due to the tremendous energy, vision and courage of its leader and fol-lowers, yet flawed because of its failure to take seriously critical and democratic sensibilities within its own operations. In fact, Jackson's attempt to gain power at the national level is a symptom of the weakness of U.S. progressive politics, and a sign that the capacity to generate extraparliamentary social motion or movements has waned. Yet given the present organizational weakness and intellectual timidity of left politics in the United States, the major option is that of multiracial grassroots citizens' participation in credible projects in which people see that their efforts can make a difference. The salutary revolutionary developments in Eastern Europe are encouraging and inspiring in this regard. Ordinary people organized can change societies.

The most significant theme of the new cultural politics of difference is the agency, capacity and ability of human beings who have been culturally degraded, politically oppressed and economically exploited by bourgeois liberal and Communist illiberal status quos. This theme neither romanticizes nor idealizes marginalized peoples. Rather, it accentuates their humanity and tries to attenuate the institutional constraints on their life-chances for surviving and thriving. In this way, the new cultural politics of difference shuns narrow particularisms, parochialisms and separatisms, just as it rejects false universalisms and homogeneous totalisms. Instead, the new cultural politics of difference affirms the perennial quest for the precious ideals of individuality and democracy by digging deep into the depths of human particularities and social specificities in order to construct new kinds of connections, affinities and communities across empire, nation, region, race, gender, age and sexual orientation.

The major impediments of the radical libertarian and democratic projects of the new cultural politics are threefold: the pervasive processes of objectification, rationalization and commodification throughout the world. The first process—best highlighted in Georg Simmel's *The Philosophy of Money* (1900)—consists of transforming human beings into manipulable objects. It promotes the notion that people's actions have no impact on the world, that we are but spectators not participants in making and remaking ourselves and the larger society. The second process—initially examined in the seminal works of Max Weber—expands bureaucratic hierarchies that impose impersonal rules and regulations in order to increase efficiency, be they defined in terms of better service or better surveillance. This process leads to disenchantment with past mythologies of deadening, flat, banal ways of life. The third and most important process—best examined in the works of Karl Marx, Georg Lukács and Walter Benjamin—augments market forces in the form of oligopolies and monopolies that centralize resources and powers and promote cultures of consumption that view people as mere spectatorial consumers and passive citizens.

These processes cannot be eliminated, but their pernicious effects can be substantially alleviated. The audacious attempt to lessen their impact—to preserve people's agency, increase the scope of their freedom and expand the operations of democracy—is the fundamental aim of the new cultural politics of difference. This is why the crucial questions become: What is the moral content of one's cultural identity? And what are the political consequences of this moral content and cultural identity?

In the recent past, the dominant cultural identities have been circumscribed by immoral patriarchal, imperial, jingoistic and xenophobic constraints. The political consequences have been principally a public sphere regulated by and for well-to-do, white males in the name of freedom and democracy. The new cultural criticism exposes and explodes the exclusions, blindnesses and silences of this past, calling from it radical libertarian and democratic projects that will create a better present and future. The new cultural politics of difference is neither an ahistorical Jacobin program that discards tradition and ushers in new self-righteous authoritarianisms, nor a guilt-ridden, leveling, anti-imperialist liberalism that celebrates token pluralism for smooth inclusion. Rather, it acknowledges the uphill struggle of fundamentally transforming highly objectified, rationalized and commodified societies and cultures in the name of individuality and democracy. This means locating the structural causes of unnecessary forms of social misery (without reducing all such human suffering to historical causes), depicting the plight and predicaments of demoralized and depoliticized citizens caught in market-driven cycles of therapeutic release—drugs, alcoholism, consumerism—and projecting alternative visions, analyses and actions that proceed from particularities and arrive at moral and political connectedness. This connectedness does not signal a homogeneous unity or monolithic totality, but rather a contingent, fragile coalition building in an effort to pursue common radical libertarian and democratic goals that overlap.

In a world in which most of the resources, wealth and power are centered in huge corporations and supportive political elites, the new cultural politics of difference may appear to be solely visionary, utopian and fanciful. The recent cutbacks of social service programs, business takebacks at the negotiation tables of workers and management, speedups at the workplace and buildups of military budgets reinforce this perception. And surely the growing disintegration and decomposition of civil society—of shattered families, neighborhoods and schools—adds to this perception. Can a civilization that evolves more and more around market activity, more and more around the buying and selling of commodities, expand the scope of freedom and democracy? Can we simply bear witness to its slow decay and doom—a painful denouement prefigured already in many poor black and brown communities and rapidly embracing all of us? These haunting questions remain unanswered, yet the challenge they pose must not remain unmet. The new cultural politics of difference tries to confront these enormous and urgent challenges. It will require all the imagination, intelligence, courage, sacrifice, care and laughter we can muster.

The time has come for critics and artists of the new cultural politics of difference to cast their nets widely, flex their muscles broadly and thereby refuse to limit their visions, analyses and praxis to their particular terrains. The aim is to dare to recast, redefine and revise the very notions of "modernity," "mainstream," "margins," "difference," "otherness." We have now reached a new stage in the perennial struggle for freedom and dignity. And although much of the First World intelligentsia adopts retrospective and conservative outlooks that defend the crisis-ridden present, we promote a prospective and prophetic vision with a sense of possibility and potential, especially for those who bear the social costs of the present. We look to the past for strength, not solace; we look at the present and see people perishing, not profits mounting; we look toward the future and vow to make it different and better.

To put it boldly, the new kind of critic and artist associated with the new cultural politics of difference consists of an energetic breed of New World *bricoleurs* with improvisational and flexible sensibilities that sidestep mere opportunism and mindless eclecticism; persons from all countries, cultures, genders, sexual orientations, ages and regions with protean identities who avoid ethnic chauvinism and faceless universalism; intellectual and political freedom fighters with partisan passion, international perspectives and, thank God, a sense of humor that combats the ever present absurdity that forever threatens our democratic and libertarian projects and dampens the fire that fuels our will to struggle. Yet we will struggle and stay, as those brothers and sisters on the block say, "out there"—with intellectual rigor, existential dignity, moral vision, political courage and soulful style.

SOURCE: From *Keeping Faith: Philosophy and Race in America,* by Cornel West, pp. 3–32. Copyright © 1993. Reproduced by permission of Routledge, Inc. Originally appeared in Russell Ferguson, Martha Gever, Trinh T. Minh-ha and Cornel West, eds., *Out There: Marginalization and Contemporary Cultures* (Cambridge, Mass.: MIT Press, 1990).

PART THREE

AMERICAN PRAGMATISM

I first studied American pragmatism in Emerson Hall at Harvard College under Professor Israel Scheffler. I was again immersed in pragmatism under Professor Richard Rorty at Princeton. Both became friends and mentors and encouraged me to develop my own sense of American pragmatism. I vowed to write a book on pragmatism that injected a sense of the tragic in this most indigenous of American philosophical traditions, and The American Evasion of Philosophy was the result. My own conception of prophetic pragmatism is what emerged when I dipped this tradition into the furnace of black suffering and resistance in America. Yet prophetic pragmatism is not my philosophy or particular vision of the world. Rather, it is a fecund discursive space in which I can put forward many voices and viewpoints. It is the philosophical space occupied by my Chekhovian Christian perspective.

Eight

WHY PRAGMATISM?

In 1977 I wrote an essay in which I predicted that Richard Rorty's then circulating manuscript, which would soon be published as Philosophy and the Mirror of Nature, *would produce a pragmatist renaissance. We read this manuscript in his Princeton seminar in the mid-1970s. In the mid-1980s I wrote a first draft of my pragmatism book, which began with Ralph Waldo Emerson and ended with Rorty. After reading the manuscript Rorty sent me a note in Paris praising the book yet advising that I omit the section on Quine and himself. He suggested I end with my own work, not his. This advice exemplifies his modesty and his steadfast support for my work over the last twenty-five years. This introduction to my book gives readers some idea of why pragmatism makes a difference in our thought and life.*

A SMALL-SCALE INTELLECTUAL renascence is occurring under the broad banner of pragmatism. The controversial works of Richard Rorty—aided by the differing views of fellow pragmatists such as Hilary Putnam, Ian Hacking and Richard Bernstein—have unsettled academic philosophy. Literary critics of the pragmatist persuasion like Frank Lentricchia and Stanley Fish have upset traditional humanists. Creative interpreters of John Dewey—like Sheldon Wolin, Michael Walzer and Benjamin Barber—who have updated radical democratic thinking now challenge liberal political theory. And pragmatist thinkers such as Jeffrey Stout are reshaping prevailing conceptions of religious thought.

Three basic issues underlie this recent renascence. First, there is a widespread disenchantment with the traditional image of philosophy as a transcendental mode of inquiry, a tribunal of reason that grounds claims about Truth, Goodness and Beauty. The professional discipline of philosophy is presently caught in an interregnum; mindful of the dead ends of analytical modes of philosophizing, it is yet unwilling to move into the frightening wilderness of pragmatism and historicism with their concomitant concerns in social theory, cultural criticism and historiography. This situation has left the discipline with an excess of academic rigor, yet bereft of substantive intellectual vigor and uncertain of a legitimate subject matter. The unwillingness of many philosophers to tread in the wilderness results from adherence to professional boundaries and academic self-understandings. To put it crudely, most philosophers are neither trained to converse with literary critics, historians and social theorists nor ready to give up the secure self-image of academicians engaged in "serious" philosophical research.

Second, the disenchantment with transcendental conceptions of philosophy has led to a preoccupation with the relation of knowledge and power, cognition and control, discourse and politics. No longer are humanistic scholars content with a historicizing of science, morality and art that shuns the ways in which sciences, moralities and the arts are inextricably linked to structures of domination and subordination. This preoccupation with the materiality of language—such as the ways in which styles of rationality and scientificity or identities and subjectivities are socially constructed and historically constituted—has focused cultural investigations on the production, distribution and circulation of forms of powers, be they rhetorical, economic or military powers.

Third, this focus on powers has returned humanistic studies to the primal stuff of human history, that is, structured and circumscribed human agency in all its various manifestations. Gone is the once fashionable poststructuralist claim to eliminate the subject. Yet also gone is the old humanist view that elevates the human agency of elite cultural creators and ignores social structural constraints, constraints that reinforce and reproduce hierarchies based on class, race, gender and sexual orientation.

It is no accident that American pragmatism once again rises to the surface of North Atlantic intellectual life at the present moment, for its major themes of evading epistemology-centered philosophy, accenting human powers and transforming antiquated modes of social hierarchies in light of religious and/or ethical ideals make it relevant and attractive. The distinctive appeal of American pragmatism in our postmodern moment is its unashamedly moral emphasis and its unequivocally ameliorative impulse. In this world-weary period of pervasive cynicisms, nihilisms, terrorisms and possible extermination, there is a longing for norms and values that can make a difference, a yearning for principled resistance and struggle that can change our desperate plight.

The irony of the contemporary intellectual scene in North America is that after an obsession with European theories and philosophies, we are discovering some of what is needed in the American heritage. This intellectual turn to our heritage ought to be neither a simplistic pro-Americanism in the life of the mind nor a naive parochialism that shuns international outlooks. But this turn is a symptom of just how blinded we often are to certain riches in the American intellectual and political past. Needless to say, we approach this past better equipped owing to European products such as Marxism, structuralism and poststructuralism. But we also acknowledge the shortcomings of these products, that is, their ultimate inability to come to terms with the specificity of our contemporary predicament. The turn to the American heritage—and especially American pragmatism—is neither a panacea for our ills nor a solution to our problems. Rather, it should be an attempt to reinvigorate our moribund academic life, our lethargic political life, our decadent cultural life and our chaotic personal lives for the flowering of many-sided personalities and the flourishing of more democracy and freedom.

My basic aim in this book is to chart the emergence, development, decline and resurgence of American pragmatism. I understand American pragmatism as a specific historical and cultural product of American civilization, a particular set of social practices that articulate certain American desires, values and responses and that are elaborated in institutional apparatuses principally controlled by a significant slice of the American middle class.

American pragmatism emerges with profound insights and myopic blindnesses, enabling strengths and debilitating weaknesses, all resulting from distinctive features of American civilization: its revolutionary beginning combined with a slave-based economy and subordination of American Indians; its elastic liberal rule of law combined with an entrenched business-dominated status quo; its hybrid culture in combination with a collective self-definition as homogeneously Anglo-American; its obsession with mobility, contingency and pecuniary liquidity combined with a deep moralistic impulse; and its impatience with theories and philosophies alongside ingenious technological innovation, political strategies of compromise and personal devices for comfort and convenience. This "hotel civilization" (to use Henry James's apt phrase), with its fusion of the uncertainty of the capitalist market with the quest for security of the home, yielded an indigenous mode of thought that subordinates knowledge to power, tradition to invention, instruction to provocation, community to personality and immediate problems to utopian possibilities.

American pragmatism is a diverse and heterogeneous tradition. But its common denominator consists of a future-oriented instrumentalism that tries to deploy thought as a weapon to enable more effective action. Its basic impulse is a plebeian radicalism that fuels an antipatrician rebelliousness for the moral aim of enriching individuals and expanding democracy. This rebelliousness, rooted in the anticolonial heritage of the country, is severely restricted by an ethnocentrism and a patriotism cognizant of the exclusion of peoples of color, certain immigrants, women, gays and lesbians, yet fearful of the subversive demands these excluded peoples might make and enact.

The fundamental argument of this book is that the evasion of epistemology-centered philosophy—from Emerson to Rorty—results in a conception of philosophy as a form of cultural criticism in which the meaning of America is put forward by intellectuals in response to distinct social and cultural crises. In this sense, American pragmatism is less a philosophical tradition putting forward solutions to perennial problems in the Western philosophical conversation initiated by Plato and more a continuous cultural commentary or set of interpretations that attempt to explain America to itself at a particular historical moment.

The pragmatists' preoccupation with power, provocation and personality—in contrast, say, to grounding knowledge, regulating instruction and promoting tradition—signifies an intellectual calling to administer to a confused populace caught in the whirlwinds of societal crisis, the cross fires of ideological polemics and the storms of class, racial and gender conflicts. This deep intellectual vocation, quite different from our sense of the emasculation of the academic profession, impels the major American pragmatists to be organic intellectuals of some sort; that is, participants in the life of the mind who revel in ideas and relate ideas to action by means of creating, constituting or consolidating constituencies for moral aims and political purposes. It is no accident that the major figures of American pragmatism use the language of crisis—hence the centrality of critical consciousness in their work—and exude urgency as they search for strategies and tactics to facilitate their exercise of intellectual and moral leadership for their constituency. And on a deeper level, these figures grapple with the problem of evil, producing ever changing yet definite ideological constructions of an American theodicy.

This book does not purport to be a comprehensive account of American pragmatism. Rather, it is a highly selective interpretation of American pragmatism in light of the present state (or my reading) of American society and culture. For instance, the omission of George Herbert Mead or C. I. Lewis is not a negative comment on their significant intellectual contributions to American pragmatism. Similarly, my focus on John Dewey at the expense of Charles Peirce and William James does not reflect my deep respect for the latter two. Rather, it expresses my sense that the thoroughgoing historical consciousness and emphasis on social and political matters found in Dewey speaks more to my purposes than the preoccupations with logic in Peirce and the obsessions with individuality in James. I consider Peirce and James as profound pioneering figures standing, in part, on the shoulders of Emerson. Yet I believe that it is with Dewey that American pragmatism achieves intellectual maturity, historical scope and political engagement. In this sense, my genealogy of American pragmatism is an explicitly political interpretation without, I hope, being pejoratively ideological.

My emphasis on the political and moral side of American pragmatism permits me to make a case for the familiar, but rarely argued, claim that Emerson is the appropriate starting point for the pragmatist tradition. Furthermore, by including treatments of a historian (Du Bois), theologian (Niebuhr), sociologist (C. Wright Mills), and literary critic (Trilling), I try to show the way in which Emersonian sensibilities and pragmatist progeny cut across the modern disciplinary division of knowledge.

In regard to method, this work is a social history of ideas. It conceives of the intellectual sphere of history as distinct, unique and personal sets of cultural practices intimately connected with concomitant developments in the larger society and culture. On the one hand, this book benefits from the groundbreaking research of social historians who delve into the institutional constraints on and agency of exploited and oppressed peoples, yet the book focuses principally on how the complex formulations and arguments of American pragmatists shape and are shaped by the social structures that exploit and oppress. On the other hand, this text learns from—without endorsing—the grand tradition of idealist historiography in that it tries to get inside the formulations and arguments of American pragmatists so that the social roles and functions of ideas do not exhaust their existence or curb intellectual curiosity. This fusion of the intrinsic interest (or hedonistic effect) and the instrumental interest (or political use) of American pragmatism is the goal of this social history of ideas.

This book also attempts to address the crisis of the American Left. It does this primarily by providing an interpretation of a progressive tradition that can inspire and instruct contemporary efforts to remake and reform American society and culture. My own conception of prophetic pragmatism—a phrase I hope is not oxymoronic to readers after elucidation and illustration—serves as the culmination of the American pragmatist tradition; that is, it is a perspective and project that speaks to the major impediments to a wider role for pragmatism in American thought.

I began this work as an exercise in critical self-inventory, as a historical, social and existential situating of my own work as an intellectual, activist and human being. I wanted to make clear to myself my own contradictions and tensions, faults and foibles as one shaped by, in part, the tradition of American pragmatism. My first book, *Prophesy Deliverance! An Afro-American Revolutionary Christianity* (1982), attempted to lay bare the oppositional potential of prophetic Christianity—especially as filtered through the best of the black church tradition. *Prophetic Fragments* (1988) followed in the same vein. My critical acceptance of certain elements of Marxist analysis linked me to the worldwide Christian anti-imperialist and anticapitalist movement often referred to as liberation theology. Yet my promotion of American pragmatism as both a persuasive philosophical perspective and an indigenous source of left politics in America perplexed many people. So just as my earlier texts emerged out of my own political praxis in and my identity with prophetic Christianity, this book consists of my attempt to come to terms with my philosophic allegiances in light of my participation in the U.S. democratic socialist movement (Democratic Socialists of America), my particular role in the American academy (Princeton University) and my existence on the margins of the black church (as a lay preacher).

This book is principally motivated by my own disenchantment with intellectual life in America and my own demoralization regarding the political and cultural state of the country. For example, I am disturbed by the transformation of highly intelligent liberal intellectuals into tendentious neoconservatives owing to crude ethnic identity-based allegiances and vulgar neonationalist sentiments. I am disappointed with the professional incorporation of former New Left activists who now often thrive on a self-serving careerism while espousing rhetorics of oppositional politics of little seriousness and integrity. More important, I am depressed about the concrete nihilism in working-class and underclass American communities—the pervasive drug addiction, suicides, alcoholism, male violence against women, "straight" violence against gays and lesbians, white violence against black, yellow and brown people and the black criminality against others, especially other black people. I have written this text convinced that a thorough reexamination of American pragmatism, stripping it of its myths, caricatures and stereotypes and viewing it as a component of a new and novel form of indigenous American oppositional thought and action, may be a first step toward fundamental change and transformation in America and the world. Like Raymond Williams's *Culture and Society* and Fredric Jameson's *Marxism and Form,* this book is, among other things, a political act.

I write as one who intends to deepen and enrich American pragmatism while bringing trenchant critique to bear on it. I consider myself deeply shaped by American civilization, but not fully a part of it. I am convinced that the best of the American pragmatist tradition is the best America has to offer itself and the world, yet I am willing to concede that this best may not be good enough, given the depths of the international and domestic crises we now face. But though this slim and slight possibility may make my efforts no more than an impotent moral gesture, nonetheless, in the heat of battle, we have no other choice but to fight.

Nine

ON PROPHETIC PRAGMATISM

This section of the last chapter of The American Evasion of Philosophy *lays bare my attempt to learn from and go beyond earlier forms of pragmatism. My text takes readers through Emerson, Peirce, James, Dewey, Hook, Mills, Du Bois, Niebuhr, Trilling, Quine and Rorty. I then situate two major thinkers influenced by pragmatism—Roberto Unger and Michel Foucault—who present alternatives to my prophetic pragmatism. My subsequent book with Unger,* The Future of American Progressivism *(1998), exemplifies our rapprochement, despite lingering tensions over my Chekhovian Christian sensibilities and his High Romantic sentiments.*

At the level of theory the philosophy of praxis cannot be confounded with or reduced to any other philosophy. Its originality lies not only in its transcending of previous philosophies but also and above all in that it opens up a completely new road, renewing from head to toe the whole way of conceiving philosophy itself . . . the whole way of conceiving philosophy has been "historicised," that is to say a new way of philosophising which is more concrete and historical than what went before it has begun to come into existence.

—ANTONIO GRAMSCI

THE MOVE FROM RORTY'S model of fluid conversation to that of the multileveled operations of power leads us back to Ralph Waldo Emerson. Like Friedrich Nietzsche, Emerson is first and foremost a cultural critic obsessed with ways to generate forms of power. For Rorty, these forms are understood as activities of conversation for the primary purpose of producing new human self-descriptions. But for Emerson, conversation is but one minor instance of the myriad of possible transactions for the enhancement of human powers and personalities. Ironically, Rorty's adoption of Michael Oakeshott's metaphor of "conversation" reflects the dominant ideal of the very professionalism he criticizes. This ideal indeed is more a public affair than are Emerson's preferred ideal transactions, e.g., gardening, walking, reading, and yet it also is more genteel and bourgeois.

The tradition of pragmatism—the most influential stream in American thought—is in need of an explicit political mode of cultural criticism that refines and revises Emerson's concerns with power, provocation and personality in light of Dewey's stress on historical consciousness and Du Bois's focus on the plight of the wretched of the earth. This political mode of cultural criticism must recapture Emerson's sense of vision—his utopian impulse—yet rechannel it through Dewey's conception of creative democracy and Du Bois's social structural analysis of the limits of capitalist democracy. Furthermore, this new kind of cultural criticism—we can call it prophetic pragmatism—must confront candidly the tragic sense found in Hook and Trilling, the religious version of the Jamesian strenuous mood in Niebuhr and the tortuous grappling with the vocation of the intellectual in Mills. Prophetic pragmatism, with its roots in the American heritage and its hopes for the wretched of the earth, constitutes the best chance of promoting an Emersonian culture of creative democracy by means of critical intelligence and social action.

The first step is to define what an Emersonian culture of creative democracy would look like, or at least give some sense of the process by which it can be created. In retrospect, it is important to note that Emerson's swerve from philosophy was not simply a rejection of the Cartesian and Kantian models of epistemology; it also was an assertion of the primacy of power-laden people's opinion (*doxa*) over value-free philosophers' knowledge (*episteme*). Emerson's swerve was a democratic leveling of the subordination of common sense to Reason. Emerson realized that when philosophers "substitute Reason for common sense, they tend to view the sense of commoners to be nonsense."[1] Emerson's suspicion of philosophy was not simply that it bewitched thinkers by means of language but, more important, that it had deep antidemocratic consequences. For Emerson, reason, formal thought, foundations, certainty were not only far removed from the dynamism of human experience; they also were human creations appearing as detached abstractions that command their creators and thereby constrain their creators' freedom. This consequence is both antilibertarian and antidemocratic in that human potential and participation are suppressed in the name of philosophic truth and knowledge. Emerson's sensibilities are echoed in our own time by Benjamin Barber:

In conquering the muddled uncertainties of politics and suborning reasonableness to rationality, they [philosophers] have served the ideal of enlightenment better than they have informed our political judgment. . . . Rights get philosophically vindicated but only as abstractions that undermine the democratic communities that breathe life into rights; justice is given an unimpeachable credential in epistemology without giving it a firm hold on action or the deliberative processes from which political action stems; talk is revivified as the heart of a political process and then recommended to citizens, but in a form that answers to the constraints not of citizenship but of philosophy; civility is celebrated, but construed as incompatible with the sorts of collective human choice and communal purposes that give civility its political meaning.[2]

To speak then of an Emersonian culture of creative democracy is to speak of a society and culture where politically adjudicated forms of knowledge are produced in which human participation is encouraged and for which human personalities are enhanced. Social experimentation is the basic norm, yet it is operative only when those who must suffer the consequences have effective control over the institutions that yield the consequences, i.e., access to decision-making processes. In this sense, the Emersonian swerve from epistemology is inseparable from an Emersonian culture of creative democracy; that is, there is political motivation and political substance to the American evasion of philosophy. "Politics is what men do when metaphysics fails. . . . It is the forging of common actuality in the absence of abstract independent standards. It entails dynamic, ongoing, common deliberation and action and it is feasible only when individuals are transformed by social interaction into citizens."[3]

The political motivation of the American evasion of philosophy is not ideological in the vulgar sense; that is, the claim here is not that philosophy is a mere cloak that conceals the material interests of a class or group. Rather, the claim is that once one gives up on the search for foundations and the quest for certainty, human inquiry into truth and knowledge shifts to the social and communal circumstances under which persons can communicate and cooperate in the process of acquiring knowledge. What was once purely epistemological now highlights the values and operations of power requisite for the human production of truth and knowledge.

The political substance of the American evasion of philosophy is that what was the prerogative of philosophers, i.e., rational deliberation, is now that of the people—and the populace deliberating is creative democracy in the making. Needless to say, this view is not a license for eliminating or opposing all professional elites, but it does hold them to account. Similarly, the populace deliberating is neither mob rule nor mass prejudice. Rather, it is the citizenry in action, with its civil consciousness molded by participation in public-interest-centered and individual-rights-regarding democracy.

Prophetic pragmatism makes this political motivation and political substance of the American evasion of philosophy explicit. Like Dewey, it understands pragmatism as a political form of cultural criticism and locates politics in the everyday experiences of ordinary people. Unlike Dewey, prophetic pragmatism promotes a more direct encounter with the Marxist tradition of social analysis. The emancipatory social experimentalism that sits at the center of prophetic pragmatic politics closely resembles the radical democratic elements of Marxist theory, yet its flexibility shuns any dogmatic, a priori or monistic pronouncements.

The encounter of prophetic pragmatism with Marxist theory can be best illustrated by an examination of the most significant and elaborate effort to put forward a Marxist-informed (though not Marxist) democratic social vision: namely, that found in Roberto Unger's multivolume work *Politics*. Unger is not a prophetic pragmatist—yet there are deep elective affinities between Unger's work and prophetic pragmatism. To put it crudely, both are noteworthy exemplars of third-wave left romanticism.

ROBERTO UNGER AND THIRD-WAVE LEFT ROMANTICISM

Roberto Unger's distinctive contribution to contemporary social thought is to deepen and sharpen in a radical manner John Dewey's notion of social experimentation in light of the crisis of Marxist theory and praxis. Unger's fundamental aim is to free Marxist conceptions of human society-making from evolutionary, deterministic and economistic encumbrances by means of Deweyan concerns with the plethora of historically specific social arrangements and the often overlooked politics of personal relations between unique and purposeful individuals. The basic result of Unger's fascinating efforts is to stake out new discursive space on the contemporary political and ideological spectrum. Prophetic pragmatism occupies this same space. This space is neither simply left nor liberal, Marxist nor Lockean, anarchist nor Kantian. Rather, Unger's perspective is both post-Marxist and postliberal; that is, it consists of an emancipatory experimentalism that promotes permanent social transformation and perennial self-development for the purposes of ever increasing democracy and individual freedom. Yet, in contrast to most significant social thinkers, Unger is motivated by explicit religious concerns, such as a kinship with nature as seen in romantic love, or transcendence of nature as manifest in the hope for eternal life. In this way, Unger highlights the radical existential insufficiency of his emancipatory experimentalism, which speaks best to human penultimate matters. For Unger, human ultimate concerns are inseparable from yet not reducible to the never ending quest for social transformation and self-development.

I shall argue three claims regarding Unger's project. First, I shall suggest that his viewpoint can be best characterized as the most elaborate articulation of a *third-wave left romanticism* now sweeping across significant segments of principally the First World progressive intelligentsia (or what is left of this progressive intelligentsia!). Second, I will show that this third-wave left romanticism—like prophetic pragmatism—is discursively situated between John Dewey's radical liberal version of socialism and Antonio Gramsci's absolute historicist conception of Marxism. Third, I shall highlight the ways in which this provocative project, though an advance beyond much of contemporary social thought, remains inscribed within a

Eurocentric and patriarchal discourse that not simply fails to theoretically consider racial and gender forms of subjugation, but also remains silent on the antiracist and feminist dimensions of concrete progressive political struggles.

The most striking impression one gets from reading Unger's work is his unabashedly pronounced romanticism. By romanticism here I mean quite simply the preoccupation with Promethean human powers, the recognition of the contingency of the self and society and the audacious projection of desires and hopes in the form of regulative emancipatory ideals for which one lives and dies. In these postmodern times of cynicism and negativism—after the unimaginable atrocities of Hitler, Stalin, Tito, Mussolini and Franco and the often forgotten barbarities committed in Asia, Africa and Latin America under European and American imperialist auspices; and during the present period of Khomeini, Pinochet, Moi and Mengistu in the Third World, bureaucratic henchmen ruling the Second World and Reagan, Thatcher, Kohl and Chirac setting the pace in the First World—Unger's romanticism is both refreshing and disturbing.

The ameliorative energies and utopian impulses that inform Unger's work are refreshing in that so many of us now "lack any ready way to imagine transformation."[4] We feel trapped in a world with no realizable oppositional options, no actualizable credible alternatives. This sense of political impotence—"this experience of acquiescence without commitment"[5]—yields three basic forms of politics: sporadic terrorism for impatient, angry and nihilistic radicals; professional reformism for comfortable, cultivated and concerned liberals; and evangelical nationalism for frightened, paranoid and accusatory conservatives. Unger's romantic sense that the future can and should be fundamentally different from and better than the present not only leads him to reject these three predominant kinds of politics, but also impels him to answer in the negative to "the great political question of our day: Is social democracy the best that we can reasonably hope for?"[6] Unger believes we can and must do better.

Yet Unger's third-wave left romanticism is disturbing in that we have witnessed—and are often reminded of—the deleterious consequences and dehumanizing effects of the first two waves of left romanticism in the modern world. The first wave—best seen in the American and French Revolutions—unleashed unprecedented human energies and powers, significantly transformed selves and societies and directed immense human desires and hopes toward the grand moral and credible political ideals of democracy and freedom, equality and fraternity. Two exemplary figures of this first wave—Thomas Jefferson and Jean-Jacques Rousseau—would undoubtedly affirm the three basic elements of Unger's conception of human activity: the contextual or conditional quality of all human activity; the possibility of breaking through all contexts of practical or conceptual activity; and the need to distinguish between context-preserving, i.e., routinized, and context-breaking, i.e., transgressive, activities.[7]

Furthermore, both Jefferson and Rousseau would agree with Unger's romantic conception of imagination as a human power that conceives of social reality from the vantage point of change and for the purposes of transformation.[8] In this regard, Unger is deeply within the North Atlantic romantic grain. Why, then, ought we to be disturbed? Despite the great human advances initiated and promoted by first wave left romanticism, its historical and social embodiments reinforced and reproduced barbaric practices: white-supremacist practices associated with African slavery and imperial conquest over indigenous and Mexican peoples; male-supremacist practices inscribed in familial relations, cultural mores and societal restrictions; and excessive business control and influence over the public interest as seen in low wages, laws against unions and government support of select business endeavors, e.g., railroads. These noteworthy instances of the underside of first-wave left romanticism should be disturbing not because all efforts to change the status quo in a progressive direction are undesirable, but rather because any attempt to valorize historically specific forms of human powers must be cognizant of and cautious concerning who will be subjected to those human powers.

The second wave of left romanticism, following upon the heels of profound disillusionment and dissatisfaction with the American and French Revolutions, is manifest in the two great prophetic and prefigurative North Atlantic figures Ralph Waldo Emerson and Karl Marx. Both were obsessed with the problem of revolution, that is, the specifying and creating of conditions for the transformation of context-preserving activities into context-breaking ones. Both had a profound faith in the capacity of human beings to remake themselves and society in more free and democratic ways. And both looked toward science—the new cultural authority on knowledge, reality and truth—as an indispensable instrument for this remaking and betterment.

Emersonian themes of the centrality of the self's morally laden transformative vocation, the necessity of experimentation to achieve the self's aims of self-mastery and kinship with nature and the importance of self-creation and self-authorization loom large in Unger's work. In fact, the penultimate paragraph of volume 1 of *Politics* reads as if it comes right out of Emerson's *Nature:*

In their better and saner moments men and women have always wanted to live as the originals that they all feel themselves to be and to cement practical and passionate attachments that respect this truth rather than submerge it. As soon as they have understood their social worlds to be made up and pasted together, they have also wanted to become the co-makers of these worlds. Some modern doctrines tell us that we already live in societies in which we can fully satisfy these desires while others urge us to give them up as unrealistic. But the first piece of advice is hard to believe, and the second is hard to practice.[9]

Similarly, Marxist motifs of the centrality of value-laden political struggle, the necessity for transformation of present-day societies and for control over nature and, most pointedly, the ability of human powers to reshape human societies against constraints always already in place play fundamental roles in Unger's project. Indeed, the last paragraph of volume 1 of *Politics* invokes the same metaphors, passions and aims as Marx's *1844 Manuscripts* and *1848 Manifesto:*

> The constraints of society, echoed, reinforced, and amplified by the illusions of social thought, have often led people to bear the stigma of longing under the mask of worldliness and resignation. An anti-naturalistic social theory does not strike down the constraints but it dispels the illusions that prevent us from attacking them. Theoretical insight and prophetic vision have joined ravenous self-interest and heartless conflict to set the fire that is burning in the world, and melting apart the amalgam of faith and superstition, and consuming the power of false necessity.[10]

The second wave of left romanticism is dominated by Emersonian ideas of America and Marxist conceptions of socialism. From roughly the 1860s to the 1940s, human hopes for democracy and freedom, equality and fraternity around the globe rested on the legacy of either Emerson or Marx. Needless to say, European efforts at nation building and empire consolidating—the major sources of second-wave right romanticism—violently opposed both the Emersonian and the Marxist legacies. Yet by the end of the World War II, with the defeat of Germany's bid for European and world domination at the hands of the Allied forces led by the United States and Russia, the second wave of left romanticism began to wane. The dominant version of the Marxist legacy—Marxist-Leninist (and at the time led by Stalin)—was believed by more and more left romantics to be repressive, repulsive and retrograde. And the major mode of the Emersonian legacy—Americanism (led then by Truman and Eisenhower)—was viewed by many left romantics as racist, penurious and hollow.

The third wave of left romanticism proceeded from a sense of deep disappointment with Marxist-Leninism and Americanism. Exemplary activistic stirrings can be found in the Third World or among people of color in the First World—Gandhi in India, Mariátegui in Peru, Nasser in Egypt and Martin Luther King, Jr., in the United States. Yet principally owing to the tragic facts of survival, myopic leadership and limited options, most Third World romanticism was diverted from the third wave of left romanticism into the traps of a regimenting Marxist-Leninism or a rapacious Americanism. The major exceptions—Chile under Salvador Allende, Jamaica under Michael Manley, Nicaragua under the Sandinistas—encounter formidable, usually insurmountable, obstacles. Needless to say, similar projects in Second World countries—Hungary in 1956, Czechoslovakia in 1968,

Poland in 1970—are tragically and brutally crushed.

The two great figures of the third wave of left romanticism are John Dewey and Antonio Gramsci. Dewey applies the Jeffersonian and Emersonian viewpoints to the concrete historical and social realities of our century. Similarly, Gramsci sharpens and revises the Rousseauistic and Marxist perspectives on these realities. As we observed earlier, in numerous essays, articles and reviews and, most important, in his texts *The Public and Its Problems* (1927), *Individualism: Old and New* (1929), *Liberalism and Social Action* (1935) and *Freedom and Culture* (1939), Dewey put forward a powerful interpretation of socialism that builds upon yet goes beyond liberalism. This interpretation highlights a conception of social experimentation that "goes all the way down"; that is, it embraces the idea of fundamental economic, political, cultural and individual transformation in light of Jeffersonian and Emersonian ideals of accountable power, small-scale associations and individual liberties. In various fragments, incomplete studies and political interventions and in works such as *The Prison Notebooks* (1929–35) and *The Modern Prince,* Gramsci sets forth a penetrating version of Marxism that rests upon yet spills over beyond Leninism. This version focuses on a notion of historical specificity and a conception of hegemony that preclude any deterministic, economistic or reductionist readings of social phenomena. In this way, Dewey and Gramsci partly set the agenda for any acceptable and viable third wave of left romanticism in our time.

Unger's provocative project occupies the discursive space between Dewey and Gramsci; it is the most detailed delineation of third-wave left romanticism we have. Like prophetic pragmatism, his work stands at the intersection of the Jefferson-Emerson-Dewey insights and the Rousseau-Marx-Gramsci formulations. Ironically, as an intellectual with Third World origins and sensibilities (Brazilian) and First World academic status and orientations (Harvard law professor for almost twenty years), Unger is much more conscious of and concerned with his Rousseau-Marx-Gramsci heritage than with his Jefferson-Emerson-Dewey sentiments. In fact, his major aim is to provide an alternative radicalism—at the levels of method and political and personal praxis—to Marxism in light of his Third World experiences and First World training.

> *Politics* is also the product of two very different experiences. One of these experiences is exposure to the rich, polished, critical and self-critical but also downbeat and Alexandrian culture of social and historical thought that now flourishes in the North-Atlantic democracies. This social-thought culture suffers from the influence of a climate of opinion in which the most generous citizens hope at best to avert military disasters and to achieve marginal redistributive goals while resigning themselves to established institutional arrangements. The other shaping experience is practical and imaginative engagement in the murky but hopeful politics of Brazil, a country at the forward edge of the Third World. There, at the

time of writing, at least some people took seriously the idea that basic institutions, practices, and preconceptions might be reconstructed in ways that did not conform to any established model of social organization.

Much in this work can be understood as the consequence of an attempt to enlist the intellectual resources of the North-Atlantic world in the service of concerns and commitments more keenly felt elsewhere. In this way I hope to contribute toward the development of an alternative to the vague, unconvinced, and unconvincing Marxism that now serves the advocates of the radical project as their *Lingua Franca*. If the arguments of this book stand up, the transformative focus of this theoretical effort has a cognitive value that transcends its immediate origins and motives.[11]

In this sense, Unger privileges Marxist discourse. On the one hand, Marxism's "structure and institutional fetishism"—its tendency to impose historical and social scripts in the name of deep-structure logics of inevitability—stand as the major impediment to Unger's radical project.[12] On the other hand, Marxism more than any other social theory contains the resources and analytical tools to resist this tendency and thereby aid and abet Unger's work.

Much of this book represents a polemic against what the text labels deep-structure social analysis. The writings of Marx and of his followers provide the most powerful and detailed illustrations of the deep-structure moves. Yet Marx's own writings contain many elements that assist the effort to free ambitious theorizing from deep-structure assumptions. People working in the Marxist tradition have developed the deep-structure approach. Yet they have also forged some of the most powerful tools with which to build a view of social life more faithful to the antinaturalistic intentions of Marx and other classic social theorists than Marx's original science of history.[13]

Unger even more closely associates his project with a particular group of Marxists (whom he dubs "political Marxists"), though he by no means affirms their efforts to stay within the Marxist explanatory framework. The major figure in this group is Antonio Gramsci. Indeed, it can be said with assurance that Gramsci's flexible Marxism, which emphasizes and explores "the relative autonomy of class situations and class consciousness from the defining features of a mode of production like capitalism," serves as the principal springboard for Unger's work.[14] His explicit acknowledgment of his debts to political Marxists such as Gramsci—a rare moment in Unger's self-authorizing texts—bears this out.

At times the political Marxists have sacrificed the development of their insights to the desire to retain a connection with the central theses of historical materialism. To them these tenets have seemed the only available basis for theoretical generalization and for critical distance from the arrangements and circumstances of the societies in which they lived. At other times, the political Marxists have simply given up on theory. . . . They have then paid the price in the loss of an ability to convey a sense of sharp institutional alternatives for past, present, and future society. The constructive theory of *Politics* just keeps going from where the political Marxists leave off. It does so, however, without either renouncing theoretical ambitions or accepting any of the distinctive doctrines of Marx's social theory.[15]

Unger believes it is necessary to go beyond Gramsci not because Gramsci is a paradigmatic Marxist "super-theorist" who generates theoretical generalizations and schemas that fail to grasp the complexity of social realities, but rather because Gramsci, despite his Marxism, is an exemplary "ultratheorist" who attempts to avoid broad explanations and theoretical systems in order to keep track of the multifarious features and aspects of fluid social realities.[16] As an unequivocal supertheorist (who tries to avoid the traps of positivism, naive historicism and deep-structure logics), Unger criticizes ultratheorists like Gramsci and Foucault for rejecting explanatory or prescriptive theories and thereby ultimately disenabling effective emancipatory thought and practice. For Unger, the ultratheorist sees a deep-structure logic inside *every* theoretical system, confuses explanatory generalizations with epistemic foundationalism and runs the risk of his work's degenerating into a nominalistic form of conventional social science. In short, the major lesson Unger learns from Gramsci is to be a more subtle, nuanced and sensitive supertheorist than Marx by building on elements in Marx and others.

Despite the prominence of certain Deweyan themes in his project, Dewey is virtually absent in Unger's text. Furthermore, the one reference to Dewey is a rather cryptic and misleading statement. After alluding to Foucault and Gramsci as major ultratheorists, Unger adds: "Moreover, it would be wrong to associate ultra-theory solely with Leftist or modernist intellectuals. Why not, for example, John Dewey (despite the gap between the commitment to institutional experimentalism and the slide into institutional conservatism)?"[17] This passage is perplexing for three reasons. First, is Unger implying that Dewey was neither a leftist nor a modernist intellectual? Second, is Unger drawing a distinction between his own social experimentalism and Dewey's institutional experimentalism? Third, in what sense and when did Dewey slide into institutional conservatism? If Unger answers the first question in the affirmative, he falls prey to the misinformed stereotypical view of Dewey as a vulgar Americanist. Dewey's sixty-five-year political record as a democratic socialist speaks for itself. And no argument is needed for Dewey's being a modernist intellectual, when he stands as the major secular intellectual of twentieth-century America. If Unger is making a distinction between his form of experimentalism and that of Dewey, its validity remains unclear unless one remains fixated on Dewey's educational reform movement and neglects the broader calls for fundamental social change put forward during the years Dewey concentrated on progressive education as well as afterward, in the late 1920s, 1930s and 1940s. And the implausible notion that Dewey slid into institutional conservatism holds only if one wrongly views his brand of anti-Stalinism in the 1940s as conservatism, for his critique of American society remained relentless to the end.

I do believe Unger has simply slipped in his brief mention of Dewey. Yet this slip is significant in that Dewey could provide Unger with some enabling insights and tools for his project. These insights and tools will not be comparable to those of Marx, for Dewey was not a social theorist. Yet Dewey's own brand of ultratheory could, like Gramsci's, chasten and temper Unger's supertheory ambitions.

For example, Unger's attempt to work out an analogical relation between scientific notions of objectivity and social conceptions of personality is prefigured—and more persuasive—in Dewey's linkage of scientific attitude (as opposed to scientific method) to democracy as a way of life. The key notions become not so much objectivity—not even Rorty's ingenious reformulation of objectivity as self-critical solidarity—as, more fundamentally, respect for the other and accountability as a condition for fallibility.[18] Similarly, Dewey's brand of ultratheory does not exclude, downplay or discourage explanatory generalizations. In fact, Dewey holds that we cannot get by without some form of supertheory, for the same reasons Unger invokes (i.e., for explaining and regulating our practices). Yet Dewey admonishes us to view supertheories as we do any other instruments or weapons we have, to use them when they serve our purposes and satisfy our interests and criticize or discard them when they utterly fail us. The significant difference between Gramsci and Dewey is not that the former accepts Marxist theory and the latter rejects it, but rather that Gramsci tenaciously holds onto Marxist theory in those areas where it fails, e.g., politics and culture. Dewey accepted much of the validity of Marxist theory and simply limited its explanatory scope and rejected its imperial, monistic and dogmatic versions. These Deweyan correctives to Unger's project point toward prophetic pragmatism.

Dewey's radical liberal version of socialism might dampen Unger's fires of utopian quest in that Dewey recognized that authoritarian communisms and liberal capitalist democracies were and are the major *credible* options in the First World and Second World at the moment. And social experimentation in the Third World remains hampered by these limits. This is not to say we ought not to dream, hope, live, fight and die for betterment, yet such romantic longings, even when dressed up in sophisticated social thought, do not alter the severe constraints of the international coordination of capital in the West and the bureaucratic stranglehold in the East. In this sense, Dewey's petit bourgeois radicalism, which is no tradition to trash despite its vast shortcomings, could not but be an incessant effort at radical reform in the West and a beacon light on repression in the East. In the same way, Gramsci's Communist party leadership, whose legacy now resides principally in Italy and Sweden, could not but comprise audacious attempts at democratization in the East and a beacon light on socially induced misery (e.g., poverty, racism) in the West. The fundamental challenge to Unger is to find space for historical maneuvering—for his emancipatory experimentalism—between Dewey and Gramsci, between petit bourgeois radicalism and Marxian socialism.

This challenge should be approached on two levels—that of highbrow academic production and consumption and that of popular political organization and mobilization. Both levels have their own kinds of significance. Universities, colleges and some professional schools, though increasingly given over to hi-tech and computers, still provide one of the few institutional arenas in which serious conversation about new ideological space can take place in liberal capitalist democracies. It indeed is no accident that much of the legacy of the New Left in the 1960s now resides in such places. Most of the consumers of Unger's project consist of these progressive professional managers who exercise some degree of cultural authority in and from these educational institutions. Their importance, especially as transmitters of elite cultural values and sensibilities, should not be overlooked. But neither should their influence be exaggerated. In fact, for the most part, what they produce and consume of a left political orientation remains within the academy. Despite Unger's admirable efforts to write in a relatively jargon-free language, this holds for his own texts. So his attempt to put forward a left project between Dewey and Gramsci will more than likely remain the property of the same disillusioned progressives he chastises. The importance of influencing the left sectors of the "downbeat and Alexandrian" intellectual culture of our time ought not to be minimized; nevertheless, Unger wants to do more than this—he wants to make a significant programmatic intervention in the real world of politics.

This brings us to the level of political organization and mobilization. Unlike Dewey and Gramsci, Unger pays little attention to the burning cultural and political issues in the everyday lives of ordinary people—issues such as religious and nationalist (usually xenophobic) revivals, the declining power of trade unions, escalating racial and sexual violence, pervasive drug addiction and alcoholism, breakdowns in the nuclear family, the cultural and political impact of mass media (TV, radio and videos) and the exponential increase of suicides and homicides. Unger invokes a politics of personal relations and everyday life, yet he remains rather vague regarding its content.

When I claim that Unger's discourse remains inscribed within a Eurocentric and patriarchal framework, I mean that his texts remain relatively silent—on the conceptual and practical levels—on precisely those issues that promote social motion and politicization among the majority of people in the country. I am not suggesting that Unger write simple pamphlets for the masses, but rather that his fascinating works give more attention to those issues that may serve as the motivating forces for his new brand of left politics. To write a masterful text of social theory and politics that does not so much as mention—God forbid, grapple with—forms of racial and gender subjugation in our time is inexcusable on political and theoretical grounds.[19] To do so is to remain captive to a grand though flawed Eurocentric and patriarchal heritage. More pointedly, it is to miss much of the new possibilities for a realizable left politics. Needless to say, to take seriously issues such as race and gender is far from a guarantee for a credible progressive politics, but to bypass them is to commit the fatal sin of supertheory: to elide the concrete at the expense of systemic coherence and consistency.

In conclusion, Unger's ambitious project warrants our close attention and scrutiny. It articulates many of the motives and ideals of the political project of prophetic pragmatism. It is, by far, the most significant attempt to articulate a third-wave left romanticism that builds on the best of the Jefferson-Emerson-Dewey and Rousseau-Marx-Gramsci legacies. Unfortunately, he remains slightly blinded by some of the theoretical and practical shortsightedness of these grand North Atlantic legacies. Yet Unger would be the first to admit that all prophets are imperfect and that all emancipatory visions and programs are subject to revision and transformation.

THE CHALLENGE OF MICHEL FOUCAULT

To praise Unger's project and that of prophetic pragmatism for their third-wave left romanticism is to go against the grain in some progressive circles owing to the influence of Michel Foucault. Foucault is the exemplary antiromantic, suspicious of any talk about wholeness, totality, telos, purpose or even future.[20] Prophetic pragmatism shares with Foucault a preoccupation with the operation of powers. It also incorporates the genealogical mode of inquiry initiated by the later phase of Foucault's work. In fact, prophetic pragmatism promotes genealogical materialist modes of analysis similar in many respects to those of Foucault.[21] Yet prophetic pragmatism rejects Foucault's antiromanticism for three basic reasons.

First, despite the profound insights and rich illuminations of Foucault's renowned archaeologies and genealogies, he remains preoccupied by one particular kind of operation of power, namely, the various modes by which human beings are constituted into subjects.[22] His powerful investigations into modes of inquiry that take the form of disciplinary powers of subjection and objectivization of human beings remain within a general Kantian framework. Foucault still asks questions such as "What are the conditions for the possibility of the constitution of the subject?" Instead of providing a transcendental response or even a historically anthropocentric answer, he gives us a genealogical account of anonymous and autonomous discourses that constitute subjects. In short, Foucault gives a Nietzschean reply to the Kantian question of the constitution of subjects.

> I wanted to see how these problems of constitution could be resolved within a historical framework, instead of referring them back to a constituent object (madness, criminality or whatever). But this historical contextualization needed to be something more than the simple relativization of the phenomenological subject. I don't believe the problem can be solved by historicizing the subject as posited by the phenomenologists, fabricating a subject that evolves through the course of history. One has to dispense with the constituent subject, to get rid of the subject itself, that's to say, to arrive at an analysis which can account for the constitution of the subject within a historical framework. And this is what I would call genealogy, that is, a form of history which can account for the constitution of knowledges, discourses, domains of objects, etc., without having to make reference to a subject which is either transcendental in relation to the field of events or runs in its empty sameness throughout the course of history.[23]

The irony of this self-description is that although Foucault's work swerves from Kantian, Hegelian, and Marxist ways of accounting for the constitution of subjects, he remains obsessed with providing such an account *by asking the Kantian question*. In fact, he is interested in the operations of power only to the degree to which he can answer this subject-centered question. In his most detailed reflections on his own work, Foucault candidly states:

> I would like to say, first of all, what has been the goal of my work during the last twenty years. It has not been to analyze the phenomena of power, nor to elaborate the foundations of such an analysis.
>
> My objective, instead, has been to create a history of the different modes by which, in our culture, human beings have been made subjects . . .
>
> Thus, it is not power but the subject which is the general theme of my research.[24]

Prophetic pragmatism objects to Foucault's project not because he has no historical sense, but rather because it remains truncated by the unhelpful Kantian question he starts with. Dewey and Rorty—as well as Wittgenstein and Heidegger—have shown that a question that begins "What are the conditions for the possibility of . . ." is misleading in that the question itself is inextricably tied to a conception of validity that stands above and outside the social practices of human beings. In this regard, Foucault's answer—anonymous and autonomous discourses, disciplines and techniques—is but the latest addition to the older ones: the dialectical development of modes of production (vulgar Marxisms), workings of the *Weltgeist* (crude Hegelians) or activities of transcendental subjects (academic Kantians).[25] All such answers shun the centrality of dynamic social practices structured and unstructured over time and space.

The second prophetic pragmatist objection is, unsurprisingly, to his reification of discourses, disciplines and techniques. By downplaying human agency—both individual and collective human actions—Foucault surreptitiously ascribes agency to discourses, disciplines and techniques. There indeed are multiple unintended consequences and unacknowledged antecedent conditions of human actions that both produce and are produced by institutions and structures. Methodological individualism in social theory, according to which isolated and atomistic individual actions fully account for humans' societies and histories, will not suffice. But the alternative is not the exclusive ascription of agency to impersonal forces, transcendental entities or anonymous and autonomous discourses. For prophetic pragmatists, human agency remains central—all we have in human societies and histories are structured and unstructured human social practices over time and space. Edward Said perceptively states regarding Foucault:

> Yet despite the extraordinary worldliness of this work, Foucault takes a curiously passive and sterile view not so much of the uses of power, but of how and why power is gained, used, and held onto. This is the most dangerous consequence of his disagreement with Marxism, and its result is the least convincing aspect of his work. . . . However else power may be a kind of indirect bureaucratic discipline and control, there are ascertainable changes stemming from who holds power and who dominates whom. . . .
>
> What one misses in Foucault is something resembling Gramsci's analyses of hegemony, historical blocks, ensembles of relationship done from the perspective of an engaged political worker for whom the fascinated description of exercised power is never a substitute for trying to change power relationships within society.[26]

Foucault is a political intellectual—a "specific" intellectual geared to and affiliated with local struggles rather than a "universal" intellectual representing and speaking for the interests of a class, nation or group—yet his Kantian questions lead him to downplay human agency, to limit the revisability of discourses and disciplines and thereby to confine his attention to a specific set of operations of power, i.e., those linked to constituting subjects. For instance, he pays little attention to operations of power in economic modes of production and nation-states.

The last prophetic pragmatist criticism of Foucault's project is that he devalues moral discourse. His fervent anti-utopianism—again in reaction to Hegelian and Marxist teleological utopianisms—rejects all forms of ends and aims for political struggle. Therefore, he replaces reform or revolution with revolt and rebellion. In this way, Foucault tends to reduce left ethics to a bold and defiant Great Refusal addressed to the dominant powers that be. Yet by failing to articulate and elaborate ideals of democracy, equality and freedom, Foucault provides solely negative conceptions of critique and resistance. He rightly suspects the self-authorizing and self-privileging aims of "universal" intellectuals who put forward such ideals, yet he mistakenly holds that *any attempt* to posit these ideals as guides to political action and social reconstruction must fall prey to new modes of subjection and disciplinary control. Foucault rightly wants to safeguard relentless criticism and healthy skepticism, yet his rejection of even tentative aims and provisional ends results in existential rebellion or micropolitical revolt, rather than concerted political praxis informed by moral vision and systemic (though flexible) analyses. In stark contrast, prophetic pragmatists take seriously moral discourse—revisable means and ends of political action, the integrity and character of those engaged and the precious ideals of participatory democracy and the flowering of the uniqueness of different human individualities.

Therefore, prophetic pragmatists reject Foucault's Kantian question, viewing it as a wheel that turns yet plays no part in the mechanism. Instead, they move directly to strategic and tactical modes of thinking and acting.[27] These modes highlight the operations of powers and the uses of provocation for the development of human personalities. Like Foucault, prophetic pragmatists criticize and resist forms of subjection, as well as types of economic exploitation, state repression and bureaucratic domination. But these critiques and resistances, unlike his, are unashamedly guided by moral ideals of creative democracy and individuality.

TRAGEDY, TRADITION AND POLITICAL PRAXIS

A major shortcoming of Emersonian pragmatism is its optimistic theodicy. The point here is not so much that Emerson himself had no sense of the tragic, but rather that the way he formulated the relation of human powers and fate, human agency and circumstances, human will and constraints made it difficult for him and for subsequent pragmatists to maintain a delicate balance between excessive optimism and exorbitant pessimism regarding human capacities. The early Emerson stands at one pole and the later Trilling at another pole. For prophetic pragmatism only the early Hook and Niebuhr—their work in the early 1930s—maintain the desirable balance.

This issue of balance raises a fundamental and long-ignored issue for the progressive tradition: the issue of the complex relations between tragedy and revolution, tradition and progress. Prophetic pragmatism refuses to sidestep this issue. The brutalities and atrocities in human history, the genocidal attempts in this century and the present-day barbarities require that those who accept the progressive and prophetic designations put forth some conception of the tragic. To pose the issue in this way is, in a sense, question begging since the very term "tragic" presupposes a variety of religious and secular background notions. Yet prophetic pragmatism is a child of Protestant Christianity wedded to left romanticism. So this question begging is warranted in that prophetic pragmatism stands in a tradition in which the notion of the "tragic" requires attention.

It is crucial to acknowledge from the start that the "tragic" is a polyvalent notion; it has different meanings depending on its context. For example, the context of Greek tragedy—in which the action of ruling families generates pity and terror in the audience—is a society that shares a collective experience of common metaphysical and social meanings. The context of modern tragedy, on the other hand—in which ordinary individuals struggle against meaninglessness and nothingness—is a fragmented society with collapsing metaphysical meanings. More pointedly, the notion of the "tragic" is bound to the idea of human agency, be the agent a person of rank or a retainer, a prince or a pauper.

> The real key, to the modern separation of tragedy from "mere suffering," is the separation of ethical control and, more critically, human agency, from our understanding of social and political life. . . .
> The events which are not seen as tragic are deep in the pattern of our own culture: war, famine, work, traffic, politics. To see no ethical content or human agency in such events, or to say that we cannot connect them with general meanings, and especially with permanent and universal meanings, is to admit a strange and particular bankruptcy, which no rhetoric of tragedy can finally hide.[28]

It is no accident that James, Hook, Niebuhr and Trilling focused on the content and character of heroism when they initially grappled with theodicy and the "tragic." Although they had little or no interest in revolution, their preoccupation with human agency, will and power resembles that of the Promethean romantics, e.g., Blake, Byron, Shelley. Yet the ideological sources of their conceptions of the "tragic" loom large in their deployment of the term.

James's focus on the individual and his distrust of big institutions and groups led him to envision a moral heroism in which each ameliorative step forward is a kind of victory, each minute battle won a sign that the war is not over, hence still winnable. Hook's early Marxism provided him with a historical sense in which the "tragic" requires a choice between a proven evil, i.e., capitalism, and a possible good, i.e., socialism. As the possible good proved to be more and more evil, the old "proven evil" appeared more and more good. The notion of the "tragic" in Hook underwent a metamorphosis such that all utopian quests were trashed in the name of limits, constraints and circumstances. The later Trilling is even more extreme, for the mere exertion of will was often seen as symptomatic of the self's utopian quest for the unconditioned.

Niebuhr held the most complex view of the "tragic" in the pragmatist tradition. Even more than the middle Trilling's intriguing ruminations on Keatsian theodicy, Niebuhr's struggle with liberal Protestantism—especially with Richard Rorty's grandfather, Walter Rauschenbusch—forced him to remain on the tightrope between Promethean romanticism and Augustinian pessimism. In fact, Niebuhr never succumbs to either, nor does he ever cease to promote incessant human agency and will against limits and circumstances. In his leftist years, mindful of the novel forms of evil in the new envisioned social order yet fed up with those in the present, he supported the insurgency of exploited workers. In his liberal years, obsessed with the evil structures in the Communist world and more and more (though never fully) forgetful of the institutional evil in American society, Niebuhr encourages state actions against the Soviet Union and piecemeal reformist practice within America.

Prophetic pragmatism affirms the Niebuhrian strenuous mood, never giving up on new possibilities for human agency—both individual and collective—in the present, yet situating them in light of Du Bois's social structural analyses that focus on working-class, black and female insurgency. Following the pioneering work of Hans-Georg Gadamer and Edward Shils, prophetic pragmatism acknowledges the inescapable and inexpungible character of tradition, the burden and buoyancy of that which is transmitted from the past to the present.[29] This process of transmittance is one of socialization and appropriation, of acculturation and construction. Tradition, in this sense, can be both a smothering and a liberating affair, depending on which traditions are being invoked, internalized and invented.

In this way, the relation of tragedy to revolution (or resistance) is intertwined with that of tradition to progress (or betterment). Prophetic pragmatism, as a form of third-wave left romanticism, tempers its utopian impulse with a profound sense of the tragic character of life and history. This sense of the tragic highlights the irreducible predicament of unique individuals who undergo dread, despair, disillusionment, disease and death *and* the institutional forms of oppression that dehumanize people. Tragic thought is not confined solely to the plight of the individual; it also applies to social experiences of resistance, revolution and societal reconstruction. Prophetic pragmatism is a form of tragic thought in that it confronts candidly individual and collective experiences of evil in individuals and institutions—with little expectation of ridding the world of *all* evil. Yet it is a kind of romanticism in that it holds many experiences of evil to be neither inevitable nor necessary, but rather the results of human agency, i.e., choices and actions.

This interplay between tragic thought and romantic impulse, inescapable evils and transformable evils makes prophetic pragmatism seem schizophrenic. On the one hand, it appears to affirm a Sisyphean outlook in which human resistance to evil makes no progress. On the other hand, it looks as if it approves a utopian quest for paradise. In fact, prophetic pragmatism denies Sisyphean pessimism and utopian perfectionism. Rather, it promotes the possibility of human progress and the human impossibility of paradise. This progress results from principled and protracted Promethean efforts, yet even such efforts are no guarantee. And all human struggles—including successful ones—against specific forms of evil produce new, though possibly lesser, forms of evil. Human struggle sits at the center of prophetic pragmatism, a struggle guided by a democratic and libertarian vision, sustained by moral courage and existential integrity and tempered by the recognition of human finitude and frailty. It calls for utopian energies and tragic actions, energies and actions that yield permanent and perennial revolutionary, rebellious and reformist strategies that oppose the status quos of our day. These strategies are never to become ends-in-themselves, but rather to remain means through which are channeled moral outrage and human desperation in the face of prevailing forms of evil in human societies and in human lives. Such outrage must never cease, and such desperation will never disappear, yet without revolutionary, rebellious and reformist strategies, credible and effective opposition wanes. Prophetic pragmatism attempts to keep alive the sense of alternative ways of life and of struggle based on the best of the past. In this sense, the praxis of prophetic pragmatism is tragic action with revolutionary intent, usually reformist consequences and always visionary outlook. It concurs with Raymond Williams's tragic revolutionary perspective:

> The tragic action, in its deepest sense, is not the confirmation of disorder, but its experience, its comprehension and its resolution. In our own time, this action is general, and its common name is revolution. We have to see the evil and the suffering, in the factual disorder that makes revolution necessary, and in the disordered struggle against the disorder. We have to recognize this suffering in a close and immediate experience, and not cover it with names. But we follow the whole action: not only the evil, but the men who have fought against evil; not only the crisis, but the energy released by it, the spirit learned in it. We make the connections, because that is the action of tragedy, and what we learn in suffering is again revolution, because we acknowledge others as men and any such acknowledgement is the beginning of struggle, as the continuing reality of our lives. Then to see revolution in this tragic perspective is the only way to maintain it.[30]

This oppositional consciousness draws its sustenance principally from a tradition of resistance. To keep alive a sense of alternative ways of life and of struggle requires memory of those who prefigured such life and struggle in the past. In this sense, tradition is to be associated not solely with ignorance and intolerance, prejudice and parochialism, dogmatism and docility. Rather, tradition is also to be identified with insight and intelligence, rationality and resistance, critique and contestation. Tradition per se is never a problem, but rather those traditions that have been and are hegemonic over other traditions. All that human beings basically have are traditions—those institutions and practices, values and sensibilities, stories and symbols, ideas and metaphors that shape human identities, attitudes, outlooks and dispositions. These traditions are dynamic, malleable and revisable, yet all changes in a tradition are done in light of some old or newly emerging tradition. Innovation presupposes some tradition and inaugurates another tradition. The profound historical consciousness of prophetic pragmatism shuns the Emersonian devaluing of the past. Yet it also highlights those elements of old and new traditions that promote innovation and resistance for the aims of enhancing individuality and expanding democracy. This enhancement and expansion constitute human progress. And all such progress takes place within the contours of clashing traditions. In this way, just as tragic action constitutes resistance to prevailing status quos, the critical treatment and nurturing of a tradition yield human progress. Tragedy can be an impetus rather than an impediment to oppositional activity; tradition may serve as a stimulus rather than a stumbling block to human progress.

Prophetic pragmatism understands the Emersonian swerve from epistemology—and the American evasion of philosophy—not as a wholesale rejection of philosophy, but rather as a reconception of philosophy as a form of cultural criticism that attempts to transform linguistic, social, cultural and political traditions for the purposes of increasing the scope of individual development and democratic operations. Prophetic pragmatism conceives of philosophy as a historically circumscribed quest for wisdom that puts forward new interpretations of the world based on past traditions in order to promote existential sustenance and political relevance. Like Emerson and earlier pragmatists, it views truth as a species of the good, as that which enhances the flourishing of human progress. This does not mean that philosophy ignores the ugly facts and unpleasant realities of life and history. Rather, it highlights these facts and realities precisely because they provoke doubt, curiosity, outrage or desperation that motivates efforts to overcome them. These efforts take the forms of critique and praxis, forms that attempt to change what is into a better what can be.

Prophetic pragmatism closely resembles and, in some ways, converges with the metaphilosophical perspectives of Antonio Gramsci. Both conceive of philosophical activity as "a cultural battle to transform the popular 'mentality.'"[31] It is not surprising that Gramsci writes: "What the pragmatists wrote about this question merits re-examination. . . . They felt real needs and 'described' them with an exactness that was not far off the mark, even if they did not succeed in posing the problems fully or in providing a solution."[32] Prophetic pragmatism is inspired by the example of Antonio Gramsci principally because he is the major twentieth-century philosopher of praxis, power, and provocation without devaluing theory, adopting unidimensional conceptions of power or reducing provocation to Clausewitzian calculations of warfare. Gramsci's work is historically specific, theoretically engaging and politically activistic in an exemplary manner. His concrete and detailed investigations are grounded in and reflections upon local struggles, yet theoretically sensitive to structural dynamics and international phenomena. He is attuned to the complex linkage of socially constructed identities to human agency while still convinced of the crucial role of the ever changing forms in class-ridden economic modes of production. Despite his fluid Leninist conception of political organization and mobilization (which downplays the democratic and libertarian values of prophetic pragmatists) and his unswerving allegiance to sophisticated Marxist social theory (which is an indispensable yet ultimately inadequate weapon for prophetic pragmatists), Gramsci exemplifies the critical spirit and oppositional sentiments of prophetic pragmatism.

This is seen most clearly in Gramsci's view of the relation of philosophy to "common sense." For him, the aim of philosophy is not only to become worldly by imposing its elite intellectual views upon people, but to become part of a social movement by nourishing and being nourished by the philosophical views of oppressed people themselves for the aims of social change and personal meaning. Gramsci viewed this mutually critical process in world-historical terms:

> From the disintegration of Hegelianism derives the beginning of a new cultural process, different in character from its predecessors, a process in which practical movement and theoretical thought are united (or are trying to unite through a struggle that is both theoretical and practical).
>
> It is not important that this movement had its origins in mediocre philosophical works or, at best, in works that were not philosophical masterpieces. What matters is that a new way of conceiving the world and man is born and that this conception is no longer reserved to the great intellectuals, to professional philosophers, but tends rather to become a popular, mass phenomenon, with a concretely world-wide character, capable of modifying (even if the result includes hybrid combinations) popular thought and mummified popular culture.
>
> One should not be surprised if this beginning arises from the convergence of various elements, apparently heterogeneous. . . . Indeed, it is worth noting that such an overthrow could not but have connections with religion.[33]

Gramsci's bold suggestion here relates elite philosophical activity to the cultures of the oppressed in the name of a common effort for social change. Prophetic pragmatist sensibilities permit (or even encourage) this rejection of the arrogant scientistic self-privileging or haughty secular self-images of many modern philosophers and intellectuals. The point here is not that serious contemporary thinkers should surrender their critical intelligence, but rather that they should not demand that all peoples mimic their version of critical intelligence, especially if common efforts for social change can be strengthened. On this point, even the nuanced secularism of Edward Said—the most significant and salient Gramscian critic on the American intellectual scene today—can be questioned.[34] For Gramsci, ideologies of secularism or religions are less sets of beliefs and values, attitudes and sensibilities and more ways of life and ways of struggle manufactured and mobilized by certain sectors of the population in order to legitimate and preserve their social, political and intellectual powers. Hence, the universities and churches, schools and synagogues, mass media and mosques become crucial terrain for ideological and political contestation. And philosophers are in no way exempt from this fierce battle—even within the "serene" walls and halls of the academy. Similar to the American pragmatist tradition, Gramsci simply suggests that philosophers more consciously posit these battles themselves as objects of investigation and thereby intervene in these battles with intellectual integrity and ideological honesty.

Prophetic pragmatism purports to be not only an oppositional cultural criticism, but also a material force for individuality and democracy. By "material force" I simply mean a practice that has some potency and effect or makes a difference in the world. There is—and should be—no such thing as a prophetic pragmatist movement. The translation of philosophic outlook into social motion is not that simple. In fact, it is possible to be a prophetic pragmatist and belong to different political movements, e.g., feminist, Chicano, black, socialist, left-liberal ones. It also is possible to subscribe to prophetic pragmatism and belong to different religious and/or secular traditions. This is so because a prophetic pragmatist commitment to individuality and democracy, historical consciousness and systemic social analyses and tragic action in an evil-ridden world can take place in—though usually on the margin of—a variety of traditions. The distinctive hallmarks of a prophetic pragmatist are a universal consciousness that promotes an all-embracing democratic and libertarian moral vision, a historical consciousness that acknowledges human finitude and conditionedness and a critical consciousness that encourages relentless critique and self-criticism for the aims of social change and personal humility.

My own version of prophetic pragmatism is situated within the Christian tradition. Unlike Gramsci, I am religious not simply for political aims, but also by personal commitment. To put it crudely, I find existential sustenance in many of the narratives in the biblical scriptures as interpreted by streams in the Christian heritage; and I see political relevance in the biblical focus on the plight of the wretched of the earth. Needless to say, without the addition of modern interpretations of racial and gender equality, tolerance and democracy, much of the tradition warrants rejection. Yet the Christian epic, stripped of static dogmas and decrepit doctrines, remains a rich source of existential empowerment and political engagement when viewed through modern lenses (indeed the only ones we moderns have!).

Like James, Niebuhr and to some extent Du Bois, I hold a religious conception of pragmatism. I have dubbed it "prophetic" in that it harks back to the Jewish and Christian tradition of prophets who brought urgent and compassionate critique to bear on the evils of their day. The mark of the prophet is to speak the truth in love with courage—come what may. Prophetic pragmatism proceeds from this impulse. It neither requires a religious foundation nor entails a religious perspective, yet prophetic pragmatism is compatible with certain religious outlooks.

My kind of prophetic pragmatism is located in the Christian tradition for two basic reasons. First, on the existential level, the self-understanding and self-identity that flow from this tradition's insights into the crises and traumas of life are indispensable *for me* to remain sane. It holds at bay the sheer absurdity so evident in life, without erasing or eliding the tragedy of life. Like Kierkegaard, whose reflections on Christian faith were so profound yet often so frustrating, I do not think it possible to put forward rational defenses of one's faith that verify its veracity or even persuade one's critics. Yet it is possible to convey to others the sense of deep emptiness and pervasive meaninglessness one feels if one is not critically aligned with an enabling tradition. One risks not logical inconsistency, but actual insanity; the issue is not reason or irrationality, but life or death. Of course, the fundamental philosophical question remains whether the Christian gospel is ultimately true.[35] And, as a Christian prophetic pragmatist whose focus is on coping with transient and provisional penultimate matters yet whose hope goes beyond them, I reply in the affirmative, bank my all on it, yet am willing to entertain the possibility in low moments that I may be deluded.

Second, on the political level, the culture of the wretched of the earth is deeply religious. To be in solidarity with them requires not only an acknowledgment of what they are up against, but also an appreciation of how they cope with their situation. This appreciation does not require that one be religious; but if one is religious, one has wider access into their life-worlds. This appreciation also does not entail an uncritical acceptance of religious narratives, their interpretations or, most important, their often oppressive consequences. Yet to be religious permits one to devote one's life to accenting the prophetic and progressive potential within those traditions that shape the everyday practices and deeply held perspectives of most oppressed peoples. What a wonderful privilege and vocation this is!

The prophetic religious person, much like C. Wright Mills's activist intellectual, puts a premium on educating and being educated by struggling peoples, organizing and being organized by resisting groups. This political dimension of prophetic pragmatism as practiced within the Christian tradition impels one to be an organic intellectual, that is, one who revels in the life of the mind, yet relates ideas to collective praxis. An organic intellectual, in contrast to traditional intellectuals, who often remain comfortably nested in the academy, attempts to be entrenched in and affiliated with organizations, associations and, possibly, movements of grassroots folk. Of course, he or she need be neither religious nor linked to religious institutions. Trade unions, community groups and political formations also suffice. Yet, since the Enlightenment in eighteenth-century Europe, most of the progressive energies among the intelligentsia have shunned religious channels. And in these days of global religious revivals, progressive forces are reaping the whirlwind. Those of us who remain in these religious channels see clearly just how myopic such an antireligious strategy is. The severing of ties to churches, synagogues, temples and mosques by the left intelligentsia is tantamount to political suicide; it turns the pessimism of many self-deprecating and self-pitying secular progressive intellectuals into a self-fulfilling prophecy. This point was never grasped by C. Wright Mills, though W. E. B. Du Bois understood it well.

Like Gramsci, Du Bois remained intimately linked with oppositional forces in an oppressed community. And in his case, these forces were (and are) often led by prophetic figures of the black Christian tradition. To be a part of the black freedom movement is to rub elbows with some prophetic black preachers and parishioners. And to be a part of the forces of progress in America is to rub up against some of these black freedom fighters.

If prophetic pragmatism is ever to become more than a conversational subject matter for cultural critics in and out of the academy, it must inspire progressive and prophetic social motion. One precondition of this kind of social movement is the emergence of potent prophetic religious practices in churches, synagogues, temples and mosques. And given the historical weight of such practices in the American past, the probable catalyst for social motion will be the prophetic wing of the black church. Need we remind ourselves that the most significant and successful organic intellectual in twentieth-century America—maybe in American history—was a product of and leader in the prophetic wing of the black church? Rarely has a figure in modern history outside of elected public office linked the life of the mind to social change with such moral persuasiveness and political effectiveness.

The social movement led by Martin Luther King, Jr., represents the best of what the political dimension of prophetic pragmatism is all about. Like Sojourner Truth, Walter Rauschenbusch, Elizabeth Cady Stanton and Dorothy Day, King was not a prophetic pragmatist. Yet like them he was a prophet, in which role he contributed mightily to the political project of prophetic pragmatism. His all-embracing moral vision facilitated alliances and coalitions across racial, gender, class and religious lines. His Gandhian method of nonviolent resistance highlighted forms of love, courage and discipline worthy of a compassionate prophet.

And his appropriation and interpretation of American civil religion extended the tradition of American jeremiads, a tradition of public exhortation that joins social criticisms of America to moral renewal and admonishes the country to be true to its founding ideals of freedom, equality and democracy. King accented the antiracist and anti-imperialist consequences of taking seriously these ideals, thereby linking the struggle for freedom in America to those movements in South Africa, Poland, South Korea, Ethiopia, Chile and the Soviet Union.

Prophetic pragmatism worships at no ideological altars. It condemns oppression anywhere and everywhere, be it the brutal butchery of Third World dictators, the regimentation and repression of peoples in the Soviet Union and Soviet-bloc countries or the racism, patriarchy, homophobia and economic injustice in the First World capitalist nations. In this way, the precious ideals of individuality and democracy of prophetic pragmatism oppose all those power structures that lack public accountability, be they headed by military generals, bureaucratic party bosses or corporate tycoons. Nor is prophetic pragmatism confined to any preordained historical agent, such as the working class, black people or women. Rather, it invites all people of goodwill both here and abroad to fight for an Emersonian culture of creative democracy in which the plight of the wretched of the earth is alleviated.

SOURCE: "Prophetic Pragmatism: Cultural Criticism and Political Engagement," *The American Evasion of Philosophy,* pp. 211–235, 269–271. Copyright © 1989. Reprinted by permission of The University of Wisconsin Press.

Ten

PRAGMATISM AND THE SENSE OF THE TRAGIC

This essay is part of a book on Josiah Royce I began writing in 1990 and have yet to finish. I will get it done one day. Royce is the only pragmatist philosopher who wrestles with the great Arthur Schopenhauer and, besides his friend William James, the only pragmatist with a tragic temperament. As seen in the recent work of James Kloppenberg on Dewey and Weber, and Eddie Glaude on Dewey and the tragic, this discussion is an exciting one. In my view, Chekhov's tragicomic sensibilities go so far beyond and cut so much deeper than anything in pragmatism that even Royce comes up short. Yet Royce should be given more prominence in the contemporary pragmatic renaissance in humanistic studies.

THE RECENT REVIVAL OF pragmatism provides a timely intellectual background for the most urgent problematic of our postmodern moment: the complex cluster of questions and queries regarding the meaning and value of democracy. No other modern philosophical tradition has grappled with the various dimensions of this problematic more than that of American pragmatism. Thomas Jefferson, Ralph Waldo Emerson and Abraham Lincoln—the grand spiritual godfathers of pragmatism—laid the foundations for the meaning and value of democracy in America and in the modern world. These foundations consisted roughly of the irreducibility of individuality within participatory communities, heroic action of ordinary folk in a world of radical contingency and a deep sense of evil that fuels struggles for justice.

Jeffersonian notions of the irreducibility of individuality within participatory communities attempt to sidestep rapacious individualisms and authoritarian communitarianisms by situating unique selves within active networks of power-sharing that protect liberties, promote prosperity and highlight accountability. In this sense, Jefferson's ideals combine much of the best of liberalism, populism and civic republicanism. Emersonian formulations of heroic action of ordinary folk in a world of radical contingency try to jettison static dogmatisms and impersonal determinisms by accenting the powers of unique selves to make and remake themselves with no original models to imitate or emulate. Emersonian ideals bring together salutary aspects of Romanticism, libertarianism and Protestantism. Lincoln's profound wrestling with a deep sense of evil that fuels the struggle for justice endeavors to hold at bay facile optimisms and paralyzing pessimisms by positing unique selves that fight other finite opponents rather than demonic foes. Lincoln's ideals hold together valuable insights of evangelical Christianity, American constitutionalism and Scottish commonsensical realism. Yet not one American *philosophical* thinker has put forward a conception of the meaning and significance of democracy in light of these foundations laid by Jefferson, Emerson and Lincoln.

If there is one plausible candidate, it would have to be John Dewey. Like Maurice Maeterlinck and Walt Whitman ("In Lincoln's lifetime Whitman was the only writer to describe him with love"),[1] Dewey understood that if one takes democracy as an object of philosophical investigation, then one must grapple with the contributions of Jefferson and Emerson. But, I suggest, Dewey failed to seriously meet the challenge posed by Lincoln—namely, defining the relation of democratic ways of thought and life to a profound sense of evil. Within the development of post-Deweyan pragmatism, only Sidney Hook's suggestive essay "Pragmatism and the Tragic Sense of Life" responds to Lincoln's challenge in a serious manner.[2] Yet it remains far from the depths of other tragic democratic thinkers like Herman Melville, F. O. Matthiessen and Reinhold Niebuhr.

There is only one great American philosopher (Alfred North Whitehead's origins exclude him) who seriously grappled with the challenge posed by Lincoln—namely, Josiah Royce. In fact, I would go as far as to claim that Royce's systematic post-Kantian idealism is primarily a long and winding set of profound meditations on the relation of a deep sense of evil to human agency. Therefore a contemporary encounter between Dewey and Royce is neither an antiquarian reconstruction of exchanges in philosophical journals nor a synoptic synthesis of instrumentalism and idealism. Rather, it is a response to the most pressing problematic of our day that creatively fuses the contributions of Jefferson, Emerson and Lincoln in our quest for the meaning and value of democracy. Since Royce viewed his project as a kind of "absolute pragmatism" (principally owing to valuable lessons learned from his close friend William James), the Dewey-Royce encounter is an affair within the pragmatist tradition. Hence, the major philosophic progeny of Jefferson, Emerson and Lincoln carry the banner of American pragmatism.

The three principal philosophic slogans of this banner are voluntarism, fallibilism and experimentalism. Both Dewey and Royce are philosophers of human will, human power and human action. Structured and unstructured social practices sit at the center of their distinct philosophic visions. In short, they agree the best characterization of pragmatism ever formulated—that of C. I. Lewis

Pragmatism could be characterized as the doctrine that all problems are at bottom problems of conduct, that all judgments are, implicitly, judgments of value, and that, as there can be ultimately no valid distinction of theoretical and practical, so there can be no final separation of questions of truth of any kind from questions of the justifiable ends of action.[3]

Dewey's stress on the primacy of human will and practice is shot through all of his major works. So his seminal conception of experience—over against that of British empiricists and Kantian transcendentalists—will suffice. It is found in one of the classic essays of modern philosophy, his "The Need for a Recovery of Philosophy" (1917):

Experience is primarily a process of undergoing: a process of standing something; of suffering and passion, of affection, in the literal sense of these words. The organism has to endure, to undergo, the consequence of its own actions. . . .

Experience, in other words, is a matter of *simultaneous* doings and sufferings. Our undergoings are experiments in varying the course of events; our active tryings are trials and tests of ourselves.[4]

Royce also puts a premium on human will and embraces this stress of James and Dewey:

No truth is a saving truth—yes, no truth is a truth at all unless it guides and directs life. Therein I heartily agree with current pragmatism and with James himself. . . .

I agree that every opinion expresses an attitude of the will, a preparedness for action, a determination to guide a plan of action in accordance with an idea. . . . There is no such thing as a purely intellectual form of assertion which has no element of action about it. An opinion is a deed. It is a deed intended to guide other deeds. It proposes to have what the pragmatists call "workings." That is, it undertakes to guide the life of the one who asserts the opinion. In that sense, all truth is practical.[5]

The voluntaristic impulse in Dewey and Royce leads to two basic notions: first, that truth is a species of the good; and second, that the conception of the good is defined in relation to temporal consequences. The first notion, that truth is a species of the good, means that our beliefs about the way the world is have ethical significance. This is what James means when he writes "our opinions about the nature of things belong to our moral life."[6] Or what Dewey highlights when he notes:

Philosophy is a form of desire, of effort at action—a love, namely, of wisdom; but with the thorough proviso, not attached to the Platonic use of the word, that wisdom, whatever it is, is not a mode of science or knowledge. A philosophy which was conscious of its own business and province would then perceive that it is an intellectualized wish, an aspiration subjected to rational discrimination and tests, a social hope reduced to a working program of action, a prophecy of the future, but one disciplined by serious thought and knowledge.[7]

Royce chimes in on the same theme in this way: "Opinions about the universe are counsels as to how to adjust your deeds to the purposes and requirements which a survey of the whole of the life whereto your life belongs shows to be the genuinely rational purposes and requirements."[8]

The second notion, that the conception of the good is defined in relation to temporal consequences, means that the future has ethical significance. In fact, the key to pragmatism, the distinctive feature that sets it apart from other philosophical traditions—and maybe its unique American character—is its emphasis on the ethical significance of the future. In a rare moment of reflection on the beginnings and traits of pragmatism in "The Development of American Pragmatism" (1922), Dewey states:

> Pragmatism, thus, presents itself as an extension of historical empiricism, but with this fundamental difference, that it does not insist upon antecedent phenomena but upon consequent phenomena; not upon the precedents but upon the possibilities of action. And this change in point of view is almost revolutionary in its consequences. An empiricism which is content with repeating facts already past has no place for possibility and for liberty. . . .
>
> Pragmatism thus has a metaphysical implication. The doctrine of the value of consequences leads us to take the future into consideration. And this taking into consideration of the future takes us to the conception of a universe whose evolution is not finished, of a universe which is still, in James' term "in the making," "in the process of becoming," of a universe up to a certain point still plastic.[9]

For pragmatists, the future has ethical significance because human will—human thought and action—can make a difference in relation to human aims and purposes. There is moral substance in the fact that human will can make the future different and, possibly, better relative to human ends and aims. As a young man of twenty-four (March 10, 1879), just beginning his assistantship in English Literature at the University of California, Berkeley, Royce outlined his system of philosophy:

Faust's contract with Mephisto is, in Goethe's view, no extraordinary act, no great crime, but simply the necessary fundament of an active life that strives for the Ideal. Here is the whole view as I just now conceive it to have been. . . .

The essence of life is found in the individual moments of accomplishment, and in those alone. . . . The individual moment is the Real; but it is so only in so far forth as it denies itself, strives to pass out over itself, to plunge on into a future. . . .

The individual moments of our lives must be full of action, the fuller the better; but they must also be, for the very same reason, full of unrest. No content of the moment, however great, must lead us to wish to remain stationary in this moment. This content in the present moment is denial of activity; it is death.[10]

More than a year later, Royce wrote in his diary (July 21, 1880): "Reflected further on the present state of the systematic development of philosophy I am undertaking. The opening and foundation thereof is surely the theory of the world of reality as a projection from the present moment" (*Fugitive Essays,* p. 35). Royce's student, editor and most able contemporary expositor, Jacob Loewenberg, comments on these fragments from the early diaries in this way: "The present—be it a present moment, a present idea, a present thought, a present self—derives its meaning from a constructive process of self-extension. And the whole technique of Royce's thinking is dominated, as we have seen, by this process" (pp. 30–31).

This preoccupation with the prospective perspective—rooted in post-Kantian idealism and given distinctive pragmatic twists by Royce and Dewey—leads Dewey to quip: "What should experience be but a future implicated in a present!"[11] Echoes of Jefferson's notion of periodic revolutions and Emerson's view of power as onward transitions and upward crossings loom large here. The pragmatic emphasis on the future as the terrain for humans-making-a-difference (including a *better* difference) results in a full-blown fallibilism and experimentalism. All facts are fallible and all experience is experimental. This is the common ground of pragmatism upon which both Dewey and Royce stand. Unique selves acting in and through participatory communities give ethical significance to an open, risk-ridden future. The slogans of voluntarism, fallibilism and experimentalism posit self-criticism and self-correction as a central component of human enterprises. The "majesty of community" and "the true spirituality of genuine doubting" combine to ensure that nothing blocks the Peircean road to inquiry.

Yet Dewey and Royce part company in response to Lincoln's challenge. The deep sense of evil affects Royce more than it does Dewey. Ironically, Royce clings to his post-Kantian idealism—even after his appropriation of Peirce's theory of interpretive communities—owing to his philosophic grappling with suffering and sorrow. Jamesian injunctions about the strenuous mood against evil do not suffice for Royce. Nor do Deweyan leaps of faith in critical intelligence. Royce holds on to his Christianlike dramatic portrait of reality—with its hope for and assurance of ultimate triumph—precisely because his sense of evil and the tragic is so deep.

What separates Royce from other American pragmatists and most American philosophers—though Arthur Danto comes to mind—is his prolonged and poignant engagement with the thought of Arthur Schopenhauer. Royce's response to Lincoln's challenge takes the form of a lifelong struggle with Schopenhauer's pessimism. The first course Royce ever taught (by choice) as a graduate fellow at Johns Hopkins University at twenty-two years of age in 1877 (January to March) was on Schopenhauer. His classic text *The Spirit of Modern Philosophy* (1892) contains thirty-three pages on Kant, twenty-eight pages on Fichte, thirty-seven pages on Hegel and thirty-six pages on Schopenhauer. I know of no other American history of modern philosophy in which Schopenhauer is treated so extensively and respectfully. For Royce, Schopenhauer is "noteworthy," "significant," "a great thinker," "a philosopher of considerable dignity," equipped with "an erudition vast rather than technical," who "enjoyed manifold labors rather than professional completeness."[12] Royce states that "Schopenhauer's principal work, *Die Welt als Wille und Vorstellung,* is in form the most artistic philosophical treatise in existence, if one excepts the best of Plato's *Dialogues*." Furthermore, Schopenhauer is the crucial transitional figure "from the romantic idealism to the modern realism."[13] In every major text of Royce—including his *Lectures on Modern Idealism,* published posthumously—Schopenhauer makes a significant appearance.

In sharp contrast, Schopenhauer—along with Lincoln's challenge of a deep sense of evil and the tragic—makes no appearances in Dewey's vast corpus. This is why I find Royce profound and poignant though ultimately unpersuasive, while I find Dewey sane and fascinating though, in the end, unsatisfactory. Like Melville, Matthiessen and Niebuhr, I believe that a deep sense of evil and the tragic must infuse any meaning and value of democracy. The culture of democratic societies requires not only the civic virtues of participation, tolerance, openness, mutual respect and mobility, but also dramatic struggles with the two major culprits—disease and death—that defeat and cut off the joys of democratic citizenship. Such citizenship must not be so preoccupied—or obsessed—with possibility that it conceals or represses the ultimate facts of the human predicament.

I will not here plunge into Royce's rich reflections on evil—ranging from his famous essays "The Problem of Job" (1897) and "The Practical Significance of Pessimism" (1879) to his treatments in his major works. Instead, I shall only sketch his notion of "irrevocable deeds" as a source of his conception of the Absolute in his most straightforward book, *Sources of Religious Insight* (1912). Royce introduces this notion in the midst of his complimentary discussion of pragmatism.

But now one of the central facts about life is that every deed once done is *ipso facto* irrevocable. That is, at any moment you perform a given deed or you do not. If you perform it, it is done and cannot be undone. This difference between what is done and what is undone is, in the real and empirical world, *a perfectly absolute difference.* The opportunity for a given individual deed returns not; for the moment when that individual deed can be done never recurs. Here is a case where the rational constitution of the whole universe gets into definite relation to our momentary experience. *And if any one wants to be in touch with the "absolute"—with that reality which the pragmatists fancy to be peculiarly remote and abstract—let him simply do any individual deed whatever and then try to undo that deed. Let the experiment teach him what one means by calling reality absolute. Let the truths which that experience teaches any rational being show him also what is meant by absolute truth.*[14]

Royce's point here is not simply to draw attention to the limits the past imposes on the future. Rather, it is to show just how concrete and practical notions of an absolute can be. His aim is to unhinge such notions from their association with impractical and inaccessible abstractions. Furthermore, he wants to better enable unique selves to act in the present and give ethical significance to the future by providing standards that transcend the present. Royce recognizes that there must be some notions of standards with regulative and critical force—though always partial and fragmentary—that sustain our strenuous mood in the perennial fight against the "capricious irrationality of the world" and the "blind irrationality of fortune."[15]

Royce defends his version of the absolute because he "looks to the truth for aid."[16] On the one hand, he accents the interplay of what he calls "the *no longer* and *not yet* of past and future, so that fulfillment never at one present instant is to be found."[17] Like Hegel's unhappy consciousness, dissatisfaction reigns and "temporal peace is a contradiction in terms." Yet he is "ready to accept the dear sorrow of possessing ideals and of taking my share of the divine task."[18] In this way,

absolute reality (namely, the sort of reality that belongs to irrevocable deeds), absolute truth (namely, the sort of truth that belongs to those opinions which, for a given purpose, counsel individual deeds, when the deeds in fact meet the purpose for which they were intended)—these two are not remote affairs invented by philosophers for the sake of "barren intellectualism." *Such absolute reality and absolute truth are the most concrete and practical and familiar of matters.* The pragmatist who denies that there is any absolute truth accessible has never rightly considered the very most characteristic feature of the reasonable will, namely, that it is always counselling irrevocable deeds, and therefore is always giving counsel that is for its own determinate purpose irrevocably right or wrong precisely in so far as it is definite counsel.[19]

On the other hand, I suspect that something deeper is going on. Royce believes more is at stake than warding off willful subjectivism and epistemic relativism. Reality and truth must, in some sense, be absolute not only because skepticism lurks about, but also, and more important, because it is the last and only hope for giving meaning to the strenuous mood, for justifying the worthwhileness of our struggle to endure. In one of the great moments in Royce's corpus—a moment not to be found in Dewey—Royce questions his idealist response to the problem of evil. After pushing pessimism to the brink, he holds on for dear life.

> For I do not feel that I have yet quite expressed the full force of the deepest argument for pessimism, or the full seriousness of the eternal problem of evil. . . .
>
> Pessimism, in the true sense, isn't the doctrine of the merely peevish man, but of the man who to borrow a word of Hegel's, "has once feared not for this moment or for that in his life, but who has feared with all his nature; so that he has trembled through and through, and all that was most fixed in him has become shaken." There are experiences in life that do just this for us. And when the fountains of the great deep are once thus broken up, and the floods have come, it isn't over this or that lost spot of our green earth that we sorrow; it is because of all that endless waste of tossing waves which now rolls cubits deep above the top of what were our highest mountains. . . .
>
> No, the worst tragedy of the world is the tragedy of brute chance to which everything spiritual seems to be subject amongst us—the tragedy of the diabolical irrationality of so many among the foes of whatever is significant. An open enemy you can face. The temptation to do evil is indeed a necessity for spirituality. But one's own foolishness, one's ignorance, the cruel accidents of disease, the fatal misunderstandings that part friends and lovers, the chance mistakes that wreck nations:—these things we lament most bitterly, not because they are painful, but because they are farcical, distracting,—not foe-men worthy of the sword of the spirit, nor yet mere pangs of our finitude that we can easily learn to face courageously, as one can be indifferent to physical pain. No, these things do not make life merely painful to us; they make it hideously petty.[20]

At this point, Royce seems to virtually throw up his hands and throw in the towel. Fresh memories of his nervous breakdown—only three years earlier—and his recovery in Australia loom large. He concludes, "From our finite point of view there is no remotely discoverable justification for this caprice." Yet he refuses to give in to Schopenhauer and holds we must "dare to hope for an answer":

> *Were* our insight into the truth of Logos based upon any sort of empirical assurance, it would surely fail us here. But now, as it is, if we have the true insight of deeper idealism, we can turn from our chaos to him . . . the suffering God . . . who actually and in our flesh bears the sins of the world, and whose natural body is pierced by the capricious wounds that hateful fools inflict upon him—it is

this thought, I say, that traditional Christianity has in its deep symbolism first taught the world, but that, in its fullness, only an idealistic interpretation can really and rationally express. . . .

What in time is hopelessly lost, is attained for him in his eternity. . . .

We have found in a world of doubt but one assurance—but one, and yet how rich! All else is hypothesis.[21]

I have quoted at length to convey Royce's implicit response to Lincoln's challenge, answering Schopenhauer. The point here is not whether his response is persuasive or convincing; rather, the point is to highlight the depths of Royce's efforts to sustain the strenuous mood in the face of the deep sense of evil. Never in the tradition of American pragmatism has Lincoln's challenge been taken so seriously. Yet the democratic legacy of Jefferson, Emerson and Lincoln in our ghastly century demands nothing less. The encounter between Dewey and Royce may help us preserve the ethical significance of *our* future.

Eleven

THE LIMITS OF NEOPRAGMATISM

This critique of contemporary pragmatisms highlights the Marxist attitude toward prag-matism: that it insufficiently grasps the role of power in dialogical and democratic prac-tices. Following the radical left pragmatist C. Wright Mills, I try to show how my prophetic pragmatism follows the Marxist critique here. In the previous essay, I high-light the existential critique of pragmatism (no serious sense of the tragic or comic). Here I pursue the political critique of pragmatism (no adequate attention to the operations of institutional or structural power).

THE RENAISSANCE OF PRAGMATISM in philosophy, literary criticism and legal thought in the past few years is a salutary development. It is part of a more gen-eral turn toward historicist approaches to truth and knowledge. I am delighted to see intellectual interest rekindled in Peirce, James and especially Dewey. Yet I sus-pect that the new pragmatism may repeat and reproduce some of the blindness and silences of the old pragmatism—most important, an inadequate grasp of the complex operations of power, principally owing to a reluctance to take traditions of historical sociology and social theory seriously. In this essay, my strategy shall be as follows. First, I shall briefly map the different kinds of neopragmatisms in relation to perspectives regarding epistemology, theory and politics. Second, I shall suggest that neopragmatic viewpoints usually fail to situate their own proj ects in terms of present-day crises—including the crisis of purpose and vocation now raging in the professions. Third, I will try to show how my conception of prophetic pragmatism may provide what is needed to better illuminate and re-spond to these crises.

Much of the excitement about neopragmatism has to do with the antifounda-tionalist epistemic claims it puts forward. The idea that there are no self-justifying, intrinsically credible or ahistorical courts of appeal to terminate chains of epis-temic justification calls into question positivistic and formalistic notions of objec-tivity, necessity and transcendentality. In this sense, all neopragmatists are an-tifoundationalists; that is, the validation of knowledge claims rests on practical judgments constituted by, and constructed in, dynamic social practices. For neo-pragmatists, we mortal creatures achieve and acquire knowledge by means of self-critical and self-correcting social procedures rooted in a variety of human processes.

Yet all neopragmatists are not antirealists. For example, Peircean pragmatists are intent on sidestepping any idealist or relativist traps, and they therefore link a social conception of knowledge to a regulative ideal of truth. This viewpoint attempts to reject metaphysical conceptions of reality *and* skeptical reductions of truth-talk to knowledge-talk. In contrast, Deweyan pragmatists tend to be less concerned with charges of idealism or relativism, owing to a more insouciant attitude toward truth. In fact, some Deweyan pragmatists—similar to some sociologists of knowledge and idealists—wrongly collapse truth claims into warranted-assertability claims or rational-acceptability claims. Such moves provide fodder for the cannons of not only Peircean pragmatists, but also old-style realists and foundationalists. To put it crudely, truth at the moment cannot be the truth about things, yet warranted-assertable claims are the only truths we can get. To miss the subtle distinction between dynamic knowledge and regulative truth is to open the door to metaphysics or to slide down the slippery slope of sophomoric relativism. Yet the antifoundationalist claims put forward by neopragmatists are often construed such that many open such doors or slide down such slopes. In short, epistemic pluralism degenerates into an epistemic promiscuity that encourages epistemic policing by realists and foundationalists.

Neopragmatists disagree even more sharply in regarding the role of theory (explanatory accounts of the past and present). All neopragmatists shun grand theory because it smacks of metaphysical posturing. Yet this shunning often shades into a distrust of theory per se—hence a distancing from revisable social theories, provisional cultural theories or heuristic historical theories. This distrust may encourage an ostrichlike, piecemeal incrementalism that reeks of a vulgar antitheoreticism. On this view, neopragmatism amounts to crude practicalism. The grand pragmatism of Dewey and especially C. Wright Mills rejects such a view. Instead, it subtly incorporates an experimental temper within theory-laden descriptions of problematic situations (for instance, social and cultural crises). Unfortunately, the pragmatist tradition is widely associated with a distrust of theory, which curtails its ability to fully grasp the operations of power within the personal, social and historical contexts of human activities.

It is no accident that the dominant form of politics in the pragmatist tradition accents the pedagogical and the dialogical. Such a noble liberalism assumes that vast disparities in resources, enormous polarizations in perceptions or intense conflicts of interests can be overcome by means of proper education and civil conversation. If persuasive historical sociological claims show that such disparities, polarizations and conflicts often produce improper agitation and uncivil confrontation, the dominant form of politics in the pragmatist tradition is paralyzed or at least rendered more impotent than it is commonly believed. One crucial theme or subtext in my genealogy of pragmatism is the persistence of the sense of impotence of liberal intellectuals in American culture and society, primarily because of unattended class and regional disparities, unacknowledged racial and sexual polarizations and untheorized cultural and personal conflicts that permeate and pervade our past and present. My view neither downplays nor devalues education and conversation; it simply highlights the structural background conditions of pedagogical efforts and dialogical events.

This leads me to my second concern, namely, the relative absence of pragmatist accounts of why pragmatism surfaces now in the ways and forms that it does. Such an account must situate the nature of pragmatist intellectual interventions—their intended effects and unintended consequences—in the present historical moment in American society and culture. I suspect that part of the renaissance of neopragmatism can be attributed to the crisis of purpose and vocation in humanistic studies and professional schools. On this view, the recent hunger for interdisciplinary studies—or the erosion of disciplinary boundaries—promoted by neopragmatisms, poststructuralisms, Marxisms and feminisms is not only motivated by a quest for truth, but also activated by power struggles over what kinds of knowledge should be given status, rewarded and passed on to young, informed citizens in the next century. These power struggles are not simply over positions and curriculums, but also over ideals of what it means to be humanistic intellectuals in a declining empire—in a first-rate military power, a near-rescinding economic power and a culture in decay.

As Henry Adams suggests, the example of a turn toward history is most evident in American culture when decline is perceived to be undeniable and intellectuals feel most removed from the action. Furthermore, pragmatism at its best, in James and Dewey, provided a sense of purpose and vocation for intellectuals who believed they could make a difference in the public life of the nation. And it is not surprising that the first perceivable consequence of the renaissance of neopragmatism led by Richard Rorty echoed James's attack on professionalization and specialization. In this sense, Rorty's *Philosophy and the Mirror of Nature* (1979) not only told the first major and influential story of analytic philosophy, but was also a challenging narrative of how contemporary intellectuals have come to be contained within professional and specialized social spaces, with little outreach to a larger public and hence little visibility in, and minimal effect on, the larger society. Needless to say, Rorty's revival of Jamesian antiprofessionalism—not to be confused with anti-intellectualism or even anti-academicism—has increased intellectuals' interest in public journalism and intensified the tension between journalists and academics.

The crisis of purpose and vocation in humanistic studies and professional schools is compounded by the impact of the class and regional disparities, racial and sexual polarizations and cultural and personal conflicts that can no longer be ignored. This impact not only unsettles our paradigms in the production of knowledge, but also forces us to interrogate and examine our standards, criteria, styles and forms in which knowledge is assessed, legitimated and expressed. At its worst, pragmatism in the academy permits us to embrace this impact without attending to the implications of power. At its best, pragmatism behooves us to critically scrutinize this impact as we promote the democratization of American intellectual life without vulgar leveling or symbolic tokenism.

But what is this "pragmatism at its best"? What form does it take? What are its constitutive features or fundamental components? These questions bring me to my third point—the idea of a prophetic pragmatist perspective and praxis. I use the adjective "prophetic" in order to harken back to the rich, though flawed, traditions of Judaism and Christianity that promote courageous resistance against, and relentless critiques of, injustice and social misery. These traditions are rich, in that they help keep alive collective memories of moral (that is, anti-idolatrous) struggle and nonmarket values (that is, love for others, loyalty to an ethical ideal and social freedom) in a more and more historically amnesiac society and market-saturated culture. These traditions are flawed because they tend toward dogmatic pronouncements (that is, "Thus saith the Lord") to homogeneous constituencies. Prophetic pragmatism gives courageous resistance and relentless critique a self-critical character and democratic content; that is, it analyzes the social causes of unnecessary forms of social misery, promotes moral outrage against them and organizes different constituencies to alleviate them, yet does so with an openness to its own blindnesses and shortcomings.

Prophetic pragmatism is pragmatism at its best because it promotes a critical temper and democratic faith without making criticism a fetish or democracy an idol. The fetishization of criticism yields a sophisticated ironic consciousness of parody and paralysis, just as the idolization of democracy produces mob rule. As Peirce, James and Dewey noted, criticism always presupposes something in place—be it a set of beliefs or a tradition. Criticism yields results or makes a difference when something significant is antecedent to it, such as rich, sustaining, collective memories of moral struggle. Similarly, democracy assumes certain conditions for its flourishing—like a constitutional background. Such conditions for democracy are not subject to public veto.

Critical temper as a way of struggle and democratic faith as a way of life are the twin pillars of prophetic pragmatism. The major foes to be contested are despair, dogmatism and oppression. The critical temper promotes a full-fledged experimental disposition that highlights the provisional, tentative and revisable character of our visions, analyses and actions. Democratic faith consists of a Pascalian wager (hence underdetermined by the evidence) on the abilities and capacities of ordinary people to participate in decision-making procedures of institutions that fundamentally regulate their lives. The critical temper motivated by democratic faith yields all-embracing moral and/or religious visions that project credible ameliorative possibilities grounded in present realities in light of systemic structural analyses of the causes of social misery (without reducing all misery to historical causes). Such analyses must appeal to traditions of social theory and historical sociology just as visions must proceed from traditions of moral and/or religious communities. The forms of prophetic praxis depend on the insights of the social theories and the potency of the moral and/or religious communities. In order for these analyses and visions to combat despair, dogmatism and oppression, the existential, communal and political dimensions of prophetic pragmatism must be accented. The existential dimension is guided by the value of *love*–a risk-ridden affirmation of the distinct humanity of others that, at its best, holds despair at bay. The communal dimension is regulated by *loyalty*–a profound devotion to the critical temper and democratic faith that eschews dogmatism. The political dimension is guided by *freedom*–a perennial quest for self-realization and self-development that resists all forms of oppression.

The tradition of pragmatism is in need of a mode of cultural criticism that keeps track of social misery, solicits and channels moral outrage to alleviate it and projects a future in which the potentialities of ordinary people flourish and flower. The first wave of pragmatism foundered on the rocks of cultural conservatism and corporate liberalism. Its defeat was tragic. Let us not permit the second wave of pragmatism to end as farce.

SOURCE: *Southern California Law Review* 63, (1990) 1747–1762. Reprinted with permission of the *Southern California Law Review*.

Twelve

NIETZSCHE'S PREFIGURATION OF POSTMODERN AMERICAN PHILOSOPHY

The most profound philosophers in and of modernity with artistic temperaments—Schopenhauer and Nietzsche—are often ignored or overlooked by American philosophers. In this highly textual essay, originally published in 1981, I try to argue that Nietzsche's perspectivalism prefigures many crucial insights of the towering contemporary American philosophers like Quine, Goodman, Sellars and Rorty. Yet the centrality of struggle in Nietzsche—lapsed Lutheran that he was—led him to call for constructive alternatives for concrete living (even if only for the cruel and courageous few in his aristocratic perfectionism).

You ask me about the idiosyncrasies of philosophers? . . . There is their lack of historical sense, their hatred of even the idea of becoming, their Egyptianism. They think they are doing a thing honour when they de-historicize it, sub specie aeterni—*when they make a mummy of it. All the philosophers have handled for millennia has been conceptual mummies; nothing actual has escaped from their hands alive. They kill, they stuff, when they worship, these conceptual idolaters—they become a mortal danger to everything when they worship. Death, change, age, as well as procreation and growth, are for them objections—refutations even. What is, does not become; what becomes, is not.*

—NIETZSCHE, *TWILIGHT OF THE IDOLS*

What I relate is the history of the next two centuries. I describe what is coming, what can no longer come differently: the advent of nihilism. This history can be related even now; for necessity itself is at work here. This future speaks even now in a hundred signs, this destiny announces itself everywhere; for this music of the future all ears are cocked even now. For some time now, our whole European culture has been moving as toward a catastrophe, with a tortured tension that is growing from decade to decade: restlessly, violently,

> headlong, like a river that wants to reach the end,
> that no longer reflects, that is afraid to reflect.
>
> NIETZSCHE, THE WILL TO POWER

Nietzsche is the central figure in postmodern thought in the West. His aphoristic style—the epigram as style—governs the elusive texts of postmodern philosophers such as Ludwig Wittgenstein and E. M. Cioran. His antihermeneutical perspectivism underlies the deconstructive stance of postmodern critics such as Jacques Derrida and Paul de Man. His genealogical approach, especially regarding the link between knowledge and power, regulates the Marxist-influenced textual practice of postmodern critic-historians such as Michel Foucault and Edward Said. And his gallant attempt to overcome traditional metaphysics is a major preoccupation of postmodern thinkers such as Martin Heidegger, Hans-Georg Gadamer and Jean-Paul Sartre.

In this essay, I will try to show the ways in which Nietzsche prefigures the crucial moves made recently in postmodern American philosophy. I will confine my remarks to two of Nietzsche's texts: *Twilight of the Idols* and *The Will to Power*.[1] The postmodern American philosophers I will examine are W. V. Quine, Nelson Goodman, Wilfred Sellars, Thomas Kuhn and Richard Rorty. The three moves I shall portray are: the move toward antirealism or conventionalism in ontology; the move toward the demythologization of the Myth of the Given or antifoundationalism in epistemology; and the move toward the detranscendentalization of the subject or the dismissal of the mind as a sphere of inquiry. I then shall claim that Nietzsche believed such moves lead to a paralyzing nihilism and ironic skepticism unless they are supplemented with a new worldview, a new "countermovement," to overcome such nihilism and skepticism. Lastly, I will suggest that postmodern American philosophy has not provided such a "countermovement," settling instead for either updated versions of scientism (Quine and Sellars), an aristocratic resurrection of pluralistic stylism (Goodman), a glib ideology of professionalism (Kuhn) or a nostalgic appeal to enlightened conversation (Rorty). Such weak candidates for a "countermovement" seem to indicate the extent to which postmodern American philosophy—similar to much of postmodern thought in the West—constitutes a dead, impotent rhetoric of a declining and decaying civilization.

ANTIREALISM

The originating figures of modern analytic philosophy—Gottlob Frege, Alexius Meinong, Bertrand Russell and G. E. Moore—are the acknowledged ancestors of postmodern American philosophers. These figures constituted a formidable realist revolt against psychologism, conventionalism and idealism.² Frege revolted against J. S. Mill's psychologism and J. Venn's conventionalism in logic; Meinong, against Franz Brentano's psychologism in object theory; Russell and Moore, against F. H. Bradley's Hegelian idealism in metaphysics and epistemology. Each separate attack shares a common theme: an attempt to resurrect realism.

There are many forms of realism in modern analytic philosophy, including naive realism, Platonic realism, critical realism and internal realism.³ The basic claims of any form of realism are that objects, things, states of affairs or the world exist externally to us and independently of our sense experience; and that these objects, things, states of affairs or this world, in some fundamental way, determine what is true, objective and real.

This two-prong definition of realism suggests two important elements of any realist position. First, it links any realist position to some notion of correspondence (or re-presenting) between either ideas and objects, words and things, sentences and states of affairs, or theories and the world. Second, this definition proposes something other than human social practice to serve as the final court of appeal determining what is and what we ought to believe. To put it crudely, realism is preoccupied with assuring us that there is an external world and with obtaining the true (accurate, objective, valid) copy of this world.

Postmodern American philosophers affirm the first prong of the definition of realism—thus bypassing idealism—but see no need to build the notion of correspondence into the way the claim is stated. In short, they are highly critical of the subject-object problematic embodied in the first prong of the definition, such that grasping reality consists of crossing the subject-object hiatus, leaving one's inner world in order to get in contact with the external world, and of one's ideas copying or corresponding to the world.

Postmodern American philosophers reject the second prong of the definition of realism—thus promoting conventionalism in ontology. They refuse to accept the view that the world determines truth or that the world is the final court of appeal that compels us to accept what is or believe as we ought.

This rejection is based on two major insights of postmodern American philosophers: the conventional character of constructing (reductionist or nonreductionist) logical systems of the world and the theory-laden character of observations. The first insight crystallized after Rudolf Carnap's highly acclaimed yet unsuccessful attempt in his *Logical Construction of the World* (1928; better known as his *Aufbau*) to rationally reconstruct the process of acquiring knowledge by reducing (or translating) statements about the world to those of immediate experience. The second insight was gained from A. J. Ayer's popular yet no less unsuccessful attempt in his *Language, Truth and Logic* (1936) to defend the verificationist theory of meaning (or roughly promoting the primacy of observational evidence for determining the meaningfulness of a sentence).

Almost a decade after his painstaking study of Carnap's *Aufbau* in his masterful work *The Structure of Appearance* (1951), Goodman concluded in his renowned essay "The Way the World Is":

> What we must face is the fact that even the truest description comes nowhere near faithfully reproducing the way the world is . . . for it has explicit primitives, routes of construction, etc., none of them features of the world described. Some philosophers contend, therefore, that if systematic descriptions introduce an arbitrary artificial order, then we should make our descriptions unsystematic to bring them more into accord with the world. Now the tacit assumption here is that the respects in which a description is unsatisfactory are *just those respects in which it falls short of being a faithful picture;* and the tacit *goal* is to achieve a description that as nearly as possible gives a living likeness. But the goal is a delusive one. For we have seen that even the most realistic way of picturing amounts merely to one kind of conventionalization. In painting, the selection, the emphasis, the conventions are different from but no less peculiar to the vehicle, and no less variable, than those of language. The idea of making verbal descriptions approximate pictorial depiction loses its point when we understand that to turn a description into the most faithful possible picture would amount to nothing more than exchanging some conventions for others.[4]

After his search for a criterion of adequacy for constructional systems, such as Carnap's phenomenalistic one, or for scientific theories, such as Einstein's special theory of relativity, Goodman held that the choice is not based primarily on mere agreement with the facts, that is, observational data, but rather on, among other things, structural simplicity. In his influential essay "The Test of Simplicity," he writes:

> Thus selection of a theory must always be made in advance of the determination of some of the facts it covers; and, accordingly, some criterion other than conformity with such facts must be applied in making the selection. After as many points as we like have been plotted by experiment concerning the correlation of two factors (for example, of time and deterioration of radioactivity), we predict the remaining points by choosing one among all the infinitely many curves that cover the plotted points. Obviously, simplicity of some sort is a cardinal factor in making this choice (we pick the "smoothest" curve). The very validity of the choice depends upon whether the choice is properly made according to such criteria. Thus simplicity here is not a consideration applicable after truth is determined but is one of

the standards of validity that are applied in the effort to discover truth.[5]

In a later essay, "Art and Inquiry," and in his most recent work, *Ways of World-making* (1978), Goodman advances the notion of fitness as appropriate to (and as replacement for) talk about truth:

> Truth of a hypothesis after all is a matter of fit—fit with a body of theory, and fit of hypothesis and theory to the data at hand and the facts to be encountered.[6]

Briefly, then, truth of statements and rightness of descriptions, representations, exemplifications, expressions—of design, drawing, diction, rhythm—is primarily a matter of fit: fit to what is referred to in one way or another, or to other renderings, or to modes and manners of organization. The differences between fitting a version to a world, a world to a version, and a version together or to other versions fade when the role of versions in making the worlds they fit is recognized. And knowing or understanding is seen as ranging beyond the acquiring of true beliefs to the discovering and devising of fit of all sorts.[7]

In his famous essay "Two Dogmas of Empiricism," Quine observed that in Ayer's attempt to correlate each meaningful sentence with observational evidence, that is, empirical confirmation, Ayer remained tied to Carnap's reductionist project by trying to reduce the meaningfulness of a sentence to its empirical import.

> But the dogma of reductionism has, in a subtler and more tenuous form, continued to influence the thought of empiricists. The notion lingers that to each statement, or each synthetic statement, there is associated a unique range of possible sensory events such that the occurrence of any of them would add to the likelihood of truth of the statement, and that there is associated also another unique range of possible sensory events whose occurrence would detract from that likelihood. This notion is of course implicit in the verification theory of meaning.
>
> The dogma of reductionism survives in the supposition that each statement, taken in isolation from its fellows, can admit of confirmation or information at all. My countersuggestion, issuing essentially from Carnap's doctrine of the physical world in the *Aufbau,* is that our statements about the external world face the tribunal of sense experience not individually but only as a corporate body.[8]

Quine extended his critique of updated empiricism to the most cherished notion of modern analytic philosophers—the notion of analyticity, the idea that a statement is true by virtue of meanings and independently of fact. Given his Duhemian holism, the idea of an isolated statement being true without empirical confirmation is as unacceptable as the idea of an isolated statement being true with empirical confirmation. His main point is that the basic "unit of empirical significance is the whole of science,"[9] namely, competing theories (versions or descriptions) of the world, not isolated statements, since the truth-value of such statements can change relative to one's theory of the world.

> If this view is right, it is misleading to speak of the empirical content of an individual statement—especially if it is a statement at all remote from the experiential periphery of the field. Furthermore it becomes folly to seek a boundary between synthetic statements, which hold contingently on experience, and analytic statements, which hold come what may. Any statement can be held true come what may, if we make drastic enough adjustments elsewhere in the system. Even a statement very close to the periphery can be held true in the face of recalcitrant experience by pleading hallucination or by amending certain statements of the kind called logical laws. Conversely, by the same token, no statement is immune to revision.[10]

Goodman and Quine are the (retired, Harvard) patriarchs of postmodern American philosophy. Their respective holistic critiques of Carnap and, to a lesser degree, Ayer constitute the emergence of postmodernity in American philosophy and mark the Americanization of analytic philosophy.[11] If Goodman and Quine are the patriarchs, then Richard Rorty and Thomas Kuhn are the renegade stepchildren. Rorty and Kuhn have followed through most thoroughly on the antirealist, historicist and conventionalist implications of the views of Goodman and the early Quine.

In his celebrated article "The World Well Lost," Rorty concludes that the theory-laden character of observations relativizes talk about the world such that appeals to "the world" as a final court of appeal to determine what is true or what we should believe is viciously circular. We cannot isolate "the world" from theories of the world, then compare these theories of the world with a theory-free world. We cannot compare theories with anything that is not a product of another theory. So any talk about "the world" is relative to the alternative theories available. In response to the second prong of the definition of realism—to the notion that the world determines truth—Rorty states:

> Now, to put my cards on the table, I think that the realistic true believer's notion of the world is an obsession rather than an intuition. I also think that Dewey was right in thinking that the only intuition we have of the world as determining truth is just the intuition that we must make our new beliefs conform with a vast

body of platitudes, unquestioned perceptual reports, and the like.[12]

Kuhn, the other stepchild of Goodman and Quine, has received more attention than any postmodern American philosopher of science primarily because he has provided a new descriptive vocabulary that gives a new perspective on a sacrosanct institution, that is, natural science, in our culture in light of the early Quine's pragmatism and Goodman's conventionalism. His controversial yet highly acclaimed book *The Structure of Scientific Revolutions* (1962) serves as a rallying point for antirealists owing to statements such as the following:

> A scientific theory is usually felt to be better than its predecessors not only in the sense that it is a better instrument for discovering and solving puzzles, but also because it is somehow a better representation of what nature is really like. One often hears that successive theories grow ever closer to, or approximate more and more closely to, the truth. Apparently generalizations like that refer not to the puzzle-solutions and the concrete predictions derived from a theory but rather to its ontology, to the match, that is, between the entities with which the theory populates nature and what is "really there."
>
> Perhaps there is some other way of salvaging the notion of "truth" for application to whole theories, but this one will not do. There is, I think, no theory-independent way to reconstruct phrases like "really there," the notion of a match between the ontology of a theory and its "real" counterpart in nature now seems to me illusive in principle.[13]

If I am right, then "truth" may, like "proof," be a term with only intra-theoretic applications.[14]

There surely have been antirealists (such as Hegel), conventionalist philosophers of science (such as Pierre Duhem) and pragmatists (such as John Dewey) prior to the rise of postmodern American philosophy. But I claim that it is Nietzsche who most openly and unequivocally prefigures the antirealist, conventionalist move made by postmodern American philosophers.

For example, in the section entitled "How the 'Real World' at Last Became a Myth" in *Twilight of the Idols*, Nietzsche comically mocks the notion of a theory-free world, a "world" that can be appealed to in adjudicating between competing theories of the world.

4. The real world—unattainable? Unattained, at any rate. And if unattained also *unknown*. Consequently also no consolation, no redemption, no duty: how could we have a duty towards something unknown?

(The grey of dawn. First yawning of reason. Cockcrow of positivism.)

5. The "real world"—an idea no longer of any use, not even a duty any longer—an idea grown useless, superfluous, *consequently* a refuted idea: let us abolish it!

(Broad daylight; breakfast; return of cheerfulness and *bon sens;* Plato blushes for shame; all free spirits run riot.)

6. We have abolished the real world: what world is left? the apparent world perhaps? . . . But no! *with the real world we have also abolished the apparent world!*

(Mid-day; moment of the shortest shadow; end of the longest error; zenith of mankind; INCIPIT ZARATHUSTRA.) (*TI*, pp. 40–41)

Nietzsche clearly subscribes to the insight of postmodern American philosophers that holds that facts are theory-laden. He writes in *The Will to Power:*

Against positivism, which halts at phenomena—"There are only *facts*"—I would say: No, facts are precisely what there is not, only interpretations. We cannot establish any fact "in itself": perhaps it is folly to want to do such a thing. (*WP*, p. 267)

There are no facts, everything is in flux, incomprehensible, elusive; what is relatively most enduring is—our opinions. (*WP*, p. 327)

Goodman's pleas for a pluralism of versions of the world as manifest in the following passages:

The movement is from unique truth and a world fixed and found to a diversity of right and even conflicting versions or worlds in the making.[15]

There are very many different equally true descriptions of the world, and their truth is the only standard of their faithfulness. And when we say of them that they all involve conventionalizations, we are saying that no one of these different descriptions is *exclusively* true, since the others are also true. None of them tells us *the* way the world is, but each of them tells us *a* way the world is.[16]

echoes Nietzsche's quip: "No limit to the ways in which the world can be interpreted; every interpretation a symptom of growth or of decline. . . . Inertia needs unity (monism); plurality of interpretations a sign of strength. Not to desire to deprive the world of its disturbing and enigmatic character!" (*WP*, p. 326)

As we saw earlier, for Goodman, this pluralism suggests multiple criteria for accepting versions of the world—in science and art.

> Truth is not enough; it is at most a necessary condition. But even this concedes too much; the noblest scientific laws are seldom quite true. Minor discrepancies are overridden in the interest of breadth or power or simplicity. Science denies its data as the statesman denies his constituents—within the limits of prudence. . . . Truth and its aesthetic counterpart amount to appropriateness under different names. If we speak of hypotheses but not works of art as true, that is because we reserve the terms "true" and "false" for symbols in sentential form. I do not say this difference is negligible, but it is specific rather than generic, a difference in field of application rather than in formula, and marks no schism between the scientific and the aesthetic.[17]

Similarly for Nietzsche, seeking after "truth" is essentially a matter of positing a goal and achieving that goal.

> The ascertaining of "truth" and "untruth," the ascertaining of facts in general, is fundamentally different from creative positing, from forming, shaping, overcoming, willing, such as is of the essence of philosophy. To introduce a meaning—this task still remains to be done, assuming there is no meaning yet. Thus it is with sounds, but also with the fate of peoples: they are capable of the most different interpretations and direction toward different goals.
>
>   On a yet higher level is to *posit a goal* and mold facts according to it; that is, active interpretation and not merely conceptual translation. (*WP*, p. 327)

Note the way in which Nietzsche's perspectivism, most clearly stated in the following passage,

> That the value of the world lies in our interpretation (—that other interpretations than merely human ones are perhaps somewhere possible—); that previous interpretations have been perspective valuations by virtue of which we can survive in

life, i.e., in the will to power, for the growth of power; that every elevation of man brings with it the overcoming of narrower interpretations; that every strengthening and increase of power opens up new perspectives and means believing in new horizons—this idea permeates my writings. The world with which we are concerned is false, i.e., is not a fact but a fable and approximation on the basis of a meager sum of observations; it is "in flux," as something in a state of becoming, as a falsehood always changing but never getting near the truth: for—there is no "truth." (*WP*, p. 330)

anticipates the early Quine's pragmatism, best articulated in this famous paragraph:

As an empiricist I continue to think of the conceptual scheme of science as a tool, ultimately, for predicting future experience in the light of past experience. Physical objects are conceptually imported into the situation as convenient intermediaries—not by definition in terms of experience, but simply as irreducible posits comparable, epistemologically, to the gods of Homer. For my part I do, qua lay physicist, believe in physical objects and not in Homer's gods; and I consider it a scientific error to believe otherwise. But in point of epistemological footing the physical objects and the gods differ only in degree and not in kind. Both sorts of entities enter our conception only as cultural posits. The myth of physical objects is epistemologically superior to most in that it has proved more efficacious than other myths as a device for working a manageable structure into the flux of experience.[18]

Note also the crucial role of utility and human interests in the early Quine's pragmatism and Nietzsche's perspectivism:

The quality of myth, however, is relative; relative, in this case, to the epistemological point of view. This point of view is one among various, corresponding to one among our various interests and purposes.[19]

The apparent world, i.e., a world viewed according to values; ordered, selected according to values, i.e., in this case according to the viewpoint of utility in regard to the preservation and enhancement of the power of a certain species of animal. . . . The perspective therefore decides the character of the "appearance"! (*WP*, p. 305)

Postmodern American philosophers, unconsciously prefigured by Nietzsche, are aptly described by Rorty when in the process of delineating what he calls "edifying" philosophers such as Dewey, Kierkegaard and the later Heidegger, he writes:

> These writers have kept alive the suggestion that, even when we have justified true belief about everything we want to know, we may have no more than conformity to the norms of the day. They have kept alive the historicist sense that this century's "superstition" was the last century's triumph of reason, as well as the relativist sense that the latest vocabulary, borrowed from the latest scientific achievement, may not express privileged representations of essences, but be just another of the potential infinity of vocabularies in which the world can be described.[20]

Nietzsche catches the flavor of this passage when he writes, "That the destruction of an illusion does not produce truth but only one more piece of ignorance, an extension of our 'empty space,' an increase of our 'desert.'" (*WP*, p. 327)

DEMYTHOLOGIZING THE MYTH OF THE GIVEN

The Myth of the Given is an attempt to secure solid foundations for knowledge claims; it is a quest for certainty in epistemology.[21] The Myth of the Given roughly holds that there is a given element—a self-justifying, intrinsically credible, theory-neutral, noninferential element—in experience that provides the foundations for other knowledge claims and serves as the final terminating points for chains of epistemic justification. Therefore the attempt of postmodern American philosophers to demythologize the Myth of the Given is a move toward antifoundationalism in epistemology. It is not surprising that such antifoundationalism is akin to the antirealism, holism and conventionalism we examined earlier.

The two major proponents of the Myth of the Given in modern analytic philosophy are C. I. Lewis, a beloved teacher of Quine and Goodman, and H. H. Price, an appreciative student of Russell.[22] For both philosophers, the given element and its interpretation constitute the basic characteristics of knowledge and experience. As Lewis states: "There are in our cognitive experience, two elements, the immediate data such as those of sense, which are presented or given to the mind, and a form, construction, or interpretation, which represents the activity of thought."[23] Price also notes after acknowledging the data of the historian, general and detective:

> But it is obvious that these are only data relatively and for the purpose of answering a certain question. They are really themselves the results of inference,

often of a very complicated kind. We may call them data *secundum quid*. But eventually we must get back to something which is a datum *simpliciter*, which is not the result of any previous intellectual process.[24]

As we said earlier, for Lewis and Price, the very foundations of knowledge are at stake in this distinction. Lewis is quite candid about this:

> If there be no datum given to the mind, then knowledge must be altogether contentless and arbitrary; there would be nothing which it must be true to. And if there be no interpretation which the mind imposes, then thought is rendered superfluous, the possibility of error becomes inexplicable, and the distinction of true and false is in danger of becoming meaningless.[25]

Similarly for Price, the phenomenological investigation of the particular modes of perception (which lies outside of science) provides the foundations for science. "Empirical Science can never be more trustworthy than perception, upon which it is based."[26]

We are fortunate to have Goodman's direct response to Lewis's two-component view of knowledge owing to a symposium in which they both (along with Hans Reichenbach) took part at an American Philosophical Association meeting at Bryn Mawr in 1951. Needless to say, Goodman is critical of Lewis's view. He replies not by denying the notion of the given, but by severing any links of a given element with notions of the true, false or certain.

> But this all seems to me to point to, or at least to be compatible with, the conclusion that while something is given, nothing given is true; that while some things may be indubitable, nothing is certain. What we have been urged to grant amounts at most to this: materials for or particles of experience are given, sensory qualities or events or other elements are not created at will but presented, experience has some content even though our description of it may be artificial or wrong and even though the precise differentiation between what is given and what is not given may be virtually impossible. But to such content or materials or particles or elements, the terms "true," or "false," and "certain" are quite inapplicable. These elements are simply there or not there. To grant that some are there is not to grant that anything is certain. Such elements may be indubitable in the vacuous sense that doubt is irrelevant to them, as it is to a desk; but they, like the desk, are equally devoid of certainty. They may be before us, but they are neither true nor false. For truth and falsity and certainty pertain to statements or judgments and not to mere particles or materials or elements. Thus, to deny that there are empirical certainties does not imply that experience is a pure fiction, that it is without content, or even that there is no given element.[27]

Five years later in his essay on Carnap, "The Revision of Philosophy," Goodman picks up the given-interpretation issue again, and this time he rejects the distinction outright:

> Any such view rests on the premise that the question "What are the original elements in knowledge?" is a clear and answerable one. And the assumption remains uncontested so long as we are dominated by the tradition that there is a sharp dichotomy between the given and the interpretation put upon it—so long as we picture the knower as a machine that is fed experience in certain lumps and proceeds to grind these up and reunite them in various ways. But I do not think this view of the matter will stand very close scrutiny.[28]

And in his latest book, the very notion of epistemological foundations and the given element in experience are dismissed and dispensed with. "With false hope of a firm foundation gone, with the world displaced by worlds that are but versions, with substance dissolved into function, and with the given acknowledged as taken, we face the questions how worlds are made, tested, and known."[29]

The most explicit attempts in postmodern American philosophy to demythologize the Myth of the Given are those of Wilfred Sellars and Richard Rorty. For Sellars, the Myth of the Given results from a confusion between the acquisition of knowledge and the justification of knowledge, between empirical causal accounts of how one comes to have a belief and philosophical investigations into how one justifies a belief one has. This confusion dissolves when one realizes that knowledge begins with the ability to justify, the capacity to use words. Everything else, he holds, is a noncognitive causal antecedent. Sellars's psychological nominalism claims that there is no such thing as prelinguistic awareness; or, to put it positively, that all awareness—of abstract and particular entities—is a linguistic affair. According to his view, "not even the awareness of such sorts, resemblances, and facts as pertain to so-called immediate experience is presupposed by the process of acquiring the use of a language."[30]

Sellars's view precludes the possibility of any form of the Myth of the Given because it rules out any self-justifying, intrinsically credible, theory-neutral, noninferential epistemic element in experience. This is so because if knowledge begins with the ability to justify, then its beginnings (or "foundations") are public and intersubjective, matters of social practice.

For example, one of the forms of the Myth of the Given subscribed to by traditional empiricist philosophers

> is the idea that there is, indeed must be, a structure of particular matter of fact such that (a) each fact can not only be noninferentially known to be the case, but presupposes no other knowledge either of particular matter of fact, or of general

truths; and (b) such that the noninferential knowledge of facts belonging to this structure constitutes the ultimate court of appeals for all factual claims—particular and general—about the world.[31]

This privileged stratum of fact is justified by appeals to prelinguistic awareness of self-authenticating, "phenomenal" qualities. Price tries to defend this view by characterizing a normal perceptual situation—of a tomato under regular circumstances of light—in which he arrives at certain indubitable beliefs:

> One thing however I cannot doubt: that there exists a red patch of a round and somewhat bulgy shape, standing out from a background of other colour-patches, and having a certain visual depth, and that this whole field of colour is directly present to my consciousness. . . . This peculiar manner of being present to consciousness is called *being given* and that which is thus present is called a *datum*. The corresponding mental attitude is called *acquaintance, intuitive apprehension,* or sometimes *having*.[32]

Sellars then replies:

> One couldn't have observational knowledge of any fact unless one knew many other things as well. . . . For the point is specifically that observational knowledge of any particular fact, e.g., that this is green, presupposes that one knows general facts of the form X is a *reliable symptom* of Y. . . . The essential point is that in characterizing an episode or a state as that of *knowing*, we are not giving an empirical description of that episode or state; we are placing it in the logical space of reasons, of justifying and being able to justify what one says.[33]

Sellars concludes that the conception of knowledge based on the Myth of the Given, along with its concomitant picture of epistemology,

> is misleading because of its static character. One seems forced to choose between the picture of an elephant which rests on a tortoise (What supports the tortoise?) and the picture of a great Hegelian serpent of knowledge with its tail in its mouth (Where does it begin?). Neither will do. For empirical knowledge, like its sophisticated extension, science, is rational, not because it has a *foundation* but because it is a self-correcting enterprise which can put any claim in jeopardy, though not *all* at once.[34]

Rorty's epistemological behaviorism extends Sellars's psychological nominalism, accenting even more the intersubjective, that is, social character, of the "foundations" of knowledge:

Explaining rationality and epistemic authority by reference to what society lets us say, rather than the latter by the former, is the essence of what I shall call "epistemological behaviorism," an attitude common to Dewey and Wittgenstein. This sort of behaviorism can best be seen as a species of holism—but one which requires no idealist metaphysical underpinnings.[35]

Following Sellars's attack on the Myth of the Given and linking this attack to Quine's holism, Rorty claims:

A holistic approach to knowledge is not a matter of antifoundationalist polemic, but a distrust of the whole epistemological enterprise. A behavioristic approach to episodes of "direct awareness" is not a matter of antimentalistic polemic, but a distrust of the Platonic quest for that special sort of certainty associated with visual perception.[36]

By combining the insights of Sellars and Quine, Rorty arrives at his own radical conclusion:

When Sellars's and Quine's doctrines are purified, they appear as complementary expressions of a single claim: that no "account of the nature of knowledge" can rely on a theory of representations which stand in privileged relations to reality. The work of these two philosophers enables us . . . to make clear why an "account of the nature of knowledge" can be, at most, a description of human behavior.[37]

In *Twilight of the Idols,* Nietzsche acknowledges that the fundamental quest in Western philosophy for self-authenticating, self-justifying, intrinsically credible beliefs and concepts must rest, to use Stanley Cavell's Wittgensteinian phrase, "outside language games."[38] For Nietzsche, as for Sellars, such beliefs and concepts must presuppose some other kind of knowledge rather than serve as the foundation of our knowledge; they are grounded on what we already know rather than serve as the grounds for all that we know. He writes in section 4 of his chapter entitled "'Reason' in Philosophy":

The *other* idiosyncrasy of philosophers is no less perilous: it consists in mistaking the last for the first. They put that which comes at the end—unfortunately! for it ought not to come at all!—the "highest concepts," that is to say the most general, the emptiest concepts, the last fumes of evaporating reality, at the beginning *as* the beginning. It is again only the expression of their way of doing reverence: the higher must not be *allowed* to grow out of the lower, must not be *allowed* to have grown at all. . . . Moral: everything of the first rank must be *causa sui.* Origin in something else counts as an objection, as casting doubt on value. (*TI,* p. 37)

Nietzsche considers the quest for certainty and the search for foundations in epistemology—any forms of the Myth of the Given—unattainable and ultimately self-deceptive. Any such quest and search must be subordinate to an inquiry as to why the will to power takes the form of such a quest and search. "It might seem as though I had evaded the question of 'certainty.' The opposite is true; but by inquiring after the criterion of certainty I tested the scales upon which men have weighed in general hitherto—and that the question of certainty itself is a dependent question, a question of second rank" (*WP*, p. 322). Any attempt to ground knowledge claims must be demystified such that the practical aims and goals concealed by such an attempt are disclosed:

> Theory and practice.—*Fateful distinction, as if there were an actual* drive for knowledge that, without regard to questions of usefulness and harm, went blindly for the truth; and then, separate from this, the whole world of *practical* interests—
>
> I tried to show, on the other hand, what instincts have been active behind all these *pure* theoreticians—how they have all, under the spell of their instincts, gone fatalistically for something that was "truth" *for them*—for them and only for them. The conflict between different systems, including that between epistemological scruples, is a conflict between quite definite instincts (forms of vitality, decline, classes, races, etc.).
>
> The so-called drive for knowledge can be traced back to a drive to appropriate and conquer. (*WP*, p. 227)

Nietzsche's rejection of foundationalism in epistemology results from his acceptance of the Heraclitean flux, of the world of becoming, which forever slips out of the arbitrary conceptual schemas through which humans come to "know" the self and world.

> The character of the world in a state of becoming as incapable of formulation, as "false," as "self-contradictory." Knowledge and becoming exclude one another. Consequently, "knowledge" must be something else: there must first of all be a will to make knowable, a kind of becoming must itself create the deception of beings. (*WP*, p. 280)

A world in a state of becoming could not, in a strict sense, be "comprehended" or "known"; only to the extent that the "comprehending" and "knowing" intellect encounters a coarse, already-created world, fabricated out of mere appearances but become firm to the extent that this kind of appearance has preserved life—only to this extent is there anything like "knowledge"; i.e., a measuring of earlier and later errors by one another. (*WP,* p. 281)

For Nietzsche, as for Quine, Goodman, Sellars and Rorty (and against Plato, Aristotle, Descartes, Kant, Kripke and Lévi-Strauss), knowledge is not a matter of grasping fixed forms, static essences or permanent substances and structures. Rather, knowledge is a matter of perceiving phenomena under a description, within a theory or in light of a version in order to, to use a Wittgensteinian phrase, "help us get about." On this point, the early Quine's pragmatism and Nietzsche's perspectivism again converge.

Each man is given a scientific heritage plus a continuing barrage of sensory stimulation; and the considerations which guide him in warping his scientific heritage to fit his continuing sensory promptings are, where rational, pragmatic.[39]

Not "to know" but to schematize—to impose upon chaos as much regularity and form as our practical needs require.

In the formation of reason, logic, the categories, it was *need* that was authoritative: the need, not to "know," but to subsume, to schematize, for the purpose of intelligibility and calculation. (*WP,* p. 278)

Nietzsche's conception of knowledge as elastic in character and creative in content is echoed in Goodman:

Furthermore, if worlds are as much made as found, so also knowing is as much remaking as reporting. All the processes of worldmaking I have discussed enter into knowing. Perceiving motion, we have seen, often consists in producing it. Discovering laws involves drafting them. Recognizing patterns is very much a matter of inventing and imposing them. Comprehension and creation go on together.[40]

Coming to know means "to place oneself in a conditional relation to something"; to feel oneself conditioned by something and oneself to condition it—it is therefore under all circumstances establishing, denoting, and making-conscious of conditions. (*WP,* p. 301)

Nietzsche debunks the Myth of the Given because, for him, knowledge is not a set of beliefs to be "grounded," but rather a series of linguistic signs that designate and describe the world in light of our evolving needs, interests and purposes. "It is an illusion that something is *known* when we possess a mathematical formula for an event: it is only designated, described; nothing more!" (*WP,* p. 335). He surely would agree with Rorty that demythologizing the Myth of the Given—and promoting antifoundationalism in epistemology—results in "preventing man from deluding himself with the notion that he knows himself, or anything else, except under optimal descriptions."[41]

DETRANSCENDENTALIZING THE SUBJECT

The last crucial move of postmodern American philosophy I will examine is the detranscendentalizing of the subject—the dismissing of the mind as a self-contained sphere of inquiry. This move is a natural consequence of the antirealism, holism, conventionalism and antifoundationalism we examined earlier.

It is important to note that notions such as the subject, self-consciousness, ego and "I" were under attack by modern analytic philosophers. Therefore this last move of postmodern American philosophers is part of the general trend of modern analytic philosophy.

For example, Quine's treatment of this matter follows, in many ways, the logical behaviorist position put forward in Gilbert Ryle's classic work, *The Concept of Mind* (1949). This position, largely intended to debunk the Cartesian myth of the "ghosts in machines," roughly holds that talk about mental states, that is, an intentional idiom, is but a clumsy and confusing way of talking about dispositions to behave in certain ways under specific circumstances, that is, a behavioristic idiom. Quine's well-known passage in his *Word and Object* (1960) summarizes his own behavioristic position:

One may accept the Brentano thesis either as showing the indispensability of intentional idioms and the importance of an autonomous science of intention, or as showing the baselessness of intentional idioms and the emptiness of a science of intention. My attitude, unlike Brentano's, is the second. To accept intentional usage at face value is, we saw, to postulate translation relations as somehow objectively valid though indeterminate in principle relative to the totality of speech dispositions. Such postulation promises little gain in scientific insight if there is no better ground for it than that the supposed translation relations are presupposed by the vernacular of semantics and intention.[42]

Underlying this viewpoint is Quine's eliminative materialist position, namely, the view that there simply are no mental states, but rather neural events. In this way, Quine detranscendentalizes any notion of the subject.

Rorty deepens this version of detranscendentalizing the subject by abandoning the very notion of mind-body identity. On his view, the social practice of speaking in neural events (by those who know neurology) and the social practice of speaking in mental states (by those who do not know neurology) "are just two ways of talking about the same thing."[43] And the "thing" being talked about in each case is that which is posited within one's theory. As Sellars points out, such thing-talk, be it neurological or commonsensical, occurs in

> a framework of "unobserved," "nonempirical" "inner" episodes. For we can point out immediately that in these respects they are no worse off than the particles and episodes in physical theory. For these episodes are "in" language-using animals as molecular impacts are "in" gases, not as "ghosts" are in "machines." They are "nonempirical" in the simple sense that they are *theoretical*—not definable in observational terms. . . . Their "purity" is not a *metaphysical* purity, but, so to speak, a *methodological* purity . . . [and] the fact that they are not introduced as physiological entities does not preclude the possibility that at a later methodological stage, they may, so to speak, "turn out" to be such.[44]

Sellars's methodological behaviorism—his way of detranscendentalizing the subject—permits him to be a behaviorist (like Quine) without thinking that all one's theoretical concepts in relation to "mental events" will turn out to refer to neurological phenomena (unlike Quine)—though, of course, they may. "The behavioristic requirement that all concepts should be introduced in terms of a basic vocabulary pertaining to overt behavior is compatible with the idea that some behavioristic concepts are to be introduced as theoretical concepts."[45]

Nietzsche's dismissal of the mind as a self-contained sphere of inquiry is illustrated in section 3 of his chapter entitled "The Four Great Errors" in *Twilight of the Idols:*

> The conception of a consciousness ("mind") as cause and later still that of the ego (the "subject") as cause are merely after-products after causality had, on the basis of will, been firmly established as a given fact, as *empiricism.* Meanwhile we have thought better. Today we do not believe a word of it. The "inner world" is full of phantoms and false lights: the will is one of them. The will no longer moves anything, consequently no longer explains anything—it merely accompanies events, it can also be absent. The so-called "motive": another error. Merely a surface phenomenon of consciousness, an accompaniment to an act, which conceals rather

than exposes the *antecedentia* of the act. And as for the ego! It has become a fable, a fiction, a play on words: it has totally ceased to think, to feel and to will! . . . What follows from this? There are no spiritual causes at all! The whole of the alleged empiricism which affirmed them has gone to the devil! (*TI*, p. 49)

Like Ryle's, Nietzsche's detranscendentalizing of the subject begins with a critique of Descartes:

"There is thinking: therefore there is something that thinks": this is the upshot of all Descartes' argumentation. But that means positing as "true a priori" our belief in the concept of substance—that when there is thought there has to be something "that thinks" is simply a formulation of our grammatical custom that adds a doer to every deed. In short, this is not merely the substantiation of a fact but a logical-metaphysical postulate. (*WP*, p. 268)

Similar to Rorty and Sellars, Nietzsche views subject-talk as mere convention, a matter of social practice rooted in our needs, interests, and purposes:

"Everything is subjective," you say; but even this is interpretation. The "subject" is not something given, it is something added and invented and projected behind what there is. (*WP*, p. 267)

However habitual and indispensable this fiction may have become by now—that in itself proves nothing against its imaginary origin: a belief can be a condition of life and nonetheless be false. (*WP*, p. 268)

He concludes that subject-talk is a linguistic social practice derived from our grammar, namely, the subject-predicate structure of our judgments.

In every judgment there resides the entire, full, profound belief in subject and attribute, or in cause and effect (that is, as the assertion that every effect is an activity and that every activity presupposes an agent); and this latter belief is only a special case of the former, so there remains as the fundamental belief that there are subjects, that everything that happens is related attributively to some subject. (*WP*, p. 294)

NIHILISM

If Nietzsche prefigures certain important developments in postmodern American philosophy, then it is appropriate to note briefly that he believed such developments ultimately lead to nihilism unless they are supplemented with a new worldview. He makes this point clearly in his Preface to *The Will to Power*:

> For one should make no mistake about the meaning of the title that this gospel of the future wants to bear. "*The Will to Power*: Attempt at a Revaluation of All Values"—in this formulation a countermovement finds expression, regarding both principle and task; a movement that in some future will take the place of this perfect nihilism—but presupposes it, logically and psychologically, and certainly can come only after and out of it. For why has the advent of nihilism become *necessary*? Because the values we have had hitherto thus draw their final consequence; because nihilism represents the ultimate logical conclusion of our great values and ideals—because we must experience nihilism before we can find out what value these "values" really had.—We require, sometime, *new values*. (*WP*, pp. 3–4)

For Nietzsche, this nihilism results from certain ideals of modern Europe, especially those ideals that presuppose belief in the categories of "aim," "unity" and "truth." Nihilism is a natural consequence of a culture (or civilization) ruled and regulated by categories that mask manipulation, mastery and domination of peoples and nature.

> Suppose we realize how the world may no longer be interpreted in terms of these three categories, and that the world begins to become valueless for us after this insight: then we have to ask about the sources of our faith in these three categories. . . .
>
> Conclusion: The faith in the categories of reason is the cause of nihilism. We have measured the value of the world according to categories *that refer to a fictitious world*.
>
> Final conclusion: All the values by means of which we have tried so far to render the world estimable for ourselves and which then proved inapplicable and therefore devaluated the world—all these values are, psychologically considered, the results of certain perspectives of utility, designed to maintain and increase human constructs of domination—and they have been falsely *projected* into the essence of things. (*WP*, pp. 13–14)

Nihilism ushers in an era in which science—the great pride of modern Europe—

provides greater and greater instrumentalities for world domination. As Maurice Blanchot observes:

> The moment Nihilism outlines the world for us, its counterpart, science, creates the tools to dominate it. The era of universal mastery is opened. But there are some consequences: first, science can only be nihilistic; it is the meaning of a world deprived of meaning, a knowledge that ultimately has ignorance as its foundation. To which the response will be that this reservation is only theoretical; but we must not hasten to disregard this objection, for science is essentially productive. Knowing it need not interpret the world, science transforms it, and by this transformation science conveys its own nihilistic demands—the negative power that science has made into the most useful of tools, but with which it dangerously plays. Knowledge is fundamentally dangerous . . . for a universe cannot be constructed without having the possibility of its being destroyed . . . [and] by making science possible, Nihilism becomes the possibility of science—which means that the human world can be destroyed by it.[46]

Nietzsche considers nihilism to be "partly destructive, partly ironic" (*WP*, p. 14). It is marked by philosophical positions of antirealism, conventionalism, relativism and antifoundationalism. We have seen that postmodern American philosophers support such positions. Quine describes himself as a "relativist,"[47] yet warns against associating him with the "epistemological nihilism"[48] of Kuhn. Goodman labels his position "as a radical relativism under rigorous restraints, that eventuates in something akin to irrealism."[49] Rorty calls himself a "historicist,"[50] and Kuhn admits to subscribing to a form of relativism.[51]

The crucial moves made by postmodern American philosophers are highly significant in that these moves disclose the unwarranted philosophical assumptions and antiquated theoretical distinctions upon which rests much of modern analytic philosophy. Yet—and in this regard they resemble their counterparts in postmodern literary criticism—postmodern American philosophers have failed to project a new worldview, a countermovement, "a new gospel of the future." Quine's and Sellars's updated versions of scientism not only reflect their positivist heritage, but, more important, reveal their homage to an outdated cultural mode of thought. Goodman's attempt to infuse the idea of style with new life is intriguing, yet ultimately resorts to an old aristocratic preoccupation. Kuhn's unequivocal promotion of the proliferation of learned societies (or groups) engaged in puzzle-solving under converging paradigms amounts to an unimaginative ideology of professionalism. And Rorty's ingenious conception of philosophy as cultured conversation rests upon a nostalgic appeal to the world of men (and women) of letters of decades past. These viewpoints do not constitute visions, worldviews or, to use Gilles Deleuze's phrase, "discourses as counter-philosophies"[52] to the nihilism to which their positions seem to lead. Instead, their viewpoints leave postmodern American philosophy hanging in limbo, as a philosophically critical yet culturally lifeless rhetoric mirroring a culture (or civilization) permeated by the scientific ethos, regulated by racist, patriarchal, capitalist norms and pervaded by debris of decay.

SOURCE: From *Early Postmodernism,* edited by Paul A. Bové (Durham, N.C.: Duke University Press, 1995), pp. 265–289.

PART FOUR

PROGRESSIVE MARXIST THEORY

In a time in which Communist regimes have been rightly discredited and yet alternatives to neoliberal capitalist societies are unwisely dismissed, I defend the fundamental claim of Marxist theory: There must be countervailing forces that defend people's needs against the brutality of profit-driven capitalism. Unfortunately, Marxists have not envisioned how these countervailing forces could be democratic ones. Hence the undemocratic Communist regimes of the past. In this section, I suggest that a progressive Marxist theory is still necessary, though not sufficient, for radical democrats.

Thirteen

THE INDISPENSABILITY YET INSUFFICIENCY OF MARXIST THEORY

Georg Lukács is the most important Marxist philosopher of this century. I included a chapter on his classic, History and Class Consciousness *(1923), in my dissertation. I also later published a long essay on his corpus—his literary criticism, Hegelian Marxism and social ontology.*

This was a fun and fascinating interview with the Hungarian philosopher Eva L. Corredor conducted in 1992. Note that although I acknowledge Lukács's immense influence on my conception of progressive Marxist theory, I unequivocally reject his teleological Hegelian Marxism and his retrograde Stalinist politics.

Eva Corredor: Thank you very much for accepting to talk to me about Lukács. What I particularly appreciated in your book *The Ethical Dimensions of Marxist Thought,* was that your approach to and interpretation of Lukács's work seemed to have an urgency and a relevance to your current preoccupations that I had not found in most other academic critics. I felt that Lukács really "spoke" to you and said something vital to you. In the introduction, which is very interesting and which is also one of your most recent texts, you mentioned that you felt "seduced" by Lukács and the Frankfurt School, and that it actually happened here at Princeton. So I should like to ask you how it happened, how you encountered Lukács, and which books you read.

Cornel West: We had a study group here in the early 1970s with a number of graduate students in philosophy, political theory and social theory. Mainly, people were studying with Sheldon Wolin. I also was close to Richard Rorty at the time, but Sheldon Wolin was the catalyst for a number of us who came together and began to read Lukács, Foucault, Deleuze, Lyotard and a host of others. We read the Frankfurt School as well, Adorno and Horkheimer. We had some real tensions in that group, and a tension primarily between those of us who thought that Hegelian versions of Marxist theory were the most interesting, and then the anti-Hegelians, mainly linked to the Parisian intellectuals, especially Foucault and Derrida, Foucault probably more than Derrida. Derrida I think is much closer to Hegel than Foucault. We had some wonderful knock-down, drag-out fights. I was always convinced that Lukács's essay on reification was the most powerful text I had read, that fused philosophical reflection with an analysis of capitalist society, as well as a sense of urgency as to how to change and transform it. So that essay for me remains one of the great essays in contemporary thought, not just in Marxist tradition, not just in Hegelian philosophy.

Corredor: So it was *History and Class Consciousness* that you read first? Had you read much of his other works, his literary analyses?

West: No, not at all. In fact I began with the 1923 collection, *History and Class Consciousness,* and then worked backwards and read *Soul and Forms* and *The Theory of the Novel,* and so on. It was primarily the philosophical Lukács, because I actually did not become preoccupied with literary criticism until the mid to late 1970s. Early on, it was primarily the history of philosophy. Actually it was Lukács who led me back to Hegel's *Phenomenology of Spirit.* I had read parts of it but I had read it in a very different way. Lukács sent me back. That was partly because Kojève was an interlocutor. We were reading Kojève's lectures on Hegel at that time.

Corredor: Was that here or in Paris?

West: No, that was here in Princeton. Not in class, just among ourselves.

Corredor: I am trying to find out how Lukács might have influenced you in your thinking and what you might have in common. I know that you describe yourself as a "prophetic, Christian, pragmatist freedom fighter" and that you are also conservative in some ways.

West: I guess so, like somebody who wants to preserve something. I would make a distinction between somebody who is in a *preservative* mode, who wants to preserve certain elements, and a *conservative,* which has the thicker ideological connotation.

Corredor: Based on Lukács's biography that was just published and some books I brought back from Hungary on Lukács's alleged messianism, one could establish a parallel between you and Lukács in the sense that Lukács can be described as a "messianic, Jewish, Marxist social critic" and also a conservative. There is the parallel with your religious side. You are a prophetic Christian, and he is said to have been very interested in messianism, especially at the beginning of his career. I am wondering whether you feel you share a prophetic-messianic religious interest or sentiment with him, or is this something that you would rather not discuss.

West: That is a very good and complex question. First, I think, in Lukács's case, here is someone who, of course early on in his career, starting with existential *Angst,* those very early essays, let us say 1910 to 1917, it is Dostoyevsky, it is the problems of life, it is the meaning of life, it is the emptiness of life, it is the spiritual sterility in life that he is grappling with, around the Stefan George Circle, an esoteric but fascinating group. There is always in Lukács an attempt to link quest for meaning with quest for freedom. And the quest for freedom is a kind of quest for deliverance, because it has quasi-religious residues in the quest for meaning. The quest for freedom has primarily a social and political character, but the individual dimension of that quest for freedom is also very important for Lukács. I think in Lukács the quest for meaning and the quest for freedom are inseparable, and that describes part of my own quest. I myself am certainly deeply influenced by Kierkegaard, deeply influenced by Dostoyevsky, by a host of persons preoccupied with the meaning of life and the absurdity of the human condition. At the same time, I am also preoccupied with the struggle against injustice and institutional and personal forms of evil, and I see that similar to Lukács's quest for freedom. So the quest for meaning in the Kierkegaardian tradition and the quest for freedom that comes out of a Marxist tradition do establish some parallel between my own pilgrimage and that of Lukács.

Corredor: In listening to you, I find a difference in your terminology and the one used by Lukács. Lukács, I believe, thought of himself as a social critic, whereas you describe yourself as a freedom fighter.

West: You are actually right, even though the meaning of an intellectual freedom fighter for me, this fusion of intellectual engagement, political transformation and existential struggle, is so tight that my first identity would be primarily that of a freedom fighter who engages in the fight for intellectual, political, social and existential freedom.

Corredor: You turn to Marxism, but you also affirm that Marxism is not a religion. And again, there is a similarity between you and Lukács that I found in your writings which I should like to quote: You speak of your own "leaps of faith" and that you are embracing "the absurdity of the human condition" (The Ethical Dimensions of Marxist Thought, p. xxvii). In Lukács's biography, which I mentioned to you earlier, the author Kadarkay says that Lukács, and in particular the young Lukács, could "arbitrarily leap from doubt into belief and find relief from the torment of doubt by affirming the absurdity of the human condition" (Kadarkay, p. 103). I think the parallel is quite striking.

West: Very, very interesting. But I tell you one fundamental divergence between my own view and that of Lukács: for me there is always a dialectic of doubt and faith, of skepticism and leap of faith, so that I am much more influenced by Pascal or Montaigne, who are both part of a particular tradition of faith but who understand that the doubt is inscribed within that faith. I am thinking of an introduction by T. S. Eliot to Pascal's *Pensées,* where he talks of how doubt and faith are intertwined, whereas with Lukács, I think, you do get a quest for certainty that would hold doubt at arm's length, and I am quite critical of something like this.

Corredor: Yes, I will have questions on this a bit later, if I may. In reading you, I felt that you described yourself primarily as a prophetic man, as a theologian. You are a believer, but you do not speak often of metaphysical things. You remain down here. In that sense, you are more a social critic than a prophet.

West: Yes. If I am in any way prophetic, I'm a prophetic thinker without a thick metaphysics. What I mean by that is that I am fairly historicist in my own formulations about how we go about understanding the Real and the Truth, and hence I talk more in terms of tradition and community than I do simply of truths and facts. So you are absolutely right, I have a *very* strong antimetaphysical bent. And again, it is very different in Lukács. Lukács would not only make some implicit metaphysical claims, but rather explicit ontological claims as well. He is much more with those who do believe that metaphysical grounding ought to be in place for claims . . . much more than someone like Dewey or Rorty.

Corredor: Another question I have relates again to both you and Lukács: You say somewhere that we have a "need for a Simmelian moment." Simmel spoke of "sinful" modern times, which Lukács picked up, in particular in his early work *The Theory of the Novel.* You yourself have written about "Nihilism in Black America: A Danger That Corrodes from Within" (*Dissent,* Spring 1992). You say that "America is in the midst of a mess of social breakdown . . . cultural decay is pervasive." Cynicism and nihilism today return very often in your accusations of modern times. The question is whether "modernism" is really sinful, again, since it was "sinful" for Simmel, it was sinful for Lukács in the early century and, listening to you it is sinful again or still a century later. Is modern age really more sinful than the previous ones?

West: No. I do not think so. I think that we have to understand modernism as a very complex, heterogeneous development with a variety of different streams and strains. The kind of attacks on modernism that Lukács puts forward, I would be quite critical of. That would be too narrow, too truncated in its reading. I think there are some insights there, there is no doubt about it, but we certainly cannot replace history with myths and turn away, internally, from the social and political and attempt to create some kind of fetish of art before which one could pay homage as in fact the social and political struggles were held at arm's length. I think that

Lukács's insights there are quite useful, but I do believe that modernism as a very complex development is not one that could be usefully described as "sinful." It has the connotation of blindness, but not sinful. We are talking about the crisis of a civilization. We are talking about the challenges of the people of color. We are talking about the inability of the elite to envision a democratic expansion. We are talking about the rise of the Soviet Union and its attempt to find an alternative to what seems to be a Western crisis in the 1920s. This was a very fascinating moment, but a moment at which it is quite understandable that someone wanted to turn away from history as some arena from which betterment could be procured. Now for me, when I talk about nihilism and cynicism or what have you, especially among the working poor and very poor in the United States, I am talking in fact about the various ways in which commodification and reification completely shattered the institutional buffers for an already devalued, despised and oppressed people, and where therefore the levels of destruction and self-destruction escalate among these people. Levels of destruction and self-destruction that call into question any sense of meaning, struggle and any sense of hope for the future, and especially for any oppressed people in the United States of African descent. The only thing we have really had is some sense of meaning and some sense of hope, and once that is gone, then we are in a living hell, in a Dantesque and most profound hell, and that is actually what we have in some parts of our country.

Corredor: I should like to come back to this a bit later and ask you here about the importance you attach to history. You say that "Rorty's historicist turn was like music to my ears." George Steiner was jestingly criticizing Lukács when he said that Lukács had sold his soul, that he had made a "devil's pact with History" because the devil had promised him the truth. . . . Again, there is in both you and Lukács this strong belief in the function of history. What do you see today as major historical conditioners? You say that you strongly believe in historical "conditionedness" of the human existence. So what is conditioning us negatively today, and what in particular is conditioning the poor? Is it capitalism, the government, the drug lords, the mafia? What do we have today that causes this nihilistic outlook and desperation?

West: Two points. One is that I do not believe in History, capital *H*. I am much closer here to Antonio Gramsci; I believe in histories with a small *h*, and therefore History with a capital *H*, associated with questions of certainty, must go. That's what Steiner means, and that is fine. But histories, with a small *h*, with all the specific ways in which over time and space human practices and social practices, both structured and unstructured, go into shaping and molding who we are, that is for me the terrain we are talking about, either progress or regress, betterment or disempowerment. Now when we look at the historical conditions of the present, again I would say one major factor is what I call, loosely, commodification. What I mean by that is simply the degree to which market forces now hold sway in every sphere of our society and in a crucial kind of way echoing Lukács's notion of reification. What happens to a society when in fact market forces saturate a society.

Corredor: So you think that the drug world is in a way reifying the young people today and making them into a commodity for capitalist exploiters?

West: They become a commodity. It generates gangster mentalities, because of the question of getting over, as they would put it, instead of getting better, and that gangster mentality promotes a war against all. And it is market driven, because it is a matter of buying and selling, in that case drugs or bodies, primarily women's bodies, but it is market driven. Now I do not want to argue that commodification is the sole force at work today. Not at all. We have got political lethargy, in terms of the political electoral system. We have got a competition between nations that impose constraints upon our economy and nation-state to create a public sphere in which there is some vitality rather than squalor. And of course, we have this massive, unprecedented redistribution of wealth from the working people to the well-to-do in the last twenty years. The withdrawal of public provisions has to do with the level of impoverishment, material impoverishment of poor people, which is a very crucial element as well in addition to the cultural consumption. There are a number of forces that act as historical conditioners, but one of the highlights I would still call the force of commodification. Again, Lukács influenced me in this as well.

Corredor: I found very interesting your periodization of history. As you know, Lukács established the periodization of literary genres, for instance, in his *Theory of the Novel.*

West: I liked that about Lukács, even though we know that it could be slightly arbitrary, but we need periodization.

Corredor: You have proposed two of them, which I found interesting, what you call "The Age of Europe," from 1492 to 1945, and then "The American Century," from then on.

West: To 1973, yes.

Corredor: At the same time, I found it interesting that, in speaking of the American century, you also attempted to show the influence of Afro-American culture, for instance, on American music and in general on

American style. I mentioned this to some of my colleagues, who said that
they had never looked at it this way. To Europeans this might be more
obvious because of the clearly non-European characteristics of American
music, dance, etc., particularly in dance, jazz and the blues. But at the
same time, and again, you are very critical of this American century and
the modern period—I know, you told me earlier, that you are not *more*
critical of this century than of previous ones. You also state that the "Age
of Europe" had a negative influence on what is happening right now,
being maybe at the root of it.

West: It does have an ambiguous legacy. The great contribution is the insti-
tutionalizing of the critiques of arbitrary power, of illegitimate forms of
authority, which arc *democratic* institutions, but, of course, there are significant racial, sexual and class constraints on those democratic practices,
and this is very important in this Age of Europe where it had been overlooked. So it is an ambiguous legacy. You've got the white supremacy,
the vicious male supremacy and class exploitation, on the one hand, and
you have the hammering out, on the ground, of democratic practices, on
the other, which are basic for the acceptability of social democracy.

Corredor: You deplore that there is no strong leadership in this world. Isn't
it that in order to be a great leader you have to have a dream or vision?
If you look back in history, great leaders usually had some vision, good
or bad, to offer to the young by which to inspire them. Martin Luther
King had a dream. How do you envisage the future? Do you have a
dream or vision for the twenty-first century? In your writings, you actually seem to refuse to voice such a dream or utopia.

West: Oh yes. I know that is true. But I am not really a dreamer. I have
strong anti-utopian elements, given my link to the skeptical tradition.
What I do have, though, is a deep, deep commitment to moral convictions and that these moral convictions can be linked to amelioration, can
be linked to social betterment, but that amelioration and social betterment are regulated more by moral ideas than a social dream, a dream of
a new society, and so forth. Of course, much of this has to do with my
own peculiar brand of Christianity. In Christianity, you have a strong
anti-utopian element in terms of talking about human history. If any
dreaming is going on at all, it has to do with the coming kingdom. This
coming kingdom is such a radical disruption with the present that it is
difficult to talk about the kingdom within the realm of human history. So
it kind of dangles like some sort of a Kantian regulative ideal.

Corredor: Let us go back to Marx. You speak critically of people who are
"trashing Marxist thought" and of contemporary critics who practice
"faddish ironic skepticism."

West: Yes, yes, and they tend to be the same people oftentimes.

Corredor: Wait, wait, one moment please, since I find that you yourself are sometimes a bit critical of people as well—and I am often sharing your criticism, especially in the case of Derrida and Foucault. In speaking of poststructuralist critics, you say that "they talk about their subtle relations of rhetoric, knowledge, power, yet they remain silent about *concrete ways by which people are empowered to resist.*" With regard to the new historicists, you say that they are "preoccupied with thick descriptions"—I love your terms!—"of the relativity of cultural products while thoroughly distrustful of social explanatory accounts of cultural practice" (p. xxii). Then you also speak of Foucault in relation to power. You say that you can learn from Foucault about power. As I remember reading Foucault, he is usually *critical* of power, he wants to undo it and show how the power of discourse, for instance, has been used to control individuals.

West: He recognizes no escape. His relational conception of power means that we are always inscribed within some matrix of power, and so we can be critical of the various forms that it takes and the manifestations that it has, but he recognizes that we are always already within a certain matrix of power relations. I think he is absolutely right about that.

Corredor: At the same time, reading you, you do not see power only as a negative; you want to empower, give power. Are you, in that sense, different from Foucault?

West: Yes and no. On the one hand, I want to talk explicitly about empowerment. Foucault would say, of course, he wants gay comrades to be empowered, if I may say so. On the other hand, though, I am, like Foucault, skeptical of any concentration of power. This is where my democratic sensibility comes in, because I do believe in fact that a concentration of power does tend to corrupt. I do believe that absolute power corrupts absolutely and hence we need democratic mechanisms for the accountability of power. But the fact that my starting point is among a relatively powerless people, I have got to be able to talk about power in a positive way, not simply in political terms but also in existential terms. We are dealing with African people whose humanity has been radically called into question. Therefore, you have to talk about empowerment in terms of taking one's humanity for granted or affirming one's humanity, or being able to accentuate one's humanity in conditions in which humanity has been so radically called into question.

Corredor: I should like to ask you about "engagement." In reading you, I felt that in some of your views you seem actually closer to Sartre than to Marx. In the *New York Times Magazine* interview that was published a few months ago (September 15, 1992), the interviewer called you a "young hip Black man in an old white Academy." Did this shock you?

West: Yes. One never knows what one's friends would talk about.

Corredor: I am picking this up because both Lukács and Sartre were criticized for being social critics, but also and maybe foremost, intellectuals and privileged people who did not get their hands dirty. Sartre, in particular, in his ivory tower wrote volume after volume about the bourgeois critic Gustave Flaubert while inciting others to engage in revolutionary action. How do *you* show your engagement beyond your teaching here at this beautiful university?

West: Right, right. I think part of it has to do with my being one of the honorary chairpersons of the Democratic Socialists of America, being part of a great legacy, of Norman Thomas and especially Michael Harrington. As honorary chairperson it forces me to be engaged with issues of labor, feminist issues, antihomophobic issues, antiracist issues. It is the leading left organization in the country, maybe the only major one, and its numbers have doubled in the last few years. In addition, of course, there is also my work in black churches, where I am in touch with ordinary black people.

Corredor: Do you talk about God at that church?

West: Oh, yes, very much so. I preach on Sundays, so I do talk about God, about social issues, and there is a long tradition of prophetic speaking in this church, the linking of the question of freedom with rich spirituality. We talk about faith and hope and service, so that I am nothing but an extension of a very long prophetic tradition. That is another reason I have a certain concern for tradition, why T. S. Eliot and others mean much to me, even though the tradition he is talking about is very different from the tradition I am talking about. But the very *concern* with tradition, also in the work of an Edward Shils, for example, means very much to me. I am deeply concerned about the dynamic character of tradition, except that for me the tradition that I am talking about comes from below and sometimes beneath modernity. It is a tradition of struggling and resisting, black people's democratic tradition, whereas the tradition they are talking about tends to be from above. But there is still so much to learn about the heroic tradition in a market society . . . we need more subversive memory. I think subversive memory is one of the most precious heritages that we have.

Corredor: This kind of thinking and feeling maybe dictates the amazing sentences you compose, of which I should like to quote a few. About Marxism, you say that "one of the major ironies of our time is that Marxist thought becomes even more relevant after the collapse of Communism in the Soviet Union and Eastern Europe than it was before." You do see the relevance of Marxism today? You are convinced that Marxist thought is an "indispensable tradition for freedom fighters" (p. xiv)?

West: Oh yes. Very much so. And the reason why that is so is that Marx was fundamentally concerned about the interlocking relation between corporate, financial and political elites who had access to a disproportionate amount of resources, power, prestige and status in society. Certainly, that is a starting point for understanding any society that we know of today, especially the United States. Once we lose sight of the very complex relations between those three sets of elites—corporate, financial-banking and political elites—and the reasons why the working people, the working poor and the very poor, find themselves with very little access to resources—once we lose sight of that, which was analyzed by the Marxist tradition (which was not the only, but the primary tradition that would analyze this), once we lose sight of this, then we have little or no analytical tools in our freedom fight. That is why I think that Marxism today becomes even more important, and this is especially so now that Eastern Europe is going to undergo a kind of "Latin Americanization" in which market forces become even more important. We see that in Latin America, where corporate America circumscribes local capital, and where the state elites go about carving up and digging up those resources among the masses that remain so tragically impoverished. I think we are going to see a certain kind of "Latin Americanization" sweeping across Eastern Europe as the corporate elites and transnational corporations hungrily go searching for markets.

Corredor: You defend Marxism and the relevance of Marxist thought, including "its ethical dimension after the Cold War as an indispensable weapon" in this freedom fight. You stress Marxist ethics. Could you explain what you understand by "Marxist ethics"?

West: Sure. First, I want to make a historical point. Marx is fundamentally a product of Romanticism, one of the great, very complex movements in modern Europe in response to the promise and tragedy of the French Revolution, or as Hazlitt put it, "the glad dawn of the morning star, the springtime of the world." That sense of hope and expectation of social transformation, which so much of Europe felt, was lost of course after the Reign of Terror. The second wave of Romanticism in which the fundamental values consisted of the many-sided development of individuals, the values of a harmonious personality that was able to flower and flourish in its own unique and singular way . . .

Corredor: This is very Lukácsean . . .

West: Oh, yes, and it comes right out of the *Letters on Aesthetic Education* by the great Schiller. Marx was deeply, deeply influenced by this. But secondly, democracy. This is why I spend so much time trying to show that when Marx defines communism as a struggle for democracy, in the *Communist Manifesto,* what he means is in fact that these ordinary people, workers, ought to have some control over the conditions of their existence, especially the conditions of their workplace. This is a profoundly democratic idea. Once you link the values of flourishing individuality, a profoundly Romantic notion, with the expansion of democratic operations and practices, I argue that you are at the ethical core of the Marxist project. As we know, Marxist-Communists, Marxist-Leninists and so forth have subverted, bastardized, violated and undermined such ethical claims. But when we look at Marx himself as a thinker in nineteenth-century Europe, driven deeply by these ethical values, although never wanting to be viewed as a moralist—he is concerned about being scientific—we know that these ethical values are deeply inscribed within his own project, and then it seems to me that we recognize that those values have much to say to us.

Corredor: Some people are opposed to the very idea of ethics, saying that ethics establish something that has to be obeyed or followed. People do not want to be told how to behave.

West: We have to make a distinction between the ethical dimension and ethics per se, because *every* social issue has an ethical dimension. What I mean by this is that there is some value judgment built into every issue, some moral vantage point from which the world is viewed. This is not solely a moral vantage point, but there is a moral dimension to the vantage point from which the world is viewed. Unfortunately, there has been a reluctance and sometimes downright refusal by Marxists to talk about ethics. I think that has been a major problem. They have tended to displace that ethical discourse with a teleological-historical discourse that is completely unconvincing, catechistic and just raw material for managerial elites to come in like Leninists and then command, regiment and repress the masses. So it seems to me that we have to talk about the ethical dimension, but also be critical of an ethics that is imposed from on high. I do agree with that kind of critique that one ought not simply impose from on high. As radical democrats, we engage in discourse in which we acknowledge the ethical dimension of what we do and try to persuade persons, one, that the values we hold are convincing, and two, that the ways in which we go about conceiving of what these values lead to regarding our politics, how society ought to be organized, are possible.

Corredor: Are your own ethics compatible with both Christian and Marxist ethics, or do you find incompatibilities with them?

West: If you believe as I do that Marxism is a particular species of second-wave Romanticism, and if you believe that Romanticism is in many ways a naturalization of much of the Christian narrative about the past and present . . . (sorry, I interrupted you here!)

Corredor: Are you treating it as a religion?

West: Well, there are religious residues. I would not say it is a religion per se, because religion for me does have something to do with God-talk or has something to do with ways of life in which the divine and the sacred are accented, whereas with the naturalization of Christianity and the Romantic movement you do get often the elimination of God-talk and you do get a displacement of the divine and sacred with the imaginative and the creative. So I would not call it a religion in that sense, but there are religious residues.

Corredor: Another approach to Marxism that I found very refreshing in your works was your use of "difference" in naming the areas in which Marxism still would have much to do. This is naturally very different from Derrida's "différance," one of the central terms in his deconstructivism. I found your use refreshing because you are coming back to the literal sense of the word in the real world after twenty years of Derridean playing with the letter *a*. So, would you say that race, gender, sexual orientation, age—all these possible differences—have assumed the place of the proletariat in Marxist theory? When you look at them, all these people, all these groups, are not the masses; they are rather marginal, they are outside, they are minorities, not the masses.

West: That is true. First of all, we have to disabuse ourselves of the notion that there ever was this proletariat as logos. The proletariat itself is a construct that is shot through with all kinds of divisions, cleavages, heterogeneities and so on, so that there is the sense that there never is any centering in a group or in the masses, even though the modes of production do create the possibility for such centering, but the notion of proletariat as center and the others as marginal we have to be suspicious of. On the other hand, certainly, we talk about gender, race and sexual orientation, which have *always* been there; therefore it upsets me when people are talking about movements among these people as *new* movements. They are *new* relative to a Marxist discourse, a working class movement. But, my God, the struggle against patriarchy predates 1789.

Corredor: There have been revolutionary women at the time of the French Revolution, like Olympe de Gouge.

West: Exactly. You take for instance David Walker's *Appeal to Colored Citizens of the World,* which is one of the most powerful critiques ever launched of white supremacy, in 1829! The young Marx is eleven years old. So the struggle has been going on, so they are not really new social movements, but they are significant social movements. I do think that we have to talk about alliance and coalition because none of these movements in and of themselves or by themselves has the power to deal with the rule of capital, that is, the rule of those interlocking elites I was talking about. Oftentimes some versions of these social movements based on race, gender and sexual orientation do not even talk about the role of corporate power, which is as limiting and limited as one can imagine.

Corredor: Are you optimistic enough to believe that this will change eventually?

West: It is open-ended. Well, it is going to be a long process. I think Raymond Williams's "long revolution" is an apt metaphor. But there are many of us who will go down fighting, trying to ensure that linkages are made, so that we can target the role of these elites not in any vulgar or immoral way, but simply acknowledge the degree to which they had this disproportionate amount of power and resources that ought to be shared and distributed within constitutional constraints.

Corredor: You are very laudatory about sophisticated Marxist theory; you say that it is indispensable, but then you also feel that it is inadequate. It is not complete. It is not enough. Where do you see its shortcomings? What else is necessary? Where do you find or get what is necessary?

West: The Marxist tradition has no serious or subtle conception of culture, and by culture I mean the sphere of desire and pleasure, the various quests for identities, e.g., nationalism. Eric Hobsbawm's recent book on nationalism is a good example of this, a good example because it shows some of the insights of Marxism on nationalism. We know that nationalism is primarily about elites carving up territories in order to control markets and control populations. That is true for any kind of bourgeoisie that casts itself on a nationalist mode. We also know about nationalists' desire for association, recognition and protection, which all has to do with desire, with how you bestow meaning upon yourself, with notions of mortality and notions of monumentality that still have a hold on people's imagination. So nationalism must be understood as a psychocultural phenomenon as well as an institutional phenomenon among elites. You see Marxism simply does not speak to the levels of psychocultural politics. You need Freud . . . and you need novels, you need the blues and spirituals, a whole host of other insights.

Corredor: I teach [at the Naval Academy] future officers, future leaders, among them there are some minorities, blacks, women. I was wondering what you would tell them. What would you tell them to read?

West: Well, one, they should read a lot of history. They could begin with Paul Kennedy's book *The Rise and Fall of Great Powers,* so that they would have a sense of where America is now, so that as future leaders they would have a sense of the general sweep of the last seventy-five or a hundred years. Second, they should read histories that help give an account of how they now have opportunities in places where once those opportunities were denied, and what the nature of those struggles was that made them gain access to such privileged spaces in American society, how difficult, protracted and sacrificial those struggles were, and then they should try to situate themselves in relation to that tradition of struggle. But that is a tough one because, you know, there are always "betwixt and betweens" at the Naval Academy and that deep conservatism, deep suspicion of any radical critique both for intellectual as well as personal and career reasons. They have to struggle with that. They've got to wrestle with that.

Corredor: I am teaching a course in French Civilization in which I sometimes speak of contemporary criticism, and I have noticed that in particular my black students are usually very interested in contemporary criticism, even in theories such as Derrida's deconstruction, when I bring in some examples as to how it could be used in social criticism concerning blacks or women in the deconstruction of established discourse. My black students are usually much more interested in this than the average white midshipman, to whom it is not of great urgency. I am thinking of one of my students in particular, to whom I sometimes talk about such theories and who seems to have questions concerning them.

West: Racism is everywhere these days, sexism is everywhere in society, so they experience themselves as *other,* as you can imagine, in some way even degraded at the Naval Academy or Princeton or any other elite place. These are theories that speak to that condition, I would imagine.

Corredor: I think it would be wonderful to have you down there, but I am sure we cannot afford you, I don't know.

West: No, no. I would love to come. I was thinking of North Carolina. But Maryland is not that far. I am going to be preaching in Annapolis this summer.

Corredor: Are you! During the summer midshipmen are not going to be there. You should come during the school year.

West: Well, maybe I'll wait until the fall. We'll work something out.

Corredor: We have a Black Studies Club at the Academy, which you could address. Now, I should like to come back to something I think is characteristic of the methodology you use in your essays on Marxist ethics. You seem to support very strongly the idea of "radical historicism" and be critical, almost in a purist fashion, of those who do not adhere to it, including Engels. In your analyses of Feuerbach, again, it is interesting to note *what* you single out for your discussion and *how* you define radical historicism. You virtually do away with the Marxist utopia. You see radical historicism as a process of which you approve, which you love, if I may say so, and which you embrace. This is, in your view, what historicism should be.

West: Yes, this is a very, very significant point. Actually I do the same thing in my essay on Jameson. I think that is just a built-in bias, and in the end it may be unjustified. That is a built-in bias against utopianism, and yet for so much of any quest for freedom the utopian dimension is crucial. I want to make a distinction between human hope and a utopian quest, because human hope for me is always being able to keep going, to sustain struggle, with ideals, but that is very different from a utopian impulse, where you try to project a whole different and better society that could be realized and actualized. I am suspicious of the latter.

Corredor: You like process, praxis and continuation. I have written down at least ten notions that you reject. Here are a few: rational necessity, universal obligation, philosophical certainty, eternal truth. How can you reconcile this with your prophetic approach?

West: That's right. It is a peculiar, peculiar kind of prophetic view, because my conception of the prophetic is not one in which one speaks from on top, which is continuous with the great and grand Jewish and Christian traditions of the prophetic that I know of, in which "Thus says the Lord" or "Eternal truth speaks from on top." My notion of the prophetic is a democratic one in which, in the midst of the quotidian, the commonplace, in the midst of the messy struggle in which one's hands are dirty, that one is holding on to moral convictions and tries to convince others that they ought to be accepted even though these moral convictions themselves can still be subject to criticism and change in vision and what-have-you.

Corredor: You are really preaching *hope,* I think.

West: That's it. That's right. But it is a hope that is grounded in a particular messy struggle, and it is tarnished by any kind of naive projections of a better future, *so that it is hope on the tightrope* rather than a utopian projection that looks over and beyond the present and oftentimes loses sight of the present.

Corredor: In many ways, you are quite Pascalian. The Pascalian wager is there and also Pascal's *"Essayons donc de bien penser."* This is really what you are preaching.

West: Exactly. You hit the nail on the head, in the sense that my Pascalian sensibility is probably my central sensibility.

Corredor: Again it is a stress on the process, the thinking, the being process. But I think, to come back to Lukács, that you credit Lukács too much for being a process theoretician. For Lukács it is very important that "what there is" today is bad, and he seems to have a definite idea of "what there ought to be." There is in him at least this teleological drive toward what there ought to be. I like your interpretation, because I think you are "updating" Lukács, in this sense you are going beyond his limitations. I have often felt that Lukács's theories were too closed, that he used too many norms, for instance, for "realism." You emphasize the importance of process. Is it a dialectic process?

West: Again, for me the dialectic is understood in a heuristic way rather than an ontological way, and what I mean by that is that it is a dialectic that is posited in order to keep the process going, rather than a dialectic that is somehow inherent in and implanted within the real. And so I want to keep the process going, and I see dialectic as a very crucial means of doing that both practically and theoretically. And, of course, what we mean by dialectic, and this is what I love about Lukács, is his concern with protracted struggle.

Corredor: In trying to identify your values, locating them in your texts, I was amazed by some of your statements that seemed almost metaphysical, for instance, when you speak of "sacrificial love" . . .

West: There is nothing metaphysical about it. It is just almost sublime, you know, because the thing about sacrificial love is that it has no metaphysical foundation for it. It is simply a leap that we make in our short lives that gives it so much meaning and infuses it with so much significance. It is a dangling experience. You take a tremendous risk, you become tremendously vulnerable, but there is no metaphysical ground. No security, nothing guaranteed, no surety whatsoever.

Corredor: There are no truths that you are clinging to. The quest for truth and philosophical certainty are anathema to the kind of radical historicism which you admire. Again, you are maybe Pascalian in the sense that you recognize an end to what humans can do and can understand, and simply subscribe to the process of life and its own limits. You affirm life and have hope and maybe faith in life.

West: Well, in addition to the Pascalian sensibility, I have a deep Chekhovian strain. What is so great about Chekhov? I think he understood this better than others, that we are able to love, care and serve others—and this is so true of his life and his art—but we are able to do that with there being no deep faith in life or human nature or history or what-have-you. And then it does not mean that we are anti-life, it does not mean that we are cynical toward it, it is simply there, and we do these things because, given our tradition that has shaped us, we do in fact feel that it does give life so much meaning and richness and so forth. Now, as a Christian, I do this against the backdrop of certain narratives, the gospel, the synoptic Gospel narratives, but again there is no metaphysical underpinning.

Corredor: In reading such ideas in your text, it made me think of Camus. Camus says that the only thing we can do is give affection, joy, and share in it. I am thinking of *The Plague,* in which the doctor continues to treat his plague-stricken patients in the midst of all hopelessness. This gives his life essence, quality. And it is not metaphysical in Camus either.

West: There are lots of parallels between him and Chekhov. I still think Chekhov had the highest expression of this deep sense of love, and care, and struggle, and service. It is just that for him, it is not against the Christian backdrop as it is for me.

Corredor: I am coming to the end of my questions. In that article in the *New York Times,* they described you as a great "synthesizer," and I see that in you as well. You bring together contradictions, you are a black star at a white academy, you are a believing Christian in a secular society, you are a progressive socialist in the age of capitalism, a cosmopolitan, public intellectual among academic specialists, a radical traditionalist. Do you see yourself in those descriptions? Do you have a calling to bring together seeming contradictions?

West: It certainly is to build on the best of Lukács, which promotes synthetic and synoptic views and visions of the past and present. In fact, one of the things I said before, one of the things I *love* about Lukács is this synecdochical mode of thinking in which you always try to relate parts to a whole, with notions of totality, even for me heuristically posited, that are very important in that they highlight interrelations and dependencies.

Corredor: Is the notion of totality important to your thinking?

West: Oh yes. Very important.

Corredor: How can you reconcile this with your admiration for Deleuze?

West: No, I think Deleuze is wrong about this. I think post-structuralists are wrong about this. I think they are right to trash certain conceptions of totality that elide and elude difference and diversity, heterogeneity and alterity, and so forth. But I think that they have done away with totalities per se. I think we need to posit totalities with all the openness and flexibility that one can muster, but we must posit totalities in order to look at the dynamic relation between parts.

Corredor: I am coming to my final question. In your present prophetic pragmatism, is there a Lukács, and where is he? What is his future there?

West: Of course, politically, there is no Lukács at all in terms of his links to Stalinism. I actually believed that there was a Luxembourgist moment in the early Lukács that has been overlooked, but the general association of Lukács with Stalinism is in fact quite empirically verifiable, and therefore there are no political links for me in this regard. Philosophically and intellectually, there are strong links, because my vantage point from looking at modern society, especially American society, remains the processes of reification and commodification. That is where I begin. So there is always a Lukácsean beginning. Methodologically, I begin with synecdochical ways of looking at the world, the relation of parts to a totality. So again, I believe, that is deeply Lukácsean, even though he has no monopoly on it, because there is the Christian view about relations of parts and whole, and there is the Hegelian one, but I mean Lukács is part of this Hegelian-Marxist sweep in terms of the relationship between the parts and the whole. The Lukácsean moment for me would be on two levels, on the methodological and the philosophical level.

The irony is, here I am, as a black Christian, deeply indebted to the Marxist tradition, to Pascal, Chekhov, the blues, spirituals, the black church and what-have-you, defending certain distinctive elements in Lukács's project and yet, at the same time, recognizing that Marxist theory and Marxist secular sensibility are both indispensable *and* inadequate, something to build on but also something to bring serious critique to bear on. The same values of individuality and democracy that I see in Marx, in Schiller and the democratic tradition, now also filter through the best of the black church, leads me to this radically secular Budapest-born Marxist, even though I come from "the hood." In this sense, the struggle for human freedom is indivisible.

Corredor: I am not surprised that you do not stop at Lukács, that you do not take him as an end in itself, nor anyone or anything else for that matter. That would be contrary to your approach to everything. Continuation and process are natural to you and your quest.

Would you like to add a final note to our discussion?

West: No, not really. I think this is one of the best interviews I have had. What you have actually led me to see in myself I rarely get a chance to think about. I am on the run all the time and do not really get a chance to think about, especially, this Pascalian-Chekhov stuff.

Corredor: Thank you very much. I hope you will come to preach in Annapolis and talk to my students.

Source: "On the Influence of Lukács: Interview by Eva L. Corredor," *Beyond Eurocentrism and Multiculturalism, Vol. 2: Prophetic Reflections* (Monroe, Me.: Common Courage Press, 1993), pp. 47–71.

Fourteen

FREDRIC JAMESON'S AMERICAN MARXISM

Fredric Jameson is the most significant Marxist thinker in American culture. We worked together for many years on Social Text—*the leading left journal in the 1980s. I shall never forget our many afternoons and nights in New York and Connecticut debating Fred C. L. R. James, Ernest Mandel, Antonio Labriola, Antonio Gramsci, Raymond Williams and others. This essay on his work ranges far and wide in the Marxist tradition—from the Frankfurt School to Walter Benjamin's messianic Marxism. This piece, published in 1982, is a pivotal work in my corpus because Jameson's work so deeply informs my conception of contemporary society and culture.*

FREDRIC JAMESON IS THE most challenging American Marxist hermeneutic thinker on the present scene. His ingenious interpretations (prior to accessible translations) of major figures of the Frankfurt School, Russian formalism, French structuralism and poststructuralism as well as of Georg Lukács, Jean-Paul Sartre, Louis Althusser, Max Weber and Louis Marin are significant contributions to the intellectual history of twentieth-century Marxist and European thought. Jameson's treatments of the development of the novel, the surrealist movement, of Continental writers such as Honoré de Balzac, Marcel Proust, Alessandro Manzoni and Alain Robbe-Grillet, and of American writers, including Ernest Hemingway, Kenneth Burke and Ursula Le Guin, constitute powerful political readings. Furthermore, his adamantly antiphilosophical form of Marxist hermeneutics puts forward an American *Aufhebung* of poststructuralism that merits close scrutiny.

In this chapter I shall highlight Jameson's impressive intellectual achievements, specific theoretical flaws, and particular political shortcomings by focusing on the philosophical concerns and ideological aims in his trilogy.[1] Jameson is first and foremost a loyal, though critical, disciple of the Lukács of *History and Class Consciousness,* in the sense that he nearly dogmatically believes that commodification—the selling of human labor power to profit-maximizing capitalists—is the primary source of domination in capitalist societies and that reification—the appearance of this relation between persons and classes as relations between things and prices—is the major historical process against which to understand norms, values, sensibilities, texts and movements in the modern world.[2]

The central question that haunts Jameson is "How can one be a sophisticated Lukácsean Marxist without Lukács's nostalgic historicism and highbrow humanism?" A more general formulation of this question is "How can one take history, class struggle and capitalist dehumanization seriously after the profound poststructuralist deconstructions of solipsistic Cartesianism, transcendental Kantianism, teleological Hegelianism, genetic Marxism and recuperative humanism?" In Anglo-American commonsense lingo, this query becomes "How can one live and act in the face of the impotence of irony and the paralysis of skepticism?" The pressing problem that plagues Jameson is whether the Marxist quest for totalization—with its concomitant notions of totality, mediation, narrative (or even universal) history, part/whole relations, essence/appearance distinctions and subject/object oppositions—presupposes a form of philosophical idealism that inevitably results in a mystification that ignores difference, flux, dissemination and heterogeneity. Jameson's work can be read as a gallant attempt at such a quest, which hopes to avoid idealist presuppositions and preclude mystifying results.

Jameson initiates this quest by examining the major European Marxist thinker for whom this problematic looms large: Jean-Paul Sartre.[3] Yet Jameson's project takes shape in the encounter with the rich German tradition of Marxist dialectical thought best exemplified in the works of Adorno, Benjamin, Marcuse, Bloch and, of course, Lukács. His dialectical perspective first tries to reveal the philosophical and political bankruptcy of modern Anglo-American thought. In the preface to *Marxism and Form* he writes:

> Less obvious, perhaps, is the degree to which anyone presenting German and French dialectical literature is forced—either implicitly or explicitly—to take yet a third national tradition into account, I mean our own: that mixture of political liberalism, empiricism, and logical positivism which we know as Anglo-American philosophy and which is hostile at all points to the type of thinking outlined here. One cannot write for a reader formed in this tradition—one cannot even come to terms with one's own historical formation—without taking this influential conceptual opponent into account; and it is this, if you like, which makes up the tendentious part of my book, which gives it its political and philosophical cutting edge, so to speak. (*MF*, p. x)

Jameson's battle against modern Anglo-American thought is aided by poststructuralism in that deconstructions disclose the *philosophical* bankruptcy of this bourgeois humanist tradition. Yet such deconstructions say little about the *political* bankruptcy of this tradition; further, and more seriously, deconstructions conceal the political impotency of their own projects. In short, Jameson rightly considers poststructuralism an ally against bourgeois humanism, yet ultimately an intellectual foe and political enemy. His tempered appreciation and subsequent rejection of structuralism and poststructuralism are enacted in his superb critical treatment of their roots and development in *The Prison-House of Language*. For example, he writes in the preface of this text:

> My own plan—to offer an introductory survey of these movements which might stand at the same time as a critique of their basic methodology—is no doubt open to attack from both partisans and adversaries alike. . . . The present critique does not, however, aim at judgments of detail, nor at the expression of some opinion, either positive or negative, on the works in question here. It proposes rather to lay bare what Collingwood would have called the "absolute presuppositions" of Formalism and Structuralism taken as intellectual totalities. These absolute pre-suppositions may then speak, for themselves, and, like all such ultimate premises or models, are too fundamental to be either accepted or rejected. (*PHL*, p. x)

Jameson's first lengthy treatment of the Marxist dialectical tradition focuses on the most intelligent thinker and adroit stylist of that tradition: Theodor Adorno.[4] Adorno presents Jameson with his most formidable challenge, for Adorno's deli-cate dialectical acrobatics embark on the quest for totalization while simultane-ously calling such a quest into question; they reconstruct the part in light of the whole while deconstructing the notion of a whole; they devise a complex con-ception of mediation while disclosing the idea of totality as illusion; and they ulti-mately promote dialectical development while surrendering to bleak pessimism about ever attaining a desirable telos. In short, Adorno is a negative hermeneuti-cal thinker, a dialectical deconstructionist par excellence: the skeleton that forever hangs in Jameson's closet.

In this way, Adorno is the most ingenious and dangerous figure for Jameson. Adorno ingeniously makes and maintains contact with the concrete in a dialecti-cal demystifying movement that begins with the art object and engages the psy-chological, which moves from the psychological and implicates the social, and then finds the economic in the social. Yet he refuses to ossify the object of inquiry or freeze the concepts he employs to interrogate the object. This intellectual en-ergy and ability is characterized by Jameson in the following way:

> It is to this ultimate squaring of the circle that Adorno came in his two last and most systematic, most technically philosophical works, *Negative Dialectics* and *Aes-thetic Theory*. Indeed, as the title of the former suggests, these works are designed to offer a theory of the untheorizable, to show why dialectical thinking is at one and the same time both indispensable and impossible, to keep the idea of system itself alive while intransigently dispelling the pretensions of any of the contingent and al-ready realized systems to validity and even to existence. . . . Thus a negative di-alectic has no choice but to affirm the notion and value of an ultimate synthesis,

while negating its possibility and reality in every concrete case that comes before it. . . . Negative dialectics does not result in an empty formalism, but rather in a thoroughgoing critique of forms, in a painstaking and well-nigh permanent destruction of every possible hypostasis of the various moments of thinking itself. (*MF*, pp. 54–55, 56)

Adorno is dangerous for Jameson because his deconstructionist strategies and political impotence resemble the very poststructuralism with which Jameson wrestles. Jameson never adequately settles this deep tension with Adorno. In his later work, he circumvents this tension by reducing Adorno's negative dialectics to an aesthetic ideal, and this reduction minimizes Adorno's philosophical challenge to Jameson's own antiphilosophical hermeneutics. Jameson tries to disarm Adorno's position by construing it as a perspective that reconfirms that status of the concept of totality by reacting to and deconstructing "totality."[5] In Jameson's view, the antitotalizing deconstructionist strategies of Jacques Derrida and Paul de Man also "confirm" the status of the concept of totality, since such strategies "must be accompanied by some initial appearance of continuity, some ideology of unification already in place, which it is their mission to rebuke and to shatter" (*PU*, p. 53). Jameson seems to be employing a rather slippery notion of how the idea of totality is confirmed, since powerful projects that "rebuke" and "shatter" this idea appear to "confirm" it. On this crucial point, Jameson presents neither a persuasive argument against deconstructionists nor a convincing case for his own position, but rather a defensive recuperative strategy that co-opts the deconstructionists in a quest for totality unbeknownst and unrecognizable to them. This ad hoc strategy reflects Jameson's unsettled tension with Adorno and his reluctance to come to terms with Paul de Man's rigorous version of deconstruction.[6]

Yet what is missing in Adorno, Jameson finds in Benjamin, Marcuse and Bloch: a theoretical mechanism that sustains hope and generates praxis in the present moment of the historical process. Such hope and praxis are promoted by a *politicized notion of desire* that is sustained by a "nostalgia conscious of itself, a lucid and remorseless dissatisfaction with the present on the grounds of some remembered plenitude" (*MF*, p. 82). For example, Jameson is attracted to Benjamin primarily because Benjamin's conception of nostalgic utopianism as a revolutionary stimulus in the present delivers Jameson from the wretched pessimism of Adorno.

For Jameson, Benjamin's notion of nostalgic utopianism—best elucidated in his masterful essay on Nikolai Leskov, "The Storyteller"—unfolds as storytelling that does justice to our experience of the past, as nonnovelistic (hence, nonindividualistic) narrative that makes contact with the concrete, with an authentic form of social and historical existence quickly vanishing owing to the reification process in late monopoly capitalism. Following Benjamin, Jameson holds that reification destroys the conditions for storytelling, for meaningful destinies and common plots that encompass the past, present and future of the human community. Therefore one-dimensional societies do not simply domesticate their opposition; they also deprive such opposition of the very means to stay in touch with any revolutionary past or visionary future. Such societies present no stories, but rather "only a series of experiences of equal weight whose order is indiscriminately reversible" (*MF*, p. 79).

Jameson conceives the politicized notion of desire—found first in Friedrich Schiller and then more fully in Herbert Marcuse—as the transformative élan repressed and submerged by the reification process in late monopoly capitalism. This conception of desire constitutes the central component of Jameson's notion of freedom, a notion that he argues can never be conceptually grasped but rather symptomatically displayed in the dissatisfaction of the present, in a Faustian Refusal of the Instant or in a Blochian ontological astonishment that renders us aware of the "not-yet" latent in the present. To put it crudely, Jameson's politicized notion of desire promises access to a revolutionary energy lurking beneath the social veil of appearances, an energy capable of negating the reified present order.

This notion of freedom—or negational activity motivated by the desire for freedom—serves as the "center" that Jameson's Marxist hermeneutics dialectically discloses and decenters. This is what makes his viewpoint *political* and *hermeneutical* as opposed to *idealistic* and *philosophical*. For example, he states:

> For hermeneutics, traditionally a technique whereby religions recuperated the texts and spiritual activities of cultures resistant to them, is also a political discipline, and provides the means for maintaining contact with the very sources of revolutionary energy during a stagnant time, or preserving the concept of freedom itself, underground, during geological ages of repression. Indeed, it is the concept of freedom which . . . proves to be the privileged instrument of a political hermeneutic, and which, in turn, is perhaps itself best understood as an interpretive device rather than a philosophical essence or idea.[7] (*MF*, p. 84)

Jameson's totalizing impulse is seen quite clearly in his claim that this political hermeneutic approach is the "absolute horizon of all reading and all interpretation" (*PU*, p. 17). This approach preserves, negates and transcends all prevailing modes of reading and interpreting texts, whether psychoanalytic, myth-critical, stylistic, ethical, structural or poststructural. Jameson unequivocally states:

> One of the essential themes of this book will be the contention that Marxism subsumes other interpretive modes or systems; or, to put it in methodological terms, that the limits of the latter can always be overcome, and their more positive findings retained, by a radical historicizing of their mental operations, such that not only the content of the analysis, but the very method itself, along with

the analyst, then comes to be reckoned into the "text" or phenomenon to be explained. (*PU,* p. 47)

This totalizing impulse can be best understood in the crucial links Jameson makes among the notions of desire, freedom and narrative. In a fascinating and important discussion of André Breton's *Manifesto,* Jameson writes:

It is not too much to say that for Surrealism a genuine plot, a genuine narrative, is that which can stand as the very *figure* of Desire itself: and this not only because in the Freudian sense pure physiological desire is inaccessible as such to consciousness, but also because in the socioeconomic context, genuine desire risks being dissolved and lost in the vast network of pseudosatisfactions which makes up the market system. In that sense desire is the form taken by freedom in the new commercial environment, by a freedom we do not even realize we have lost unless we think of it in terms, not only of the stilling, but also of the awakening, of Desire in general. (*MF,* pp. 100–101)

In Jameson's sophisticated version of Lukácsean Marxism, narrative is the means by which the totality is glimpsed, thereby preserving the possibility of dialectical thinking. This glimpse of totality—disclosed in a complex and coherent story about conflicting classes and clashing modes of production—constitutes the "very figure of Desire" in the present, a desire that both enables and enacts the negation of the present. Jameson understands this notion, unlike the function of the notion of desire in poststructuralism, to result in a will to freedom, not in a will to presence. In fact, Jameson's conception of the function of desire is much closer to the Christian view of a will to salvation than the deconstructionist "will to presence"; that is, Jameson's perspective more closely resembles a transcendental system that regulates human action than a rhetorical system that circumscribes epistemological moves.

Jameson's American Marxist *Aufhebung* of poststructuralism posits the major terrain—the primal scene—of contemporary criticism not as epistemology, but as ethics. Instead of focusing on the numerous Sisyphean attempts to construct a metaphysics of presence, he highlights the various efforts to negate the present and shows how such negations point toward a society of freedom. For example, Jacques Derrida, the preeminent deconstructionist, brilliantly unmasks the binary oppositions in traditional and contemporary Western thought, such as speech and writing, presence and absence and so forth. Yet Derrida remains oblivious to similar binary oppositions in ethics, such as good and evil.

To move from Derrida to Nietzsche is to glimpse the possibility of a rather different interpretation of the binary opposition, according to which its positive and negative terms are ultimately assimilated by the mind as a distinction between good and evil. Not metaphysics but ethics is the informing ideology of the binary opposition: and we have forgotten the thrust of Nietzsche's thought and lost everything scandalous and virulent about it if we cannot understand how it is ethics itself which is the ideological vehicle and the legitimation of concrete structures of power and domination. (*PU*, p. 114)

Jameson's attempt to shift the fierce epistemological and metaphysical battles in contemporary Continental philosophy and criticism to ethics is invigorating and impressive. This shift is prompted by his de-Platonizing of the poststructuralist notion of desire—which freely floats above history like a Platonic form only to be embodied in various versions of metaphysics of presence—and his placing it in the underground of history that emerges in the form of a negation of the present, as an "ontological patience in which the constraining situation itself is for the first time perceived in the very moment in which it is refused" (*MF*, pp. 84–85). Of course, Jameson recognizes that this shift replaces one metaphysical and mythical version of desire with his own. Yet, in his view, his politicized notion of desire has crucial historical consequences and therefore it is more acceptable than the poststructuralist conception of desire.

Yet, it will be observed, even if the theory of desire is a metaphysic and a myth, it is one whose great narrative events—repression and revolt—ought to be congenial to a Marxist perspective, one whose ultimate Utopian vision of the liberation of desire and of libidinal transfiguration was an essential feature of the great mass revolts of the 1960s in Eastern and Western Europe as well as in China and the United States. (*PU*, p. 67)

Jameson's project of politicizing the notion of desire is rooted in Schiller's *Letters on the Aesthetic Education of Mankind*, which sidesteps the Kantian epistemological question of the necessary conditions for the possibility of experience, and instead raises the more political question of the speculative and hypothetical (or utopian) conditions for the possibility of a free and harmonious personality. In attempting to answer this question, Schiller presents analogies between the psyche and society, between the mental divisions of impulses (*Stofftrieb, Formtrieb* and *Spieltrieb*) and the social divisions of labor (Work, Reason and Art). In the same vein, Jameson's reading of Marcuse's *Eros and Civilization* sees Marcuse as replacing Freud's inquiry into the structure of actual mental phenomena with an inquiry into the speculative and hypothetical conditions for the possibility of an aggression-free society in which work is libidinally satisfying. As in Benjamin's nostalgic utopianism, the primary function of memory is to serve the pleasure principle; the origin of utopian thought resides in the remembered plenitude of psychic gratification. Jameson quotes Marcuse's famous formulation of the origins of thought. "The memory of gratification is at the origin of all thinking, and the impulse to recapture past gratification is the hidden driving power behind the process of thought."[8] Jameson then adds:

> The primary energy of revolutionary activity derived from this memory of a prehistoric happiness which the individual can regain only through its externalization, through its reestablishment for society as a whole. The loss or repression of the very sense of such concepts as freedom and desire takes, therefore, the form of a kind of amnesia or forgetful numbness, which the hermeneutic activity, the stimulation of memory as the negation of the here and now, as the projection of Utopia, has as its function to dispel, restoring to us the original clarity and force of our own most vital drives and wishes. (*MF*, pp. 113–114)

It should be apparent that Jameson is, in many ways, a traditional hermeneutical thinker; that is, his basic theoretical strategy is that of recuperation, restoration and recovery.[9] Furthermore, his fundamental aim is to preserve the old Christian notion—and Marxist affirmation—that history is meaningful:

> Only Marxism can give us an adequate account of the essential *mystery* of the cultural past, which, like Tiresias drinking blood, is momentarily returned to life and warmth and allowed once more to speak, and to deliver its long-forgotten message in surroundings utterly alien to it. This mystery can be reenacted only if the human adventure is one. . . . These matters can recover their original urgency for us only if they are retold within the unity of a single great collective story; only if, in however disguised and symbolic form, they are seen as sharing a single fundamental theme—for Marxism, the collective struggle to wrest a realm of Freedom from a realm of Necessity; only if they are grasped as vital episodes in a single vast unfinished plot. (*PU*, pp. 19–20)[10]

Jameson recognizes the deep affinity of his Marxist project with religious *Weltanschauungen*. And since he is not afflicted with the petty, antireligious phobia of scientistic Marxists, Jameson develops his affinity by juxtaposing the medieval Christian allegorical method and Northrop Frye's interpretive system with his own project.[11] In fact, the system of four levels—the literal, allegorical, moral and anagogical levels—of medieval Christian allegorical interpretation constitutes a crucial component of his theoretical framework. This model provides him a means by which to come to terms with the persistent problem for Marxism: the problem of mediation, the task of specifying the relationship between various levels and of adapting analyses from one level to another in light of a meaningful story of the past, present and future of the human community.

The first (or literal) level permits Jameson to retain the historical referents of events and happenings—such as human suffering, domination and struggle—and the textual referents of books and works—such as conflict-ridden historical situations, class-ridden social conditions and antinomy-ridden ideological configurations. In this way, Jameson accepts the antirealist arguments of poststructuralists, yet rejects their textual idealism.[12] He acknowledges that history is always already mediated by language, texts and interpretations, yet he insists that history is still, in some fundamental sense, "there." He conceives of history as an "absent cause" known by its "formal effects." In the crucial paragraph that directly replies to textual idealists and completes his theoretical chapter in *The Political Unconscious* he writes:

> History is therefore the experience of Necessity, and it is this alone which can forestall its thematization or reification as a mere object of representation or as one master code among many others. Necessity is not in that sense a type of content, but rather the inexorable *form* of events; it is therefore a narrative category in the enlarged sense of some properly narrative political unconscious which has been argued here, a retextualization of History which does not propose the latter as some new representation or "vision," some new content, but as the formal effects of what Althusser, following Spinoza, calls an "absent cause." Conceived in this sense, History is what hurts, it is what refuses desire and sets inexorable limits to individual as well as collective praxis, which its "ruses" turn into grisly and ironic reversals of their overt intention. But this History can be apprehended only through its effects, and never directly as some reified force. This is indeed the ultimate sense in which History as ground and untranscendable horizon needs no particular theoretical justification: we may be sure that its alienating necessities will not forget us, however much we might prefer to ignore them. (*PU*, p. 102)

The second (or allegorical) level sets forth the interpretive code, which is for Jameson the mediatory code of the reification process in capitalist societies.[13] This mediatory code takes the form of a genealogical construction characterized by neither genetic continuity nor teleological linearity, but rather by what Bloch called *Ungleichzeitigkeit*, or "nonsynchronous development." This conception of history and texts as a "synchronic unity of structurally contradictory or heterogeneous elements, genetic patterns, and discourses" allows Jameson to identify and isolate particular aspects of the past as preconditions for the elaboration of reifying elements in the present.[14]

The third (or moral) level constitutes an ethical or psychological reading in which, following Althusser's conception of ideology, representational structures permit individual subjects to conceive their lived relationships to transindividual realities such as the destiny of humankind or the social structure. The fourth (or anagogical) level–which is inseparable from the third level–provides a political reading for the collective meaning of history, a characterization of the transindividual realities that link the individual to a fate, plot and story of a community, class, group or society.

Jameson's appropriation of the medieval system leads him to redefine the activity of interpretation in allegorical terms; that is, his own political allegorical machinery, with its aims of ideological unmasking and utopian projection, dictates the way in which interpretation and criticism ought to proceed.

> We will assume that a criticism which asks the question "What does it mean?" constitutes something like an allegorical operation in which a text is systematically *rewritten* in terms of some fundamental master code or "ultimately determining instance." On this view, then, all "interpretation" in the narrower sense demands the forcible or imperceptible transformation of a given text into an allegory of its particular master code or "transcendental signified": the discredit into which interpretation has fallen is thus at one with the disrepute visited on allegory itself.
>
> Yet to see interpretation this way is to acquire the instruments by which we can force a given interpretive practice to stand and yield up its name, to blurt out its master code and thereby reveal its metaphysical and ideological underpinnings. (*PU,* p. 58)

Jameson's redefinition of the allegorical model also draws him closer to Northrop Frye. In *Marxism and Form,* Jameson invokes, in a respectful yet somewhat pejorative manner, Frye's interpretive system as "the only philosophically coherent alternative" to Marxist hermeneutics.[15] In a later essay, "Criticism in History," Jameson harshly criticizes Frye's system as ahistorical and guilty of presupposing an unacceptable notion of unbroken continuity between the narrative forms of "primitive" societies and those of modern times.[16] Yet in *The Political Unconscious,* there is some change of heart:

> In the present context, however, Frye's work comes before us as a virtual contemporary reinvention of the four-fold hermeneutic associated with the theological tradition. . . .
>
> The greatness of Frye, and the radical difference between his work and that of the great bulk of garden-variety myth criticism, lies in his willingness to raise the issue of community and to draw basic, essentially social, interpretive consequences from the nature of religion as collective representation. (*PU,* p. 69)

In fact, Jameson's central concept of the political unconscious–though often defined in Lévi-Straussian language as a historical *pensée sauvage* and influenced by the Feuerbachian and Durkheimian conceptions of religion–derives from Frye's notion of literature (be it a weaker form of myth or a later stage of ritual) as a "symbolic meditation on the destiny of community."[17] What upsets Jameson about Frye is no longer simply Frye's ahistorical approach, but, more important, Frye's Blakean anagogy–the image of the cosmic body–which Jameson claims privatizes a political anagogy and hence poses the destiny of the human community in an individualistic manner, in terms of the isolated body and personal gratification.[18]

Frye's conflation of ethics and politics gives Jameson the opportunity both to congratulate and to criticize him. Jameson congratulates Frye–the North American liberal version of structuralism–because Frye conceives the central problematic of criticism to be not epistemological, but rather ethical, namely, the relation of texts to the destiny of human communities. In this sense, Frye is preferable to the French structuralists and poststructuralists, since he understands that there is a crucial relationship among desire, freedom and narrative.

Jameson criticizes Frye because Frye understands this relationship too idealistically and individualistically. In this sense, Frye stands halfway between the *Platonized* notion of desire employed by those who deconstruct the metaphysics of presence and the *politicized* notion of desire promoted by Jameson's Marxist hermeneutics. Frye's *moralized* notion of desire dictated by his "anatomy of romance" (to use Geoffrey Hartman's phrase) constitutes a halfway house.[19] As Jameson notes: "Frye's entire discussion of romance turns on a presupposition– the ethical axis of good and evil–which needs to be historically problematized in its turn, and which will prove to be an ideologeme that articulates a social and historical contradiction" (*PU,* p. 110).

By contrast, the principal attraction of Jameson to the project of Gilles Deleuze and Félix Guattari in *Anti-Oedipus* is precisely their *politicized* notion of desire, which does not simply relegate it to the subjective and psychological spheres. Jameson acknowledges that the "thrust of the argument of the *Anti-Oedipus* is, to be sure, very much in the spirit of the present work, for the concern of its authors is to reassert the specificity of the political content of everyday life and of individual fantasy-experience" (*PU,* p. 22). But Jameson objects to their Nietzschean perspectivist attack on hermeneutic or interpretive activity, and hence their antitotalizing orientation and micropolitical conclusions.

The major problem with Jameson's innovative Marxist hermeneutics is that, like Frye's monumental liberal reconstruction of criticism or M. H. Abrams's magisterial bourgeois reading of romanticism, his viewpoint rests on an unexamined metaphor of translation, an uncritical acceptance of transcoding. In this sense, Geoffrey Hartman's incisive criticisms of Frye and J. Hillis Miller's notorious attack on Abrams render Jameson's project suspect.[20] In an interesting manner, the gallant attempts of Frye to resurrect the romance tradition and the

Blakean sense of history, of Abrams to recuperate the humanist tradition and the bourgeois conception of history, and of Jameson to recover the Marxist tradition and the political meaning of history, all ultimately revert to and rely on problematic methodological uses of various notions of analogy and homology.[21]

For example, Jameson presupposes homologous relations between ethics and epistemology. This presupposition permits him to distinguish himself from Frye by articulating the differences between moralizing and politicizing the notion of desire. As I noted earlier, Jameson ingeniously shifts the primal scene of criticism from epistemology to ethics. Yet his attempt to historicize the moralistic elements of Frye encourages him to follow the Nietzschean strategies of the poststructuralists in the realm of ethics. Therefore he arrives at the notion that he must go beyond the binary opposition of good and evil in order to overcome ethics and approach the sphere of politics. This notion leads him to the idea that such overcoming of ethics is requisite for a "positive" hermeneutics and a nonfunctional or anticipatory view of culture.

Three principal mistakes support Jameson's presupposition that analogous and homologous relations obtain between ethics and epistemology. First, he believes that the epistemological decentering of the bourgeois subject can be smoothly translated into the moral sphere as an attack on individualistic ethics of bourgeois subjects. This plausible case of analogy seems to warrant, in his view, more general considerations about the homologous relation between ethics and epistemology. Second, he assumes that the poststructuralist attacks on epistemological and metaphysical binary oppositions can be simply transcoded en bloc to ethical binary oppositions. This assumption rests on the notion that these attacks are merely "misplaced,"[22] rather than misguided. Third, Jameson misreads three important moments in modern philosophy, namely, Nietzsche's ill-fated attempt to go beyond good and evil, Hegel's critique of Kantian morality and Marx's rejection of bourgeois ethics.

There is a fundamental link between the epistemological decentering of the subject and an attack on the individualistic ethics of bourgeois subjects, for the arguments by Spinoza and Hegel against individualistic ethics were accompanied by epistemological hostility to the isolated subject. And as Jameson rightly argues, the distinctive Marxist contribution to the current discourse, which takes "decentering" as its center, is to show that both the subject decentered and the decentering itself are modes of ideological activity that are always already bound to particular groups, communities and classes at specific stages of capitalist development.

In my view, Jameson goes wrong in trying to relate epistemological moves to ethical ones in ideological terms without giving an account of the collective dynamics that accompany these moves. From the Marxist perspective, all metaphysical, epistemological and ethical discourses are complex ideological affairs of specific groups, communities and classes in or across particular societies. These discourses must not be understood in their own terms (which Jameson rightly rejects), nor may one discourse become primary and consequently subordinate other discursive nets (which Jameson often insinuates). Rather, the Marxist aim is to disclose the ideological function and class interest of these evolving discourses in terms of the collective dynamics of the pertinent moment in the historical process. Jameson moves two steps forward by eschewing the metaphysical and epistemological terrains of the poststructuralists; his strategy discredits rather than defeats them, which is appropriate since poststructuralist defeatism is impossible to defeat on its own grounds. Yet Jameson moves a step backward by shifting the battleground to ethics. This shift, as I shall show later, prevents him from employing the Marxist logic of collective dynamics and leads him to call for a "new logic of collective dynamics" (*PU*, p. 294).

Jameson's second mistake is to believe that the poststructuralist attacks on binary oppositions are enacted in the wrong terrains, rather than being wrong attacks. Instead of calling into question the very theoretical attitude or unmasking the ideological activity of "going beyond" binary oppositions, Jameson appropriates the same machinery and directs it to ethical binary oppositions. In this way, his project is akin to poststructuralist ones in the bad sense—or akin to idealist projects in the Marxist sense. Jameson mistakenly does not object to deconstructionist strategies, but rather to where they have been applied. In short, his critique does not go deep enough; that is, he does not disclose *the very form of the strategies themselves as modes of ideological activity* that both conceal power relations and extend mechanisms of control by reproducing the ideological conditions for the reproduction of capitalist social arrangements.

Jameson's third mistake is a threefold misreading: of Nietzsche's attempt to go beyond good and evil, of Hegel's critique of Kantian morality and of Marx's rejection of bourgeois ethics. For Jameson, Nietzsche's attempt to go beyond good and evil is the ethical analogue to the poststructuralist attempt to go beyond the binary oppositions in metaphysics and epistemology. But surely this is not so. Nietzsche's attempt to go beyond good and evil is, as the subtitle of his text states, *"Vorspiel einer Philosophie der Zukunft"* (Prelude to a Philosophy of the Future). Nietzsche hardly rests with the aporias of deconstructionists, but rather aligns himself with the genealogical concerns of the "historically minded" in order to get his own positive project off the ground. His profound transvaluation of values is not enacted in order to transcend the moral categories of good and evil, but rather to unmask them, disclose what they conceal, and build on what underlies such categories. And for Nietzsche, the "reality" that lies beneath these categories is the will to power. *Ressentiment* is one particular expression of the will to power of the weak and oppressed toward the strong and the oppressors within traditional Judeo-Christian culture and, to a certain extent, modern bourgeois European culture.[23] Unlike the deconstructionists, Nietzsche aims to debunk and demystify in order to build anew—and the springboard for his "countermovement," his "new gospel of the future," is the will to power.

> Suppose, finally, we succeeded in explaining our entire instinctive life as the development and ramification of *one* basic form of the will—namely, of the will to power, as *my* proposition has it; suppose all organic functions could be traced back to this will to power and one could also find in it the solution of the problem of procreation and nourishment—it is *one* problem—then one would have gained the right to determine *all* efficient force univocally as—*will to power*. The world viewed from inside, the world defined and determined according to its "intelligible character"—it would be "will to power" and nothing else.[24]

Jameson's emulation of poststructuralist strategies in the realm of ethics leads him to root Nietzsche's project in the isolated subject of bourgeois epistemology and to offer the doctrine of eternal recurrence as the Nietzschean solution to the problem of good and evil. He writes:

> Briefly, we can suggest that, as Nietzsche taught us, the judgmental habit of ethical thinking, of ranging everything in the antagonistic categories of good and evil (or their binary equivalents), is not merely an error but is objectively rooted in the inevitable and inescapable centeredness of every individual consciousness or individual subject: what is good is what belongs to me, what is bad is what belongs to the Other. . . . The Nietzschean solution to this constitutional ethical habit of the individual subject—the Eternal Return—is for most of us both intolerable in its rigor and unconvincingly ingenious in the prestidigitation with which it desperately squares its circle. (*PU,* p. 234)

It is necessary to note four points against Jameson, however. First, like Marx, Nietzsche realizes that all ethical discourse is a communal affair; ethics is a group response to particular historical circumstances. Therefore, bourgeois ethics (tied to the individual subject) is but one communal response among others and certainly not identical or even similar to expressions of traditional Christian morality.[25] Second, Nietzsche's doctrine of eternal recurrence grounds his affirmative attitude toward life (an alternative to that of Christianity, in his view); it is itself an expression of his will to power, but not a "solution" to the binary opposition of good and evil. Third, Nietzsche acknowledges that his "going beyond" good and evil does not result in transcending morality, but rather in establishing a new morality that rests upon precisely that which former moralities concealed and precluded: a will to power that generates a creative, self-transforming, life-enhancing morality. Fourth, Nietzsche, again like Marx, holds that "going beyond" good and evil is not a philosophical or even hermeneutical issue, but rather a genealogical matter linked to a historical "countermovement" that contains a vision of the future. Going beyond good and evil will not result in finding new categories untainted by the double bind, but rather new distinctions of good and evil tied to building new communities or, for Nietzsche, building new "selves."

This building of new communities leads us directly to Jameson's misunderstanding of Hegel's critique of Kantian morality and Marx's rejection of bourgeois ethics. Jameson rightly notes that

> one of the great themes of dialectical philosophy, the Hegelian denunciation of the ethical imperative, [is] taken up again by Lukács in his *Theory of the Novel*. On this diagnosis, the *Sollen,* the mesmerization of duty and ethical obligation, necessarily perpetuates a cult of failure and a fetishization of pure, unrealized intention. For moral obligation presupposes a gap between being and duty, and cannot be satisfied with the accomplishment of a single duty and the latter's consequent transformation into being. In order to retain its own characteristic satisfactions, ethics must constantly propose the unrealizable and the unattainable to itself. (*PU,* p. 194)

But Jameson then problematically adds that dialectical philosophy addresses itself to the matter of "going beyond" good and evil and, in contrast to Nietzsche, "proposes a rather different stance (this time, outside the subject in the transindividual, or in other words in History) from which to transcend the double bind of the merely ethical" (*PU,* p. 235).

The problem here is that Jameson reads Hegel through poststructuralist lenses in which "the double bind of the merely ethical" is a philosophical problem that demands categorical transcendence, rather than through Marxist lenses in which "the double bind of the merely ethical" is an ideological activity to unmask and transform by collective praxis. This Marxist reading of Hegel is necessary in order to grasp the depths of Marx's rejection of bourgeois ethics. Hegel's disenchantment with Kant's morality was not simply because he believed that the categorical imperative was empty or that the moral ought was unattainable. But rather, more important, Hegel was disenchanted because the way in which Kant separates the real from the ideal requires a philosophical projection of an impossible ideal that both presupposed and concealed a particular social basis, namely, Kant's own specific time and place.[26] In other words, Hegel saw Kant's morality as a *Moralität*–a first-personal matter–that was derivative from a *Sittlichkeit*–a communal matter.

The Hegelian critique of Kantian morality opens the door to a Marxist viewpoint on ethics in two respects. First, it rejects the Kantian conception of what a theory about the nature of ethics must be. Second, it imposes severe limits on the role and function of ethical discourse (which is not reducible to moral con-victions) in social change. As David Hoy rightly points out, "in giving up the Kantian metaphilosophical view about what theories of morality can and should do, Hegel is giving up the dream of ideal resolutions of moral conflicts. Conflicts are matters of weighing obligations, and moral obligations have no au-tomatic priority."[27]

On this view, Marx's rejection of bourgeois ethics bears little resemblance to poststructuralist attempts to go beyond good and evil. Rather, Marx's rejection is based on giving up the Kantian dream of ideal resolutions of moral conflicts, giv-ing up the Hegelian dream of philosophical reconciliation of the real and the ideal and surrendering the poststructuralist dream of philosophical transcendence of metaphysical, epistemological and ethical double binds.[28] The Marxist concern is with practically overcoming historical class conflicts. Therefore, the Marxist rejec-tion of bourgeois ethics has less to do with attacks on binary oppositions such as good and evil and more to do with the Hegelian subordination of *Moralität* to *Sit-tlichkeit*. The Marxist aim is to discern an evolving and developing *Sittlichkeit* in the womb of capitalist society, a *Sittlichkeit* whose negative ideal is to resist all forms of reification and exploitation and whose positive ideals are social freedom and class equality.

The Marxist lesson here is that only if one has taken metaphysics, epistemol-ogy and ethics seriously, will one be attracted by Heideggerian rhetoric about going beyond metaphysics or Nietzschean rhetoric about going beyond good and evil. If one, instead, takes history seriously—as do Marx after 1844 and American pragmatism at its best—then metaphysics, epistemology and ethics are not formi-dable foes against which to fight, nor are the Ali-like shuffles of the deconstruc-tions that "destroy" them impressive performances. On this view, deconstruction-ists become critically ingenious yet politically deluded ideologues who rightly attack bourgeois humanism, yet who also become the ideological adornments of late monopoly-capitalist academies.

Analogies and homologies, no matter how sophisticated and refined, between epistemology and ethics, metaphysics and morals, make sense as long as one clings to the notion that there are two such interrelated yet distinct spheres, disci-plines or discourses. One rejects this notion neither by enabling interdisciplinary moves nor by questing "beyond" both spheres, but rather by viewing the histori-cal process outside the lenses of traditional or contemporary metaphysical, episte-mological and ethical discourses. That is, our history has not posed metaphysical, epistemological and ethical problems that need to be solved or "gone beyond"; rather, it has left us these problems as imaginative ideological responses to once pertinent but now defunct problematics.

To resurrect the dead, as bourgeois humanists try to do, is impossible. To at-tack the dead, as deconstructionists do, is redundant and, ironically, valorizes death. To "go beyond" the dead means either surreptitiously recuperating previous "contents" of life in new forms (Nietzsche) or else deceptively shrugging off the weight of the dead, whether by promoting cults of passive, nostalgic "dwelling" (Heidegger) or by creative self-rebegetting and self-redescribing (Emerson, Harold Bloom, Richard Rorty).

What is distinctive about the Marxist project is that it neither resurrects, attacks nor attempts to "go beyond" metaphysical, epistemological and ethical discourses. It aims rather at transforming present practices—the remaining life—against the backdrop of previous discursive and political practices, against the "dead" past. Marxism admonishes us to "let the dead bury the dead," acknowledges that this "dead" past weighs like an incubus upon prevailing practices and accents our capacities to change these practices. Marx ignores, sidesteps and avoids discussions of metaphysical, epistemological and ethical issues not because he shuns his inescapable imprisonment in binary oppositions, remains insulated from metaphysical sedimentations, or hesitates to make knowledge claims and moral judgments, but rather because, for him, the bourgeois forms of discourse on such issues are "dead," rendered defunct by his particular moment in the historical process. The capitalist mode of production—with its own particular mystifying forms of social relations, technologies and bureaucracies and its aim of world domination—requires forms of theoretical and practical activity and modes of writing, acting and organizing heretofore unknown to the "dead" past.

From this Marxist view, the deconstructionist disclosing and debunking of the binary oppositions in the Western philosophical tradition is neither a threat to European civilization nor a misplaced critique better enacted against the binary oppositions in ethics. Rather, deconstructions are, like the left Hegelian critiques of Marx's own day, interesting yet impotent bourgeois attacks on the forms of thought and categories of a "dead" tradition, a tradition that stipulates the lineage and sustains the very life of these deconstructions. My claim here is not simply that these attacks valorize textuality at the expense of power, but, more important, that they are symbiotic with their very object of criticism; that is, they remain alive only as long as they give life to their enemy. In short, deconstructionist assaults must breathe life into metaphysical, epistemological and ethical discourses if their critiques are to render these discourses lifeless.[29]

The major ideological task of the Marxist intervention in present philosophical and critical discussions becomes that of exposing the reactionary and conservative consequences of bourgeois humanism, the critical yet barren posture of poststructuralist skepticism and deconstructionist ironic criticism, and the utopian and ultimately escapist character of the Emersonian gnosticism of Bloom and the Emersonian pragmatism of Rorty. The negative moment of Jameson's Marxist hermeneutics initiates this urgent task. The basic problem with the positive moment in his project is precisely its utopianism, especially in linking the Nietzschean quest beyond good and evil to Marxist theory and praxis. In a crucial passage, Jameson writes:

> It is clear, indeed, that not merely Durkheim's notion of collective "consciousness," but also the notion of "class consciousness," as it is central in a certain Marxist tradition, rests on an unrigorous and figurative assimilation of the consciousness of the individual subject to the dynamics of groups. The Althusserian and post-structuralist critique of these and other versions of the notion of a "subject of history" may readily be admitted. The alternatives presented by the Althusserians, however, . . . have a purely negative or second-degree critical function, and offer no new conceptual categories. What is wanted here—and it is one of the most urgent tasks for Marxist theory today—is a whole new logic of collective dynamics, with categories that escape the taint of some mere application of terms drawn from individual experience (in that sense, even the concept of praxis remains a suspect one). (*PU,* p. 294)

It comes as little surprise that Jameson's plea for a "new logic" resembles Jacques Derrida's call for a "new reason," since Jameson enacts the deconstructionist strategy of going beyond binary oppositions. At this level of comparison, the major difference is that Jameson banks his positive hermeneutics on this "new logic," whereas Derrida merely invokes "new reason" in his rhetoric before returning to his negative antihermeneutical activity. Yet, from a Marxist perspective, Jameson's basis for a positive hermeneutics is utopian in the bad sense, for it is a utopianism that rests either on no specifiable historical forces potentially capable of actualizing it or on the notion that every conceivable historical force embodies it. Jameson clearly favors the latter formulation.

> The preceding analysis entitles us to conclude that all class consciousness of whatever type is Utopian insofar as it expresses the unity of a collectivity; yet it must be added that this proposition is an allegorical one. The achieved collectivity or organic group of whatever kind—oppressors fully as much as oppressed—is Utopian not in itself, but only insofar as all such collectivities are themselves *figures* for the ultimate concrete collective life of an achieved Utopian or classless society. Now we are in a better position to understand how even hegemonic or ruling-class culture and ideology are Utopian, not in spite of their instrumental function to secure and perpetuate class privilege and power, but rather precisely because that function is also in and of itself the affirmation of collective solidarity. (*PU,* pp. 290–291)

This exorbitant claim illustrates not only utopianism gone mad, but also a Marxism in deep desperation, as if any display of class solidarity keeps alive a discredited class analysis. Even more important, this claim, similar to the thin historicism and glib optimism of Bloom's Emersonian gnosticism and Rorty's Emersonian pragmatism, reflects the extent to which Jameson remains within the clutches of American culture. Given the barbarous atrocities and large-scale horrors inflicted by hegemonic ruling classes in Europe, Africa, Asia and Latin America, only a Marxist thinker entrenched in the North American experience could even posit the possibility of ruling-class consciousness figuratively being "in its very nature Utopian" (*PU,* p. 289). Benjamin's tempered utopianism or Bloch's doctrine of hope certainly do not support such Marxist flights of optimism or lead to such an American faith in the future.

Jameson's bad utopianism is but a symptom of the major political shortcoming of his work: His texts have little or no political consequences. On the one hand, his works have little or no political praxis as texts; that is, they speak, refer or allude to no political movement or formation in process with which his texts have some connection.[30] They thus remain academic Marxist texts that, for the most part, are confined to specialists and antispecialists, Marxists and anti-Marxists, in the academy. On the other hand, his works have little or no political praxis in yet another sense: They provide little or no space for either highlighting issues of political praxis within its theoretical framework or addressing modes of political praxis in its own academic setting.[31]

Jameson's works are therefore too theoretical; his welcome call for a political hermeneutics is too far removed from the heat of political battles. By their failure sufficiently to reflect, and reflect on, the prevailing political strife, Jameson's works reenact the very process of reification that they condemn. Surely, the present fragmentation of the North American Left, the marginalization of progressive micropolitical formations and the rampant mystification of North American life and culture impose severe constraints on Jameson's textual practice; nonetheless, more substantive reflections on "practical" political strategies seem appropriate. My plea here is not anti-intellectual or antitheoretical, but rather a call for more sophisticated theory aware of and rooted in the present historical and political conjuncture in American capitalist civilization.

Of course, Jameson's own social positioning—an American professor of French writing Marxist hermeneutical works—solicits expectations of self-obsession, political isolation and naive optimism. Yet Jameson's texts are not self-obsessed, though his style of elusive, elliptical sentences (which appear more contrapuntal than dialectical) borders on a Frenchifying of English prose. Jameson's texts are not isolated, monadic works, despite the consistent absence of any acknowledgments to fellow critics or colleagues in his prefaces, yet they direct us to look at France rather than at ourselves. Hence his critical treatments of Sartre, Lévi-Strauss, Althusser, Lacan, Bénichou, Deleuze, Guattari and Lyotard are nearly hermetic, and he is relatively silent on distinguished American critics such as his former Yale colleague Paul de Man or noteworthy historically minded critics like R. P. Blackmur, Philip Rahv or Irving Howe. Jameson is not a naive optimist, but his sophisticated utopianism finally seems to be part and parcel of the American penchant for unquenchable faith in history and irresistible hope for romantic triumph.

My main point here is not simply that Jameson should write less Frenchified, expand his fascinating Marxist discourse to include talented American friends and foes and situate himself more clearly within the American Marxist tradition. Rather, Jameson's own historical predicament—his own conceptual tools, academic audience, utopian proclivities and political praxis—should become more an object of his dialectical deliberations. Nevertheless, Jameson has done more than any other American hermeneutical thinker in achieving intellectual breakthroughs and accenting theoretical challenges of the Marxist tradition in our postmodern times. The path he has helped blaze now awaits those, including himself, who will carry on with the urgent tasks not simply of taking seriously history and politics, but, more specifically, of taking seriously our intellectual, American and socialist identities as writers of texts, shapers of attitudes, beneficiaries of imperialist fruits, inheritors of hegemonic sensibilities and historical agents who envision a socialist future.

I would like to extend my gratitude to Jonathan Arac, Stanley Aronowitz, Paul Bové, Fredric Jameson, David Langston, Michael Sprinker and Anders Stephanson for their incisive comments and criticisms of an earlier version of this essay.

SOURCE: From *Keeping Faith: Philosophy and Race in America,* by Cornel West, pp. 165–91, 302–306. Copyright © 1993. Reproduced by permission of Routledge, Inc.

Fifteen

RACE AND SOCIAL THEORY

This is one of my initial attempts at a theoretical framework for explaining the complex phenomena of racism. It maps existing theories, incorporates their insights, discards their shortcomings and ends with my own genealogical materialist theory, one that confronts the psychosexual dimension of race. I intend to develop this framework further in the future.

In this field of inquiry, "sociological theory" has still to find its way, by a difficult effort of theoretical clarification, through the Scylla of a reductionism which must deny almost everything in order to explain something, and the Charybdis of a pluralism which is so mesmerized by "everything" that it cannot explain anything. To those willing to labour on, the vocation remains an open one.

—STUART HALL

WE LIVE IN THE midst of a pervasive and profound crisis of North Atlantic civilization whose symptoms include the threat of nuclear annihilation, extensive class inequality, brutal state repression, subtle bureaucratic surveillance, widespread homophobia, technological abuse of nature and rampant racism and patriarchy. In this essay, I shall focus on a small yet significant aspect of this crisis: the specific forms of African American oppression. It is important to stress that one can more fully understand this part only in light of the whole crisis, and that one's conception of the whole crisis should be shaped by one's grasp of this part. In other words, the time has passed when the so-called race question can be relegated to secondary or tertiary theoretical significance. In fact, to take seriously the multileveled oppression of peoples of color is to raise fundamental questions regarding the very conditions for the possibility of the modern West, the diverse forms and styles of European rationality and the character of the prevailing modern secular mythologies of nationalism, professionalism, scientism, consumerism and sexual hedonism that guide everyday practices around the world.

My strategy in this essay will be as follows. First, I will examine briefly the major conservative, liberal and left-liberal conceptions of African American oppression.

Second, I shall point out the distinctive strengths of adopting a refined Marxist methodology and analytical perspective. I then will sketch four influential Marxist attempts to understand African American oppression. Last, I shall argue that if we are to arrive at a more adequate conception of African American oppression, we must build upon and go beyond the Marxist tradition with the help of neo-Freudian investigations (especially those of Otto Ranke, Ernest Becker and Joel Kovel) into the modern Western forms of isolation and separation, as well as through poststructuralist reflections (by Jacques Derrida, Paul de Man, Michel Foucault and Edward Said) on the role and function of difference, otherness and marginality in contemporary philosophical discourse. I will sketch such a genealogical materialist position.

CONSERVATIVE VIEWS OF AFRICAN AMERICAN OPPRESSION

We begin with conservative conceptions of African American oppression primarily because we live in a country governed by those who accept many of these conceptions. Conservative perspectives focus on two terrains: *discrimination in the marketplace* and *judgments made in the minds of people*. It is no accident that conservatives tend to valorize neoclassical economics and utilitarian psychology. The basic claim is that differential treatment of black people is motivated by the "tastes" of white employers and/or white workers. Such "tastes," for instance, aversion to black people, may indeed be bad and undesirable—that is, if it can be shown that such "tastes" are based on faulty evidence, unconvincing arguments or irrational impulse. Yet it is possible that such "tastes" may be rational choices made by white people owing to commitments to high levels of productivity and efficiency in the economy, or due to evidence regarding the inferior capacities and/or performances of blacks.

There are three basic versions of conservative views of African American oppression: the *market* version, the *sociobiologist* version and the *culturalist* version. The market version—best represented by Milton Friedman's classic *Capitalism and Freedom* (1962) and his student Gary Becker's renowned *The Economics of Discrimination* (1957)—holds that it is not in the economic interests of white employers and workers to oppose black employment opportunities. Friedman and Becker claim that such racist behavior or "bad taste" flies in the face of or is an extraneous factor mitigating against market rationality, that is, the maximizing of profits. In this way, both understand "racist tastes" as the irrational choice of white employers and workers that sidetracks market rationality in determining the best economic outcomes. The practical policy that results from this market perspective is to educate and persuade white employers and workers to be more rational or attuned to their own self-interests. The underlying assumption here is that "pure" market mechanisms (as opposed to government intervention) will undermine "racist tastes." Another basic presupposition here is that market rationality, along with undermining "racist tastes," is in the interest of white employers *and* white workers *and* black people.

The sociobiologist version—put forward by Arthur Jensen (*Harvard Educational Review,* Winter 1969) and Richard Hernstein (*Atlantic Monthly,* September 1971)—suggests that prevailing evidence leads to the conclusion that blacks are, in some sense, genetically inferior. Blacks' IQ performance, which allegedly "measures" intelligence, that is, the capacity for acquiring knowledge and solving problems, is such that the "racist tastes" of white employers and workers may be justified—not on the basis of aversion to blacks, but due to group performance attainment. Unlike Friedman and Becker, Jensen and Hernstein consider the "racist tastes" of white employers and workers as rational choices made on "scientific" grounds. In this way, African American oppression is not a changeable and eradicable phenomenon, but rather part of "the natural order of things."

Last, the culturalist version—as seen in Edward Banfield's *The Unheavenly City* (1965) and Thomas Sowell's *Race and Economics* (1975)—holds that the "racist tastes" of white employers and workers can be justified on cultural rather than biological grounds. They argue that the character and content of African American culture inhibits black people from competing with other people in American society, be it in education, the labor force or business. For Banfield and Sowell, the necessary cultural requisites for success—habits of hard work, patience, deferred gratification and persistence—are underdeveloped among African Americans. Therefore African American oppression will be overcome only when these habits become more widely adopted by black people.

Although these three versions of conservative views of African American oppression differ among themselves, they all share certain common assumptions. First, they view market rationality (or marginal productivity calculations) as the sole standard for understanding the actions of white employers and workers. Second, this market rationality presupposes an unarticulated Benthamite felicific calculus or Hobbesian psychological egoistic model that holds self-interest to be the dominant motivation of human action. Third, this calculus or model is linked to a neoclassical economic perspective that focuses principally upon individuals and market mechanisms, with little concern about the institutional structure and power relations of the market and limited attention to social and historical structures, for instance, slavery, state repression and second-class citizenship. Last, all agree that government intervention into the marketplace to enhance the opportunities of African Americans does more harm than good.

Liberal Views of African American Oppression

Liberal conceptions of African American oppression are under severe intellectual and political assault, yet they remain inscribed within our laws and are still, in some ways, observed. It is crucial to acknowledge that liberal viewpoints adopt the same neoclassical economic perspective and egoistic model as those of conservatives. Yet unlike conservatives, liberals highlight racist institutional barriers that result from the "racist tastes" of white employers and workers. Liberals reject mere persuasion to change these "tastes" and attack genetic inferiority claims as unwarranted and arbitrary. Liberals focus on two domains: *racist institutional barriers in the marketplace* and *inhibiting impediments in African American culture*. Those liberals who stress the former can be dubbed "market liberals," and those who emphasize the latter, "culturalist liberals." Market liberals, such as Gunnar Myrdal and Paul Samuelson, claim that African American oppression can be alleviated if the state intervenes into racist structures of employment practices and thereby ensures, coercively if necessary, that fair criteria are utilized in hiring and firing black people. Of course, what constitutes "fair criteria" can range from race-free standards to race-conscious ones. Furthermore, culturalist liberals like Thomas Pettigrew hold that government programs should be established to prepare people, especially blacks, for jobs. These programs can range from educational efforts such as Head Start to direct training and hiring to the now defunct Job Corps projects. School integration efforts going back to the gallant struggles of the NAACP decades ago are part of this culturalist liberal position. In fact, it is fair to say that the vast majority of black public officials are culturalist and/or market liberals.

As I noted earlier, both conservatives and liberals subscribe to market rationality as the primary standard for understanding and alleviating African American oppression. Both groups assume that "rough justice" between blacks and white Americans can be achieved if black productivity is given its rightful due, namely, if there is close parity in black and white incomes. At the level of public policy, the important difference is that liberals believe this "rough justice" cannot be achieved without state intervention to erase racist institutional barriers, especially in employment and education.

LEFT-LIBERAL VIEWS OF AFRICAN AMERICAN OPPRESSION

It is important that we do not confuse left liberals with liberals—just as we should not confuse conservatives with neoconservatives (the latter tend to be market liberals and culturalist conservatives). This is so because left liberals have what most liberals and conservatives lack: *a sense of history*. This historical consciousness of left liberals makes them suspicious of abstract neoclassical economic perspectives and sensitive to the role of complex political struggles in determining the predominant economic perspective of the day. In other words, left liberals recognize that classical economic views shifted to neoclassical ones (from Adam Smith and David Ricardo to Alfred Marshall and Stanley Jevons) not only because better arguments emerged, but also because those arguments were about changing realities of nineteenth-century industrial capitalism and inseparable from clashing political groups in the midst of these changing realities. Similarly the versions of market liberalism associated with Franklin Roosevelt in regard to state-economy relations and John Kennedy in regard to state-economy-race relations were transformations of neoclassicism in the face of the Depression, the rise of organized labor and the struggles of Southern blacks under evolving capitalist conditions. Left liberals understand African American oppression as an ever changing historical phenomenon and a present reality. They locate the "racist tastes" of white employers and workers and the racist institutional barriers of American society within the historical contexts of over two hundred years of slavery and subsequent decades of Jim Crow laws, peonage, tenancy, lynchings and second-class citizenship. It is no surprise that left liberals remain in dialogue with Marxist thinkers and, in many cases, are deeply influenced by sophisticated forms of Marxist historical and social analysis.

Left liberals, such as William Julius Wilson (*The Declining Significance of Race*, 1978) and Martin Kilson (*Neither Insiders nor Outsiders*, forthcoming), who think seriously about African American oppression are usually Weberians or followers of contemporary Weberians like Talcott Parsons and Robert Merton. The major theoretical models they adopt and apply are not those of neoclassical economics, but rather structural-functionalist sociology. This difference is not as broad as it may seem, but the historical orientation of left liberals radically separates them from most liberals and conservatives. In fact, this sense of history constitutes a kind of "crossing of the Rubicon" by left liberals. After such a crossing there can be no return to ahistorical conceptions of African American oppression.

Left liberals tend to be a rather eclectic lot who borrow insights from conservatives (for instance, a stress on black self-reliance and the need to acquire efficacious habits for black upward social mobility) and from liberals (for instance, the necessity for government action to regulate employment practices and enhance African American cultural deprivation). They acknowledge the crucial structural social constraints upon African Americans and, like Weber, conceptualize these constraints in terms of groups competing for prestige, status and power over scarce economic resources. For left liberals, strata and social position supersede class location, and financial remunerations at the workplace, that is, income, serves as the basic measure of societal well-being. The major index of African American oppression for left liberals is that black incomes remain slightly less than 60 percent of white incomes in the United States. The public policies they support to alleviate African American oppression focus upon full employment, public works programs and certain forms of affirmative action.

MARXIST VIEWS OF AFRICAN AMERICAN OPPRESSION

We come now to Marxist conceptions of African American oppression. And one may ask, given the conservative tenor of the times, why Marxist theory at all? Is not Marxism an outdated and antiquated tradition that: (1) has tragically produced widespread unfreedom in the Communist East; (2) utterly failed to attract the working classes in the capitalist West; (3) primarily served the purposes of anticolonial mythologies in the Third World that mask the butchery of present-day national bourgeoisies in parts of Africa, Asia and Latin America; and (4) is presently overwhelmed by information, communication and technological revolutions as well as nonclass-based movements like feminism, gay and lesbian rights, ecology and the various movements among people of color in the First World? These questions are serious indeed, and must be confronted by anyone who wishes to defend the continuing vitality and utility of the Marxist tradition.

I shall begin by making some basic distinctions between *Marxist thought* as a monocausal, unilinear philosophy of history that accurately predicts historical outcomes; *Marxism* as it is exemplified in diverse "actually existing" Communist regimes in the Soviet Union, China, Cuba, Poland and so forth; and *Marxist theory* as a methodological orientation toward the understanding of social and historical realities. Needless to say, I readily reject Marxist thought as a monocausal, unilinear, predictive science of history or a homogeneous, teleological narrative of past and present events. Such infantile Marxism has been subjected to persuasive criticism by Karl Popper, John Plamenatz, John Dewey and Raymond Aron from outside the Marxist tradition, and by members of the Frankfurt School (Adorno, Horkheimer, Marcuse), Raymond Williams and Antonio Gramsci from within. I also reject, although not without sympathy for, the undemocratic regimes that regiment and dominate their peoples in the name of Marxism. As a democratic and libertarian socialist, I find these regimes morally repugnant, yet I wish to stress that detailed historical analysis of why they evolved as they have is required if we are to grasp their tragic predicament. Such analysis does not excuse the atrocities committed, yet it does give us a realistic sense of what these regimes have been up against.

Despite rejecting Marxist thought as a philosophy of history and Marxism as it has appeared in diverse "actually existing" Communist regimes, I hold that Marxist theory as a methodological orientation remains indispensable—although ultimately inadequate—in grasping distinctive features of African American oppression. As a methodological orientation, Marxist theory requires that we begin from two starting points.

First, the *principle of historical specificity* impels us to examine the various conditions under which African American oppression emerged, the ever-changing structural constraints under which African Americans have accommodated and resisted multiple forms of oppression, and the crucial conjunctural opportunities (for instance, those in the 1870s, 1920s and 1960s) that African Americans have either missed or seized. This historicizing approach entails that we highlight economic, political, cultural and psychosexual conflicts over resources, power, images, language and identities between black and other people as among black people themselves.

The second starting point for Marxist theory is the *principle of the materiality of structured social practices over time and space*. This principle maintains that extradiscursive formations such as modes of production, state apparatuses and bureaucracies, and discursive operations such as religions, philosophies, art objects and laws not only shape social actions of individuals and groups, but possess historical potency and effectivity in relation to, but not reducible to, each other. Marxist theory is materialist *and* historical to the degree that it attempts to understand and explain forms of oppression in terms of the complex relation of extradiscursive formations to discursive operations. Classical Marxists view this relation in terms of a more or less determining base and a more or less determined superstructure, whereas neo-Marxists understand this relation as (in Raymond Williams's famous phrase) "the mutual setting of limits and exerting of pressures." The explanatory power of Marxist theory resides precisely in the specifying of the complex relation of base and superstructure, limits and pressures, extradiscursive formations and discursive operations, that is, in establishing with precision the nature of determination. This problem remains unresolved in the Marxist tradition, while the most impressive efforts remain those enacted in the best of Marx's own textual practices.

Marx's own effort to account for determination highlights the multileveled interplay between historically situated subjects who act and materially grounded structures that circumscribe, that is, enable and constrain, such action. This human action constitutes structured social practices that are reducible neither to context-free discrete acts of individuals nor to objective structures unaffected by human agency. The dialectical character of Marxist theory resides precisely in the methodological effort to view the interplay of subject and structure in terms of dynamic social practices during a particular time and in a specific space. The aim of Marxist theory is to view each historical moment as a multidimensional transaction between subjects shaped by antecedent structures and traditions and prevailing structures and traditions transformed by struggling subjects. As Perry Anderson has recently put it, Marxism is "the search for subjective agencies capable of effective strategies for the dislodgement of objective structures."

Each evolving society then becomes—as an object of investigation—a "complex articulated totality" produced by social practices (including those that constitute the investigation itself) shot through with relations of domination and conflict in an overdetermined economic sphere and relatively autonomous political, cultural, theological and psychic spheres. By "complex articulated totality" I mean that the specific conflicts on the various levels of society are linked to one another, while the specificity of one level is neither identical with nor reducible to a mirror image of the specificity of another level. Yet the articulation of these specific conflicts within and across the various spheres constitutes a "totality" because the relations of these conflicts are not arbitrary or capricious, as Marxist theorists attempt to show. These accounts or explanations privilege the economic sphere without viewing the other spheres as mere expressions of the economic. In other words, Marxist theory claims that social and historical explanation must view, in some discernible manner, the economic sphere as the major determining factor in accounting for the internal dynamics (or synchronicity) and historical change (or diachronicity) of human (and especially capitalist) societies. It should be apparent that Marxist conceptions of African American oppression reject the "bad tastes" starting point of conservatives, the "racist institutional barriers" starting point of liberals and the Weberian views about the economic sphere of left liberals, that is, the stress on strata and status. Nonetheless, there remains considerable controversy among Marxist theorists about how to construe the economic sphere, whether as a mode of production, as merely the forces of production, or as primarily a mode of surplus extraction or form of appropriation of surplus value. Consensus has been reached only insofar as all hold that the economic sphere is constituted by conflict-ridden classes characterized by their relation (ownership, effective control or lack thereof) to the means of production.

Unfortunately—and largely due to the European character of Marxist scholarship on race—there exists a paucity of sophisticated Marxist treatments of racially structured societies. Outside the historical work of W. E. B. Du Bois, the grand efforts of Oliver Cox and C. L. R. James, and the pioneering recent writings of Eugene Genovese, Stuart Hall, Cedric Robinson and Orlando Patterson, the richness of the Marxist methodological orientation and analytical perspective in relation to race remains untapped. Instead, Marxist theorists of African American oppression have put forward rather bland and glib views. For example, *class reductionists* have simply subsumed African American oppression under class exploitation and viewed complex racist practices as merely conscious profiteering—or a divide-and-conquer strategy—on behalf of capitalists. Although this view captures a practical truth about racist employers' practices during a particular period in racially fractured capitalist societies, it inhibits more thorough theoretical investigation into other crucial aspects, features and functions of racist practices. Furthermore, it tacitly assumes that racism is rooted in the rise of modern capitalism. Yet it can be easily shown that although racist practices were appropriated and promoted in various ways by modern capitalist processes, racism predates capitalism. Racism seems to have its roots in the early encounter between the civilizations of Europe, Africa and Asia, encounters that occurred long before the rise of modern capitalism. The very category of "race"—denoting primarily skin color—was first employed as a means of classifying human bodies by François Bernier, a French physician, in 1684. The first substantial racial division of humankind is found in the influential *Natural System* (1735) of the preeminent naturalist of the eighteenth century, Carolus Linnaeus. Yet both instances reveal racist practices—in that both degrade and devalue non-Europeans—at the level of intellectual codification. Xenophobic folktales and mythologies, racist legends and stories—such as authoritative church fathers' commentaries on the Song of Solomon and the Ywain narratives in medieval Brittany—were operating in the everyday lives of ordinary folk long before the seventeenth and eighteenth centuries. In fact, Christian anti-Semitism and European antiblackism were rampant throughout the Middle Ages. In short, the class reductionist viewpoint rests upon shaky theoretical and historical grounds.

The other simplistic Marxist conceptions of African American oppression are those of the *class super-exploitationist* perspective and the *class nationalist* view. The former holds that African Americans are subjected to general working-class exploitation and specific class exploitation owing to racially differential wages received and/or to the relegation of black people to the secondary sector of the labor force. Again the claim is that this is a conscious divide-and-conquer strategy of employers to fan and fuel racial antagonisms between black and white workers and to "bribe" white workers at the expense of lower wages for black workers. Again, this perspective contains a practical truth about the aims of white employers during a particular period of particular capitalist societies, yet the "bribe" thesis is a weak reed upon which to hang an account of the many levels on which racism works. More important, this position still views race solely in economic and class terms.

The class nationalist viewpoint is the most influential, widely accepted and hence unquestioned among practicing black Marxists. It understands African American oppression in terms of class exploitation and national domination. The basic claim is that African Americans constitute or once constituted an oppressed nation in the Southern Black Belt and, much like Puerto Ricans, form an oppressed national minority within American society. There are numerous versions of this so-called Black Nation thesis. Its classical version was put forward in the Sixth Congress of the Third International in 1928, slightly modified in its 1930 resolution and codified in Harry Haywood's *Negro Liberation* (1948). Subsequent versions abound on the sectarian black Left—from Nelson Peery's *The Negro National Colonial Question* (1978), James Forman's *Self-Determination and the African-American People* (1981) to Amiri Baraka's formulations in his journal, *The Black Nation*. More refined conceptions of the class nationalist view were put forward in the form of an internal colony thesis by Harold Cruse in *The Crisis of the Negro Intellectual* (1967) and Robert Allen in *Black Awakening in Capitalist America* (1969); yet even in these two seminal texts of the 1960s the notion of African America as an internal colony remains a mere metaphor without serious analytical content. Ironically, the most provocative and persistent proponent of a class nationalist perspective is Maulana Karenga, who arrived at his own self-styled position that infuses a socialist analytical component within his cultural nationalism. His *Essays in Struggle* (1978) and *Kawaida Theory* (1981) stand shoulders above much of the theoretical reflections on African Americans' oppression proposed by the black Marxist Left.

On the practical level, the class nationalist perspective has promoted and encouraged impressive struggles against racism in the United States. But with its ahistorical racial definition of a nation, its flaccid statistical determination of national boundaries and its illusory distinct black economy, the Black Nation thesis serves as a misguided attempt by Marxist-Leninists to repudiate the class reductionist and class super-exploitationist views of African American oppression. In short, it functions as a poor excuse for the absence of a viable Marxist theory of the specificity of African American oppression.

Such a theory is, however, in the making. The recent efforts of Howard Winant and Michael Omi to develop a *class racialist* position contribute to such a theory. As I noted earlier, the pioneering work of Eugene Genovese, Stuart Hall and Orlando Patterson is also quite promising in this regard. The Marxist conception of racially structured capitalist societies as "complex articulated totalities," buttressed by flexible historical materialist analysis, looms large in their work. Genovese is deeply influenced by Gramsci's nuanced conception of hegemony; Hall, by Althusser and Gramsci's notion of articulation; and Patterson by Marx's own concept of domination, by a homespun existentialism and by recent studies of Rytina and Morgan in demography. A distinctive feature of these class racialist (or class ethnic) views is that they eschew any form of reductionism, economism and a priorism in Marxist theory. Furthermore, they attempt to give historically concrete and sociologically specific Marxist accounts of the racial aspects of particular societies. This means that they accent the different forms of racial domination and reject racism as a universal and unitary transhistorical phenomenon, for instance, as a prejudicial proclivity of individual psychology or race instinct.

In this way, recent forms of Marxist theory demystify the *conservative* idea of "bad tastes" by historically situating the emergence of these "tastes" as socially pertinent, functional and potent; they structurally circumscribe the *liberal* notion of "racist institutional barriers" by viewing such mechanisms within the operations of racially fractured and fractionated capitalist modes of production; and they contest the Weberian assumptions of *left liberals* by linking struggles for prestige and status to changing class conflicts and by stressing people's empowerment (participation in decision-making processes) rather than mere increased financial remuneration at the workplace (higher incomes). In stark contrast to vulgar Marxist views, this body of Marxist theory holds racism to be neither a mere conspiracy or ideological trick from above, nor a divide-and-conquer strategy of capitalists, but rather a complex cluster of structured social practices that shape class relations and create a crucial dimension in the lives of individuals throughout capitalist societies. The linchpin in this refined Marxist view is that the economic sphere is the ultimate determining explanatory factor for grasping the role and function of racism in modern societies. My own somewhat hesitant rejection of this linchpin leads me to build upon, yet go beyond, this last incarnation of Marxist theory.

Toward a Genealogical Materialist Analysis

In this last section, I shall set forth a schematic outline of a new conception of African American oppression that tries to bring together the best of recent Marxist theory and the invaluable insights of neo-Freudians (Ranke, Becker, and Kovel) about the changing forms of immortality quests and perceptions of dirt and death in the modern West, along with the formulations of the poststructuralists (Derrida, de Man, Foucault, Said) on the role of difference, otherness and marginality in discursive operations and extradiscursive formations.

My perspective can be characterized as a genealogical materialist analysis, that is, an analysis that replaces Marxist conceptions of history with Nietzschean notions of genealogy, yet preserves the materiality of multifaceted structured social practices. My understanding of genealogy derives neither from mere deconstructions of the duplicitous and deceptive character of rhetorical strategies of logocentric discourses, nor from simple investigations into the operations of power of such discourses. Unlike Derrida and de Man, genealogical materialism does not rest content with a horizon of language. In contrast to Foucault and Said, I take the challenge of historical materialism with great seriousness. The aspects of Nietzsche that interest me are neither his perennial playfulness nor his vague notions of power. What I find seductive and persuasive about Nietzsche is his deep historical consciousness, a consciousness so deep that he must reject prevailing ideas of history in the name of genealogy. It seems to me that in these postmodern times, the principles of historical specificity and the materiality of structured social practices—the very founding principles of Marx's own discourse—now require us to be genealogical materialists. We must become more radically historical than is envisioned by the Marxist tradition. By becoming more "radically historical" I mean confronting more candidly the myriad effects and consequences (intended and unintended, conscious and unconscious) of power-laden and conflict-ridden social practices—for instance, the complex confluence of human bodies, traditions and institutions. This candor takes the form of a more theoretical open-endedness and analytical dexterity than Marxist notions of history permit—without ruling out Marxist explanations a priori.

Furthermore, a genealogical materialist conception of social practices should be more materialist than that of the Marxist tradition, to the extent that the privileged material mode of production is not necessarily located in the economic sphere. Instead, decisive material modes of production at a given moment may be located in the cultural, political or even the psychic sphere. Since these spheres are interlocked and interlinked, each always has some weight in an adequate social and historical explanation. My view neither promotes a post-Marxist idealism (for it locates acceptable genealogical accounts in material social practices), nor supports an explanatory nihilism (in that it posits some contingent yet weighted set of material social practices as decisive factors to explain a given genealogical configuration, that is, set of events). More pointedly, my position appropriates the implicit pragmatism of Nietzsche for the purposes of a deeper, and less dogmatic, historical materialist analysis. In this regard, the genealogical materialist view is both continuous and discontinuous with the Marxist tradition. One cannot be a genealogical materialist without (taking seriously) the Marxist tradition, yet allegiance to the methodological principles of the Marxist tradition forces one to be a genealogical materialist. Marxist theory still may provide the best explanatory account for certain phenomena, but it also may remain inadequate to account for other phenomena—notably here, the complex phenomenon of racism in the modern West.

My basic disagreement with Marxist theory is twofold. First, I hold that many social practices, such as racism, are best understood and explained not only or primarily by locating them within modes of production, but also by situating them within the cultural traditions of civilizations. This permits us to highlight the specificity of those practices that traverse or cut across different modes of production, for example, racism, religion, patriarchy, homophobia. Focusing on racist practices or white-supremacist logics operative in premodern, modern and postmodern Western civilization yields both racial continuity and discontinuity. Even Marxist theory can be shown to be both critical of and captive to a Eurocentrism that can justify racist practices. And though Marxist theory remains indispensable, it also obscures and hides the ways in which secular ideologies—especially modern ideologies of scientism, racism and sexual hedonism (Marxist theory does much better with nationalism, professionalism and consumerism)—are linked to larger civilizational ways of life and struggle.

Second, I claim that the Marxist obsession with the economic sphere as the major explanatory factor is itself a reflection of the emergence of Marxist discourse in the midst of an industrial capitalism preoccupied with economic production; and, more important, this Marxist obsession is itself a symptom of a particular Western version of the will to truth and style of rationality that valorizes control, mastery and domination of nature and history. I neither fully reject this will to truth, nor downplay the crucial role of the economic sphere in social and historical explanation. But one is constrained to acknowledge the methodological point about the degree to which Marxist theory remains inscribed within the very problematic of the unfreedom and domination it attempts to overcome.

Genealogical materialist analysis of racism consists of three methodological moments that serve as guides for detailed historical and social analyses:

1. A *genealogical* inquiry into the discursive and extradiscursive conditions for the possibility of racist practices, that is, a radically historical investigation into the emergence, development and sustenance of white-supremacist logics operative in various epochs in the modern Western (Eastern or African) civilization.

2. A *microinstitutional* (or localized) analysis of the mechanisms that promote and contest these logics in the everyday lives of people, including the ways in which self-images and self-identities are shaped and the impact of alien, degrading cultural styles, aesthetic ideals, psychosexual sensibilities and linguistic gestures upon peoples of color.

3. A *macrostructural* approach that accents modes of overdetermined class exploitation, state repression and bureaucratic domination, including resistance against these modes, in the lives of peoples of color.

The first moment would, for example, attempt to locate racist discourses within the larger Western conceptions of death and dirt, that is, in the predominant ways in which Western peoples have come to terms with their fears of "extinction with insignificance," of existential alienation, isolation and separation in the face of the inevitable end of which they are conscious. This moment would examine how these peoples have conceptualized and mythologized their sentiments of impurity at the visual, tactile, auditory and, most important, olfactory levels of experience and social practice.

Three white-supremacist logics—the battery of concepts, tropes and metaphors constituting discourses that degrade and devalue people of color—operative in the modern West may shed some light on these issues. The *Judeo-Christian racist logic,* which emanates from the biblical account of Ham looking upon and failing to cover his father Noah's nakedness, thereby provoking divine punishment in the form of blackening his progeny, links racist practices to notions of disrespect for and rejection of authority, to ideas of unruly behavior and chaotic rebellion. The *"scientific" racist logic,* which promotes the observing, measuring, ordering and comparing of visible physical characteristics of human bodies in light of Greco-Roman aesthetic standards, associates racist practices with bodily ugliness, cultural deficiency and intellectual inferiority. And the *psychosexual racist logic* endows black people with sexual prowess, views them as either cruel, revengeful fathers, frivolous, carefree children or passive, long-suffering mothers. This logic—rooted in Western sexual discourses about feces and odious smells—relates racist practices to bodily defecation, violation and subordination, thereby relegating black people to walking abstractions, lustful creatures or invisible objects. All three white-supremacist logics view black people, like death and dirt, as Other and Alien.

An important task of genealogical inquiry is to disclose in historically concrete and sociologically specific ways the discursive operations that view Africans as excluded, marginal and other and to reveal how racist logics are guided (or contested) by various hegemonic Western philosophies of identity and universality that suppress difference, heterogeneity and diversity. Otto Ranke and Ernest Becker would play an interesting role here, since their conception of societies as codified hero-systems or as symbolic-action systems that produce, distribute and circulate statuses and customs in order to cope with human fears of death or extreme otherness may cast light on modern Western racist practices. For example, with the lessening of religious influence in the modern West, human immortality quests were channeled into secular ideologies of science, art, nation, profession, race, sexuality and consumption. The deep human desire for existential belonging and for self-esteem—what I call the need for and consumption of *existential capital*—results in a profound, even gut-level, commitment to some of the illusions of the present epoch. None of us escapes. And many Western peoples get much existential capital from racist illusions, from ideologies of race. The growing presence of Caribbean and Indian peoples in Britain, Africans in Russia, Arabs in France and black soldiers in Germany is producing escalating black/white hatred, sexual jealousy and intraclass antagonisms. This suggests that the means of acquiring existential capital from ideologies of race is in no way peculiar to the two exemplary racist Western countries, the United States and South Africa. It also reminds us that racist perceptions and practices are deeply rooted in Western cultures and become readily potent in periods of crisis, be that crisis cultural, political or economic.

The second moment, the microinstitutional or localized analysis, examines the elaboration of white-supremacist logics within the everyday lives of people. Noteworthy here is the conflict-ridden process of identity formation and self-image production by peoples of color. The work of Goffman and Garfinkel on role-playing and self-masking, the insights of Althusser, Kristeva and Foucault on the contradictions shot through the process of turning individual bodies into ideological subjects (for instance, "colored," "Negro," "black" subjects) and the painful struggle of accepting and rejecting internalized negative and disenabling self-conceptions (for instance, pervasive lack of self-confidence in certain activities, deep insecurities regarding one's capacities) among people of color, as highlighted in Memmi and Fanon, are quite useful to this analysis.

The third (and last) moment, the macrostructural analysis, deepens the historical materialist analyses of Genovese, Hall and Patterson, with the proviso that the economic sphere may, in certain cases, not be the ultimate factor in explaining racist practices. As I noted earlier, there is little doubt that it remains a crucial factor in every case.

SOURCE: From *Keeping Faith: Philosophy and Race in America,* by Cornel West, pp. 251–270. Copyright © 1993. Reproduced by permission of Routledge, Inc.

PART FIVE

RADICAL DEMOCRATIC POLITICS

The major challenge for radical democrats is to connect our theories of in-justice and social misery to credible programs that can organize and gal-vanize people. In this section, I pursue broad possibilities for change and promote specific policies that can make a difference in everyday people's lives. Intellectual work for radical democrats must always link the vi-sionary to the practical.

Sixteen

THE ROLE OF LAW IN PROGRESSIVE POLITICS

This essay was published in David Kairys's best-seller The Politics of Law, *which is used in law schools and classes around the country. It provides a historical perspective on the role of law in progressive politics and concrete advice for lawyers interested in progressive social change. It is one of the most requested essays in my corpus.*

WHAT IS THE ROLE and function of the law in contemporary progressive politics? Are legal institutions crucial terrain on which significant social change can take place? If so, how? In which way? What are progressive lawyers to do if they are to remain relatively true to their moral convictions and political goals?

In this chapter I shall attempt to respond to these urgent questions. This response will try to carve out a vital democratic left space between the Scylla of upbeat liberalism, which harbors excessive hopes for the law, and the Charybdis of downbeat leftism, which promotes exorbitant doubts about the law. My argument rests upon three basic claims. First, the fundamental forms of social misery in American society can be neither adequately addressed nor substantially transformed within the context of existing legal apparatuses. Yet serious and committed work within this circumscribed context remains indispensable if progressive politics is to have any future at all. Second, this crucial work cannot but be primarily defensive unless significant extraparliamentary social motion or movements bring power and pressure to bear on the prevailing status quo. Such social motion and movements presuppose either grassroots citizen participation in credible progressive projects or rebellious acts of desperation that threaten the social order. Third, the difficult task of progressive legal practitioners is to link their defensive work within the legal system to possible social motion and movements that attempt to transform American society fundamentally.

Any argument regarding the role of law in progressive politics must begin with two sobering historical facts about the American past and present. First, American society is disproportionately shaped by the outlooks, interests and aims of the business community—especially that of big business. The sheer power of corporate capital is extraordinary. This power makes it difficult even to imagine what a free and democratic society would look like (or how it would operate) if there

were publicly accountable mechanisms that alleviated the vast disparities in resources, wealth and income owing in part to the vast influence of big business on
the U.S. government and its legal institutions. This is why those who focus on
forms of social misery—such as the ill-fed, ill-clad and ill-housed—must think in
epochal, not apocalyptic, terms.

The second brute fact about the American past and present is that this society
is a *chronically* racist, sexist, homophobic and jingoistic one. The complex and tortuous quest for American identity from 1776 to our own time has produced a culture in which people define themselves physically, socially, sexually and politically
in terms of race, gender, sexual orientation and "anti-American" activities. One
unique feature of the country among other modern nations—with the embarrassing exceptions of South Africa and Hitler's Germany—is that race has served as
the linchpin in regulating this national quest for identity. A detailed genealogy of
American legal discourse about citizenship and rights, as initiated by the late
Robert Cover of Yale, bears out this inescapable reality. The historical articulation
of the experiential weight of African slavery and Jim Crowism to forms of U.S.
patriarchy, homophobia and anti-American (usually Communist and socialist) repression or surveillance yields a profoundly conservative culture.

The irony of this cultural conservatism is that it tries to preserve a highly dynamic corporate-driven economy, a stable election-centered democracy and a precious liberties-guarding rule of law. This irony constitutes the distinctive hybridity
of American liberalism (in its classical and revisionist versions) and the debilitating dilemma of American radicalism (in its movements for racial, class and sexual
equality). In other words, American liberalism diffuses the claims of American
radicals by pointing to long-standing democratic and libertarian practices, despite
historic racist, sexist, class and homophobic constraints. Hence, any feasible
American radicalism seems to be but an extension of American liberalism. Needless to say, the sacred cow of American liberalism—namely, economic growth
achieved by *corporate* priorities—is neither examined nor interrogated. And those
that do are relegated to the margins of the political culture.

My first claim rests upon the assumption that the extension of American liberalism in response to movements for racial, class and sexual equality is desirable yet insufficient. This is so because the extension of American liberalism
leaves relatively untouched the fundamental reality that undergirds the forms of
social misery: *the maldistribution of resources, wealth and power in American society.* Yet
the extension of American liberalism in regard to race, labor, women, gays, lesbians and nature *appears* radical on the American ideological spectrum principally because it goes against the deeply entrenched cultural conservatism in the
country. In fact, this extension—as seen, for example, in the 1930s and 1960s—
takes place by means of insurgent social motion and movements convincing political and legal elites to enact legislation or judicial decrees over the majority of

the population. In short, the very extension of American liberalism has hardly ever been popular among the masses of American people primarily owing to a pervasive cultural conservatism.

The law has played a crucial role in those periods in which liberalism has been extended precisely because of the power of judicial review and an elected body of officials responding to social movements—not because cultural conservatism has been significantly weeded out. The effects of these laws and policies over time have attenuated some of the more crude and overt expressions of cultural conservatism, yet the more subtle expressions permeate the culture. The existing legal apparatuses cannot adequately address or substantially transform the plight of the racially and sexually skewed ill-fed, ill-clad or ill-housed not only because of the marginalizing of perspectives that highlight the need for a redistribution of resources, wealth and power, but also because of the perception that the extension of American liberalism is the most radical option feasible within American political culture.

Is this perception true? Is it the case that all workable radical alternatives must presuppose economic growth achieved by corporate priorities? These questions are especially acute given the collapse of social Keynesianism in the mid-1970s— that "magic" Fordist formula of mass production undergirded by mass consumption alongside government provisions to those with no access to resources, which sustained economic growth in the postwar period. The conservative project of supply-side economics and military Keynesianism of the 1980s yielded not simply a larger gap between the haves and have-nots, but also a debt-financed public sphere and a more corporate-dominated economy—all in the name of "free enterprise."

If the extension of American liberalism is the only feasible radical option within American political culture, then the defensive role of progressive lawyers becomes even more important. Their work constitutes one of the few buffers against cultural conservatism, which recasts the law more in its own racist, sexist, antilabor and homophobic image. Furthermore, the work within the existing legal system helps keep alive a memory of the social traces left by past progressive movements of resistance, a memory requisite for future movements. This defensive work, though possibly radical in intent, is *liberal* practice in that it proceeds from within the legal system in order to preserve the effects of former victories threatened by the conservative offensive. Yet this same defensive work has tremendous radical potential, especially within the context of vital oppositional activity against the status quo. This is why the distinction between liberal and radical legal practice is not sharp and rigid; rather, it is fluid and contingent due to the ever changing larger social situation. Needless to say, the crucial role of this kind of legal practice—be it to defend the rights of activists, secure permits to march or dramatize an injustice with a class suit—is indispensable for progressive politics. Yet in "cold" moments in American society—when cultural conservatism and big business fuse with power and potency—radical lawyers have little option other than defensive work. This work is often demoralizing, yet it serves as an important link to past victories and a basis for the next wave of radical action.

In our present period, radical legal practice takes two main forms: theoretical critiques of liberal paradigms in the academy that foster subcultures of radical students and professors or participation in radical organizations that engage in extraparliamentary social motion. It is no accident that the first form consists of a pedagogical reform movement within elite institutions of the legal academy. This critical legal studies (CLS) movement is symptomatic of a pessimism regarding feasible radical options in American political culture and a distance between radical legal critiques and radical legal action vis-à-vis the courts. This sense of political impotence and gulf between radical professors of law and radical lawyers results not because CLS consists of insular bourgeois theorists with little grasp of political reality. In fact, their understanding of this reality is often acute. Yet some of the CLS trashing of liberalism at the level of theory spills over to liberal legal practice. This spillover is myopic, for it trashes the only feasible progressive practice for radical lawyers vis-à-vis the courts. This myopia becomes downright dangerous and irresponsible when aimed at civil rights lawyers for whom the very effort to extend American liberalism may lead to injury or death in conservative America.

Is there any way out of this impasse? Can progressive legal practice be more than defensive? My second claim holds that there are but two ways out. In situations of sparse resources along with degraded self-images and depoliticized sensibilities, one avenue for poor people is existential rebellion and anarchic expression. The capacity to produce social chaos is the last resort of desperate people. It results from a tragic quest for recognition and survival. The civic terrorism that haunts our city streets and the criminality that frightens us is, in part, poor people's response to political neglect and social invisibility. Like most behavior in American society, it is directly linked to market activity—the buying and selling of commodities. In this case, the commodities tend to be drugs, alcohol and bodies (especially women's bodies). These tragic forms of expression have yet to take on an explicitly political character, yet they may in the near future. If and when they do, the prevailing powers will be forced to make *political* responses, not simply legal ones that lead to prison overcrowding.

One major challenge for progressive politics is to find a way of channeling the talent and energy of poor people into forms of social motion that can have impact on the powers that rule. This second way out of the impasse is the creation of organized citizen participation in credible progressive projects. Yet American political culture mitigates against this. The status quo lives and thrives on the perennial radical dilemma of disbelief: It is hard for ordinary citizens to believe their actions

can make a difference in a society whose resources, wealth and power are disproportionately held by the big-business community.

The best project progressive politics offered in recent decades was the courageous and exciting 1980s presidential campaigns of the charismatic spokesperson
seeking acceptance and respect within the Democratic party: the prophetic witness of the Reverend Jesse Jackson. Yet his two campaigns reveal the weakness of
American progressive politics: the obsession with televisual visibility alongside little grassroots organizing beyond elections and the inability to generate social motion outside electoral politics. In Jackson's case, it also discloses the refusal to promote democratic practices within one's own organization. Jackson has had a
significant and, for the most part, salutary effect on American progressive politics.
The major contribution of his efforts is that they were the first serious attempt-
since the Poor People's Campaign of Martin Luther King, Jr., to constitute a multiracial coalition to raise the issue of the maldistribution of resources, wealth and
power. Yet, unlike King's, Jackson's attempt to highlight this crucial issue was
often downplayed or jettisoned by his quest for entry into the elite groupings of
the centrist Democratic party. Social motion and movements in America tend to
be neither rooted in nor sustained by campaigns for electoral office, no matter
how charismatic the leader.

There can be no substantive progressive politics beyond the extension of American liberalism without social motion or movements. And despite the symbolic
and cathartic electoral victories of liberal women and people of color, all remain
thoroughly shackled by corporate priorities in the economy and in debt-ridden
administrations. Under such conditions, the plight of the ill-fed, ill-clad and ill-
housed tends to get worse.

With the lethargic electoral system nearly exhausted of progressive potential—
though never to be ignored owing to possible conservative politicians eager for
more power—we must look toward civil society, especially to mass media, universities, religious and political groupings and trade unions. Despite the decline of
popular mobilization and political participation and the decrease of unionized
workers and politicized citizens, there is a vital and vibrant culture industry, religious life, student activism and labor stirrings. In the midst of a market-driven
culture of consumption—with its spectatorial passivity, pervasive banality and
modes of therapeutic release—there is an increasing sense of social concern and
political engagement. These inchoate progressive sentiments are in search of an
effective mode of organized expression. Until we create some channels, our progressive practice will remain primarily defensive.

How do we go about creating these channels of resistance and contestation to
corporate power? What positive messages do we have to offer? What programs
can we put forward? This brings me to the third claim regarding the role of law
in progressive politics. In a society that suffers more and more from historical

amnesia—principally due to the dynamic, past-effacing activities of market forces—
lawyers have close contact with the concrete traces and residues of the struggles
and battles of the past. This is in part what Alexis de Tocqueville had in mind
when he called the legal elites America's only aristocracy. Needless to say, he understood continuity with the past in terms of social stability. I revise his formulation to connect continuity with the memory of the effects of progressive victories
of the past inscribed in the law of a society whose link with the past is tenuous
and whose present is saturated with flashing images, consumer and hedonistic
sensibilities and quick information (much of it disinformation dispensed by unre-
liable corporate cartels).

The role of progressive lawyers is not only to engage in crucial defensive practices—liberal practice vis-à-vis the courts—but also to preserve, recast and build on
the traces and residues of past conflicts coded in laws. This latter activity is guided
by a deep historical sensibility that not only deconstructs the contradictory character of past and present legal decisions or demystifies the power relations operative in such decisions; it also concocts empowering and enabling narratives that
cast light on how these decisions constitute the kind of society in which we live
and how people resist and try to transform it. Progressive lawyers can be politically engaged narrators who tell analytically illuminating stories about how the
law has impeded or impelled struggles for justice and freedom. Like rap artists of
the best sort, progressive lawyers can reach out to a demoralized citizenry to energize them with insights about the historical origins and present causes of social
misery in light of visions, analyses and practices to change the world. Lawyers
can perform this role more easily than others due to the prestige and authority of
the law in American society. Progressive lawyers can seize this opportunity to
highlight the internal contradictions and the blatant hypocrisy of much of the law
in the name of the very ideals—fairness, protection and formal equality—heralded
by the legal system. This kind of progressive legal practice, narrative in character
and radical in content, can give visibility and legitimacy to issues neglected by
and embarrassing to conservative administrations as well as expose and educate
citizens regarding the operations of economic and political powers vis-à-vis the
courts. In this regard, historical consciousness and incisive narratives yield immanent critiques, disclose the moral lapses and highlight the structural constraints of
the law while empowering victims to transform society.

Without this kind of historical consciousness and analytical storytelling, it is
difficult to create channels for resistance and challenge to corporate power. In addition, there must be an accent on the moral character of the leaders and followers in the past and present who cared, sacrificed and risked for the struggle for
justice and freedom. Progressive lawyers must highlight the *ethical* motivations of
those who initiated and promoted the legal victories that furthered struggles for
racial, sexual and class equality within the limiting perimeters of American law.

The CLS movement is significant primarily because it introduced for the first time in legal discourse a profoundly historicist approach and theoretical orientation that highlights *simultaneously* the brutal realities of class exploitation, racial subordination, patriarchal domination, homophobic marginalization and ecological abuse in the American past and present. By historicist approach, I mean a candid recognition that the law is deeply reflective of—though not thoroughly determined by—the political and ideological conflicts in American society. By theoretical orientation, I mean a serious encounter with social theories that accent the structural dynamics of the economy, state and culture that shape and are shaped by the law.

Legal formalism, legal positivism and even legal realism remained relatively silent about the brutal realities of the American past and present. This silence helped American liberalism remain for the most part captive to cultural conservatism. It also limited radical alternatives in legal studies to extensions of American liberalism. The grand breakthrough of CLS was to expose the intellectual blinders of American liberal legal scholarship and to link these blinders to the actual blood that has flowed owing to the realities hidden. It calls attention to the human costs paid by those who suffer owing to the institutional arrangements sanctioned by liberal law in the name of formal equality and liberty.

Yet CLS has not been and cannot be more than a progressive movement within a slice of the professional managerial strata in American society without connections to other social motions in American society. Academic leftist subcultures have a crucial role to play, yet they do not get us beyond the impasse.

It may well be that American culture does not possess the democratic and libertarian resources to bring about racial, sexual and class equality. Its cultural conservatism and big-business influences may impose insurmountable constraints for such a radical project. Lest we forget, there are roughly three reactionaries (Klansmen, John Birchers and so on) for every leftist in America. Yet it is precisely this kind of cynical—or is it realistic?—outlook that often confines radicalism to extensions of American liberalism. How does one combat or cope with such an outlook?

There is no definitive answer to this question. The enabling and empowering response that avoids illusions is to sustain one's hope for social change by keeping alive the memory of past and present efforts and victories and to remain engaged in such struggles owing principally to the *moral* substance of these efforts. As Nietzsche noted (with different aims in mind), subversive memory and other-regarding morality are the principal weapons for the wretched of the earth and those who fight to enhance their plight. This memory and morality in the United States consists of recurring cycles of collective insurgency and violent repression, social upsurge and establishmentarian containment. The American Left is weak and feeble during periods of social stability owing to the powers of big business and cultural conservatism; it surfaces in the form of social movements (usually led by charismatic spokespersons) to contest this stability due to their moral message that borrows from the nation's collective self-definition (as democratic and free) and due to cleavages within big business and culturally conservative groups. The social movements do not, and cannot, last long; they indeed change the prevailing status quo, but rarely fundamentally rearrange the corporate priorities of American society. In this regard, American radicalism is more than an extension of American liberalism when it constitutes a serious and concrete threat to big business, usually in the call for substantial redistribution of resources, wealth and power. Yet this threat, though significant, is short-lived owing to repression and incorporation. After such social movements, American radicalism is relegated to a defensive posture, that is, trying to preserve its victories by defending extensions of American liberalism.

If this crude historical scenario has merit, the major role of the law in progressive politics is threefold. First, past victories of social movements encoded in the law must be preserved in order to keep alive the memory of the past, struggle in the present and hope for the future. Second, this preservation, though liberal in practice, is radical in purpose in that it yearns for new social motion and movements that can threaten the new social stability of big business and cultural conservatism long enough to enact and enforce more progressive laws before repression and incorporation set in. In this regard, radical American legal practice is a kind of Burkean project turned on its head. It fosters tradition not for social stability, but to facilitate threats to the social order; it acknowledges inescapable change not to ensure organic reform, but to prepare for probable setbacks and defeats of social movements. Third, the new memories and victories inscribed in new laws are kept alive by the defensive work of progressive lawyers in order to help lay the groundwork for the next upsurge of social motion and movements.

The interplay between the work of progressive lawyers and social movements is crucial. In some cases, it is a matter of life or death for charismatic leaders or courageous followers. In other instances, it is a question of serving as the major buffer between the unprincipled deployment of naked state power and "principled" use of the courts against social movements. Such a buffer may prolong these movements and increase their progressive impact on society and culture. The moral character of these movements is important precisely because it may make repressive attackers less popular and will more than likely help sustain the memory of the movement more easily. One of the reasons the civil rights movement led by Martin Luther King, Jr., is remembered more than, say, other equally worthy ones such as the CIO-led unionization movement or the feminist movement is that its moral vision was central to its identity and accented by its major spokesperson. Needless to say, this vision appealed to the very ideals that define the national identity of many who opposed the movement.

How do progressive lawyers articulate ideals that may subvert and transform the prevailing practices legitimated by limited liberal versions of these ideals? Progressive legal practice must put forward interpretations of the precious ideal of democracy that call into question the unregulated and unaccountable power of big business; it also must set forth notions of the precious ideal of liberty that lay bare the authoritarian attitudes of cultural conservatism. This two-pronged ideological strategy should consist of an unrelenting defense of substantive democracy (in a decentralized, nonstatist fashion) and all-inclusive liberty (as best articulated in the Bill of Rights). This defense is utopian in that it tries to keep alive the possibility of social movements; it is realistic in that it acknowledges the necessity of liberal legal practices for radical lawyers to preserve the gains after social movements have been crushed or absorbed.

With solid yet insular academic leftist subcultures, eager yet sober black, brown, Asian and red Lefts, a battered yet determined labor movement (especially organized public-sector workers), beleaguered yet bold feminist and womanist progressives, scarred though proud gay and lesbian Lefts and the growing number of green and gray activists, united social motions and movements are in the making. What is needed is neither a vanguard party nor purist ideology, but rather a coming together to pursue the common goals of radical democratic and libertarian projects that overlap, especially locally and regionally and not simply within electoral politics. Democratic leadership of and by ordinary citizens in extraparliamentary modes must flourish. The social stability of the conservative and moderate administrations must be bombarded and shaken by democratic demands and libertarian protections. The profits and investments of big businesses should be scrutinized for public accountability and civic responsibility. The xenophobia and jingoism of cultural conservatives have to be morally rejected and judicially checked. A new world is in the making. Let us not allow the lethargy of American politics, the predominance of big business and the pervasiveness of cultural conservatism to blunt the contributions we can make, especially if some of us choose the law as the vocational terrain for progressive politics.

Seventeen

THE POLITICAL INTELLECTUAL

My close friend and brother Anders Stephanson, distinguished professor of history at Columbia University—conducted this interview for the international art magazine Flash Art in 1987. He and I go back over twenty years of intense dialogues about culture, international relations (his book on George Kennan is a gem) and politics. We even wrote a joint essay on Perry Anderson, the towering Marxist intellectual. This interview is one of the best I've done because he asked such challenging questions.

Anders Stephanson: Philosophically speaking, you come out of the American tradition of pragmatism. In everyday parlance, pragmatism is often understood as adjusting in an almost opportunistic manner to existing circumstances. Philosophical pragmatism is something quite different.

Cornel West: When philosophers talk about pragmatism, they are talking about Charles Peirce, William James and John Dewey. For me, it is principally Dewey. Three theses are basic: (1) antirealism in ontology, so that the correspondence theory of truth is called into question and one can no longer appeal to Reality as a court of appeal to adjudicate between conflicting theories of the world; (2) antifoundationalism in epistemology, so that one cannot in fact invoke noninferential, intrinsically credible elements in experience to justify claims about experience; and (3) detranscendentalizing of the subject, the elimination of mind itself as a sphere of inquiry. These three theses (mainly Dewey's) are underpinned by the basic claim that social practices—contingent, power-laden, structured social practices—lie at the very center of knowledge. In other words, knowledge is produced, acquired and achieved. Here, the link to the Marxist tradition, especially that of Antonio Gramsci, looms large for me.

Stephanson: These claims also have similarities with some poststructuralist theory.

West: Very much so. Detranscendentalizing the subject is, in Derrida's case, of course, a matter of the decentering of the subject, and in that regard his deconstruction clearly converges with Dewey's three basic theses of long ago. Derrida is more than a skeptical footnote to Husserl, but he can be viewed as that; and when he is, his deconstruction is a problematization of Husserl's quest for certainty within the interior monologue, within the self-presence of consciousness, within the mental theater.

Stephanson: There is obviously no pragmatic agreement on what Derrida at times is erroneously understood to be arguing, the absurd idea that there is nothing outside the text.

West: He can actually be understood to claim that there is nothing outside social practices: intertextuality is a differential web of relations shot through with traces, shot through with activity. For a pragmatist, that activity is always linked to human agency and the context in which that agency is enacted. If he is read that way, I am in agreement.

Stephanson: Poststructuralism is a critique of Marxism insofar as it undermines "the worldliness of the text"; but what also stands out is the attack on totalizing and totality. In the French context, this seems in part an effort to escape from Sartre's shadow, in part a general reaction against the postwar dominance of Marxism within the intelligentsia. In the "totalizing heterogeneity" of the United States one might well feel more inclined to retain some notion of totality.

West: I agree. Without "totality," our politics become emaciated, our politics become dispersed, our politics become nothing but existential rebellion. Some heuristic (rather than ontological) notion of totality is in fact necessary if we are to talk about mediations, interrelations, interdependencies, about totalizing forces in the world. In other words, a measure of synecdochical thinking must be preserved, thinking that would still invoke relations of parts to the whole, as for example the Gramscian articulation of spheres and historical blocs. It is true, on the other hand, that we can no longer hang on to crude orthodox "totalities" such as the idea of superstructure and base.

Stephanson: It is curious that French poststructuralism in a way shares its fixation on language with Habermas, an antagonistic thinker thoroughly mired in "modernity." I find the idea of language as a model for social and political theorizing quite suspect.

West: Language cannot be a model for social systems, since it is inseparable from other forms of power relations, other forms of social practices. I recognize, as Gadamer does, the radical linguisticality of human existence; I recognize, as Derrida does, the ways in which forms of textualization mediate all our claims about the world; but the linguistic model itself must be questioned. The multilevel operations of power within social practices—of which language is one—are more important.

Stephanson: This is why you describe yourself as a "neo-Gramscian pragmatist."

West: Gramsci's notion of hegemony is an attempt to keep track of these operative levels of power, so one does not fall into the trap of thinking that class relations somehow can be understood through linguistic models, so one does not fall into the trap of thinking that state repression that scars human bodies can be understood in terms of linguistic models. Power operates very differently in nondiscursive than in discursive ways.

Stephanson: The earlier Foucaultian distinction between discursive and nondiscursive formations remains valid for you then?

West: He should have held on to it, just as Habermas should have held on to his earlier notion of interaction—a notion rooted in the Marxist talk about social relations of production—rather than thinning it out into some impoverished idea of communication. Both can be seen as a move toward linguistic models for power.

Stephanson: Even in the case of Foucault? His pan-power theories are, after all, discursive rather than purely *linguistic*.

West: True. The later, genealogical Foucault would not make claims on linguistic models, but he remained more interested in power as it relates to the constitution of the subject than in power as such. Now, the structure of identity and subjectivity is important and has often been overlooked by the Marxist tradition; but forms of *subjection* and *subjugation* are ultimately quite different from "thick" forms of oppression like economic *exploitation* or state *repression* or bureaucratic *domination*. At any rate, "the conditions for the possibility of the constitution of the subject" is a Kantian question to which there is no satisfactory answer. To answer it, as Heidegger said in his self-critique, is to extend the metaphysical impulse in the name of an attack on metaphysics. From that viewpoint, Foucault's notion of anonymous and autonomous discourses is but one in a series of attempts going back to Kant's transcendental subject and Hegel's transindividual world spirit.

Stephanson: What if Foucault would have said that he recognized the existence of other types of oppression, but that his field of analysis was simply different?

West: I would have replied: "Fine, but that sounds more like the language of an academic than a political intellectual." It would have been to fall into the same traps of disciplinary division of labor he was calling into question. If, in fact, one is writing texts that are strategic and tactical in relation to present struggles, then it is difficult for me to see how one can be counterhegemonic without actually including "thick" forms.

Stephanson: At any rate, the poststructuralist problematic seems now to have been engulfed by the general debate on postmodernism. A certain confusion of terminology marks this debate. Conceptual pairs like *moder-*

nity/postmodernity and *modernism/postmodernism* mean very different things depending on country and cultural practice.

West: Three things are crucial in clearing that up: historical periodization, demarcation of cultural archives and practices, and politics/ideology. Take history and demarcation, for example. It is clear that "modern" philosophy begins in the seventeenth century, well before the Enlightenment, with the turn toward the subject and the new authority, the institutionalization, of scientific reason. What we call postmodern philosophy today is precisely about questioning the foundational authority of science. This trajectory is very different from that of modernist literary practices, which in turn is quite different from that of architecture: the former, to simplify, attacks reason in the name of myth, whereas the latter valorizes reason together with technique and form. These problems of periodization and demarcation are often ignored. For instance, Portoghesi's work on postmodern architecture seems to assume that his historical framework is an uncontroversial given.

Stephanson: In this sense, Lyotard's initial theorization of the postmodern condition is profoundly marked by its French provenance.

West: Yes. His book, in many ways an overcelebrated one, is really a French reflection on the transgressions of *modernism* that has little to do with *postmodernism* in the American context. In France, modernism still appears to be the *centering* phenomenon. Figures like Mallarmé, Artaud, Joyce and Bataille continue to play a fundamental role. In the United States, as Andreas Huyssen has emphasized, postmodernism is an avant-garde–like rebellion against the modernism of the museum, against the modernism of the literary and academic establishment. Note, too, the disjunction here between cultural postmodernism and postmodern politics, for Americans are politically always already in a condition of postmodern fragmentation and heterogeneity in a way that Europeans have not been; and the revolt against the center by those constituted as marginals is an *oppositional* difference in a way that poststructuralist notions of difference are not. These American attacks on universality in the name of difference, these "postmodern" issues of Otherness (Afro-Americans, Native Americans, women, gays) are in fact an implicit critique of certain French postmodern discourses about Otherness that really serve to hide and conceal the power of the voices and movements of Others.

Stephanson: From an American viewpoint, the debate between Lyotard and Habermas is thus rather off the mark.

West: Interesting *philosophical* things are at stake there, but the politics is a family affair, a very narrow family affair at that. Habermas stands for the grand old tradition of the Enlightenment project of *Vernunft*. I have some affinities with that tradition, but there is nothing new about what he has to say. Lyotard's attack on Habermas comes out of a valorization of the transgression of modernism vis-à-vis an old highbrow, Enlightenment perspective. All this is very distant from the kind of debates about post-modernism we have in the States, though of course one has to read it, be acquainted with it.

Stephanson: Agreed, but the debate has not been without effect here either. For instance, it is now often felt necessary in architectural discussions to make references to Lyotard.

West: It has become fashionable to do so because he is now a major figure, but I am talking about *serious* readings of him. Anyone who knows any-thing about Kant and Wittgenstein also knows that Lyotard's readings of them are very questionable and wrenched out of context. When these readings then travel to the United States, they often assume an authority that remains *uninterrogated*.

Stephanson: A case in point is the concept of "life-world," now freely bandied about and most immediately originating in Husserl. In the later Habermas it fulfills an important function as the site of colonization for the "systems-world." This, roughly, seems to combine Weber with Husserl, but the result is in fact nothing so much as classic American so-ciology.

West: When Habermas juxtaposes the life-world with the colonizing sys-tems, it strikes me as a rather clumsy Parsonian way of thinking about the incorporation of culture into advanced capitalist cycles of production and consumption. On the one hand, Habermas has in mind the funda-mental role that culture has come to play, now that the commodification process has penetrated cultural practices that were previously relatively autonomous; on the other hand, he is thinking of how oppositional forces and resistance to the system (what I call the process of commodi-fication) are on the wane. This is simply a less effective way of talking about something that Marxists have been talking about for years.

Stephanson: Yet, it is obvious that both Lyotard and Habermas must have done something to fill a kind of lack somewhere—otherwise their recep-tion here would be inexplicable.

West: True. These remarks do not explain why Habermas and Lyotard have gained the attention they have. Habermas, of course, speaks with the status of a second-generation Frankfurt School theorist; and he has become such a celebrity that he can drop a number of terms from a num-ber of different traditions and they take on a salience they often do not deserve. More fundamentally, his encyclopedic knowledge and his obsession with the philosophical foundations of democratic norms also satisfy a pervasive need for left academic intellectuals—a need for the professional respectability and rigor that displace political engagement and this-worldly involvement. At the same time, his well known, but really tenuous, relation to Marxism provides them with an innocuous badge of radicalism. All of this takes place at the expense of an encounter with the Marxist tradition, especially with Gramsci and the later Lukács of the ontology works. In this sense, Habermas unwittingly serves as a kind of opium for some of the American left academic intelligentsia. The impact of Lyotard, on the other hand, is probably the result of the fact that he was the first serious European thinker to address the important question of postmodernism in a comprehensive way. Deleuze, to take a related philosopher, never did, though he is ultimately a more profound poststructuralist who should get more attention than he does in the United States. His early book on Nietzsche is actually an original text.

Stephanson: Why?

West: Because Deleuze (and Levinas) was the first to think through the notion of difference independent of Hegelian ideas of opposition, and that was the start of the radical anti-Hegelianism that has characterized French intellectual life in the last decades. This position—the trashing of totality, the trashing of mediation, the valorization of difference outside the subject-object opposition, the decentering of the subject—all these features we now associate with postmodernism and poststructuralism go back to Deleuze's resurrection of Nietzsche against Hegel. Foucault, already assuming this Deleuzian critique, was the first important French intellectual who could *circumvent,* rather than confront, Hegel, which is why he says that we live in a "Deleuzian age." To live in a Deleuzian age is to live in an anti-Hegelian age so that one doesn't have to come to terms with Lukács, Adorno or any other Hegelian Marxists.

Stephanson: Nietzsche's ascendancy was not without maleficent effects when French theory was imported into the United States.

West: It was unfortunate for American intellectual life, because we never had the Marxist culture against which the French were reacting. Nor was it a culture that took Hegel seriously; the early John Dewey was the only left Hegelian we ever had. Nietzsche was received, therefore, in the context of analytic philosophy, and you can imagine the gaps and hiatuses, the blindness that resulted when Nietzsche entered narrow Anglo-American positivism. In literary criticism, on the other hand, Nietzsche was part of the Derridean baggage that the "New Critics" were able easily (and often uncritically) to assimilate into their close readings. As a result, we now have a "Tower of Babel" in American literary criticism.

Stephanson: The current, however, does not run in only one direction. Is the present French interest in "postanalytic" philosophy an indication that intellectual life is being reoriented toward the United States, at least in terms of objects of inquiry?

West: No doubt. French society has clearly come under the influence of Americanization, and West Germany, always somewhat of a fifty-first state, has moved in this direction as well. More immediately, now that the university systems in Europe no longer have the status or financial support they once had, American universities are pulling in the European intellectuals, offering money and celebrity status but also a fairly high level of conversation.

Stephanson: Features of what we associate with the concept of postmodernism have been part of American life for a long time: fragmentation, heterogeneity, surfaces without history. Is postmodernism in some sense really the codification of life in Los Angeles?

West: Only in one form and specifically at the level of middlebrow culture. The other side is the potentially oppositional aspect of the notion. Postmodernism ought never to be viewed as a homogeneous phenomenon, but rather as one in which political contestation is central. Even if we look at it principally as a form of Americanization of the world, it is clear that within the United States there are various forms of ideological and political conflict going on.

Stephanson: The black community, for example, is more "contestational" than average America.

West: The black political constituency still has some sense of the reality of the world, some sense of what is going on in the Third World. Look at the issues Jesse Jackson pressed in 1984 and now in 1988, and you find that they were issues normally reserved for the salons of leftist intellectuals. Bringing that on television had a great impact.

Stephanson: Yet, the black American condition, so to speak, is not an uplifting sight at the moment.

West: Not at all. There is increasing class division and differentiation, creating, on the one hand, a significant black middle class, highly anxiety-ridden, insecure, willing to be co-opted and incorporated into the powers that be, concerned with racism to the degree that it poses constraints on upward social mobility; and, on the other, a vast and growing black underclass, an underclass that embodies a kind of *walking nihilism* of pervasive drug addiction, pervasive alcoholism, pervasive homicide and an exponential rise in suicide. Now, because of the deindustrialization, we also have a devastated black industrial working class. We are talking here about tremendous hopelessness.

Stephanson: Suicide has increased enormously?

West: It has increased exponentially in the last decades for black males like myself who are between eighteen and thirty-five. This is unprecedented. Afro-Americans have always killed themselves less than other Americans, but this is no longer true.

Stephanson: What does a black oppositional intellectual do in these generally dire circumstances?

West: One falls back on those black institutions that have attempted to serve as resources for sustenance and survival, the black churches being one such institution, especially their progressive and prophetic wing. One tries to root oneself organically in these institutions so that one can speak to a black constituency, while maintaining a conversation with the most engaging political and postmodernist debates on the outside so that the insights they provide can be brought in.

Stephanson: That explains why you are, among other things, a kind of lay preacher. It does not explain why you are a Christian.

West: My own left Christianity is not simply instrumentalist. It is in part a response to those dimensions of life that have been flattened out, to the surface-like character of a postmodern culture that refuses to speak to issues of despair, that refuses to speak to issues of the absurd. To that extent I still find Christian narratives and stories *empowering and enabling*.

Stephanson: What does it mean to a black American to hear that, in Baudrillard's language, we are in a simulated space of hyperreality, that we have lost the real?

West: I read that symptomatically. Baudrillard seems to be articulating a sense of what it is to be a French, middle-class intellectual, or perhaps what it is to be middle class generally. Let me put it in terms of a formulation from Henry James that Fredric Jameson has appropriated: There is a reality *that one cannot not know*. The ragged edges of the Real, of *Necessity*, not being able to eat, not having shelter, not having health care, all this is something that one cannot not know. The black condition acknowledges that. It is so much more acutely felt because this is a society where a lot of people live a Teflon existence, where a lot of people have no sense of the ragged edges of necessity, of what it means to be impinged upon by structures of oppression. To be an upper-middle-class American is actually to live a life of unimaginable comfort, convenience and luxury. Half of the black population is denied this, which is why they have a strong sense of reality.

Stephanson: Does that make notions of postmodernism meaningless from a black perspective?

West: It must be conceived very differently at least. Take Ishmael Reed, an exemplary postmodern writer. Despite his conservative politics, he cannot deny the black acknowledgment of the reality one cannot not know. In writing about black American history, for instance, he has to come to terms with the state-sponsored terrorism of lynching blacks and so on. This is inescapable in black postmodernist practices.

Stephanson: How is one in fact to understand black postmodernist practices?

West: To talk about black postmodernist practices is to go back to bebop music and see how it relates to literary expressions like Reed's and Charles Wright's. It is to go back, in other words, to the genius of Charlie Parker, John Coltrane and Miles Davis. Bebop was, after all, a revolt against the middle-class "jazz of the museum," against swing and white musicians like Benny Goodman, who had become hegemonic by colonizing a black art form. What Parker did, of course, was to Africanize jazz radically: to accent the polyrhythms, to combine these rhythms with unprecedented virtuosity on the sax. He said explicitly that his music was not produced to be accepted by white Americans. He would be suspicious if it were. This sense of revolt was to be part and parcel of the postmodern rebellion against the modernism of the museum.

Stephanson: To me, bebop seems like a black cultural avant-garde that corresponds historically to abstract expressionism in painting—the last gasp of modernism—on which indeed it had some considerable influence.

West: Certainly they emerge together, and people do tend to parallel them as though they were the same, but abstract expressionism was not a revolt in the way bebop was. In fact, it was an instance of modernism itself. Bebop also had much to do with fragmentation, with heterogeneity, with the articulation of difference and marginality, aspects of what we associate with postmodernism today.

Stephanson: Aspects of the cultural dominant, yes; but these elements are also part of modernism. Surely one can still talk about Charlie Parker as a unified subject expressing inner *angst* or whatever, an archetypal characteristic of modernism.

West: True, but think too of another basic feature of postmodernism, the breakdown of highbrow and pop culture. Parker would use whistling off the streets of common black life: "Cherokee," for instance, was actually a song that black children used to sing when jumping rope or, as I did, playing marbles. Parker took that melody of the black masses and filtered it through his polyrhythms and technical virtuosity, turning it into a highbrow jazz feature that was not quite highbrow anymore. He was already calling into question the distinction between high and low culture, pulling from a bricolage, as it were, what was seemingly popular and relating it to what was then high. Yet, I would not deny the modernist impulse, nor would I deny that they were resisting jazz as commodity, very much like Joyce and Kafka resisted literary production as commodity. In that sense bebop straddles the fence.

Stephanson: The ultimate problem, however, is whether it is actually useful to talk about someone like Charlie Parker in these terms.

West: It is useful to the degree that it contests the prevailing image of him as a modernist. As you imply, on the other hand, there is a much deeper question as to whether these terms *modernism/postmodernism* relate to Afro-American cultural practices in any illuminating way at all. We are only at the beginning of that inquiry.

Stephanson: Was there ever actually a mass black audience for bebop?

West: Yes, Parker's was the sort of music black people danced to in the 1940s. Miles's "cool" stage was also big in the 1950s with albums like "Kinda Blue," though it went hand in hand with the popularity of Nat King Cole and Dinah Washington.

Stephanson: What happened to this avant-garde black music when Motown and Aretha Franklin came along?

West: It was made a fetish for the educated middle class, principally, but not solely, the white middle class. In absolute terms, its domain actually expanded because the black audience of middle-class origin also expanded. But the great dilemma of black musicians who try to preserve a tradition from mainstream domestication and dilution is in fact that they lose contact with the black masses. In this case, there was eventually a move toward "fusion," jazz artists attempting to produce objects intended for broader black-and-white consumption.

Stephanson: Miles Davis is the central figure of that avant-garde story.

West: And he crossed over with the seminal record *Bitches Brew* in 1970, accenting his jazz origins while borrowing from James Brown's polyrhythms and Sly Stone's syncopation. *Bitches Brew* brought him a black mass audience that he had lost in the 1960s—certainly one that Coltrane had lost completely.

Stephanson: Crossover artists, in the sense of having a racially mixed mass audience, are not very numerous today.

West: No, but there are more than ever: Whitney Houston, Dionne Warwick, Lionel Richie, Diana Ross and Anita Baker. Baker is a very different crossover artist, because she is still deeply rooted in the black context. Michael Jackson and Prince are crossover in another sense; their music is less rooted in black musical traditions and much more open to white rock and so forth.

Stephanson: In Prince's case it has to do with the fact that he is not entirely from a black background.

West: Still, he grew up in a black foster home and a black Seventh Day Adventist church, but in Minneapolis, which is very different from growing up like Michael Jackson in a black part of Gary, Indiana. Minneapolis has always been a place of cultural cross-fertilization, of interracial marriages and relationships. The early Jackson Five, on the other hand, were thoroughly ensconced in a black tradition, and Michael began his career dancing like James Brown. Now he is at the center of the black-white interface.

Stephanson: Prince never really played "black" music as one thinks of it. His music was "fused" from the start.

West: To be in a black context in Minneapolis is already to be in a situation of fusion, because the blacks themselves have much broader access to mainstream white culture in general. You get the same thing with other black stars who have come out of that place.

Stephanson: Michael Jackson, by contrast, is now a packaged middle-American product.

West: A nonoppositional instance of commodification in black skin that is becoming more and more like candy, more radical than McDonald's, but not by much. It is watered-down black music, but still with a lot of the aggressiveness and power of that tradition.

Stephanson: Music is *the* black means of cultural expression, is it not?

West: Music and preaching. Here, rap is unique because it combines the black preacher and the black music tradition, replacing the liturgical-ecclesiastical setting with the African polyrhythms of the street. A tremendous *articulateness* is syncopated with the African drumbeat, the African funk, into an American postmodernist product; there is no subject expressing original anguish here, but a fragmented subject pulling from past and present, innovatively producing a heterogeneous product. The stylistic combination of the oral, the literate and the musical is exemplary as well. Otherwise, it is part and parcel of the subversive energies of black underclass youth, energies that are forced to take a cultural mode of articulation because of the political lethargy of American society. The music of Grandmaster Flash and the Furious Five, Kurtis Blow, and Sugar Hill Gang has to take on a deeply political character because, again, they are in the reality that the black underclass *cannot not know*—the brutal side of American capital, the brutal side of American racism, the brutal side of sexism against black women.

Stephanson: I always thought rap was too indigenous a black form of expression to make it in the general marketplace. Run/DMC has proven me wrong on this.

West: Indeed. Run/DMC is as indigenous as you can get. Upper-middle-class white students at Yale consume a lot of Run/DMC.

Stephanson: Yet, the constitutive elements of rap seemed to me too fixed for it to become a permanent presence on the crossover scene, more anonymous and less easily assimilated into existing white concepts of melody and structure. This, too, is probably wrong.

West: People said the same thing about Motown in 1961, the same thing about Aretha Franklin, who is about as organic as you can get. She is not as accepted by mainstream white society as the smoother and more diluted Warwick and Ross, but she *is* accepted. That, from the perspective of 1964–1965, is unbelievable. The same thing could happen with rap music, since the boundaries are actually rather fluid. But it won't remain the same.

Stephanson: Where will rap end up?

West: Where most American postmodern products end up: highly packaged, regulated, distributed, circulated and consumed.

Stephanson: Preaching, as you said, is obviously a cultural form of expression, but is it a specifically *artistic* form?

West: Sure. The best preachers are outstanding oral artists, performance artists. Martin Luther King, Jr., gave white America just a small taste of what it is to be an artistic rhetorician in the black churches. Tremendous gravity and weight are given to these artistic performances, because people's *lives* hang on them. They provide some hope from week to week so that these folk won't fall into hopelessness and meaninglessness, so that they won't kill themselves. The responsibility of the black preacher-artist is, in that sense, deeply functional, but at the same time it entails *a refinement of a form* bequeathed to him by those who came before. Black preaching is inseparable here from black singing. Most secular black singers come out of the choir, and the lives of the congregation hang on how they sing the song, what they put into the song, how passionate, how self-invested they are. Preaching is just less visible to the outside as an art form because words uttered once don't have the same status as cultural products; but the black preachers are artists with a very long tradition.

Stephanson: Since it does not lend itself to mechanical reproduction, preaching is also hard to destroy by turning it into a business. How is this artistic form of expression actually evaluated?

West: In terms of the impact the preacher has on the congregation. This impact can take the form of cantankerous response, or the form of existential empowerment, the convincing of people to keep on keeping on, to keep on struggling, contesting and resisting.

Stephanson: It is Kant's acrobat who intervenes constantly to transform an otherwise unstable equilibrium into another equilibrium.

West: Well put. Black sermonic practices have not received the attention they deserve. As a matter of fact, black linguistic practices as such need to be examined better, because they add a lot to the American language.

Stephanson: Black language creates a wealth of new words, which are then quickly picked up by the mainstream.

West: Usually with significant semantic changes. Stevie Wonder's "Everything is alright, uptight, out of sight" is a string of synonyms. *Uptight,* when I was growing up, meant smooth, cool, everything is fine. By the time it got to middle America, *uptight* meant anxiety-ridden, the inability of everything to be fine. Similar semantic shifts, though perhaps less drastic, take place with *chilling out, mellowing out* and other black expressions. *Chilling out* meant letting things be, a sort of Heideggerian notion of *aletheia,* letting the truth reveal itself, letting it shine, letting it come forth.

Stephanson: Given the social circumstances of which it is a product, black American language seems to me, on the outside, not to allow very easily for prevalent white orders of theoretical reflection.

West: It is a hustling culture, and a hustling culture tends to be *radically* "practicalist," deeply pragmatic, because the issue is always one of surviving, getting over.

Stephanson: This, I imagine, demands some sharp linguistic twists for you.

West: I am continually caught in a kind of "heteroglossia," speaking a number of English languages in radically different contexts. When it comes to abstract theoretical reflection, I employ Marx, Weber, Frankfurt theorists, Foucault and so on. When it comes to speaking with the black masses, I use Christian narratives and stories, a language meaningful to them but filtered through and informed by intellectual developments from de Tocqueville to Derrida. When it comes to the academy itself, there is yet another kind of language, abstract but often atheoretical, since social theorizing is mostly shunned. Philosophers are simply ill-equipped to talk about social theory—they know Wittgenstein but not Weber, they know J. L. Austin but not Marx.

Stephanson: Apart from the musician and the preacher, black culture exhibits a third artist of great importance: the athlete. There is enormous emphasis on aesthetic execution in black sports.

West: You can see this in basketball, where the black player tries to *style* reality so that he becomes spectacle and performance, always projecting a sense of self, whereas his white counterpart tends toward the productivistic and mechanistic. A lot of time, energy and discipline also go into it, but usually with a certain *investment of self* that does not express the work ethic alone. Ali was, of course, exemplary in this respect. Not only was he a great boxer, but a stylish one as well—smooth, clever, rhythmic, and syncopated.

Stephanson: Whence comes this emphasis on spectacle?

West: Originally, it derives from an African sense of pageantry, the tendency to project yourself *in performance* in a way so that you are at one with a certain flow of things. By "one," I do not mean any romantic kind of unity between subject and object or pantheistic unification with nature, but at one with the craft and task at hand. It is also to risk something. Baraka has spoken of the African *deification of accident,* by which he indicated the acknowledgment of risk and contingency: to be able to walk a tightrope, to be able to do the dangerous and to do it well. But it is a form of risk-ridden execution that is *self-imposed.*

Stephanson: Among the various black modes of cultural expression, pictorial art has not, with all due allowances for graffiti art, been much in evidence. The black middle class seems uninterested and so does the underclass; art as a practice is esoteric and largely without rewards.

West: Access to the kinds of education and subcultural circles is much less available to potential black artists. In addition to the racism in the avantgarde world, painting and sculpture are not as widely appreciated as they ought to be in black America. Therefore, pictorial black artists are marginal. They deserve more black support—and exposure.

Stephanson: Beyond impediments of entry, is there not also some indigenous cultural element at work here? There are, after all, many black writers and dancers.

West: The strong, puritanical Protestantism of black religion has not been conducive to the production of pictures. For the same reason, there is a great belief in the *power of the word,* in literate acumen. In fact, writers are sometimes given too much status and become "spokespeople" for the race, which is ridiculous. Yet there is an openness, diversity, multiplicity of artistic sensibility when developed and cultivated in the black community. Realist modes of representation are, for example, not inherently linked to Afro-American culture. The pioneering artwork of Howardina Pindell, Emma Amos, Benny Andrews and Martin Puryear are exemplary in this regard.

Stephanson: It is a cliché to say that we live in a society of images, but we obviously do. Blacks watch more television than the average. Do they appropriate these images differently?

West: There is an element of scrutiny involved. The images have been so pervasively negative, so degrading and devaluing of black people—especially of black women—that the process has always been one tied to some skepticism and suspicion.

Stephanson: Images are seen through a skeptical racial grid?

West: A racial grid as transmitted from one generation to the next. This does not mean it is always critical. Think, for example, of all the Italian pictures of Jesus that hang in black churches at this very moment, pictures of Michelangelo's uncles when the man was actually a dark Palestinian Jew. Such images are widely accepted. But that particular one is, of course, different because it is sacred and therefore much more difficult to question. There is a much more critical attitude toward television. With the exception of the new phenomenon of the *Cosby Show* and *Frank's Place,* black folk are still usually depicted there as buffoons, black women as silly.

Stephanson: Images of blacks are sometimes produced by blacks, as in many music videos. Those I have watched tend to be either sentimental ones about people yearning for the "right one" or highly charged ones featuring minutely choreographed movement.

West: You also find a lot of conspicuous consumption—a lot of very expensive cars, furs, suits and so forth. The American dream of wealth and prosperity remains a powerful carrot, because television producers are aware of the reality that the black audience cannot not know. Another big problem is the relation between black men and women. Different kinds of women are projected as objects of desire and quest, but they are downright white women, or blacks who look entirely white, or very light-skinned black women. Rarely do you find any longing for the really *dark* woman. And when a black woman is the star, she is usually yearning for a black man who is light—never a white man, but a black man who is light.

Stephanson: Black culture is, of course, as sexist as the rest.

West: In a different way. The pressure on Afro-Americans as a people has forced the black man closer to the black woman—they are in the same boat. But they are also at each other's throats. The relation is internally hierarchical and often mediated by violence: black men over black women.

Stephanson: Is it not more unabashedly sexist in its macho version? For even though popular culture as such is deeply infused with macho imagery, it seems to me that the black ditto is more *overtly* so.

West: Black society shows the typical range from the extreme machismo of any patriarchy to a few egalitarian relations. Nonetheless, what you say is probably true, and there are simply no excuses for the vicious treatment of black women by these men. Yet interaction between the sexes in the black community is unintelligible without highlighting the racist and poverty-ridden circumstances in which so many blacks live. Machismo is itself a bid for power by relatively powerless and degraded black men. Remember, too, that the white perception here is principally informed by interracial relations between black men and white women, relations in which black machismo is particularly pronounced. There is also an *expectation* among large numbers of white folk that black men be macho, and black men then tend to fulfill that expectation. Those who do not are perceived as abnormal. A crucial part of this phenomenon is the question of sexual prowess; if you're not a "gashman," your whole identity as a black male becomes highly problematic. So, to a degree, the process is a self-fulfilling prophecy.

Stephanson: There has been an extreme destruction of the family within the black underclass. Aside from the obvious causes, why is this?

West: Aside from the changes in society as a whole, developments like hedonistic consumerism and the constant need of stimulation of the body, which make any qualitative human relationships hard to maintain, it is a question of a breakdown in cultural resources, what Raymond Williams calls structures of meaning. Except for the church, there are few potent traditions on which one can fall back in dealing with hopelessness and meaninglessness. There used to be a set of stories that could convince people that their absurd situation was one worth coping with, but the passivity is now overwhelming. Drug addiction is only one manifestation of this—you live a life of living death, of slower death, rather than killing yourself immediately. I recently spoke at a high school in one of the worst parts of Brooklyn, and the figures were staggering: almost 30 percent had attempted suicide, 70 percent were deeply linked to drugs. This is what I mean by "walking nihilism." *It is the imposing of closure on the human organism, intentionally, by that organism itself.* Such nihilism is not *cute.* We are not dancing on Nietzsche's texts here and *talking* about nihilism; we are in a nihilism that is *lived.* We are talking about real obstacles to the sustaining of a *people.*

Stephanson: Which is not quite how Nietzschean nihilism is normally conceived.

West: There are a variety of nihilisms in Nietzsche, and this is not so much one in which meaning is elusive, certainly not one with a surplus of meaning. What we have, on the contrary, is not at all elusive—*meaninglessness,* a meaningless so well understood that it can result in the taking of one's own life.

SOURCE: From *Beyond Eurocentrism and Multiculturalism, Vol. 2: Prophetic Reflections* (Monroe, Me.: Common Courage Press, 1993), pp. 81–102. Originally appeared in *Flash Art* in 1987.

Eighteen

A WORLD OF IDEAS

This interview was my first television appearance in America. Of course, Bill Moyers is a master interviewer. He teased out features of my style and substance often overlooked by others. He and I have precious roots in Texas, are shaped by Baptist church experiences and are deeply concerned about race and injustice in America. This was an ideal place for me to express my beliefs to a television audience for the first time. My audience base rose quickly after this interview.

Bill Moyers: You've been seen in some very unusual places for an intellectual: the storefronts and streets of Harlem, the shanty-towns of South Africa, one of the worst high schools in one of the worst districts in Brooklyn. Why? Those are so far from Princeton, so far from the ivory tower.

Cornel West: I understand the vocation of the intellectual as trying to turn easy answers into critical questions and putting those critical questions to people with power. The quest for truth, the quest for the good, the quest for the beautiful all require us to let suffering speak, let victims be visible and let social misery be put on the agenda of those with power. So to me, pursuing the life of the mind is inextricably linked with the struggle of those who have been dehumanized on the margins of society.

Moyers: One black intellectual said you make him uncomfortable with your ease out there on the street.

West: Certainly I have tried, on the one hand, to uphold the discipline of the life of the mind, but, on the other hand, to keep track of other people's humanity, their predicaments and plights. I want to empathize and sympathize with them the best that I possibly can.

Moyers: Many Americans believe that a substantial portion of the black community in the inner cities is simply saying yes now to death, violence and hate. What do you find when you go there?

West: I do find a lot of meaninglessness and hopelessness, but at the same time I find people who are struggling, trying to survive and thrive under excruciating conditions. So the question becomes: How does one attempt to transform this meaninglessness and hopelessness into a more effective kind of struggle and resistance? It's a very difficult task, but there are many highly courageous people, working people, ordinary people, who are trying to hold on to meaning and value in a society that revolves more and more around the market mentality, the market ethos that permeates almost every sphere of this society.

Moyers: What does that ethos do to a community?

West: It makes it very difficult to hold on to nonmarket values, such as commitment in relationships, solidarity, community, care, sacrifice, risk and struggle. Market values encourage a preoccupation with the now, with the immediate.

Moyers: The future is now.

West: That's exactly right. What that means, then, is people feel they no longer have to work or sacrifice. Why? Because the big money can be achieved right now. In the black community market activity is at its most pernicious and vicious right now in the drug industry. Young people want to make the easy buck now. In many ways they are mirroring what they see in society at large, what they see on Wall Street. It makes it very difficult for them to take not only commitment and caring and sacrificing, but ultimately human life itself seriously. Profits become much more important than human life. What we see is a very cold-hearted meanspiritedness throughout these communities. I think again it reflects so much of our own culture and civilization. It's quite frightening.

Moyers: You've been making a lot of speeches to young people in the high schools like those in Brooklyn, where the situation is fairly miserable. What do you say to those young people?

West: I tell them we live in a society that suffers from historical amnesia, and we find it very difficult to preserve the memory of those who have resisted and struggled over time for the ideals of freedom and democracy and equality. Then I provide some historical background of people who displayed this kind of courage in its highest form—people like Martin Luther King, Jr., Michael Harrington, Ida B. Wells-Barnett and other freedom fighters. Then I move up to the present and talk about how many of their parents and brothers and sisters in some way extend that kind of tradition. And I ask the kids: "Are you going to be part of this tradition? What's going to happen to this tradition? How can we keep it alive? How can we keep it vital and vibrant?"

Moyers: You're suggesting that each one of them can matter, and yet they're living in communities where the institutions have broken down, where the family is fragmented, where chaos is all around them. Don't they need institutions that will nurture them? Institutions they can hold on to for the message of self-worth and self-determination to take hold?

West: Oh, very much so. In fact, when I talk about the historical leaders, I talk about the institutions that produced them—the families, the schools, the colleges, the churches, the synagogues and the temples. It's true that many American families, neighborhoods and associations are undergoing a kind of disintegration and decomposition, but it's not thorough. There are still some American families and some black families that are holding together. There are still some neighborhoods, black, white, brown and Asian, that are holding together.

Moyers: What do you tell them about how to signify?

West: They have to hope. They have to hold on to some notion that the future can be different if they sacrifice, if they fight, if they struggle. This is an old message. I learned this message in the black church years ago. I'm very much a product of a loving black family and a caring black church. And more than anything else, the church taught me the lesson of the cross. The only way to hope, to faith, to life is through the blood. The cross is a symbol of the impossible possibility, to use Karl Barth's language, the impossible possibility of holding on to faith, hope, and love in the kind of world in which we live, the kind of world in which blood is in fact always flowing.

Moyers: Once upon a time the church did provide that kind of lesson, it did provide that kind of community. But a poll I saw just recently said that in the black community, the church is less and less a part of the life of young people. Do you find that so?

West: The influence of the black church is declining, as are churches around the country. But I do think that the message of the church remains relevant, even among those who are not Christians. The value of service to others, the value of caring for others, the value of attempting to keep one's eye on the forms of social misery, inadequate housing, health care, child care, unemployment and underemployment—religion has no monopoly on these kinds of values. Religion may help motivate persons to act on these values in light of the stories within their traditions, but neither Christians nor Jews nor Muslims nor Hindus have a monopoly on this.

Moyers: I've always been curious why so many blacks, when they were brought to this country, adopted Christianity, which was the religion that often defended the slavery that imprisoned them. How do you explain that?

West: I think large numbers of black people turned to Christianity for three basic reasons. The first had to do with issues of meaning and value. Black people arriving here 371 years ago had to come to terms with the absurd in the human condition in America, the place of enslavement.

Moyers: So that image of the Exodus, of the slaves freeing themselves, was especially appealing to black slaves in America.

West: Yes. The God of history who sides with the oppressed and the exploited, a God who accents and affirms one's own humanity in a society that is attacking and assaulting black intelligence and black beauty and black moral character, namely, white-supremacist ideology—this message spoke very deeply at the level of meaning and value. But Christianity is also important institutionally because black people appropriated primarily the left wing of the Reformation. The Baptists and the Methodists are much more democratically structured than the Catholics. The preachers are immediately accountable to the congregation, and the pew has access to leadership. Black humanity at the level of both leadership and followership could be accented.

Then I think there was also a political reason. Black people could engage in a form of critique of slavery, of Jim Crowism, of second-class citizenship, while holding on to the humanity of those who they opposed. This is the great lesson of Martin Luther King, Jr., who is a product of this tradition.

Moyers: We have opponents, but not enemies.

West: That's exactly right. Actually, the enemy is oppression and exploitation. It's legitimate to abhor and hate oppression and exploitation, but we cannot lose sight of the humanity of those who are perpetuating it. This is a very difficult and complex doctrine, because it seems to promote a kind of a masochistic love of oppressor.

Moyers: The negative side of religion was that it could breed apathy and compliance. Also, the black church could even become a haven for charismatic con men, as modern-day television is to some evangelists.

West: Sure. I think Karl Marx's critique of religion as an impotent form of protest against suffering has an element of truth. Religion has tended to legitimize and to undergird forms of oppression precisely because it provided a critique that remained spiritual and had very little understanding of the social, economic and political conditions that were sustaining the oppression. At its best, religion can provide us with the vision and the values, but it doesn't provide the analytical tools. One doesn't look to the Bible to understand the complexity of the modern industrial and postindustrial society. It can give us certain insights into the human condition, certain visions of what we should hope for, but we also need the tools. They are found outside of religious texts and outside of religious sensibilities. We move to the social sciences for some handle on the maldistribution of resources, wealth, income, prestige and influence in our society. So all forms of prophetic religion must be linked in some sense with a set of analytical tools.

Moyers: But there is still in that old scripture a very powerful moral message. You end one of your books, *Prophesy Deliverance,* with a quote of Jesus from Luke 4:18: "The spirit of the Lord is upon me because he has anointed me to preach good news to the poor. He has sent me to proclaim release to the captives and recovering of sight to the blind, to set at liberty those who are oppressed." Do you think that message still means anything in urban areas where you visit often?

West: Yes, I do. I think it means that there is still someone who cares for those who are socially invisible and politically marginalized. The spirit of the Lord is still empowering to those who have been cast aside to struggle, enabling those who've been cast aside to not lose hope.

Moyers: You have been on a long intellectual odyssey yourself. Are you still an active Christian?

West: Very much so. Jesus' words, along with many others, have helped sustain me as I encountered for myself the absurdity of being an American and a person of African descent. W. E. B. Du Bois talked about this years ago in his American classic *Souls of Black Folk.* "All that people of a darker hue have ever wanted to be," he said, "is human beings who could be both American and also acknowledge their African heritage." This double consciousness, of living in many ways *in* America but not still fully *of* it, is a tension, I think, that all of us forever grapple with. Those words allow me to hold on to my sense of possibility.

Moyers: You have talked about combative spirituality. What do you mean by that?

West: I mean a form of spirituality—of community and communion—that preserves meaning by fighting against the bombardments of claims that we are inferior or deficient. Combative spirituality sustains persons in their humanity, but also transcends solely the political. It embraces a political struggle, but it also deals with issues of death or dread, of despair or disappointment. These are the ultimate facts of existence and they're filtered through our social and political existence. Ultimately all of us as individuals must confront these, and a combative spirituality accents a political struggle, but goes beyond it by looking death, dread, despair, disappointment and disease in the face and saying that there is in fact a hope beyond these.

Moyers: But isn't that hope deferred again? Isn't that justice deferred? Isn't that saying, "You have to put up with the miserable conditions in Brooklyn today, in Harlem, because one day there'll be a reward?"

West: No, because it calls into question all illusions that there'll be a utopia around the corner. When you talk about hope, you have to be a long-distance runner. This is again so very difficult in our culture, because the quick fix, the overnight solution, mitigates against being a long-distance runner in the moral sense, the sense of fighting because it's right, because it's moral, because it's just. That kind of hope linked to combative spirituality is what I have in mind.

Moyers: So combative spirituality is that sense of subversive joy, as you once called it?

West: Subversive joy is the ability to transform tears into laughter, a laughter that allows one to acknowledge just how difficult the journey is, but also to acknowledge one's own sense of humanity and folly and humor in the midst of this very serious struggle. It's a joy that allows one both a space, a distance from the absurd, but also empowers one to engage in the struggle again when the time is necessary.

Moyers: Some of that has come, has it not, from black music, from gospel and jazz and blues?

West: Yes.

Moyers: What about rap? Does rap have any of that spiritual energy in it?

West: Oh, very much so. I mean, black rap music is the most important popular musical development in the last ten years. It is a profound extension of the improvisational character of what I call the Afro-American spiritual blues impulse, which is an attempt to hold at bay the demons and devils. What rap has done is to allow a kind of marriage between the rhetorical and the musical by means of some of the most amazing linguistic virtuosities we have seen in the language, the lyrics, the quickness, the speaking.

Moyers: You have said that rap music is part and parcel of the subversive energies of the youthful black underclass. What do you mean by subversive energies?

West: They respond to their sense of being rejected by the society at large, of being invisible in the society at large, with a subversive critique of that society. It has to do with both the description and depiction of the conditions under which they're forced to live, as well as a description and depiction of the humanity preserved by those living in such excruciating conditions. It then goes beyond to a larger critique of the power structure as a whole. It is international in terms of its link to struggles in South Africa, so that in that sense it's part of a prophetic tradition. But I should say that what is lacking in rap music is vision and analysis. It's fun, it's entertaining, it helps sustain the rituals of party-going on the weekends, but it still lacks a vision. This is where again the church plays an important role, you see, because otherwise, it's quite easy to channel these energies into very narrow, chauvinistic, xenophobic forms that lack vision, that have no moral content or ethical substance.

Moyers: Blacks have made an enormous contribution in this country through preaching, through music, through sports, yet we still see the black underclass sinking in a quagmire. Almost every analyst I know says nothing is helping, not black rap music, not the black church, not social programs, not capitalist economics. Nothing is helping this black underclass. And yet you still trumpet hope.

West: Yes, I do. I mean, the condition of the black underclass is tragic, but they are still human beings who are getting about. Many are still making sense of the world. Many are actually still escaping. I don't want to lose sight of them. Many are still in churches trying to hold on to their moral character. Many are outside of churches trying to hold on to their moral character. I don't want to view the black underclass as a monolithic or homogeneous entity. These are actual human beings, children of God. Some are losing, many are losing, some are winning in terms of holding on to their sense of self and holding on to their sense of vitality and vibrancy.

That in no way excuses the structural and institutional forces that are at work: the unemployment, the failed educational system, the consumer culture that bombards them. The black underclass still has to contend with all of these in addition to the larger racist legacy. But it's not only about race. As we know, there are other factors as well, so that certainly a description of their conditions must include this. But I hold up hope. I'm talking about my cousins and friends and relatives who are seemingly locked into this condition, yet change can indeed come about.

Moyers: Where is the moral outrage in society today? Do you see it?

West: Not enough. There's been a kind of anaesthetizing, I think, in the 1980s toward forms of social misery. But there's the National Coalition of the Homeless. There's the NAACP and DSA, Democratic Socialists of America, of which I'm an honorary chair. There's a whole host of groups that have been trying to sustain some moral outrage, filtered through a systemic analysis of our situation and regulated by a vision. It hasn't taken the way it has in past decades, but I think the 1990s will be different.

Moyers: The conundrum is that if you are morally outraged today, you're relegated to the margins of society. It's almost considered out of the norm to be concerned about social misery. To be mature today means you're supposed to say we can't ameliorate certain circumstances in life.

West: But I think the important point there is that we have to understand why this is so. Why has cynicism become so pervasive over the past ten years for those who wanted to focus on social misery? And I see that cynicism more and more on the wane. I think Eastern Europe is providing us with a different lesson, you see. Up until the last few months, people did not believe that ordinary human beings organized could fundamentally change society. We had scholars around the world saying that the very notion of revolution was outdated and antiquated. We could not even imagine a transfer of power that we have witnessed in Eastern Europe in the past month and a half. So all of those assumptions and presuppositions are now being called into question, which means that the focus of ordinary people organizing, mobilizing, having impact on powers that be, once again moves to the center of the agenda.

SOURCE: From *Beyond Eurocentrism and Multiculturalism, Vol. 2: Prophetic Reflections* (Monroe, Me.: Common Courage Press, 1993), pp. 103–112.

Nineteen

THE DILEMMA OF THE BLACK INTELLECTUAL

This essay, written in 1985, is the most widely quoted and controversial piece I have published. It has been reprinted many times in a variety of places—especially by the younger generation of intellectuals of all colors. This popularity reflects a deep crisis of vocation among black intellectuals. bell hooks's "Black Women Intellectuals"—in our book Breaking Bread (1991)—is a devastating critique of this piece. I recommend that people read them together.

The peculiarities of the American social structure, and the position of the intellectual class within it, make the functional role of the negro intellectual a special one. The negro intellectual must deal intimately with the White power structure and cultural apparatus, and the inner realities of the Black world at one and the same time. But in order to function successfully in this role, he has to be acutely aware of the nature of the American social dynamic and how it monitors the ingredients of class stratifications in American society. . . . Therefore the functional role of the negro intellectual demands that he cannot be absolutely separated from either the Black or White world.

—HAROLD CRUSE
The Crisis of the Negro Intellectual (1967)

The contemporary black intellectual faces a grim predicament. Caught between an insolent American society and insouciant black community, the Afro-American who takes seriously the life of the mind inhabits an isolated and insulated world. This condition has little to do with the motives and intentions of black intellectuals; rather, it is an objective situation created by circumstances not of their own choosing. In this meditative essay, I will explore this dilemma of the black intellectual and suggest various ways of understanding and transforming it.

ON BECOMING A BLACK INTELLECTUAL

The choice of becoming a black intellectual is an act of self-imposed marginality; it assures a peripheral status in and to the black community. The quest for literacy indeed is a fundamental theme in Afro-American history and a basic impulse in the black community. But for blacks, as with most Americans, the uses for literacy are usually perceived to be for more substantive pecuniary benefits than those of the writer, artist, teacher or professor. The reasons some black people choose to become serious intellectuals are diverse. But in most cases these reasons can be traced back to a common root: a conversion-like experience with a highly influential teacher or peer that convinced one to dedicate one's life to the activities of reading, writing and conversing for the purposes of individual pleasure, personal worth and political enhancement of black (and often other oppressed) people.

The way in which one becomes a black intellectual is highly problematic. This is so because the traditional roads others travel to become intellectuals in American society have only recently been opened—and remain quite difficult. The main avenues are the academy or the literate subcultures of art, culture and politics. Prior to the acceptance of black undergraduate students to elite white universities and colleges in the late 1960s, select black educational institutions served as the initial stimulus for potential black intellectuals. And in all honesty, there were relatively more and better black intellectuals then than now. After a decent grounding in a black college, where self-worth and self-confidence were affirmed, bright black students then matriculated to leading white institutions to be trained by liberal sympathetic scholars often of renowned stature. Stellar figures such as W. E. B. Du Bois, E. Franklin Frazier and John Hope Franklin were products of this system. For those black intellectuals-to-be who missed college opportunities for financial or personal reasons, there were literate subcultures—especially in the large urban centers—of writers, painters, musicians and politicos for unconventional educational enhancement. Major personages such as Richard Wright, Ralph Ellison and James Baldwin were products of this process.

Ironically, the present-day academy and contemporary literate subcultures present more obstacles for young black intellectuals than those in decades past. This is so for three basic reasons. First, the attitudes of white scholars in the academy are quite different than those in the past. It is much more difficult for black students, especially graduate students, to be taken seriously as *potential scholars and intellectuals,* owing to the managerial ethos of our universities and colleges (in which less time is spent with students) and to the vulgar (racist!) perceptions fueled by affirmative-action programs, which pollute many black student–white professor relations.

Second, literate subcultures are less open to blacks now than they were three or four decades ago, not because white avant-garde journals or leftist groups are more racist today, but rather because heated political and cultural issues, such as the legacy of the black power movement, the Israeli/Palestinian conflict and the invisibility of Africa in American political discourse, have created rigid lines of demarcation and distance between black and white intellectuals. Needless to say, black presence in leading liberal journals like the *New York Review of Books* and the *New York Times Book Review* is negligible—nearly nonexistent. And more leftist periodicals such as *Dissent, Socialist Review, The Nation* and *Telos* or avant-garde scholarly ones like *Diacritics, Salmagundi, Partisan Review* and *Raritan* do not do much better. Only *Monthly Review, Massachusetts Review, Boundary 2* and *Social Text* make persistent efforts to cover black subject matter and have regular black contributors. The point here is not mere finger-pointing at negligent journals (though it would not hurt matters!), but rather an attempt to highlight the racially separatist publishing patterns and practices of American intellectual life, which are characteristic of the chasm between black and white intellectuals.

Third, the general politicization of American intellectual life (in the academy and outside), along with the rightward ideological drift, constitutes a hostile climate for the making of black intellectuals. To some extent, this has always been so, but the ideological capitulation of the significant segment of former left liberals to the new-style conservatism and old-style imperialism has left black students and black professors with few allies in the academy and in influential periodicals. This hostile climate requires that black intellectuals fall back upon their own resources—institutions, journals and periodicals—which, in turn, reinforces the de facto racially separatist practices of American intellectual life.

The tragedy of black intellectual activity is that the black institutional support for such activity is in shambles. The quantity and quality of black intellectual exchange is at its worst since the Civil War. There is no major black academic journal, no major black intellectual magazine, no major black periodical of highbrow journalism, not even a major black newspaper of national scope. In short, the black infrastructure for intellectual discourse and dialogue is nearly nonexistent. This tragedy is, in part, the price for integration—which has yielded mere marginal black groups within the professional disciplines of a fragmented academic community. But this tragedy also has to do with the refusal of black intellectuals to establish and sustain their own institutional mechanisms of criticism and self-criticism, organized in such a way that people of whatever color would be able to contribute to them. This refusal over the past decade is significant in that it has lessened the appetite for, and the capacity to withstand, razor-sharp criticism among many black intellectuals whose formative years were passed in a kind of intellectual vacuum. So, besides the external hostile climate, the tradition of serious black intellectual activity is also threatened from within.

The creation of an intelligentsia is a monumental task. Yet black churches and colleges, along with significant white support, served as resources for the first black intellectuals with formal training. The formation of high-quality habits of criticism and international networks of serious intellectual exchange among a relatively isolated and insulated intelligentsia is a gargantuan endeavor. Yet black intellectuals have little choice: either continued intellectual lethargy on the edges of the academy and literate subcultures unnoticed by the black community, or insurgent creative activity on the margins of the mainstream ensconced within bludgeoning new infrastructures.

BLACK INTELLECTUALS AND THE BLACK COMMUNITY

The paucity of black infrastructures for intellectual activity results, in part, from the inability of black intellectuals to gain respect and support from the black community—and especially the black middle class. In addition to the general anti-intellectual tenor of American society, there is a deep distrust and suspicion of the black community toward black intellectuals. This distrust and suspicion stem not simply from the usual arrogant and haughty disposition of intellectuals toward ordinary folk, but, more important, from the widespread refusal of black intellectuals to remain, in some visible way, organically linked with Afro-American cultural life. The relatively high rates of exogamous marriage, the abandonment of black institutions and the preoccupations with Euro-American intellectual products are often perceived by the black community as intentional efforts to escape the negative stigma of blackness or as symptoms of self-hatred. And the minimal immediate impact of black intellectual activity on the black community and American society reinforces common perceptions of the impotence, even uselessness, of black intellectuals. In good American fashion, the black community lauds those black intellectuals who excel as *political activists* and *cultural artists;* the life of the mind is viewed as neither possessing intrinsic virtues nor harboring emancipatory possibilities—solely short-term political gain and social status.

This truncated perception of intellectual activity is widely held by black intellectuals themselves. Given the constraints on black upward social mobility and the pressures for status and affluence among middle-class peers, many black intellectuals principally seek material gain and cultural prestige. Since these intellectuals are members of an anxiety-ridden and status-hungry black middle class, their proclivities are understandable and, to some extent, justifiable, since most intellectuals are in search of recognition, status, power and often wealth. For black intellectuals this search requires immersing oneself in and addressing oneself to the very culture and society that degrade and devalue the black community from whence one comes. And, to put it crudely, most black intellectuals tend to fall within the two camps created by this predicament: "successful" ones, distant from (and usually condescending toward) the black community, and "unsuccessful" ones, disdainful of the white intellectual world. But both camps remain marginal to the black community—dangling between two worlds with little or no black infrastructural base. Therefore, the "successful" black intellectual capitulates, often uncritically, to the prevailing paradigms and research programs of the white bourgeois academy, and the "unsuccessful" black intellectual remains encapsulated within the parochial discourses of Afro-American intellectual life. The alternatives of meretricious pseudocosmopolitanism and tendentious, cathartic provincialism loom large in the lives of black intellectuals. And the black community views both alternatives with distrust and disdain—and with good reason. Neither alternative has had a positive impact on the black community. The major black intellectuals from W. E. B. Du Bois and St. Clair Drake to Ralph Ellison and Toni Morrison have shunned both alternatives.

This situation has resulted in the major obstacle confronting black intellectuals: the inability to transmit and sustain the requisite institutional mechanisms for the persistence of a discernible intellectual tradition. The racism of American society, the relative lack of black community support and hence the dangling status of black intellectuals have prevented the creation of a rich heritage of intellectual exchange, intercourse and dialogue. There indeed have been grand black intellectual achievements, but such achievements do not substitute for tradition.

I would suggest that there are two *organic* intellectual traditions in Afro-American life: *the black Christian tradition of preaching and the black musical tradition of performance*. Both traditions, though undoubtedly linked to the life of the mind, are oral, improvisational and histrionic. Both traditions are rooted in black life and possess precisely what the literate forms of black intellectual activity lack: institutional matrices over time and space within which there are accepted rules of procedure, criteria for judgment, canons for assessing performance, models of past achievement and present emulation and an acknowledged succession and accumulation of superb accomplishments. The richness, diversity and vitality of the traditions of black preaching and black music stand in strong contrast to the paucity, even poverty, of black literate intellectual production. There simply have been no black literate intellectuals who have mastered their craft commensurate with the achievements of Louis Armstrong, Charlie Parker or Rev. Manuel Scott—just as there are no black literate intellectuals today comparable to Miles Davis, Sarah Vaughan or Rev. Gardner Taylor. This is so not because there have been or are no first-rate, black, literate intellectuals, but rather because without strong institutional channels to sustain traditions, great achievement is impossible. And, to be honest, black America has yet to produce a great, literate intellectual, with the sole exception of Toni Morrison. There indeed have been superb ones—Du Bois, Frazier, Ellison, Baldwin, Hurston—and many good ones. But none can compare to the heights achieved by black preachers and, especially musicians.

What is most troubling about black literate intellectual activity is that, as it slowly evolved out of the black Christian tradition and interacted more intimately with secular Euro-American styles and forms, it seemed as if, by the latter part of the twentieth century, maturation would set it. Yet, as we approach the last few years of this century, black literate intellectual activity has declined in both quantity and quality. As I noted earlier, this is so primarily because of relatively greater black integration into postindustrial capitalist America with its bureaucratized, elite universities, dull middlebrow colleges and decaying high schools, which have little concern for and confidence in black students as potential intellectuals. Needless to say, the predicament of the black intellectual is inseparable from that of the black community—especially the black middle-class community—in American society. And only a fundamental transformation of American society can possibly change the situation of the black community and the black intellectual. And though my own Christian skepticism regarding human totalistic schemes for change chasten my deep socialist sentiments regarding radically democratic and libertarian socioeconomic and cultural arrangements, I shall forego these larger issues and focus on more specific ways to enhance the quantity and quality of black literate intellectual activity in the United States. This focus shall take the form of sketching four models for black intellectual activity, with the intent to promote the crystallization of infrastructures for such activity.

THE BOURGEOIS MODEL: THE BLACK INTELLECTUAL AS HUMANIST

For black intellectuals, the bourgeois model of intellectual activity is problematic. On the one hand, the racist heritage—aspects of the exclusionary and repressive effects of white academic institutions and humanistic scholarship—puts black intellectuals on the defensive: There is always the need to assert and defend the humanity of black people, including their ability and capacity to reason logically, think coherently and write lucidly. The weight of this inescapable burden for black students in the white academy has often determined the content and character of black intellectual activity. In fact, black intellectual life remains largely preoccupied with such defensiveness, with "successful" black intellectuals often proud of their white approval and "unsuccessful" ones usually scornful of their white rejection. This concern is especially acute among the first generation of black intellectuals accepted as teachers and scholars within elite white universities and colleges, largely a post–1968 phenomenon. Only with the publication of the intimate memoirs of these black intellectuals and their students will we have the gripping stories of how this defensiveness cut at much of the heart of their intellectual activity and creativity within white academic contexts. Yet, however personally painful such battles have been, they had to be fought, given the racist milieu of American intellectual and academic life. These battles will continue, but with much less negative consequences for the younger generation because of the struggles by the older black trailblazers.

On the other hand, the state of siege raging in the black community requires that black intellectuals accent the practical dimension of their work. And the prestige and status, as well as the skills and techniques provided by the white bourgeois academy, render it attractive for the task at hand. The accentuation

of the practical dimension holds for most black intellectuals regardless of ideological persuasion—even more than for the stereotypical, pragmatic American
intellectual. This is so not simply because of the power-seeking lifestyles and
status-oriented dispositions of many black intellectuals, but also because of their
relatively small number, which forces them to play multiple roles vis-à-vis the
black community and, in addition, intensifies their need for self-vindication—the
attempt to justify to themselves that, given such unique opportunities and privileges, they are spending their time as they ought—which often results in activistic and pragmatic interests.

The linchpin of the bourgeois model is academic legitimation and placement.
Without the proper certificate, degree and position, the bourgeois model loses
its *raison d'être*. The influence and attractiveness of the bourgeois model permeate the American academic system; yet the effectiveness of the bourgeois model
is credible for black intellectuals only if they possess sufficient legitimacy and
placement. Such legitimacy and placement will give one access to select networks and contacts that may facilitate black impact on public policies. This
seems to have been the aim of the first generation of blacks trained in elite white
institutions (though not permitted to teach there), given their predominant interests in the social sciences.

The basic problem with the bourgeois model is that it is existentially and intellectually stultifying for black intellectuals. It is existentially debilitating because it
not only generates anxieties of defensiveness on the part of black intellectuals; it
also thrives on them. The need for hierarchical ranking and the deep-seated
racism shot through bourgeois humanistic scholarship cannot provide black intellectuals with either the proper ethos or conceptual framework to overcome a defensive posture. And charges of intellectual inferiority can never be met upon the
opponent's terrain—to try to do so only intensifies one's anxieties. Rather the terrain itself must be viewed as part and parcel of an antiquated form of life unwor-
thy of setting the terms of contemporary discourse.

The bourgeois model sets intellectual limits, in that one is prone to adopt uncritically prevailing paradigms predominant in the bourgeois academy because of
the pressures of practical tasks and deferential emulation. All intellectuals pass
through some kind of apprenticeship stage in which they learn the language and
style of the authorities, but when they are already viewed as marginally talented,
they may be either excessively encouraged or misleadingly discouraged to critically examine paradigms deemed marginal by the authorities. This hostile environment results in the suppression of their critical analyses and in the limited use
of their skills in a manner considered legitimate and practical.

Despite its limitations, the bourgeois model is inescapable for most black intellectuals. This is so because most of the important and illuminating discourses in
the country take place in white bourgeois academic institutions and because the

more significant intellectuals teach in such places. Many of the elite white universities and colleges remain high-powered schools of education, learning and training principally due to large resources and civil traditions that provide the leisure time and atmosphere necessary for sustained and serious intellectual endeavor. So, aside from the few serious autodidactic black intellectuals (who often have impressive scope, but lack grounding and depth), black intellectuals must pass through the white bourgeois academy (or its black imitators).

Black academic legitimation and placement can provide a foothold in American intellectual life so that black infrastructures for intellectual activity can be created. At present, there is a small yet significant black presence within the white bourgeois academic organizations, and it is able to produce newsletters and small periodicals. The next step is to more broadly institutionalize black intellectual presence, as the Society of Black Philosophers of New York has done, by publishing journals anchored in a discipline (crucial for the careers of prospective professors), yet relevant to other disciplines. It should be noted that such a black infrastructure for intellectual activity should attract persons of whatever hue or color. Black literary critics and especially black psychologists are far ahead of other black intellectuals in this regard with journals such as the *Black American Literature Forum,* the *College Language Association* and the *Journal of Black Psychology.*

Black academic legitimation and placement also can result in black control over a portion of, or significant participation within, the larger white infrastructures for intellectual activity. This has not yet occurred on a broad scale. More black representation is needed on the editorial boards of significant journals so that more black intellectual presence is permitted. This process is much slower and has less visibility, yet, given the hegemony of the bourgeois model, it must be pursued by those so inclined.

The bourgeois model is, in some fundamental and ultimate sense, more part of the problem than the "solution" in regard to black intellectuals. Yet, since we live our lives daily and penultimately within this system, those of us highly critical of the bourgeois model must try to transform it, in part from within the white bourgeois academy. For black intellectuals—in alliance with nonblack progressive intellectuals—this means creating and augmenting infrastructures for black intellectual activity.

THE MARXIST MODEL: THE BLACK INTELLECTUAL AS REVOLUTIONARY

Among many black intellectuals, there is a knee-jerk reaction to the severe limitations of the bourgeois model (and capitalist society)—namely, to adopt the Marxist model. This adoption satisfies certain basic needs of the black intelligentsia: the need for social relevance, political engagement and organizational involvement. The Marxist model also provides entry into the least xenophobic white intellectual subculture available to black intellectuals.

The Marxist model privileges the activity of black intellectuals and promotes their prophetic role. As Harold Cruse has noted, such privileging is highly circumscribed and rarely accents the theoretical dimension of black intellectual activity. In short, the Marxist privileging of black intellectuals often reeks of condescension that confines black prophetic roles to spokespersons and organizers; only rarely are they allowed to function as creative thinkers who warrant serious critical attention. It is no accident that the relatively large numbers of black intellectuals attracted to Marxism over the past sixty years have yet to produce a major black Marxist theoretician. Only W. E. B. Du Bois's *Black Reconstruction* (1935), Oliver Cox's *Caste, Class and Race* (1948) and, to some degree, Harold Cruse's *The Crisis of the Negro Intellectual* (1967) are even candidates for such a designation. This is so not because of the absence of black intellectual talent in the Marxist camp, but rather because of the absence of the kind of tradition and community (including intense critical exchange) that would allow such talent to flower.

In stark contrast to the bourgeois model, the Marxist model neither generates black intellectual defensiveness nor provides an adequate analytical apparatus for short-term public policies. Rather, the Marxist model yields black intellectual self-satisfaction, which often inhibits growth; it also highlights social structural constraints with little practical direction regarding conjunctural opportunities. This self-satisfaction results in either dogmatic submission to and upward mobility within sectarian party or pre-party formations, or marginal placement in the bourgeois academy equipped with cantankerous Marxist rhetoric and sometimes insightful analysis utterly divorced from the integral dynamics, concrete realities and progressive possibilities of the black community. The preoccupation with social structural constraints tends to produce either preposterous, chiliastic projections or paralyzing, pessimistic pronouncements. Both such projections and pronouncements have as much to do with the self-image of black Marxist intellectuals as with the prognosis for black liberation.

It is often claimed that "Marxism is the false consciousness of the radicalized, bourgeois intelligentsia." For black intellectuals, the Marxist model functions in a more complex manner than this glib formulation permits. On the one hand, the Marxist model is liberating for black intellectuals in that it promotes critical consciousness and attitudes toward the dominant bourgeois paradigms and research programs. Marxism provides attractive roles for black intellectuals—usually highly visible leadership roles—and infuses new meaning and urgency into their work. On the other hand, the Marxist model is debilitating for black intellectuals because the cathartic needs it satisfies tend to stifle the further development of black critical consciousness and attitudes.

The Marxist model, despite its shortcomings, is more part of the "solution" than part of the problem for black intellectuals. This is so because Marxism is the brook of fire—the purgatory—of our postmodern times. Black intellectuals must pass through it, come to terms with it and creatively respond to it if black intellectual activity is to reach any recognizable level of sophistication and refinement.

THE FOUCAULTIAN MODEL: THE BLACK INTELLECTUAL AS POSTMODERN SKEPTIC

As Western intellectual life moves more deeply into crisis, and as black intellectuals become more fully integrated into intellectual life—or into "the culture of careful and critical discourse" (as the late Alvin Gouldner called it)—a new model appears on the horizon. This model, based primarily upon the influential work of the late Michel Foucault, unequivocally rejects the bourgeois model and eschews the Marxist model. It constitutes one of the most exciting intellectual challenges of our day: the Foucaultian project of historical nominalism. This detailed investigation into the complex relations of knowledge and power, discourses and politics, cognition and social control compels intellectuals to rethink and redefine their self-image and function in our contemporary situation.

The Foucaultian model and project are attractive to black intellectuals primarily because they speak to the black postmodern predicament, defined by the rampant xenophobia of bourgeois humanism predominant in the whole academy, the waning attraction to orthodox reductionist and scientific versions of Marxism and the need for reconceptualization regarding the specificity and complexity of Afro-American oppression. Foucault's deep antibourgeois sentiments, explicit post-Marxist convictions and profound preoccupations with those viewed as radically "other" by dominant discourses and traditions are quite seductive for politicized black intellectuals wary of antiquated panaceas for black liberation.

Foucault's specific analyses of the "political economy of truth"—the study of discursive ways in which and institutional means by which "regimes of truth" are constituted by societies over space and time—result in a new conception of the intellectual. This conception no longer rests upon the smooth transmittance of "the best that has been thought and said," as in the bourgeois humanist model, or on the utopian energies of the Marxist model. Rather, the postmodern situation requires "the specific intellectual" who shuns the labels of scientificity, civility and prophecy and, instead, delves into the specificity of the political, economic, and cultural matrices within which regimes of truth are produced, distributed, circulated and consumed. No longer should intellectuals deceive themselves by believing—as do humanist and Marxist intellectuals—that they are struggling "on behalf" of the truth; rather, the problem is the struggle over the very status of truth and the vast institutional mechanisms that account for this status. The favored code words of "science," "taste," "tact," "ideology," "progress" and "liberation" of bourgeois humanism and Marxism are no longer applicable to the self-image of postmodern intellectuals. Instead, the new key terms become those of "regime of truth," "power/knowledge" and "discursive practices."

Foucault's notion of the specific intellectual rests upon his demystification of conservative, liberal and Marxist rhetorics that restore, resituate and reconstruct intellectuals' self-identities so that they remain captive to and supportive of institutional forms of domination and control. These rhetorics authorize and legitimate, in different ways, the privileged status of intellectuals, which not only reproduces ideological divisions between intellectual and manual labor, but also reinforces disciplinary mechanisms of subjection and subjugation. This self-authorizing is best exemplified in the claims made by intellectuals that they "safeguard" the achievements of highbrow culture or "represent" the "universal interests" of particular classes and groups. In Afro-American intellectual history, similar self-authorizing claims such as "the talented tenth," "prophets in the wilderness," "articulators of a black aesthetic," "creators of a black renaissance" and "vanguard of a revolutionary movement" are widespread.

The Foucaultian model promotes a leftist form of postmodern skepticism; that is, it encourages an intense and incessant interrogation of power-laden discourses in the service of neither restoration, reformation nor revolution, but rather of revolt. And the kind of revolt enacted by intellectuals consists of the disrupting and dismantling of prevailing "regimes of truth"—including their repressive effects—of present-day societies. This model suits the critical, skeptical and historical concerns of progressive black intellectuals and provides a sophisticated excuse for ideological and social distance from insurgent black movements for liberation. By conceiving of intellectual work as oppositional political praxis, it satisfies the leftist self-image of black intellectuals, and, by making a fetish of critical consciousness, it encapsulates black intellectual activity within the comfortable bourgeois academy of postmodern America.

THE INSURGENCY MODEL: THE BLACK INTELLECTUAL AS CRITICAL, ORGANIC CATALYST

Black intellectuals can learn much from each of the three previous models, yet should not uncritically adopt any one of them. This is so because the bourgeois, Marxist and Foucaultian models indeed relate to, but do not adequately speak to, the uniqueness of the black intellectual predicament. This uniqueness remains relatively unexplored, and will remain so until black intellectuals articulate a new "regime of truth" linked to, yet not confined by, indigenous institutional practices permeated by the kinetic orality and emotional physicality, the rhythmic syncopation, the protean improvisation and the religious, rhetorical and antiphonal elements of Afro-American life. Such articulation depends, in part, upon elaborate black infrastructures that put a premium on creative and cultivated black thought; it also entails intimate knowledge of prevailing Euro-American "regimes of truth," which must be demystified, deconstructed and decomposed in ways that enhance and enrich future black intellectual life. The new "regime of truth" to be pioneered by black thinkers is neither a hermetic discourse (or set of discourses), which safeguards mediocre black intellectual production, nor the latest fashion of black writing, which is often motivated by the desire to parade for the white bourgeois intellectual establishment. Rather it is inseparable from the emergence of new cultural forms that prefigure (and point toward) a post- (not anti-) Western civilization. At present, such talk may seem mere dream and fantasy. So we shall confine ourselves to the first step: black insurgency and the role of the black intellectual.

The major priority of black intellectuals should be the creation or reactivation of institutional networks that promote high-quality critical habits primarily for the purpose of black insurgency. An intelligentsia without institutionalized critical consciousness is blind, and critical consciousness severed from collective insurgency is empty. The central task of postmodern black intellectuals is to stimulate, hasten and enable alternative perceptions and practices by dislodging prevailing discourses and powers. This can be done only by intense intellectual work and engaged insurgent praxis.

The insurgency model for black intellectual activity builds upon, yet goes beyond, the previous three models. From the bourgeois model, it recuperates the emphasis on human will and heroic effort. Yet the insurgency model refuses to conceive of this will and effort in individualistic and elitist terms. Instead of the solitary hero, embattled exile and isolated genius—the intellectual as star, celebrity, commodity—this model privileges collective intellectual work that contributes to communal resistance and struggle. In other words, it creatively accents the voluntarism and heroism of the bourgeois model, but it rejects the latter's naïveté about society and history. From the Marxist model, it recovers the stress on structural constraints, class formations and radical democratic values. Yet the insurgency model does not view these constraints, formations and values in economistic and deterministic terms. Instead of the a priori privileging of the industrial working class and the metaphysical positing of a relatively harmonious socialist society, there is the wholesale assault on varieties of social hierarchy and the radical democratic (and libertarian) mediation, not elimination, of social heterogeneity. In short, the insurgency model ingeniously incorporates the structural, class and democratic concerns of the Marxist model, yet it acknowledges the latter's naïveté about culture.

Last, from the Foucaultian model, the insurgency model recaptures the preoccupation with worldly skepticism, the historical constitution of "regimes of truth" and the multifarious operations of "power/knowledge." Yet the insurgency model does not confine this skepticism, this truth-constituting and detailed genealogical inquiry to micronetworks of power. Instead of the ubiquity of power (which simplifies and flattens multidimensional social conflict) and the paralyzing overreaction to past utopianisms, there is the possibility of effective resistance and meaningful societal transformation. The insurgency model carefully highlights the profound Nietzschean suspicion and the illuminating oppositional descriptions of the Foucaultian model, though it recognizes the latter's naïveté about social conflict, struggle and insurgency—a naïveté primarily caused by the rejection of any form of utopianism and any positing of a telos.

Black intellectual work and black collective insurgency must be rooted in the specificity of Afro-American life and history; but they also are inextricably linked to the American, European and African elements that shape and mold them. Such work and insurgency are explicitly particularist though not exclusivist—hence they are international in outlook and practice. Like their historical forerunners— black preachers and black musical artists (with all their strengths and weaknesses)—black intellectuals must realize that the creation of "new" and alternative practices results from the heroic efforts of collective intellectual work and communal resistance that shape and are shaped by present structural constraints, workings of power and modes of cultural fusion. The distinctive Afro-American cultural forms such as the black sermonic and prayer styles, gospels, blues and jazz should inspire, but not constrain, future black intellectual production; that is, the process by which they came to be should provide valuable insights, but they should serve as models to neither imitate nor emulate. Needless to say, these forms thrive on incessant critical innovation and concomitant insurgency.

THE FUTURE OF THE BLACK INTELLECTUAL

The predicament of the black intellectual need not be grim and dismal. Despite the pervasive racism of American society and anti-intellectualism of the black Community, critical space and insurgent activity can be expanded. This expansion will occur more readily when black intellectuals take a more candid look at themselves, the historical and social forces that shape them and the limited though significant resources of the community from whence they come. A critical "self-inventory"—which this essay schematically sets forth—that scrutinizes the social positions, class locations and cultural socializations of black intellectuals is imperative. Such scrutiny should be motivated by neither self-pity nor self-satisfaction. Rather, this "self-inventory" should embody the sense of critique and resistance applicable to the black community, American society and Western civilization as a whole. James Baldwin has noted that the black intellectual is "a kind of bastard of the West." The future of the black intellectual lies neither in a deferential disposition toward the Western parent nor a nostalgic search for the African one. Rather, it resides in a critical negation, wise preservation and insurgent transformation of this hybrid lineage that protects the earth and projects a better world.

SOURCE: From *Breaking Bread: Insurgent Black Intellectual Life,* by bell hooks and Cornel West (Cambridge, Mass.: South End Press, 1991), pp. 131–146. Originally appeared in *Cultural Critique* 1, no. 1 (1985).

Twenty

AMERICAN PROGRESSIVISM REORIENTED

I remember hearing about Roberto Unger, the Brazilian intellectual wonder tenured at Harvard Law School in his mid-twenties, in 1976, and I attended his famous dramatic lectures on Marx, Weber, Durkheim and others soon after. I first met him in a Habermas seminar on American philosophy in Frankfurt, Germany, in 1987. Our common friend and connection was Richard Rorty. We met in New York City a few times in the years that followed, and when I arrived at Harvard in 1994, we decided to teach courses together on race, nation and democracy—as well as American democracy— at the law school. After three years of discussion, we published The Future of American Progressivism *(1998). This section from the book puts forward a full-fledged set of programs that could get us beyond the present impasse of a neoliberal Democratic party and conservative Republican party. Unger's democratic experimentalism and my radical democracy come together in a fascinating way.*

THE WORK OF AMERICAN progressivism today is to democratize the market economy and energize representative democracy. Progressives should build the link between economic reforms designed to challenge the stark divisions between vanguards and rearguards, and political reforms intended to quicken democratic politics in America.

The program we outline opposes dualism, the division of the economy into a rigid contrast of advanced and backward sectors, and proposes a deepening of democracy: strengthening the tools for the collective discussion and solution of collective problems. It is, therefore, a productivist program, rooting a bias toward more equality of income and wealth in a set of economic arrangements and a strategy of economic growth, rather than merely attempting, through retrospective and compensatory tax-and-transfer, to undo part of what the economy has wrought. It rejects the simple contrast between governmental activism and free enterprise not because it wants to have a little of each, but because it insists upon having more of both. To this end, our program offers to renovate the institutional machinery for a decentralized and experimental partnership between government and business. It seeks to extend the rights of labor, increasing the wage take from national income. The point is to do so in ways that serve the interests of the working people of the country as a whole rather than benefit the relatively privileged and organized workers in capital- and technology-rich industries. It goes beyond the fight against racial discrimination to the redress of racial injustice while recognizing that the problems of racial injustice are inseparable from the problems of class injustice. Our program defends a refinancing of the government on a basis that reconciles a high tax yield—and therefore a more effective governmental ability to invest in people's capabilities—with the need to preserve, indeed to strengthen, incentives to work, save and invest. It both exemplifies and encourages the master practice of democratic experimentalism: motivated, sustained and cumulative tinkering with the institutional arrangements of the government and the economy. It relies on a more engaged and informed citizenry rather than on a more enlightened technocratic elite. And it maps out the steps that make possible the gradual emergence of a lasting transracial progressive majority in American politics as both the condition and the consequence of the democratizing changes it proposes. It is not the humanization of the inevitable; it is the alternative to an unnecessary and unacceptable fate. It is the American religion of possibility translated into a plan for the next step.

A key assumption of this proposal is that the focus of ideological controversy and institutional innovation throughout the world has shifted. The old conflict between market and command, progovernment and antigovernment, is dead or dying. The days of pitting state planning against laissez-faire policies are over. They are giving way to a new contest between the alternative institutional forms of representative democracies, market economies and free civil societies. The institutional arrangements for political, economic and social pluralism now established in the North Atlantic world will turn out to be a subset of a larger set of institutional and social possibilities. We must now look to a democratic civilization that embraces new ways of organizing and deepening political, economic and social freedom.

Institutions house civilizations. Ideals live in practices. By pursuing divergent institutional pathways, according to their own needs and strivings, countries will reveal the vital role of national distinctions in a world of democracies: to develop the powers and possibilities of humanity in different directions. The United States—the most experimentalist of modern nations—has the most to gain, spiritually as well as practically, from this rebirth of its religion of human possibility on a global scale. The doctrine of the one true way flatters the country, and betrays it.

Here are some of the planks in a progressive platform faithful to these ambitions. They are meant to mark a path rather than to define a blueprint. Each of their elements is controversial. Each element could be replaced by equivalent devices. Taken together, they nevertheless indicate a way to begin from where we are now. This path can lead, by small, incremental steps, into a society that is more democratic and more innovative. In that society the grid of class, gender and race weighs less heavily upon our life in common.

TAXES: FROM LIBERAL PIETIES TO REDISTRIBUTIVE REALITIES

The United States has the lowest aggregate tax take of any of the major industrial countries: the revenues of the federal government amount to 20 percent of GDP and the revenues of all three levels of American government to 36 percent GDP (as contrasted, for example, with 47 percent of GDP in France in a recent year). A considerable body of evidence shows that people in many countries support a high tax base tenaciously as long as its improved social, educational and health benefits are palpable. To be sure, we must not kill the goose that lays the golden eggs, dampening incentives to work, save and invest. One solution may be to reform taxation so that it falls on consumption rather than on income.

Progressives regularly oppose consumption taxes, particularly when they apply to transactions (as in a sales tax) rather than to individuals. Such taxes are admittedly regressive because they hit the poor proportionately more than the rich. Business interests, for the same reason, favor them. The business interests and the progressives are both mistaken. The most important lesson of comparative tax experience of First World nations is that redistribution takes place much more on the spending side of the budget than on its revenue-raising side. In other words, it matters less how fair the raising of revenue is than how much the government takes if it can use what it takes to help the people who most need help. The United States has on paper one of the most progressive tax systems in the industrialized world, and the greatest levels of social and economic inequality. Despairing of a political economy that would achieve real redistribution, American progressives today prefer to genuflect to progressive pieties than to achieve progressive results.

Broad-based taxation of consumption (as through the so-called comprehensive, flat-rate, value-added tax) can make it possible to increase revenues while easing the burden of taxation upon saving and investment. It is a money machine. In a second stage, once tax reform has secured the basis of a strong revenue flow friendly to economic growth, we can begin to give a larger role to two sets of redistributive taxes. One would be the direct taxation, on a steeply progressive scale, of what an individual spends on his own consumption with a basic level of spending left untaxed—like an income tax with an exemption for saving. The other would be taxes on the accumulation of wealth and on its transmission through family inheritance and family gifts.

American democracy should work toward the generalization of a principle of social inheritance. Everyone should be able to count on a minimum of resources. These resources are the tools of self-reliance, not an alternative to self-reliance. People should have a social-endowment account, so that society can do for everyone a little bit of what family inheritance does for a few. At major moments in their lives—when they go to college, make a down payment on a house, or open a business—they should be able to draw on this account. The minimum account should increase according to two countervailing principles: compensation for special need or handicap according to predefined criteria and reward for special capacity, competitively demonstrated.

Pensions, Saving and Investment: The Resources for Growth

Capital is now supposed to be globalized. It is not. The truth is that only a small portion of investment funds crosses national frontiers, and in doing so sometimes makes a big ruckus. The architects of the new, neoliberal world economy are building, in the name of economic freedom, an order that allows capital to roam all over the globe and imprisons labor in the nation-state. Most capital nevertheless stays at home.

For a long time, the United States has fallen into the habit of depending upon other people's money: Foreigners put their money in the United States, buy the public debt of the American government and even hold—abroad—most of the paper currency. Like many pieces of undeserved good fortune, this one has its dark side. It helps keep the United States from facing the full consequences, or recognizing the full dimensions, of its low saving level. Gross domestic saving in the United States is 15 percent of GDP, well below what it is in many other rich economies. Dependence upon foreign saving limits the freedom of maneuver in American economic policy and makes economic growth in America hostage to events in other parts of the world.

The need to raise the level of saving in order to ensure sustained economic progress is an opportunity as well as a problem, for it can help push the country in a direction in which it has other reasons to travel. It provides a context in which to reconcile faster economic growth with a more equal distribution of national wealth.

A shift to consumption-based taxation may help raise the saving level by exempting saving from taxation as well as by helping the federal government avoid future deficits. However, the greatest, because most direct, boost to saving is likely to come from a system for the public organization of compulsory private saving. The most important setting in which to introduce such a system is Social Security and private-pension reform. The United States hardly needs the astronomical saving rate (51 percent) that tiny Singapore has achieved under an unnecessarily bureaucratic and centralized version of such a system of required private saving. All it needs is to do better, socially as well as economically, than it has.

The law would require everyone to save in special pension funds a certain percentage of their incomes, defined on a progressive scale according to income levels. Middle-level income earners would keep what they get. High earners would have some of what they save redistributed away from them into the accounts of low earners. Low earners, demonstrating either that they work or that they suffer from a problem that prevents them from working, would have money distributed into their accounts (simply an extension of the principal of the earned-income tax credit, which long enjoyed bipartisan support).

The money would be paid into a broad range of independently managed and competitive funds—not just conventional mutual funds, investing in the established equity and bond markets, but mixed public-private venture-capital funds, investing in new business. Many of these venture-capital funds would be chartered to invest in a diversified mix of start-up firms, and some would get matching or contributory funds or credit enhancements from government to invest in the small and medium-sized businesses of the economic rearguard. Once fully developed, such a system would replace both Social Security and private pensions.

Is this proposal a pay-as-you-go redistributive pension scheme like Social Security? Or a get-what-you-saved saving scheme like private pensions? It combines the market orientation of the latter with the equalizing commitments of the former. Is it a marginal improvement to the existing conduit between saving and productive investment offered by banks and stock markets? Or is it the beginning of an attempt to build, alongside banks and stock markets, an additional bridge between saving and productive investment? We cannot tell beforehand, and it hardly matters.

In the United States, as in other industrial economies, an average of 80 percent of investment in production by businesses of all sizes comes from "retained earnings," what companies save from profits. Most of what individuals save disappears into a financial casino, a money-filled black hole with haphazard, uneven relevance to the funding of production and innovation. Venture capital—the financing of new enterprise by outside investors—remains a tiny sideshow to the operations of this casino. In the spirit of democratic experimentalism, we should try to find a way to tap more of the productive potential of saving by innovating in the economic arrangements that make saving available to enterprise. We should do so in ways that help anchor, in the core institutions of the economy, a bias toward greater equality of access and greater freedom of initiative.

CHILDREN AND EDUCATION: THE FUTURE FIRST

The top priority of social legislation in the United States today, and the greatest justification for a high tax take, should be child protection. The law must ensure food and medical and dental support through families or neighborhoods to every child who needs them.

Thirty-eight percent of poor people in the United States are children. The contrast between the relative generosity for the old—through Social Security and Medicare—and the cruel and stupid abandonment of the young is one of the great injustices of American life. Frustration with the results of programs like Aid to Families with Dependent Children has now prompted Democrats to join with Republicans in broadening what was already a tremendous gap.

Experience throughout the world has taught us that such support is more effective when families and community groups share in the formulation as well as the implementation of programs, turning public-resource transfers into devices of social solidarity and triggers for social organization. A parent movement that enables the nurturers of our society to come through for their children is a good start. The partnership of a weakened family with a welfare bureaucracy falls short. It must be backed up, and transformed, by the action of neighborhood associations and family networks. Cooperative, supervised preschooling and after-school care can form part of their job.

Social supports for children can serve as the front line in the development of social rights for everyone. For example, the sensible and characteristically American way to introduce universal, publicly backed health insurance would be to begin by guaranteeing health insurance to all children. In the setting of child support, we could try out different mixes of public funding and private payment, of public oversight and private management. The successful models in universal health insurance for children could then be extended, by incremental steps, to the adult population.

The child crisis converges with the failure of the American public school system to accomplish a central part of the mission of schools in a democracy: to rescue children from the limitations of class and family situation, giving them access to a world of longer memory, broader imagination and stronger ambition. The professional and business class avoids this failure either by living in upscale neighborhoods, with better than average public schools, or by sending their children to private schools. The majority of public schools become both a source and a mirror of social apartheid in America. This crisis is not the inevitable price of political and economic freedom; it is simply the result of bad arrangements, bad ideas and bad politics.

With the strengthening of a national focus upon the future, and therefore upon children, we can address anew the reform of public education. Three principles should guide our efforts.

The first principle is that, in a democracy, the child must be available to the school; it is not enough for the school to be available to the child. To exercise effectively the right to a public education, children need ample support, if necessary, from the government and, if possible, in their families.

The second principle is that everyone should master a core set of generic conceptual and practical skills, getting ready for a life of instability, learning and innovation. Specialized study and vocational training should supplement rather than replace education in these basic, multipurpose skills. What begins in childhood should extend throughout life in the form of continuing adult education.

The third principle is that, if democracy is to triumph, localism in education should be contained. Schools should be able to rely upon state and national as well as local finance so that they do not reproduce the economic advantages and disadvantages of their communities. Nor should their curricula passively reflect community attitudes. If parent participation is important, so is the role of the school as a counterweight to the limitations of local opinion and family circumstance.

The school in a democracy should take no part in delivering to children the ancient message of the family or the local community: Become like me. It has a bigger job—to equip children with the means to think and to stand on their own feet, bringing the ideas and experiences of far away or long ago to bear upon the understanding and the criticism of the here and now. The school should examine possibilities of imagination and of life that the surrounding society is unable or unwilling to countenance. It should be the voice of the future—of alternative futures—within the present, and it should recognize in children, the future workers and citizens, little prophets.

Thus, we need to prevent any one level of government and any one form of connection between school, community and family from having the definitive say over what goes on in the classroom. A system of multiple accountability, multiple guidance and multiple funding—from federal, state and municipal levels of government—will help liberate the public schools from exclusive dependence upon local control and give them the economic and cultural resources with which to form free people.

RACIAL DISCRIMINATION AND CLASS INJUSTICE: HOW NOT TO FORGET ABOUT ONE WHILE DEALING WITH THE OTHER

Racial antagonisms hurt American democracy in two ways: first, by the evils of racial discrimination and segregation and, second, by the obstacles they create to the redress of class injustice. Working Americans remain divided by race, struggling under the injustices of racial oppression and resentful of what often seem to be the unjust effects of policies designed to right racial wrongs. These divisions have helped keep them from uniting around leaders, organizations, policies and programs committed to loosen the constraints that class status imposes on the life chances of individuals. The present body of antidiscrimination law and policy—including affirmative action—has become both part of the solution and part of the problem.

The flaw in the conventional approach to racial discrimination and affirmative action today is that it sits uncomfortably between two missions, accomplishing neither fully and making the execution of the one seem a hindrance to the achievement of the other. One goal is the struggle against racial discrimination; the other is the improvement of the circumstances of a racially marked underclass.

The legal and political triumphs of the civil rights movement, in and outside government, have succeeded in diminishing the force of racial discrimination throughout American life. It would be perverse to belittle this achievement. Nevertheless, the antidiscrimination law we now have may be too little to combat the hardened, substantial forms of racial prejudice that remain. In some areas—affirmative action first among them—established law and practice go beyond antidiscrimination to some element of active preferment in jobs and education in favor of blacks and other groups that continue to suffer from racial oppression. However, law and practice move toward this goal without either reaching or acknowledging it; the majority of the country and its jurists reject a policy of race-based compensatory privileges. In the meantime, however, this confused, halfhearted policy produces some benefits—captured disproportionately by the elites of the favored groups (the black professional and business class, for example)—and countless resentments—felt by the white losers, real or imagined. These resentments help prevent the development of the transracial progressive majority we need.

The solution is to cut boldly through this tangle of inhibiting confusions, clearly distinguishing antidiscrimination from the larger effort to redress the difficult mixture of racial and class injustice—and devising means suited to each of these two objectives.

Progressives should confront racial discrimination as a distinct evil. They should persuade Americans to follow the example of some other countries, criminalizing its most serious instances. At the same time we should insist upon creating many more situations in American life where people of different races work, study and live together, discovering in their human individualities likenesses and differences that cut across racial divisions. Now that there is disappointment with the cause of racial desegregation, the case for pressing it as a tonic to American democracy has never been stronger.

The suffering of a black and Latino underclass that combines racial stigma with class subjugation presents a different problem, requiring different solutions. We do need a policy of active preferment in education and jobs in favor of those caught in entrenched situations of social disadvantage and exclusion from which they cannot escape, readily or at all, by their own initiative. However, we should not base this preferment solely on race, for race is typically just one element, although often a major one, of the social disablement we seek to repair.

The law should develop standards to give a special push in schooling and employment—and therefore also in admissions and hirings—to those who suffer from an accumulation of forms of disadvantage from which they cannot be expected to escape on their own. Prominent among these sources of subjugation are class, race, gender and handicap. We know for a fact that it is the convergence of some of these factors in the life situation of individuals that may prevent them from seizing upon the opportunities of American society. Placed in this context, the offer of preferment loses its invidious, narrowly racial character. We can defend it, as a matter of the law and the Constitution (although it would surely require a change of present constitutional understandings), because it helps make feasible the demand for individual self-reliance. It helps keep the promise of equal opportunity for all.

Such an effort is useful and even necessary. It is, however, no substitute for the broader attempt to democratize the market economy in America, narrowing the gap between vanguard and rearguard. We must take it for what it is: a subsidiary tool of social policy, but a major vindication of justice for the individual.

Economic Vanguardism Outside the Vanguard: Narrowing the Gap Between the Advanced and Backward Sectors of the Economy

The most important issue of political economy today in the United States, as throughout the world, is not deficits, taxes, saving or even, in the conventional sense, jobs. It is the social form that will be taken by a way of working together and producing goods and services that is beginning to reconstruct economies all over the globe. A method of collaboration rather than a technology of production lies at the heart of this advanced economy, although technologies of information and communication have helped equip it. It is a method of flattened hierarchies and permanent innovation, of fluid job definitions and constant reshaping of products, services and practices. It combines teamwork with competition. It is production as learning. It can be carried out by decentralized big businesses or by cooperative-competitive networks of small and medium-sized businesses. It thrives under particular conditions: a background of community life and good government, especially good local government—able to ensure high-quality basic education, opportunities for continuous reskilling, dense networks of association and the high trust such networks breed—as well as first-rate transport and communication facilities. It is not just for making computers and software or for supplying highly paid professional services; it is for doing anything. Flexible, high-technology, and knowledge-rich production is here to stay.

Where such conditions are largely present, national government can take a back seat. Without intervention, economic vanguardism flourishes in an isolated, advantaged part of the economy. That is the situation we see emerging in America as elsewhere: a world of advanced sectors and regions connected with one another and weakly linked to the backward sectors and regions of their own societies.

The reordering of production as learning will happen one way or another. The crucial issue is whether it will happen in forms that are more or less socially inclusive. The work of progressives must be to steer it in an inclusive direction. To that end, we need to fashion the instruments for decentralized, participatory and experimentalist styles of partnership between government and business. To push economic vanguardism beyond the social and geographic frontiers of the conventional vanguards, we need national and local governments able to help create the missing conditions and to help form the missing agents.

We should reject the false choice between the idea of arms'-length government (embraced by free-market orthodoxy) and the contrasting practice (exemplified by some of the northeast Asian "tiger economies") of a centralized economic bureaucracy formulating industrial and trade strategy, subsidizing credit and rewarding promise or success with favor. Instead, we should develop a broad-based and market-friendly effort to lift up the rearguard.

Such an effort would have four elements. The first element is the focus on child protection and educational renewal and the use of child-centered support programs to encourage the development of community groups. Without an organized local society, able to take care of its children, vanguardism outside the vanguard has no chance. A second element is the creation of technical support centers, reskilling services and small-business incubators to assist private initiative outside the advanced sectors of the economy. A major responsibility of such centers would be to help identify and propagate successful work and business practices as they emerged. A third element is the organization of associations among firms. The associated businesses would pool financial, commercial and technical resources in some areas while competing with one another in others. A fourth element is the broadening of access to finance and technology through the establishment of independently administered venture-capital funds, chartered to invest in the rearguard and to conserve and grow the resources with which they would be endowed. Experience suggests that, with accountable but independent management and properly diversified investment portfolios, such funds can achieve high rates of return on their endowments.

Different kinds of property relations between the funds and their client firms would develop over time. Some funds would keep a distance from their clients, auctioning capital off to a diversified group of entrepreneurs with the best prospects of making good on the investment and taking equity stakes in the firms they helped start, as any venture capitalist would. Other funds would nurture close and lasting relations with a group of similar small businesses, becoming the financial and technical brain and arm of a little confederation of firms. Property would be divided up in different ways between funds and firms, and different regimes of private and social property and decentralized initiative would begin to coexist experimentally within the economy.

The outcome of such experiments is not the suppression of the market; it is the democratizing and diversification of the market. It is the road to closing the gap between vanguard and rearguard. It is the refusal to let the global reshaping of production continue on an exclusive and divisive course.

AN ORGANIZED SOCIETY AND AN EMPOWERED LABOR FORCE: THE TOOLS AND RESOURCES OF ASSOCIATION

A disorganized society cannot generate conceptions of its alternative futures or act on them. Organization is power, a power essential to a vigorous democracy. Disorganization is surrender to drift, to accident, to fate. America has always been famous for its wealth of voluntary associations. Today, however, Americans are more disassociated than ever before: living alone, often without friends, and less engaged in unions, clubs, fraternal orders and even local government or parent-teacher associations. Only in church, synagogue and mosque attendance do the numbers seem to hold up, faith in God having outlived, for many Americans, hope in society.

It is not enough to call for a rebirth of the spirit of voluntary association, for although we may call the spirit, it may not come. Instead, we need to reexamine and reconstruct the institutional setting in which association thrives. Reforms in labor law, local government law and federal tax law can help renew the force and democratize the scope of associational activity in America.

Such reforms can also diminish the force of a striking and troubling feature of associational life in all contemporary industrial democracies. The associations with a message for society at large—clubs and churches as well as political parties—remain detached from the everyday world of work and production. Practical associations involved in this everyday world—firms and unions—lack such a message; their job is to make money and defend the interests of their members. If the established rules of contract and corporate law that people use to create and maintain practical associations are indeed like a language, capable of expressing any thought, then the problem is that those who speak this language may have little to say, while those who have something to say are unable to speak it.

Society should be independently organized outside the government—a simple idea with complicated and controversial implications. One major site of organization is work. Labor laws need to be strengthened not to deepen divisions between a minority of relatively privileged workers in traditional industry and everyone else, but to facilitate unionization everywhere. As temporary work increases in many sectors of the economy, we need to reform the labor laws to encourage the unionization of temporary workers and to ensure the blend of legal regulation of the employment relation and collective bargaining with the employer that is appropriate to their circumstances. More generally, we have to create a structure in which union representation of workers and collaborative profit sharing with workers come to be seen as complementary rather than incompatible approaches. Otherwise, we shall have allowed a contest between cooperation at work and association among workers to develop at the heart of industry, threatening the project of greater economic democracy in America.

An emphasis on early and continuing education and reskilling rather than on job tenure, the development of varied forms of worker protection suited to the circumstances of a segmented labor force and a commitment to generalize the principle of worker participation in company profits can combine to reverse one of the most antidemocratic trends in recent American life: the decrease of the wage take from national income. Moreover, this trend can be reversed without threatening the high employment levels the United States has happily achieved. The ability to raise the real value of wages, without threatening jobs and economic growth or risking inflation, will be further strengthened if we succeed in replacing all payroll taxes by the consumption-oriented taxation we advocate.

What we must resist at any cost is the entrenchment of stark divisions between insiders—relatively privileged, organized workers with jobs in the capital- and knowledge-rich sectors of the economy—and outsiders—workers with unstable, dead-end jobs in the capital- and knowledge-poor sectors. It is a division that has helped bring European social democracy to grief.

Traditional social democrats often fight for something close to job tenure for workers with the good jobs and promote, under the slogan of stakeholding, a mini-constitutionalism of the firm: Consumer groups and local communities as well as workers would have a say or even a veto over management decisions. It is a formula that sets up a tension between defending workers' rights and promoting economic flexibility and innovation. Moreover, it is predicated on a division between insiders and outsiders and can help reinforce it. Instead of enshrining job tenure, we want to enhance the capabilities of workers through devices such as government-supported continuous reskilling and social-endowment accounts. Instead of a rigid scheme of checks and balances in corporate governance, we propose radically to decentralize and democratize access to productive resources and opportunities through means such as the public-private venture-capital funds and technical support centers we earlier described.

If work is one site of voluntary association, community life is another. We could, for example, create legal mechanisms for the selection of community councils or neighborhood associations outside the structure of local government. Such councils could be elected on a neighborhood basis to engage individual citizens as well as community groups in the solution of the social—not the physical or financial—problems of the neighborhood, for example, working with the police to set up community policing, identifying children in trouble and referring them or their families to the right sources of public or private assistance and intervening with hospitals, insurers, and bureaucracies when the old and the sick need help. This work would be neither continuous nor paid. It would be a form of social leadership, somewhere in between private charity and public office. Those who performed it would have, as a matter of law, only advisory power but, as a matter of practical effect, as much influence as their organizing efforts allowed them to exert.

Private philanthropy has been a powerful engine of voluntary action in the United States. It survives, however, on a tax favor. Thus, its consequence is to magnify the voice of the rich, allowing them to ride their social and cultural hobbyhorses. Thanks to the tax laws, their poorer fellow citizens co-sign these gifts whether they want to or not and whether they know it or not. Why not democratize the tax favor? For every tax-deducted dollar the donor were allowed to use as he or she wished, a certain portion of the donor's dollars would have to go into a common fund, with the percentage calculated to preserve the force of the tax incentive. That fund, with decentralized governance and independent trustees drawn from every walk of American life, would finance social groups who applied to it for help—through, for example, matching funds or matching commitments of free labor time—to carry out their own charitable activities. The disincentive to private contributions would be limited; the impact upon the resource base of voluntary action in America, immense.

POLITICS, MONEY AND MEDIA: QUICKENING THE TEMPO OF DEMOCRACY

For better and worse, Americans revere their Constitution. They early rejected Thomas Jefferson's advice to replace the Constitution completely every few generations. As a result, they hesitate to fiddle with the setup of the government, and they often prefer to revise (or rather to let Supreme Court justices revise) their Constitution by reinterpreting it rather than by changing it outright.

There are many constitutional reforms that would be worth discussing if the American antipathy to constitutional redesign were less severe. Consider one such example. Admittedly outside the agenda of feasible contemporary concerns, it nevertheless suggests both the price of constitutional conservatism and the possible direction of political reform. Moreover, it clarifies the vision underlying the here-and-now political innovations we do propose further ahead.

Madison's scheme for the Constitution combined two principles: an insistence upon the dispersal of political power and a plan to slow politics down by establishing a rough correspondence between the transformative reach of a political project and the severity of the constitutional obstacles it has to overcome in the course of its execution. Both principles combine in the system of "checks and balances" among branches of government: Franklin Roosevelt, for example, had to wage a tremendous struggle until he got the Supreme Court as well as the Congress on his side, and he had an economic and social disaster working for him.

These two principles—the fragmentation of political power and the slowing down of political change—could, however, be disconnected in the interests of a deepened democracy. We might want to keep the first principle and rid ourselves of the second. For example, think of the following way to combine characteristics of the presidential and parliamentary systems of government. If the president and the Congress disagree about a program of reform for the country, either of the two elected branches of government can call early elections, but then both branches have to run. The idea is to resolve the impasse quickly through the prompt engagement of the electorate in its resolution, rather than to perpetuate it in divided government until the next regular election.

To follow the logic of the remedy, we might make voting mandatory, as it is in many contemporary democracies, with the penalty of a fine for the violation of the duty. Failure to vote would, therefore, be sanctioned less severely than, for example, refusal to do jury duty. The obligation to come to the polling station, however, is intended to achieve a good that is at least as great as serving on juries: to prevent the government from being elected by a minority, given that over half the adult citizenry now fails to vote in the United States. That a citizen should have to turn his or her mind for a few moments, every now and then, to the affairs of the Republic—with the privilege of abstaining in the voting booth—seems a tiny measure of intrusion to accept in exchange for a huge advance in civic engagement. Comparative experience suggests that, once the law directs people to vote, they get into the habit. In no democracy that has adopted such a rule has there ever been a majority in favor of its revocation.

The combined effect of these changes would be to quicken the tempo and raise the energy level of American democracy, while maintaining or even strengthening the fundamental mechanism for making governmental power decentralized and accountable. It will not happen, at least not anytime soon, but it points in a direction. We offer four connected proposals to move American democracy in this direction.

First, establish public financing of political campaigns. Public financing is more effective than the attempt to tighten the policing of private money, especially when combined with our next suggestion, extended free access to television time. It is a minor expense, with vast equalizing and limit-breaking potential for American politics. The best criterion for the distribution of such public funding is a standard intermediate between the present representation of the political parties at the level of government—federal, state or local—at which they are running and a standard of arithmetical equality—the same for all.

Second, give the political parties and their candidates ample free time on television. Fight in the legislatures and the courts to get this time freely given by the networks and channels, as a condition of their license rather than as a service to be paid by the taxpayers. Americans need a public space in which to discuss their shared problems, and television has become the space that matters most. In Brazil, for example, fifty minutes a day of television and radio on all channels are blocked out for the parties and candidates forty-five days before an election. The primitive technology and the indifferent content of many of the political talks have not prevented the campaign programs from maintaining a substantial audience. The voters learn, and so do the politicians. The perversity of the sound bite is reversed when candidates for major national office are required to spend many hours on the air; in the surprisingly intimate medium of television, it is hard to disguise yourself for long.

Third, lower the legal, constitutional and ideological barriers to experimental, localized and temporary reversals and combinations of governmental and private responsibilities. If, for example, municipal sanitation services can be contracted out to private business, research and development can also be conducted by joint ventures of governmental agencies, nonprofit organizations such as universities and private businesses. Venture capital—investment in start-up firms—can be arranged by decentralized funds and support centers, with independent management, a mixed public-private character and special responsibility for the development of the economic rearguard.

Many such reversals and combinations of function should be tried out locally and temporarily. Different trial solutions to the same problems should be allowed to coexist. How else can we find out what works? Much more is at stake here than efficiency of public administration. The point is to tap the repressed potential for decentralized partnership among individuals, government and business, rejecting the model of arms'-length regulation as the only acceptable way in which government can relate to society. One project will lead to another. Small successes will give impulse to larger ambitions. American federalism—far from being a pretext to stop social experiments in the name of "states' rights"—will turn out to be a special case of the larger idea of "many laboratories."

Fourth, change the attitudes and the practices about party politics so that the political parties—the two big parties as well as emerging third parties—can become the authors and agents of real alternatives. We need not choose between the political party as the disciplined instrument of a purist ideology and the political party as a syndicate of professional office-seekers catering to an amorphous assortment of special interests. Americans are unlikely ever to adopt proportional representation—the electoral system that distributes legislative seats in proportion to votes for parties. They are even less likely to embrace the closed-list version of such systems—where the voter votes only for a party and the parties determine the priority of the candidates on its slate. However, the present scheme of election primaries in the United States makes sense only if Americans have given up on political parties and the coherent options that it would be the task of the parties to forge and implement. Adopted in the name of grassroots democracy, this scheme robs the parties of any prospect of strong internal organization and programmatic definition.

Who knows the name of the chairman of either major political party in the United States? He or she is invariably a creature of the president in office or a caretaker until the next presidential candidate shows up and, in either event, a hapless hustler for money. Members of Congress are routinely reelected, although the electorate professes disgust with the political class, because the public expects from them little more than service to local interests and conformity to certain minimum ideological tests in their voting behavior. The result is that, although Americans are able to discuss, for example, an isolated issue, like whether to allow physicians to help the terminally ill commit suicide, they lack the political instruments with which to define, collectively, different roads for their country to take. Should such a demarcation of national possibilities be just the work of a clever politician, sensing a change in national mood and grasping at the latest fashions from the universities? Or should it result from a more inclusive and sustained conversation in the country?

The political parties should assert greater authority over slates, candidates, candidate selection and party platforms. At the same time, however, they should open themselves up to internal democracy, organizing national elections among their members to choose their leaders and directions. The shift from an emphasis upon candidate-by-candidate choice through primaries to an emphasis upon party democracy and party leadership would trigger the organization of movements and factions within each party to contest such party elections. The defeated groups would clamor for minority representation in the party councils or establish third parties. The temperature of American politics would rise, and its repertory of programmatic alternatives broaden.

In this great country every privilege is suspect, and ordinary men and women are known to be not so ordinary after all. Tinkering is both a habit and a creed, and experimentalism joins hands with democracy. An America triumphant in the world nevertheless seems unable to solve its own problems. Class injustice, racial hatred and rationalized selfishness thrive today in a climate of disillusionment and feed on an experience of disengagement and disconnection. In this circumstance, the work of the progressives is to speak, within and outside the Democratic party, for a clear alternative. Not for some impossible, romantic dream of a different "system." Not for the last-ditch defense of every part of the New Deal compromise in American politics. Not for the Republican agenda—or the doctrine of the one true way—with a human face. Not for the humanization of the inevitable. But for a practical view of how, step by step and piece by piece, to democratize the American economy and reenergize American democracy.

To understand your country you must love it. To love it you must, in a sense, accept it. To accept it as it is, however, is to betray it. To accept your country without betraying it, you must love it for that in it which shows what it might become. American—this monument to the genius of ordinary men and women, this place where hope becomes capacity, this long halting turn of the no into the yes—needs citizens who love it enough to reimagine and remake it.

SOURCE: From *The Future of American Progressivism: An Initiative for Political and Economic Reform,* by Roberto Mangabeira Unger and Cornel West (Boston: Beacon Press, 1998), pp. 56–93.

Twenty One

PARENTS AND NATIONAL SURVIVAL

In 1993 Senator Bill Bradley, William Bennett and David Gergen brought together progressive and conservative intellectuals for a dialogue in Aspen, Colorado. It was at this meeting that I met the progressive and feminist economist Sylvia Ann Hewlett. A product of working-class Wales, Cambridge University and Harvard University, she had taught at Barnard and written books on Latin American economies and workplace issues. In 1994 I joined her National Parents' Association and became co-chair of its Task Force. We started writing our book, The War Against Parents, *in 1995 and published it in 1998. After forty-five lectures in thirteen states, the book received much attention—resulting in our being summoned to the White House for meetings with President Bill Clinton, First Lady Hillary Rodham Clinton and Domestic Adviser Bruce Reed. This brief excerpt from the book gives one a sense of what we are up to—stealing the thunder from the Right on family issues and establishing progressive policies for working parents. Some left critics trashed the book primarily owing to our attention to fathers and dads, including our critical yet subtle treatments of Promise Keepers and the Nation of Islam. With the rise of progressive Working Family parties in New York and other places, we are vindicated.*

WHATEVER THEIR POLITICAL ORIENTATION, our leaders seem to have little understanding of how much the decks are stacked against parents in our materialistic, individualistic age. At the heart of the matter is the fact that from a purely economic standpoint, raising a child has become the ultimate nonmarket activity as various types of market logic have moved against mothers and fathers. Adults have never viewed children solely or even primarily as financial assets, but through history and across cultures, parents have often reaped at least some material reward from raising children—help with planting or harvesting, support in old age and so on. None of these economic reasons for raising children hold true today. On the contrary, in the modern world children are hugely expensive and yield little in the way of economic return to the parents. Estimates of the costs of raising a child to age eighteen are now in the $145,000 range—and this figure does not include college or graduate school![1] Despite this significant investment, the grown-up child rarely contributes earnings—or any other kind of material support—to the parental household. In the late twentieth century, children "provide love, smiles, and emotional satisfaction, but no money or labor."[2]

Of course, large numbers of well-meaning moms and dads may still elect to invest large quantities of money and time in child-raising, but for the first time in history their loving energies are not reinforced by enlightened self-interest. Instead, they must rely entirely on large reserves of altruistic love—large enough to last for more than two decades per child. This is a tall order in a society that venerates the market. We are asking parents to ignore the logic of their pocketbooks and buck the dominant values of our age. If they routinely fall down on the job, who can blame them? Contemporary moms and dads are trapped between the escalating requirements of their children, who need more resources (in terms of both time and money) for longer periods of time than ever before, and the signals of a culture that is increasingly scornful of effort expended on others. Parents often feel as though they are expected to read from two or three scripts that diverge completely in terms of how they lead their lives. Should they take on a second job to pay for college, or should they stay home in the evening to do a little bonding and turn off the TV? Or should they do neither of the above, but instead work two jobs and spend the extra income on health-club membership? Life is short, and paying at least some attention to oneself is a good idea. Besides, a trimmer figure might make all the difference in the next round of promotions. It is easy for a bewildered parent to become paralyzed as he or she is besieged by a host of contradictory demands.

FREE FEMALE LABOR

For more than a century, a variety of scholars and social commentators have paid tribute to the nonmarket work done by women in American society. In the 1880s and 1890s, the social feminist Jane Addams stressed the moral heft of women's traditional roles. Indeed, much of her political activism was directed toward securing for women the right to stay at home and care for their children rather than being forced into the labor market. She saw "the home as the original center of civilization."[3]

Much more recently, the psychologist Carol Gilligan has made a distinction between the voices of men and women. In her highly acclaimed 1982 book, *In a Different Voice,* she describes how men gravitate toward the instrumental and the impersonal and emphasize abstract principles, while women lean toward intimacy and caring and give priority to human relationships. Gilligan points out that the female "care" voice is not inferior to the male "instrumental" voice, as it is often treated in psychological theory; it is simply different—different and enormously important. Over the decades this voice of care has played a critical role in producing a healthy equilibrium between individual and community in American society. Because it balances self with other and tempers market values with non-market values, it has gone some distance toward redeeming the urgent greed that is the spirit of capitalism.

Prior to the 1960s, when more families were organized along traditional lines than is true today, women provided this voice of care, which knitted together family and community. At least in the middle classes, a clear division of labor between the sexes allowed women to devote huge amounts of time to nourishing and nurturing: They read bedtime stories, helped with homework, wrapped presents, attended parent-teacher conferences and taught Sunday school. But in the 1970s, myriad selfless tasks that were the stuff of raising kids and building communities went by the board as American society underwent a sea change. Traditional patterns were broken by a liberation movement that often encouraged women to clone the male competitive model in the marketplace and by a new set of economic pressures that increasingly required both parents to be in the paid labor force to sustain any semblance of middle-class life.

Before getting too nostalgic about traditional roles, however, we should remember that the sacrificial load carried by at-home women was often hard to bear. Many spent their entire lives laboring to serve the needs of others. Gilligan tells us that the main change wrought by feminism was that it "enabled women to consider it moral to care not only for others but also for themselves." She quotes Elizabeth Cady Stanton telling a reporter in 1848 "to put it down in capital letters: SELF-DEVELOPMENT IS A HIGHER DUTY THAN SELF-SACRIFICE."[4] Despite her appreciation of the importance of women's traditional roles, Jane Addams was also convinced that women must undergo a struggle for identity and recognition. She thought that the great challenge facing women was to hold in fruitful tension the "I" of the self, the "us" and "ours" of the family and the "we" of citizens of the wider civic world.[5] Nora struggled with this challenge in Ibsen's *A Doll's House* (1879), and women have been struggling with it ever since.

The insights of Addams and Gilligan reflect the lives of middle-class white women and have little to do with the lives of poor women, particularly poor black women. Since the beginning of this nation, women of color have toiled both in the workplace—often in a white woman's kitchen—and in their own homes. In a very real sense, their contribution to family and community has been even more heroic than that of middle-class women. In sustained and steadfast ways, they have looked after the children of affluent white women in addition to their own, and they have received very little in the way of recompense or recognition. Black women thus have done double duty and been doubly invisible.

This brief historical excursion helps explain why the shortcomings of our nation on the parent-support front were until recently cloaked by the existence of a deep and largely invisible reservoir of free female labor. For generations women spent huge chunks of their lives making the nonmarket investments in family and com-

munity that underpin our nation. By nurturing children and by nourishing a web of
care that included neighborhood and township, women created the competence
and character upon which our democracy and our economy depended. Thus, the
invisible labor of women comprised nothing less than the bedrock of America's
prosperity and power. In addition, as women grew and tended our stock of human
and social capital, they masked the contradictions inherent in our political culture.
Conservatives had the luxury of cultivating a blind faith in markets because women
(unacknowledged and unappreciated though they were) provided the all-important
nonmarket work. And liberals had the luxury of cultivating a taste for self-fulfill-
ment—at least white men did—because women reached out to others.

As we move into the twenty-first century, it is clear that relying on free and invisible female labor as the wellspring of our social and human capital no longer
works. Modern women are intent on a fair measure of self-realization, and besides, the economic facts of family life preclude a return to traditional structures.
Falling male wages and sky-high rates of single parenthood make it hard to spin
out a scenario in which large numbers of women (or men) have the option of staying home on a full-time basis.

It is ironic to note that the nurturing, caring roles that are so underappreciated
by contemporary culture are very much factored in by the market. Career inter-
ruptions triggered by childbirth and the special demands of the early childhood
years cost women dearly in terms of earning power. A study by the Rand Corporation shows that a two- to four-year break in employment lowers lifetime income by 13 percent, while a five-year break lowers it by 19 percent.[6] Of course, if
we were to expand our programs of family support—paid parenting leave, job
sharing and the like—more women would be able to stay on their career ladders
during the childbearing years.

FATHERS UNDER SIEGE

The inability of our nation to give value to or even to recognize the work of parents has penalized men and women in different ways. If the work done by mothers has been rendered invisible—or used to exact a price in the labor market—fathers have come under special attack by programs and policies oblivious to the
importance of the father-child bond. Over the last thirty years, divorce reform
and the enormous expansion of our welfare system have conspired to make it extremely difficult for a large proportion of American men—somewhere between a
third and a half—either to live with or to stay in effective touch with their children.
Aid to Families with Dependent Children is a case in point. In retrospect, it seems
clear that AFDC, the nationwide program that for three decades provided the
lion's share of income support for poor families, was set up so as to deliberately
exclude fathers. The rules held that if an "able-bodied man" resided in a house-

hold, a woman with dependent children was unable to claim benefits for herself and her children.[7] This caused men to be literally pushed out of the nest. Not only did these AFDC regulations create a huge disincentive to marry; they made it extremely difficult for poor men to become fathers to their children. These government-sponsored rules help explain why out-of-wedlock births in the black community leapt from 21 percent in 1960 to 69.8 percent in 1996.[8]

In recent years men have experienced a tremendous loss of power in the workplace and in the family, which is a large part of the reason why millions of men are turning to Promise Keepers and the Nation of Islam. Demoralized, displaced men are seeking solace in brotherhood and turning inward to their gods. Jesus or Allah might just come through for them in a way that is increasingly problematic for employers or government.

The antifather bias in our public policies has found its clearest expression in the demonization of deadbeat dads. Public outrage on this subject was triggered by a 1989 Census Bureau report entitled "Child Support and Alimony," which described how more than a quarter of all noncustodial fathers were absent from their children's lives and paid nothing in the way of child support.[9] Shocking and shameful as these findings are, some factors were overlooked. To begin with, almost 40 percent of the "absent fathers" described in this report had neither custody nor visitation rights and therefore no ability to connect with their children. It seems odd to call them by the pejorative term "absent" when they have no right to be present. In addition, a little-known study by the Department of Health and Human Services shows that noncustodial mothers have a far worse record of child-support compliance than noncustodial fathers—almost half of all noncustodial mothers pay nothing toward the support of their children.[10] It seems that once a parent—male or female—has lost touch with a child, that parent is unlikely to contribute financial support. It is probably unrealistic to think we can keep in place all the obligations of traditional parenthood without its main reward: loving contact with a child.[11] Yet, rather than create policies that help noncustodial parents connect with their children, all we seem capable of doing is cracking down some more on deadbeat dads—thin stuff in a country that leads the world in fatherlessness.

One thing we do know: The huge increase in fatherlessness goes some distance toward explaining why so many youngsters are out of control. There is now a weight of evidence connecting fatherlessness to child poverty, juvenile crime and teen suicide.

The Parent-Child Bond

This brings us to the heart of the matter: If the center of this nation is to hold, we have to learn to give new and self-conscious value to the art and practice of parenting. It can no longer be left to invisible female labor or the tender mercies of the market. Make no mistake about it, the work of moms and dads is of utmost importance to our nation. At a fundamental level of analysis, the parent-child bond is the strongest and most primeval of all human attachments. When it weakens and frays, devastating consequences ripple through our nation, because this elemental bond is the ultimate source of connectedness in society.

H. F. Harlow, the animal psychologist, demonstrated in a famous series of studies of infant monkeys the extraordinary importance of parental love. Taking a group of newborn monkeys from their parents, he placed them with artificial surrogates—a wire mesh "mommy" and a terry-cloth "mommy." Despite the fact that the infant monkeys were supplied with all the ingredients for physiological development—nourishment, water, proper temperature and protection against disease—they failed to flourish. In Harlow's study, the deprived infants became zombies, developing odd, autistic behavior of the kind one sees in severely retarded persons. To Harlow, they did not seem fully alive. And while the baby monkeys enormously preferred the terry-cloth mommy to the wire-mesh mommy, avoiding the cold wire mesh and clinging fiercely to the warm, cuddly terry cloth, even the terry-cloth mommy was a long way from being enough.

These artificial surrogates failed to provide loving, tender, responsive care, and thus the baby monkeys grew up not knowing the give-and-take of talk and touch, of feeding and fondling, of learning and playing. The infants survived and eventually grew into adults, but strange, abnormal adults who could not relate to their own kind or reproduce.[12] The implication of Harlow's research for humans is clear: The mere fact of physical survival does not guarantee a person. The full development of a human being requires something much deeper and more complicated than food and water; it requires sustained and sustaining love. According to the psychiatrist Willard Gaylin, "It is necessary to care for a child with love, in order to initiate a similar capacity in the child."[13]

Who will provide this transforming love? The obvious candidates are parents, because it is mothers and fathers, above other adults, who tend to fall crazily in love with their children. As the child psychologist Urie Bronfenbrenner has shown, children thrive on huge amounts of "irrational, emotional attachment," most often the gift of a mother or a father but in exceptional cases provided by a devoted grandparent or some other caregiver.[14] This is the magical force that provides the basis for self-love and self-esteem. And once a child has learned to love himself or herself, that child is able to care deeply about others. Thus parental love not only contributes powerfully to the development of a fully human being, it also nourishes and sustains the larger society. The connections are straightforward enough: Caring about the well-being of others is the foundation of compassion, conscience and citizenship. When a child is deprived of parental love, that youngster is liable to grow up in an infantilized state—very much like Harlow's zombies—never developing a love of self, never developing the ability to reach out to others. This is a recipe for violence, against oneself and against others, for anger and aggression remain raw and exposed, untempered by a commitment to anyone or anything. It is also a recipe for civic collapse. How do you persuade a young person who is profoundly careless of his own or of others' well-being to join a Boys and Girls Club or to vote in our democracy?

Cornel West: I remember meeting one of these disconnected, tortured youngsters at a talk I gave at a community center in Newark, New Jersey. After the event, a young man sixteen or seventeen years old came up to me and said, "Professor West, I hear you're a pretty smart brother, you write this deep stuff, it must take a lotta talent and a lotta work to do something like that. Well, I've got talent too. I'm the smartest guy in my class. But the rub is, I can't find any motivation. I don't see why I should try to do what you do. More and more I feel I belong on the streets, hustling, dealing and hurting like everyone else. That's the way to survive where I live."

He then asked a question. "Brother, what made you want to keep doing all that hard work, what made you believe in some kind of different future?" So I talked about my dad encouraging and disciplining me, my mom reading poetry to me, my older brother helping me with my homework, and my younger sisters cheering me on. The young man listened closely and then, in obvious pain, said, "Here's the score—I'm in this world by myself. My mother's strung out and tuned out. I have brothers, but I don't know them, and as for my father, where he is nobody knows. I sure have never seen him."

I remember feeling totally helpless. I had no recipe to heal these open wounds. The only thing I could think of doing was to bow before the enormity of his misery, kiss the young brother's hand and mumble some words of empathy. "My God, I can't imagine—it's beyond my experience. You've got things you can teach me—you've been somewhere I've never been. I've read a ton of books on alienation, but I cannot grasp what you are living. . . . I cannot understand what it must be like to have never been loved." I then simply told him to stay strong and don't forget to pray.

This bleak and bitter encounter in Newark reflects the agony of a child who was born without a skin, without the tender love of an attentive parent. For this young man, the parent-child bone—the relationship that transmits self-love and the capacity to love others—had never developed, and the consequences were quite deadly.

A WORLD UPSIDE DOWN

This young man is not alone. In modern America, across race, gender and class, millions of children are in terrible trouble. Consider the following facts:

- The homicide rate for children aged fourteen to seventeen has risen 172 percent since 1985.
- One fifth (20.5 percent) of all children are growing up in poverty—a 36 percent increase since 1970.
- The number of homeless children has tripled since the late 1980s.
- The use of illicit drugs among high-school seniors is up 44 percent since 1992.
- SAT scores have slipped 27 points since the early 1970s.
- The rate of suicide among black teenagers has more than tripled since 1980.
- Obesity among children aged twelve to seventeen has doubled since 1970.[15]

Some of these statistics (poverty, homelessness) describe the pain of disadvantaged kids; others (obesity, SAT scores) describe the anguish of middle-class kids. Problems triggered by divorce, teen pregnancy, school failure and substance abuse are no longer confined to the ghetto. They reach deep into the middle class; they belong to "us" as well as to "them." Out-of-control children aren't always other people's kids. They come in all sizes, shapes and colors and from affluent neighborhoods as well as down-at-the-heel city 'hoods. Kids who do bad things have highly educated parents as well as barely literate ones. A recent Carnegie Corporation report describes the depth and reach of our child-related problems: "Nearly half of American adolescents are at high or moderate risk of seriously damaging their life chances. The damage may be near term and vivid, or it may be delayed, like a time bomb set in youth."[16]

The enormous surge in youth violence is perhaps the most cruel—and most costly—manifestation of our inability to nurture our young. Children are now responsible for a staggering 20 million crimes a year. Between 1985 and 1994, among those aged fourteen to seventeen, arrests for murder increased by 172 percent, and for other violent crimes (rape, robbery and aggravated assault) by 46 percent. And while violent crime among teenagers has been escalating, comparable crime rates for adults have been falling quite rapidly: Between 1990 and 1994, homicide rates among adults aged twenty-five and older declined 18 percent.[17] There are now two crime trends in America, one for adults and one for children, and they are moving in opposite directions. One poorly understood fact is the hefty price tag attached to juvenile crime, as society ends up paying for a lifetime spent in and out of jail. A recent study estimates the cost to taxpayers of one violent young person at $1.5 million.[18]

In a day and age when we associate crime with young black men, it is important to stress that increases in juvenile crime apply across the board, in "all races, social classes, and lifestyles." Although young black males are four to five times more likely to be arrested for violent crime than white youths of the same age, the increase in the rate of arrests is far higher for white youths than for black: a 44 percent increase compared to a 19 percent increase between 1988 and 1993.[19]

Daphne Abdela, age fifteen, moved in a private-school underworld in New York City where belonging means playing thug, getting wasted and committing crimes. In her case, these crimes might well have included murder. In June 1997, she and her buddy Chris Vasquez, also fifteen, were arraigned in connection with the stabbing death of a forty-four-year-old real estate agent named Michael McMorrow. The killing occurred in the vicinity of the stately apartment building on Central Park West where Daphne lived. Daphne reportedly told the police that after the murder she and Chris mutilated the body, cutting off the dead man's nose and almost severing a hand in an attempt to hide his identity. Then they tried to sink McMorrow's 220-pound frame in the park's lake, gutting it first, Daphne told police, "because he was a fatty."

Daphne cannot claim to be black, brown or disadvantaged. She is a highly privileged youngster, even by the standards of Manhattan. Before her arrest she lived in a $3 million home and was driven to school by the family chauffeur.[20]

When we look into the future, the picture becomes bleaker still. Demographic trends indicate that when it comes to juvenile crime, the worst may be yet to come. A "baby boomlet" in the late 1980s and early 1990s means that there are now 40 million children under age ten in the United States. We can therefore expect the adolescent population to swell by a quarter over the next decade. Since so many of these children are growing up below the poverty line in fragmented families, there is every reason to expect a new surge in juvenile crime.

If thousands of American youngsters are being killed or injured at the hands of their peers, thousands more are lost in their own nightmares. These are the children who self-destruct, seeing suicide as their only way out. Their numbers too are soaring. Between 1960 and 1994, the suicide rate among teens nearly tripled, making suicide the third leading cause of death for young people. Black children and very young children seem to be at risk in new and dreadful ways: The suicide rate among black males aged ten to fourteen went up a staggering 240 percent between 1980 and 1995.[21]

A particularly shameful fact is that the United States has the highest percentage of children living in poverty of any rich nation: 20.5 percent, a figure that represents a 36 percent increase since 1970 and compares with 9 percent in Canada, 4 percent in Germany and 2 percent in Japan.[22] Children quite simply have not shared in America's prosperity in recent years. Very young children are particu larly badly off: For those under six years of age, the poverty rate is 23 percent, which means that over 5 million preschoolers now live below the poverty line.[23] Bad as these figures are, they are expected to get considerably worse as the effects of welfare reform kick in. The Urban Institute predicts an additional 1.1 million children will have slithered into poverty in 1997 alone. Black and Hispanic children are disproportionately represented in the poor population—47 percent of black children and 34 percent of Latino children are poor—but in recent years the poverty rate has grown twice as fast among whites as among blacks. Significantly, in 1996, 69 percent of poor children lived in families where at least one adult was at work—up from 61 percent in 1993.[24] In the late 1990s, getting a job does not necessarily pull a family out of poverty.

Substance abuse is also on the increase among teens. The use of illegal drugs by adolescents increased significantly between 1992 and 1995. This represents a reversal of earlier downward trends. In 1996 the government reported troubling increases in drug use in all age groups. For example, between 1992 and 1995 the use of marijuana by high-school seniors increased by 63 percent, while the use of inhalants such as glues, aerosols and solvents by eighth graders increased 28 percent.[25]

On the educational front the news is equally grim, since underachievement and failure continue to dog the steps of American youngsters. Across the nation, combined average Scholastic Aptitude Test (SAT) scores have fallen significantly since 1972, despite a recent recentering exercise, which had the effect of raising nominal scores. Data collected by the National Assessment of Educational Progress, which has been testing national samples of students aged nine, thirteen and seventeen each year since 1969, show "few indications of positive trends" in reading and writing.[26] American children are also at or near the bottom in most international surveys measuring educational achievement, coming in seventh out of ten countries in physics and tenth—dead last—in average mathematics proficiency.

Another disturbing fact is that only 69.7 percent of American students who enter ninth grade earn a high-school diploma four years later, a figure that has slipped seven percentage points since 1970.[27] Most policymakers see this as a national disgrace in an age where other advanced nations have nearly universal secondary-school education. In Japan, for example, 90 percent of seventeen-year-olds graduate from high school.

Not only is a large proportion of American youth growing up badly educated and ill prepared for the world of work, but a significant number are further handicapped by increasingly serious emotional problems. According to the Carnegie Corporation, today's youngsters are having trouble coping with stresses in their lives: "Many are depressed, and about a third of adolescents report they have contemplated suicide."[28] Since 1971, the number of adolescents admitted to private psychiatric hospitals has increased fifteenfold. Experts in the field explain this alarming trend by pointing to a constellation of pressures ranging from long workdays to divorce to absent fathers, which have left many parents too thinly stretched to provide consistent support for their children. The pressures on single mothers are particularly severe. Indeed, in many instances the stress is so great that parenting breaks down and becomes inconsistent and erratically punitive.

One thing seems clear enough from this brief survey: Not only are American children failing to thrive; in several critical respects, their condition and life circumstances are steadily deteriorating. Overall, they lead more dangerous and more poverty-stricken lives than children did thirty, twenty or even five years ago. They are also less likely to succeed in school and more likely to experiment with drugs, and many are depressed and seriously self-destructive. It is particularly distressing to realize that children in America are at much greater risk than children elsewhere in the advanced industrial world. Although the United States ranks second worldwide in per capita income, this country does not even make it into the top ten on any significant indicator of child welfare.

Twenty Two

ON THE 1980S

This brief piece is my interpretation of the decade of the 1980s as requested by Newsweek magazine for its anniversary issue. My respondent was Secretary James Baker of the Reagan administration. Based on the letters I received, this essay saw good use in high-school social studies classes across the nation. This kind of journalistic writing is risky, because it can become too simplistic, flat or clever. In fact, I gave up journalism a few years later. Now I only give lectures, write books and read voraciously.

THE 1980S WERE NOT simply a decade of glitz and greed. More important, they ushered in a new era of American history—the triumphant conservatism of Reagan, Rambo and retrenchment. The Reagan revolution was a full-blown ideological response to the anemic liberalism of the Carter presidency, which faltered in the face of runaway inflation, sluggish economic growth, the Iranian hostage crisis and the relative erosion of America's place in the global economy. The Rambo mentality harked back to a gunfighter readiness to do battle with an "evil" empire at nearly any cost. And the unapologetic retrenchment took the form of making people more comfortable with their prejudices and reducing public focus on the disadvantaged. The 1980s discouraged a serious national conversation on the deep problems confronting us.

For the first time since the 1920s, the political Right—along with highly organized conservative corporate and bank elites—boldly attempted to reform American society. The aim of Reaganomics—couched in the diverse languages of supply-siders (Arthur Laffer), single-minded monetarists (Paul Volcker) and budget balancers (Alan Greenspan)—was to give new life to the utopian ideology of laissez-faire capitalism. This ideology cast high taxes, regulation and welfare assistance to the poor as the major impediments to economic growth and prosperity. Low taxes, deregulation and cutbacks in liberal social programs were viewed as a means to curtail inflation and generate an economic boom.

The decade brought us the largest peacetime military buildup in American history (about 28 percent of the federal budget in 1988!); it brought us the short-sighted choices of highly compensated corporate executives to consume, acquire and merge rather than invest, research and innovate. Together these developments caused high levels of public and private debt and the starvation of the public sector. There was little money for roads, railways, community development, housing, education, neighborhood improvement and, above all, decent-paying jobs for those displaced by industrial flight.

In the 1980s, the expansion of unfettered markets produced great wealth for the top 1 percent of the population, impressive income for the top 20 percent and significant decline in real wages for the bottom 40 percent. For example, the top 1 percent owned 44 percent of the household net wealth in 1929 and 36 percent in 1989 (in 1976, it dropped to 20 percent). By 1989, the top 1 percent of families owned 48 percent of the total financial wealth in the country. Of course, income inequality is less extreme than wealth inequality—yet the significant increase of both in the 1980s reveals the fundamental virtues and vices of unbridled capitalist markets. These markets yield *efficiency* and *ingenuity* in regard to what consumers desire and what products cost. At the same time they increase *inequality* and *isolation* in regard to what the most vulnerable people need and which basic social goods are available to them.

The major *economic* legacy of Reaganomics was to increase the disparity between rich and poor and to downsize the American middle class. Our social structure began to look less like a diamond and more like an hourglass. More hours of work were required to sustain a decent standard of living even as an undeniable decline in the quality of life set in—with increased crime, violence, disease (e.g., AIDS), tensions over race, gender and sexual orientation, decrepit public schools, ecological abuse and a faltering physical infrastructure. In short, Reaganomics resulted in waves of economic recovery, including millions of new jobs (many part-time), alongside a relative drop in the well-being of a majority of Americans.

The unintended *cultural* consequence of this economic legacy was a spiritual impoverishment in which the dominant conception of the good life consists of gaining access to power, pleasure and property, sometimes by any means. In other words, a fully crystallized market culture appeared in which civic institutions such as families, neighborhoods, unions, churches, synagogues, mosques held less and less sway, especially among young people. Is it a mere accident that nonmarket values like loyalty, commitment, service, care, concern—even tenderness—can hardly gain a secure foothold in such a market culture? Or that more and more of our children believe that life is a thoroughly hedonistic and narcissistic affair?

One of the telling moments of the 1980s came when a member of the Federal Communications Commission boasted that when television was deregulated, "the marketplace will take care of children." And, to a significant degree, this unintentionally sad and sobering prophecy has come true. The entertainment industry, with its huge doses of sex and violence, has a disproportionate and often disgusting influence over us and our children. A creeping Zeitgeist of cold-heartedness and mean-spiritedness accompanies this full-blown market culture.

Everything revolves around buying and selling, promoting and advertising. This logic leads ultimately to the gangsterization of culture—the collapse of moral fabric and the shunning of personal responsibility in both vanilla suburbs and chocolate cities. Instead of reviving traditional values, the strong patriotism and social conservatism of the 1980s has ironically yielded a populace that is suspicious of the common good and addicted to narrow pleasures.

The 1980s came to a close with the end of the Cold War—yet the culture wars of a racially torn and market-driven American society loom large. A strategy of "positive polarization" (especially playing the racial card) has realigned the electorate into a predominantly white conservative Republican party and a thoroughly bewildered centrist Democratic party. This has helped produce a disgruntled citizenry that slouches toward cynicism, pessimism and even fatalism. Nearly half of all black children and 20 percent of all American children grow up in poverty, trapped in a cycle of despair and distrust.

The major paradox of the 1980s is that the decade ended with the collapse of moribund Communist regimes of repression and regimentation—as well as the advent of more than 40 new social experiments in democracy around the world—just as American democracy is quietly threatened by internal decay. In other words, the far-reaching insights of Adam Smith's defense of the role of markets loom large in the eyes of former Communist societies just as the cultural inanities of capitalism pointed out by Karl Marx become clearer in rich capitalist democracies—especially in the United States.

The market magic of the triumphant conservatism of the 1980s did help squeeze out fat and make American business more competitive in the brutal global economy. But we have yet to come to terms with the social costs. Confused citizens now oscillate between tragic resignation and vigorous attempts to hold at bay their feelings of impotence and powerlessness. Public life seems barren and vacuous. And gallant efforts to reconstruct public-mindedness in a balkanized society of proliferating identities and constituencies seem far-fetched, if not futile. Even the very art of public conversation—the precious activity of communicating with fellow citizens in a spirit of mutual respect and civility—appears to fade amid the noisy backdrop of name-calling and finger-pointing in flat sound bites.

The new decade of the 1990s begins with Americans hungry to make connections, to communicate their rage, anger, fury and hope. The new popularity of radio and TV talk shows is one symptom of this populist urge. Rap—the major form of popular music among young people—is another. The great American novel of the 1980s, the Nobel Prize laureate Toni Morrison's *Beloved,* yearns to tell a "story not to be passed on"—a story of a great yet flawed American civilization afraid to confront its tragic past and fearful of its frightening future.

This fear now permeates much of America—fear of violent attack or vicious assault, fear of indecent exposure or malicious insult. Out of the 1980s came a new kind of civic terrorism—physical and psychic—that haunts the public streets and private minds of America.

Race sits at the center of this terrifying moment. Although a small number of black men—who resemble myself or my son in appearance—commit a disproportionate number of violent crimes, the unfair stereotype of all black men as criminals persists. And despite the fact that most of these crimes are committed against black people, the national focus highlights primarily white victims.

Yet we all must assume our share of responsibility for the despair and degradation. The generational layers of social misery that afflict poor communities were rendered invisible in the 1980s not just by our government, but by ourselves. Economic desperation coupled with social breakdown now threatens the very existence of impoverished communities in urban areas—with growing signs of the same forces at work in rural and suburban America. The drug and gun cultures among youth are the most visible symptoms of this nihilism. If we are to survive as a nation, the 1990s must be a decade in which candid and critical conversation takes place about race and poverty, rights and responsibilities, violence and despair.

The great comeback pop singer of the 1980s Tina Turner tragically croons, "What's Love Got to Do With It?" In a decade of glitz and greed, "Who needs a heart when a heart can be broken?" And the most talented songwriting team in American popular music of the 1980s, Babyface and L. A. Reid, nod in their classic song, "My, My, My." Maybe in the 1990s we can bring back some love, justice, humor and community.

SOURCE: From *Newsweek,* January 3, 1994, pp. 48–49. Copyright © 1994 Newsweek, Inc. All rights reserved. Reprinted by permission.

Twenty Three

MICHAEL HARRINGTON, DEMOCRATIC SOCIALIST

As a member of Democratic Socialists of America—the largest left organization in the country—for seventeen years, a member of its National Political Action committee for six years and now one of its honorary chairs, I have a close connection to Michael Harrington's legacy. We worked closely together and traveled the country as spokespersons for the organization in the 1980s. So I was honored when The Nation *magazine asked me in 1990 to write an essay just after he lost his battle with cancer. I tried to do it with insight and love for him as well as critical challenge to the American Left. His bold thought and gallant efforts will live forever in the annals of freedom fighters everywhere.*

THE DEATH OF MICHAEL Harrington is the end of an era in the history of American socialism. He was the socialist evangelist of our time—the bearer of the mantles of Eugene Debs and Norman Thomas. Unlike Debs and Thomas, however, Harrington was a serious intellectual. His first book, *The Other America* (1962)—with a boost from Dwight Macdonald's famous review in the *New Yorker*—thrust him into the limelight and prompted the Kennedy administration's campaign against poverty. His fifteen other books ranged from solid history of Western socialist movements (*Socialism,* 1972), to analysis of advanced capitalist societies (*Twilight of Capitalism,* 1976), to autobiographical reflections (*The Long-Distance Runner,* 1988) to broad pronouncements about the prevailing crisis of Western civilization (*The Politics at God's Funeral,* 1984). Though far from original works, these books guided and inspired many progressives in their struggles for freedom, solidarity and justice.

Like the late Raymond Williams in Britain and the late C. P. Macpherson in Canada, Harrington carved out a vital democratic socialist space between the Scylla of Stalinism and the Charybdis of liberalism. With his early roots in Irish Catholicism, he was a Pascalian Marxist who wagered boldly on the capacity of ordinary men and women to create and sustain a socialist future. Harrington was also a socialist in the American grain: experimental in method, moral in motivation and optimistic in outlook. Like Walt Whitman, John Dewey and C. Wright Mills, he believed in the possibility of social betterment by means of creative intelligence, moral suasion and political struggle. Yet he was the first great democratic socialist in the United States to be well read in the Marxist classics (his translation of Georg Lukács's "What Is Orthodox Marxism?" thirty-years ago was the first in this country) *and* to have mastered the details of progressive public policy. Endowed with great ambition, talent, discipline and curiosity—but no Ph.D.—he became the shining knight and activist intellectual of the democratic Left for nearly three decades.

Harrington was the product of two distinct intellectual subcultures: those of the artistic bohemian radicals (centered at the White Horse tavern in Greenwich Village) and the anti Stalinist socialists of the late 1950s and early 1960s. The former changed him from a follower of Dorothy Day's Catholic social gospel (after college at Holy Cross, a year at Yale Law School and an M.A. in English at the University of Chicago) into a secular proponent of sexual freedom and racial equality; the latter turned him into a self-styled Marxist with deep democratic sentiments. Both left subcultures were thoroughly New Yorkish and disproportionately Jewish, and thus permeated by intense conversation, bookish knowledge, oppositional outlooks and identification with the oppressed and exploited. Harrington's superb oratorical skills, voracious reading and links with the progressive wing of the labor movement were fundamentally shaped by these subcultures—which are no longer available to young intellectuals. His charisma as a progressive leader and his heritage as a public intellectual bore this particular historical stamp and reflected as well his good nature and his ability to reconcile opposing people and ideas.

In his last book, *Socialism: Past and Future,* Harrington grapples with the most fundamental questions facing democratic socialists: Is socialism more than "the hollow memory of a passionate youth" or "humankind's most noble and useful political illusion"? Can the socialist ideal once again become credible and desirable, given its heavy "baggage of historic failure" in the form of command economies, bureaucratic authoritarian elites and repressive regimentation of ordinary people in the "actually existing" Communist countries? What are the analytical contents, practical socioeconomic arrangements and moral values that define the term "socialism"? Does the term obstruct and obscure the very ideals it purports to promote? What does it mean to be a democratic socialist today?

Harrington's attempt to reply to these pressing questions constitutes not only a reevaluation of the socialist life he led, but also a projection of his legacy. The book was begun the day he was told that he had inoperable cancer and a limited time to live. And the text is vintage Harrington—lucid, candid, tempered, yet upbeat. His basic argument is that the hope for human freedom and justice in the future rests upon the capacity of people to choose and implement democratic forms of socialization in the face of "irresponsible," "unthinking" and "unsocial" versions of corporate socialization. Harrington defines corporate socialization as a

fusion of Weber's notion of rationalization, or the expansion of bureaucratic hierarchies that impose impersonal rules and regulations in order to increase efficiency,
and Marx's idea of commodification, or the globalization of capital. (This takes the
form of centralizing corporations that concentrate power and wealth and render
people increasingly dependent on market forces to satisfy their needs and desires.)
For Harrington, the fundamental choice is not between rigid command economies
and "free markets," or between bureaucratic collectivist regimes and capitalist
democracies. Rather, the basic choice in the future will be between a democratic,
or "bottom-up," socialization and a corporate, or "top-down," socialization. This
choice is much more complex than it appears on the surface and is a far cry from
the classic Marxist choice between socialism and barbarism posed by Rosa Lux-
emburg.

First, Harrington's notion of democratic socialization has nothing to do with
nationalization or state control of economic enterprises. Nor is it associated with
a socialist "negation" of capitalism. Instead, it is a process in which social forces—
especially those brought to bear by progressive groups, associations and organizations—try to broaden the participation of citizens in the economic, cultural and
political spheres of society and thus control the conditions of their existence. At
present these forces are weak compared with those of corporate socialization. Orthodox Marxist-Leninists have made the fatal mistake of reducing democratic socialization to elitist nationalization, creating monstrosities that are neither socialist
nor capitalist, neither free nor efficient.

Second, Harrington shows that the reality of corporate socialization can be separated from the rhetoric about "free markets" or the absence of state intervention
in the economy. As Reagan and Thatcher illustrated, corporate socialization, despite conservative pieties about "laissez-faire" capitalism, is deeply statist, with its
military buildups, socially authoritarian regimentation of the labor force, moral
strictures on individual (especially women's) choices and a debt-financed public
sphere.

Third, democratic socialization, in Harrington's view, entails more than workers' participation in investment decisions (including access to relevant knowledge
and information) and the use of markets for nonmarket purposes. It also requires
a new culture, a new civilization. Harrington's attempt to define this "new socialism" harks back to the best of the nineteenth-century utopian socialists, such as
Charles Fourier, Robert Owen and the Saint-Simonians. Although Harrington
shuns their naïveté, moralism and messianism, he accents their feminist, commu-
nitarian and cultural radicalism. He then adds a strong antiracist and ecological
consciousness that calls for a new global civilization in which wealth is distributed
more equally and life is lived more meaningfully.

Harrington's project is indeed visionary. Yet he struggles to make it appear to
be more than mere fantasy. So he accepts the sacred cow of the present capitalist

structure of accumulation—namely, economic growth—and attempts to show how it can be channeled toward qualitative living, not merely quantitative consuming. He proposes replacing the gross national product with a new set of statistics, the qualitative national (and international) product, which would subtract from the GNP environmental degradation, premature death, wasteful packaging and un-informative advertising in order to keep track of the quality of life. Further, Harrington suggests a restructuring of the United Nations and its related economic institutions—such as the World Bank and the International Monetary Fund—in order to transfer resources from North to South and promote cultural differences. He emphatically points out that Third World debt not only forces cutbacks in crucial social services for the countries' poor people, but also prevents the South from consuming First World goods—consumption that could fuel economic growth in both North and South. And his trenchant critique of the calculated dependence of the export-led economies of the Four Tigers (Taiwan, South Korea, Hong Kong and Singapore)—the showcase countries for conservative economists—reveals the fragility of the present international economic order. His discussion is extremely relevant to Eastern Europeans clamoring for the "free market"—that is, full integration into the corporate-dominated economic order of the West.

How will democratic socialization come about? How do we radically reform a system while working within it? How can democratic socialist practices be more than a social democracy in which corporate priorities operate within a public sector organized by liberals and managed by bureaucratic elites? And given the fragmentation and casualization of the labor force—the de-skilling and re-skilling of workers due to the automation, computerization and robotization in the workplace—who will be the major agents of social change?

Harrington approaches these questions with candor and caution. First, he assumes that any socialist conception of social change must be epochal, not apocalyptic. He finds it impossible to conceive the triumph of democratic socialization in the next fifty years. Second, he presents Sweden's social democratic order as the major inspiration—not the utopian model or flawless example—for figuring out how to overcome the most inegalitarian effects of corporate socialization. Sweden's policy of "collective capital formation," which links growth to efficiency and democratic management, and solidaristic wage demands that first reward those at the bottom of the labor force fall far short of his vision. Yet they show what can be done when pressure is brought to bear on capital in the interests of social justice and democratic participation. Harrington acknowledges the precious gains achieved by reformers as well as the structural constraints on reform. His notion of "visionary gradualism" is an attempt to walk this tightrope of short-term strategies and tactics and long-term aims.

But is he successful? Does he remain blind to possible new social forces or silent about new strategies for change? It is extremely difficult to know how to measure "success" here. Certainly social movements he did not foresee may emerge. New cleavages in the fragile conservative camp could weaken the right offensive, and structural transformations could threaten the present forms of corporate socialization. Yet it would be unfair to blame Harrington for failure to predict such events.

The major problem I have with Harrington's impressive project is that it remains too far removed from lived experience in advanced capitalist societies. Despite his call for a new culture, he does not discuss the civic terrorism that haunts our city streets; the central role of TV, video, radio and film in shaping the perceptions of citizens; the escalating violence against women, gays and lesbians; the racial and ethnic polarization or the slow decomposition of civil society (families, schools, neighborhoods and associations). There are no reflections in the book about the impact of the plagues of drugs and AIDS on a terrified populace or the entrenchment of jingoistic patriotism and nationalism. Although he invokes Gramsci, Harrington is more interested in the notion of "historic blocs"—coalition politics—than in the actual operations of hegemony that mobilize people's "consent" (in the forms of indifference or passivity) to the "fate" of corporate socialization. Subtle investigations into such cultural, experiential and existential realities—as intimated in the works of Georg Simmel, Lukács, Walter Benjamin, Siegfried Kracauer and other cultural critics—are needed before democratic socialization can become more than a noble ideal.

Harrington combined many of the best qualities of the old Left and a genuine openness to some of the insights of the New Left. In his life and work, the fist and rose begin to come together. With the historic merger of his organization, the Democratic Socialist Organizing Committee, with the New American Movement in 1982, this unity-in-process, though full of tension, was manifest. His mere presence gave the new group, Democratic Socialists of America, a visibility and legitimacy in progressive circles far beyond its numbers (roughly 7,000).

Because the Left is organizationally weak and intellectually timid relative to its conservative counterparts (it is armed more with journals and gestures than with programs and politicians), it has tended to rely on charismatic spokespersons and insurgent movements. Harrington's death makes this situation more apparent. The splitting of the old and New Lefts from the black, brown, yellow and red Lefts—dating back to the mid-1960s—exacerbates the predicament of progressives. This is why Jesse Jackson's Rainbow politics is so refreshing. It is a new multiracial attempt to channel the inchoate left-liberal sentiments of ordinary people into an electoral campaign of national scope. Yet the legacy of Harrington, as well as those of Martin Luther King, Jr., Fannie Lou Hamer and Malcolm X, as well as the efforts of feminists, greens, the Gray Panthers and gays and lesbians, deserves a movement with deeper roots. Jackson's courageous attempt to gain power at the national level is a symptom of the weakness of the Left—a sign that its capacity to generate extraparliamentary social motion or movements has waned. The best way to keep the legacy of Harrington alive is to go beyond it by building from grassroots citizens' participation in credible progressive projects in which activists see that their efforts can make a difference. In this way, the crucial difference that Michael Harrington made in many of our lives can become contagious.

SOURCE: "Michael Harrington, Socialist," *Beyond Eurocentrism and Multiculturalism, Vol. 1: Prophetic Thought in Postmodern Times* (Monroe, Me.: Common Courage Press, 1993), pp. 181–188.

PART SIX

PROPHETIC CHRISTIAN THOUGHT

Despite the challenges presented by the widespread trivialization and dilution of the Christian gospel, I remain committed to its fundamental claim: To follow Jesus is to love your way through the darkness of the world. This love appears absurd—in fact pure folly in the face of much of the world's misery—and yet it yields indescribable levels of sorrow and joy, sadness and ecstasy. To be a Christian is to look at the world through the lens of the cross and thereby keep one's focus on human suffering and struggle. Unfortunately, much of American religion is market religion—such as our pervasive postresurrection Christianity—which identifies with the world's "winners" based on health and wealth. In my view, to be a serious Christian is to live dangerously against the grain of the world. For too much of American Christianity, to follow Jesus is to seek comfort devoid of courageous compassion and bold witness for "the least of these." This section gives readers a taste of why the love ethic of Jesus remains central to my Chekhovian Christian and radical democratic way of being in—and against—the world.

Twenty Four

THE CRISIS IN CONTEMPORARY AMERICAN RELIGION

These introductory remarks to my second book, Prophetic Fragments *(1988), convey my moral outrage at the relative indifference of American religion to the challenge of social justice beyond charity. The Christian Right is a glaring example of this tendency. Yet I view myself as neither a self-righteous prophet railing at those gone astray nor an elevated elitist who brings the Truth to the benighted masses. To be a part of a prophetic tradition is not to be a prophet or elitist. Rather, it is humbly to direct your strongest criticisms at yourself and then self-critically speak your mind to others with painful candor and genuine compassion.*

THE CRISIS IN CONTEMPORARY American religious life is profound and pervasive. The crisis is profound in that it deepens as Americans turn more desperately toward religion. The crisis is pervasive in that it affects every form of religiosity in the country—from Christianity to Buddhism, from reform Judaism to Islam. To put it bluntly, American religious life is losing its prophetic fervor. There is an undeniable decline in the clarity of vision, complexity of understanding and quality of moral action among religious Americans. The rich prophetic legacies of Sojourner Truth, Walter Rauschenbusch, Dorothy Day, Abraham Heschel, and Martin Luther King, Jr., now lay nearly dormant—often forgotten—and the possession of a marginal few. Political and cultural conservatism seems to have silenced most of the prophetic religious voices and tamed the vast majority of churches, temples, synagogues and mosques. Prophetic religion indeed is at the crossroads in present-day America.

The principal aim of *Prophetic Fragments* is to examine and explore, delineate and demystify, counter and contest the widespread accommodation of American religion to the political and cultural status quo. This accommodation is suffocating much of the best in American religion; it promotes and encourages an existential emptiness and political irrelevance. This accommodation is, at bottom, idolatrous—it worships the gods created by American society and kneels before the altars erected by American culture.

American religious life—despite its weekly rituals and everyday practices—is shot through with existential emptiness. This emptiness—or lack of spiritual depth—results from the excessive preoccupation with isolated personal interests and atomistic individual concerns in American religious life. These interests and concerns unduly accommodate the status quo by mirroring the privatism and careerism rampant in American society. Like so much of American culture, exorbitant personalistic and individualistic preoccupations in American religion yield momentary stimulation rather than spiritual sustenance, sentimental self-flagellation rather than sacrificial self-denial. Needless to say, these accommodationalist forms of religion fit well with the thriving consumerism, narcissism and hedonism in the country. Religion becomes but one more stimulant in a culture addicted to stimulation—a stimulation that fuels consumption and breeds existential emptiness. In this way, postmodern American culture attempts to eliminate spiritual depth, disseminate stimulatory surfaces, flatten out transcendence into titillation and replace the sense of the mystery of existence with that of the self's feelings of intensity (usually of the orgiastic sort). Accommodationalist forms of religion usually aid and abet this postmodern condition, thereby surreptitiously prohibiting the very existential state they claim to promote—namely, spiritual depth.

Furthermore, American religious life—notwithstanding its vast philanthropic networks and impressive charitable record—lacks a substantive social consciousness. This is so because, like so much of American life, it suffers from social amnesia. American religious people have little memory of or sense for collective struggle and communal combat. At the level of family and individuals, this memory and sense lingers. But at the level of larger social groups and institutions, this memory and sense of struggle evaporates. This social amnesia prevents systemic social analysis of power, wealth and influence in society from taking hold among most religious Americans. Instead, the tendency is to fall back on personalistic and individualistic explanations for poverty, occupational mobility or social catastrophe.

For instance, moralistic acts are often conflated with moral actions. Yet the former proceed from sheer sentimental concern—for example, pity—whereas the latter flow from an understanding of the larger context in which the action takes place and of the impact of the action on the problem. In short, moralistic acts rest upon a narrow, parochial anti-intellectualism that sees only pitiful individuals, whereas moral action is based on a broad, robust prophetism that highlights systemic social analysis of the circumstances under which tragic persons struggle. It is no accident that the moralistic, anti-intellectualistic forms of American religion thoroughly trash modernity and secularity, yet revel in the wonders of technology and in the comfortable living of modern prosperity. This flagrant hypocrisy—simply highlighted in the events in recent months, yet true for all of the big-time, narrow TV evangelists—is overcome only when one adopts a principled prophetism, that is, a prophetic religion that incorporates the best of modernity and secularity (tolerance, fallibilism, criticism), yet brings prophetic critique to bear upon the idols of modernity and secularity (science, technology and wealth).

I live, work and write out of a particular religious perspective—namely, that of the prophetic stream of the Christian tradition. I first encountered this stream in the bosom of the black Baptist heritage in America, and this stamp is still felt and seen in my own religious outlook. Yet I am concerned with the prophetic potential of all religions (such as Buddhism, Hinduism, Judaism and Islam) and the progressive possibilities of all secular ideologies (including feminism, Marxism, anarchism and liberalism). My prophetic outlook is informed by a deep, historical consciousness that accents the finitude and fallenness of all human beings and accentuates an international outlook that links the human family with a common destiny; an acknowledgment of the inescapable yet ambiguous legacy of tradition and the fundamental role of community; a profound sense of the tragic character of life and history that generates a strenuous mood, a call for heroic, courageous moral action always against the odds; and a biblically motivated focus on and concern for the wretched of the earth that keeps track of the historic and social causes for much (though by no means all) of their misery.

On the one hand, I assume that religious traditions are, for the most part, reactionary, repressive and repulsive without heavy doses of modern formulations of rule of law, gender and racial equality, tolerance and, especially, substantive democracy. On the other hand, such modern formulations can be based on or derived from the best of religious traditions. To be a contemporary religious intellectual—and person—is to be caught in this creative tension on the boundary between past and present, tradition and modernity—yet always mounted in the barricades on this battlefield on which life is lived and history is made. Prophetic thought and action is preservative in that it tries to keep alive certain elements of a tradition bequeathed to us from the past and revolutionary in that it attempts to project a vision and inspire a praxis that fundamentally transforms the prevailing status quo in light of the best of the tradition and the flawed yet significant achievements of the present order. These fragments—which feebly reflect the Christian faith that shores me up against the ruins in our world—are linked together by my response to one basic question: How does a present-day Christian think about and act on enhancing the plight of the poor, the predicament of the powerless and the quality of life for all in a prophetic manner?

SOURCE: "Introduction: The Crisis in Contemporary American Religion," *Prophetic Fragments* (Grand Rapids, Mich.: Wm. B. Eerdmans Publishing Co., 1988), pp. ix–xi.

Twenty Five

THE HISTORICIST TURN IN PHILOSOPHY OF RELIGION

This ambitious essay is a philosophical inquiry into the limits of philosophic reflections on religion—especially in America. It reflects my skepticism about any claims of religious certainty or dogmatic pronouncements about the nature of God. Yet I remain skeptical about skepticism, since we must not only think and question, but also live and love—and die. My Chekhovian Christian way of being is peppered by skepticism, but not paralyzed by it. I live on the treacherous and tortuous terrain between doubt and faith, at the bloody crossroads of despair and hope.

———————

From the disintegration of Hegelianism derives the beginning of a new cultural process, different in character from its predecessors, a process in which practical movement and theoretical thought are united (or are trying to unite through a struggle that is both theoretical and practical).... Out of the critique of Hegelianism arose modern idealism and the philosophy of praxis. Hegelian immanentism becomes historicism, but it is absolute historicism only with the philosophy of praxis.... One should not be surprised if this beginning arises from the convergence of various elements, apparently heterogeneous.... Instead, it is worth noting that such an overthrow could not but have connections with religion.

—ANTONIO GRAMSCI, *PRISON NOTEBOOKS*

IN THE PAST FEW decades philosophy of religion has suffered decline as a discipline. Consider the towering figures in the field: The synoptic vision of Edgar Sheffield Brightman, the tough-minded empiricism of Henry Nelson Wieman and the magisterial metaphysics of Alfred North Whitehead are now distant memories for present-day participants in this discipline. Here I shall sketch a brief account of this decline and, more important, suggest a new conception of philosophy of religion that warrants serious attention. This new conception promotes a historicist turn in philosophy of religion that remains within yet deepens the American grain—empirical, pluralist, pragmatic and activist.[1]

The Golden Age of Philosophy of Religion

The Enlightenment critiques of religious thought—such as David Hume's *Dialogues Concerning Natural Religion* and Immanuel Kant's chapter "The Ideal of Pure Reason" in his *Critique of Pure Reason*—set the terms for the modern philosophical debate concerning the status of religious beliefs. These terms accepted the subjectivist turn that puts philosophical reflection first and foremost within the arena of immediate awareness or self-consciousness. Undergirded by the rising authority of science—with its probabilistic reasoning and fallibilistic conclusions—post-Humean and post-Kantian philosophers of religion were forced either to give up or to redefine the scientific character of religious beliefs and thereby to conceptually redescribe such beliefs in moral, affective, aesthetic or existential terms. In other words, one became a neo-Kantian, Schleiermachean, Hegelian or Kierkegaardian. Whether such descriptions yielded epistemic status to religious beliefs became the question for modern philosophy of religion.

Yet this question was not the central issue for the masters of European philosophy in the late nineteenth century. Karl Marx, John Stuart Mill and Friedrich Nietzsche were obsessed primarily with the nature of modern science and the character of modern society and culture. Modern theologians were preoccupied with the epistemic status of religious beliefs, but this preoccupation signified their marginality in European intellectual life.

In stark contrast to their European counterparts, religious concerns loomed large in the first significant American philosophical response to modernity. The first generation of American pragmatists, especially Charles Peirce and William James, attempted not only to demythologize modern science, but also to update religion. For American pragmatists, religious beliefs were not simply practical postulates for moral behavior, pietistic modes of self-consciousness, pictorial representations of absolute knowledge or anxiety-ridden, self-involving choices. Religious beliefs were on the same spectrum as any other beliefs—always linked to experience. The pragmatism of Peirce and James incredibly seized the imagination of a whole generation of American philosophers, including idealist philosophers like Josiah Royce, William Ernest Hocking and Edgar Sheffield Brightman—thereby initiating the Golden Age of philosophy of religion in modern Euro-American thought.

Nowhere in the modern world did philosophers take religion more seriously than in the United States between 1900 and 1940. No other national philosophical tradition compares with the set of American texts such as William James's *The Varieties of Religious Experience* (1902), John Elof Boodin's *Truth and Reality* (1911), William Ernest Hocking's *The Meaning of God in Human Experience* (1912), Josiah Royce's *The Problem of Christianity* (1913), Douglas Clyde MacIntosh's *Theology as an Empirical Science* (1919), Henry Nelson Wieman's *Religious Experience and Scientific*

Method (1926), Alfred North Whitehead's *Process and Reality* (1929), Shailer Mathews's *The Growth of the Idea of God* (1931), John Dewey's *A Common Faith* (1934) and Edgar Sheffield Brightman's *A Philosophy of Religion* (1940).

There are complex sociological and historical reasons that account for this phenomenon. My basic point is simply that for the first four decades of this century most of the major American philosophers were philosophers of religion and that the Golden Age of philosophy of religion in the modern West was primarily an American affair.

This American predominance in philosophy of religion produced profound philosophical breakthroughs. First, major American philosophers, starting with Peirce, radically questioned the subjectivist turn in philosophy. They attacked the notion that philosophical reflection begins within the inner chambers of mental episodes. American pragmatists promoted an intersubjectivist turn that highlighted the communal and social character of acquiring knowledge. American process philosophers accented a primordial form of experience, for example, causal efficacy, which disclosed the often overlooked interpretive and abstract status of sense perception.

These two diverse critiques of the fundamental starting point for European Enlightenment philosophy undermined the relational framework of mind-objects-God. The pragmatists' move led toward a focus on the social practices—from verification procedures to communal values—that produced knowledge about minds, objects and God. The process strategy yielded a new complicated vocabulary that rejected lines of demarcation between consciousness, world and the divine. Furthermore, the legacies of both pragmatic and process thought reclaimed the epistemic and scientific status of religious beliefs as well as their practical value. In short, the major movements in the Golden Age of philosophy of religion undercut the three basic pillars of modern European philosophy.

The distinctive feature of the most influential American philosophies of religion—pragmatism and process thought—is that they defend religious experience and beliefs under the banners of radical empiricism, open-ended pragmatism and ethical activism. Radical empiricism tries to stay in tune with the complex plurality and fluid multiplicity of experience on the individual and corporate levels. Open-ended pragmatism accentuates the various problems motivating logical inquiry and reflective intelligence. Ethical activism links human responsibility and action to the purposeful solving of problems in the personal, cultural, ideological, political, economic and ecological spheres of human and natural activities. In this sense, the major American philosophers prior to World War II did not succumb to the secular insularity of their European counterparts; nor did they cater to the irrational impulses of parochial religious and ideological thinkers: Their plebeian humanism—more democratic than Matthew Arnold's bourgeois humanism and more individualistic than Marx's revolutionary humanism—encouraged them to view sympathetically, though critically, the lives of common people and hence take religion seriously in their sophisticated philosophical reflection.

THE DECLINE OF PHILOSOPHY OF RELIGION

As I noted earlier, the Golden Age of philosophy of religion is long past. The flowering of American philosophy—with its deep religious concerns—was cut short. The political and military crisis in Europe resulted in intellectual émigrés to the United States who changed the academic discipline of philosophy. This change was inextricably bound to the increasing professionalization of the discipline of philosophy.

The advent of logical positivism—with its diverse versions of atomism, reductionism and narrow empiricism—put an end to the Golden Age of philosophy of religion. This Viennese-style positivism, though popularized in America by A. J. Ayer's *Language, Truth, and Logic* (1936), brought with it all the old European Enlightenment baggage pragmatism and process thought had discredited: the subjectivist starting point, subject/object relations and the philosophical trashing of religion. As Dewey's long and languishing star faded in New York and Whitehead's legacy courageously persisted in relative isolation at Chicago, the positivism of Rudolf Carnap, Carl Hempel and others spread like wildfire throughout elite graduate schools in philosophy—especially Harvard, UCLA and Minnesota. By the death of Whitehead in 1947, few graduate students in philosophy at influential schools had heard of Hocking and Brightman, had read Wieman or grappled with Whitehead (besides, maybe, his *Principia Mathematica*). James was deemed a cultural critic who lacked philosophical rigor; Dewey, a mere social activist with scientistic sentiments and fuzzy philosophical meditations. Technical argumentation, logical notation and rigorous analysis—with their concomitant subfields of logic, epistemology and methodology in the natural sciences—had seized center stage.

To put it crudely, logical positivism was based on three fundamental assumptions. First, it assumed a form of sentential atomism that correlates isolated sentences with either possible empirical confirmation (as in the sciences), logical necessity (as in mathematics and logic) or emotion (as in ethics, religion and the arts). Second, it emerged with a kind of phenomenalist reductionism that translates sentences about physical objects into sentences about actual and possible sensations. Third, it presupposed a version of analytical empiricism that holds observational evidence to be the criterion for cognitively meaningful sentences and hence the final court of appeal in determining valid theories about the world. These crucial assumptions, which constitute independent yet interrelated doctrines, were held at various times by the leading logical positivists. More important, they were guided by fundamental distinctions between the analytic and the synthetic, the linguistic and the empirical, theory and observation.[2]

The immediate consequence of logical positivism on philosophy of religion was the near collapse of the latter as a serious academic discipline, or even a subfield within philosophy. This consequence had a devastating effect: During the early stages of the professionalization of philosophy after World War II, philosophy of religion had little or no academic legitimacy. Therefore most of those interested in philosophy with religious concerns were forced to study in graduate programs of divinity schools or seminaries such as Yale, Chicago or Union. Furthermore, since American philosophies of religion also were forms of social and cultural criticism, the near collapse of philosophy of religion was a symptom of the narrow mode of philosophizing promoted by logical positivists. Needless to say, as philosophers had less and less to say about religion, politics, ethics, the arts and the normative role of science in the world, and more and more to say about analytical sentences, methodological operations in physics and the reducibility of objects to sense data, the literate populace lost interest in the intellectual activity of philosophers. In other words, philosophy in America was losing touch with American philosophy.

THE RESURGENCE OF AMERICAN PHILOSOPHY

The major tragedy of contemporary philosophy of religion is that the resurgence of American philosophy occurred at the time when most American theologians were being seduced either by the antiphilosophical stance of Karl Barth or by the then fashionable logical positivism and linguistic analysis. The great contributions of W. V. Quine, Nelson Goodman and Wilfred Sellars, which undermined Viennese-style positivism and Oxford-inspired linguistic philosophy, were made just as A. J. Ayer, J. L. Austin and Ludwig Wittgenstein or Karl Barth and Emil Brunner were becoming prominent on the American theological scene. The result of this situation is that Quine, Goodman and Sellars are relatively alien to most contemporary religious thinkers, and that either refined forms of German idealism, as with Paul Tillich, heuristic mythological versions of Christianity, as in Reinhold Niebuhr, and indigenous updates of process philosophy, as in Schubert Ogden and John B. Cobb, Jr., constitute the most significant contributions of philosophy of religion in America after World War II.

The resurgence of American philosophy was enacted by the powerful critiques of logical positivism launched by Quine, Goodman and Sellars. Quine's epistemological holism, which heralded systems of sentences (or theories) as opposed to isolated sentences as the basic units of empirical significance, discarded sentential atomism. Furthermore, his methodological monism, which rejected the analytic-synthetic distinction, rendered unacceptable the positivist classificatory criterion for tautological and meaningful sentences.[3] Goodman's postempiricist antireductionism highlighted the theory-laden character of observation and undercut the narrow empiricist standard for adjudicating between conflicting theories of the world. And his ontological pluralism relegated the idea of truth to that of fitness and promoted diverse true versions of the world instead of a fixed world and unique truth. He thus called into question the monocosmic naturalism of logical positivism (a radical move which even Quine resisted owing to his ontological allegiance to physics—a lingering trace of positivism in the great critic of positivism).[4]

Lastly, Sellars's epistemic antifoundationalism precluded any "given" elements as acceptable candidates that serve as the final terminating point for chains of epistemic justification—thereby condemning any form of empiricist grounding of knowledge claims.[5] The Quine-Goodman-Sellars contributions, though related in complex and often conflicting ways and still questionable in some philosophical circles, signify the American takeover of analytical philosophy—a takeover that has led to the demise of analytical philosophy.[6]

The Quine-Goodman-Sellars insights bear striking resemblances to the viewpoints of earlier American pragmatists. The resurgence of American philosophy is, in part, the recovery of the spirit and temper of American pragmatism reflected in Charles Peirce's first rule of reason: Do not block the way of inquiry.[7] Yet this resurgence is silent regarding the status and role of religion (and social and cultural criticism) in philosophical reflection. Contemporary American philosophy is postanalytic philosophy, with deep debts to pragmatism, yet little interest in religious reflection.

This is so principally because postanalytic philosophy has been preoccupied with the secular priesthood, the sacred institution in modern culture: the scientific community and its practice. Thomas Kuhn's influential book *The Structure of Scientific Revolutions* (1962) can be viewed as the grand postanalytic philosophical text written for the positivist philistines—the great popularization of the implications of the Quine-Goodman-Sellars contributions for the paradigm of rationality in modern culture, that is, the practices of scientists. Paul Feyerabend, who describes himself as a "church historian," deepens these implications (in the political and ideological spheres) regarding the demystification of scientific method and practices in *Against Method* (1975) and *Science in a Free Society* (1978). In short, the philosophy and history of science function in contemporary American philosophy as did the philosophy and history of religion in the Golden Age of American philosophy. The gain is a more sophisticated dialogue concerning the content and character of rationality in modernity; the loss is a less engaged relation with the wider culture and society.

This situation is exemplified in Richard Rorty's masterful manifesto of American postanalytic philosophy, *Philosophy and the Mirror of Nature* (1979), and Richard Bernstein's learned meditations on the role of philosophy after Rorty in *Beyond*

Objectivism and Relativism (1983). Despite their Kuhnian perspectives regarding the social character of rationality, both focus their philosophical concerns almost exclusively on philosophy of science and say nothing about philosophy of religion. And this latter silence is accompanied by a glaring absence of sustained social and cultural criticism. The salutary contributions of Rorty and Bernstein are that (like Hegel and Marx at their best) they make historical consciousness central to their philosophical reflections, without falling into the transcendentalist trap of making historical consciousness the new candidate for philosophically grounding knowledge claims (as did Hegel and Marx at their worst). Yet Rorty and Bernstein put forward "thin" historical narratives that rarely dip into the complex world of politics and culture. Both remain seduced by a kind of Lovejoy-like history of ideas far removed from concrete historical processes and realities. "Thick" historical narratives, such as those of Karl Marx, Max Weber, Simone de Beauvoir, W. E. B. Du Bois and Antonio Gramsci, elude them.

In other words, Rorty and Bernstein hold at arm's length serious tools of social theory and cultural criticism. Presently, Rorty's self-styled neopragmatism—much like Jacques Derrida's poststructuralism—is creating waves in the academy. But these waves remain those of departmental internecine struggles between old-style empiricists and new-style pragmatists, argumentative realists and narrativistic historicists, establishmentarian humanists and the professional posthumanists. These noteworthy conflicts within the discipline of philosophy in the academy have yet to spill over into serious cultural and political debates regarding the larger issues of public concern.

THE THEOLOGICAL DISCOVERY OF HISTORY

While professional philosophers lingered under the spell of the grand Quine-Goodman-Sellars breakthroughs, and academic theologians nested in Barthian cocoons or emulated logical positivists and linguistic analysts, liberation theologians discovered history. This discovery did not consist of systematic reflections on historicity, which has been long a priority of German-trained theologians and Heideggerian-influenced philosophers, but rather of linking historical processes in society to political praxis. In this sense the theological discovery of history by Gustavo Gutiérrez, Mary Daly and James Cone was qualitatively different from the recovery of historicism by Richard Rorty and Richard Bernstein.[8] The former was philosophically underdeveloped yet politically engaged and culturally enlightening; the latter, politically and culturally underdeveloped and philosophically enlightening. Gutiérrez was responding, in part, to the hegemony of Jacques Maritain's integral humanism among liberal Latin American Catholic elites and the "developmentalism" of U.S. foreign policy which masks corporate interests and Latin American social misery. Daly and Cone were recuperating the experiential and activist dimensions of American thought. The early works of Daly are not simply religious critiques of ecclesiastical and cultural patriarchy; they also explore—at the behest of Whitehead and James—primordial forms of female experience that may empower victims of sexist oppression. Even in her post-Christian texts, these experiential and activist dimensions remain. Similarly, the initial works of Cone are not only sustained diatribes against Euro-American racism; they also probe into the degraded and devalued modes of African American experience that promote and encourage resistance against white-supremacist practices. Yet, for many of us, Daly's neo-Thomist metaphysics loomed too large and Cone's Barthian Christocentrism was too thick—and their early one-dimensional social analyses were too parochial.

Notwithstanding their philosophical and social-analytical limitations, liberation theologians put historical processes, social analyses and political praxis at the center of theological discourse in seminaries and divinity schools. Their linking of historical consciousness to present-day political struggles—to anti-imperialist, feminist and black freedom movements—galvanized new intellectual energies throughout the religious academy. This intellectual upsurge caught many neoorthodox theologians and liberal philosophers of religion unaware and unequipped to respond adequately. Yet it is no accident that the two major theological responses to liberation theology have come from process theologians: Schubert Ogden's *Faith and Freedom* and John B. Cobb, Jr.'s *Process Thought and Political Theology*.

Just as Rorty's and Bernstein's historicism is philosophically groundbreaking yet lacking in serious political substance, Gutiérrez's, Daly's and Cone's liberation perspectives are theologically groundbreaking yet lacking in serious philosophical substance. For example, Gutiérrez's conception of Marxist science is quite positivist, Daly's ontological arguments often slide into mere cathartic assertions and Cone's religious claims reek of a hermetic fideism. Unfortunately, the nonexistent dialogue between academic philosophers and theologians nearly ensures an intellectual estrangement that permits the political insouciance of American neopragmatists and promotes the philosophical insularity of liberation theologians. What is needed is a rapprochement of the philosophical historicism of Rorty and Bernstein and the moral vision, social analysis and political engagement of the liberation perspectives of Gutiérrez, Daly and Cone.

The Present Need for the Philosophy of Religion

American philosophy at its best has taken the form of philosophy of religion. This is so not because philosophy of religion possesses some special privilege or wisdom as a discipline, but rather because of the particular character of American philosophical thought. For complex national reasons, when American philosophers turn their backs on religion, they turn their eyes toward science. This usually results in muting their social and political concerns. My point here is not that American philosophers become religious, but rather that they once again take religion seriously, which also means taking culture and society seriously.

The contemporary tasks of a responsible and sophisticated philosophy of religion are threefold. First, it must deepen the historicist turn in philosophy by building upon the Quine-Goodman-Sellars contributions, and "thickening" the "thin" historicism of Rorty's and Bernstein's neopragmatism by means of undogmatic social analysis and engaged cultural criticism. Second, it should put forward moral visions and ethical norms that regulate the social analysis and cultural criticism drawn from the best of available religious and secular traditions bequeathed to us from the past. Third, it should scrutinize in a rational manner synoptic worldviews of various religious and secular traditions in light of their comprehensive grasp of the complexity, multiplicity and specificity of human experiences, and their enabling power to motivate human action for the negation and transformation of structures of oppression.

The historicist turn in philosophy of religion must steer clear of the Scylla of transcendental objectivism and the Charybdis of subjectivist nihilism. My particular version of philosophical historicism is neither the neo-Kantian historicism (à la Wilhelm Dilthey) that presupposes a positivist conception of the *Naturwissenschaften* nor the Popperian-defined historicism that possesses magic powers of social prediction and projection. Rather, the historicism I promote is one that understands transient social practices, contingent cultural descriptions and revisable scientific theories as the subject matter for philosophical reflection. Hence, social analysis and cultural criticism are indispensable components of such reflection.

On the one hand, transcendental objectivism is precluded by rejecting all modes of philosophical reflection that invoke ahistorical quests for certainty and transhistorical searches for foundations—including most realist moves in ontology, foundationalist strategies in epistemology and mentalistic discourses in philosophical psychology. On the other hand, subjectivist nihilism is avoided by condemning all forms of philosophical activity that devalue and disregard possibilities, potentialities and alternatives to prevailing practices. Wholesale leveling and trashing of standards, criteria and principles that facilitate dialogue, conversation and exchange result from subjectivist nihilism. Such nihilism is not simply parasitic on the failures of transcendental objectivism; it also shuns historical consciousness and thereby remains captive to the subjectivist turn. In this way transcendental objectivism is delusory though not necessarily socially pernicious, whereas subjectivist nihilism is inescapably insidious.

My version of historicism flows from the tradition of mitigated skepticism signified by Sebastian Castellio of Basel, William Chillingworth and Pascal at the birth of modern conceptions of knowledge and science. It is deepened and enriched by the tempered Pyrrhonism of David Hume, the Hegelian-inspired historicisms of Kierkegaard and Marx, the demystifying perspectivalism of Nietzsche and the enabling pragmatism of James and Dewey. Like Gadamer, my version of historicism acknowledges the unavoidable character and central role of tradition and prejudice, yet it takes seriously the notion of sound human judgment relative to the most rationally acceptable theories and descriptions of the day. In this way, the historicism I promote is akin to that of Rorty and Bernstein—and especially that of Jeffrey Stout.[9]

My philosophical historicism is inextricably bound to undogmatic social analysis and engaged social criticism, because if one is not nihilistic about history, one must be open to new possibilities, potentialities and alternatives to present practices. In this view, the major role of social analysis and cultural criticism is to understand these practices and discern forces for betterment. Therefore, philosophical historicism—if logically consistent and theoretically coherent—leads to "thick" historicism, to social and heterogeneous narratives that account for the present and project a future.

Although social analysis and cultural criticism play central roles in my historicist philosophy of religion, some forms of such analyses and criticisms are not acceptable. Adequate social analyses and cultural critiques must be regulated by moral visions and ethical norms that are ensconced in religious or secular traditions—shot through with their own set of presuppositions, prejudgments and prejudices. A historicist philosophy of religion is not limited in an a priori manner to religious traditions. Yet in its attempts to take seriously the human dimensions of ultimacy, intimacy and sociality, it usually incorporates elements from religious traditions. Secular traditions are indispensable, yet they have had neither the time nor the maturity to bequeath to us potent cultural forms of ultimacy, intimacy and sociality comparable to older and richer religious traditions.

Acceptable modes of social analysis and cultural criticisms are guided by moral visions and ethical norms that flow from synoptic worldviews, including such crucial matters as the ideal of what it is to be human, the good society, loving relationships and other precious conceptions. These worldviews are to be rationally scrutinized in light of their capacity to illuminate the complexity, multiplicity and specificity of human experiences and their ability to enable oppositional activity against life-denying forces, be they biological, ecological, political, cultural or economic forces.

Since I believe that the major life-denying forces in our world are economic exploitation (resulting primarily from the social logic of capital accumulation), state repression (linked to the social logic of state augmentation), bureaucratic domination (owing to the social logic of administrative subordination), racial, sexual and heterosexual subjugation (due to the social logics of white, male and heterosexual supremacist practices) and ecological subjection (resulting, in part, from modern values of scientistic manipulation), I entertain a variety of social analyses and cultural critiques that yield not merely one grand synthetic social theory, but rather a number of local ones that remain international in scope and historical in content. My general social-analytical perspective—deeply neo-Gramscian in spirit—is more influenced by the Marxist tradition than by any other secular tradition, but it also acknowledges the severe limitations of the Marxist tradition. By claiming that the Marxist tradition is indispensable yet inadequate, my social-analytical perspective is post-Marxist without being anti-Marxist or pre-Marxist; that is, it incorporates elements from Weberian, racial, feminist, gay, lesbian and ecological modes of social analysis and cultural criticism.

I arrive at these analyses because the moral vision and ethical norms I accept are derived from the prophetic Christian tradition. I follow the biblical injunction to look at the world through the eyes of its victims, and the Christocentric perspective that requires that one see the world through the lens of the Cross—and thereby see our relative victimizing and relative victimization. Since we inhabit different locations on the existential, socioeconomic, cultural and political scales, our victim status differs, though we all, in some way, suffer. Needless to say, the more multilayered the victimization, the more suffering one undergoes. And given the predominant forms of life-denying forces in the world, the majority of humankind experiences thick forms of victimization.

The synoptic vision I accept is a particular kind of prophetic Christian perspective that comprehensively grasps and enables opposition to existential anguish, socioeconomic, cultural and political oppression and dogmatic modes of thought and action. I do not believe that this specific version of the prophetic Christian tradition has a monopoly on such insights, capacities and motivations. Yet I have never been persuaded that there are better traditions than the prophetic Christian one.

My acceptance of the prophetic Christian tradition is rational in that it rests upon good reasons. These reasons are good ones not because they result from logical necessity or conform to transcendental criteria. Rather, they are good in that they flow from rational deliberation that perennially scrutinizes my particular tradition in relation to specific problems of dogmatic thought, existential anguish and societal oppression.

My reasons may become bad ones. For example, I would give up my allegiance to the prophetic Christian tradition if life-denying forces so fully saturated a situation that all possibility, potentiality and alternatives were exhausted, or if I became convinced that another tradition provides a more acceptable and enabling moral vision, set of ethical norms and synoptic worldview. I need neither metaphysical criteria nor transcendental standards to be persuaded, only historically constituted and situated reasons.

Yet, presently, I remain convinced by prophetic Christian tradition. Its synoptic vision speaks with insight and power to the multiform character of human existence and to the specificity of the historical modes of human existence. Its moral vision and ethical norms propel human intellectual activity to account for and transform existing forms of dogmatism, oppression and despair. And the historicist turn in philosophy of religion helps us understand that we are forced to choose, in a rational and critical manner, some set of transient social practices, contingent cultural descriptions and revisable scientific theories by which to live. This historicist stress on human finitude and human agency fits well, though it does not justify, my Christian faith. And, to put it bluntly, I do hope that the historicist turn in philosophy of religion enriches the prophetic Christian tradition and enables us to work more diligently for a better world.

SOURCE: From *Keeping Faith: Philosophy and Race in America,* by Cornel West, pp. 119–134, 298–299. Copyright © 1993. Reproduced by permission of Routledge, Inc. Originally appeared in Leroy S. Rouner, ed., *Knowing Religiously* (Boston University Studies in Philosophy and Religion, Volume 7). Copyright © 1985 The University of Notre Dame Press.

Twenty Six

RELIGION AND THE LEFT

This essay was the lead piece of a special double issue of Monthly Review *(1984) on religion and the Left. This issue was important because it marked the first time this leading Marxist journal—secular and atheistic—had seriously broached the subject of religion. Ironically,* Monthly Review *was initially funded primarily by money inherited by the great F. O. Matthiessen from his father. And Matthiessen was not only one of the towering literary critics of this century (and Harvard professor for decades), but also a Christian socialist whose struggle over his homosexuality led to suicide.*

NOTWITHSTANDING THE SECULAR SENSIBILITIES of most leftist intellectuals and activists, religion permeates and pervades the lives of the majority of people in the capitalist world. And all signs indicate that the prevailing crisis in the capitalist world is not solely an economic or political one. Recent inquiries into the specificity of racism, patriarchy, homophobia, state repression, bureaucratic domination, ecological subjugation and nuclear exterminism suggest that we need to understand this crisis as that of capitalist civilization. To extend leftist discourses about political economy and the state to a discourse about capitalist civilization is to accent a sphere rarely scrutinized by Marxist thinkers: *the sphere of culture and everyday life.* And any serious scrutiny of this sphere sooner or later must come to terms with religious ways of life and religious ways of struggle.

In this chapter I shall pose three crucial questions to contemporary Marxism regarding religion. First, how are we to understand the character and content of religious beliefs and practices? Second, how are we to account for the recent religious upsurges in Latin America, the Middle East, Asia, Africa, Eastern Europe and the United States? And third, in which ways can these upsurges enrich and enhance—or delimit and deter—the international struggle for human freedom and democracy? In the present historical moment, these queries strike me as inescapable and important.

RELIGION AND MARXIST THEORY

The classical Marxist understanding of religion is more subtle than is generally acknowledged. Crude Marxist formulations of religion as the opium of the people in which the religious masses are viewed as passive and ignorant objects upon which monolithic religious institutions impose fantasies of other-worldly fulfillment reveal more about Enlightenment prejudices and arrogant self-images of petit bourgeois intellectuals than the nature of religion. Contrary to such widespread crypto-Marxist myths about religion, Marx and Engels understood religion as a profound human response to, and protest against, intolerable conditions. For Marx and Engels, religion as an opium of the people is not a mere political pacification imposed from above, but rather a historically circumscribed existential and experiential assertion of being (or somebodiness) by dehumanized historical agents under unexamined socioeconomic conditions. Marx and Engels characterized religion as alienation not primarily because it is "unscientific" or "premodern," but rather because it often overlooks the socioeconomic conditions that shape and mold its expression and thereby delimits human powers and efforts to transform these conditions. In short, the classical Marxist critique of religion is not an a priori philosophical rejection of religion; rather, it is a social analysis of and historical judgment upon religious practices.

For Marx and Engels, religion often overlooks the socioeconomic circumstances that condition its expression, principally because the religious preoccupation with cosmic vision, ontological pronouncements on human nature and personal morality hold at arm's length social and historical analysis. Hence religion at its worst serves as an ideological means of preserving and perpetuating prevailing social and historical realities and at its best yields moralistic condemnations of and utopian visions beyond present social and historical realities—with few insights regarding what these realities are and how to change them. The Marxist point here is not simply that religion alone is an impotent and inadequate form of protest, but also that without a probing and illuminating social and historical analysis of the present, even the best-intentioned religionists and moralists will impede fundamental social and historical transformation. In stark contrast to crude Marxists, Marx and Engels do not claim that only a substitution of a rigid Marxist science of society and history for false religion and glib moralism can liberate humankind, but rather that a Marxist social and historical analysis can more effectively guide transformative human praxis motivated, in part, by moral and/or religious norms of human freedom and democracy.

This more nuanced understanding of religion has rarely surfaced in the Marxist tradition, primarily owing to the early Eurocentric development of Marxism. In Europe—where the Enlightenment ethos remained (and still remains) hegemonic among intellectuals and the literate middle classes—secular sensibilities were nearly prerequisite for progressive outlooks, and religious beliefs usually a sign of political reaction. The peculiar expression of critical consciousness in Europe focused on a corrupt and oppressive feudal order which the institutional church participated in, firmly supported and buttressed. And though the advent of Marxism itself bears traces of this Enlightenment legacy, the deep sense of historical consciousness nurtured and promoted by Marx and Engels led them to understand religious beliefs as first and foremost cultural practices generated from conflictual and contradictory socioeconomic conditions, rather than as ahistorical sets of philosophical arguments. Of course, Kant, Fichte and especially Hegel and Feuerbach contributed to such an understanding.

The Marxism of the Second International—with its diverse forms of economic determinism, Kantian moralism and even left social Darwinism—viewed cultural and religious issues in a crude and reductionist manner. Karl Kautsky's monumental work *The Foundations of Christianity* (1908) is an exemplary text in this regard. The major antireductionist voices in this deterministic wilderness were those of the Italian Marxist Antonio Labriola and the Irish Marxist James Connolly. Lenin and Trotsky indeed undermined the crudity and reductionism of the Second International, but they confined their efforts to the realms of politics and the arts. Neither provided serious and sustained antireductionist formulations in regard to ethics and religion. In fact, the Third International remained quite reductionist on such matters.

The centrality of morality and religion loom large in the works of Antonio Gramsci. For the first time, a major European Marxist took with utter seriousness the cultural life-worlds of the oppressed. Though still tied to a rationalist psychology that neglected unconscious impulses and a revolutionary teleology that uncritically privileged industrial working-class agency, Gramsci highlighted the heterogeneous elements comprising the cultural ways of life of oppressed people and the fragile, ever changing character of these elements in response to contradictory socioeconomic circumstances.

Gramsci understood culture as a crucial component of class capacity. Like James Connolly before him and Raymond Williams in our own time, Gramsci examined the ways in which cultural resources enabled (and disenabled) political struggle among the exploited and excluded in capitalist societies. While Lukács disclosed the reified character of contemporary capitalist culture—the way in which processes of commodification and thingification permeate bourgeois thought, art and perception—Gramsci focused on the cultural means by which workers and peasants resisted such reification. While Karl Korsch enunciated his principle of historical specificity—the need to acknowledge the materiality of ideology and the diversity of conflicting social forces in a particular historical moment—Gramsci applied this principle and specified the nature of these conflicting social forces with his complex notions of hegemony and historical blocs.

Ironically, the major figures of so-called Western Marxism were preoccupied with culture—but none was materialist enough to take religion seriously. Whether it was Adorno and Marcuse on the subversive character of highbrow music and poetry, Sartre and Althusser on the progressive possibilities of avant-garde prose and theater or Benjamin and Bakhtin on the revolutionary potential of film and the novel—all rightly viewed the cultural sphere as a domain of ideological contestation. Yet none highlighted religion as a crucial component of this cultural sphere.

It is important to note that it has been primarily Third World Marxists—for whom issues of praxis and strategy loom large—who have confronted the religious component of culture in a serious way. Peru's José Carlos Mariátegui, China's Mao Tse-tung, and Guinea-Bissau's Amilcar Cabral were trailblazers on such matters. All three shunned the reductionism of the Second International, eschewed the excessive hostility toward religion of the Third International and transcended the Enlightenment prejudices of the Western Marxists. Mariátegui, Mao and Cabral—whose cultural concerns inspire black Marxists, feminist Marxists, gay and lesbian Marxists in the First World—recovered and refined the classical Marxist insights regarding the materiality and ambiguity, the relative autonomy and empowering possibilities of cultural and religious practices by grasping the existential and experiential content of such practices under capitalist conditions. In our own time, such Marxist historians as Christopher Hill and E. P. Thompson in England, W. E. B. Du Bois and Eugene Genovese in the United States, Marc Bloch and Henri Lefebvre in France, Manning Clarke in Australia and Enrique Dussel in Mexico have begun to come to terms with the complex relation of religious practices to political struggle. In other words, the age of crude Marxist reductionist treatments of religion—along with European secular condescending attitudes that undergird them—is passing. Concrete social and detailed historical analyses of the relation of religion to revolutionary praxis is now a major issue on the agenda for contemporary Marxism.

RELIGION AND MARXIST POLITICS

The fundamental challenge of religion for Marxist politics is how we should understand religious practices as specific forms of popular opposition and/or subordination in capitalist societies. Recent religious upsurges around the world—in postindustrial, industrial and preindustrial capitalist countries—call into question bourgeois theories of secularization and crude Marxist theories of modernization. The world-historical social processes of rationalization, commodification and bureaucratization have generated neither a widespread "disenchantment with the world," a "polar night of icy hardness and darkness" nor a revolutionary class consciousness among industrial workers. Instead, we have witnessed intense revivals of nationalism, ethnicity and religion. Modern capitalist processes indeed have transformed traditional religious worldviews, intimate *Gemeinschaft*-like arrangements and customary social bonds, but these processes have not eliminated the need and yearning for such worldviews, arrangements and bonds. Recent nationalist, ethnic and religious revivals constitute new forms of these worldviews, arrangements and bonds, with existential intensity and ideological fervor.

There are three basic reasons for this. First, the culture of capitalist societies has, for the most part, failed to give existential moorings and emotional assurance to their inhabitants. The capitalist culture of consumption—with its atomistic individualism, spectatorial passivity and outlooks of therapeutic release—does not provide meaningful sustenance for large numbers of people. So in First World countries, religious responses—often in nostalgic forms, but also in utopian ones—are widespread. Given the relative lack of long standing ties or traditional links to a religious past, these responses are intertwined with the prevailing myths of European modernity: nationalism, racism, anti-Semitism, sexism, anti-Orientalism and homophobia. This is why religious (as well as nationalist and ethnic) revivals are usually dangerous—though they also can be occasions of progressive opportunity. Such opportunity is significant in that religious impulses are one of the few resources for a moral and political commitment beyond the self in the capitalist culture of consumption. These impulses often require commitments to neighbor, community and unknown others—though such commitments are ideologically circumscribed.

The second reason religious revivals emerge is that they constitute popular responses to intense capitalist domination of more traditional societies. This is especially so in Third World countries in which the cultural forms are either indigenous or colonial and the capital is primarily external or international. The boom-town character of industrialization, urbanization and proletarianization demands that cultural ways of life, usually religious, provide strategies for new personal meaning, social adjustment and political struggle.

The emergence of the most important Third World development in religious practices—the liberation theology movement—consists of such strategies of new personal meaning, social adjustment and political struggle. This movement began in Latin America primarily in response to rapid capitalist penetration, quick yet painful industrial class formation, rampant state repression and bloated urbanization. This response was not only rooted in Christian thought and practice; it also flowed from the major "free" space in these repressive regimes, the church. And given the overwhelming Roman Catholic character of this movement—with the monumental reforming impetus of Vatican II (1962–1965) and the groundbreaking counterhegemonic posture of the Medellín Latin American bishops' meeting (1968)—these new strategies became more open to personal meanings, social adjustments and political struggles informed by prophetic elements in the Scriptures and ecclesiastical tradition as well as progressive social and historical analyses.

Liberation theology in Latin America—embodied in the works of Gustavo Gutiérrez, Reuben Alves, Hugo Asmann, José Miguez-Bonino, Victorio Araya, Ernesto Cardenal, Paulo Freire, Elsa Tamez, José Miranda, Pablo Richard, Juan

Luis Segundo, Enrique Dussel, Beatrice Couch, and others—is generated and sustained by popular religious opposition to the consolidation of capitalist social processes in Latin America. It is, in part, an anti-imperialist Christian mode of thought and action. Similar liberation theology outlooks—with their own contextual colorings—are found in Africa (especially South Africa), Asia (especially the Philippines and South Korea), the Caribbean (especially Jamaica) and the United States (especially among blacks and feminists). Yet in terms of widespread concrete praxis, none yet rivals that of Latin America.

The last reason such religious revivals emerge is that they constitute anti-Western forms of popular resistance to capitalist domination. This is especially so in those Third World countries (or pockets in the First World, as with indigenous peoples) in which a distinct cultural and religious way of life still has potency and vitality compared to Western modes of religion. For example, in the Middle East and parts of Asia and Africa, Islam, Buddhism, Hinduism or traditional religions still have substance and life. Hence these religions serve as cultural sources against not simply Western imperialism, but also much of Western civilization—especially Western self-images, values and sensibilities. Such resistance, like all forms of resistance, can be restorative and reactionary (as in Iran) or progressive and prophetic (as among many Palestinians).

In short the religious revivals, along with nationalistic and ethnic ones, fundamentally result from the inability of capitalist civilization to provide contexts and communities wherein meaning and value can be found to sustain people through the traumas of life. And since there can be no potent morality without such contexts and communities, these religious revivals represent an ethical challenge to Marxism. Instead of the promised autonomy and progress of the European Enlightenment, the modern West has bequeathed to the world—besides ingenious technological innovations, personal liberties for some and comfortable living for the few—mere fragments and ruins of a decaying and declining civilization. This decay and decline owes much to the captivity of its ways of life to class exploitation, patriarchy, racism, homophobia, technocratic rationality and the quest for military might. Of course, many of these remarks—and even more so in the realm of personal liberties—can be made of "actually existing socialist" civilization. But our focus here is the capitalist world. And as this capitalist world continues its deterioration, religious revivals will more than likely persist. The great question is: Will such revivals enable or disenable the Left in its struggle for human freedom and democracy?

RELIGION AND MARXIST STRATEGY

Religious upsurges in the Third World (and Second World, as in Poland) may quite clearly contribute to the building of a left movement. As we have seen in

Latin America—where over two hundred thousand base Christian communities exist as concrete praxis centers for social change, communal support and personal sustenance—and parts of Africa and Asia, religion plays an important role in liberation struggles. The prophetic church in Nicaragua, with its tensions (both healthy and unhealthy) with the state, is the best recent example of this crucial role.

The major contribution religious revivals can make to left strategy is to demand that Marxist thinkers and activists take seriously the culture of the oppressed. This fundamental shift in the sensibilities and attitudes of Marxists requires a kind of desecularizing and de-Europeanizing of Marxist praxis, a kind of laying bare and discarding of the deep-seeded Enlightenment prejudices that shape and mold the perspectives and perceptions of most Marxists. This shift does not demand a softening of critical consciousness, but rather a deepening of it. It does not result in an antiscience stance, but rather in antiscientism (the idolizing of science). It does not yield an antitechnology viewpoint, but rather an antitechnologism. Nor does it produce a rejection of reason, but rather a specifying of liberating forms of rationality.

Such a shift is necessary because after over a century of heralding the cause of the liberation of oppressed peoples, Marxists have little understanding and appreciation of the culture of these people. This means that though Marxists have sometimes viewed oppressed people as political or economic agents, they have rarely viewed them as *cultural* agents. Yet without such a view there can be no adequate conception of the capacity of oppressed people—the capacity to change the world and sustain the change in an emancipatory manner. And without a conception of such capacity, it is impossible to envision, let alone create, a socialist society of freedom and democracy. It is, in part, the European Enlightenment legacy—the inability to believe in the capacities of oppressed people to create cultural products of value and oppositional groups of value—that stands between contemporary Marxism and oppressed people. And it is the arrogance of this legacy, the snobbery of this tradition, that precludes Marxists from taking seriously religion, a crucial element of the culture of the oppressed.

Needless to say, shedding the worst of the Enlightenment legacy does not entail neglecting the best of this European tradition. Relentless criticism and historical consciousness remain the crucial ingredients of any acceptable emancipatory vision—just as protracted class struggle and an allegiance to socialist democracy remain indispensable features of any recognizable Marxism. So the call for an overcoming of European bourgeois attitudes of paternalism toward religion does not mean adopting religious viewpoints. Religious affiliation is neither the mark of ignorance nor of intelligence. Yet it is the mark of wisdom to understand the conditions under which people do or do not have religious affiliation. In this sense, science neither solves nor dissolves the issue of religious beliefs. Instead, history provides us with traditions against which we must struggle, yet in which we must critically abide. The grand quest for truth is a thoroughly historical one that takes the form of practical judgments inseparable from value judgments on, and social-analytical understandings of, prevailing socioeconomic realities. There indeed are standards of adjudication, but such historically constituted standards include multiple viewpoints worthy of adoption. Hence, the quest for truth continues with only human practice providing provisional closure.

If Marxists are to go beyond European bourgeois attitudes toward the culture of the oppressed without idealizing or romanticizing these cultures, it is necessary to transcend a hermeneutics of suspicion and engage in hermeneutical combat. In other words, Marxists must not simply enact *negative* forms of subversive demystification (and, God forbid, more bourgeois forms of deconstruction!), but also *positive* forms of popular revolutionary construction of new personal meanings, social adjustments and political struggles for human freedom and democracy. These new forms can emerge only after traversing, transforming and building upon the crucial spheres in society—religion, family, labor process, state apparatuses—in order to consolidate and unite multiple organizational groupings for fundamental social change.

So to take seriously the culture of the oppressed is not to privilege religion, but to enhance and enrich the faltering and neglected utopian dimension of left theory and praxis. It is to believe not simply in the potential of oppressed peoples, but also to believe that oppressed people have already expressed some of this potential in their actual products, their actual practices. To be a person of the Left is not only to envision and fight for a radically free and democratic society; it is also to see this society-in-the-making as manifest in the abilities and capacities of flesh-and blood people in their struggles under conflictual and contradictory socioeconomic conditions not of their own choosing. This is the fundamental message regarding the relation of religious practices to a revolutionary praxis beyond capitalist civilization.

SOURCE: From *Prophetic Fragments* (Grand Rapids, Mich.: Wm. B. Eerdmans Publishing Co., 1988), pp. 13–21. Originally appeared in *Monthly Review*, July–August 1984.

Twenty Seven

ON ELISABETH SCHÜSSLER FIORENZA'S IN
MEMORY OF HER

Elisabeth Schüssler Fiorenza has been influential because of her ability to bring rigorous feminist theory to religious studies. In Memory of Her *(1983), Schüssler Fiorenza's masterpiece, shows her profound commitment to the full-fledged humanity of women and to a view of Jesus as a "woman-identified man." And her scholarship is magisterial. Ten years after this essay appeared, I am blessed to be a close colleague and friend of Elisabeth at Harvard, where we still fight the battle for feminist scholarship and radical Christian love.*

ELISABETH SCHÜSSLER FIORENZA'S *In Memory of Her* is a groundbreaking work. For the first time, we have a powerful defense of new theological emancipatory models of hermeneutics, critical method and historical reconstruction and an application of these models in one book. This intentional traversing of academic disciplines—theology, ethics, church history and biblical studies—for the pursuit of knowledge and empowerment of women represents a coming of age for liberation theology. In this chapter I shall focus solely on Schüssler Fiorenza's hermeneutical and methodological formulations, without losing sight of her broader concerns.

Any major challenge to prevailing paradigms in scholarship must build upon the profound and persuasive insights generated by mainstream scholars, yet call into question their uncritically accepted presuppositions, prejudgments and prejudices that deter new breakthroughs. Schüssler Fiorenza adopts this strategy with great effectiveness. She begins by accepting the starting point of biblical historical criticism: the acknowledgment of biblical texts as neither verbally inspired revelation nor doctrinal stipulations, but rather as historical responses within the context of religious communities over time and space. Following the feminist claim that such contexts are patriarchal and androcentric, Schüssler Fiorenza demystifies mainstream biblical scholarship by revealing its captivity to androcentrism—its relative silence on and marginalization of women's lives in the past and present—and by disclosing the oppositional Christian women's culture concealed by traditional church his-story.

Schüssler Fiorenza moves from this "hermeneutics of suspicion" to hermeneutical combat by putting forward an alternative model of interpretive criteria and methodological orientation for unearthing, understanding and undergirding women's individual and collective agency in the past and present. This move is neither a glib attack on the cult of objectivity in the academy nor a vulgar call for women's freedom. Rather, it is a sophisticated fusing of hermeneutics, social theory, Christian ethics and church history that specifies standards for evaluation and appropriation of past texts and histories, highlights gender system (women's oppression and resistance) as a fundamental category of historical and social analysis and promotes Christian women's heritage.

Schüssler Fiorenza's feminist critical hermeneutics quickly dismisses the doctrinal and historical exegetical models of biblical interpretation by rejecting the former's ahistorical claim of revelational immediacy in the Bible and the latter's positivistic commitment to "value-free" inquiry. Of course, Schüssler Fiorenza realizes that both models have been severely criticized and thoroughly discarded by most twentieth-century biblical scholars—yet residues such as the quest for timeless truth and an allegiance to detached, value-neutral investigation persists. The model of dialogical-hermeneutical interpretation is predominant in biblical scholarship. The philosophical influence of Heidegger, Gadamer and Ricoeur ensures biblical interpretive sensitivity to the "otherness" of the text, the inescapable prejudices of the interpreter and the pervasive web of language, tradition and community. For Schüssler Fiorenza, this model is important, yet limited. It is important because it takes *historicity* seriously by acknowledging the temporal situating of the interpreter and the illuminating potential of the interpreter's biases. Yet it is limited in that it does not take *history* seriously; that is, the model refuses to dig into the depths of the cultural, political and societal contexts of texts and interpreters. Heidegger, Gadamer and Ricoeur have taught biblical scholars to accent the existential interestedness of interpreters while listening to the "strangeness" of past texts; but this important insight does not encourage biblical scholars to examine also the social, political and economic interests of interpreters contained in texts. The model of liberation theology highlights these interests and brings to the surface the ideological commitments of interpreters and texts within the context of class struggle, cultural/racial conflict and feminist resistance.

Schüssler Fiorenza suggests that feminist Christian scholars—since Elizabeth Cady Stanton's monumental *The Women's Bible* (1895)—have appropriated liberation themes without critically examining the problems of the hermeneutical models they adopt. She focuses on two such models: the neoorthodox model and the sociology-of-knowledge model. Feminists such as Letty Russell, Phyllis Trible and Rosemary Ruether have put forward influential claims regarding the patriarchal language of the Bible while holding that there is a nonpatriarchal content therein.

This apologetic move presupposes fundamental distinctions between revelatory essence and historical accident, timeless truth and culturally conditioned language, constant Tradition and changing traditions. The aim of such neoorthodoxy is to confront candidly the specter of historical conditionedness without succumbing to historical relativism and to specify the biblical grounds for Christian identity (by preserving Christocentric revelation) in the face of objections by natural theologians.

Schüssler Fiorenza's critique of feminist neoorthodoxy is threefold. First, she argues that neoorthodox models ultimately put the burden of historical agency on God, not women. The worldly skepticism of neoorthodoxy can accommodate liberation themes, but it cannot rest transformative powers in the praxis of oppressed peoples. Therefore the reinterpretation of the gospel from a liberationist perspective can yield, at most, a moral ideal and an abstract prophetic tradition with little grounding in the flesh-and-blood past and present of struggling peoples. Second, this model—against the intentions of its feminist representatives—idealizes the biblical and prophetic traditions by refusing to come to terms with the oppressive androcentric elements of these traditions. This idealization produces rather romanticist claims about the "liberating" effects of recuperating past prophetic traditions. The intent is admirable; yet the effect is rather empty. To put it crudely, the model yields theological critique, moral outrage and ahistorical tradition posturing, but not engaged empowerment of the downtrodden. Third, neoorthodoxy posits an "Archimedean point" that attempts to meet secular (or religious post-Christian) feminist objections regarding the patriarchal and even misogynist character of Christianity: This "Archimedean point"—divine revelation in Jesus Christ—preserves the liberating kernel within the patriarchal husk.

The sociology-of-knowledge model, best exemplified in Mary Daly's work, accents the overwhelming sexism shot through biblical texts and church traditions. This model holds that reconstruction and revision of such texts and traditions is anachronistic. Instead of disclosing a liberating essence in such texts and traditions, the model calls for new construction and new vision: the creation of feminist life-centers that will generate alternative ways of naming reality and modes of women's empowerment. It assumes that the medium is the message, that patriarchal language can yield only patriarchal content. Therefore new mediums and languages must be constructed by feminists. Schüssler Fiorenza is enchanted by the audacity of this model, especially with its willingness to push Christian feminists to the edge with its sober assessment of patriarchy in Christian texts and traditions. Yet she refuses to construe complex Christian practices as mere patriarchal enactments. Since the model focuses primarily on sexist language and sado-ritual repetitions of Goddess repression and murder, it provides shock effects to the novices (feminists-to-be). Yet it does not deal in any serious manner with concrete socioeconomic structures of oppression and feminist opposition to these structures. The model opts for marginality, "Otherworld sisterhood" and "sacred space," which reinforces the peripheral status imposed upon women in patriarchal society and gives the "center," the "old territory," namely, human history, to oppressive men and subjugated women. This model surely heightens feminist awareness of patriarchy in history, but it elides specific historical forms of patriarchy, abstracts from the social and historical relations that shape these forms and, most important, denies the protracted struggles of women at the "center," in the "old territory," within human history.

Schüssler Fiorenza's new model of feminist critical hermeneutics of liberation moves the focus from questions concerning the authority of biblical revelation to discussions regarding feminist historical reconstruction of the background conditions under which biblical texts were constituted—from androcentric texts to patriarchal-historical contexts in which women contest and resist as well as defer and lose. Such reconstruction proceeds not only by delving into the liberating impulse within the biblical texts, but, more important, by going beyond the texts to examine women's struggle against patriarchal canonization. Since these texts are not objective, factual reports of the past, but rather pastorally engaged responses to particular circumstances, it is not surprising that they represent the views of (and for?) the "historical winners." By critically scrutinizing the canonization process itself, Schüssler Fiorenza goes beyond the neoorthodox model as well as that of liberation theology. No longer can one simply turn to the canonical Christian texts for insights and even imperatives for present social and political struggles. Rather, the formation of the biblical texts becomes a terrain of ideological and historical contestation. To start with the biblical texts, the final canon, and infer liberation themes, deliverance motifs and salvific principles that then serve as sources to criticize the texts themselves still dehistoricizes and depoliticizes the canonization process.

For Schüssler Fiorenza, the revelatory criteria for theological evaluation and appropriation of the Christian past and present is transbiblical, that is, linked to biblical texts yet substantively beyond them. At times, Schüssler Fiorenza nearly excludes the biblical texts and offers only Christian women's struggle for liberation from patriarchal oppression. At other times, she admits that this struggle in the past produced nonpatriarchal elements in the biblical texts. This ambiguity is seen in her metaphor for biblical revelation as a historical prototype, not a mythic archetype—as an all-too-human process open to critique and change rather than an ideal, timeless form. The ambiguity arises in that if one locates revelation first and foremost in the Christian (or non-Christian) feminist struggle for freedom, and if the biblical texts are fundamentally androcentric, it is unclear why the adjective "biblical" is used in "biblical revelation."

This dilemma haunts Schüssler Fiorenza's hermeneutical and methodological discussion. Her critiques of the prevailing interpretive models are often persuasive.

And her attempt to analyze seriously the historical context with gender system as a fundamental category as well as highlight the ideological conflicts within the canonization process is welcome. Yet her model seems to lead her into feminist history about Christian women rather than *Christian* feminist historical reconstruction. Does she pull the Christian rug from under her project and relegate her work to historical inquiry on Christian feminist women by failing to generate Christian normative criteria to regulate her interpretation and appropriation of the past? I think not. She pushes us to the edge of the Christian tradition precisely to help us understand it as a deeply historical yet revelatory phenomenon.

Schüssler Fiorenza's conception of truth and justification–her implicit ontology and epistemology–within her new hermeneutical model provides us with clues to her Christian identity. In contemporary hermeneutics there are three basic philosophical strategies regarding the separate yet related problems of truth and justification. The first strategy follows Hegel by discerning Truth within the depths of the historical process. This discernment consists of keeping track of the active, reflective, autonomizing *Weltgeist* who ultimately overcomes the historical process in order to achieve absolute self-consciousness and self-transparency. Refined versions of this perspective–put forward in religious form by Wolfgang Pannenberg and in Marxist form by Georg Lukács–holds that every hermeneutics requires some degree of transcendental, that is, totalistic viewpoint. Therefore every hermeneutics, if honest about itself, presupposes a philosophy of history and hence is but a disguised form of Hegelianism.

The second strategy incorporates Kierkegaardian insights regarding the radical transiency of historical claims and the ultimate mystery (or utter "absurdity") of God's self-disclosure in Jesus Christ. This strategy, developed by Barth and others, sits at the center of the neoorthodox model. It employs sophisticated modes of historicist argumentation and, contrary to Schüssler Fiorenza's claim (culled from Peter Berger) that it invokes an "Archimedean point," refuses to look at the world *sub specie aeternitatis*. Yet this strategy claims that the existential power and worldview generated by an encounter with Jesus Christ in the preached Word of the Christian community warrants the truth-status of Christian revelation.

The last strategy rests on Gadamer's historicist perspective, which understands Truth as revealment *and* concealment, as part and parcel of the perennial process of cultivating and refining inescapable traditions in relation to particular situations and circumstances. On this view there can be no transcendental standpoint, but there indeed are transcending possibilities that build upon prevailing finite standpoints. The criterion for Truth here resides neither in Hegelian transcendentalism nor in Kierkegaardian fideism, but rather in the regulative ideal of the *Vorgriff der Vollkommenheit* ("anticipation of perfection")–the openness to newness and novelty on the way to a perennially deferred unity. Like Dewey's pragmatism, this strategy shuns a Derridean unregulated free play of truth-effacing that lacks an applicatory praxis dimension and any form of closure. Instead, this strategy promotes regulated historical praxis with only provisional closure without a constitutive telos.

This third strategy runs deep throughout Schüssler Fiorenza's philosophical discussion. Her fundamental concern with human agency, the dialectical interplay of revealment and concealment, the situating of texts within *Wirkungsgeschichte* (continuously operative and influential history) shot through with social conflict and the conception of biblical texts and subsequent interpretations as human practices are all compatible with Gadamer's historicism. Yet Schüssler Fiorenza refuses to go all the way down the historicist road. And if she did so, the Christian locus of truth and justification would be sacrificed. Contrary to the perceptions of many, the consequences of full-blown historicism are neither nihilistic relativism nor promiscuous pluralism; but for the Christian, such historicism does result in a radical depriveleging of Jesus Christ as rendered in the biblical texts. One can surely follow the historicism of Gadamer and Dewey and sidestep vulgar relativistic traps. But for Christians to follow such paths means giving up the unique status of Jesus Christ. This is so because if one's historicism "goes all the way down" (like Hegel's) but resists Neoplatonic-like epistrophes (unlike Hegel's and like Gadamer's), then Jesus Christ becomes not only a historical person but also permeated by contradiction and imperfection. For the Christian, the historical status of Jesus is crucial, but mere peer status of Jesus Christ is ultimately to reject the Hegelian and Gadamerian strategies—and remain on Kierkegaardian terrain. This does not mean subscribing to a neoorthodox model, simply that a neoorthodox element sustains one's Christian identity.

The privileged status of Jesus Christ looms large in Schüssler Fiorenza's text. Given her shift from androcentric texts to patriarchal contexts, one would expect a thorough interrogation of the patriarchal sensibilities and practices of Jesus, in and beyond the biblical texts. Instead, we are offered a view of Jesus as a "woman-identified man" with a *basileia* vision of a discipleship of equals, as if a reincarnate Jesus would join the contemporary feminist struggle against patriarchy. Such a presentist reading of the synoptic Gospels reeks of Christian confessionalism and ahistorical moralism—the very charges Schüssler Fiorenza makes against feminist neoorthodox Christian scholars.

My point here is neither to promote a secular depriveleging of Jesus Christ nor to return to prefeminist readings of biblical texts and the Christian tradition. Rather, my point is to acknowledge the degree to which the Kierkegaardian-Barthian touchstone of modern Christian identity remains intact in Schüssler Fiorenza's work. I applaud this element in her text, but I remain unconvinced that it follows from her new hermeneutical model. The irreducible life, death and resurrection of Jesus Christ—whose power and perspective is always found in human communities in dialogical form—is the mark of modern Christian identity.

Schüssler Fiorenza's presentist portrait of Jesus Christ affirms this mark. Given her deep feminist commitments, this portrait becomes her way of preserving the privileged status of Jesus Christ. Without this status, the struggle for women's liberation has no Christian normative source. The struggle may warrant support, but there would be no Christian grounds to arrive at this conclusion. I believe that Christian texts and traditions—without a presentist reading of Jesus Christ yet while preserving the irreducibility of Jesus Christ—justify feminist liberation movements. But this justification is a historically informed moral one.

Is it contradictory and disempowering that Jesus Christ (male in human form) normatively grounds women's fight for freedom? I think not. Just as it is not contradictory that Jesus Christ (Jewish in ethnic origins) normatively grounds Arabs' struggle for human dignity in Israel—even as it grounds any struggle for human dignity. Only in an age obsessed with articulations of particularities (e.g., gender, race, nation) often relegated to the margins by false universalities (e.g., technocratic rationality, value-free and value-neutral inquiry) could such questions arise with potency. And only with a sophisticated emancipatory hermeneutics can a new conception of differential universality emerge that provides the framework for new perspectives and practices. Schüssler Fiorenza's powerful Christian interpretation and reconstruction of the biblical texts and early church move us closer to such a conception.

SOURCE: *Prophetic Fragments* (Grand Rapids, Mich.: Wm. B. Eerdmans Publishing Co., 1988), pp. 250–256. Originally appeared in *Religion Studies Review*, January 1985; review of Elisabeth Schüssler Fiorenza, *In Memory of Her: A Feminist Theological Reconstruction of Christian Origins* (New York: Crossroad, 1983).

Twenty Eight

ON LESZEK KOLAKOWSKI

Leszek Kolakowski's radical Pascalian Christian views overlap with my own Chekhovian Christian way of being—though my sense of the comic wards off some of his unbearably sad religion. His best book on his own constructive work is Religion: If There Is No God . . . On God, the Devil, Sin and Other Worries of the So-called Philosophy of Religion *(1982). I also highly recommend his recent book* God Owes Us Nothing *(1997).*

LESZEK KOLAKOWSKI IS A unique and fascinating figure on the American intellectual scene. Born in Poland, he was expelled from Warsaw University in 1968 owing to his self-styled humanist Marxism and oppositional political commitments—represented in his influential book *Towards a Marxist Humanism*. His writings cover a broad range of subjects, from Spinoza, Husserl, Anglo-American positivism and seventeenth-century sectarian movements to his recent controversial three-volume history of Marxist thought. He also has written three books of tales and some plays.

Since the early 1970s, Kolakowski has energetically and persistently defended religious experience within the secular world of English-speaking highbrow intellectual culture. In valuable contributions to *Encounter, London Times Literary Supplement, Salmagundi* and numerous other periodicals, he has tried to convince his peers that religious insights are indispensable for understanding the major events of this century.

In his book *Religion: If There Is No God . . . On God, the Devil, Sin and Other Worries of the So-called Philosophy of Religion* (Oxford, 1982), Kolakowski makes his strongest case for religious experience. Although the book appears in Frank Kermode's *Masterguides* series and is intended to be an introductory treatment of the discipline of philosophy of religion, Kolakowski puts a deeply personal stamp on it. In fact, the book is not so much a standard introduction to philosophy of religion as a collection of philosophical fragments on being religious. The text indeed provides illuminating encounters with classical perspectives in the Western and Eastern traditions of religious thought. But it also contains brilliant existential insights and words of wisdom about life. There are few sustained positive philosophical arguments primarily because Kolakowski spends much time attempting to show why philosophical arguments are inappropriate for understanding religious experience. In short, this text is in the tradition of Montaigne, Pascal and Kierkegaard, not Descartes, Kant and Hegel.

For Kolakowski, the primary task of philosophy of religion is neither rationally to ground particular religious beliefs nor comprehensively to systematize existing religious doctrines. Rather, the role of the philosopher of religion is to preserve the integrity and irreducibility of forms of "socially established worship of eternal reality," that is, religion. This task of preservation entails sidestepping the dilemmas created by both religious liberals and fundamentalists and showing how the major religions speak to the most basic feature of human existence, namely, the need to cope with powerlessness, helplessness, weakness and frailty.

Kolakowski does not believe that philosophical inquiry can persuade or dissuade one from adopting particular religious worldviews. But rational discourse can help in pointing out what is at stake in adopting one worldview over another.

> I rather tend to accept the law of the infinite cornucopia which applies not only to philosophy but to all general theories in the human and social sciences: it states that there is never a shortage of arguments to support any doctrine you want to believe in for whatever reasons. These arguments, however, are not entirely barren. They have helped in elucidating the *status quaestionis* and in explaining why these questions matter, and this is what I am concerned with here. (p. 16)

What is ultimately at stake is one's sanity, that is, the ability to make sense of a deeply tragic and flawed existence without succumbing to meaninglessness and hopelessness. Kolakowski's defense of religious experience holds that human beings must learn how to be failures and how to cry for help while acknowledging that this very capacity to learn and wisdom to cry out is a form of empowerment from a Reality greater than human beings that keeps people struggling and living. The major foes are self-deception, for example, forms of happiness that are really types of bad faith, and self-deification, for example, the refusal to acknowledge the need for divine help or aid.

From the vantage point of this Augustinian framework, Kolakowski examines the question of evil in the world, the various gods of the philosophers, mystical traditions in Christianity, Judaism, Islam and Eastern religions, the relation between fear of death and religious faith and the uniqueness of the language of the Sacred within the context of worship. Kolakowski is most provocative and profound on the issues of theodicy and mysticism. Both sections are powerful *tours de force* in and of themselves.

Kolakowski links the religious conception of learning how to be a failure yet avoiding insanity to God's inability to commit suicide. This crucial divine inability (even Nietzsche has God killed by humans!) confines evil to a separation from

God—that is, Sin—that is moral, not ontological. The world is viewed as essentially good, yet existentially evil. On this Christian view, a deep sense of the tragic is required, yet the world is not inherently tragic.

For religious traditions, be they Christian, Islamic, Buddhist or whatever, the problem of evil cannot be "solved" or even understood theoretically. Rather, it can only be met with a practical response: trust God or go insane. This basic trust or confidence is based neither on an objective reading of history nor the workings of nature. Rather, it is an unconditional trust, a nonfalsifiable assent that ensures continued sanity, that is, meaning and hope. In other words, some form of such trust is requisite for psychic health, yet there are no philosophical grounds for such trust.

> To summarize this part of the discussion: an acceptance of the world as a divinely ordered cosmos wherein everything is given a meaning is neither self-contradictory nor inconsistent with empirical knowledge, and yet it can never be a consequence of such knowledge, however vastly expanded. Both moral evil and human suffering, including everybody's inevitable failure in life, can be accepted and mentally absorbed, but it would be preposterous to pretend that, starting with the terrifying chaos of life, we can, as a result of logically admissible procedures, end up with a cosmos full of sense and of purpose. The act of faith and trust in God has to precede the ability to see His hand in the course of events and in the sadness of human history. In brief: *credo ut intelligam.* (pp. 53–54)

Kolakowski highlights the anthropocentric character of Judaic and Christian thought on evil and suffering. Eastern traditions affirm the unity and sanctity of all life, whereas Jews and Christians uphold the dignity of human life while promoting the human right to master and exploit nonhuman organisms, especially animals. Furthermore, Christian perspective implies that there is some unredeemable evil, that some forms of suffering and hardship stand outside the domain of redemption and punishment. In this regard, the absurdity of the world or insanity in life seeps in even from a religious (in this case, Christian) perspective.

In the section on mysticism, Kolakowski reaches an interesting conclusion: "that it is not inconsistent or monstrous to be a sceptic and a mystic at the same time" (p. 145). In epistemological matters, both skeptic and mystic claim that knowledge is essentially a practical, not cognitive, affair; that is, silence is the appropriate response to whether we can really know that we know, yet since out of necessity we must speak and act knowledge becomes a tool to cope with reality, not a mirror that depicts reality.

Kolakowski's experiential attitude and skeptical approach to religious experience would seem to imply that he is either a closet pragmatist stripped of the privileging of the scientific method in all cognitive matters or a full-blown conventionalist informed by a sociology of knowledge. Yet one would be wrong to accept such implications. Kolakowski indeed possesses a deep sense of historical contingency and a critical disposition toward all philosophical traditions. But he also is fearful of relativism, nihilism and cynicism. At moments in his text he moves toward a philosophical transcendentalism in order to defend the possibility of God's existence. At the heart of the book, he claims:

> I will try to argue for the following, quasi-Cartesian assertion: Dostoyevski's famous dictum, "If there is no God, everything is permissible," is valid not only as a moral rule but also as an epistemological principle. This means that the legitimate use of the concept "truth" or the belief that "truth" may even be justifiably predicted of our knowledge is possible only on the assumption of an absolute Mind. (p. 82)

> Thus I follow the Cartesian formula insofar as it asserts that human claims to truth are empty without reference to the divine being. No reference to God's veracity is thereby implied; but I admit that the predicate "true" has no meaning unless referred to the all-encompassing truth, which is equivalent to an absolute mind. The transcendental approach is thus far vindicated.
>
> The argument has nothing to do however with the proofs of God's reality: it can neither reinforce nor enfeeble any of the arguments in existence. Its aim is not to show that God does exist, but to expose the dilemma which we seem to face when we cope with the question of truth and of the very possibility of an epistemology: either God or a cognitive nihilism, there is nothing in between. (Pp. 90–91)

Yet he finally must reject any such philosophical transcendentalism, since we have no access to an Archimedean point that would permit us to adjudicate rationally between the conflicting perspectives: "My point is negative: since we have no key to the treasury of transcendental rationality, all restrictions imposed on the implicit everyday criteria of meaning are royal commands issued *ex nihilo* by philosophers and carry no other legitimacy; they are enforceable only to the extent of the philosophers' sheer power" (p. 164).

I suggest that Kolakowski's struggle between the Scylla of transcendentalism and the Charybdis of nihilism yields a unique philosophical position—a religious form of cultural ontology that shuns a glib objectivism and stresses the contingency of human cultural practices, yet holds out for convergence and unity in the long run. This convergence and unity is not simply a regulative ideal, but rather features of a humanly incomprehensible God. Like Charles Peirce's conservative version of pragmatism (and similar to Hilary Putnam's recent work), Kolakowski wants to preserve a bedrock notion of Reality and Truth by means of an eschatology. Unlike Peirce and Putnam, his eschatology is not a matter of the scientific community ultimately grasping Truth, that is, convergence as rational agreement, but rather of religious persons ultimately "being in Truth," that is, convergence as existential deliverance. I find the makings of such a viewpoint in the following statements.

> Jesus' saying that the truth will make us free does not mean that the mastery of technical skills will lead to a desirable result; for Him, and for all great religious teachers, people realize the nature of their bondage in the same act of illumination that includes the means of shaking it off and the understanding of the divinely ordained destiny of the world. . . .
>
> No philosophical speculation can perform this task. In spite of the claims of philosophical transcendentalism it is only by reference to the all-knowing and eternal mind that the convergence of goals and knowledge is attainable. . . .
>
> It would be utterly wrong to infer from the foregoing discussion that the conflict between the Reason of the Enlightenment and religious certitudes or, on a larger scale, between the Profane and the Sacred, may be in my view explained in terms of logical mistakes, conceptual confusion or misconceived ideas about borderlines between knowledge and faith. Such an approach would appear to me grotesquely inadequate. The conflict is cultural, not logical, and it is arguably rooted in the persistent, irreconcilable claims imposed on us by various forces within human nature. . . . Do we have to do with an accidental collision or rather with a fundamental conflict which might have remained latent here and there yet was bound to emerge as a result of the sheer growth in human abilities to master the world?
>
> The factual elements which are required to answer such a question would encompass the complete history of all religions, whereas its unavoidable speculative components must necessarily be derived from the ontology of culture. (pp. 219, 220, 224)

This embryonic religious version of cultural ontology builds on the best of the skeptical, pragmatic and historicist traditions without succumbing to theoretical self-contradiction or internal inconsistency. It is neither tied to a particular religious set of doctrines nor even confined to Western forms of religiosity—yet it preserves the integrity and irreducibility of religious experience.

I find this perspective highly attractive. Yet I remain unconvinced that this view can do anything more than project possible kinds of convergence and unity—hence function essentially as regulative ideals. Favoring Dewey's version of pragmatism over that of Peirce, I hold that there can be no ontological assurance of convergence and unity without our reading into cultural practices the very projected convergence and unity presupposed by our own perspectives, that is, vicious circularity. So all we can have, as cultural agents and historical beings, is regulative ideals of convergence and unity dependent on our own perspectives. This view still avoids vulgar relativism and nihilism, but it stops short of any sort of ontology. It keeps us in history and culture without history and culture—as Kolakowski rightly desires—disposing and casting our dignity and worth "in the wanton and boundless sea of chance." In this way, Kolakowski helps us deepen the historicist turn in philosophy of religion while holding on to the profound insights of the multiple religious traditions of humankind.

SOURCE: "On Leszek Kolakowski's *Religion*," *Prophetic Fragments* (Grand Rapids, Mich.: Wm. B. Eerdmans Publishing Co., 1988), pp. 216–221. Originally appeared in *Old Westbury Review*, Fall 1986; review of Leszek Kolakowski, *Religion* (Oxford: Oxford University Press, 1982).

Twenty Nine

ON LIBERATION THEOLOGY: SEGUNDO AND HINKELAMMERT

Liberation theology—the view that God sides with the struggles of oppressed peoples to free themselves—is one of the most gallant efforts to keep alive the prophetic Christian witness in this century. First put forward by black American James Cone and joined by Latin American thinkers like Gustavo Gutiérrez, Juan Luis Segundo, Hugo Assman, Rosemary Ruether, Franz Hinkelammert and others, this worldly theology changed the landscape of twentieth-century theological education, especially in the Western Hemisphere. I spent the summer of 1980 teaching in the famous Departmento Ecumenico de Investigaciones in San Jose, Costa Rica—and in dialogue with the leading liberation theologians in Latin America. I also lectured throughout Brazil and Jamaica, further rooting myself in the soil of liberation theology.

On Juan Luis Segundo's *Faith and Ideologies*

LIBERATION THEOLOGIES ARE THE principal forms of Christian prophetic thought and action in our contemporary age. They present the ways of life and struggle of Christians around the world who have convinced remnants of the church to open its eyes to human misery and oppose socioeconomic systems and political structures that perpetuate such misery. Like all serious modes of inquiry, liberation theologies are predicated on crisis—on human situations of tremendous danger and incipient possibility. Such concrete crises invariably generate forms of critical consciousness. Liberation theologies are the predominant forms of critical consciousness within the Christian church that respond to the dangers of class, racial and sexual privilege and project the possibility of class, racial and sexual equality.

Black, feminist, Native American, Hispanic and especially Latin American versions of liberation theology have made major contributions to Christian thought and the life of the church. The theological theme of God's identification with the poor and oppressed now resounds throughout out seminaries, takes shape in some of our ecclesiastical agencies and regulates the practices in a select few of our churches. The methodological mandate for systemic social analysis of structures of domination in light of the good news of Jesus Christ is forcing many theologians, preachers and laity to take seriously the works of Karl Marx and Max Weber, Simone de Beauvoir and W. E. B. Du Bois, Anthony Giddens and Christopher Lasch. In short, liberation theologies have pushed religious thinkers beyond their usual parochial concerns and challenged churches to become more enlightened participants in the great political and economic issues of our time.

But beneath this intense intellectual ferment and heated political discourse lurks a hidden truth: *The high moment of liberation theology has passed.* Original texts of James Cone, Mary Daly and Gustavo Gutiérrez spawned widely diffused and dispersed theological currents. As with all groundbreaking upsurges, liberation theologies emerged with impressive power and insight and presently have evolved in diverse and multiple forms.

This evolution of liberation theologies is particularly noteworthy in that these theologies ushered forth from an academic discipline that suffers from an immense identity crisis. Hence, the early enthusiasm for liberation theologies can be attributed not only to the relevance of their perspectives for the oppressed, but also to the hope that these theologies would breathe new life into a fading and faltering mode of intellectual reflection. To put it crudely, liberation theologies were expected to both change the world and keep theology alive.

Yet as the zenith of liberation theological reflection fades, we witness the proliferation of philosophical investigations, cultural critiques, social analyses and historical reconstructions from Christian liberationist perspectives. The theological concerns of liberation theology are now shifting to their philosophical, cultural, social-analytical or historical concerns. This move requires not only rigorous interdisciplinary tools, but also more intense interaction with secular colleagues—thereby facilitating more religious participation within the larger public conversation in society and culture at large.

This positive dialogue and candid alliance with both the academy and political movements helps break down the walls of demarcation between divinity schools and universities, preachers and political activists. But it also could result in a new kind of theological evasion, a refusal to take seriously the difficult task of specifying Christian identity in a pluralistic world. And as the tentacles of secular professionalism and vulgar politicization further pervade our seminaries and divinity schools, even the theological task itself could become passé.

In regard to this precarious though pregnant situation, liberation theologies more than likely will move in one of four directions. They will: (1) relapse into traditional kinds of systematic theology equipped with new themes, motifs and insights—as in Jon Sobrino's *Christology at the Crossroads;* (2) retreat into versions of philosophical anthropology (i.e., a philosophy of human existence) that appeal to Kant, Hegel, Feuerbach or the early Marx and thereby subvert systematic theology—as in Juan Luis Segundo's *The Liberation of Theology;* (3) spill over into social theory, cultural criticism and historical reconstruction, which may take either

Christian or post-Christian forms—as in Elisabeth Schüssler Fiorenza's *In Memory of Her* or Mary Daly's *Gynecology,* respectively; or (4) resort to practical writings in journalistic styles that attempt to reach the general literate laity and clergy—as in James Cone's *My Soul Looks Back.*

The first alternative is essential but limited; it preserves precious links with elements of the tradition and church, but at the inescapable expense of intellectual marginality in our secular intellectual milieu. The second option, philosophic anthropology, is a trap to be avoided by both theologians and philosophers alike; it succumbs to a seductive quest for universal categorical schemas that yield either formal results too empty for usefulness or transcendental frameworks that conceal their historicity. The third line of development is the most fruitful and challenging; it sidelines many narrowly trained theologians and gives prominence to Christian and secular social theorists, cultural critics and historians. The last direction performs a crucial propagandistic role, but provides little, if any, intellectual depth.

Juan Luis Segundo's *Faith and Ideologies* exemplifies the second option. This book builds on his earlier work and puts forward a full-blown philosophical anthropology—a detailed specification of "the universal dimensions of human beings." Segundo is the most ambitious and audacious of the Latin American liberation religious thinkers. He disregards the traditional intellectual division of labor in the university and eagerly pursues a daring idea, no matter how half-baked that idea may be. In this book, Segundo's ambition and audacity lead to organizational fragmentation and philosophical confusion.

Segundo's aim in this text is threefold: first, to infuse new content in the categorical notions of faith and ideology; second, to explore how these two ideas relate to one another, using Christianity and Marxism as interlocutors; and third, to examine the concrete situation of present-day Latin America in light of his philosophical perspective. Like Immanuel Kant and Matthew Arnold, Segundo wants to preserve the transcendent character of moral conduct, yet create a comprehensive secular discourse that subsumes religion. In short, his primary intention is to displace theology and put forward a new philosophical anthropology.

But in Chapter 1, entitled "Toward a New Statement of the Problem," it becomes quite clear that Segundo's philosophical anthropology is not new at all. Rather, it is a warmed-over version of neo-Kantianism—much less refined than those found in Wilhelm Dilthey or Jürgen Habermas. Segundo's two "basic anthropological dimensions" are faith and ideology. He understands "faith" to be the human acquisition of meaning and value principally by means of socialization. "Ideology" is taken to be the human techniques of efficacy and predictability necessary to actualize one's value-laden ends or goals.

Following Gregory Bateson's *Steps to an Ecology of Mind,* Segundo defines faith as a "partially self-validating" set of "epistemological and ontological premises" which human beings impose on "the flux of happenings" for purposes of order and coherence. Since these "premises" circumscribe the limits of human knowledge, they are immune from rational validation, hence "self-validating." Yet Segundo also defines faith as a "certain type of knowledge." Here confusion sets in. Can faith be a set of "premises" that delimit what we can and do know and also be a certain type of knowledge? Is the latter a transcendental form of knowledge, a special kind of knowledge that enables us to know the premises that constitute preconditions for knowledge? Is this not viciously circular? Or does Segundo mean that the premises are socially derived and hence we know them through social and historical analysis? If so, then can he consistently claim that faith is "an anthropological dimension as universal as the human species itself"? Surely not. He must either fall back on neo-Kantianism and provide an account of faith as an anthropological dimension or adopt a Mannheimian sociology of knowledge and give up talk about such dimensions. At one point in his text, Segundo endorses Mannheim's "real sociology of knowledge," yet still characterizes the indispensable unconditional absolute as a value, a "transcendent datum." Like Kant of the *Critique of Practical Reason,* philosophical anthropology has solely a self-validating, that is, a moral basis. But, following Mannheim, if morality is socially constituted, philosophical anthropology is undercut.

To add more confusion, Segundo understands faith as "the fund of saved energy on which all human planning is based." In addition to this technocratic image of faith, Segundo's attempt to link this conception of faith to his overarching theory of evolution—with its desirable homeostatic mechanisms and the "best energy calculus"—is utterly unconvincing. Owing to his imprecise and amorphous definitions of faith, it is difficult to follow his comparative criticisms of Pannenberg's notion of trust and Tracy's conception of religion.

In his discussion of faith, Segundo relies upon a pre-Wittgensteinian view of language; that is, in contrast to Wittgenstein's view that language constitutes our social world, Segundo holds that language expresses private worlds. In order to make clear how people "express in words their values-structure, their meaning-world," Segundo engages in some close readings of poems—especially Gustavo Adolfo Bécquer's famous *Rima.* After a rather idiosyncratic though interesting interpretation, Segundo highlights human "access, through the medium of language, to the vast, structured realm of meaning and values." This neo-Kantian vocabulary, found in Ernst Cassirer and Susanne K. Langer, is highly suspect. Yet, ironically, Segundo persists with this expressivist view of language even after invoking the work of the later Wittgenstein, which precludes any such view. At this point one is forced to conclude that Segundo's intellectual project yields philosophical confusion.

Similar to Habermas, Segundo fears that meaning-structures (faith) are "structured in terms of efficacy (ideology) alone"; That is, issues involving value are reduced to technical matters. And this fear is justified. But is not his own technocratic conception of faith a reduction of meaning to mere use, planning and efficacy? If so, he promotes the very program he fears. Segundo rightly exposes the dimension of faith in modern and postmodern science—a point noted by David Hume and refined by Michael Polanyi—yet his means-ends mode of philosophical and political analysis reeks of technocratic rationality. Even John Dewey, no friend of modern Luddites like Martin Heidegger, grappled more seriously with the reductionist implications and managerial consequences of crude means-ends analyses.

The second and third parts of Segundo's book are much better than the first. The section on Christianity and Marxism is, though far from original, competent. His claims regarding Marx's rejection of philosophy for science and opposition to ontological materialism are persuasive. Yet his defense of Erich Fromm's claim that Marx put forward a philosophical anthropology—which is true for the early Marx, but rejected by the later Marx—is perplexing. Segundo rightly suggests that the continuity between the early and later Marx consists of his "ideal conception of the human being." But does such an ideal constitute a philosophical anthropology? Does the mere possession of values mean that one adheres to a philosophical anthropology? Surely not. So why defend Fromm's exorbitant claim?

The last section of Segundo's book is a sketch of "a Latin American anthropology"—a reading of Latin American realities from 1950 to 1975 in light of his philosophical perspective. After brief generalizations of the periods of consciousness-raising, violent action and repression, Segundo tries to go beyond mere economic and political analysis and accents "the ecological state of human beings" in relation to nature, the state and class exploitation. He ends his book calling for the creation of "an effective cultural tradition"—a task to be achieved only if the supreme evolutionary quality, flexibility, is internalized and transmitted to the younger generation of freedom fighters.

In stark contrast to *The Liberation of Theology*, Segundo's *Faith and Ideologies* is more a phenomenon than an event, a symptom of the second alternative in the evolution of liberation theologies rather than a mover and shaker on the contemporary scene. His book illustrates the severe limitations of opting for a full-blown philosophical anthropology. And even if one decides to do so, it is better to revise already refined versions rather than create one's own out of thin air or derived from anthropologists and psychologists.

In my opinion, the major intellectual task of liberation theologians is to continue to reexamine and reshape the traditional doctrines of the church, engage in more serious efforts of social theory, cultural criticism and historical reconstruction and write palpable and intelligible essays and texts for the nonacademic literate laity and clergy. Needless to say, these three activities require different persons working on different terrains. Church theologians are not likely to put forward sophisticated social analyses, just as more broadly engaged social theorists cannot possibly do justice to the complexities of church theology—though both can write for a wider audience.

Furthermore, if liberation theologies have taught us anything, it is that Christian thinkers must be organically linked with prophetic churches and progressive movements. An uncommitted and detached liberation theologian is a contradiction in terms. Without some form of ecclesiastical and political praxis, critical consciousness becomes as sounding brass and theological reflection a tinkling cymbal.

ON FRANZ HINKELAMMERT'S *THE IDEOLOGICAL WEAPONS OF DEATH*

Liberation theology at its best is a worldly theology—a theology that not only opens our eyes to the social misery of the world, but also teaches us better to understand and transform it. Academic theology in the First World, true to its priestly role, remains preoccupied with doctrinal precision and epistemological pretension. It either refuses to get its hands dirty with the ugly and messy affairs of contemporary politics or pontificates at a comfortable distance about the shortcomings of theoretical formulations and practical proposals of liberation theologians. Yet for those Christians deeply enmeshed in and united with poor people's struggles, theology is first and foremost concerned with urgent issues of life and death, especially the circumstances that dictate who lives and who dies.

Franz Hinkelammert's *The Ideological Weapons of Death* marks a new point of departure for liberation theology. First, it is the first product of a unique institutional setting—the renowned Departmento Ecumenico de Investigaciones (DEI) in San Jose, Costa Rica—that is intentionally interdisciplinary and explicitly political. Shunning the narrow confines of the intellectual division of labor in academic institutions, DEI rejects the compartmentalized disciplines of our bureaucratized seminaries and divinity schools. Instead DEI promotes and encourages theological reflection that traverses the fields of political economy, biblical studies, social theory, church history and social ethics. In this way, DEI reveals the intellectual impoverishment of academic theologies that enact ostrichlike exercises in highly specialized sand—with little view to the pressing problems confronting ordinary people in our present period of crisis.

Second, Hinkelammert's book is significant in that it tries to ground liberation theology itself in a more detailed social-analytical viewpoint and a more developed biblical perspective. For too long liberation theologians have simply invoked Marxist theory without a serious examination of Marx's own most fecund analysis of capitalist society—namely, his analysis of fetishism. As Georg Lukács noted in his influential book *History and Class Consciousness* (1923), the Marxist analysis of fetishism in *Capital* brings to light hidden and concealed effects of commodity relations in the everyday lives of people in capitalist societies. These effects result from the power-laden character and class-ridden structure of capitalist societies which make relations between people appear as relations between things. This deceptive appearance presents capitalist realities as natural and eternal. A Marxist analysis of this veil of appearance discloses these realities to be transient historical products and results of provisional social struggles.

Hinkelammert's book takes as its point of analytical departure the three central stages of Marx's analysis of fetishism—the commodity fetishism, money fetishism and capital fetishism. The magical power people ascribe to commodities produced, money acquired and capital expanded has idolatrous status in capitalist societies—a status not only rarely questioned, but, more important, hardly analyzed and understood by Christians. Too often Christians merely condemn seductive materialism or pervasive hedonism with little or no grasp of the complex relations of the conditions under which commodities are produced, the ways in which money is acquired and the means by which capital is expanded. Positing these complex relations as objects of theological reflection is unheard of in contemporary First World theology. Yet, if theologians are to come to terms with life-and-death issues of our time, there is no escape from reflecting upon and gaining an understanding of these complex relations.

Such a monumental step requires a grounding in the history of economic thought and contemporary social theory. In this regard, working knowledge of the classical economic theories of Adam Smith and David Ricardo, the neoclassical economic formulations of Alfred Marshall and Stanley Jevons, the intricate debates between followers of Karl Marx, Max Weber and Émile Durkheim in social theory and the present-day viewpoints of Milton Friedman, Paul Samuelson and Ernest Mandel become requisite for serious theological engagement with the burning life-and-death issues of our day. Needless to say, the immediate intellectual risk is a debilitating dilettantism that obfuscates rather than illuminates. Yet to refuse the risk is to settle for an arid academicism that values professional status and career ambitions at the expense of trying to lay bare the richness of the Christian gospel for our time. Therefore Hinkelammert's text may seem strange to First World Christians—with his analyses of the links between Milton Friedman's thought and the economic policies of the Chilean dictator Pinochet or his critique of the Trilateral Commission's recommendations for the Third World. In fact, many First World academic theologians may balk at such exercises that seem to fall outside more tame theological investigations. Yet, it should be apparent after reading Hinkelammert's text that he simply is attempting to come to terms with the array of ideological weapons of death deployed against the wretched of the earth—and the books and blueprints of academic and political elites are not spared.

His critiques also apply to contemporary biblical scholarship in the First World. This culturally homogeneous guild of highly trained yet narrowly socialized academicians have, in many ways, yet to enter the postmodern age of epistemo-logical disarray, cultural upheaval and ideological contestation. This guild remains the last bastion of First World male hegemony over the methods and results of a branch of theological investigations. Most biblical scholars remain uncritically and unjustifiably wedded to sophisticated models of research—models that emerged from problematics of a bygone period. Hinkelammert boldly contests the compla-cency of this guild by putting forward a highly controversial and provocative read-ing of Pauline conceptions of life and death in light of his own analysis of fetishism. Whatever one's views are on the complexity of Pauline theology, this perspective cannot but broaden the conversation in New Testament studies and thereby deepen our readings of Paul's Letters.

Last, Hinkelammert examines the implications of his views on modern Catholic thought. Recent pastoral letters from the Catholic and Methodist churches in the United States have alerted us to the crucial role of denominational pronouncements on social and political issues. These pronouncements cannot be fully understood without some knowledge of the history of the churches' social teachings. This is especially so in regard to the issue of private property—an often uncritically examined cornerstone of much of these teachings. As Hinkelammert notes, the aim is not simply to substitute socialist notions of property for earlier conceptions of private property, but rather to interrogate the very act of hyposta-sizing property as such. Historical questions concerning how private property be-came an unquestioned presupposition of Christian social ethics, the relation of churches to social systems based on slave and wage labor and theoretical issues about the relation of conceptions of personhood to private property and the links between slaves and women to rights of property possession loom large here.

Hinkelammert's book provides neither full-fledged solutions nor panaceas to the broad range of issues it raises. Rather, it is a groundbreaking work-in-progress that alerts us to contemporary forms of captivity to which most First World theologies are bound. Like the first wave of liberation theologies from Latin America, Asia, Africa and First World women and minorities (especially Afro-Americans), his book opens new discursive space in our theological work. The seriousness with which Hinkelammert takes Marxist analyses of fetishism, biblical studies, modern Catholic social ethics and the current shortcomings of liberation theologies indeed may initiate a second wave—I hope a tidal wave—that fundamentally transforms how we do theology and act out our precious Christian faith.

SOURCE: "On Juan Luis Segundo's *Faith and Ideologies*," *Prophetic Fragments* (Grand Rapids, Mich.: Wm. B. Eerdmans Publishing Co., 1988), pp. 197–202; originally appeared in *Commonweal,* January 27, 1984; review of Juan Luis Segundo, *Faith and Ideologies* (Maryknoll, N.Y.: Orbis, 1983). "On Franz Hinkelammert's *The Ideological Weapons of Death*," *Prophetic Fragments* (Grand Rapids, Mich.: Wm. B. Eerdmans Publishing Co., 1988), pp. 203–206; originally appeared as the foreword to the Orbis edi-tion, 1986.

Thirty

CHRISTIAN LOVE AND HETEROSEXISM

The evils of heterosexism and homophobia, strongly supported by institutional religion, are two of the most difficult and delicate issues of our time. After lecturing around the country in churches and participating in the historic film All God's Children, *I sat down and reflected at length on these issues in my life and our society with Mary Kenyatta and others at the Harvard School of Education. This is my clearest statement on the plight of gay brothers and lesbian sisters (of all colors) and the responsibility of so-called straight folk like myself. My stance has generated anger and rage from many Christians, including those who agree with me on many issues. But I do not write or act to win popularity contests.*

IN THE FALL OF 1995, *deep in the midst of shaping and developing this special issue, several* Harvard Educational Review *editorial board members had the opportunity to hear philosopher and scholar Dr. Cornel West speak at the Harvard Graduate School of Education. They enthusiastically reported back to us that in his talk, West, who is professor of Afro-American Studies and of the philosophy of religion at Harvard, drew explicit and repeated connections between white supremacy, patriarchy and heterosexism. At the time, we were searching for an article that would illuminate the deep ties between different forms of oppression in the United States. We envisioned an article that would serve as a bridge from the diverse topics represented within this special issue to broad systems of power, privilege and domination. Inspired by Dr. West's articulation of the above issues, as well as by his focus on democratic struggles for liberation, we asked him if he would be willing to be interviewed for our special issue.*

Dr. West agreed, but he expressed concern that, as a heterosexual, he not displace "any of the gay, lesbian, or transgender voices." He went on to say:

> For me it is a privilege and really a blessing to be part of the issue, because the issue that you're raising is very important. But as you know, it's important as well that one not come in from the outside, as it were. It is important not to push aside any of the voices that come from inside of the movement itself.

It was precisely his respectful concern that compelled us to request an interview with Dr. West. In addition, we found it very powerful, particularly in light of our largely heterosexual readership, that a heterosexual activist and scholar would repeatedly take a strong position against het-

erosexism. When cast in a way that made clear that this was an opportunity to reach out to other heterosexuals and say to them, "If you're serious about being a democrat or a radical, then this piece of our struggle is essential," West readily agreed to participate.

In this interview with HER editorial board members Vitka Eisen and Mary Kenyatta, Cornel West offers a vision of a democratic struggle that is inclusive of lesbian, gay, bisexual and transgender people. He places heterosexism within the context of capitalism, establishing connections to other forms of oppression. He also reminds us that, as democratic educators, we continually have to examine the ways in which we may internalize, and therefore perpetuate, patriarchy and homophobia in our lives and our teaching. West shares some of his personal struggle facing his own homophobia, and he emphasizes the importance of so-called straight people joining their gay and lesbian brothers and sisters in the effort to dismantle heterosexism and other systems of oppression.

Vitka Eisen and Mary Kenyatta: We've often heard you speak about the connections among homophobia, patriarchy and racism. Why do you talk about these issues, and how do you see them linked? And would you also talk about some of the personal challenges you face as a heterosexual black man, in taking such a vocal stance against heterosexism?

Cornel West: My own understanding of what it means to be a democrat (small *d*), partly what it means to be a Christian, too, but especially what it means to be a democrat, is that you're wrestling with particular forms of evil.[1] It seems to me that to talk about the history of heterosexism and the history of homophobia is to talk about ways in which various institutions and persons have promoted unjustified suffering and unmerited pain. Hence, the questions become: How do we understand heterosexism? Why is it so deeply seated within our various cultures and civilizations? We could talk primarily about America, but we can talk globally as well. I think it fundamentally has to do with the tendency human beings have to associate persons who are different with degradation, to associate those who have been cast as marginal with subordination and devaluation. So in order to be morally consistent and politically consistent, I think democrats have to focus on particular forms of unjustified suffering across the board, be it patriarchy, vast economic inequality, white supremacy or male supremacy or heterosexism. It's just a matter of trying to be true to one's own sense of moral integrity.

Eisen and Kenyatta: You've taken a very visible, very public stance against heterosexism and homophobia. Are there personal challenges for you in taking that stance?

West: Well, no doubt, no doubt. Any time you offer a serious critique of the systems of power and privilege, be it compulsory heterosexuality, be it white supremacy or what have you, you're going to catch some hell. There's no doubt, both within the black community and the black church, as well as outside, that I tend to catch hell on this issue. There's no doubt about it. But for me, it's fundamentally a matter of trying to highlight the moral ideals that serve as a basis of the critique of homophobic behavior, heterosexism as a whole, as well as their political consequences. I don't think that one can actually engage in serious talk about the fundamental transformation of American society—that is, the corporate elites, the bank elites, the white supremacists, the male supremacists, as well as the heterosexists—without talking about hitting the various forms of evil across the board. The interesting thing is that some of the critiques almost have to take an *ad hominem* form. A person might think, wait a minute, why is he so concerned about homophobia? There must be something going on in his personal life, and so forth.

My view is that I have to recognize deep homophobia inside of me, because I grew up in the black community, in the black church, on the black block, and there's a lot of homophobia in all three sites. So I'm quite candid about the internal struggle that I undergo because of my own homophobic socialization. How do you deal with the feelings of either threat or fear—and, I think, for many homophobes—outright hatred? I don't think I ever, even as a young person, hated gay brothers or lesbian sisters. I think I did associate it early on with something that was alien. And I've often, even in movies, seen lesbian love as very different. I think that, in a patriarchal society, for a man to see two women involved in lesbian activity is less threatening than seeing two men involved in gay activity. When I've seen gay activity on the screen, for example, it does hit me viscerally as very alien and different. That's where my moral struggle comes into play, in terms of acknowledging that difference from my perspective, but not associating it with degradation or disgust. Rather, it is just a particular mode of human expression that I have been taught to associate with degradation. I simply acknowledge it as different, but I don't have to make that connection with degradation per se. And in doing so, I have been honest with myself. In an interesting way, people say, well, you're so interested in this issue, maybe you've got a secret life or something. And I say, you know, if one is gay or lesbian, one should be proud of it. There's nothing to hide in that regard, it seems to me. And if one isn't gay or lesbian, one may just acknowledge that others make certain kinds of choices and have different orientations, and so forth. So-called straight persons can go on about the business of living and still fight an antihomophobic struggle along with gay and lesbian comrades.

Eisen and Kenyatta: Your earlier comment about the homophobia you witnessed growing up in the black community reminds me that there's a certain lore about communities of color—not all communities of color, but particularly religious communities of color—that suggest that there is more overt homophobia within these communities than in dominant white communities. Can you speak about this perception? How much of this lore is an attempt on the part of the Right to force divisions where there might be alliances?

West: Yeah, that's a tough question. That's a very tough question, because degrees of intolerance and tolerance and degrees of hatred and openness are very difficult to measure. I know when I was growing up in the black community, most people knew that, let's say, the brother who played the organ in the church was a gay brother. People would say, oh, that's so-and-so's child. You know, he's that way. And they'd just keep moving. There wasn't an attempt to focus on his sexuality; he was an integral part of the community. It wasn't a matter of trying to target him and somehow pester him or openly, publicly degrade him. Those who said he's "that way" didn't believe that way was desirable, but they just figured that's just the way he was, that's just his thing, you know. But one of the ways in which he chose to function was to be part of his community. People knew it, but he just didn't make a big deal out of it.

For me, however, it's very important that even closeted sexuality be something that's seriously interrogated, because it can lead toward a kind of internalized homophobia within gay or lesbian persons themselves. I think you get some of that in the great James Baldwin, in his struggles over whether he wants to be gay in identity or to highlight his particular sexual orientation as a public feature of his identity. And that's a tough question. But when I was growing up that tended to be the attitude.

I had always thought that even though homophobia was thick, it was dealt with in such a way that it did not disunite the black community because this was a community under siege, dealing with institutional terrorism, Jim Crow, Jane Crow, and so forth—you had to accent commonality. At the same time, we have seen an increase in so-called gay bashing and lesbian bashing in the country as a whole, including the black community and other communities of color. Here, of course, as you get a slow shattering of community, in this case the black community, then a lot of the paranoid dispositions become more salient and more visible. One of those forms is violence against gays and women, and this is also the case when we consider violence against sisters in the black community. We've always had that, but we've seen also an exponential increase in this violence as the community disintegrates. So I'm a little reluctant to say homophobia is actually more rampant in the black community than it is in the larger white community. My hunch is that it runs pretty deep in both. But in the past, it was cast in such a way that it was subordinate to the survival of the black community as a whole. As that community now undergoes a very, very deep crisis, if not slow dissolution, we see the scapegoating of the most vulnerable: black women, gays, and lesbians.

Eisen and Kenyatta: With highly charged political and moral issues such as sexuality, how do democratic educators balance a respect for diverse community values with respect for their own democratic ideals, particularly where community values may run counter to them?

West: I think it's a tough call. Partly it's just a matter of a certain kind of practical wisdom, because I don't think there are any abstract principles that would allow us to make various judgments in each case. There are going to be tensions anytime you're dealing with very rich notions of individuality. And by individuality I don't mean the rugged, ragged, rapacious individualism of American capitalism, but of free choices that people make that help them make and remake themselves as persons within a community. Individuality within a community always has a certain kind of tension. I think as democrats, as radical democrats, it's very important that we keep alive a subversive memory of critique and resistance and therefore, when we talk about sexuality, we understand it as a particular discourse, a particular institutional practice over time and space that has reinforced certain systems of power and privilege. At the same time, there's a tradition of resistance against that system of power and privilege.

Foucault and others have pointed out that the very construct of homosexuality itself comes from the medical community (you know, Westphal's work in 1870) and, as such, is constituted as a disease and, of course, as a crime, legally and politically.[2] This is a shift from the discourse of sodomy, which was viewed as a sin against nature. Now this is a very important move because it's an attempt by a set of elites to exert a certain kind of control over how people view their bodies, what they do with their bodies, what the state does with their bodies and how those bodies are scarred and bruised, internally and externally. But this shift is also connected to other systems of power and privilege, white supremacists, the rule of capital and so on.

What you actually have then is an attempt to keep alive a certain subversive memory for a democrat. For me it's impossible to be a democrat and not have a very deep sense of remembrance of the freedom fighters who came before and what they were up against. What was the nature of the systemic oppression that they were responding to? And at the same time you've got a number of these different traditions, each with its strengths and its weaknesses. You've got the black freedom struggle that has historically focused on white supremacy; it has not said enough on issues of vast economic inequality and has hardly said enough when it comes to homophobia and heterosexism. Then you've got a gay/lesbian freedom struggle that has focused primarily on heterosexism and homophobia and at times has not said enough about white supremacy.

I think in the U.S. context there's always tension when it comes to the legacy of white supremacy, which cuts through every tradition of resistance and critique. That's why somebody like Audre Lorde for me was, and in memory is, such a towering figure. It's so rare to have such a deep artist, on the one hand, and a sophisticated political activist, on the other. She was also a progressive humanitarian who could speak to the depths of human suffering and pain that cut across the various forms of oppression and create a common space, a radical democratic common space. That doesn't happen too often; it doesn't happen often at all. To think through the notion of difference in such a way that it becomes a source of strength, rather than a set of obstacles and impediments that reinforce our own paranoid disposition, is rare. We all have the paranoid dispositions. For me the important thing, as a Christian, is to recognize that the evil is inside each and every one of us, in part because of that treacherous terrain called history that has shaped, socialized and acculturated us. Consequently, it's not ever a matter of one group feeling as if they don't have some white supremacy, male supremacy, or homophobia inside of them. Because we've been socialized in the white-supremacist, patriarchal society, those residues are there no matter how liberated one thinks one actually is. It's a perennial struggle, and that's one of the reasons why there has to be a collectivity. You have to organize and mobilize to keep each other accountable. That's part of the democratic ethos within radical democratic groups, because we have to prefigure, in some way, the kind of society that we're talking about within our own movement. The only way we deal with these evils inside of us is to keep each other accountable. I'm not sure we ever fully eliminate them. Audre Lorde says, look inside and then name the forms of oppression working therein, and, at the same time, never be paralyzed by them, never be debilitated by them. She's so honest about her internal struggle against oppression.

Eisen and Kenyatta: What do you see as the limits of identity politics and the struggle for democratic ideals, and what are the strengths? How can people mobilize across and through identity politics?

West: I think identity politics, on the one hand, are inescapable and, on the other hand, still too limited. It's inescapable primarily because we have such underdeveloped class-based politics in America. The power of corporate and bank elites is such that it has made it very difficult for fellow citizens to believe that class-based politics can be sustained in a way that these politics would actually meet head-on the tremendous entrenched power of the rule of capital. Consequently, a person falls back on her or his own particular ethnic, racial, sexual identities as a way of sustaining some critique against this deeply conservative society, in which the rule of capital is almost a precondition for democracy to flower and flourish. On the other hand, we have a society that has been so deeply rooted in white supremacy that it makes it very difficult to talk about class-based politics without talking about just how central race and racism have been in the constitution of American identity, culture and society.

You get a lot of reductionist formulations from the Left about this issue. The argument goes: it's really a class issue, it's got to be just a class issue. To engage in that reductionist formulation is partly an attempt to sidestep the challenge of race when we've had this long history of race-based slavery and race based Jim Crow.

And so I think identity politics have lost sight of a class-based analysis, which makes it impossible for people to conceive of a fight for the fundamental democratic transformation of American society toward more egalitarian distribution of goods and resources. It's impossible to conceive of that fight without beginning with one's own conception of one's pain and suffering as it relates to the most visible scars. The most visible source of those scars for people of color are white supremacists. For women, it has been patriarchy. For gays and lesbians, it has been heterosexism and homophobia. Although beginning there, I think one ultimately has to reach a space where there's some overlapping consensus regarding the way in which these various systems of oppression operate. In the economic sphere, you have to have coalition because the powers that be are so strong that individuals will be crushed. We've seen that over and over and over again. For example, anytime a gay or a lesbian activist attempts both to accent the critique of heterosexism and homophobia and then to link them to other oppressions, the powers that be become even more hostile. That is true of the black movement, and it is true of the feminist and womanist movement. Democracy—radical democracy in all of its forms—tries to accent the variety of institutional and individual forms of evil and constitutes the most formidable threat to the powers that be. Very much so. And the powers that be are quite serious. No doubt about that. They've got a lot of resources at their disposal to crush people. No doubt.

Eisen and Kenyatta: The question about identity politics is linked to a question about destructive divisions between liberation struggles for people of color and liberation struggles for gays and lesbians. The hierarchy of oppressions—"my oppression is worse than your oppression"—gets in the way of coalition building. What can be done to foster coalition?

West: I think the fundamental issue is the difficulty of forging bonds of trust between various communities of resistance. The reason why it's difficult to generate those bonds of trust is, I think, precisely because, at the psychocultural level, the forms of fear and insecurity and anxiety associated with others come from the prevailing systems that socialize us in a way that reinforces the fears and anxieties and insecurities associated with the "other," for example, gay, lesbian, black, brown, red, and so forth. The powers that be know that as long as there are no bonds of trust or very, very weak bonds of trust, there won't be any effective coalition-building or any substantive alliances among communities of resistance. And they're right. The only way bonds of trust can be forged is when you have enough courageous activists, so-called leaders and so-called followers, who are willing to violate prevailing lines of demarcation that are in place. But to violate and transgress those lines of demarcation means that those persons have to struggle deeply within themselves to wrestle honestly with their own insecurities and the anxiety that they associate with other people. There's a certain kind of existential honesty and intellectual candor that must go with political courage, both with leadership and so-called followership, if we're ever going to forge the kinds of bonds of trust necessary to create the coalitions that can present at least a substantive challenge to the powers that be. There's still no guarantee even after the bonds of trust are forged—they've got armies and tanks and a whole lot of other things—but at least the chances are better.

Eisen and Kenyatta: What does that candor look like?

West: The candor? Well, it's painful, it's very painful. When I start with the homophobia in me, it's painful. One is ashamed of oneself in terms of how one has been socialized. How does one attempt to overcome it? I would think in white brothers and sisters, when they actually look at the white supremacy in them, it's got to be painful if they're serious democrats, if they're serious about struggle. You overcome it by not just wrestling with it, but also by fusing with others in a context that will keep you accountable in such a way that you will remain vulnerable and, hence, open for growth and development, rather than simply debilitated, paralyzed and therefore frozen. I think this is true in a variety of the different contexts that we've talked about: the patriarchy inside of us, the class arrogance inside of us and the homophobia inside of us.

Eisen and Kenyatta: All of that requires a certain level of political courage. So where's the base?

West: That's very true. I think the political courage is based on a profound commitment. If you're fundamentally committed to dealing with the suffering and pain, you will be willing to put yourself through some processes. One sign of commitment, for me, is always the degree to which one is willing to be self-critical and self-questioning, because that's a sign that you're serious about generating the conditions for the possibility of overcoming the suffering that you're after. Commitment is fundamentally about focusing on the suffering and trying to overcome it, trying to understand where it comes from, its causes, its effects. At the same time, it is about trying to prepare oneself to sacrifice and to serve in such a way that one attempts to overcome the suffering.

In addition to that, there is a serious intellectual dimension, and that has to do, again, with historical consciousness and that dangerous memory, that subversive memory. Because one of the ways in which one views oneself in process is to realize that you're part of a larger process and tradition that has been going on, and that persons who have raised the same kind of questions you raise struggle in their own ways. You can see it in their lives, their growth, their development and their conscienticization. It is a complex and a perennial process, but it's worth it. I think one of the things we have to convey is that even given all the pain and suffering associated not just with being victimized, but also with being agents against that victimization, is that there's also a deep joy and ecstasy in struggle. It is a desirable way of being in the world, because it does, in fact, give you a sense of meaning and purpose. It gives you a sense of camaraderie, connectedness and relatedness. And a decadent civilization such as our own suffers from what Arthur Miller called the disease of unrelatedness, where people quest for relations and intimacy and suffer a lack of community and solidarity. It's just a spiritually impoverished way of being in the world. My good friend Stanley Hauerwas says that capitalism tends to produce rather s-h-i-t-t-y people, and he's absolutely right. He's absolutely right. Nonmarket values of love and care and service and laughter and joy run counter to that seriousness of maximizing personal preferences and maximizing profits. It's just a very impoverished way of being human, you see. I think that one of the things we democrats, radical democrats, have to acknowledge is this joy and ecstasy in pain-ridden struggles. So you get this fascinating juxtaposition of the joy and the pain and the despair and the hope all linked together. But that's what it begins with anyway.

Eisen and Kenyatta: Living out paradox . . .

West: That's exactly right. Living in time and space, and that's where for me, the Christian perspective comes in, you see. To my mind, the best of Christianity has been that of a quest to be an existential democrat. See, what the Palestinian Jew named Jesus was all about was, "I'm going to overturn various forms of hierarchy that stand in the way of being connected with you compassionately." You see? And so the common eating, wherein all hierarchies of cuisine are called into question. Everybody come. Everybody use your hands. The same was true of free healing.

The ruling elite in the Roman Empire had to put him to death for a political crime. Why? Because he went straight to the temple. The temple was the center of life. And he turned the tables on the money lenders. Why? Because this market activity, this buying and selling, was getting in the way of a loving, compassionate, sympathetic, empathetic relation with human beings. And you know, he knew he was in trouble; he was in deep trouble. He's got the Roman elites. He's got the top slice of Jewish aristocracy. He's violating their laws and he's speaking to their working classes, right there in the midst of the exploitation of the peasants occurring there across the board, among Jews and non-Jews. So you get this particular Jewish figure who comes in and reforms a dominant tradition of Judaism, provides a critique of the Roman Empire, and ends up on a cross. And his followers come up with a narrative that says that cross is based on his blood that flows, which is that pain and suffering. But love still seems to be piercing through, even at a moment when it seems God is silent and the good is impotent. It still seems to pierce through. And for democrats, existential democrats, that's all we have. The question is: How do we keep that love piercing through our communities in our attempts to create full solidarity? To keep alive traditions of resistance and critique, so that from Stonewall in June 1969, a high moment, a transformation of consciousness, a certain tradition has been kept alive that had been inchoate, but now it's consolidated in a new kind of way, you see.[3] There's this wonderful book by Robert Goss, called *Jesus Acted Up,* that talks about this conception of God, love-making and just doing, in light of this tradition that I'm talking about.[4] It's one of the most powerful statements that I've read that links my own conception of what it means to be an existential democrat and a radical democrat from the Christian point of view, to the context of the gay/lesbian liberation movement. But Christians have no monopoly on this. The questions are: How do I endure compassionately? How do I continue to bring critique to bear in a loving way with no naive utopian notions that somehow things are going to get better without struggle, or that somehow struggle itself can produce perfectibility, but still be sustained in the midst of very, very dark and difficult times? And, of course, secular traditions have as much access to that compassionate love as religious traditions do, just as religious and secular traditions also bastardize and reinforce systemic oppression.

Eisen and Kenyatta: So how do you reconcile your Christianity with the contemporary Christianity that says love the sinner, hate the sin, when sin is read as "queer"?

West: Well, you do have to go back to the various claims to authority that are invoked. That means going back to the Scripture, going back to the church fathers, and looking at all of the various ways in which the richness of Christianity has been so thoroughly debased and bastardized in the name of promoting forms of unjustified suffering. For example, in the Scripture itself, when one actually looks at the nine references to so-called homosexuality or sodomy, most of them allude to male, same-sex sexual activities—there is only one reference to female. And part of these references are to tribal proscriptions, and part of them refer to male prostitution within Canaanite cults vis-à-vis Judaism. But, at the same time, there are deeply patriarchal, as well as homophobic, elements shot through those who wrote the text. That homophobia has to be teased out as well, in light of the claims of mercy and the claims of justice that are also in the text. As such, the text itself, of course, is polyvalent; it is ambiguous in that regard. For example, the apostle Paul is concerned about lust and concerned about dehumanized relationships—no matter whether gay or lesbian, or so-called straight. This makes good sense. You want to treat each other as ends rather than means. There's no doubt about it. But, on the other hand, Paul himself is shot through with deeply patriarchal and homophobic sensibilities, being the person he was in his particular time. Now, of course, what's interesting is that most of the religious Right, and the religious persons who use Scripture to justify homophobia, don't like to admit that Jesus is not only silent on the issue, but he goes about engaging in forms of touch and intimate relation, not sexual that we know of, but in intimate relation in the best sense of sensual, across the board, from Mary to Lazarus, you see. People have said, well, if homosexuality is such a burning issue, how come Jesus doesn't say anything about it? Because if he did, it would have been at least constituted within the writings of the synoptic Gospels, you see. And that's very upsetting, very upsetting indeed to right-wing Christian brothers and sisters!

Eisen and Kenyatta: You could catch hell for this one too.

West: If Jesus was proclaiming a certain kind of love-centered state of existence that is impinging upon the space and time in which we live, impinging upon history, and if this issue of homosexuality and homoeroticism was such a fundamental sin, he certainly would have highlighted it. And so again, what we get, as in so many other cases, is an attempt to project various conceptions of the gospel that followed after the life and death and resurrection of Jesus, in an attempt to reinforce the very thing that he himself was fighting against. That goes from empire, to vast economic inequality, to the good Samaritan. My God, people don't realize how subversive that was in his day. That's like treating "niggers," gays and lesbians and so forth as if they're really part of the family. Now you see, that's just too big a challenge for most Christians who are holding on to such thin and impoverished conceptions of the gospel. And yet, if Jesus would come back and say that the good Samaritan in the latter part of the twentieth century was treating these so-called niggers, and treating these gays and lesbians, and treating these poor white brothers whom you associate with trash as part of the family, he would then reveal the depths of their idolatry. He would show that, in fact, what they're really tied to is a set of idols rather than that blood that flowed at that cross from the body of Jesus. It is a very important dialogue in which I think people like Peter Gomes and others have played a very important role: highly visible persons of integrity who bring critique to bear on this particular form of evil.[5]

Eisen and Kenyatta: The last question we have for you is, what do you think a lesbian and gay struggle brings to the struggle for a radical democracy?

West: There's a new dimension that gay brothers and lesbian sisters bring to the struggle, and that is a conception of the erotic linked to bodies that forces us to accent the cultural as well as the political and economic dimensions of our radical democratic movement. You see, America itself, of course, begins with indigenous peoples being dispossessed of their land, the subordination of indigenous peoples, and hence an attempt to create a puritanically based conception of a nation with a city on a hill that's special and exceptional. Since the very beginning, Americans have been very, very uneasy with their bodies, and have associated the erotic with the different, the other, the alien. That attempt to escape from one's body and to be open to the variety of different pleasures that can flow from that body has always been associated with anarchy and disorder. This Puritanical culture cuts across race and class and region in America; and even though it has undergone a fundamental transformation, it's still around.

Even when you had a Marxist-based movement, they didn't want to talk about the erotic; the Communist party was often as Puritanical as the YMCA. The big difference was that they allowed for so-called cross-racial relations, which was subversive, culturally subversive. But it still wasn't as subversive as allowing the erotic itself to play a fundamental role. It is partly because the erotic itself has this Dionysian energy that overflows beyond the rational. In that regard, the erotic offers a much deeper critique of radicalisms that are linked to the Enlightenment. To be a serious gay and lesbian activist, or to have learned from gay and lesbian liberation movements, is to engage at this level of a critique of Enlightenment sensibility thinking that it's all about rational control and a rational project. I'm not trashing reason, or trashing the rational. However, the erotic forces us to acknowledge that our radicalism ought to be much more open and much more self-critical. Now there's a sense in that the black movement brought this to bear as well, with the crucial role of the body, partly as a result of an African culture that is much less uncomfortable with the body than a Puritanical one. But, even the African and Afro-American traditions did not accent the degree to which the erotic could be found in same-sex relationships. And that, to me, is a crucial contribution, and also to someone like myself, a challenge, a crucial challenge. Here again, Audre Lorde and others have noted the ways in which the erotic can be empowering and ennobling, enabling and ennobling, and can actually release in us energies that, I think in the end, are indispensable for struggle because they also become forces for hope in a situation in which there is not a lot of hope.

The interesting question is the relationship between the ethical and the erotic. The erotic without the ethical can become just thoroughly licentious in the most flat hedonistic sense. But the erotic fused with the ethical means there is respect for the other, and that respect for the other also means being attentive to the needs of the other given their erotic energies. These kinds of issues seem to me to be fundamental ones because, of course, they affect every relationship. I mean, even in friendships that are nonsexual, there's an erotic dimension. And as teachers of students we know there's an erotic dimension, but it has got to be severed from any use of power for subordination, sexual pleasure, sexual manipulation and so forth. But if one is honest in one's own humanity and is concerned with a qualitative relation with any significant other, I think one has to acknowledge that there is an erotic dimension. And it's precisely this dimension, among others, but especially within this dimension, that I think gay and lesbian movements have made a major, major advance in radical thought and in radical action.

Eisen and Kenyatta: Thank you so much for contributing to this special issue on lesbians, gays, bisexuals and transgender people and education. We acknowledge your courage and integrity, and we appreciate your commitment to a democratic struggle for social transformation that includes lesbians, gays, bisexuals and transgender people as well as all other oppressed people.

SOURCE: The Editors, "Cornel West on Heterosexism and Transformation: An Interview," *Harvard Educational Review* 66, no. 2 (Summer 1996), pp. 356–367. Copyright © 1996 by the President and Fellows of Harvard College. All rights reserved.

Thirty One

A PHILOSOPHICAL VIEW OF EASTER

This piece is a favorite of mine, even though I now reject wholeheartedly its salvation-history perspective. The centrality of Good Friday—and especially Holy Saturday, when God is as dead for Christians as God was for Nietzsche—for me now prevents me from embracing Easter too quickly. The condemnation of one thief may lead to despair—just as we are condemned to life and death. The salvation of the other thief may lead to hope—just as we are saved every day from life and death. But within this paradox hang we suffering, shuddering and struggling creatures.

I

THE JOYFUL ATTITUDE OF a Christian toward the resurrection claim that "Jesus arose from the dead" seems to preclude the philosophical dispositions of disinterest, detachment and distance. Yet, as a Christian and philosopher, I believe that the resurrection claim can be both dispassionately defended and enthusiastically exalted. In this brief chapter I will suggest philosophical strategies for such a defense and existential reasons for such an exaltation. In my treatment of the resurrection claim, I shall move from its philosophical testability to my own personal testimony.

There are three basic aspects of the resurrection claim, namely, its truth-value, its epistemic status and its significance. First, we must ask what it means to say that the resurrection claim is true or false. Second, how do we know whether the resurrection claim is true or false? Third, what significance should the resurrection claim have for us as Christians?

II

Before we begin to examine what it means to say that the resurrection claim is true or false, we must have some idea of what it means to say that any claim is true or false. A commonsensical view would be that a claim is true or false if it can be correlated with a particular set of experiences or observations such that all and only members of that set are evidence for or against the claim. For example, the resurrection claim would be true if we could persuasively demonstrate that reliable observers saw Jesus physically dead, put in Joseph's tomb and either arise from the dead or alive after his death.

There are two major problems with this commonsensical view. First, it rests upon the reliability of those friends and disciples of Jesus who are purported to have made observations that may serve as evidence for the veracity of the resurrection claim. David Hume's powerful essay on miracles convincingly renders this reliability problematic. Second, this view assumes that the resurrection claim is the kind of claim whose truth-value can be determined by a particular set of observations. This assumption is questionable because it presupposes the dogma of sentential reductionism, namely, the view that sentences have their evidence for or against their truth or falsity isolated from and independent of other sentences.

I will suggest that the truth-values of crucial claims or important sentences in the two major kinds of descriptions, versions or theories of the self, world and God—religion and science—can be determined neither in isolation from other sentences nor by a particular set of observations. My suggestion rests upon the insight put forward by the Catholic philosopher of science Pierre Duhem and popularized in our time by W. V. Quine and Thomas Kuhn: that the truth-value of our claims about the self, world and God are determined by marshaling evidence for or against the descriptions, versions or theories of which these claims are a part. This insight leads us to examine the truth-value of particular descriptions, versions or theories of the self, world and God, not isolated claims or sentences within these particular descriptions, versions or theories.

If we hold to the dogma of sentential reductionism and observational criterion in determining the truth-value of claims or sentences in scientific descriptions, versions or theories of the self, world and God, we reach the same dead end that Hume reached in his narrow dogmatic rejection of the resurrection claim in Christian descriptions, versions or theories. The dogma of sentential reductionism for scientific descriptions amounts to the claim that any scientific statement could be reduced to an equivalent statement consisting solely of observation terms or observables. But the most important sentences in any scientific description, version or theory contain nonobservation terms, such as disposition terms, metrical terms and theoretical terms. For example, terms such as *recessive trait, conductor of heat, magnetic* or *elastic* are not observable characteristics of objects, but rather dispositions of objects to behave in certain ways under specific circumstances. Terms such as *length, mass, temperature* or *electric charge* are numerically measurable quantities that also cannot be reduced to observable attributes of objects. And terms such as *force, pressure, electron* or *black holes* are neither observable characteristics of objects nor observable objects, but rather theoretical constructs whose positing within a theory is warranted by the explanatory and predictive power the theory yields.

I suggest that just as it is inappropriate to apply the dogma of sentential reductionism and the observational criterion to the most important claims or sentences in scientific descriptions, so it is inappropriate to apply this dogma and criterion to the resurrection claim in Christian descriptions. We must acknowledge that truth-values pertain to bodies of knowledge, descriptions, versions or theories of the self, world and God, not to atomic sentences, autonomous statements or isolated claims. If we do not acknowledge this Duhemian insight, then we must admit that it is impossible to determine the truth-value of scientific laws (which contain nonobservation terms) in scientific theories and the resurrection claim in Christian descriptions.

So, in reply to our first question about what it means to say that the resurrection claim is true or false, we conclude that to raise the question of the truth-value of this claim is to raise the question of the truth-value of Christian descriptions, versions or theories of the self, world and God of which the resurrection claim is central.

III

Now that we have some idea of what it means to say that the resurrection claim is true or false, how do we know whether the resurrection claim is true or false? Since the truth-value of the resurrection claim is inseparable from the truth-value of particular Christian descriptions, versions or theories of which this claim is central, the crucial question becomes, how do we know particular Christian descriptions are true or false?

It is important to point out here different senses of "know" or kinds of knowledge in the various scientific and religious language games we play. For example, when one puts forward knowledge claims from the viewpoint of a scientific description, version or theory about the self, world and God, one is attempting to support or defend a particular description, version or theory that tries to provide reliable predictions and trustworthy explanations of future experience in light of past experience. When one puts forward knowledge claims from the vantage point of a religious description, version or theory about the self, world and God, one is attempting to support or defend a particular description, version or theory that tries to promote the valuing of certain insights, illuminations, capacities and abilities in order honestly to confront and effectively to cope with the inevitable vicissitudes and unavoidable limit situations in life.

In drawing this distinction between scientific "knowing" and religious "knowing," I do not want to suggest that science and religion require different methodologies or different standards by which to adjudicate conflicting descriptions. Rather, I am suggesting that both consist of social practices and human activities with different aims to achieve and different problems to address. I make this distinction between scientific practices and religious practices in order to avoid category mistakes, such as asking science to achieve the aims or address the problems of religion or vice versa.

In coming to terms with the question of how we know particular Christian descriptions, versions or theories of the self, world and God are true or false and hence whether the resurrection claim within these descriptions, versions or theories is true or false, we are forced to acknowledge that there are no *ultimate* courts of appeal presently available to us. Every penultimate court of appeal is linked to a particular description, version or theory of the self, world and God. To confine ultimate courts of appeal to the spheres of either science or religion is reductionistic. To believe that Truth is a property solely of scientific theories that yield reliable predictions and trustworthy explanations is to fall prey to a narrow positivism. To believe that Truth is an attribute solely of religious descriptions that promote certain insights and capacities for living is to fall prey to an expedient existentialism. And to believe that there is a description-free, version-free, theory-free standard that enables us to choose the true descriptions, versions or theories in science and religion is to fall prey to an Archimedean objectivism.

Since we should neither reduce Truth to the spheres of either science or religion nor assume we can view the world *sub species aeternitatis,* we must acknowledge our finitude, fallenness and sinfulness as human beings. This acknowledgment entails that when we say we "know" that a particular scientific or religious description, version or theory of the self, world and God is true, we are actually identifying ourselves with a particular group of people, community of believers or tradition of social practices. There indeed may be good reasons why we identify ourselves with particular groups, communities or traditions. But there are, ultimately, no reasons with the force of logical necessity or universal obligation that could rationally compel others to join us. In this sense, there is no true description, version or theory of the self, world and God that all must and should acknowledge as inescapably true, but rather particular descriptions, versions or theories put forward by various people, groups, communities and traditions in order (usually) to make such views attractive to us.

At this point, it is appropriate for me to cast off my dispassionate philosophical disposition and openly acknowledge my own membership in the Christian community. This "casting off" is essentially a rejection of the conception of philosophy, which does not permit one openly to acknowledge the particular tradition and community from which one speaks. By accepting a particular (i.e., Kierkegaardian) Christian description and therefore accenting our fallenness, I am led to adopt a radical historicist view that renders all "truth-talk" a contextual affair, always related to human aims and human problems, human groups and human communities.

As a self-avowed Christian, it seems redundant to say that a particular Christian description of the self, world and God is true. But, more important, it is misleading to say this. Christians believe in various Christian descriptions that do not claim their descriptions are true, but rather that these descriptions are acceptable and possibly sufficient for their aims. Christian descriptions hold that our fallenness will never permit our Christian descriptions to grasp the Truth. This is so because, for Christians, Jesus Christ is the Truth, and Jesus Christ always rests outside our particular Christian descriptions.

The philosophical implication of this view is that, for Christians, Truth is not a characteristic of a description, not even of a Christian description. Rather, Jesus Christ is the Truth or Reality and can only be existentially appropriated by fallen human beings caught in their finite descriptions. And the fact that this view itself is but part of a finite Christian description only further accents our fallenness and supports the view.

I am suggesting that the primary test for the "truth-value" of particular Christian descriptions and their resurrection claim is their capacity to facilitate the existential appropriation of Jesus Christ. This means that any "true" Christian description makes the Reality of Jesus Christ available, that it promotes and encourages the putting of oneself on the line, going to the edge of life's abyss and finding out whether the Reality of Jesus Christ, though understood through one's finite Christian description, can sustain and support, define and develop oneself in one's perennial struggle of becoming a fuller and more faithful self in Christ.

So, in reply to our second question about the epistemic status of the resurrection claim or how we know that particular Christian descriptions and their resurrection claim are true or false, we conclude that truth claims about descriptions in science and religion are contextual and that for Christians "truth-talk" precludes disinterest, detachment and distance because Jesus Christ is the Truth, the Truth which cannot be theoretically reified into a property of an abstract description, but only existentially appropriated by concrete human beings in need.

IV

What significance should the resurrection claim within particular Christian descriptions of the self, world and God have for us as Christians? This question can be adequately addressed only after we have some notion of what the biblical understanding of the resurrection claim is. How did the first Christians view the resurrection claim? What significance did it have for them?

These questions take us into the muddy waters of New Testament scholarship. But this need not discourage us, for such controversy indicates that first-rate Christian minds are still grappling with the meaning of the resurrection claim. Following the powerful and penetrating 1955 Ingersoll Lecture by Oscar Cullmann, I believe it is first important to point out that the resurrection claim should not be confused with the Greek claim about the immortality of the soul. The Christian resurrection claim assumes that the sting of death was once deadly, that its power was once definitive, whereas the Greek immortality claim presupposes that the soul is intrinsically eternal, hence death is a release, a liberation for the soul out of the prison of the body. On the Christian view, the sting and power of death is conquered and overcome by the death and resurrection of Jesus Christ. On the Greek view, this victory over death is superfluous and unnecessary since the soul has always belonged to the eternal world, the world of Being and Essence.

The radical character of the Christian resurrection claim is found in its salvation-history perspective. The Christian claim that "Jesus arose from the dead" or that Jesus is "the firstborn from the dead" is a proclamation of a divine miracle of creation in that God has called back to life a new creature from the old, a new creation from the old, a new history from the old. In this sense, the resurrection claim essentially refers to the inauguration of a new future, a future that promises redemption and deliverance.

The resurrection claim should mean to us that Jesus' victory over death ushered in a new age, an age in which the almighty power of God is already fulfilled but not yet consummated, an age in which death is conquered but not yet abolished. This new age is an interim period in which this divine power in the form of the Holy Spirit is at work among us. In this interim period, this Holy Spirit can be understood as the Reality of Jesus Christ to be existentially appropriated by fallen human beings for life sustenance, self-formation, self-maturation and societal transformation.

The significance of the resurrection claim within "true" Christian descriptions of the self, world and God is that, despite how tragic and hopeless present situations and circumstances appear to be, there is a God who sits high and looks low, a God who came into this filthy, fallen world in the form of a common peasant in order to commence a new epoch, an epoch in which Easter focuses our attention on the decisive victory of Jesus Christ and hence the possibility of our victory over our creaturehood, the old creation and this old world, with its history of oppression and exploitation. So to be a Christian is to have a joyful attitude toward the resurrection claim, to stake one's life on it and to rest one's hope upon its promise—the promise of a new heaven and a new earth.

SOURCE: From *Prophetic Fragments* (Grand Rapids, Mich.: Wm. B. Eerdmans Publishing Co., 1988), pp. 260–266. Originally appeared in *Dialog: A Journal of Theology*, Winter 1980.

Thirty Two

ON GIBSON WINTER'S ECOLOGICAL ECUMENISM

One of the major lacunae in my work is the crucial ecological challenges of our time—abuse of nature, cruelty to sentient nonhumans, possible nuclear annihilation. In this essay, I examine the fascinating project of Gibson Winter, "Hope for the Earth." Winter is one of the few Christian thinkers to confront ecological issues with a deeply philosophical and broadly historical perspective.

GIBSON WINTER'S "HOPE FOR the Earth: A Hermeneutic of Nuclearism in Ecumenical Perspective" is the most provocative and powerful meditation I have read on the urgent issues of possible nuclear annihilation and actual nuclear weaponry buildup. Based on his ontological framework set forth in *Liberation Creation: Foundations of Religious Social Ethics,* Winter argues that nuclearism is not simply a logical consequence of Western technological development; it also is an effect of the modern Western way of *Dasein-in-der-Welt* ("being-in-the-world"). This fundamental insight permits Winter to go beyond the usual confinement of nuclearism to the concerns of peace activists and move toward making crucial links to U.S. and Soviet forms of imperialism and colonialism. Furthermore, like Nietzsche, Winter discerns a basic will to power at the heart of the modern Western project that posits an autonomous, calculating Subject that defies and degrades historicity, temporality, spatiality and sociality for the purposes of mastery and manipulation.

The work of Robert J. Lifton, Richard Falk, George Kennan and Jonathan Schell have informed and alerted the public to various dimensions of nuclearism. Winter's reflections move to the archaeological dimension of this matter; that is, he provides a philosophical excavation of the ontological terrain wherein the hegemony of modern European *techne* has reigned since Descartes and Hobbes. Winter's inquiry cuts deeper than a mere history of ideas, depiction of possible nightmares and prescriptions of *Realpolitik* primarily because it attempts to lay bare the hermeneutical horizons and existential symbols that promote and encourage dispositions of destruction and annihilation. His perspective not only provides a profound characterization of the philosophical depths of nuclearism; it also suggests a new way of Being-in-the World which takes seriously openness to the disclosure of Divine Mystery, thereby facilitating a *periagoge* ("turning") toward a historically informed humility, a spatially anchored sociality and an ecumenically oriented communality.

I applaud Winter's motivations. For too long the political and moral aspects of nuclearism have been accented at the expense of its religious aspects. Surely, issues concerning the common good and normative character of nuclear weaponry warrant close attention. Yet our conceptions of goodness, power and ultimacy in relation to nuclearism also demand our rational scrutiny. In this regard, Winter has performed a valuable service.

I also deeply resonate with Winter's intentions. His attempt to elevate the dialogue to a more sophisticated level of investigation is salutary. And I believe he has succeeded well in rearranging the domain in which discourses on nuclearism take place.

Yet, I disagree in significant ways with Winter's perspective. First, my conception of the Western project is more radically pluralist and heterogeneous than his. I find the roots of Western nuclearism in far more than the mechanistic tradition of Descartes and Hobbes. In fact, I find some of these roots in the organicist tradition of which Winter is a product. Second, I am not persuaded that the valorization of a root metaphor of *poesis* or *phronesis* avoids the Western will to power. Third, the particular way in which *periagoge* comes about in Winter's perspective remains quite vague, with hints of mere moral persuasion and idealist reflection.

Winter is right to ground the modern Western will to power in the disembodied and deracinated *cogito* of Descartes and in the psychological hedonism of Hobbes. The autonomous world-seeking and power-hungry Subjects of the exemplary early modern thinkers indeed constitute a kind of prototype of the destructive monstrous forces now haunting us—as Mary Wollstonecraft Shelley's *Frankenstein* illustrates. But I suggest that there are many other possible grounds for the modern Western will to power. These grounds include the organicist and historicist traditions.

The organicist tradition—from Herder to Hitler, Hegel to Heidegger—usually incorporates a mystical dimension, which promotes an openness to the mystery of *Geist, Volk,* Being, Presence or the Whole that sits well with authoritarian subordination and passive submission. My point here is not that Winter's beloved Heidegger was a Nazi for a few months, but rather that the organicist tradition bears as much intellectual responsibility for our present predicament as the mechanistic tradition of Descartes and Hobbes. In his book, Winter calls for a new synthesis of the creative powers of the mechanistic tradition and the participatory communitarianism of the organicist tradition. Yet, I remain unconvinced that the kind of radical democratic participatory values Winter and I favor are rooted in the organicist tradition. As Jacques Derrida, Gilles Deleuze and Michel Foucault have pointed out, organicist notions of unity, harmony and totality have led not only to the unhappy consciousness of the modern West, but also to premature closures and debilitating constraints that are but forms of the Western will to power. Such dangerous notions often elude and elide difference and heterogeneity (the very ingredients for radical participatory democracy), which results in dominating and destructive dispositions.

Similarly, the historicist tradition—from Nietzsche to Gadamer, Marx to Gramsci—which tries to take seriously historicity, sociality and community bears some culpability for nuclearism. The discovery of history in the modern West—principally a nineteenth-century affair—meant the control of and mastery over historical forces. As Engels noted, freedom is the recognition of necessity and necessity is history as *Ananke,* as preexistent material to shape and mold for human purposes. Again the modern Western will to power looms large.

In short, I am not disagreeing with Winter's powerful critique of the mechanistic tradition. I am merely extending it to other precious traditions in the modern West, including his own. My point here is simply that the major traditions in the modern West fall prey to his critique—none are free of spot or wrinkle. Furthermore, these traditions (though some more than others) contain elements useful for launching such critiques. For example, the mechanistic tradition—though worthy of devastating criticism and ultimate rejection—produced Hume's associationism, which bequeathed to us a valuable mitigated skepticism that promoted a fallibilism requisite for an acceptable historicism. The organicist tradition—though limited and romantic—yielded the rich system of Hegel and the profound insights of Heidegger, which made possible penetrating critiques of technological rationality. Lastly, the historicist tradition—which I prefer, though still criticize—gave us Marx's illuminating social analyses and Gramsci's revisions, which still partly guide our conception of and activities against modern forms of oppression. Yet, despite these grand contributions, these traditions contribute in significant ways to the modern European will to power and our present nuclear predicament.

I support Winter's claim that the complex linking of Cartesian and Hobbesian epistemologies to modern *techne* more readily results in dominating dispositions. But I am not convinced—by either Winter, MacIntyre, Gadamer or Bernstein—that its replacement by some notion of *poesis* or *phronesis* will in itself necessarily or probably void the Western will to power or dilute the nuclearism in our world. In fact, Nietzsche may be right: the very attempt to recover and recuperate our Greek heritage—both pre-Socratic and post-Socratic notions—is debilitating and reveals our parochialism. I do not follow Nietzsche in such a direction, but his radical viewpoints warrant serious attention. To put my cards on the table, I hold that a particular religious and political form of *phronesis*—a practical wisdom linked to specific prophetic religious and progressive political movements—might redirect the Western will to power and constrain the nuclearism in our world. But this position remains a hope and a risk. Even openness to the disclosure of Divine Mystery does not guarantee it. For there is, in my Christian view, the slight chance that Christianity might be false.

In other words, Winter must spell out in more detailed terms the concrete political content of his alternative to Cartesian and Hobbesian *technes*. I find his characterization of the effects of these *technes* persuasive. But precisely what the relation of "dwelling" is to political praxis and "sharing" is to movement building remains unclear. Furthermore, I think such praxis and movement building can be done without assuming that "the rhythms and energies of the play of life lend a common base to human aspirations and struggles." Such romantic naturalism is not warranted by the commonsensical or scientific evidence we have, and surely no transcendental justification can stand the scrutiny of Winter's historicist sentiments. So what does sustain such an optimistic assumption? Like Whitehead's consequent nature of God, it is an understandable but unacceptable naturalist leap of faith. The impossible possibility of Divine Grace might sustain and enable such a leap, but not "the relational processes of species life."

Lastly, Winter's account of how the *periagoge* is to take place is underdeveloped. At one point, he suggests this to be the role of the "servant church." Yet "in the Between" even this cloud of witnesses "has no special protection from the painful rupture of power and goodness." At another point, he suggests that the choice of life over death "*can* come when people begin to reflect on where the path of deterrence is leading."

My point here is not that Winter should put forward elaborate strategies and tactics to resist and overthrow nuclearism, but rather that he must specify more clearly the conditions under which new ways of being-in-the-world—with their concomitant new hermeneutical horizons and existential symbols—come about. To put it bluntly, the pedagogical dimension of his perspective remains vague—and there can be no *periagoge* without a distinct *paideia*.

In conclusion, Winter's essay elevates the contemporary discourse on nuclearism in an admirable and impressive manner. His critique is powerful—yet its scope needs broadening. His alternative is pregnant—though it lacks historical concreteness. And his pedagogy is perspicacious—but it remains rudimentary. We all should be grateful to Professor Winter for his meditation—his grand vision, acute analysis and propitious praxis—because he surely helps us to think more clearly and work more effectively for the preservation and humanization of the earth.

SOURCE: "Winter in the West," *Prophetic Fragments* (Grand Rapids, Mich.: Wm. B. Eerdmans Publishing Co., 1988), pp. 246–249. Originally appeared in *Religion and Intellectual Life*, Spring 1984.

Thirty Three

PROPHETIC CHRISTIAN AS ORGANIC INTELLECTUAL: MARTIN LUTHER KING, JR.

I delivered this address at the unveiling of a bust of Martin Luther King, Jr., at the U.S. Capitol in October 1986. This poignant moment in my life provided an occasion to reflect on the exemplary prophetic Christian of our time. I shall never forget the firm and affirming handshake of Coretta Scott King immediately after my presentation—a soft and sweet gesture to cement a rededication to the legacy of this organic intellectual in the prophetic Christian and democratic tradition.

I hate, I despise your feast days, and I will not smell in your solemn assemblies. Though ye offer me burnt offerings and your meat offerings, I will not accept them: Neither will I regard the peace offerings of your fat beasts. Take thou away from me the noise of thy songs; for I will not hear the melody of thy viols. But let justice run down as waters, and righteousness as a mighty stream.

—Amos 5:21–24

The Spirit of the Lord is upon me, because he hath anointed me to preach the gospel to the poor; he hath sent me to heal the broken-hearted, to preach deliverance to the captives, and recovering of sight to the blind, to set at liberty them that are bruised.

—Luke 4:18

I've seen the lightning flash, I've heard the thunder roll, I've felt sin breakers dashing trying to conquer my soul. But I heard the voice of Jesus saying still to fight on. He promised never to leave, never to leave me alone.

—Negro Spiritual

MARTIN LUTHER KING, JR., was the most significant and successful organic *intellectual* in American history. Never before in our past has a figure outside of elected public office linked the life of the mind to social change with such moral persuasiveness and political effectiveness. An adequate account of why and how King emerged as such a figure must consider the distinctive historical conditions of post–World War II America—with its supreme world-power status, unprecedented economic boom and apartheid-like structures of racial domination in the South—that set the stage for the moral vision, personal courage and political determination of King and those who struggled alongside him.

In this essay, I shall focus principally on the intellectual and existential sources that inform King's thought—that is, intellectual and existential sources that are preeminently religious in character and prophetic in content. I suggest that there are four major sources in King's thought. The first—and most important—source was *the prophetic black church tradition* that initially and fundamentally shaped King's worldview. The second consisted of a *prophetic liberal Christianity* King encountered in his higher education and scholarly training. The third source was a *prophetic Gandhian method of nonviolent social change* that King first encountered in a sermon by Mordecai Johnson (president of Howard University) and that he later used in his intense intellectual struggle with the powerful critiques of the Christian love ethic by Karl Marx and Friedrich Nietzsche. The last source was that of *prophetic American civil religion*, which fuses secular and sacred history and combines Christian themes of deliverance and salvation with political ideals of democracy, freedom and equality. I shall argue that these four religious sources constitute the major pillars of Martin Luther King, Jr.'s, thought. Let us start at King's beginnings—that is, in the bosom of the black Baptist church.

The black church—a shorthand rubric that refers to black Christian communities of various denominations that came into being when African American slaves decided, often at the risk of life and limb, to "make Jesus their choice" and to share with one another their common Christian sense of purpose and Christian understanding of their circumstances—is unique in American culture. This is so because it is the major institution created, sustained and controlled by black people themselves; that is, it is the most visible and salient cultural product of black people in the United States. The profound insights *and* petty blindnesses, immeasurable depths *and* immobilizing faults, incalculable richness *and* parochial impoverishment of that complex hybrid people called Afro-Americans surface most clearly in the black church.

And let us be very clear and let us never forget that the great American prophetic figure of our time, Martin Luther King, Jr., was a child of the black church—an individual product of the major institutional product of black people in this country. The black church was created under economic conditions of preindustrial slavery and socioeconomic circumstances of "natal alienation" (Orlando Patterson's term in *Slavery and Social Death* to describe a form of social death in which people have no legal ties of birth in both ascending and descending generations, no right to predecessors or progeny). Hence black people were *confined* to a perpetual and inheritable state of domination and *defined* as dishonored persons with no public worth, social standing or legal status—only economic value, mere commodities to be bought, sold or used. In this regard, the black church signified and signifies the collective effort of an exploited and oppressed, degraded and despised, dominated and downtrodden people of African descent to come to terms with the absurd *in* America and the absurd *as* America. The black church was a communal response to an existential and political situation in which no penultimate reasons suffice to make any kind of sense or give any type of meaning to the personal circumstances and collective condition of Afro-Americans.

With the "death of the African gods" (to use Albert Raboteau's phrase in his book *Slave Religion*), black people creatively appropriated a Christian worldview—mainly from such dissenters in the American religious tradition as Baptists and Methodists—and thereby transformed a prevailing absurd situation into a persistent and present *tragic* one, a kind of "Good Friday" state of existence in which one is seemingly forever on the cross, perennially crucified, continuously abused and incessantly devalued—yet sustained and empowered by a hope against hope for a potential and possible triumphant state of affairs. The ground of this hope was neither rationally demonstrable nor empirically verifiable. Rather, it was existentially encountered in an intense *personal* relationship with Jesus Christ, whose moral life, agonizing death and miraculous resurrection literally and symbolically enacted an ultimate victory over evil—collective slavery and personal sin—a victory that had *occurred* but was not yet *consummated*, with evil *conquered* but not yet *abolished*. The Christocentric language of the black church—of Jesus as the bright and morning star against the backdrop of the pitch darkness of the night, as water in dry places, a companion in loneliness, a doctor to the sick, a rock in a wearied land—exemplifies the intimate and dependent personal relationship between God and individual and between God and a world-forsaken people.

The important point here is not simply that this is the broad black Christian worldview that King heard and adopted at his father's church, Ebenezer Baptist Church in Atlanta, Georgia, but also that this worldview put the pressing and urgent problem of evil—the utterly and undeniably *tragic* character of life and history—at its center. Furthermore, the major focus of the *prophetic* black Christian worldview was neither an escapist pie-in-the-sky heaven nor a political paradise on earth. Rather, the stress was on marshaling and garnering resources from fellowship, community and personal strength (meditation, prayer) to cope with overwhelmingly limited options dictated by institutional and personal evil. In short, this black Christian perspective indeed affirmed a sustaining eschatology (that is, a heaven-orientation) and a moral critique of pervasive white racism—but its emphasis was on survival and struggle in the face of an alternative of absurdity and insanity.

The principal African resources in black Christianity were threefold. First, a *kinetic orality* permeated black sermons and songs, black prayers and hymns. A sense of community was constituted and reinforced by an invigorated rhetoric, rhythmic freedom and antiphonal forms of interaction. Fluid, protean and flexible oral stylizations of language gave black church life a distinctively African American stamp— a stamp that flowed from black cultural agency in a society that tried to deny and downplay any form of black agency and black creativity. Second, a *passionate physicality* accented black control and power over the only social space permitted to them in American society—that is, their bodies. Self-assertion of *somebodiness* enacted by bodily participation in stylized forms of spiritual response in black church liturgy signified a sense of *homefulness* for an exilic people. Last, a *combative spirituality* was promoted and promulgated by the central roles of preacher, deacon and choir. Each had to meet a weekly challenge of feeding the flock, encouraging the discouraged and giving hope to the downhearted. This stress on the performative and the pragmatic, on pageantry and the histrionic put a premium on prospective moral practice or forward-looking ethical struggle for black Christian parishioners. This sense of struggle paradoxically cultivated a historical patience and subversive joy, a sober survival ethic and an openness to seize credible liberation opportunities.

The theology of the black church was, for the most part, traditionally Augustinian with an African American difference. It accented the traditional Protestant Christian doctrines of divine majesty, sovereignty, mystery, sin and grace, forgiveness and love filtered through the black experience of oppression. This filtering linked God's plan of salvation to black liberation—inseparable, though not identical—and bestowed upon black people a divine source for self-identity—for example, as children of God—that stood in stark contrast to the cultural perceptions and social roles imposed upon them by a racist American society.

This African American difference not only highlighted the dignity of a people (as unique individuals) denied such dignity in their surroundings, but also accented the strong universalist and egalitarian Christian *imago dei* notion of all persons having equal value and significance in the eyes of God. In this way, the black church put forward perspectives that encouraged both individuality and community fellowship, personal morality and antiracist political engagement, a grace-centered piety and a stress on Christian good works. To put it crudely, the black church attempted to provide a theological route through the Scylla of a quietistic, priestly American Christianity that legitimated racism and the Charybdis of a secular (self-righteous) Promethean view that elevated human powers at the expense of divine grace and divine aid. The black church tried to hold together both the dignity and depravity of persons in such a way that God–like Yahweh with the children of Israel–identifies with the disinherited and downtrodden, yet even the disinherited and downtrodden are sinners in need of conversion and sanctification. Human beings can change and be changed–both individuals and societies– yet no individual or society can *fully* conform to the requirements of the Christian gospel, hence the need for endless improvement and amelioration.

This complex dialectical interplay of human finitude and human betterment in predominant black church theological perspectives makes Afro-American Christianity more evangelical than fundamentalist. This is so because fundamentalist Christianity is preoccupied with the claims of science and historical criticism of biblical texts; it views the Bible not only in literalist terms, but, more important, in the form of propositions in light of a notion of *closed* revelation–only certain biblically derived propositions constitute divine revelation. By contrast, black evangelical Christianity is primarily concerned with human fallenness, including our readings of the Bible. Biblical texts indeed remain the authoritative guide to Christian life, yet the focus is on moral conduct and spiritual development in light of *continued* revelation–that is, openness to divine purpose, especially through the Holy Spirit–grounded in the Bible *and* appropriated by individuals and communities in the present. In short, fundamentalist Christianity is *rationalistic* in orientation and *legalistic* in effect, hence it leans toward bibliolatry, whereas black evangelical Christianity is *dramatic* in orientation and *moralistic* in effect, hence it affirms a biblically informed perspective.

My claim is that black church viewpoints not only fundamentally shaped King's thought, but also regulated the themes and motifs, aspects and elements he accentuated in his encounters with liberal Christianity (at Morehouse College, Crozer Theological Seminary, the University of Pennsylvania, Boston University and Harvard University), Gandhian conceptions of love and social change and American civil religion. In this way, the black church's influence on King's views is the most *primordial* and *decisive* source of his thought. In his own writings and sermons, he simply presupposed this influence and always assumed that his being a black Baptist minister spoke for itself regarding this black church influence. For example, his choice of Georg Wilhelm Hegel as his favorite philosopher was not because King was convinced of the necessary developments of the *Weltgeist* put forward in *The Phenomenology of Spirit,* but rather because Hegel held that "growth comes through struggle"–a view King was quite disposed to, given his formation in the black church. Furthermore, King's preferred method of looking for partial truths in opposing positions, in rejecting extremes and affirming a creative synthesis of opposing views in a tension-ridden harmony is, on the surface, Hegelian. But it is, on a deeper level, rooted in the dialectical mediation of the dualistic character of the self (spirit/nature) and world (history/eternity)–a mediation both King (in an Afro-American context) and Hegel (in a German Lutheran context) inherited from Christian thought. The point is not that King did not learn much from Hegel, but rather that Hegel was a *supplement* to King's black church influence.

This supplementary character of intellectual sources subsequent to King's black church formation can be seen quite clearly in his encounter with liberal Christianity in his formal higher education and training. For example, at Morehouse College, King's concentration in sociology reinforced his theological and moral condemnation of the hypocrisy of Southern white racist Christians and their alleged adherence to the Christian gospel. Walter Chivers, his sociology professor, conducted detailed empirical investigation of lynchings in the South in light of a self-styled ethical critique of American capitalism. More pointedly, under George D. Kelsey (head of the Department of Religion) and Dr. Benjamin Mays (Morehouse College president), King's black church prospectives were refined. By avoiding fundamentalist traps, shedding parochial images of mere cathartic preaching and linking sophisticated intellectual pursuit to serious Christian commitment, King became convinced at Morehouse that his vocation lay in becoming a minister in the black Baptist tradition.

King's response to the Euro-American Christian academic world was to select those viewpoints that gave philosophical and theological articulation to deeply held themes and beliefs he acquired in the black church. The four central religious themes were the dignity and sanctity of human persons; the moral obligation and social responsibility of Christians to resist institutional evils such as racist segregation; the significance of personal immortality; and the power of Christian love to make a difference in personal *and* social life. At Crozer, King took nearly one-third of his courses under George Davis. In a way similar to black church perspectives, Davis conceived of God as a deity intimately and intricately involved in human history—a "working, toiling God" who labors through human beings to realize the ultimate end and aim of history. This end and aim was the recognition and appreciation of the value of human personality and the brotherhood of man. Influenced by the social gospel of Walter Rauschenbusch, Davis linked his personalism to political and social engagement.

Yet it was the work of L. Harold DeWolf at Boston University that provided the liberal Christian resources most congenial and amenable to King's refined black church perspectives. In his six courses with DeWolf and in writing his doctoral dissertation (on the conception of God in Paul Tillich and Henry Nelson Wieman) under the guidance of DeWolf, King found an acceptable and respectable academic theology that best expressed the major themes and beliefs of his black church background. DeWolf's personalism provided King with a professional theological language that put forward the four basic themes King had inherited from the black church tradition. During his years in graduate school, King did tentatively adopt limited liberal Christian ideas about the natural goodness of people and the progressive direction of human history. Yet later in the heat of battle, King fell back on more classical Christian ideas of sin, grace and hope within the context of the black struggle for freedom. In short, Davis and DeWolf *supplemented* King's black church viewpoints, supplements that resulted in slight revisions, emendations and new academic forms for his evangelical content. King indeed called himself an evangelical liberal—an apt description after adopting Kelsey's nonliteralist, dramatic reading of the biblical texts, Mays's Christian modernist view of educated and engaged black ministers, Davis's stress on human history as the crucial terrain for divine activity and DeWolf's full-blown personalism that undergirded a social gospel.

The major challenges to King's black church formation came from the critiques of religion put forward by Karl Marx and Friedrich Nietzsche as, for example, Marx's claim (based on Ludwig Feuerbach's views) that religion was the opiate of the people—the instrument of those who rule in that it disinvests people of their own powers by investing God with all power and thereby rendering them submissive and deferential toward the status quo. Furthermore, Marx's claim of the vast economic disparity between the rich and poor—for instance, the *class inequality* in America between 1 percent of the population who owned 28 percent of the wealth and the bottom 45 percent of the population who owned 2 percent of the wealth—made an important impact on King. King's black church formation led him to conclude that many forms of religion did render people submissive, but also that *prophetic* Christianity could *empower* people to fight against oppression and struggle for freedom and justice. King remained convinced all of his life that there was a need for a redistribution of wealth and a deemphasis on material possessions in a profit-oriented capitalist society. And later in life, King endorsed some forms of (indigenous) American democratic and libertarian socialism that preserved a constitutional rule of law and protected individual liberties in order to secure and promote a "person-centered rather than property-centered and profit-centered" economy. In regard to his response to Marx, King wrote:

> I read Marx as I read all of the influential historical thinkers—from a dialectical point of view, combining a partial yes and a partial no. Insofar as Marx posited a metaphysical materialism, an ethical relativism, and a strangulating totalitarianism, I responded with an unambiguous "no"; but insofar as he pointed to weaknesses of traditional capitalism, contributed to the growth of a definite self-consciousness in the masses, and challenged the social conscience of the Christian churches, I responded with a definite "yes."

In short, King succumbed to neither a knee-jerk negative reaction to Marx without reading and grappling with him nor an uncritical acceptance of Marx's atheism, which overlooked the contribution of prophetic religious people to struggles for freedom.

Nietzsche's view of Christian love as a form of resentment and revenge of the powerless and impotent toward the powerful and the strong led King briefly to "despair of the power of love in solving social problems." Following both the black church tradition and liberal Christianity, King had concluded that the Christian love ethic applied only to individuals' relationships—not to group, nation or class conflicts. And if Nietzsche was correct, even individual relationships of love were but power struggles masquerading as harmonious interactions. The Gandhian method of love-motivated (agapic) nonviolent resistance provided King with a response to Marx and an answer to Nietzsche. The love ethic of Jesus Christ was a moral and practical method—a way of life and way of struggle in which oppressed people could fight for freedom without inflicting violence on the oppressor, humiliating the opponent, and hence possibly transform the moral disposition of one's adversary.

For King, this method of nonviolent resistance required more internal *moral discipline* than that of Marxist revolutionaries, because one had to accept suffering without retaliation, to receive blows without striking back. For him, this was not cowardice but courage, not fear but fortitude. Nonviolent resistance also went beyond Nietzschean resentment and revenge in that resistance was directed at the forces of evil, rather than against persons who commit the evil. The enemy is injustice and oppression, not those who perpetuate the injustice and oppression.

Needless to say, this Gandhian viewpoint goes against our common instincts and moral intuitions. In this sense, the application of the love ethic of Jesus Christ in the social sphere requires not only tremendous moral discipline and fortitude, but also *profound trust* in the redemptive power of love and in the salvific plan of God. This trust presupposes that the unearned suffering of agapic nonviolent resisters can educate, transform and even convert one's opponents. The aim is not simply to rely on the moral sense or conscience of the adversary but, if need be, to force the adversary to develop such a sense and conscience. And if one concludes that no such development is possible, then we simply must admit that we are doomed to an unending cycle of violence and oppression—with the old victims of violence soon to become new perpetrators of violence. Such a nightmare—an inevitable conclusion for Marx and Nietzsche in King's view—radically calls into question the very power of the love ethic of Jesus Christ. For King, if one accepts such a nightmare, then only self-destruction awaits us. To accept such a view—for individuals, groups or nations—is to acquire and preserve "power without compassion, might without morality, and strength without sight."

The last major resource for King's thought was American civil religion—that complex web of religious ideals of deliverance and salvation and political ideals of freedom, democracy and equality that constitute the evolving collective self-definition of America. This first new nation—born liberal, born modern and born bourgeois—gave birth to a grand social experiment unprecedented in human history. Its Declaration of Independence constituted, for King, a great moral event and document. King's appropriation and interpretation of American civil religion led him creatively to extend the tradition of American jeremiads—a tradition of public exhortation that joins social criticisms of America to moral renewal and calls America back to its founding ideals of democracy, freedom and equality. King was convinced that, despite the racism of the founding fathers, the ideals of America were sufficient if only they were taken seriously in practice. Therefore, King's condemnation of and lament for America's hypocrisy and oppression of poor whites, indigenous peoples, Latinos and black people was put forward in the name of reaffirming America's mission of embodying democracy, freedom and equality. King did not support and affirm the bland American dream of comfortable living and material prosperity. Rather, he put forward his own dream—grounded and refined in the black church experience, supplemented by liberal Christianity and implemented by Gandhian methods of nonviolent resistance—rooted in the American ideals of democracy, freedom and equality.

King's thought remains a challenge to us principally in that he accented the anticolonial, anti-imperialist and antiracist consequences of taking seriously the American ideals of democracy, freedom and equality. He never forgot that America was born out of revolutionary revolt and subversive rebellion against British colonialism and imperialism and that although much of white America viewed the country as the promised land, black slaves saw it as Egypt, that just as Europe's poor huddled masses were attracted to America, the largest black mass movement (led by Marcus Garvey) was set on leaving America! Through his prophetic Christian lens, King saw just how far America had swerved away from its own revolutionary past. In its support of counterrevolution in Vietnam, Guatemala, Colombia, Jamaica and South Africa—and today we can add Chile, Nicaragua and South Korea—the United States betrayed its own ideals. King acutely observed in 1968:

> The greatest irony and tragedy of all is that our nation, which initiated so much of the revolutionary spirit of the modern world, is now cast in the mold of being an arch anti-revolutionary. We are engaged in a war that seems to turn the clock of history back and perpetuate white colonialism.

King's universal and egalitarian religious and moral commitments, as well as his historical consciousness, led him to *internationalize* the American ideals of democracy, freedom and equality and thereby measure not only domestic policies, but also U.S. foreign policy by these ideals. And he found both sets of policies wanting. He knew some progress had been made—yet so much more progress was needed, and even present gains could be reversed, as we have witnessed in the past few years. Regarding the domestic front, King proclaimed: "If the problem [of injustice to the poor and blacks] is not solved, America will be on the road to its self-destruction." And on the eve of his murder, he again warned regarding the international scene: "And also in the human rights revolution, if something isn't done, and in a hurry, to bring the colored peoples of the world out of their long years of poverty, their long years of hurt and neglect, the whole world is doomed."

The unique status and legacy of Martin Luther King, Jr., is that, as a black Baptist minister, he embodies the best of American Christianity; as an organic intellectual, he exemplifies the best of the life of the mind involved in public affairs; as a proponent of nonviolent resistance, he holds out the only slim hope for social sanity in a violence-ridden world; as an American prophet, he commands the respect even of those who opposed him; and as an egalitarian internationalist, he inspires all oppressed peoples around the world who struggle for democracy, freedom and equality. What manner of man was he, this child and product of the black church open enough to learn from others and rooted enough in his own tradition to grow, who now belongs to the nation and the world—a nation and world still "not able to bear all his words" even as they try to honor him?

SOURCE: "Martin Luther King, Jr.: Prophetic Christian as Organic Intellectual," *Prophetic Fragments* (Grand Rapids, Mich.: Wm. B. Eerdmans Publishing Co., 1988), pp. 3–12. An address delivered at a King symposium at the U.S. Capitol, October 1986.

Thirty Four

SUBVERSIVE JOY AND REVOLUTIONARY PATIENCE IN BLACK CHRISTIANITY

I wrote this piece for a French audience. It highlights the tragic elements of Afro-American Christianity and the liminal dimensions of black music. I see in retrospect that in 1984 my struggle with the tragicomic character of black life and the human predicament was central to my work.

PROFOUND PREOCCUPATION WITH THE Christian gospel is a distinctive feature of Afro-American culture. This near obsession with the "good news" proclaimed by Jesus of Nazareth is rooted in the unique Afro-American encounter with the modern world. And like every understanding of the gospel, the black Christian perspective is shaped by a particular history and culture.

The trauma of the slave voyage from Africa to the New World and the Euro-American attempt systematically to strip Africans of their languages, cultures and religions produced a black experience of the absurd. This state of "natal alienation"—in which Africans had no right to their past or progeny—prevented wide spread transmittance of tradition to American-born Africans. Such alienation was more pervasive in the United States than in other parts of the New World principally because of a low ratio of blacks to whites, which facilitated more frequent and intense black-white interaction. Only 4.5 percent of all Africans imported to the New World came to North America, though an incredibly high rate of slave reproduction (or induced breeding) soon quadrupled this percentage figure. Therefore second- and third-generation Africans in the United States made sense of and gave meaning to their predicament without an immediate relation to African worldviews and customs.

With the slow but sure "death of the African gods," many blacks creatively appropriated the Christian gospel peddled by religious dissenters in American life, that is, by Methodists and Baptists. The evangelical outlook of these denominations stressed the conversion experience, equality of all people before God and institutional autonomy. The conversion experience often resembled African novitiate rites in which intense emotional investment and ecstatic bodily behavior signified vital faith. This experience equalized the status of all before God, thereby giving the slaves a special self-identity and self-esteem in stark contrast with the

inferior roles imposed upon them in American society. Institutional autonomy ensured black control over the central organization in the Afro-American community—a crucial characteristic that sets blacks in the United States apart from other
New World Africans in Catholic Latin America and the Anglican Caribbean.

The black interpretation of the Christian gospel accented the tragedy in the
struggle for freedom and the freedom in a tragic predicament. The African slaves'
search for collective identity could find historical purpose in the exodus of Israel
out of slavery and personal meaning in the bold identification of Jesus Christ with
the lowly. Furthermore, the slaves empathized with the senseless persecution of
Job and the deep despair of Ecclesiastes. Afro-American Christianity is Christocentric to the core—yet Jesus Christ is not simply understood as an agent of deliverance, but also a human exemplar of pain and agony. The crucified Christ
looms as large as the risen Christ.

The conception of freedom prevalent in Afro-American Christianity possesses
three dimensions: the existential, the social and the eschatological. Existential
freedom is a mode of being-in-the-world that resists dread and despair. It embodies an ecstatic celebration of human existence without affirming prevailing reality.
Like many pagan religions, this celebration consists of a rejoicing in the mere fact
of being alive; yet like Christianity, it contains a critical disposition toward the
way the world is.

Existential freedom in black Christianity flows from the kinetic orality and affective physicality inherited from West African cultures and religions. This full-
fledged acceptance of the body deems human existence a source of joy and gaiety. Physical participation and bodily involvement in religious rituals epitomizes
this kind of freedom. In short, black Christianity has a strong Dionysian
element.

The tension and anxiety produced by the harsh conditions of oppression accentuates this Dionysian aspect. Rhythmic singing, swaying, dancing, preaching,
talking and walking—all features of black life—are weapons of struggle and survival. They not only release pressures and desperation, they also constitute bonds
of solidarity and sources for individuality. For example, the famous loud "cry" of
black religious and secular singers or the guttural "shout" of preachers are simultaneously groans of hurt, acts of communal catharsis and stylizations of unique
vocal techniques. The heartfelt groans acknowledge the deplorable plight of a
downtrodden people. The cathartic acts provide emotional and physical relief
from the daily scars of humiliation and degradation. The individual stylistic vocals assert the sense of "somebodiness" in a situation that denies one's humanity.

The first artistic gift of Afro-Americans to the world—the spirituals—exemplify
existential freedom in action. At the level of form, these "sorrow songs" contain
subtle rhythmic elements alongside brooding melodies. They invoke deep passions not of self-pity or self-hatred, but of lament and hope. The spirituals give

artistic form to the frustrations and aspirations of a battered people constantly under siege with few human allies. The lyrical focus is often the liberating power of God, but the stylistic forms stress the self-invested moan, the risky falsetto and the nuanced syncopation. Often confused with mere circumlocution and repetition, the lyrics and styles of the spirituals directly confront existential dread and despair with the armor of vocal virtuosity, rhythmic facility and faith in God. Subsequent developments such as the blues, jazz and gospel music may reject or revise the Christian commitment, vocalize instruments and add more complex rhythms, but the cultural crucible of such developments rests in the distinct musical articulation of Afro-American Christianity.

Religion, rhythm and rhetoric have been the three spheres in which Afro-American existential freedom has taken root. Oppression excluded other areas. Black preaching of the gospel is rhythmic, cathartic and full of moans and groans. Black rhythm is rooted in religiosity, liminality and full of call and response. And the gospel is understood in terms of existential self-involvement, moral flexibility and political improvisation.

The social dimension of the freedom predominant in black Christianity does not primarily concern political struggle, but rather cultural solidarity. The politics of the black church is highly ambiguous, with a track record of widespread opportunism. Yet the cultural practices of the black church embody a basic reality—sustained black solidarity in the midst of a hostile society. Black Christianity is not merely a reaction to white exclusion; rather, it is a distinct culture that revels in its own uniqueness. This uniqueness—displayed in black existential freedom—is the mark of black identity and a guide for future black church development. Black people do not attend churches, for the most part, to find God, but rather to share and expand together the rich heritage they have inherited. This heritage, sustained by close familial relationships and friendships, evolves around a personal dependence on God that facilitates a communal fellowship. The common black argument for belief in God is not that it is logical or reasonable, but rather that such belief is requisite for one's sanity and for entrée to the most uplifting sociality available in the black community.

The eschatological aspect of freedom in black Christianity is the most difficult to grasp. It is neither a glib hope for a pie-in-the-sky heaven nor an apocalyptic aspiration that awaits world destruction. Rather, it is a hope-laden articulation of the tragic quality of everyday life of a culturally degraded, politically oppressed and racially coerced labor force. Black Christian eschatology is anchored in the tragic realism of the Old Testament wisdom literature and the proclamation of a coming kingdom by Jesus Christ. Anthropologists have observed that there is a relative absence of tragic themes in the ancient oral narratives of West Africa. Is it no accident that the black understanding of the gospel stresses this novel motif, the utterly tragic character of life and history?

Yet the black Christian conception differs from more traditional tragic perspectives. It promotes a tragic sense of life that affirms the workings of evil forces beyond human control while promoting struggle against particular forms of evil in the world. In sharp contrast to notions of tragedy that yield conservative politics, the black Christian tragic sense of life focuses on resistance and opposition in the here and now against overwhelming odds. The regulative ideal for such resistance is a kingdom beyond history, but this kingdom is ultimately brought about by divine intervention. So this tragic sense of life, with deferred triumph, vastly differs from either Greek conceptions of tragedy or modern notions of the tragic vision.

Tragedy is, of course, a literary form inherited from the Greeks. It usually entails an initial act of shame or horror that violates the moral order. This act results in conscious and intense suffering that yields some transcendent knowledge of what it is to be human. This knowledge—often an affirmation of the ultimate worthwhileness of life and a perception of the objective character of the moral order—is the only saving grace for the hero, who is crushed by the intractable limits of his or her situation. The basic assumptions are that there is a moral order, that suffering is meaningful and that heroic effort is noble. For black Christianity, this perspective is unacceptable because its mode of closure elevates Fate and its positive form of knowledge remains contemplative.

The modern tragic vision is a truncated version of Greek tragedy. The purpose of suffering is rendered problematic and the knowledge resulting from suffering is suspect. The very notion of a moral order is called into question and displaced by a preoccupation with the consciousness occupying the suffering, the details of the context in which the suffering occurs and the ways in which suffering is evaded or tolerated. This viewpoint has little persuasive power for black Christianity in that its rejection of any end or aim of human existence discourages purposeful struggle, especially communal and collective struggle. Such a viewpoint tends to presuppose luxury in that it may stimulate the ironic consciousness of a declining petite bourgeoisie, but it spells suicide for the downtrodden. Like Greek tragedy, it may generate profound insights, but it is disenabling for degraded and oppressed peoples.

The tragic sense of life in black Christian eschatology views suffering as a stepping-stone to liberation. Yet liberation does not eradicate the suffering in itself. Therefore suffering is understood only as a reality to resist, an actuality to oppose. It can neither be submitted to in order to gain contemplative knowledge nor reified into an object of ironic attention. Rather, it is a concrete state of affairs that produces discernible hurt and pain, hence requiring action of some sort. Black Christian eschatology focuses on praxis against suffering, not reflection upon it, personal and collective resistance to suffering, not a distancing from it. And ultimately, with the aid of divine intervention, suffering is overcome.

The radically comic character of Afro-American life—the pervasive sense of play, laughter and ingenious humor of blacks—flows primarily from the profound Afro-American Christian preoccupation with the tragedy in the struggle for freedom and the freedom in a tragic predicament. This comic release is the black groan made gay. Yet this release is neither escapist nor quietistic. Rather, it is *engaged gaiety, subversive joy* and *revolutionary patience,* which works for and looks to the kingdom to come. It is utopian in that it breeds a defiant dissatisfaction with the present and encourages action. It is tragic in that it tempers exorbitant expectations. This perspective precludes political disillusionment and its product, misanthropic nihilism.

The gospel in Afro-America lauds Calvinistic calls to transform the world, yet shuns puritanical repression. It promotes the Pascalian wager, yet transcends Jansenist self-obsession. Life is viewed as both a carnival to enjoy and a battlefield on which to fight. Afro-American Christianity promotes a gospel that empowers black people to survive and struggle in a God-forsaken world.

SOURCE: From *Prophetic Fragments* (Grand Rapids, Mich.: Wm. B. Eerdmans Publishing Co., 1988), pp. 161–165. Originally appeared in *Le Monde Diplomatique*, October 1984.

PART SEVEN

THE ARTS

My own feeble attempt to speak truths, expose lies and bear witness aspires to the condition of the arts, especially music. As Kafka rightly notes, art "is a hand outstretched in the darkness, seeking for some touch of grace which will transform it into a hand that bestows gifts." I intend neither to make the arts an idol, nor to render them fetishes. Yet I come close. I cannot conceive of any theory or even language adequate to the impact on me of Sophocles, Dante, Shakespeare, Mozart, Racine, Faulkner, Morrison, O'Neill, Armstrong, Vaughan or Coltrane. In this regard, Schopenhauer is right. There is a mystery to great art and the magnitude of that mystery is too much for our words to capture. Yet we do speak and write about art. I hope with humility!

Thirty Five

CRITICAL REFLECTIONS ON ART

This essay appeared in Art Forum *in 1989. It attempted to address the crisis in art criticism as the tides of new historicism and poststructuralism escalated. My aim was to preserve the integrity of art, to keep track of its powers in academic discussions of its historical contexts and political uses. I also had a chance to inject Harold Rosenberg, the powerful art critic of days past, into the discussion.*

> *Knowledge of art is not enough to make one a critic, any more than knowledge of art is enough to make one an artist. The student who turns to art in order to avoid reflecting upon his condition may become a specialist, a scholar, a connoisseur, but not a critic. For the latter exists through curiosity, indignation, and the widest practice of intellectual freedom.*

> —HAROLD ROSENBERG

THE DAYS OF ART criticism's eclectic and accessible generalists–like Clement Greenberg and Harold Rosenberg–are long gone. Certainly this has something to do with the increasing professionalization of the practice of criticism in general, for the funneling of the creative energy of young critics through academic channels has tended to produce specialists with little sense of (or interest in) synthetic perspectives. And needless to say, this academicization is related in complex ways to the commercialization of art, the ubiquitous commodification of culture in our day.

Yet even given the deadening potential of these processes in all fields, art criticism has lagged behind the theoretical moves made in other branches of cultural criticism. In recent years, there simply have not emerged art critics who have commanded serious intellectual attention on a par with their colleagues in the literary arena. The predominance and preeminence of the grand art historians (E. H. Gombrich, for example) in the highbrow humanist mode has cast a long and troublesome shadow. While literary critics, from the beginning of our century, could draw energy from the erudite analyses of T. S. Eliot and Ezra Pound, springboards that freed them (from old historicist encumbrances) to leap boldly into the Modernist literature of their own day, art critics like Roger Fry, Wyndham Lewis and Herbert Read remained tethered, despite their admirable attempts to engage with the present, to a backward-looking glance. It is no accident that many noteworthy nonacademic art critics—those who wrote for a wider public, not only for "trade" journals—took their inspiration from Eliot.

This problem was exacerbated after World War II, as the center of the art world shifted from Paris to New York—to a country whose Puritan origins and instrumentalist bent ill equipped its intelligentsia to take painting, photography and sculpture seriously. It is not surprising, then, that the first generation of formidable modern art critics in America were recent European immigrants or the products of immigrant subcultures—like Greenberg and Rosenberg. And these critics looked to European resources—Trotsky, Freud, Rimbaud, Baudelaire, Picasso—to grasp the new developments in postwar American art.

The entrance of art critics into the academy produced a generation crippled by a collective inferiority complex vis-à-vis the scholarly humanist tradition of old-style art historians, art critics who stood by in utter amazement at the self-confidence of post-Eliot literary critics. And since the slow demise of New Criticism, the brief moment of Northrop Frye's myth criticism and the French invasion of Jacques Derrida and Michel Foucault in literary criticism, art critics have principally played catch-up. Yet seeking to overthrow, or to undermine, the received tenet that the work of art is, at some fundamental level, independent of the social, political, psychological world in which its creator operates (certainly a worthy goal), the basic thrust of contemporary art criticism has been to deaestheticize (or historicize, sociologize or psychologize) art objects in order to render them worldly. Hence the major battles in aesthetic theory have been those that pit Kantians of various stripes against different kinds of Hegelians, Marxists or Freudians. These debates have been and can be fascinating and illuminating—but in the end they prove simply parochial and provincial.

This is so because they presuppose contexts and consensuses that no longer exist. The received modern world of differentiated autonomous spheres, a teleology based on Eurocentric notions of history, determining productive forces and ego-centered subjects—once legitimate assumptions from which to proceed—has now given way to a world characterized by global commodification; postcolonial and New World histories; nationalist, religious, and xenophobic revivals; and hybrid subjects with shattered superegos. Thus we must now proceed as did Kant, Hegel, Marx, and Freud in their day, namely, by acknowledging the ways in which the very act of criticism must construct the new contexts and consensuses in which we should operate. As Rosenberg warned in "Criticism and Its Premises:"

Unless critical discussion achieves the intellectual scale of our revolutionary epoch, it cannot be taken seriously. In practical fact, current writing on art consists largely of opportunistic sponsorship of trivial novelties and of assertions of per-

sonal tastes for which support is sought in pedantic references to art history. . . .
As a result, art criticism today is looked down upon by other forms of critical
thinking as an unintelligible jargon immersed in an insignificant aestheticism.[1]

Young art critics today would, no doubt, contest Rosenberg's claim by trotting
out their new historicism and discursive materialism, inspired by Foucault, Clifford Geertz, Julia Kristeva and others. And one does find in the recent work of art
critics obligatory appeals to history, society, culture and the role of power. Yet I
suggest that this new wave of art criticism is itself another form of aestheticism in
disguise. This is so not only because the ironic consciousness that informs this decentering, deconstructing and dismantling of highbrow European art objects and
perspectives is the reflection, in part, of an aestheticizing of art history through the
cloudy lens of liberal anti-imperialist guilt, but, more important, because it refuses
to give an account of how the present historical context shapes its own "historicizing" efforts. If most of our art critics offered such an account, it would be quite
apparent that they are actually recycling new forms of Eurocentric parochialism
and provincialism in the name of a professional avant-gardism—and one far removed from much of the interesting work of contemporary artists themselves.

The fervent post-Modernism debate in art criticism is a good example of how
new historicists, textualists and materialists wax eloquent about power and subordination, yet provide no analyses of their own deployment of power in regard
to what their debate excludes or is silent about. Robert Storr rightly notes:

> To be sure, much postmodernist critical inquiry has centered precisely on the is-
> sues of "difference" and "otherness." On the purely theoretical plane the explo-
> ration of these concepts has produced some important results, but in the absence
> of any sustained research into what artists of color and others outside the main-
> stream might be up to, such discussions became rootless instead of radical.[2]

We might add that the rootlessness—that is, the ahistorical character—of the post-
Modernism debate dovetails neatly with aestheticist "weightlessness"—namely, the
failure to examine who bears the cost of the "absences" present in one's discourses and in one's exercise of authority and power.

Part of the problem here is simply the rather racially segregated and discriminatory practices of the art world—much more so than the literary world—which
make it much riskier for critics to take seriously art outside the white mainstream.
Yet the aesthetic historicism of the new wave of art criticism—which refuses to examine the operations of power at the present historical juncture and what role
their own ironic stance is playing in this juncture—tends to reduce this kind of demand to mere moral finger-pointing and pleas for inclusion (as does the belletris-
tic stance of "give-us-back-the-good-old-days" critics like Hilton Kramer).

My point here is not to trash the new historicists—they are often insightful and instructive. Rather, my aim is to emphasize that to be a critic is to do more than reinterpret isolated historical moments with dazzling descriptions or to cull other disciplines for stunning juxtapositions of cultural and artistic practices. To be a critic is to muster the available resources to respond to the crisis of one's own time—in light of one's view of the past.

The challenge is a formidable one. Walking the tightrope between the Scylla of aestheticism and the Charybdis of reductionism is difficult. And those few critics who pull it off do so when they are summoned by the power of the art objects that engross their curiosity, not when they follow the dictates of even the most subtle methodology. In this sense, evaluation is never an end in itself (to preserve some eternal canon or further a political cause), but rather an integral by-product of a profound understanding of an art object, of how its form and content produce the multiple effects they do and of the role it plays in shaping and being shaped by the world of ideas, political conflicts, cultural clashes and the personal turmoils of its author and audience.

The future of art criticism, then, lies in a more thorough turn toward history, with each step in this turn making possible the next. First, we must require of ourselves a more ambitious structural analysis of the present cultural situation (embracing a wholesale inquiry into both the personal and the institutional operations of power within the academy, the mass media and the museum and gallery networks). Only then can we focus on the specific art object, according creativity its integrity while conceiving of each artwork's distinctive form and style as a response to the cultural present *and* to past artistic styles. And finally, in examining how significant art objects (those that are accorded stature in the articulated canon and those that are not) offer insights into the human condition in *specific* times and places, but also shape our view of the current cultural *crisis,* we will hear the silences and see through the blind spots that exist alongside those insights. Art criticism *is* art history, but much intellectual baggage must be shed if we are to have a criticism commensurate with the complexities and challenges of our epoch, if we are to make history as well as to mine it.

SOURCE: *Artforum,* November 1989, "Critical Reflections on Art," by Cornel West.

Thirty Six

HORACE PIPPIN'S CHALLENGE TO ART CRITICISM

Music often overshadows painting in American culture, and this is especially so in the black American arts world. So I jumped at the opportunity to write about a major black painter, Horace Pippin, when Judith Stein asked me to contribute to her catalogue for the Pippin exhibition at the Pennsylvania Academy of the Fine Arts. In this essay, I situate Pippin within the Emersonian grain of American culture and use his rich work to reevaluate the Harlem Renaissance and elevate his artistic soul mates like Sterling Brown and Bessie Smith. This piece also exemplifies my belief that superb art—refined, sophisticated wrestlings with form and content in serious depictions of the world—is to be found among everyday folk.

THE ART OF HORACE Pippin poses grave challenges to how we appreciate and assess artworks in late twentieth-century America. A serious examination of Pippin's place in art history leads us into the thicket of difficult issues that now beset art critics. What does it mean to talk about high art and popular culture? Do these rubrics help us to evaluate and understand visual artifacts? Is folk art an illuminating or oxymoronic category? Can art be more than personal, racial or national therapy in American culture? Has the commercialization of art rendered it a mere commodity in our market-driven culture? Can the reception of the work of a black artist transcend mere documentary, social pleading or exotic appeal?

These complex questions often yield Manichaean responses—self-appointed defenders of high culture who beat their breasts in the name of craftsmanship and quality, and self-styled avant-gardists who call for critique and relevance. The former tend to use the monumental touchstones of the recent past—especially those of high modernism—to judge the present. The latter reject monumentalist views of art history even as they sometimes become highly paid celebrities in the art world. Pippin's work shows this debate to be a sterile exchange that overlooks much of the best art in the American grain: high-quality craftsmanship of art objects that disclose the humanity of people whose plight points to flaws in American society. Pippin's paintings are neither monumentalist in the modernist sense nor political in a postmodernist way. Rather, they are expressions of a rich Emersonian tradition in American art that puts a premium on the grandeur in the commonplace, ordinary and quotidian lives of people. This tradition promotes neither a glib celebration of everyday experiences nor a naive ignorance of the tragic aspects of our condition. Rather, Pippin's Emersonian sensibility affirms what John Dewey dubbed "experience in its integrity."[1] Pippin's so-called folk art boldly exclaims with Emerson: "I ask not for the great, the remote, the romantic; what is doing in Italy or Arabia; what is Greek art, or Provencal minstrelsy; I embrace the common, I explore and sit at the feet of the familiar, the low. Give me insight into day and you may have the antique and future worlds."[2]

This artistic affirmation of everyday experiences of ordinary people is anti-elitist, but not anti-intellectual—that is, it shuns a narrow mentality that downplays the joys and sufferings of the degraded and despised, yet it heralds high standards for how these joys and sufferings are represented in art. Pippin's paintings—as a grand instance of the Emersonian tradition in American art—attempt to democratize (not denigrate) the aesthetic by discerning and displaying tragedy and comedy in the ordinary experiences of common folk. In this way, his work echoes the Emersonian sensibility of John Dewey:

> In order to *understand* the aesthetic in its ultimate and approved forms, one must begin with it in the raw; in the events and scenes that hold the attentive eye and ear of man, arousing his interest and affording him enjoyment as he looks and listens. . . . The sources of art in human experience will be learned by him who sees how the tense grace of the ball-player infects the onlooking crowd; who notes the delight of the housewife in tending her plants, and the intent interest of her goodman in tending the patch of green in front of the house; the zest of the spectator in poking the wood burning on the hearth and in watching the darting flames and crumbling coals.[3]

We see such precious moments in Pippin's *Harmonizing* (1944), with black men *joyfully* singing on the block, or in *Domino Players* (1943), with black women *enjoying* a domino game. We also realize that Pippin's link to Abraham Lincoln is not so much a link to the president as emancipator of black people or to the president as hypocrite, but rather to Abe as the folk hero who is believed to have said that God must have loved common folk since he made so many of them. *Abe Lincoln, The Good Samaritan* (1943) fuses this Emersonian sensibility of Lincoln with a Christian theme of concern for the disadvantaged ("Let Christianity speak ever for the poor and the low").[4]

Yet Pippin's Emersonian practice—which sidesteps the sterile "quality versus diversity" debate—lends itself to establishmentarian abuse. A genuine artistic concern with the common easily appears as an aspiration for authenticity—especially for an art establishment that puts a premium on the "primitive" and hungers for the exotic. The relative attention and support of the self-taught Pippin at the expense of academically trained black artists reflects this establishmentarianism abuse. This situation is captured by Richard J. Powell in his pioneering book *Homecoming: The Art and Life of William H. Johnson,* when he discusses the response of Alain Locke and a local critic to Johnson's new "primitive" works in the summer of 1940 at the Exhibition of the Art of the American Negro (1851–1940) for the American Negro Exposition in Chicago:

> For both the reviewer in Chicago and Alain Locke, Johnson's flirtation with images and forms that suggested naiveté was symptomatic of the art world's then-current fascination with self-trained "daubers," "scribblers," and "whittlers," whose creative lives had been spent (for the most part) outside of the art world proper. One of the most celebrated of these folk artists, black American painter Horace Pippin, worked in a somewhat similar manner to Johnson, with oil paints applied in a thick, impasto consistency, and visual narratives punctuated by strong, solid areas of pure color. Schooled and dedicated artists like Johnson must have felt a little envious of these self-taught painters such as Pippin who, in only a few years, had several museum and gallery exhibitions to their credit.
>
> As Johnson's past comments about primitivism and folk culture demonstrate, he acknowledged the innate power and spirituality that emanated from the art of common people and had decided to allow that part of his own folk heritage to assert itself in his work. Although no less eager to have his own work seen and appreciated, Johnson no doubt accepted the broad appeal of those folk artists then deservedly enjoying the art world's spotlight.[5]

This institutional dilemma regarding the dominant white reception of Pippin's work raises crucial issues about the trials and tribulations of being a black artist in America. In Pippin's case, being a self-taught black artist in America in the Emersonian tradition complicates the matter. On the one hand, a professional envy among highly trained black (and white) artists is understandable, given the limited slots of visibility—and given the history of racist exclusion of black artists in the art world. On the other hand, the absence of professional training does not mean that there is no quality in Pippin's art. Even Alain Locke, the elitist dean of African American art in mid-century America, described Pippin as "a real and rare genius, combining folk quality with artistic maturity so uniquely as almost to defy classification."[6] Yet the relation of the politics of artistic visibility to the quality of visible artworks requires critical scrutiny. As James Clifford rightly notes, "The fact that rather abruptly, in the space of a few decades, a large class of non-Western artifacts came to be redefined as art is a taxonomic shift that requires critical historical discussion, not celebration."[7] Clifford does not have Pippin's work in mind here—especially since Pippin's art was recognized as such, as seen in the inclusion of four of his works in a Museum of Modern Art exhibit called Masters of Popular Painting in 1938.[8] But Pippin's works can easily be tarred with the brush of "primitivism," even "exoticism," highlighting his lack of schooling and his subject matter, rather than the quality of his art.

In her discussion of the Primitivism show at the Museum of Modern Art in 1984, Michele Wallace shows how these issues surrounding the reception of Pippin's work remain alive in our time:

> Black criticism was blocked from the discussions of Modernism, which are defined as exclusively white by an intricate and insidious cooperation of art galleries, museums and academic art history, and also blocked from any discussion of "primitivism," which has been colonized beyond recognition in the space of the international and now global museum. At this juncture one is compelled to ask, "Is multiculturalism, as it is being institutionally defined, occupying the same space as 'primitivism' in relationship to Post-modernism?" For me, a response to such a question would need to include a careful scrutiny of the history of black popular culture and race relations, and account for the sexualization of both, thus defining the perimeters of a new knowledge which I can only name, at this point, as the problem of the visual in Afro-American culture.[9]

Is a black artist like Pippin caught in a catch-22 dilemma—unjustly excluded owing to his blackness *qua* "inferior" (artist) or suspiciously included due to his blackness *qua* "primitive" (artist)? Is this especially so for those black artists in the Emersonian tradition, such as Sterling Brown in poetry or Bessie Smith in music? These questions get at the heart of what it is to be a black artist in America.

To be a black artist in America is to be caught in what I have called elsewhere "the modern black diasporan problematic of invisibility and namelessness."[10] This problematic requires that black people search for validation and recognition in a culture in which white-supremacist assaults on black intelligence, ability, beauty and character circumscribe such a search. Pippin's example is instructive in that, unlike the other two celebrated mid-century black artists in this country—Richmond Barthé and Jacob Lawrence—Pippin lived and functioned outside the cosmopolitan art world. Like the early blues and jazz artists in American music, Pippin's art remained rooted in black folk culture, yet also appealed to the culture industry of his day. He indeed gained significant validation and recognition from the white art establishment—but at what personal and artistic cost? Do all American artists in our market culture bear similar costs?

Unlike William H. Johnson and Beauford Delaney, Pippin did not go mad. But his wife did spend her last months in a mental institution after a breakdown. Pippin did drink heavily—yet we do not know whether this was related directly to his art career. So in regard to the personal costs, our answer remains open-ended.

The artistic cost paid by Pippin is best summed up in this brief characterization of his career by a leading art historian in 1956:

> Horace Pippin (1888–1946), an unschooled Negro of West Chester, Pennsylvania, unfitted for labor by a war wound, turned to painting. "Pictures just come to my mind," he explained, "and I tell my head to go ahead," an explanation of his innocent art which needs no further comment. His discovery and exploitation as a painter in 1937 did not change his art, although it was too much for him as a human being.[11]

This view of Pippin as an "innocent autodidact" chimes well with the image of the black artist lacking sophistication and subtlety. We cannot deny the poignant simplicity of Pippin's art—yet simplicity is neither simplistic nor sophomoric. Rather, Pippin's burden of being a black artist in America required that he do battle with either primitivist designations or inferiority claims about his art. This struggle is best seen in the words of one of Pippin's black artistic contemporaries, William H. Johnson, quoted by the distinguished abstract sculptor of African descent, Martin Puryear: "I myself feel like a primitive man—like one who is at the same time both a primitive and a cultured painter."[12]

This sense of feeling like a primitive and modern person-artist is one form of the black mode of being in a white-supremacist world—a world in which W. E. B. Du Bois claimed that the black person and artist is

> born with a veil, and gifted with second-sight in this American world,—a world which yields him no true self-consciousness, but only lets him see himself through the revelation of the other world. It is a peculiar sensation, this double-consciousness, this sense always looking at one's self through the eyes of others, of measuring one's soul by the tape of a world that looks on in amused contempt and pity. One ever feels his twoness,—an American, a Negro; two souls, two thoughts, two unreconciled strivings; two warring ideals in one dark body, whose dogged strength alone keeps it from being torn asunder.
>
> The history of the American Negro is the history of this strife—this longing to attain self-conscious manhood, to merge his double self into a better and truer self. In this merging he wishes neither of the older selves to be lost. He would not Africanize America, for America has too much to teach the world and Africa. He would not bleach his Negro soul in a flood of white Americanism, for he knows that Negro blood has a message for the world. He simply wishes to make it possible for a man to be both a Negro and an American, without being cursed and spit upon by his fellows, without having the doors of Opportunity closed roughly in his face.[13]

This classic characterization of being black in xenophobic America means that black artists are always suspect for not measuring up to rigorous standards or made to feel exotic in a white world that often associates blackness with bodily energy, visceral vitality and sexual vibrancy. Pippin's art is a powerful expression of black spiritual strivings to attain self-conscious humanhood—to believe truly one is fully human and to believe truly that whites can accept one's black humanity. This utopian endeavor indeed is crippled by black self-hatred and white contempt, yet the underlying fire that sustains it is not extinguished by them. Rather, this fire is fueled by the dogged fortitude of ordinary black folk who decide that if they cannot be truly free, they can, at least, be fully themselves. Pippin's art portrays black people as "fully themselves"—that is, as they are outside of the white normative gaze that requires elaborate masks and intricate posturing for black survival and sanity. This does not mean that behind the masks one finds the "real faces" of black folk or that beneath the posturing one sees the "true gestures" of black bodies. Instead, Pippin's art suggests that black people within the white normative gaze wear certain kinds of masks and enact particular kinds of postures, and outside the white normative gaze wear other kinds of masks and enact different sorts of postures. In short, black people tend to behave differently when they are "outside the white world"—though how they behave within black spaces is shaped by their battles with self-hatred and white contempt.

As I noted earlier, Pippin's art reminds one of Sterling Brown's poetry or Bessie Smith's music, in that all three artists reject the two dominant models of black art in the *white* world at the time: black art as expressive of the "new Negro" and black art as protest. Instead, they build on the major paradigm of black art in the *black* world: black art as healing, soothing yet humorously unsettling illuminations of what it means to be human in black skin in America.

Pippin's work appears a decade or so after the celebrated Harlem Renaissance. This fascinating moment in black culture remains a highly contested one in regard to what it was and what it means. A renaissance is a rebirth by means of recovering a classical heritage heretofore overlooked or ignored. Do the works of the major artists of the Harlem Renaissance—Countee Cullen, Claude McKay, Nella Larsen, Jessie Fauset, Rudolf Fisher, Wallace Thurman, early Aaron Douglas and others—engage in such a recovery? I think not. Instead of serious and substantive attempts to recover the culturally hybrid heritage of black folk, we witnessed the cantankerous reportage of a black, middle-class identity crisis. The Harlem Renaissance was not so much a genuine renaissance, but rather a yearning for a renaissance aborted by its major artists owing to a conscious distance from the very cultural creativity they desired. In this sense, the Harlem Renaissance was a self-complimentary construct concocted by rising black middle-class artistic figures to gain attention for their own anxieties at the expense of their individual and social identities, and to acquire authority to impose their conceptions of legitimate forms of black cultural productions on black America.

The dominant theme of romanticizing the "primitivism" of poor black folk and showing how such "primitivism" fundamentally affects the plights and predicaments of refined and educated black middle-class individuals (Claude McKay's best-seller *Home to Harlem* is paradigmatic here) looms large in the Harlem Renaissance. This theme fits in well with the crisis in European and American civilization after World War I. The war was the end of an epoch—an epoch regulated by nineteenth-century illusions of inevitable progress and perennial stability for emerging industrial societies. With the shattering of European self-confidence—as history is viewed no longer as a train for smooth amelioration, but rather as Joyce's "nightmare" or Eliot's "immense panorama of futility and anarchy"—appetites for "primitivism" were whetted. With the rise of non-Western nations—Japan's victory over Russia (1905), revolutions in Persia (1905), Turkey (1907), Mexico (1911), China (1912)—ferocious nationalisms appealed to machismo-driven myths of virility and vitality as Woodrow Wilson's Fourteen Points squared off against Lenin's doctrine of national self-determination. The economic boom in the United States, facilitated by economic expansionism abroad (especially the takeover of Latin American markets from Britain after the war) and protectionism at home, ushered in mass communications (radio, phonograph and talking film) and mass culture for the middle classes—a mass culture already saturated with black cultural products. The great talents of George Gershwin, Jerome Kern, Benny Goodman and Paul Whiteman rest in large part on the undeniable genius of Louis Armstrong, Duke Ellington, Bessie Smith and Ma Rainey. Lastly, the great migration of black people from the Jim and Jane Crow South to the industrial urban centers of the North produced not only social dislocation, cultural disorientation and personal disillusionment; it also contributed to the makings of a massive political movement (Marcus Garvey's Universal Negro Improvement Association) and the refinement of the great black cultural renaissance actually taking place far removed from most of the Harlem Renaissance artists and critics—the evolution of jazz in New Orleans, St. Louis, Memphis and Chicago.

Like its European counterpart in France (the Negritude movement led by Léopold Senghor), the Harlem Renaissance conceived of black art as the refined expressions of the new Negro. In the exemplary text of the Harlem Renaissance, *The New Negro* (1925)—"its bible," as rightly noted by Arnold Rampersad[14]—black art is conceived to be the imposition of form on the rich substance of black folk culture. Influenced by the high modernisms of Europe and suspicious of art forms already operative in black folk culture (e.g. blues, dance, sermon, sports—none of which are examined in *The New Negro*) Locke states: "There is ample evidence of a New Negro in the latest phases of social change and progress, but still more in the internal world of the Negro mind and spirit. Here in the very heart of the folk-spirit are the essential forces, and folk interpretation is truly vital and representative only in terms of these."[15] These "essential forces" of the folk, primitive, raw, coarse, and unrefined, require the skills of cultivated and educated artists to disclose black life to the world.

In the only essay on jazz in *The New Negro,* J. A. Rogers's "Jazz at Home," this Lockean aesthetic attitude is amplified:

> Yet in spite of its present vices and vulgarizations, its sex informalities, its morally anarchic spirit, jazz has a popular mission to perform. Joy after all, has a physical basis. . . . Moreover, jazz with its mocking disregard for formality is a leveller and makes for democracy. The jazz spirit, being primitive, demands more frankness and sincerity. . . . And so this new spirit of joy and spontaneity may itself play the role of reformer. Where at present it vulgarizes, with more wholesome growth in the future, it may on the contrary truly democratize. At all events, jazz is rejuvenation, a recharging of the batteries of civilization with primitive new vigor. It has come to stay, and they are wise, who instead of protesting against it, try to lift and divert it into nobler channels.[16]

For Rogers, jazz is not a distinct art form with its own integrity and cultivated artists. Instead it is a primitive energy in search of political funnels that will expand American democracy. In fact, he claims that jazz is popular because, after the horrors of the war, "in its fresh joyousness men found a temporary forgetfulness, infinitely less harmful than drugs or alcohol."[17] Locke would not go this far in his therapeutic view of folk culture and his modernist conception of art—yet Locke and Rogers agree that popular culture is not a place where art resides, but rather provides raw material for sophisticated artists (with university pedigrees and usually white patrons) to create expressions of the "New Negro."

Pippin's Emersonian sensibility rejects this highly influential view of black art—a view that shaped the crucial activities of the Harmon Foundation.[18] And although Locke recognized Pippin's genius in 1947, it is doubtful whether he would have in 1925.[19] Like Sterling Brown or Bessie Smith, Pippin is less concerned about expressing the sense of being a "New Negro" and more focused on artistic rendering of the extraordinariness of ordinary black folk then and now. The "New Negro" still seems too preoccupied with how black folk appear to the white normative gaze, too obsessed with showing white people how sophisticated they are, how worthy of white validation and recognition. For Pippin, such validation and recognition is fine, yet only if it does not lead him to violate the integrity of his art or blind him to the rich experiences of ordinary black folk while trying to peddle "the black experience" to white America.

The next dominant conception of black art as protest emerged after the collapse of the Harlem Renaissance, principally owing to the depression. The great black literary artwork of protest was Richard Wright's *Native Son* (1940). This conception of black art displaced the sophisticated and cultivated New Negro with the outraged and angry Mad Negro. Gone were the attempts to distance oneself from the uncouth, "primitive" black masses. In place of the sentimental journeys behind the veil to see how black folk live and are, we got the pervasive physical and psychic violence of black life turned outward to white America.

The irony of the view of black art as protest—as description of the inhumane circumstances of much of black life and as heartfelt resistance to these circumstances—is that it is still preoccupied with the white normative gaze, and it reduces black people to mere reactors to white power. Pippin's *Mr. Prejudice* (1942) contains protest elements, yet it refuses to view the multilayered character of black life as a reaction to the sick dictates of xenophobic America. Pippin's Emersonian orientation refuses to cast art as a primary agent for social change or a central medium for protest—even when he shares the values of those seeking such change or promoting such protest. This kind of redemptive culturalism—the notion that culture can yield political redemption—flies in the face of Pippin's view of black art as those ritualistic activities that heal and soothe, generate laughter and unsettle dogmas with such style and form that they constitute black ways of being human. To pursue such a conception of black art in a white world obsessed with black incapacities and atavistic proclivities means to run the risk of falling into the traps of "primitivism."

Nearly fifty years after his death, Pippin's art still reminds us of how far we have *not* come in creating new languages and frameworks that do justice to his work, account for his narrow receptions and stay attuned to the risks he took and the costs he paid. The Horace Pippin exhibition (January 1994) courageously and meticulously mounted by the Pennsylvania Academy of Fine Arts once again puts American art criticism on trial—not for its verdict on Horace Pippin, but for how our understandings of Pippin's art force us to reconceive and reform the art world as it now exists.

SOURCE: From *Keeping Faith: Philosophy and Race in America,* by Cornel West, pp. 55–66, 295–296. Copyright © 1993. Reproduced by permission of Routledge, Inc. Originally appeared in *I Tell My Heart: The Art of Horace Pippin* (Universe Publishing, 1993); copyright © Pennsylvania Academy of the Fine Arts, Philadelphia, 1993.

Thirty Seven

RACE AND ARCHITECTURE

I spent more time on this essay than on any other piece in this volume—I worked on it for over five years. I delivered earlier versions in architecture departments at Harvard, Princeton, UCLA, Montreal and Chicago and incorporated critical responses to it. My friends Darell Fields, Kevin Fuller and Milton Curry at Appendix, *the only journal of black architectural theory, encouraged me to think about the connection between power/authority and architecture. I believe I make crucial connections between black bodies and European edifices in this piece, yet I have not been able to pursue this subject further. This essay was sheer fun to write.*

THERE IS A NEW energy and excitement among the younger generation of architectural critics. Theory is now fashionable, and interdisciplinary studies an absolute necessity. The next decade promises to be a period of intellectual ferment in precincts once staid and serene.

Architecture—the "chained and fettered art"[1]—is the last discipline in the humanities to be affected by the crisis of the professional and managerial strata in American society. This crisis is threefold—that of political legitimacy, intellectual orientation and social identity. Like their counterparts in critical legal studies in law schools, feminists, poststructuralists and Marxists in universities and liberation theologians in seminaries, oppositional architectural critics are turning to the works of Antonio Gramsci, Raymond Williams, Stuart Hall, Michel Foucault, Edward Said, Sheila Rowbotham and other cultural critics to respond to this crisis. And though we are in the embryonic stage of this response, intense interrogations of architectural practices will deepen.

The political legitimacy of architecture is not a question of whether and why buildings should be made. Rather, it has to do with how authority warrants or does not warrant the way in which buildings are made. Architecture—viewed as both rigorous discipline (science) and poetic buildings (art)—is often distinguished from other arts by its direct dependence on social patronage and its obligation to stay in tune with the recent developments in technology.[2] Yet architectural critics are reluctant to engage in serious analyses of the complex relations between corporate firms, the state and architectural practices. The major fear is that of falling into the trap of economic determinism—of reducing the grandeur of precious architecture to the grub of pecuniary avidity. And surely the forms, techniques and styles of architecture are not reducible to the needs and interests of public or private patrons. But this deadly reductionist trap should not discourage architectural critics from pursuing more refined investigations into how economic and political power help shape how buildings are made—and not simply how they come to be. Needless to say, Manfredo Tafuri's *Architecture and Utopia: Design and Capitalist Development* (1973) is a move in this direction, yet even this work stays a bit too far removed from the ground where detailed historical work should focus.

A plausible objection to this line of reasoning is that architectural critics do not have the historical and analytical training to do such analyses. So it is better to leave this work to be done by cultural historians and even economists. This objection leads us to the crucial issue of the political legitimacy of architectural critics—namely, why are they trained as they are, how are they reproduced, and what set of assumptions about history, economics, culture and art inform the curriculum and faculties that educate them? Gone are the days of Montgomery Schuyler, George Shepperd Chappell and the great Lewis Mumford. The professionalization of architectural criticism—which has its own traps of insular jargon, codes and etiquette for the initiated—requires genealogies of the changing frameworks and paradigms that become dominant at particular historical moments and of how these frameworks and paradigms yield insights and blindnesses for those who work within them. These genealogies should highlight not simply the dynamic changes of influential critical perspectives in the academy, but also how these perspectives shape and are shaped by the actual building of edifices and how these perspectives relate to other significant cultural practices, for instance, painting in Le Corbusier's early work and populism in Venturi's thought. What Aaron Betsky calls "the trivialization of the architectural profession" and James Wines dubs its "failure of vision"[3] must be unpacked by means of structural and institutional analyses of what goes into molding architects and their critics.

In this way, the issue of the political legitimacy of architecture is posed neither in a nostalgic, moralistic manner that translates the will of an epoch into space, nor in a sophomoric, nihilistic mode that promotes an easy and lucrative despair. Rather, the challenge is to try to understand architectural practices as power-laden cultural practices that are deeply affected by larger historical forces, for instance, markets, the state, the academy, but also as practices that have their own specificity and social effects—even if they are not the kind of effects one approves of. This is why the kind of Miesian nostalgia of Roger Kimball will not suffice.[4]

The political legitimacy of architecture is linked to an even deeper issue: the intellectual crisis in architectural criticism. The half-century predominance of the international styles in architecture left critics with little room to maneuver. Robert Venturi's groundbreaking *Complexity and Contradiction* (1966)—with its empirical, relativistic and anti-Platonic approach—created new space for critics. Yet its treatment of the semantic dimension of architecture remained wedded to the Olympian Platonism of the great modernists; that is, his truncated perspective covered only the conventional styles and "extrinsic" factors such as poor design. As Alan Colquhoun perceptively notes, "The book does not exclude the possibility that the general principles of the modern movement were sound and might still form the basis of a complex and subtle architecture."[5] Yet Venturi indeed opened Pandora's box. Architectural criticism has been a Towel of Babel ever since.

The intellectual crisis in architectural criticism is primarily rooted in the modernist promotion of what Lewis Mumford called "the myth of the machine." This myth is not simply an isolated aesthetic ideology, but rather a pervasive sociocultural phenomenon that promotes expert scientific knowledge and elaborate bureaucratic structures that facilitate five P's—power, productivity for profit, political control and publicity.[6] Architecture is distinct from the other arts in that it associated its own modernist avant-garde movements—its formalism and newness—with the myth of the machine. For Colquhoun, "Modern architecture conflated absolute formalism with the actual productive forces of society. There was in Modern architecture an overlap between nineteenth-century instrumentalism and modernist formalism which did not occur in any of the other arts."[7]

This is why modernism in architecture enthusiastically embraced technology in an excessive utopian manner, whereas modernism in literature put a premium on myth (over against science and technology) in a dystopian way. Le Corbusier—with his complex bundle of tensions between architecture as machine production and architecture as intuitive expression—proclaimed in his epoch-making manifesto *Towards a New Architecture* (1923): "The Modern age is spread before them [engineers and others], sparkling and radiant."[8] Yet James Joyce's Stephen in *Ulysses* (1922) sees history as a nightmare from which he is trying to awake and T. S. Eliot perceives, in his review of Joyce's text, modern history as an "immense panorama of futility and anarchy."

My point here is not simply that the early Le Corbusier and fellow Modernists in architecture were naive and duped, but, more important, that the distinctive development of architecture produced such an idealizing of technology and industry. The subsequent collapse of this utopianism into a sheer productivism with a Platonic formalism that sustains an architectural monumentality (as in the genius of Ludwig Mies van der Rohe, transplanted from Germany to Chicago) set the framework of our present intellectual crisis in architectural criticism.[9] Needless to say, the call for irony and ambiguity that focuses on the symbolic content (not space or structure) in the populism of Robert Venturi, the forms of historical eclecticism in the postmodernism of Charles Jencks, or the plea for communication in the public art of James Wines's de-architecture provide inadequate responses to this crisis.[10] This is primarily because all three provocative responses fail to grasp on a deep level the content and character of the larger cultural crisis of our time.

The recent appropriations of the ironic skepticism of Jacques Derrida (as in the provocative writings of Peter Eisenman) and the genealogical materialism of Michel Foucault (as with the criticism of Anthony Vidler and Michael Hayes) can be viewed as the awakening of architectural criticism to the depths of our cultural crisis. Although deconstructivist architecture is, as Mark Wrigley rightly observes, more an extension of and deviation from Russian constructivism than a blanket architectural application of Derrida's thought,[11] it does force architectural critics to put forward their own conception of the current cultural crisis—even if it seems to amount to mere sloganeering about "the end of Western metaphysics" or the omnipresence of "the disciplinary order." In short, the French invasion of architectural criticism—twenty years after a similar affair in literary criticism—has injected new energy and excitement into a discipline suffering a cultural lag. Yet this invasion has led many architectural critics to the most deadly of traps: *the loss of identity as architectural critics.*

The assimilation of architectural criticism into literary criticism or the immersion of architectural objects into larger cultural practices has led, in many cases, to a loss of the specificity of architectural practices and objects. Such a loss results in the loss of the *architectural* dimension of what architectural critics do. The major virtue of the French invasion is that new possibilities, heretofore foreclosed, are unleashed; the vice is that architectural critics lose their identity and focus primarily on academicist perspectives on the larger crisis of our culture—a focus that requires a deeper knowledge of history, economics, sociology and so on than most architectural critics have or care to pursue. My point here is not that this task should be abandoned by architectural critics. Rather, I am claiming that what architectural critics do know—the specificity of the diverse traditions of architectural practices (from the nitty-gritty matters of calculations to artistic styles, perspectives, visions and links to structures of power)—should inform how we understand the present cultural crisis.

None of us have the definitive understanding of the complex cultural crisis that confronts us, though some views are better than others. My own view is that an appropriate starting point is a reexamination of what the modernists valorized: the myth of the machine. Hence, the work of Lewis Mumford is indispensable. Yet, since faith in progress by means of expanding productive forces—be it the liberal or Marxist version—is a secular illusion, the myth of the machine must be questioned in new ways. This questioning must go far beyond a playful explosion of modernist formalism that heralds ornamentation and decoration of past heroic efforts. It also must be more than a defense of the autonomy of architectural discourse in the guise of its textualization—an outdated, avant-gardist gesture in a culture that now thrives and survives on such fashionable and faddish gestures.

Rather, the demystifying of the machine can proceed—thanks, in part, to the insights of poststructuralist analyses—by examining the second term in the binary opposition of machine-nature, civilized-primitive, ruler-ruled, Apollonian-Dionysian, male-female, white-black in relation to architectural practices. This examination should neither be a mechanical deconstructive operation that stays on the discursive surfaces at the expense of an analysis of structural and institutional dynamics of power, nor should it result in a mere turning of the tables that trashes the first terms in the binary oppositions. Rather, what is required is a sophisticated, architectural-historical inquiry into how these notions operate in the complex formulations of diverse and developing discourses and practices of actual architects and critics. Such an inquiry presupposes precisely what contemporary architectural criticism shuns: *a distinctive architectural historiography that sheds light on the emergence and development of the current cultural crisis as it shapes and is shaped by architectural practices.* As Mark Jarzombek rightly states:

> Architects have read too many history books and have not done enough on-location history of their own. It used to be, from the Renaissance on, that architects told the historians what was important about a building of the past and what was not. Now it is historians who tell architects. That architects so willingly give up their birthright marks, perhaps, the dawning of a new age in architectural history. The Pre-modern Post-modern used the past to create a historiographic understanding of the present. Once the ancient ruins had all been studied and the archaeologists took over, the modernists were free to turn the same historiographic principles used by earlier generations against history itself. The post-modern historicists now use history to kill historiography. There may not be much left to talk about when the next generation of architects comes along.[12]

These remarks hold from the Adorno-informed pessimism of Tafuri through the presentist populism of Venturi to the "classical" postmodernism of Jencks.

The major challenge of a new architectural historiography is that its conception of the "past" and "present" be attuned to the complex role of difference—nature, primitive, ruled, Dionysian, female, black and so on. In this sense, the recent talk about the end of architecture, the exhaustion of the architectural tradition, the loss of architecture as a social force and so on is a parochial and nostalgic talk about a particular consensus—and its circumstances—that indeed no longer exists. This consensus rests upon certain governing myths (machine), narratives (Eurocentric ones), design strategies (urban building efforts) and styles (phallocentric monuments) that no longer aesthetically convince or effectively function for us. This "us" is a diverse and heterogeneous one—not just architects and their critics.

The case of the great Le Corbusier may serve as an illustration. His serious grappling with the binary oppositions above reaches a saturation point in his critique of the classical theory of architectural design (Vitruvius) in the form of the Modulor. This new form of measure derived not just from the proportions of the human figure but, more specifically, from women's bodies—especially fat, "primitive," "uncivilized," non-European, Dionysian-driven, black, brown and red women's bodies. It is no secret that Le Corbusier's paintings and pencil sketches in the early 1930s began to focus on the shapes of women's bodies, highlighting the curves of buttocks and shoulder arches. This preoccupation is often viewed as a slow shift from a machine aesthetic to a nature aesthetic. Like Picasso's use of "primitive" art to revitalize the art of the new epoch, Le Corbusier turns toward female and Third World sources for demystifying—not simply displacing—the myth of the machine he had earlier heralded. Le Corbusier's move toward these sources was not a simple rejection of the myth of the machine. As Charles Jencks notes: "Le Corbusier found in Negro music, in the hot jazz of Louis Armstrong, 'implacable exactitude,' 'mathematics, equilibrium on a tightrope' and all the masculine virtues of the machine."[13] And in regard to Josephine Baker's performance on board the *Julius Caesar* on a trip to South America in 1929, Le Corbusier writes:

> In a stupid variety show, Josephine Baker sang "Baby" with such an intense and dramatic sensibility that I was moved to tears. There is in this American Negro music a lyrical "contemporary" mass so invincible that I could see the foundation of a new sentiment of music capable of being the expression of the new epoch and also capable of classifying its European origins as stone age—just as has happened with the new architecture.[14]

Although Baker is, for Le Corbusier, "a small child pure, simple and limpid," more than mere European male paternalism is at work here. Rather, he also is in search of new forms of space, proportion, structure and order in light of the products, bodies and sensibilities of those subsumed under the second terms of the aforementioned binary oppositions—natural, primitive, ruled, Dionysian, female and people of color. "I look for primitive men not for their barbarity but for their wisdom."[15] "The columns of a building should be like the strong curvaceous thighs of a woman."[16] "I like the skin of women."[17]

Le Corbusier's Ronchamp chapel in eastern France, the Unité at Marseille and his Carpenter Center at Harvard all bear this so-called brutalist stamp. Like Mumford's subtle nostalgia for the medieval "Garden Village," Le Corbusier's search for non-European and female sources was intimately linked to his conception of architectural practices as forms of and means for collective life—a life he associated first and foremost with hierarchical religious communities such as the monastic order of the Carthusians.

The efforts of Le Corbusier's "middle" period can be neither imitated nor emulated. Yet his gallant yet flawed attempt to come to terms with difference—with those constituted as Other—must inform any new architectural historiography in our postcolonial world and postmodern culture of megamachines, multinational corporations, nation-states and fragmented communities. Where then do we go from here?

The future of architectural criticism rests on the development of a refined and revisionist architectural historiography that creatively fuses social histories of architectural practices and social histories of technology in light of sophisticated interpretations of the present cultural crisis. This historiography must be informed by the current theoretical debates in the larger discourse of cultural criticism. Yet the benefits of these debates are in the enabling methodological insights that facilitate history writing and cultural analyses of specific past and present architectural practices, not ontological and epistemological conclusions that promote mere avant-gardist posturing. Theory is not historiography, though no historiography escapes theory. Yet the present obsession with theory must now yield to theory-laden historiography if architectural criticism is to have any chance of grasping the impasse that now engulfs us. There are no guarantees for any resolutions, but there are certain routes that weaken our efforts to move beyond this fascinating, and possibly fecund, moment in architectural criticism.[18]

Thirty Eight

THE SPIRITUALS AS LYRICAL POETRY

In this piece written for my friend and brother Richard Newman's Go Down, Moses *(1998), I examine the tragic elements of exemplary spirituals in light of two lyrical giants of European poetry—Russia's Fyodor Tyutchev and Italy's Giacomo Leopardi. Both Tyutchev and Leopardi—from the margins of Western Europe—add new existential darkness and historical substance to the lyrical genre in poetry. The spirituals also do so as poetry and music.*

THE AFRICAN AMERICAN SPIRITUAL is the unique cultural creation of New World modernity. As the distinguished historian Richard Newman (my friend and brother) rightly notes, the spirituals of American slaves of African descent constitute the first expression of American modern music. How ironic that a people on the dark side of modernity—dishonored, devalued and dehumanized by the practices of modern Europeans and Americans—created the fundamental music of American modernity. Yet we still wonder and wrestle with what it is that makes these songs so *modern*—so powerful and poignant, so upsetting and unsettling, so soothing and comforting—to us late moderns.

As I grow older, I find it more and more difficult to read the heart-piercing lyrics of the spirituals. They not only invoke precious memories of beloved family and friends in those soul-stirring moments of my black church life; these songs also remind me of how difficult it is to engage in a deep-sea diving of the soul—a diving that may yield, if one is strong enough, bloodshot eyes and a tear-stained hope. When the slaves sang "Go Down, Moses," they put forward a political message of freedom and a hope for endurance in the face of death and despair *after* one arrives in the penultimate promised land of these United States. In short, the spirituals challenge any Enlightenment notion of human autonomy. They force us to confront the paradox of human freedom: We must be strong enough to resist the prevailing forms of bondage, yet honest enough to acknowledge our weaknesses in the face of death and disappointment. This honesty about our weakness is itself a supreme form of strength that precludes paralysis and impotence.

Even more than the incredible blues and jazz of black people, the spirituals enact the initial "soul-making" of New World Africans. I deliberately use the Keatsian term here because the spirituals embody the creativity of courageous human beings who engaged the world of pain and trouble with faith, hope, spirit—and a kind of existential freedom even in slavery. The great W. E. B. Du Bois was the first public intellectual to grasp the significance of this complex "soul-making" of a people. In the last chapter of his classic *The Souls of Black Folk* (1903), Du Bois probed the character of "the sorrow songs." He found a depth of articulate anguish unbeknownst in early American history. He also discovered a level of questioning about the nature of suffering that was alien to American culture. Du Bois was on the right track. The spirituals not only reveal the underside of America—in all of its stark nakedness; they also disclose the night side of the human condition—in all of its terror and horror. But they do so through an unequivocal Christian lens. So we often leap to the religious consolation of the spirituals without lingering for long on sadness and melancholia.

The African American spirituals constitute the most sustained phenomenology of New World evil. In stark contrast to most artists and intellectuals of European descent, the illiterate, articulate slaves were obsessed with the problem of evil as it pertained to the most undeniable darkness of America—slavery. And though their resources were primarily religious, their existential insights go far beyond Christian dogma and doctrine.

Like Shakespeare's *Hamlet,* the spirituals are preoccupied with the memory of those beloved ones who have died and the desire for revenge against those who prosper from their evildoings. The major themes consist of mourning, suffering, resisting. Yet unlike Hamlet, who after much soul-searching commits murder, the heroes of the spirituals—namely, Jesus, Daniel, and Moses—triumph because they find great strength in an all-embracing love and mercy.

The spirituals have perplexed critics primarily because of this uncanny tension between a profound pagan sense of the tragic and a deep Christian sense of justice. Ironically, both understandings assume the intractability of white supremacy in American life—be it slavery, Jim Crow, or postmodern cultural put-down—and view the preservation of the human soul under such dishonored conditions as the major challenge. Emerson was concerned with developing the human character through self-reliance within an American context of numbing conformity; the spirituals, on the other hand, focus on forging human integrity through self-respect within an American context of white hatred and fear of black folk.

I find it useful to compare the spirituals—the grand lyrical expressions at the initial moments of American self-definition—with the great lyrical poets of marginalized European peoples. In fact, two of the greatest lyrical poets of modern Europe—Fyodor Tyutchev of Russia and Giacomo Leopardi of Italy—have fascinating elective affinities with the spirituals. Both are rooted in Christian soils—Russian Orthodoxy and Roman Catholicism—yet sprout their poetic wings far above it. Both are distrustful of European arrogance and Enlightenment illusions and are obsessed with the night side of Western civilization. In regard to form, both deploy a kind of rhythmic repetition that plays with linguistic pacing, revealing an obsession with human time. This obsession often yields a privileging of silence by means of poetry, a call for music and song that goes beyond mere language.

The slaves' own self-conscious grasp of their inability to capture in language the depths of "Deep River" resonates with the spirit of Tyutchev's classic "Silentium!" (1829).

> *Speak not, lie deep, do not reveal*
> *Things that you wish or things you feel;*
> *Within your soul's protected mine*
> *Let them ascend and then decline*
> *Like silent stars in heaven bleak;*
> *Admire their sheen—but do not speak.*

> *How can a heart be put in words?*
> *By others—how can one be heard?*
> *Will people know what you live by?*
> *A thought expressed becomes a lie.*
> *Don't muddy springs that are unique:*
> *Drink from their depth—but do not speak.*

> *Live only in yourself encased;*
> *Your soul contains a world of chaste,*
> *Mysterious thoughts, which outside noise*
> *Robs of their magic and destroys;*
> *The rays of morning make them weak—*
> *Enjoy their song but do not speak!. . .*

Tyutchev's animation of nature and celebration of the landscape seem to suggest a latent pantheism alien to the spirituals. But Tyutchev neither worships nature nor equates God with it. Like the spirituals, he uses the majesty of God manifest in nature to highlight the misery of humankind. Like his friend and intellectual mentor Friedrich Schelling, all forms of idealism, romanticism or pantheism run headlong into the bedrock, the recalcitrant reality, of evil. Tyutchev's poetry wrestles with the dark questions of Schelling's classic work on theodicy, *On the Essence of Human Freedom* (1809): Does the seeming ineradicability of the non-rational signify the triumph of the absurd? Does the apparent intractability of the unfathomable point to the victory of evil? Are there countervailing forces—divine and human—that offset and overcome "the veil of sadness which is spread over all nature, the deep, unappeasable melancholy of all life"?

These foundation shaking queries rendered Schelling silent for over forty years, pushed some slaves to sing sorrow songs and drove Tyutchev to write in "Our Age" (1851):

> *Not flesh but spirit is depraved today,*
> *And Man feels miserable and tormented . . .*
> *He hates his darkness, tries to break away,*
> *But, once in daylight, riots discontented.*

> *The unendurable he must endure,*
> *From lack of faith as in a desert burning . . .*
> *He perishes . . . but, weak and insecure,*
> *He will not pray for faith, despite his yearning.*

> *He will pronounce, repenting, nevermore*
> *The words, "O Everlasting One! I ask you,*
> *For I believe in Thee, unlock this door*
> *And, in my disbelief, come to my rescue! . . . "*

If Fyodor Tyutchev represents a useful comparison to the religious nature of the spirituals, then Giacomo Leopardi may yield insights into the tragic nature of the spirituals. Haunted by a sense of his own ugliness (he was a disfigured hunchback) and overwhelmed by unrequited love, Leopardi's poetry—like the spirituals—soars to the sky on the wings of incredible grief and unbearable sorrow. He begins his famous "Night Song of a Nomadic Shepherd in Asha" (1830):

> *Moon, moon of silence, what are you doing,*
> *Tell me what you're doing in the sky?*

Later in the poem he writes:

> *A man comes struggling into the world;*
> *His birth is in the shadow of death;*
> *Pain and suffering*
> *Are his first discoveries;*
> *And from that point*
> *His mother and father try*
> *To console him for having been born.*

Leopardi ends the poem with echoes of Sophocles, Job and the slave author of "Am I Born to Die?"

> *Perhaps if I had wings to soar*
> *Over the clouds and count the stars,*
> *Or run like thunder from peak to peak,*
> *I'd be happier, my gentle flock,*
> *I would be happier, radiant moon.*
> *Or maybe I simply miss the truth*
> *In thinking of other lives like this:*
> *Perhaps whatever form it takes*
> *Or wherever it comes to pass—*
> *Lair of beast or baby's cradle—*
> *To that creature being born*
> *Its birth day is a day to mourn.*

Similar to the slave author's lament "Lord, I wish I had never been born," Leopardi pursues this tragic theme in "Sappho's Last Song" (1822):

> *What offence, what loathsome crime marked me*
> *Before I was born, making Heaven and the fall*
> *Of Fortune frown as they did? What sin*
> *Did I commit as a child—when one can know*
> *No wrong at all—that my iron-dark thread of life,*
> *Lacking all the summer colors of youth,*
> *Lay twisted on Fate's implacable spindle? Reckless*
> *Words fly from your mouth: A hidden purpose*
> *Fashions whatever has to happen. Everything is hidden*

Except our pain. We come, a forsaken race,
Crying into the world, and the gods
Keep their own counsel . . .

Leopardi's pagan humanism departs from the Christian sense of providence found in the spirituals. Yet the passionate questioning and desperate seeking of the spirituals reveal, at times, an anger with God. For Leopardi, this anger fueled by unjustified grief yields a spiritual humility in a godless universe, an eternal silence in an infinite space. In "Dream" (1828), he cries:

And random suffering cancels all
Such raw, unripened knowledge.—Hush,
I said, my poor dear, hush . . .

. . . But alas, what is
This thing called death? It seems, if ever,
I should be able this day to say for sure, and so
Guard this helpless self against heartless stars.

For the spirituals, this anger fanned by unmerited misery offers a spiritual humility in a Christian world, an uncanny spirit of combat on a treacherous terrain ruled by a majestic yet mysterious God of love and mercy. Just as the epigraph of Leopardi's masterpiece, "Broom or the Flower of the Desert" (1836), is John 3:19, "And men loved darkness rather than light," so the epigraph of one the greatest spirituals, "Didn't My Lord Deliver Daniel," could be John 3:16, "God so loved the world that He sent His only begotten son . . ." The spirituals knew that humans loved darkness yet they held out for a light of deliverance in a vanquishing and vanishing world. Says Leopardi in "Broom":

Nothing but ruins now left
Where this sweet flower takes root
And, it seems, takes pity
On the suffering of others, filling
The air with fragrance, a touch
Of consolation in the wasteland . . .

For the slaves, God's revelation in Christ is the sole flickering candle against the darkness of American slavery and human finitude. Their social "blackness" (shame) and existential "emptiness" (anxiety) find help only in divine deliverance (Christ). For Leopardi, only empathy and social solidarity can push back the darkness of oppression and death, yet even heroic efforts may be "built on sand." Speaking to both deserted persons and desert flowers, Leopardi concludes his greatest poem:

> *'Til that time comes you won't bow down*
> *Like cowards before the one who'll destroy you,*
> *Seeking your salutation in vain; and you won't*
> *Raise vainglorious heads to the stars*
> *Or up above this wasteland where*
> *By chance and not by choice you have*
> *Your birthplace and your home; and still*
> *You're wiser and that much less weak*
> *Than man, inasmuch as you don't believe*
> *These delicate stems of yours have been,*
> *By yourself or the fatal scheme*
> *Of things, fashioned for immortality.*

The greatest spiritual, "Nobody Knows the Trouble I See, Lord," speaks to dishonored persons whose humanity had been rendered invisible by physical chains and psychic blinders. As in Leopardi, this human condition is one of darkness. The spiritual explicitly asks for prayer—for empathy and social solidarity—"to drive old Satan away." This kind of support, one that constitutes a loving tradition of resistance, yields a joy and even ecstasy because it is undergirded by a Lord who is able to deliver Daniel. "Glory Hallelujah!" Yet prayer for the slaves was much like the songs themselves—an artistic expression that gives form to the cry for help in the midst of great trials and tribulations. Prayers, poetry, spirituals—all are passionate acts of will that honestly express the human need for help and support. The towering literary artist of our own blood-drenched century, Franz Kafka, notes: "Art, like prayer, is a hand outstretched in the darkness, seeking for some touch of grace which will transform it into a hand that bestows gifts."

Is it mere accident that "A Love Supreme" (1964)—the masterpiece of the greatest musical artist of our time and the grand exemplar of twentieth-century black spirituality, John Coltrane—is cast in the form of prayer? The slave authors of the spirituals, Fyodor Tyutchev, Giacomo Leopardi, Franz Kafka and John Coltrane all engaged in a Keatsian "soul-making" in that they courageously confronted the darkness in and of modernity with artistic integrity and genuine spirituality. They did so with, in the words of William James: "Not the conception or the intellectual perception of evil, but the grisly blood-freezing heart-palsying sensation of it close upon one. . . . How irrelevantly remote seem all our usual refined optimisms and intellectual and moral consolations in presence of a need of help like this! Here is the real core of the religious problem: Help! Help!"

The African American spiritual—with its motifs of homelessness, namelessness and hope against hope—is the first modern artistic expression of this human out-cry in the New World.

SOURCE: "Foreword," *Go Down, Moses,* by Richard Newman, pp. 9–17. Foreword copyright © 1998 by Cornel West. Reprinted by permission of Clarkson N. Potter Publishers, a division of Crown Publishers, Inc.

Thirty Nine

IN MEMORY OF MARVIN GAYE

I was a regular columnist and reviewer for Christianity and Crisis *for a few wonderful years. The moment I heard of the great Marvin Gaye's sad death I wrote this piece. Since then I have received letters from teachers of writing exposition saying that they use it in their classes to provoke and challenge their students. Since his death, Marvin Gaye has been immortalized by the hip-hop generation. And rightly so.*

MUCH OF THE SIGNIFICANT truth about the career of the Afro-American singer Marvin Gaye may be obscured by the problems of his later life and the manner of his dying (he was shot to death by his father April 1, 1984, in a tragic, and as yet unexplained, incident).

First and foremost, Gaye was a Christian artist. He was also one of the most gifted performers produced by the Afro-American religious experience. Raised in his father's Pentecostal church, located in the East Capitol projects in Washington, D.C., Gaye was imbued with a deep spiritual sensitivity anchored in a Christ-centered ethic of love. Initially this sensitivity was expressed in his instrumental virtuosity—especially on the organ, piano and drums. Although Gaye sang in the church choir, his vocal talent did not surface until he filled the first-tenor slot of Harvey Fuqua's Moonglows, a smooth-harmony rhythm and blues group. When Gaye's silky and soulful voice caught the attention of Berry Gordy, Jr.—the founder of Motown Recording Company—in a Detroit nightclub in 1961, he was immediately offered a contract. The public career of Marvin Gaye had begun.

Motown was the Jackie Robinson of black popular music: after crossing the color line in its field, it went on to excel and to win the hearts of vast numbers of nonblack Americans. As with other Motown stars—Diana Ross, Lionel Richie and Michael Jackson—Gaye's relationship with Motown enabled his talent to become visible to the world. Unlike these other artists, Gaye's musical and philosophical roots remained in the Afro-American Christian tradition. His first classic recordings were neither adolescent, rhythmic dance records (as with the Supremes and the Jackson Five) nor funky rock renderings (as with Lionel Richie's Commodores). Rather, Gaye's great early achievements—sung with the incomparable Tammi Terrell—were poignant and powerful love songs, written by the team of Nickolas Ashford and Valerie Simpson of White Rock Baptist Church in New

York City. These classics—such as "Your Precious Love," "Ain't Nothing Like the Real Thing," "You're All I Need to Get By" and "Ain't No Mountain High Enough"—were the pivotal songs that directed the Christian religiosity of black church music into the secular spirituality of Afro-American popular music. For the first time in American history, the musical depth of the black church was let loose into the mainstream of American society. And American popular music would never again be the same.

Upon the tragic death of Tammi Terrell, who collapsed in Gaye's arms during a performance in 1967, Gaye went into hiding. Despite his success as a solo performer ("I'll Be Doggone," "Ain't That Peculiar," and "I Heard It Through the Grapevine" all reached the Top Ten), Gaye became reclusive, melancholic and deeply dissatisfied with his music. He would not perform publicly for five years.

"WHAT'S GOING ON"

Yet Gaye's tortuous struggle with the sudden death of Tammi Terrell, his younger brother Frankie's firsthand accounts of atrocities in Vietnam, the escalation of the civil rights movement into black power advocacy, the widespread invasion of drugs among unemployed black youth and the rise of ecological consciousness produced the greatest album in Afro-American popular music: *What's Going On* (1971). This groundbreaking album was not only the first conceived and enacted by the artist (as opposed to studio staffers), but also the first concept album that hung together by means of a set of themes—themes concerned with socio-economic critique and Christian outlook.

Gaye's critique of American society was explicit. "Rockets, moon shots," he wrote in "Inner City Blues," "Spend it on the have-nots." With "radiation underground and in the sky," he saw birds and animals dying in "Mercy, Mercy Me (The Ecology)." Instead of brutality, he asked attention: "Talk to me, so you can see" ("What's Going On"). And in such songs as "Save the Children," "God Is Love" and "Wholly Holy," he explicitly evoked the love ethic of Jesus Christ as the basis for negating and transforming the world: If we learn from the book Jesus left us, we can rock the world, we can "holler love across the nation."

What's Going On was not only the best-selling album in Motown history at the time; it also set standards of Afro-American popular music that remain unequaled. Only Gaye's marvelously gifted pupil, Stevie Wonder, has attempted to exceed such standards by fusing the spiritual richness of Afro-American music, the sense of social engagement and the love ethic of Jesus Christ.

What's Going On was the peak of Gaye's career. He continued to produce popular albums and hits. Yet, principally owing to two painful divorces, Oedipal obsessions, paranoiac fits and suicidal impulses, Gaye became captive to a form of bondage he admonished others to avoid: drugs. His songs still portrayed a longing for transcendence, but instead of the agapic praxis of communities he high-lighted erotic communion—as in his albums *Let's Get It On* (1973) and *I Want You* (1976) and his Grammy Award single "Sexual Healing" (1982).

In his last years, Gaye oscillated between earthly pessimism and eschatological hope: from the notion that nuclear holocaust was imminent to a faith that only Jesus can save us. During his sporadic bouts with suicide, Gaye is reported to have viewed Jesus and sins that would never be forgiven as the primary motivations to live. And, at the height of this turmoil, the last words he wrote for his last album, *Midnight Love* (1982), were "I still love Jesus, all praises to the Heavenly Father." May this troubled musical genius, deeply immersed in the Afro-American religious experience and genuinely sensitive to the harsh realities of American society, rest in peace. And may his artistic Christian witness live forever.

SOURCE: From *Prophetic Fragments* (Grand Rapids, Mich.: Wm. B. Eerdmans Publishing Co., 1988), pp. 174–176. Originally appeared in *Christianity and Crisis*, June 11, 1984.

Forty

ON AFRO-AMERICAN MUSIC: FROM BEBOP TO RAP

This essay has had an amazing life of its own. Originally written for the avant-garde journal Semiotexte *(1982), then extended for the French paper for which I wrote as an American correspondent for four years,* Le Monde Diplomatique *(1983), this piece has been reprinted in numerous collections and anthologies on American music. I thoroughly enjoyed writing it, but it just skimmed the surface of what I wanted to say. With such fine music critics as Peter Guralnick, Stanley Crouch, Nelson George, Armond White, Brian Ward, Michael Eric Dyson, Jon Spencer and others, I have little need to say more.*

THE SALIENT FEATURE OF popular music in First World capitalist and Third World neocolonialist societies is the appropriation and imitation of Afro-American musical forms and styles. The Afro-American spiritual-blues impulse—with its polyphonic, rhythmic effects and antiphonal vocal techniques, kinetic orality and affective physicality—serves as a major source for popular music in the West. This complex phenomenon, the Afro-Americanization of popular music, prevails owing to three basic reasons. First, the rise of the United States as a world power focused international attention more pointedly on native U.S. cultural forms and styles. Second, vast technological innovations in mass media and communications facilitated immediate and massive influence of certain forms and styles upon others. Third, and most important, Afro-American music is first and foremost, though not exclusively or universally, a countercultural practice with deep roots in modes of religious transcendence and political opposition. Therefore it is seductive to rootless and alienated young people disenchanted with existential meaninglessness, disgusted with flaccid bodies and dissatisfied with the status quo.

Afro-American popular music constitutes a crucial dimension of the background practices—the ways of life and struggle—of Afro-American culture. By taking seriously Afro-American popular music, one can dip into the multileveled lifeworlds of black people. As Ralph Ellison has suggested, Afro-Americans have had rhythmic freedom in place of social freedom, linguistic wealth instead of pecuniary wealth. I make no attempt here to come to terms with the complexity of the evolving forms and content of Afro-American popular music. Rather, I simply try to provide a cognitive mapping of the major breaks and ruptures in Afro-American popular music in light of their changing socioeconomic and political contexts from bebop to rap, from Charlie Parker to the Sugarhill Gang.

Our starting point is the grand break with American mainstream music, especially imitated and co-opted Afro-American popular music, by the so-called bebop jazz musicians—Charlie Parker, Theolonius Monk, Dizzy Gillespie and others. Their particular way of Africanizing Afro-American jazz—with the accent on contrasting polyrhythms, the deemphasis of melody and the increased vocalization of the saxophone—was not only a reaction to the white-dominated, melody-obsessed "swing jazz"; it also was a creative musical response to the major shift in sensibilities and moods in Afro-America after World War II. Through their technical facility and musical virtuosity, bebop jazz musicians expressed the heightened tensions, frustrated aspirations and repressed emotions of an aggressive yet apprehensive Afro-America. Unlike the jazz of our day, bebop jazz was a popular music, hummed on the streets, whistled by shoeshine boys and even danced to in the house parties in urban black communities.

Yet the bebop musicians, like Thomas Pynchon in our time, shunned publicity and eschewed visibility. Their radical nonconformist stance—often misunderstood as a repetition of the avant-garde attitude of the *fin de siècle* artists—is reflected in their famous words "We don't care if you listen to our music or not." Their implicit assumption was that, given the roots of their music, black folk could not *not* listen to it and others had to struggle to do so. Yet as the ferment of the short-lived "bebop era" subsided into the "cool" style of the early 1950s, it was clear that bebop had left an indelible stamp on Afro-American popular music. Despite the brief ascendancy of black "cool" artists such as (the early) Miles Davis and John Lewis and white "cool" musicians like Chet Baker and David Brubeck, the Afro-American spiritual-blues impulse (always alive and well in Count Basie's perennial band) surfaced quickly in the sounds of Charles Mingus, Ray Charles and Art Blakey's hard bebop Jazz Messengers, who all paved the way to the era of soul and funk.

Needless to say, most black folk in the 1950s listened weekly to spiritual and gospel music in black churches—sung by young choir members such as Sam Cooke, Curtis Mayfield, Dionne Warwicke, Aretha Franklin, Gladys Knight and Lou Rawls. With increased strata and class differentiation in the ever blackening urban centers throughout the United States, secular attitudes proliferated and financial rewards for nonreligious and nonjazz black popular music escalated. On the one hand, jazz—under the influence of John Coltrane, Miles Davis, Ornette Coleman and others—became more and more a kind of highbrow, "classical" avant-garde music its originators and innovators abhorred. On the other hand, black churches turned their theological guns on "the devil's music" (traditionally pointed at the blues), resulting in more and more marginality for black religious music. So the stage was set for a black popular music that was neither jazz nor gospel: soul music.

Soul music is more than either secularized gospel or funkified jazz. Rather, it is a particular Africanization of Afro-American music with intent to appeal to the black masses, especially geared to the black ritual of attending parties and dances. Soul music is the populist application of bebop's aim: racial self-conscious assertion among black people in light of their rich musical heritage. The two major artists of soul music—James Brown and Aretha Franklin—bridge the major poles in the Afro-American experience by appealing to agrarian and urban black folk, the underclass and working class, religious and secular men and women. Only the black upper middle class of long standing—and most of white America—initially rejected them. Ironically, though unsurprisingly, none of James Brown's and few of Aretha Franklin's gold records were or are played by nonblack-oriented radio stations. Yet their influence, including white appropriations and imitations, flourished.

As the black baby boom catapulted and black entrepreneurial activity in mass communications expanded, it became apparent that a youthful black market could support a black recording industry. In the South, Otis Redding, the great soul singer, had moved far along on this road, yet white power stubbornly resisted. So when in 1958 Berry Gordy, a black industrial worker in one of Detroit's Ford plants, decided to establish Motown, black popular music took a tremendous leap forward. Far ahead of black literary artists and scholars in this regard, major black popular musicians, writers, singers and producers could now work in a production unit owned by and geared toward black people.

Motown was the center of Afro-American popular music in the 1960s and early 1970s—with the phenomenal success of over 75 percent of its records reaching the Top Ten rhythm and blues tune charts in the mid-1960s. The musical genius of Stevie Wonder, Michael Jackson and Lionel Richie; the writing talents of Smokey Robinson, Nicholas Ashford, Valerie Simpson, Norman Whitfield, Barrett Strong, Eddie and Brian Holland, Lamont Dozier and Marvin Gaye; and the captivating performances of the Temptations, the Miracles, the Supremes, the Four Tops, Gladys Knight and the Pips, the Jackson Five and the Commodores set Motown far above any other recording company producing Afro-American popular music.

Motown was the Jackie Robinson of black popular music: It crossed the color line for the first time, then proceeded to excel and thereby win the hearts and souls of vast numbers of nonblack folk. The most successful Motown figures—Diana Ross, Stevie Wonder, Michael Jackson and Lionel Richie—now have secure status in mainstream American popular music. And outside of Motown, the only black singers or groups to achieve such transracial acceptance are Nat King Cole, Louis Armstrong, Johnny Mathis, Dionne Warwicke, Jimi Hendrix, Sly and the Family Stone, Lou Rawls and Earth, Wind and Fire.

Like Jackie Robinson, Motown reflected the then stable, persevering, upwardly mobile working class in Afro-America. At its height, Motown produced smooth, syncopated rhythms, not funky polyrhythms (like James Brown or the Watts 103rd Street Rhythm Band); restrained call-and-response forms, not antinomian antiphonal styles (as with Aretha Franklin or the late Donny Hathaway); and love-centered romantic lyrics, not racially oriented social protest music (like Gil-Scott Heron or Archie Shepp). Yet Motown delicately and wisely remained anchored in the Afro-American spiritual-blues impulse.

There is little doubt that Motown produced some of the great classics in Afro-American and American popular music. The Temptations' "My Girl," "Since I Lost My Baby," "You're My Everything"; the Miracles' "OOO Baby Baby," "Choosey Beggar," "Here I Go Again"; Marvin Gaye and Tammi Terrell's "Your Precious Love," "If This World Were Mine," "Ain't Nothing Like the Real Thing"; Stevie Wonder's "For Once in My Life," "My Cherie Amour," "You Are the Sunshine of My Life"; and Gladys Knight and the Pips' "Neither One of Us" all will stand the test of time.

As Motown became more commercially successful with the larger white American audience, it began to lose ground in Afro-America. On two musical fronts—fast funk and mellow soul—Motown faced a serious challenge. On the first front, Motown had never surpassed James Brown. Yet Motown had produced music for Afro-America to dance—to twist, jerk, boogaloo, philly dog and skate. With the appearance of George Clinton's innovative Funkadelic and Parliament, a new wave of funk appeared: technofunk. Never before had black folk heard such deliberately distorted voice and contrapuntal rhythmic effects filtered through electronic instrumentalities. Building principally on James Brown, the Funkadelic's "I Wanna Know If It's Good to You," "Loose Booty" and "Standing on the Verge of Getting It On" sounded musically revolutionary to the ears of the masses of black folk. Motown quickly moved into technofunk with the Temptations' successful "Cloud Nine," "I Can't Get Next to You" and "Psychedelic Shack," but it was clear that the change of image (and personnel) could not give Motown hegemonic status on fast funk.

On the second front, that of mellow soul, Motown had no peer until the rise—precipitated by the roaring success of the Delfonics—of the Philly Sound at Sigma Sound Studio in Philadelphia. The poignant music and lyrics of Kenneth Gamble and Leon Huff, Thom Bell and Linda Creed, Joseph Jefferson, Bruce Hawes and Yvette Davis, Norman Harris and Allen Felder surfaced in the late 1960s and early 1970s with force and potency, as witnessed by the popular songs sung by the O'Jays, the Spinners, Harold Melvin and the Blue Notes, Blue Magic, Teddy Pendergrass, Major Harris, the Jones Girls, Lou Rawls and even Johnny Mathis. Furthermore, the noteworthy presence of Harlem's Main Ingredient, Chicago's Chi-Lites, Detroit's (non-Motown) Dramatics, Jersey City's Manhattans and Los Angeles's Whispers on this front yielded a more diverse situation.

The early 1970s witnessed slightly more political overtones in Afro-American popular music. Surprisingly, the political ferment of the late 1960s did not invoke memorable musical responses on behalf of popular Afro-American musicians, with the exception of James Brown's "Say It Loud I'm Black and I'm Proud." The youthful black market thrived on music for dance and romance; and such music was the mainstay of the late 1960s. As the Vietnam War intensified (with over 22 percent of its U.S. victims being black), the drug culture spread and black elected officials emerged, recordings such as the Temptations' "Ball of Confusion," the Chi-Lites' "Give More Power to the People," James Brown's "Funky President (People, It's Bad)" and the Isley Brothers' "Fight the Power" revealed more explicit concern with the public life and political welfare of Afro-America. Ironically, this concern was exemplified most clearly in the greatest album produced by Motown: Marvin Gaye's *What's Going On.* True to their religious roots, Afro-American popular musicians and writers couched their concerns in highly moralistic language, devoid of the concrete political realities of conflict and struggle. Marvin Gaye's classical recording openly evoked Christian apocalyptic images and the love ethic of Jesus Christ.

The watershed year in Afro-American popular music in this period was 1975. For the first time in Afro-American history, fast funk music seized center stage from mellow soul music. In the past, it was inconceivable that a black rhythm and blues group or figure—no matter how funk-oriented—not possess a serious repertoire of slow mellow, often ballad, music. It is important to remember that James Brown's early hits were mellow soul, such as "Please, Please, Please," "Bewildered," "It's a Man's World." Given the demand for nonstop dance music in discotheques in the early 1970s and the concomitant decline of slow dancing and need for mellow soul, black dance music became dominant in Afro-American popular music. Barry White's sensual upbeat tunes, Brass Constructions' repetitive syncopations, Kool and the Gang's distinctive Jersey funk and Nile Rogers and Bernard Edwards's classy chic are exemplary responses to the disco scene. Yet the most important Afro-American response to this scene occurred in 1975 when George Clinton and William "Bootsy" Collins released two albums: Parliament's *Chocolate City* and *Mothership Connection.*

By building directly upon Clinton's Funkadelic, such as deploying the same musicians, Parliament ushered forth the era of black technofunk—the creative encounter of the Afro-American spiritual-blues impulse with highly sophisticated technological instruments, strategies and effects. Parliament invited its listeners, especially the dwellers of "Chocolate cities" and to a lesser extent those in the "Vanilla suburbs," to enter the "Fourth World," the world of black funk and star wars, of black orality, bodily sensuality, technical virtuosity and electronic adroitness. The cover of the first Parliament album, *Chocolate City,* portrayed Washington, D.C.'s Lincoln Memorial, Washington Memorial, Capitol Building and

White House melting presumably under the heat of black technofunk and the increasing "chocolate" character of the nation's capital. The album contained only one mellow soul song ("I Misjudged You"), a mere ritualistic gesture to the mellow pole of Afro-American popular music. The second album, *Mothership Connection*—now joined with the leading saxophonists of James Brown's band, Maceo Parker and Fred Wesley—literally announced the planetary departure to the "Fourth World" on the mothership, with not one earthbound mellow love song.

The emergence of technofunk is not simply a repetition of black escapism or an adolescent obsession with "Star Trek." In addition to being a product of the genius of George Clinton, technofunk constitutes the second grand break of Afro-American musicians from American mainstream music, especially imitated and co-opted Afro-American popular music. Like Charlie Parker's bebop, George Clinton's technofunk both Africanizes and technologizes Afro-American popular music—with polyrhythms on polyrhythms, less melody and freaky electronically distorted vocals. Similar to bebop, technofunk unabashedly exacerbates and accentuates the "blackness" of black music, the "Afro-Americanness" of Afro-American music—its irreducibility, inimitability and uniqueness. Funkadelic and Parliament defy nonblack emulation; they assert their distinctiveness—and the distinctiveness of "funk" in Afro-America. This funk is neither a skill nor an idea, not a worldview or a stance. Rather, it is an existential capacity to get in touch with forms of kinetic orality and affective physicality acquired by deep entrenchment in—or achieved by pretheoretical styles owing to socialization in—the patterns of Afro-American ways of life and struggle.

Technofunk is a distinctive expression of postmodern black popular music; it constitutes a potent form of the Afro-American spiritual-blues impulse in the pervasive computer phase and hedonistic stage of late capitalist U.S. society. Ironically, the appeal of black technofunk was not a class-specific phenomenon. Technofunk invigorated the "new" politicized black middle class undergoing a deep identity crisis, the stable black working class fresh out of the blues-ridden ghettos, the poor black working class hungry for escapist modes of transcendence and the hustling black underclass permeated by the drug culture. Black technofunk articulated black middle-class anxieties toward, yet fascination with, U.S. "hi-tech" capitalist society; black working-class frustration of marginal inclusion within and ineffective protest against this society; and black underclass self-destructive dispositions owing to outright exclusion from this society. For black technofunk, in a period of increasing black strata and class divisions, there are no fundamental cleavages in Afro-America, only the black nation. The cover of George Clinton's 1978 Funkadelic album, *One Nation Under a Groove,* portrays black folk from all walks of life hoisting up Marcus Garvey's Afro-American liberation flag (of red, black, and green stripes) with "R & B" printed on it—the initials not for "rhythm and blues," but "rhythm and business." In vintage black nationalist patriarchal fashion, the inside of the album contains a beautiful naked black woman lying on her back, signifying the biological source and social "backbone" of the black nation.

Again like bebop, technofunk's breakthrough was brief. Its intensely Africanizing and technologizing thrust was quickly diluted and brought more and more into contact with other nonblack musical currents, as witnessed in Prince's creative Minneapolis sound and Midnight Star's "freakazoid funk." Since 1975, four noteworthy trends have surfaced: the invasion of Afro-American popular music by ex-avant-garde jazz musicians, the meteoric rise of Michael Jackson (aided by Rod Temperton and especially Quincy Jones) as a solo performer, the refreshing return of gospel music, and the exuberant emergence of black rap music.

Miles Davis's canonical album, *Bitches Brew,* in 1970 already displayed the influence of soul music on jazz; his admiration of the California funk of Sly and the Family Stone is well known. Yet by the late 1970s the influx of bona fide jazz musicians—most notably George Benson, Quincy Jones, Herbie Hancock and Donald Byrd—into Afro-American popular music (rhythm and blues) was phenomenal. The motivation was not simply financial; it also was symptomatic of perceived sources of vitality and vigor in black music in late capitalist U.S. society and culture. In avant-garde jazz, Ornette Coleman's and John Coltrane's free jazz—like Arnold Schoenberg's atonal music in the Western classical tradition—symbolized both grand achievements and dead ends. For example, Pharaoh Sanders, who briefly upheld the rich legacy of Coltrane's "new wave" jazz, was soon recording with B. B. King, the great blues singer and musician, at the Fillmore East. In short, jazz musicians were not only making a monetary bid for musical popularity; more important, they were acknowledging the legitimacy of the music of the black masses. In short, they were reaffirming the original vision of the great revolutionary figure in jazz, Louis Armstrong. White middlebrow audiences and black old-timers continued to support the great jazz singers—such as Ella Fitzgerald, Sarah Vaughan, Carmen McRae, Billy Eckstine and Joe Williams—but jazz instrumentalists could hardly make it. In many ways, this continues to be so, though the youthful genius of Wynton Marsalis may rearrange the terrain of jazz itself. Notwithstanding the present predicament of jazz musicians, George Benson, a superb jazz guitarist, acquired immediate fame as a Motown-like smooth, mellow soul singer; Herbie Hancock, a "cool" jazz pianist with the early Miles Davis, moved into his own brand of technofunk; and the Van Gelder studio group—Bob James, Grover Washington, Eric Gale and others—produced an ingenious "pop jazz," often based on rhythm and blues tunes. The most successful jazz musician turned rhythm and blues producer, Quincy Jones, joined his immense talent with that of the leader of the most beloved of black singing groups—Michael Jackson of the Jackson Five.

The distinctive talent of Michael Jackson is that he combines the performative showmanship of James Brown (whom he imitated in his first 1968 exhibition to gain a contract with Motown), the lyrical emotional intensity of Smokey Robin-son, the transracial appeal of Dionne Warwicke and the aggressive though atten-uated technofunk of the Isley Brothers. In this regard, Michael Jackson stands shoulders above his contemporaries. He is the musical dynamo of his generation. This became quite clear with his highly acclaimed 1979 *Off the Wall* album and fur-ther confirmed by his record-setting 1982 *Thriller* album. The point here is not simply that the albums sell millions of copies and stay on top of the tune charts for several months. Rather, the point is that Michael Jackson is the product of the Afro-American spiritual-blues impulse, which now has tremendous international influence, thereby serving as a major model for popular music in the world, espe-cially First World capitalist and Third World neocolonialist countries. Like Muhammed Ali—and unlike most of his musical contemporaries—Michael Jack-son is an international star of grand proportions, the most prominent world-historical emblem of the Afro-American spiritual-blues impulse.

Ironically, and unlike the only other comparable figure, Louis Armstrong, Michael Jackson is not a musical revolutionary within Afro-American history. Rather, he is a funnel through which flow many of the diverse streams and cur-rents of the Afro-American musical tradition. It is precisely his versatility and di-versity—from old funk, technofunk and mellow soul to ballads with the ex-Beatle Paul McCartney—that marks his protean musical identity. The only contempo-rary figure comparable to Michael Jackson is Stevie Wonder, and though Stevie Wonder is more musically talented and daring (as well as more politically en-gaged), Jackson possesses a more magnetic magic on stage and in the studio. Yet neither Wonder nor Jackson explore the musical genre that exploded on the scene in the late 1970s and early 1980s: gospel music.

The black church, black-owned and black-run Christian congregations, is the fountainhead of the Afro-American spiritual-blues impulse. Without the black church, with its African roots and Christian context, Afro-American culture—in fact, Afro-America itself—is unimaginable. Yet, as should be apparent, the black church has suffered tremendous "artistic drainage." The giant talents of Mahalia Jackson, James Cleveland and Clara Ward prove that the black church can keep some of its sons and daughters in the artistic fold, but for every one who stayed with the gospels, there have been four who went to rhythm and blues. In the late 1960s Edwin Hawkins's "Oh Happy Day" received national visibility, but the gospel explosion—partly spawned by the Pentecostal thrust in the black religious community—did not take off until the reunion of James Cleveland and Aretha Franklin in their historic 1972 double album set *Amazing Grace*. The towering suc-cess of this live concert at the New Temple Missionary Baptist Church in Los An-geles convinced many reluctant recording companies that gospel music was mar-ketable. And soon superb albums such as Andraè Crouch's *Take Me Back* and Walter Hawkins's (Edwin's brother) *Love Alive* and *Love Alive II* proved them correct. Although gospel music remains primarily a black affair—written and performed by and for black people—the recent Christian conversions of the popular Deneice Williams and disco queen Donna Summers may broaden the scope.

The most important development in Afro-American popular music since 1979 is black rap music. This music has been performed on ghetto streets and between stage acts during black concerts for many years. In 1979, Sylvia Robinson, the major songwriter for the mellow soul group *The Moments* (recently renamed Ray, Goodman and Brown), decided to record and release "Rapper's Delight" by Harlem's Sugarhill Gang. Within months, black rap records were filling record shops around the country. Most of the first black rap records were musically derived from big hits already released and lyrically related to adolescent love affairs. Yet as more sophisticated rap performers, such as Kurtis Blow and Grandmaster Flash and the Furious Five, emerged, the music became more original and the lyrics more graphic of life in the black ghetto. Kurtis Blow's "The Breaks" and "125th Street" and Grandmaster Flash and the Furious Five's "The Message" and "New York, New York" are exemplary in this regard.

Black rap music is more important than the crossover of jazz musicians to rhythm and blues, the rise of the "older" Michael Jackson and the return of gospel music because, similar to bebop and technofunk, black rap music is emblematically symptomatic of a shift in sensibilities and moods in Afro-America. Black rap music indeed Africanizes Afro-American popular music—accenting syncopated polyrhythms, kinetic orality and sensual energy in a refined form of raw expressiveness—while its virtuosity lies not in technical facility, but rather street-talk quickness and linguistic versatility. In short, black rap music recovers and revises elements of black rhetorical styles—some from black preaching—and black rhythmic drumming. In short, it combines the two major organic artistic traditions in black America—black rhetoric and black music. In this sense, like bebop and technofunk, black rap music resists nonblack reproduction, though such imitations and emulations proliferate.

Yet unlike bebop and technofunk—and this is a crucial break—black rap music is primarily the musical expression of the paradoxical cry of desperation and celebration of the black underclass and poor working class, a cry that openly acknowledges and confronts the wave of personal coldheartedness, criminal cruelty and existential hopelessness in the black ghettos of Afro-America. In stark contrast to bebop and technofunk, black rap music is principally a class-specific form of the Afro-American spiritual-blues impulse that mutes, and often eliminates, the utopian dimension of this impulse. The major predecessors of black rap music were the political raps of Gil-Scott Heron and the powerful musical poems of the Last Poets over a decade ago; their content was angry, funky and hopeful. Black rap music is surely grounded in the Afro-American spiritual-blues impulse, but certain versions of this music radically call into question the roots of this impulse, the roots of transcendence and opposition. Without a utopian dimension—without transcendence from or opposition to evil—there can be no struggle, no hope, no meaning.

Needless to say, the celebratory form of black rap music, especially its upbeat African rhythms, contains utopian aspirations. But this form is often violently juxtaposed with lyrical hopelessness of the oppressed poor people of Afro-America. My hunch is that the form (the funky rhythms) have basically a ritualistic function: music for cathartic release at the black rituals of parties and dances. In short, even the rhythms conceal the unprecedented phenomena in Afro-American life of the slow but seemingly sure genocidal effects upon the black underclass and poor working class in late capitalist U.S. society and the inability of poor black folk to muster spiritual, let alone political and economic, resources to survive. This is especially so for young black people. The black suicide rate among eighteen to thirty year olds has tripled in the past two decades; black homicide is the leading cause of death among young black men; over 50 percent of black households are headed by abandoned and abused young black women; the black prison population has doubled since the 1960s; and black churches, led by either rip-off artists like Rev. Ike, devout denominational leaders such as Rev. Jemison of the National Baptist Convention or dedicated prophets like Rev. Daughtry of the National Black United Front—do not reach the vast majority of young black people.

Black rap music is the last form of transcendence available to young black ghetto dwellers, yet it, tellingly, is often employed to subvert, undermine and parody transcendence itself. Such artistic strategies—play, silence, and performance—are typical postmodern ones in which petit bourgeois artists, philosophers and critics wallow. Yet the indigenous proliferation of these strategies among the (once most religious) now most degraded and oppressed people in the urban centers of the richest country in the history of humankind signifies a crisis of enormous proportions for Afro-America.

It is ironic that the Afro-Americanization of popular music around the world occurs at the time that the transcendent and oppositional roots of the Afro-American spiritual-blues impulse are radically challenged from within the Afro-American musical tradition. This challenge occurs not simply because of lack of will or loss of nerve, but primarily because of treacherous ruling-class policies, contemptuous black middle-class attitudes and the loss of existential moorings due to the relative collapse of family structures and supportive networks. To put it bluntly, the roots of the Afro-American spiritual-blues impulse are based on the supposition that somebody—God, Mom or neighbors—cares. Some expressions of black rap music challenge this supposition. The future of the Afro-American spiritual-blues impulse may well hang on the quality of the response to this challenge. In this sense, the vitality and vigor of Afro-American popular music depends not only on the talents of Afro-American musicians, but also on the moral visions, social analyses and political strategies that highlight personal dignity, provide political promise and give existential hope to the underclass and poor working class in Afro-America.

SOURCE: "On Afro-American Popular Music: From Bebop to Rap," *Prophetic Fragments* (Grand Rapids, Mich.: Wm. B. Eerdmans Publishing Co., 1988), pp. 177–187. Originally appeared in *Semiotexte* (1982).

Forty One

ON ANNA DEAVERE SMITH'S FIRES IN THE MIRROR

Anna Deavere Smith is one of the towering artists of our time. Her work explores the human dimensions of dehumanizing situations—from black-Jewish hostilities in Brooklyn and riotous animosities in Los Angeles to presidential scandals in Washington, D.C. I was honored to write the foreword to her powerful drama Fires in the Mirror.

THE CONTEMPORARY BLACK-JEWISH dialogue suffers from three basic shortcomings. First, we often appeal to an abstract humanism and faceless universalism that refuse to confront the concrete conflicts that divide us. Second, we usually conduct the conversation as if the tensions between black and Jewish *men* are exactly the same as those between black and Jewish *women*. Third, we attempt to conduct the exchange in a public space equally appealing to both blacks and Jews—yet fail to recognize that Jews seem to be much more eager to inhabit this public space than blacks.

Anna Deavere Smith's powerful work, *Fires in the Mirror*, is the most significant artistic exploration of black-Jewish relations in our time, precisely because she takes us beyond the three basic shortcomings. In the midst of the heated moment of murder, mayhem and madness of the Crown Heights crisis, she gives us poignant portraits of the everyday human faces that get caught up in the situation. Her sensitive renderings of the tragic and comic aspects of the reactions and responses of blacks and Jews to the Crown Heights crisis give our universal moral principles a particular heartfelt empathy. Her ability to move our passions not only takes us beyond any self-righteous condescension toward parochial Hasidism and provincial black urbanites, but also forces us to examine critically our own complicity in cultural stereotypes that imprison our imaginations and thereby make *us* parochial and provincial. In the best tradition of tragedy, Smith explores the possibilities of human choices in an urgent crisis that yields limited options. Not to choose "sides" is itself a choice—yet to view the crisis as simply and solely a matter of choosing sides is to reduce the history and complexity of the crisis in a vulgar Manichaean manner. In the best tradition of comedy, Smith exposes the ordinary foibles of human responses to this serious crisis, which signify our own imperfect and tension-ridden views about the Crown Heights episode. Her funny characterizations—that for some border on caricatures—provoke genuine laughter even as we know that laughter is an inadequate response to the pain, cruelty and sheer absurdity of the crisis. We laugh, not only because her characters are in some fundamental ways like us—human, all-too-human—but also because we refuse to give pain, cruelty and absurdity the last word. Once again, *Fires in the Mirror* is testimony to how art can take us beyond ourselves as we examine ourselves even in an ugly moment of xenophobic frenzy.

For too long the black-Jewish dialogue has been cast in masculine terms by principally male interlocutors. Is it no accident that the major issues of contention—affirmative action and the security of the state of Israel—tend to highlight the power struggles of men in the public spaces of jobs and the military? Smith explodes this narrow framework by taking us into the private spheres of American society where the complex discourses of women often take place in patriarchal America. This is especially so in Hasidic and black America where the access of women to public space—especially major leadership roles—is frowned upon. Yet Smith neither romanticizes nor idealizes Hasidic, black or secular Jewish women. Instead, she humanizes the black-Jewish dialogue by including the diverse and often conflicting voices within black and Jewish America. This kind of polyphony of perspectives is rarely aired and heard in the black-Jewish dialogue. It should not surprise us that most Jewish women are less disposed to oppose affirmative action than many Jewish men, that strong Jewish women's voices are heard in the Peace Now movement in Israel or that black women's critiques of black nationalist Sonny Carson are persuasive. In short, the gendered character of the black-Jewish dialogue often produces obstacles that compound the problems and render us more paralyzed. Smith's deepening of this dialogue by *de-patriarchalizing* our conversation is a major contribution in this regard.

Fires in the Mirror is a grand example of how art can constitute a public space that is perceived by people as empowering rather than disempowering. What I mean by this is that many blacks are deeply suspicious—or even downright pessimistic—about entering a black-Jewish dialogue. This is especially so for young black people who are reluctant to engage with Jews who often perceive themselves as underdogs yet who usually are middle-class Americans. This issue of Jews as victims in an American context unsettles many African Americans. Needless to say, the Jewish experience in America is quite atypical in Jewish history. Yet, for many black people, the Jewish experience in America is *the* Jewish experience that counts most in the present situation. And since the black experience in America is much worse than the Jewish experience in America, the notion of two oppressed groups in America coming together for dialogue smacks of a dishonesty and even a diversion.

And, to complicate the situation even more, the degradation of the public sphere by conservative elites in the past two decades has exacerbated distrust between any group or constituency—especially progressive ones. This degradation has principally taken the form of associating the public sphere with the faults of black people. For example, public housing, public education and even public transportation are associated in the American mind with the faults of black people. Is it not the case that the very mention of public provisions—not tax breaks or subsidies for corporate America, but subsistence support—evokes images of lazy black men and welfare queens? The political success of playing this insidious racial card has led to a large-scale gutting of public life that has yielded a balkanized populace with little sense of public-mindedness and a narrow obsession with one's constituency and identity. If one cannot trust people as citizens in the public sphere, one must close ranks and trust only those in one's tribe, and tribal strife in America is usually racial in content.

In black America, this tribal mentality has often focused on those who are the public face of the larger system. The relatively invisible WASP corporate and bank elites are rarely targeted since they are so far removed from the everyday life of black people. Instead, the most visible beneficiaries of black consumption, e.g., shop owners and landlords in black communities, or the most vociferous critics of black strategies for progress, e.g., conservative opponents of affirmative action, loom large as objects of black rage.

In Jewish America, this tribal mentality has often highlighted those who make the loudest noise about Jewish conspiracy and Jewish control. The relatively quiet, covert anti-Semites in high places in American life tend to receive more genteel treatment, while the most vocal anti-Semites garner the bulk of Jewish rage.

In this scenario, WASP corporate and bank elites receive little attention regarding how they promote policies and programs that contribute to black poverty, and covert anti-Semitic elites get off relatively scot-free in regard to maintaining impediments to Jewish mobility. And since the public sphere is racialized, any entry of black people in a public dialogue often means that they—we—are on the defensive. So black people must give an account of our faults, condemn some of our xenophobic spokespersons, explain the "silence" of black moral voices and so on. This sense of black people having to do much of the "work" and bear most of the burden in public dialogues generates a deep distrust of any such public dialogue for many black people. Furthermore, any hint of a double standard at work in such a public dialogue spoils the conversation. This is why those black people who do enter public dialogues are eager to hear the faults, e.g., xenophobia, of other communities as well as that of black communities.

Smith's *Fires in the Mirror* is not only aware of this delicate set of issues, but also responds to them with the kind of risk and sensitivity that sets black people at ease. She lets black people know that a fair treatment of all our faults will transpire—so we can confront, examine, parody and maybe begin to overcome these faults. And she is keenly aware that these activities will never get off the ground without a clearing of the air so that bonds of trust can be forged.

As a citizen, Smith knows that there can be no grappling with black anti-Semitism and Jewish anti-black racism without a vital public sphere and that there can be no vital public sphere without genuine bonds of trust. As an artist, she knows that public performance has a unique capacity to bring us together—to take us out of our tribal mentalities—for self-critical examination and artistic pleasure. *Fires in the Mirror* is one sure sign, an oasis of hope, that human art can triumph in the face of a frightening urban crisis—a crisis symptomatic of a national tragedy. It provides us with a glimpse of what we need and what we must do if we are ever to overcome the xenophobic cancer that threatens to devour the soul of the precious yet precarious democratic experiment called America.

Forty Two

ON WALT WHITMAN

This short piece on the greatest American poet was written for a French audience—one whose perspective on the riches of Whitman's free verse and variable foot is often hampered by a neoclassical lens that favors the fixed foot of the ancient line. This brief essay reflects a distinct change in my view of Whitman compared to the one put forward in my initial reading of him in my first book. The powerful work of Professor George Kateb at Princeton led to a deeper appreciation of Whitman's genius. Needless to say, Whitman's Democratic Vistas *remains the secular bible for radical democrats.*

WALT WHITMAN IS NOT only America's most original poet; more important, he is, in the words of David Thoreau, "the greatest democrat the world has ever seen." His most profound and poignant poems—"Song of Myself," "To Think of Time," "Crossing Brooklyn Ferry," "Out of the Cradle Endlessly Rocking" and his famous homage to Abraham Lincoln, "When Lilacs Last in the Dooryard Bloomed"—enact the heroic endeavor to make and remake a dynamic and empathetic self. They attempt to sing in his words, "the song of a great composite *democratic individual*." Similarly, his prosaic masterpiece of cultural criticism, *Democratic Vistas* (1871), is the landmark text in modern democratic thought. It belongs alongside John Stuart Mill's *On Liberty* (1859), W. E. B. Du Bois's *The Souls of Black Folk* (1903) and John Dewey's *The Public and Its Problems* (1927) as a classic in the defense of individuality and social justice.

What sets Whitman the poet apart from his nineteenth-century contemporaries is his uncanny ability to perfect the Wordsworthian revolution of writing poetry based on the spoken language and everyday life. And what sets Whitman the critic apart from his fellow men and women of letters is his enervating faith in democracy as a way of life and mode of being in the world—not simply as a form of governance. It was only Whitman in his day who took up the exciting yet frightening risk of living, thinking and feeling democratically; for him, democracy had deep ontological, existential and social implications.

The unique experience of reading Whitman's poetry is that of a heartfelt presence of intimacy solicited by a powerful voice that fuses soul, mind and body. His poetry resembles an oracular epic that deploys dramatic speech, gesture and tone without any vulgar sense of the didactic and sermonic. Yet it aims to convince and convert as well as to energize and provoke. Whitman's intention is to release the creative powers of his readers to make and remake themselves, just as his poetic style exemplified this creative process in Whitman himself. It is no accident that his artistic models tended to be drawn not from literature, but rather the theater, music (especially Italian opera and other popular forms) and, to some extent, charismatic religious rhetoric (of the prophetic sort). He writes as if literature did not exist, with no quotations, no references to any other writers or allusions to the classics or ancients. And he realizes that such writing has to be an extremely self-conscious act of high craftsmanship to achieve this effect—the effect of touching the hearts, moving the souls and changing the lives of his readers.

Like Nietzsche, Whitman associated this effect with life-enhancing self-scrutiny and heightened self-creation. Unlike Nietzsche, Whitman located this effect in the moral and intellectual capacities of common people. Similar to fellow countryman Ralph Waldo Emerson, Whitman believed that every person was a potential Prometheus, a possible Napoleon of the spirit. His democratic faith rests upon the pillars of voluntarism, fallibilism and experimentalism. His kind of voluntarism accented a willful self-making and self-mastery that required great discipline and energy. His kind of fallibilism stressed the Peircean slogan of never blocking the road to inquiry or, in the words of George Kateb, "Nothing is for keeps." Lastly, his kind of experimentalism promoted an existential risk that wagered on the abilities of common people to control their own individual and collective destinies. In this sense, democracy for Whitman was never a static end in itself, but rather a dynamic means for the cultivation and encouragement of the potentialities and possibilities of unique individuals. In *Democratic Vistas* he states:

> For it is not that democracy is of exhaustive account, in itself. It is that, as we see, it is the best, perhaps only, fit and full means, formulator, general caller-forth, trainer, for the million, not for grand material personalities only, but for immortal souls. To be a voter with the rest is not so much; and this, like every institute, will have its imperfections. But to become an enfranchised man, and now, impediments removed, to stand and start without humiliation, and equal with the rest; to commence or have the road clear'd to commence, the grand experiment of development, whose end, (perhaps requiring several generations) may be the forming of a full-grown man or woman—that is something . . . the democratic formula is the only safe and preservative one for coming times.

For Whitman, our present-day capitalist democracies—now in a self-congratulatory mood after the collapse of repressive Communist regimes in Eastern Europe—are but initial steps in his adventure of democracy, because too many "impediments," e.g., class, racial and sexual ones, to self-development remain. Hence, his democratic challenge to us still requires a substantive response.

SOURCE: From *Beyond Eurocentrism and Multiculturalism, Vol. 1: Prophetic Thought in Postmodern Times* (Monroe, Me.: Common Courage Press, 1993), pp. 167–169.

PART EIGHT

RACE AND DIFFERENCE

This section highlights highly controversial aspects of race matters in American life. It examines issues of public policy like affirmative action, the burning tensions between black and brown brothers and sisters, the intricate and painful realities of black sexuality, black male-female relations, the misunderstandings of black nationalism and my own frustrations with some Jewish intellectuals past and present.

Forty Three

ON AFFIRMATIVE ACTION

My friend and brother George Curry—visionary and courageous editor of Emerge
*magazine—convinced me to write this essay for his volume on affirmative action (the best
such volume we have!). Affirmative-action policies, I believe, are inadequate, yet they
remain one of the most significant ways of confronting the ugly legacy of white supremacy
in American life. I thought it urgent to provide a historical perspective on affirmative
action because our public discussion had ignored why it emerged and also had reduced
it to "unqualified people of color getting jobs or slots they didn't deserve." I felt it was
important to shatter such amnesia and mendacity.*

TODAY'S AFFIRMATIVE-ACTION POLICY is not the appropriate starting point
for a substantive debate on affirmative action. Instead, we must begin with the
larger historical and moral context of the recent controversy. Why was the policy
established in the first place? What were the alternatives? Who questioned its operation, and when? How did it come about that a civil rights initiative in the
1960s is viewed by many as a civil rights violation in the 1990s? Whose civil
rights are we talking about? Is there a difference between a right and an expectation? What are the limits of affirmative action? What would the consequences be
if affirmative action disappeared in America?

THE AIM OF AFFIRMATIVE ACTION

The vicious legacy of white supremacy—institutionalized in housing, education,
health care, employment and social life—served as the historical context for the
civil rights movement in the late 1950s and 1960s. Affirmative action was a *weak*
response to this legacy. It constituted an imperfect policy conceded by a powerful
political, business and educational establishment in light of the pressures of organized citizens and the disturbances of angry unorganized ones.

The fundamental aim of affirmative action was to put a significant dent in the
tightly controlled networks of privileged white male citizens who monopolized the
good jobs and influential positions in American society. Just as Catholics and Jews
had earlier challenged the white Anglo-Saxon Protestant monopoly of such jobs
and positions, in the 1960s blacks and women did also. Yet since the historical

gravity of race and gender outweighs that of religion and ethnicity in American society, the federal government had to step in to facilitate black and female entry into the U.S. mainstream and malestream. This national spectacle could not but prove costly under later, more hostile circumstances.

The initial debate focused on the relative lack of fairness, merit and public interest displayed by the prevailing systems of employment and education, principally owing to arbitrary racist and sexist exclusion. In the 1960s, class-based affirmative action was not seriously considered, primarily because it could easily have been implemented in such a way as to perpetuate exclusion, especially given a labor movement replete with racism and sexism. Both Democratic and Republican administrations supported affirmative action as the painful way of trying to create a multiracial democracy in which women and people of color were not second-class citizens. Initially, affirmative action was opposed by hard-line conservatives, usually the same ones who opposed the civil rights movement led by Dr. Martin Luther King, Jr. Yet the pragmatic liberals and conservatives prevailed.

THE NEOCONSERVATIVE OPPOSITION

The rise of the neoconservatives unsettled this fragile consensus. By affirming the principle of equality of opportunity yet trashing any mechanism that claimed to go beyond merit, neoconservatives drove a wedge between civil rights and affirmative action. By claiming that meritocratic judgments trump egalitarian efforts to produce tangible results, neoconservatives cast affirmative-action policies as reverse racism and the major cause of racial divisiveness and low black self-esteem in the workplace and colleges.

Yet even this major intellectual and ideological assault did not produce a wholesale abandonment of affirmative action on behalf of business, political and educational elites. The major factor that escalated the drive against affirmative action was the shrinking job possibilities—along with stagnating and declining wages—that were squeezing the white middle class. Unfortunately, conservative leaders seized this moment to begin to more vociferously scapegoat affirmative action and to seek its weakening or elimination.

Their first move was to define affirmative action as a program for "unqualified" women and, especially, black people. Their second move was to cast affirmative action as "un-American," a quota system for groups rather than a merit system for individuals. The third move was to claim that antidiscrimination laws are enough, given the decline or end of racism among employers. The latest move has been to soothe the agonized consciences of liberals and conservatives by trying to show that black people are genetically inferior to whites in intelligence; hence, nothing can be done.

The popularity—distinct from the rationality—of these moves has created a climate in which proponents of affirmative action are on the defensive. Even those of us who admit the excesses of some affirmative-action programs—and therefore call for correcting, not eliminating, them—give aid and comfort to our adversaries. This reality reveals just how far the debate has moved in the direction of the neoconservative and conservative perceptions in the country. It also discloses that we need far more than weak policies like affirmative action to confront the legacies of white supremacy and corporate power in the United States—legacies visible in unemployment and underemployment, unaffordable health care and inadequate child care, dilapidated housing and decrepit schools for millions of Americans, disproportionately people of color, women and children.

The idea that affirmative action violates the rights of fellow citizens confuses a right with an expectation. We all have a right to be seriously and fairly considered for a job or position. But calculations of merit, institutional benefit and social utility produce the results. In the past, those who were never even considered had their rights violated; in the present, those who are seriously and fairly considered yet still not selected do not have their rights violated but rather have their expectations frustrated.

For example, if Harvard College receives more than ten thousand applications for fourteen hundred slots in the freshman class and roughly four thousand meet the basic qualifications, how does one select the "worthy" ones? Six thousand applicants are already fairly eliminated. Yet twenty-six hundred still will not make it. When considerations of factors other than merit are involved, such as whether candidates are the sons or daughters of alumni, come from diverse regions of the country or are athletes, no one objects. But when racial diversity is involved, the opponents of affirmative action yell foul play. Yet each class at Harvard remains about 5 to 7 percent black—far from a black takeover. And affirmative action bears the blame for racial anxiety and division on campus in such an atmosphere. In short, neoconservatives and conservatives fail to see the subtle (and not so subtle) white-supremacist sensibilities behind their "color-blind" perspectives on affirmative action.

THE LIMITS OF AFFIRMATIVE ACTION

Yet it would be myopic of progressives to make a fetish of affirmative action. As desirable as those policies are—an insight held fast by much of corporate America except at the almost lily-white senior-management levels—they will never ameliorate the plight and predicament of poor people of color. More drastic and redistributive measures are needed in order to address their situations, measures that challenge the maldistribution of wealth and power and that will trigger cultural renewal and personal hope.

If affirmative action disappears from the American scene, many blacks will still excel and succeed. But the larger signal that sends will be lethal for the country. It is a signal that white supremacy now has one less constraint and black people have one more reason to lose trust in the promise of American democracy.

SOURCE: "Affirmative Action in Context," by Cornel West, in *The Affirmative Action Debate,* edited by George E. Curry, pp. 31–35. Copyright © 1996 by George E. Curry. Reprinted by permission of Perseus Books Publishers, a member of the Perseus Books Group.

Forty Four

ON BLACK-BROWN RELATIONS

Black-brown relations will continue to pose a major challenge for American race matters in the next century. In Los Angeles, New York City and Washington, D.C., my friend and brother Professor Jorge Klor de Alva and I engaged in public dialogues about these urgent issues. This Harper's Magazine *interview, conducted in April 1996, generated great controversy.* Harper's *was flooded with letters accusing Jorge of stripping me of my blackness and claiming I gave too much weight to racism in American life.*

THIS CONVERSATION TOOK PLACE *at the Colombe d'Or restaurant in Manhattan.*

Jorge Klor de Alva is the Class of 1940 Professor of Comparative Ethnic Studies and Anthropology at the University of California at Berkeley. He is the author or editor of fourteen books on anthropology, history and interethnic relations in the Americas. He is presently at work on The Norton Anthology of Indigenous Mesoamerican Literature.

Earl Shorris is a contributing editor of Harper's Magazine *and the author of ten books, including* Latinos: A Biography of the People; Ofay, *a 1966 novel about a black-white love affair; and* Under the Fifth Sun: A Novel of Pancho Villa.

Cornel West is a professor of Afro-American Studies and Philosophy of Religion at Harvard University. He is the author of eleven books on philosophy, African-American studies and religion, including Race Matters. *His latest book is* The Future of the Race, *coauthored with Henry Louis Gates, Jr.*

Earl Shorris: To begin, would you both answer one question with a yes or no, no more than that? Cornel, are you a black man?

Cornel West: Yes.

Shorris: Jorge, do you think Cornel is a black man?

Jorge Klor de Alva: No, for now.

Shorris: Apparently we have something to talk about. Jorge, can you tell me why you say, "No, for now"?

Klor de Alva: To identify someone as black, Latino or anything else, one has to appeal to a tradition of naming and categorizing in which a question like that can make sense—and be answered with a yes or a no. In the United States, where unambiguous, color-coded identities are the rule, Cornel is clearly a black man. Traveling someplace else, perhaps in Africa, Cornel would not necessarily be identified as black. He might be seen as someone of mixed African descent, but that's different from being identified as black. Cornel is only black within a certain reductionist context. And that context, where color is made to represent not so much the hue of one's skin as a set of denigrated experiences—and where these experiences are applied to everyone who ever had an African ancestor—is one I consider to be extremely negative.

West: I think when I say I am a black man, I'm saying first that I am a modern person, because black itself is a modern construct, a construct put forward during a particular moment in time to fit a specific set of circumstances. Implicit in that category of "black man" is American white supremacy, African slavery and then a very rich culture that responds to these conditions at the level of style, mannerism, orientation, experimentation, improvisation, syncopation—all of those elements that have gone into making a new people, namely, black people.

A hundred years ago I would have said that I was a "colored man." But I would still have been modern, I'd still have been New World African, I'd still have been dealing with white supremacy and I would still have been falling back on a very rich culture of resistance, a culture that tried to preserve black sanity and spiritual health in the face of white hatred and job ceilings. I think Jorge and I agree that we're dealing with constructs. And I think we agree in our objections to essentialist conceptions of race, to the idea that differences are innate and outside of history.

Klor de Alva: What advantage has it been, Cornel, for blacks to identify themselves as blacks?

West: For one, that identification was imposed. We were perceived as a separate people—enslaved, Jim Crowed and segregated. To be viewed as a separate people requires coming to terms with that separateness. This category "black" was simply a response to that imposition of being a separate people, and also a building on one's own history, going back to Africa, yes, but especially here in the United States. So when I say, for example, that jazz is a creation of black people, I'm saying that it's a creation of modern people, New World African people. And we've come up with various categories, including black, as a way of affirming ourselves as agents, as subjects in history who create, initiate and so forth. So in that sense there have actually been some real benefits.

Klor de Alva: When the Europeans arrived in Mexico, they confronted people whose level of social organization was not unlike that of the Romans. Before millions died from newly introduced diseases, the Europeans called them *naturales,* or "natural people." Afterwards the survivors came to be called "Indians," a term the natives did not use until the nineteenth century, preferring to identify themselves by their tribal group. And to the extent that they were able to do that, they managed to maintain a degree of cultural integrity as separate groups. When that ended, they were all seen as despised Indians.

The general label only helped to promote their denigration. Now, I agree that group designations help build a sense of community, but as free and enslaved Africans took on the general labels that oppressed them, they also helped to legitimize their being identified as one irredeemable people. In the United States this unwillingness to challenge what has come to be known as the one-drop rule—wherein anyone who ever had an African ancestor, however remote, is identifiable only as black—has strengthened the hand of those who seek to trap them, and other so-called people of color, in a social basement with no exit ladder.

West: When we talk about identity, it's really important to define it. Identity has to do with protection, association and recognition. People identify themselves in certain ways in order to protect their bodies, their labor, their communities, their way of life; in order to be associated with people who ascribe value to them, who take them seriously, who respect them; and for purposes of recognition, to be acknowledged, to feel as if one actually belongs to a group, a clan, a tribe, a community. So that anytime we talk about the identity of a particular group over time and space, we have to be very specific about what the credible options are for them at any given moment.

There have been some black people in America who fundamentally believed that they were wholehearted, full-fledged Americans. They have been mistaken. They tried to pursue that option—Boom! Jim Crow hit them. They tried to press that option—Boom! Vanilla suburbs didn't allow them in. So they had to then revise and recast their conception of themselves in terms of protection, association and recognition. Because they weren't being protected by the police and the courts. They weren't welcome in association. Oftentimes they were not welcome in white suburbs. And they weren't being recognized. Their talents and capacities were debased, devalued and degraded. "Black" was the term many chose. Okay, that's fine, we can argue about that. But what are the other options? "Human being?" Yes, we ought to be human beings, but we know that's too abstract and too vague. We need human communities on the ground, not simply at the level of the ideal.

CONSTRUCTING HUMANS

Klor de Alva: Nobody is born black. People are born with different pigmentation, people are born with different physical characteristics, no question about that. But you have to learn to be black. That's what I mean by constructedness.

West: But are people born human? Is "human" itself constructed, as a category?

Klor de Alva: Certainly as a category, as a social, as a scientific category, of course it's a construct. The species could have been identified in some other fashion. Since Columbus's landfall you had very extensive debates as to whether indigenous peoples in the Americas were human, like Europeans, or not. The priest Montesinos posed that question to the Spanish colonists in 1511, and Las Casas, a fellow priest, and the theologian Sepúlveda debated the issue at mid-century before Emperor Charles V.

West: You see, this historical process of naming is part of the legacy not just of white supremacy, but of class supremacy. Tolstoy didn't believe his peasants were actually human until after he underwent conversion. And he realized, "My God, I used to think they were animals; now they're human beings. I have a different life and a new set of lenses with which to view it." So it is with any talk about blackness. It's associated with subhumanness, and therefore when we talk about constructed terms like "black" or "peasant" or "human," it means that the whole thing's up for grabs in terms of constructedness. And if that's so, then all we have left is history.

Klor de Alva: All identities are up for grabs. But black intellectuals in the United States, unlike Latino intellectuals in the United States, have an enormous media space within which to shape the politics of naming and to affect the symbols and meanings associated with certain terms. Thus, practically overnight, they convinced the media that they were an ethnic group and shifted over to the model of African-American, hyphenated American, as opposed to being named by color. Knowing what we know about the negative aspects of naming, it would be better for all of us, regardless of color, if those who consider themselves, and are seen as, black intellectuals were to stop participating in the insidious one-drop-rule game of identifying themselves as black.

West: If you're saying that we are, for the most part, biological and cultural hybrids, I think you're certainly right. But at the same time there's a danger in calling for an end to a certain history if we're unable to provide other options. Now, because I speak first and foremost as a human being, a radical Democrat and a Christian, I would be willing to use damn near any term if it helped to eliminate poverty and provide adequate health care and child care and a job with a living wage, some control at the workplace and some redistribution of wealth downward. At that point, you can call all black people colored. That's fine with me.

Shorris: Are you saying that you're willing to disappear?

West: Well, I would never disappear, because whatever name we would come up with, we're still going to have the blues and John Coltrane and Sarah Vaughan and all those who come out of this particular history. And simply because we change the name wouldn't mean that we would disappear.

Klor de Alva: I think that's the wrong emphasis. I think what has happened is that much of the cultural diversity that Cornel mentions has, in fact, disappeared behind this veil that has transformed everybody with one drop of African blood into black. That reductionism has been a much more powerful mechanism for causing diversity to disappear.

West: Well, what do you mean by disappearance at this point?

Klor de Alva: Let me answer your question from a slightly different perspective. We have, in the United States, two mechanisms at play in the construction of collective identities. One is to identify folks from a cultural perspective. The other is to identify them from a racial perspective. Now, with the exception of black-white relations, the racial perspective is not the critical one for most folks. The cultural perspective was, at one time, very sharply drawn, including the religious line between Catholics and Protestants, Jews and Protestants, Jews and Catholics, Jews and Christians. But in the course of the twentieth century, we have seen in the United States a phenomenon that we do not see anyplace else in the world—the capacity to blur the differences between these cultural groups, to construct them in such a way that they became insignificant and to fuse them into a new group called whites, which didn't exist before.

West: Yes, but whiteness was already in place. I mean, part of the tragedy of American civilization is precisely the degree to which the stability and continuity of American democracy has been predicated on a construct of whiteness that includes the subordination of black people, so that European cultural diversity could disappear into American whiteness while black folk remain subordinated.

Klor de Alva: But everything, even whiteness, must be constructed and is therefore subject to change.

West: Categories are constructed. Scars and bruises are felt with human bodies, some of which end up in coffins. Death is not a construct. And so, when we're talking about constructs having concrete consequences that produce scars and bruises, these consequences are not constructed, they're felt. They're very real. Now, in light of that, I would want to accent the strengths of the history of black resistance. One of the reasons why black people are so integral a part of American civilization is because black people have raised a lot of hell. That's very important, especially in a society in which power and pressure decide who receives visibility. By raising hell I mean organization, mobilization, chaos-producing capacity, as in rebellion. That's a very important point. Why is it important? It's important for me because what's at stake is the quality of American civilization, whether it actually survives as a plausible idea.

That's why a discourse on race is never just a discourse on race. Richard Wright used to say that the Negro is America's metaphor. It means you can't talk about one without talking about the nature of the other. And one of the reasons we don't like to talk about race, especially as it relates to black folk, is because we're forced to raise all the fundamental questions about what it means to be an American, what it means to be a part of American democracy. Those are exhausting and challenging questions.

The best of the black intellectual and political tradition has always raised the problem of evil in its concrete forms in America. People like Frederick Douglass, Martin Luther King, Jr. and Ella Baker never focused solely on black suffering. They used black suffering as a springboard to raise issues of various other forms of injustice, suffering and so forth that relate to other groups—black, brown, white workers, right across the board, you see. During the '80s, the major opposition to right-wing Reaganism was what? Jesse Jackson's campaigns. Opening up to workers, gay brothers, lesbian sisters, right across the board. Black suffering was a springboard. Why? Because a question of evil sits at the heart of the American moral dilemma. With the stark exception of its great artists—Melville, Faulkner, Elizabeth Bishop, Coltrane, Toni Morrison—American society prefers to deny the existence of its own evil. Black folk historically have reminded people of the prevailing state of denial.

ANGLOS MAY BE OF ANY RACE

Shorris: We've just demonstrated one of the tenets of this conversation. That is, we have discussed almost exclusively the question of blacks in this society. But we started out saying we would have a black-brown dialogue. Why does that happen? And not only in the media. Why did it happen here, among us?

Klor de Alva: Part of the answer, as Cornel was pointing out, is that blacks are the central metaphor for otherness and oppression in the United States. Secondly, in part I take your question, when focused on Latinos, to mean, Don't Latinos have their own situation that also needs to be described if not in the same terms, then at least in terms that are supplementary?

I'm not sure. The answer goes to the very core of the difference between Latinos and blacks and between Cornel and myself: I am trying to argue against the utility of the concept of race. Why? Because I don't think that's the dominant construct we need to address in order to resolve the many problems at hand. Cornel wants to construct it in the language of the United States, and I say we need a different kind of language. Do you know why, Earl? Because we're in the United States and blacks are Americans. They're Anglos.

West: Excuse me?

Klor de Alva: They're Anglos of a different color, but they're Anglos. Why? Because the critical distinction here for Latinos is not race, it's culture.

West: Speaking English and being part of American culture?

Klor de Alva: Blacks are more Anglo than most Anglos because, unlike most Anglos, they can't directly identify themselves with a nation-state outside of the United States. They are trapped in America. However unjust and painful, their experiences are wholly made in America.

West: But that doesn't make me an Anglo. If I'm trapped on the underside of America, that doesn't mean that somehow I'm an Anglo.

Klor de Alva: Poor whites similarly trapped on the underside of America are also Anglos. Latinos are in a totally different situation, unable to be captured by the government in the "five food groups" of racial classification of Americans. The Commerce Department didn't know what to do with Latinos; the census takers didn't know what to do with Latinos; the government didn't know what to do with Latinos, and so they said, "Latinos can be of any race." That puts Latinos in a totally different situation. They are, in fact, homologous with the totality of the United States. That is, like Americans, Latinos can be of any race. What distinguishes them from all other Americans is culture, not race. That's where I'm going when I say that Cornel is an Anglo. You can be a Latino and look like Cornel. You can be a Latino and look like you, Earl, or like me. And so, among Latinos, there's no surprise in my saying that Cornel is an Anglo.

West: But it seems to me that "Anglo" is the wrong word.

Klor de Alva: Hey, I didn't make it up, Cornel.

West: "Anglo" implies a set of privileges. It implies a certain cultural formation.

Klor de Alva: I'm trying to identify here how Chicanos see "Anglos."

West: But I want to try and convince those Latino brothers and sisters not to think of black folk as Anglos. That's just wrong. Now, they can say that we're English-speaking moderns in the United States who have yet to be fully treated as Americans. That's fine.

Klor de Alva: My friend, Cornel, I was speaking of one of the more benign Latino names for blacks.

West: Let's hear some of the less benign then, brother.

WHAT COLOR IS BROWN?

Klor de Alva: Do you think of Latinos as white?

West: I think of them as brothers and sisters, as human beings, but in terms of culture, I think of them as a particular group of voluntary immigrants who entered America and had to encounter this thoroughly absurd system of classification of positively charged whiteness, negatively charged blackness. And they don't fit either one: They're not white, they're not black.

Shorris: What are they?

West: I see them primarily as people of color, as brown people who have to deal with their blackness-whiteness.

Shorris: So you see them in racial terms.

West: Well, no, it's more cultural.

Shorris: But you said "brown."

West: No, it's more cultural. Brown, for me, is more associated with culture than race.

Shorris: But you choose a word that describes color.

West: Right. To say "Spanish-speaking" would be a bit too vague, because you've got a lot of brothers and sisters from Guatemala who don't speak Spanish. They speak an indigenous language.

Klor de Alva: You have a lot of Latinos who aren't brown.

West: But they're not treated as whites, and "brown" is simply a signifier of that differential treatment. Even if a Latino brother or sister has supposedly white skin, he or she is still Latino in the eyes of the white privileged, you see. But they're not treated as black. They're not niggers. They're not the bottom of the heap, you see. So they're not niggers, they're not white, what are they? I say brown, but signifying culture more than color. Mexicans, Cubans, Puerto Ricans, Dominicans, El Salvadorans all have very, very distinctive histories. When you talk about black, that becomes a kind of benchmark, because you've got these continuous generations, and you've got very common experiences.

Now, of course, blackness comprises a concealed heterogeneity. You've got West Indians, you've got Ethiopians. My wife is Ethiopian. Her experience is closer to browns'. She came here because she wanted to. She was trying to get out from under a tyrannical, Communist regime in Ethiopia. She's glad to be in a place where she can breathe freely, not have to hide. I say, "I'm glad you're here, but don't allow that one side of America to blind you to my side."

So I've got to take her, you know, almost like Virgil in Dante's *Divine Comedy,* through all of this other side of America, so that she can see the nightmare as well as the dream. But as an Ethiopian, she came for the dream and did a good job of achieving it.

Klor de Alva: So you are participating in the same process as the other Americans, other Anglos—to use that complicated term—that same song and dance of transforming her into a highly racialized American black.

West: It wasn't me. It was the first American who called her "nigger." That's when she started the process of Americanization and racialization. She turned around and said, "What is a nigger?"

Klor de Alva: And you're the one who explained it.

LBJ's Other Dilemma

Shorris: How do you see yourself, Jorge?

Klor de Alva: I'm an American citizen. What are you, Cornel?

West: I am a black man trying to be an American citizen.

Klor de Alva: I'm an American citizen trying to get rid of as many catc gories as possible that classify people in ways that make it easy for them to be oppressed, isolated, marginalized. Of course, I'm a Chicano, I'm a Mexican-American. But for me to identify myself that way is not much help. More helpful is my actually working to resolve the problems of poor folks in the United States.

If I were black, I would heighten the importance of citizenship. Why? Because every time we've seen huge numbers of immigrants enter the United States, the people most devastated by their arrival, in terms of being relegated to an even lower rung on the employment ladder, have been blacks.

Shorris: Are you defining "black" and "Latino" as "poor"?

Klor de Alva: No, no. I'm not defining them that way at all.

West: What's fascinating about this issue of race is the degree to which, in the American mind, black people are associated with instability, chaos, disorder—the very things that America always runs from. In addition, we are associated with hypersexuality, transgressive criminal activity—all of the various stereotypes and images.

Shorris: We all know LBJ's comment about affirmative action. He said that it's the right thing to do but that it will destroy the Democratic party. There certainly is every likelihood that it has destroyed the Democratic party as it's traditionally been understood, that the Democratic party's base in the South has disappeared, that the white South now votes Republican and many blacks don't vote at all. What does this mean about America and the likelihood of any kind of affirmative action, or any program for social justice, succeeding, either for blacks or for Latinos?

Klor de Alva: No matter what kind of policy you set in place, there has to be something in it for everybody or the policy is not going to last very long. And I'm not even going to get into the issue that affirmative action has been essentially an African American thing, not a Latino thing.

West: But who have the major beneficiaries been? White women. And rightly so. More of them have been up against the patriarchy than black and brown people have been up against racism.

Klor de Alva: If you're right that white women are the main beneficiaries, and if I'm right that African Americans were meant to be the primary beneficiaries, then we have to ask if affirmative action is an effective strategy for the resolution of the Latinos' problems. And has the failure of class organization been due primarily to the racial divisions in the society? If so, then race is a lamentable category for any kind of progressive organization, and we need an alternative to affirmative action. I would remove the government from participation in the naming game and its divisive racializing of identities.

West: To the degree to which the Democratic party cuts against a strong white-supremacist grain in America and identifies with black people unequivocally, it will be destroyed. That's essentially what the Republican strategy has been since 1968. The question then becomes, How do we talk about these issues of class while also recognizing that any silence with respect to the de facto white supremacy results in institutions that ought to be changed because they have little moral content to them? If you're going to have a spineless, milquetoast Democratic party that can't say a word against racism, it doesn't deserve to exist anyway.

Klor de Alva: Affirmative action has had the capacity to create a black middle class. Many of these folks also have been the dominant group in the civil rights arena and in other human rights areas. The net effect has been to create a layer, essentially of African Americans, within the public sphere that has been very difficult for Latinos to penetrate and make their complaints known.

West: That's true, and I think it's wrong. But at the same time, blacks are more likely to register protests than Latinos are. That's what I mean by raising hell, you see. Black people are more likely to raise hell than brown people.

Klor de Alva: But having been blocked from the public sector, I am concerned that Latinos turning to the private one will buy deeply into U.S. concepts of race and will be even less willing than Anglos to employ blacks. So for me, any new social or public policy must begin with dismantling the language of race.

West: It's important not to conflate overcoming racial barriers with dismantling racial language. I'm all for the former; I'm not so sure about the latter, because it ignores or minimizes the history of racism. Most of human history is a history of oligarchs, unaccountable elites, manipulating anger, rage, setting working people against one another to enable those elites to maintain their position. That's why democracies are so rare in human history.

Shorris: Let me ask you a question about oligarchies. There are wealthy blacks, middle-class blacks and many poor blacks. There are wealthy browns, middle-class browns many poor browns. Are we talking about two groups or six? Are we talking about economic self-interest being greater than any kind of cultural or racial self-interest?

West: There is always going to be self-interest operating. The question is, How does it relate to the common good and contribute to the production, distribution and consumption of goods and services so that there's some relative equality? Now, the six groups that you're talking about have to do with class divisions within brown and black America. The class divisions are there. And they're going to increase, there's no doubt about that. We're going to see more conservatives in black America, more conservatives in brown America, because the country in general is tilting in that direction and it's nice to be on the bandwagon. Even though we claim to be with the underdog, it's very American to want to be with the winners. So as those class divisions escalate, you're going to get class envy and class hatred within brown America as well as within black America. One of the purposes of a black-brown dialogue is to head off precisely these kinds of hatreds and various forms of bigotry.

Klor de Alva: At the level of the working class, we're seeing a great deal of cooperation, but as you move up the economic scale, you have progressively more turf wars—how many slots blacks get for this, how many slots Latinos get for that. Once you get to mayors of towns or cities, you have Latinos who aren't going to do terribly much for the black community or, if they're black, not very much for the Latino community.

Hence my emphasis on a solution that addresses economics rather than race.

West: We do have some data in terms of voting behavior when it comes to brown-black contrast. Ninety percent of whoever votes in the black community still votes Democratic, right? Cubans, a million Cubans in America, vote for Republicans. We have 2.8 million Puerto Ricans. They vote Democratic roughly 60–40. We have 17.1 million Mexicans. They vote, the majority, for the Democratic party. Black Americans tilt much more toward the Democratic party than any other group, à la LBJ's idea: It's going to destroy this party, all these black folk over here. You see, once you get that racial divide, you can promote white anxieties and white fears, and you can use that for all it's worth. And the Republicans are going to use that into the twenty-first century. There's no doubt about it.

Klor de Alva: Cornel, you're going back to the question of this evil empire.

West: No, it's not evil. It's a civilization in which there is a problem of evil.

Klor de Alva: All civilizations have a problem with evil.

West: But some—like the United States—are in sustained denial even as they view themselves as the embodiment of good.

Klor de Alva: I don't agree with that. I would say that one of the significant ideological possibilities, a door that's always open in the United States— and it goes back to that old contrast between Mexico and the United States—is that the United States has an epic vision, a vision of good against evil. Latinos supposedly have a tragic vision—a conflict between two goods. But in the United States, evil is always right there, and its defeat, like its creation, can therefore be imagined. Cornel, you represent evil if you take off your three-piece suit and walk out into the street at three o'clock in the morning.

West: Brother, I represent evil now, as a savage in a suit. Because this is black skin, what we started with. So I don't need to take off my suit. But the difference is this: The tragic view—of Unamuno or Melville or Faulkner or Morrison or Coltrane—is a much more morally mature view of what it is to be human. The triumphant view of good over evil, which is Manichaean, is sophomoric, childish. It has been dominant in America because our civilization is so spoiled.

Klor de Alva: I would like to agree with you, were it not for the fact that that tragic vision is also a kind of Hamlet vision. It makes it very difficult to move, to overcome evil.

West: But better Hamlet than Captain Ahab in *Moby-Dick*. And that's precisely what Melville was getting at—this tremendous voluntaristic view of the world in which a will to power, based on an absolute conception of good over evil, allows one to lead toward what? Nihilism, self-destruction. I'd go with Hamlet any day.

Klor de Alva: Not me, not at the price of indecision and paralysis.

West: Now, Martin Luther King, Jr. was neither Hamlet nor Captain Ahab, you see. King was something else. King actually comes out of a black tradition with a profound sense of the tragic. When he has Mahalia Jackson sing "Precious Lord," that's not triumphalism. That is the deepest sense of the tragic nature of this civilization, the same tragic sense at work in the spirituals and the blues and jazz. King was not in any way a triumphalist. The great King insight is that, because he rejects triumphalism, he knows that the evil is not simply external, that it's in him. He knew that there was white supremacy in him. That's what allowed him to love Bull Connor even as he opposed Connor's white supremacy. That's the great Christian insight.

Klor de Alva: I agree with you. The evil is here in the United States, but it can be challenged.

One Night of Love

Shorris: Cornel, what do you most worry about in the future?

West: I think my fundamental concern is the disintegration of American civilization as black people become more and more insulated, isolated, targeted and hence subjected to the most brutal authoritarian rule in the name of democracy. And that's exactly where we're headed, so it's not just a fear.

Klor de Alva: I would say that what you've described for America would be true of just about any nation I know, particularly any multicultural nation. It's not something that's unique to the United States. My biggest fear, as this nation moves into an inevitable browning, or hybridization, is that there will be a very powerful minority, overwhelmingly composed of Euro-Americans, who will see themselves in significant danger as a consequence of the way democracy works: winner-take-all. And they will begin to renege on some of the basic principles that created the United States and made it what it is.

Shorris: We've been talking about conflicts. Let's stipulate, unless you disagree, that the advantage to the people in power of keeping those at the bottom at each other's throats is enormous. That's the case in all societies. So we have blacks and browns, for the most part, at the bottom. And they are frequently at each other's throats. They're fighting over immigration, fighting over jobs and so on. A group of young people comes to you and says, "Tell us how to make alliances, give us a set of rules for creating alliances between blacks and browns." What would you answer?

West: I'd appeal to various examples. Look at Ernesto Cortés and the Industrial Areas Foundation in Texas or the Harlem Initiatives Together in New York City, which have been able to pull off black-brown alliances of great strength, the "breaking bread" events of the Democratic Socialists of America. Or I'd talk about Mark Ridley-Thomas in south-central Los Angeles and look at the ways in which he speaks with power about brown suffering as a black city councilman, the way in which he's able to build within his own organization a kind of black-brown dialogue. Because what you really see then is not just a set of principles or rules, but some momentum at work.

Shorris: But how do you do that? What's the first step?

West: Well, it depends on what particular action you want to highlight. You could, say, look at the movement around environmental racism, where you have a whole host of black-brown alliances. With Proposition 187 you had a black-brown alliance among progressives fighting against the conservatives who happened to be white, black and brown. In the trade-union movement, look at 1199, the health-care workers union, here in New York City. You've got brown Dennis Rivera at the top, you've got black Gerry Hudson third in charge, running things. That's a very significant coordinated leadership of probably the most important trade union in the largest city in the nation. So it depends on the particular issue. I think it's issue by issue in light of a broad vision.

Shorris: What is the broad vision?

West: Democracy, substantive radical democracy in which you actually are highlighting the empowering of everyday people in the workplace and the voting booth so that they can live lives of decency and dignity. That's a deeply democratic sensibility. And I think that sensibility can be found in both the black and brown communities.

Klor de Alva: Unless there's a dramatic shift in ideology, linkages between people who are identified as belonging to opposing camps will last only for the moment, like the graffiti I saw during the L.A. riots: "Crips. Bloods. Mexicans. Together. Forever. Tonite [*sic*]," and then next to that, "LAPD" crossed out and "187" underneath. That is, the alliances will work only as long as there's a common enemy, in this case the LAPD, whose death the graffiti advocated by the term "187," which refers here to the California Criminal Code for homicide.

As long as we don't have a fundamental transformation in ideology, those are the kinds of alliances we will have, and they will be short-lived and not lead, ultimately, to terribly much. Clearly, the progressive forces within the United States must be able to forge ideological changes that would permit lasting linkages. At the core of that effort lies the capacity to address common suffering, regardless of color or culture. And that cannot be done unless common suffering, as the reason for linkages across all lines, is highlighted in place of the very tenuous alliances between groups that identify themselves by race or culture.

Shorris: Let's see if anything happened in this conversation. Cornel, are you a black man?

West: Hell yes.

Shorris: Jorge, is he a black man?

Klor de Alva: Of course not.

SOURCE: "Our Next Race Question: The Uneasiness Between Blacks and Latinos." Copyright © 1996 by *Harper's Magazine*. Reproduced from the April issue by special permission.

Forty Five

ON BLACK SEXUALITY

In 1993 I published the best-seller Race Matters *a book that has now sold nearly 400,000 copies. This text appeared owing to the editorial genius of Deb Chasman of Beacon Press. My favorite chapter is about the often overlooked issue of black sexuality—the elephant in the room no one dares mention. Yet race and sexuality have always been linked in loaded ways. We will never understand and change the experiences and perceptions of black bodies in our world until we break the taboo of confronting candidly black sexuality and its myths.*

"Here," she said, "in this here place, we flesh; flesh that weeps, laughs; flesh that dances on bare feet in grass. Love it. Love it hard. Yonder they do not love your flesh. They despise it. They don't love your eyes; they'd just as soon pick em out. No more do they love the skin on your back. Yonder they flay it. And O my people they do not love your hands. Those they only use, tie, bind, chop off and leave empty. Love your hands! Love them. Raise them up and kiss them. Touch others with them, pat them together, stroke them on your face 'cause they don't love that either. You got to love it, You! . . . This is flesh I'm talking about here. Flesh that needs to be loved."

—TONI MORRISON, *BELOVED* (1987)

AMERICANS ARE OBSESSED WITH sex and fearful of black sexuality. The obsession has to do with a search for stimulation and meaning in a fast-paced, market-driven culture; the fear is rooted in visceral feelings about black bodies fueled by sexual myths of black women and men. The dominant myths draw black women and men either as threatening creatures who have the potential for sexual power over whites or as harmless, desexed underlings of a white culture. There is Jezebel (the seductive temptress), Sapphire (the evil, manipulative bitch) or Aunt Jemima (the sexless, long-suffering nurturer). There is Bigger Thomas (the mad and mean predatory craver of white women), Jack Johnson (the super performer—be it in athletics, entertainment or sex—who excels over others naturally and prefers women of a lighter hue), or Uncle Tom (the spineless, sexless—or is it impotent?—sidekick of whites). The myths offer distorted, dehumanized creatures whose bodies—color of skin, shape of nose and lips, type of hair, size of hips—are already distinguished from the white norm of beauty and whose feared sexual activities are deemed disgusting, dirty or funky and considered less acceptable.

Yet the paradox of the sexual politics of race in America is that, behind closed doors, the dirty, disgusting and funky sex associated with black people is often perceived to be more intriguing and interesting, while in public spaces talk about black sexuality is virtually taboo. Everyone knows it is virtually impossible to talk candidly about race without talking about sex. Yet most social scientists who examine race relations do so with little or no reference to how sexual perceptions influence racial matters. My thesis is that black sexuality is a taboo subject in white and black America and that a candid dialogue about black sexuality between and within these communities is requisite for healthy race relations in America.

The major cultural impact of the 1960s was not to demystify black sexuality, but rather to make black bodies more accessible to white bodies *on an equal basis.* The history of such access up to that time was primarily one of brutal white rape and ugly white abuse. The Afro-Americanization of white youth—given the disproportionate black role in popular music and athletics—has put white kids in closer contact with their own bodies and facilitated more humane interaction with black people. Listening to Motown records in the 1960s or dancing to hip-hop music in the 1990s may not lead one to question the sexual myths of black women and men, but when white and black kids buy the same billboard hits and laud the same athletic heroes, the result is often a shared cultural space where some humane interaction takes place.

This subterranean cultural current of interracial interaction increased during the 1970s and 1980s even as racial polarization deepened on the political front. We miss much of what goes on in the complex development of race relations in America if we focus solely on the racial card played by the Republican party and overlook the profound multicultural mix of popular culture that has occurred in the past two decades. In fact, one of the reasons Nixon, Reagan and Bush had to play a racial card, that is, had to code their language about race, rather than simply call a spade a spade, is due to the changed *cultural* climate of race and sex in America. The classic scene of Senator Strom Thurmond—staunch segregationist and longtime opponent of interracial sex and marriage—strongly defending Judge Clarence Thomas—married to a white woman and an alleged avid consumer of white pornography—shows how this change in climate affects even reactionary politicians in America.

Needless to say, many white Americans still view black sexuality with disgust. And some continue to view their own sexuality with disgust. Victorian morality and racist perceptions die hard. But more and more white Americans are willing to interact sexually with black Americans *on an equal basis*—even if the myths still persist. I view this as neither cause for celebration nor reason for lament. Anytime two human beings find genuine pleasure, joy and love, the stars smile and the universe is enriched. Yet as long as that pleasure, joy and love is still predicated on myths of black sexuality, the more fundamental challenge of humane interaction remains unmet. Instead, what we have is white access to black bodies on an equal basis—but not yet the demythologizing of black sexuality.

This demythologizing of black sexuality is crucial for black America, because much of black self-hatred and self-contempt has to do with the refusal of many black Americans to love their own black bodies—especially their black noses, lips, lips and hair. Just as many white Americans view black sexuality with disgust, so do many black Americans—but for very different reasons and with very different results. White-supremacist ideology is based first and foremost on the degradation of black bodies in order to control them. One of the best ways to instill fear in people is to terrorize them. Yet this fear is best sustained by convincing them that their bodies are ugly, their intellect is inherently underdeveloped, their culture is less civilized and their future warrants less concern than that of other peoples. Two hundred and forty-four years of slavery and nearly a century of institutionalized terrorism in the form of segregation, lynchings and second-class citizenship in America were aimed at precisely this devaluation of black people. This white-supremacist venture was, in the end, a relative failure—thanks to the courage and creativity of millions of black people and hundreds of exceptional white folk like John Brown, Elijah Lovejoy, Myles Horton, Russell Banks, Anne Braden and others. Yet this white dehumanizing endeavor has left its toll in the psychic scars and personal wounds now inscribed in the souls of black folk. These scars and wounds are clearly etched on the canvas of black sexuality.

How does one come to accept and affirm a body so despised by one's fellow citizens? What are the ways in which one can rejoice in the intimate moments of black sexuality in a culture that questions the aesthetic beauty of one's body? Can genuine human relationships flourish for black people in a society that assaults black intelligence, black moral character and black possibility?

These crucial questions were addressed in those black social spaces that affirmed black humanity and warded off white contempt—especially in black families, churches, mosques, schools, fraternities and sororities. These precious black institutions forged a mighty struggle against the white-supremacist bombardment of black people. They empowered black children to learn against the odds and supported damaged black egos so they could keep fighting; they preserved black sanity in an absurd society in which racism ruled unabated; and they provided opportunities for black love to stay alive. But these grand yet flawed black institutions refused to engage one fundamental issue: *black sexuality*. Instead, they ran from it like the plague. And they obsessively condemned those places where black sexuality was flaunted: the streets, the clubs and the dance halls.

Why was this so? Primarily because these black institutions put a premium on black survival in America. And black survival required accommodation with and acceptance from white America. Accommodation avoids any sustained association with the subversive and transgressive—be it communism or miscegenation. Did not the courageous yet tragic lives of Paul Robeson and Jack Johnson bear witness to this truth? And acceptance meant that only "good" Negroes would thrive—especially those who left black sexuality at the door when they "entered" and "arrived." In short, struggling black institutions made a Faustian pact with white America: avoid any substantive engagement with black sexuality and your survival on the margins of American society is, at least, possible.

White fear of black sexuality is a basic ingredient of white racism. And for whites to admit this deep fear even as they try to instill and sustain fear in blacks is to acknowledge a weakness—a weakness that goes down to the bone. Social scientists have long acknowledged that interracial sex and marriage is the most *perceived* source of white fear of black people—just as the repeated castrations of lynched black men cries out for serious psychocultural explanation.

Black sexuality is a taboo subject in America principally because it is a form of black power over which whites have little control—yet its visible manifestations evoke the most visceral of white responses, be it one of seductive obsession or downright disgust. On the one hand, black sexuality among blacks simply does not include whites, nor does it make them a central point of reference. It proceeds as if whites do not exist, as if whites are invisible and simply don't matter. This form of black sexuality puts black agency center stage with no white presence at all. This can be uncomfortable for white people accustomed to being the custodians of power.

On the other hand, black sexuality between blacks and whites proceeds based on underground desires that Americans deny or ignore in public and over which laws have no effective control. In fact, the dominant sexual myths of black women and men portray whites as being "out of control"—seduced, tempted, overcome, overpowered by black bodies. This form of black sexuality makes white passivity the norm—hardly an acceptable self-image for a white-run society.

Of course, neither scenario fully accounts for the complex elements that determine how any particular relationship involving black sexuality *actually* takes place. Yet they do accent the crucial link between black sexuality and black power in America. In this way, to make black sexuality a taboo subject is to silence discussion of a particular kind of power black people are perceived to have over whites. On the surface, this "golden" side is one in which black people simply have an upper hand sexually over whites given the dominant myths in our society.

Yet there is a "brazen" side—a side perceived long ago by black people. If black sexuality is a form of black power in which black agency and white passivity are interlinked, then are not black people simply acting out the very roles to which the racist myths of black sexuality confine them? For example, most black churches shunned the streets, clubs and dance halls in part because these black spaces seemed to confirm the very racist myths of black sexuality to be rejected. Only by being "respectable" black folk, they reasoned, would white America see their good works and shed its racist skin. For many black church folk, black agency and white passivity in sexual affairs was neither desirable nor tolerable. It simply permitted black people to play the role of the exotic "other"–closer to nature (removed from intelligence and control) and more prone to be guided by base pleasures and biological impulses.

Is there a way out of this catch–22 situation in which black sexuality either liberates black people from white control in order to imprison them in racist myths or confines blacks to white "respectability" while they make their own sexuality a taboo subject? There indeed are ways out, but there is no one way out for all black people. Or, to put it another way, the ways out for black men differ vastly from those for black women. Yet, neither black men nor black women can make it out unless both get out, since the degradation of both are inseparable though not identical.

Black male sexuality differs from black female sexuality because black men have different self-images and strategies of acquiring power in the patriarchal structures of white America and black communities. Similarly, black male heterosexuality differs from black male homosexuality owing to the self-perceptions and means of gaining power in the homophobic institutions of white America and black communities. The dominant myth of black male sexual prowess makes black men desirable sexual partners in a culture obsessed with sex. In addition, the Afro-Americanization of white youth has been more a male than a female affair, given the prominence of male athletes and the cultural weight of male pop artists. This process results in white youth–male and female–imitating and emulating black male styles of walking, talking, dressing and gesticulating in relation to others. One irony of our present moment is that just as young black men are murdered, maimed and imprisoned in record numbers, their styles have become disproportionately influential in shaping popular culture.

For most young black men, power is acquired by stylizing their bodies over space and time in such a way that their bodies reflect their uniqueness and provoke fear in others. To be "bad" is good not simply because it subverts the language of the dominant white culture, but also because it imposes a unique kind of order for young black men on their own distinctive chaos and solicits an attention that makes others pull back with some trepidation. This young black male style is a form of self identification and resistance in a hostile culture; it also is an instance of machismo identity ready for violent encounters. Yet in a patriarchal society, machismo identity is expected and even exalted–as with Rambo and Reagan. Yet a black machismo style solicits primarily sexual encounters with women and violent encounters with other black men or aggressive police. In this way, the black male search for power often reinforces the myth of black male sexual prowess—a myth that tends to subordinate black and white women as objects of sexual pleasure. This search for power also usually results in a direct confrontation with the order-imposing authorities of the status quo, that is, the police or criminal justice system. The prevailing cultural crisis of many black men is the limited stylistic options of self-image and resistance in a culture obsessed with sex, yet fearful of black sexuality.

This situation is even bleaker for most black gay men who reject the major stylistic option of black machismo identity, yet who are marginalized in white America and penalized in black America for doing so. In their efforts to be themselves, they are told they are not really "black men," not machismo-identified. Black gay men are often the brunt of talented black comics like Arsenio Hall and Damon Wayans. Yet behind the laughs lurks a black tragedy of major proportions: the refusal of white and black America to entertain seriously new stylistic options for black men caught in the deadly endeavor of rejecting black machismo identities.

The case of black women is quite different, partly because the dynamics of white and black patriarchy affect them differently and partly because the degradation of black female heterosexuality in America makes black female lesbian sexuality a less frightful jump to make. This does not mean that black lesbians suffer less than black gays—in fact, they suffer more, principally owing to their lower economic status. But this does mean that the subculture of black lesbians is fluid and the boundaries are less policed precisely because black female sexuality in general is more devalued, hence more marginal in white and black America.

The dominant myth of black female sexual prowess constitutes black women as desirable sexual partners—yet the central role of the ideology of white female beauty attenuates the expected conclusion. Instead of black women being the most sought after "objects of sexual pleasure"—as in the case of black men—white women tend to occupy this "upgraded," that is, degraded, position primarily because white beauty plays a weightier role in sexual desirability for women in racist patriarchal America. The ideal of female beauty in this country puts a premium on lightness and softness mythically associated with white women and downplays the rich stylistic manners associated with black women. This operation is not simply more racist to black women than that at work in relation to black men; it also is more devaluing of women in general than that at work in relation to men in general. This means that black women are subject to more multilayered bombardments of racist assaults than black men in addition to the sexist assaults they receive from black men. Needless to say, most black men—especially professional ones—simply recycle this vulgar operation along the axis of lighter hues that results in darker black women bearing more of the brunt than their already devalued lighter sisters. The psychic bouts with self-confidence, the existential agony over genuine desirability and the social burden of bearing and usually nurturing black children under these circumstances breeds a spiritual strength of black women unbeknownst to most black men and nearly all other Americans.

As long as black sexuality remains a taboo subject, we cannot acknowledge, examine or engage these tragic psychocultural facts of American life. Furthermore, our refusal to do so limits our ability to confront the overwhelming realities of the AIDS epidemic in America in general and in black America in particular. Although the dynamics of black male sexuality differ from those of black female sexuality, new stylistic options of self image and resistance can be forged only when black women and men do so together. This is so not because all black people should be heterosexual or with black partners, but rather because all black people—including black children of so-called mixed couples—are affected deeply by the prevailing myths of black sexuality. These myths are part of a wider network of white-supremacist lies whose authority and legitimacy must be undermined. In the long run, there is simply no way out for all of us other than living out the truths we proclaim about genuine humane interaction in our psychic and sexual lives. Only by living against the grain can we keep alive the possibility that the visceral feelings about black bodies fed by racist myths and promoted by market-driven quests for stimulation do not forever render us obsessed with sexuality and fearful of each other's humanity.

SOURCE: "Black Sexuality: The Taboo Subject," *Race Matters* (Boston: Beacon Press, 1993), pp. 83–91.

Forty Six

ON BLACK NATIONALISM

In 1989 Michael Lerner invited me to a conference in New York City sponsored by his prophetic Jewish magazine, Tikkun. *We became close friends and genuine brothers. We worked together with the marvelous Jane Isay for three years on our book,* Jews and Blacks: Let the Healing Begin *(1995). In black churches, Jewish synagogues and colleges around the country we conducted candid dialogues on black-Jewish relations. We remain special soul mates. In this exchange we explore the complex meaning of black nationalism—a subject often ignored or misconstrued by much of America, owing to white fears of black rage and revenge.*

IN THE PERIOD AFTER the decline of the civil rights movement and the alliance it generated between blacks and Jews, nationalist forces in each community have pushed against greater cooperation and toward separation. In this chapter we explore the meaning of black nationalism and its role in this dynamic.

Lerner: How do you think the Christian-Jewish dynamic relates to the black-Jewish one?

West: It's like this. In the black Christian world there is in a significant sense an accent on a love that is universalistic and internationalist. This is a quite different emphasis from most or much Christianity in the United States, and opens up the possibility of multiracial alliances. King's movement was one manifestation of this. It's Christianity's universalistic ethic that enables it to make it in the jaws of defeat and still afford some sense of agency or possible moral action, which is important since the black sense of the tragic is very much at the center of black Christianity.

I don't expect to see racism eliminated in American life, but we still fight against it. Never give up combat till the end. Betterment is always possible. And no matter how secular Jews are, they still have core elements of a progressive worldview that means they would not want to give up on human amelioration in history. There's no doubt in my mind that those who will be on the cutting edge of black-Jewish dialogue on the ground will be the prophetic black churches.

Lerner: The black churches have elements of black nationalism in them also, don't they?

West: Not too much. We have to make a distinction between black cultural distinctiveness and black nationalism.

Lerner: Tell me about that. What is black cultural distinctiveness?

West: It's a history of black styles and mannerisms: ways of singing, praying, worshipping and communicating that have created a certain sense of community and sustained sanity. There's no doubt that in syncopated styles, rhythmic styles and repetitive and antiphonal styles one sees a distinctiveness among black folk in the United States. The black church plays a crucial role in the creation of these styles and mannerisms. This is not black nationalism because nationalism is an ideology.

Louis Armstrong had a black style. How he walked, talked, blew his horn and so forth: but he wasn't a black nationalist. Wynton Marsalis in the same way comes deeply out of a tradition of black cultural distinctiveness. In many ways he recognizes the degree to which black styles and mannerisms have influenced his sense of who he is, but he's not a black nationalist. You can't assume that anybody who revels in black cultural distinctiveness is a black nationalist.

Lerner: So a black nationalist is usually somebody who says what?

West: A black nationalist is somebody who says that black people must close ranks, be suspicious of others and even hold them at arm's length. Primarily they stress black unity, solidarity, togetherness in a quest for a black nation—a place of black safety and self-determination. It's probably a good thing to have a certain healthy suspicion of others, because black people can be used and abused, but if you want to get people to change, you have to give openness a chance.

Lerner: Many people say that a primary task for blacks in this period is to discover their own black authenticity and their own identity. That the primary way in which blacks have been undermined, and continue to be undermined, is by the cultural materialism of the dominant society. And that black nationalists are taking a leadership role in trying to reestablish a struggle for black authenticity. I wonder if that's true. Where does this struggle for black authenticity and black identity fit into your picture of what needs to happen for blacks?

West: Where I agree with black nationalism unequivocally and wholeheartedly is the attempt to provide a sense of the history of African people—a history that's either been denied, marginalized, degraded or denigrated. In that regard, black nationalists are certainly attacking the vicious legacy of white supremacy, and I agree with that entirely, as would you yourself. We want to strip the past of white-supremacist lies that have so often regulated much of Western historiography about people of color who come to America—especially Africans.

Now of course in a market culture where a sense of history is increasingly farfetched and distant, it's no accident that the sense of history can easily be displaced by very crude nostalgic myths about the past. Some black nationalists have fallen into this trap: of just generating romantic conceptions of the past to undergird self-esteem. I think that's short-sighted, and I think it undermines the capacity of black people to critically confront our past.

This sense of history that the black nationalists call for, I agree with it, very much so. I don't like the term "black authenticity" because it implies that's there has been and is one black essence, one black core, one black center—and that one group has a monopoly on that center. That's precisely what history is not. History is about the multiple strands of various traditions, about communities clashing, quarreling, appropriating. Talking about "authenticity" is a way of trumping any serious discussion about the black condition, past and present. Black nationalists can fall into traps of nostalgia and romanticism as they attempt to generate their own myths, their own fictions.

Lerner: We have those same things in certain versions of Zionism.

West: It's true in every group, every tribe and every nation. Look at the history of America in terms of all the celebratory lies that tried to hide the realities, truths and facts they didn't want to confront.

Lerner: The question is: What can replace that nationalism and still retain a commitment to validating the needs of people for a cultural identity that is not defined solely in terms of their relationship with the capitalist market? What's the answer to that? It seems to me that the consciousness of the black community today is unbelievably permeated by the capitalist market—and this gets reflected in popular culture in an obsession with fancy clothes, sexuality turned into a commodity and salvation through consumption—with the possible exception of the black churches.

West: Yes, we have in the black churches a community that sustains members. We have a style, form, and level of content, definitely so. But as you know, it isn't completely unaffected by the market. There's a lot of market religion in both the Jewish and the black community. T. S. Eliot was absolutely right when he said you don't inherit a tradition, you have to obtain it by great labor. The only way you preserve a sense of history is to have a community and tradition struggling in the present to keep the best of the past alive. That's one of the real paradoxes in our understanding of the past: It stays alive only to the degree to which persons in the present keep it alive. Many church communities in the black community and religious communities in the Jewish community are able to do that. Not them alone, but they are the dominant ones. Needless to say, market religion that effaces the past is growing in both black and Jewish communities.

The struggle is amplified by the degree to which market forces become more and more powerful, more and more erosive of historical memory. In place of historical memory you get either nostalgia, a "fossil-collecting," antiquarian sensibility, or a kind of icon selection of the past, where you simply talk about the "greatest hits"—the great figures who come back out of context solely as the icons before whom you worship, rather than as live figures whom you learned from, criticized and sympathized with.

Although it's sometimes hard to acknowledge it amongst narrow black nationalists, there is actually such a thing as progressive black nationalism.

Lerner: What's the distinction?

West: A progressive black nationalist is like a progressive Zionist. They have a real solidarity with their people, but they also want to accent the humanity of others who are engaging in humane interaction across groupings. Their nationalism has an internationalist, universalistic dimension. However, there's a big tension between the universalism they expound and the nationalism they are forced to defend, so they are rarely the ones in power. They are, rather, the prophetic critics of their fellow nationalists.

Lerner: How can we get people to spend less time listening to Farrakhan and more time listening to progressive people?

West: We've got to institutionalize progressive voices in both communities so that they become more visible and effective. There are a number of persons who right now sympathize with and even follow Minister Farrakhan, who in the early part of the twenty-first century will be radical democrats. These people are fundamentally concerned about black suffering; they go into Farrakhan's organization because they are concerned about this suffering and in the end they feel that it doesn't provide enough vision and insight and analysis. So they end up as progressives. This is the trajectory of persons such as Malcolm X, Amiri Baraka, Sonia Sanchez. There is a struggle going on over the minds, bodies and souls of young black Americans, some of whom will go through Minister Louis Farrakhan's organization and end up as progressives. How soon? It's hard to say. The progressive black nationalist position is the closest I come to, although I personally don't consider myself a nationalist of any sort.

Lerner: Can you summarize your position on that?

West: Any kind of nationalism, for the most part, will be used in a way that ends up dehumanizing folk. We all need recognition and some form of protection, but usually in these dominant forms the quest for group unity results in attacking someone else. The history of nationalism seems to be part and parcel of the history of tribalism. It tends to be deeply patriarchal and homophobic with little sense of our common humanity. Black nationalism has come to be problematic because every black nationalist has to sooner or later have some relation with territory or land. Black people in America are a people without land, that's part of our heritage.

Lerner: Do you ever have a longing for land?

West: Yes. We have a house in Ethiopia. When I go to Ethiopia I feel in some sense at home. I could certainly envision living there, because racial tension is virtually nonexistent. It's not romantic, because tribal strife does exist; it's just a question of being in a country where black humanity is taken so utterly for granted. But I'm still an outsider there.

Lerner: American Jews have programs whereby they can go to Israel for a year, or maybe just for the summer. What would be wrong with having similar institutionalized ways of bringing folk over to Africa?

West: I rather like that idea. But there is a trap of which I'm leery. There are very positive things about Africa in terms of being comfortable, but negative things in terms of being New Worlders in the Old World. A lot of blacks have romantic notions of Africa, and I would want to fight against that. It's the same with Jews. You think you can go to Israel and, lo and behold, all the tensions of being Jewish in Chicago or New York disappear. Or it's a guilt trip, almost an appeal to machismo: "Come to where the real action is." This is an idolatrous trap, because of course you want to contribute to Jewish survival, but it's easy to cheapen that and not recognize that all of us are born into circumstances not of our choosing. You can't leapfrog out of your circumstance in order to grab hold of some easy identity.

Lerner: So, on a personal level, do you feel you can be part of this society?

West: Yes and no. After 244 years of slavery and 87 years of Jim Crow, I think black people in America will always have some sense of being outsiders. Yet there's a sense in which I am a part of it, because the nation is unimaginable without black people in the culture, either past or present. It's the tension between being an outsider and being more integral to America than 90 percent of Americans. It's what Du Bois called "double consciousness." I'm thirteenth-generation American! That's about as integral as you can get.

Lerner: The twentieth century has been full of horrendous and disgusting national struggles. Right now we have a picture in our mind of Serbs and Bosnians killing each other, and we see the possibility of the same thing reemerging throughout Eastern Europe. A progressive person might explain black nationalism as a response to the failure of society to give blacks equality: a distorted response, but one they can understand. When black nationalism pops up in America today and manifests in anti-Semitic ways, Jews have a lot of questions about it. Was black nationalism flourishing when blacks were slaves? Was there nationalism in Africa?

West: Nationalism per se is a modern phenomenon. It's a post-Napoleonic development in modern Europe. Once organizing activity began to take place for the purpose of promoting self-determination among black people, nationalism became one of the more attractive ideologies that could attempt to mobilize them.

Lerner: When did it happen, this activity to organize black people?

West: Slave insurrections, hundreds of them. They were proto–black nationalist efforts. But organizationally speaking, black nationalism doesn't really take off till you get Chief Sam's "back to Africa" movement in Oklahoma trying to constitute a nation in a serious sense. By "serious" I mean talking about land and territory, because so much of black nationalism avoids this fundamental issue. Chief Sam's movement organized people to go back to Africa; they actually went back to Sierra Leone.

Lerner: When was this?

West: Right after the attempt by a group of blacks to make Oklahoma an all-black state between 1900 and 1905. It wasn't successful, but it left a legacy. The first part of the legacy was black municipalities scattered all over Oklahoma. The second part was the founding in 1896 of a black/Judaic religious institution. That institution in Boley, Oklahoma, still exists today, but it isn't as visible because of the black Hebrews in the urban centers. That black/Judaic movement had a significant impact on black group thinking. It was nationalist thinking, but it used a Jewish model for organizing black people, with their own Temple, their own rabbis and so forth.

Lerner: They self-consciously modeled themselves on Jews?

West: It was very much based on the Old Testament—they shunned the New Testament. Curtis Caldwell is writing the history of this fascinating group. Now as I said before, Chief Sam was the third part of the legacy of the attempt to make Oklahoma an all-black state. He had a real impact on Marcus Garvey, who reached the conclusion all black nationalists reach, which is deep pessimism regarding America's will toward racial justice. They give up on the possibility of ever living lives of dignity and decency in America, and they leave. This brother, Chief Sam, organized folk in such a way that he took off in a boat with sixty-five people—which means he was more successful than Marcus Garvey. Garvey never saw Africa, though he talked about it every day. But when Garvey arrived in the States in 1915, he put together the largest mass movement among black people ever. And it happened to be a thorough-going black nationalist movement.

Lerner: Why did it catch on?

West: Garvey was able to speak to the deep sense of disillusionment and disappointment of uprooted black people after their participation in the First World War. Many had risked their lives. Of course we can't forget the major race riot in East St. Louis, July 1917. Tulsa, Oklahoma, 1921, another race riot. In fact in the summer of 1919 there were over twenty major race riots. Now keep in mind that at this period, "race riot" means white Americans murdering, pillaging and plundering in black communities.

Lerner: Not like today's race riots, which are largely blacks acting in response to their oppression.

West: You started getting blacks on the aggressive on a grand scale with Watts in August 1965. Though it's true there were exceptions, as in Harlem in 1943. Or, in Tulsa, Oklahoma, you had a number of black soldiers who organized and began shooting at policemen. This was just mind-boggling for most of white America. Anyway, there were black people becoming progressively disillusioned in terms of the promise of American democracy, and giving up.

Lerner: After the compromise of 1876, when Reconstruction was dismantled, why were blacks disillusioned then?

West: There was a majority of black people in the South, but it was difficult, if not impossible, to organize politically, because they were silenced by terrorism. A number of voices emerged, but they ended up swinging on trees. The level of terrorism was instilling fear into black hearts and black souls, so that it was impossible to overcome it in order to get them to organize. That is one of the reasons why Garvey's movement was centered in New York and the North. Garvey himself had to meet the Ku Klux Klan in order to let them know that there were going to be some Universal Negro Improvement Association branches in the South, and they ought not to mess with those branches. Because these branches were afraid to meet. The NAACP, too; it was basically an illegal organization, and if they met, the white reactionary forces would come down hard.

Lerner: I'm not sure I understand. What do you mean, "if they met"?

West: If you formed an NAACP branch in one of a large number of Southern cities, the space would be torched, the individuals would be hunted down.

Lerner: So why would the Klan listen to Garvey?

West: Well, that's very interesting. In some ways they were similar. Both believed in segregation; both believed blacks ought to leave the country. Garvey continually made the same three points. One: "You are a mighty race, you can do what you will." Two: "Our basic problem is disorganization. Black people must organize and mobilize." Three: "Don't ever be duped into believing that your white allies are reliable. Under conditions of economic, social, political and sexual competition, every white person is a potential Klansman." When he invited the Klan and the Anglo-Saxon Club to Liberty Hall in Harlem he said, "This is what white Americans really think. Liberals don't want to believe it, but you push them far enough or desire their daughters and they'll say the same things." So Garvey's appeal to blacks' postwar pessimism came at a propitious moment. Black nationalism was predicated on deep pessimism, and on black people understanding self-determination in a mode in which the issue of land was never seriously addressed. Garvey wanted to but could not really address the issue of land. He would either have to talk about colonizing Africa, the way it had been done with Liberia; or about getting the Africans who were there to invite the African Americans over; or he had to go symbolic and talk about a state of mind rather than a nation-state, which is primarily what he did. "Decolonize your mind, your body, your soul." Which was very positive in terms of affirmation, and Garvey was not a black supremacist. Garvey's movement, of course, was crushed by the U.S. government and the disillusionment remained, to emerge again with Elijah Muhammad's movement.

Lerner: You seem to be giving black nationalism a pivotal role here.

West: Black nationalism is an integral part of black history, but I don't believe it is central to it. That is because the pessimism on which black nationalism was predicated was never fully embraced in an organizational sense. Black people usually still maintain some possibility for a multiracial coalition, for trying to extend the scope of democracy in America. I think the role of the black church has been crucial in this, because what it has done historically is steal the thunder from the black nationalists. It highlights black cultural distinctiveness and, despite calling for group cohesiveness, its message is universalistic. It has always been open to others willing to work with us. By saying that self-love and self-affirmation are key, it took center ground over black nationalism. So the black church is much more central to black history than black nationalism.

SOURCE: "Black Nationalism," *Jews and Blacks: A Dialogue on Race, Religion, and Culture in America,* by Michael Lerner and Cornel West, pp. 91–114. Used by permission of Putnam Berkley, a division of Penguin Putnam Inc.

Forty Seven

TENSIONS WITH JEWISH FRIENDS AND FOES

In 1997, my friend and brother Jack Salzman and I published a coedited scholarly collection of new essays (Struggles in the Promised Land) *exploring the vexed history of black-Jewish relations, from the curse of Ham to Jews in the slave trade, coalitions in the civil rights and left movements, blacks and Jews in Hollywood and tensions over affirmative action and Israel. My essay represents my first and only response to vicious attacks on my work and life by a few Jewish journalists and writers. I received strong support from many Jewish intellectuals and solid backing from most of the black intelligentsia.*

I GREW UP IN a black world without Jews. Yet my evolving worldview about life and love, faith and struggle was and is deeply shaped by the Jewish world—be it the Bible, Marx, Durkheim, Freud, Kafka, Wittgenstein or Lukács. Most of the flesh-and-blood Jews I have encountered are descendants of Eastern European immigrants who arrived in America at the turn of the century. And the vast majority of my Jewish friends tend to be progressive intellectuals and activists. So my personal reflections on black-Jewish relations preclude any broad generalizations or monolithic formulations.

My first significant and sustained interaction with Jews—especially in college and graduate school—was exciting and exhilarating. I had never been so impressed with such an engaging group of white Americans so deeply concerned about white supremacy and other social evils. In our numerous discussions in study groups, classes, cafés and political organizations, we informed and inspired one another in regard to our democratic socialist visions, analyses and strategies for social change. We also reveled in critical evaluations of artists and writers in highbrow and popular culture. And though we never worshiped the New York intellectuals, I always had a good word and strong argument for my favorites—Delmore Schwartz, Dwight Macdonald, Harold Rosenberg, Irving Howe and Michael Harrington (two non-Jews out of five). Yet none of these figures compared to my major intellectual heroes at this young age—Turgenev, Kierkegaard, Marx, Chekhov, Niebuhr, Wittgenstein, Du Bois, Baldwin, Ellison, Schopenhauer and Nietzsche (two Jews out of eleven).

This period lasted roughly from the late 1960s to the mid-1970s. The rise of visible Jewish neoconservative thinkers shattered my parochial perceptions of the Jewish intelligentsia. In stark contrast to the cosmopolitan sensibilities of my Jewish progressive friends, I detected a strong dose of tribalism in the complex, convoluted and hardly convincing arguments of Jewish neoconservatives. Ironically, this postwar quest (1967, 1973 wars against Israel) for Jewish identity was influenced by the post–civil rights quest for black identity—a quest predominant among my black intellectual friends and comrades. On the domestic front, the astonishing entry of many American Jews into the middle class produced a new cultural situation. Increasing exogamous marriages, diluted Jewish rituals and dull suburban life raised crucial issues of Jewish continuity and identity. On the Israeli front, the very survival of the country was at stake, and U.S. support—financial and military—was indispensable for its sustenance. The pressing issues of affirmative action (the relative weighing of merit, fairness and public interest) and Zionism (the relative weighing of Jewish survival, secular democracy and Palestinian subordination) loomed large—even among my Jewish progressive friends.

This painful and poignant struggle in the Jewish world perplexed me for two reasons. First, I considered affirmative action neither a panacea to vicious racist practices of the past nor a fetish to wipe clean class constraints in American life. Instead, I viewed affirmative action as a weak strategy to break the back of a tight, well-to-do white male network that had disproportionate access to power, wealth, status and influence. So retreat on affirmative action was a sure sign of a progressive or liberal failure of nerve and commitment. Second, I was never a Zionist (like Martin Luther King, Jr., Bayard Rustin and W. E. B. Du Bois). I strongly believe that Jewish survival depends on statehood for security. But I also believe that in the long run only a secular democratic state—with no special Jewish character—can secure Jewish survival. Hence, I was confused by the intense secular argument for a full-fledged meritocracy in America and the heartfelt Zionist claims for a Jewish state in Israel. As a radical democrat, my dilemma was how to fight the subtle forms of white and male supremacy still operating alongside affirmative action, shatter the silence on class constraints and put forward a moral critique of Zionism without downplaying the need for Jewish survival or falling into anti-Semitic traps. Needless to say, most of my Jewish leftist friends were progressive Zionists. So we argued intensely and respectfully as comrades.

In parts of the black world, my position was viewed with great suspicion: Why do you spend so much time with Jewish progressives who will soon betray you on the altar of Jewish interests and networks? Are not black-Jewish alliances the occasion for black deference and Jewish paternalism? Why do you engage Jewish Zionists in such a charitable manner when you put forward such harsh criticisms of black nationalists? Is it possible to forge black-Jewish coalitions with integrity without attempting to create conditions under which black progressives, liberals and nationalists can coalesce?

Since I take seriously the dual strategies of black operational unity and multiracial democratic alliance, I struggled with these challenging questions. How does one remain true to radical democratic ideals that oppose all forms of xenophobia and target corporate power for downward redistribution of wealth, while always acknowledging the tremendous weight of white supremacy in American society? I have worked with black nationalists since the late 1960s—in black united fronts, black political parties and black religious formations—precisely because they rightly target the most explosive issue and rawest nerve in American life: white supremacy. Yet I do so as a radical democrat, not as a black nationalist. Nationalism of any form is for me a species of tribalism that warrants moral rejection. And since all forms of nationalism I know are deeply patriarchal and homophobic, I have great suspicions of them. Just like organized religion. Yet some good can come from them, so I selectively work with them.

My dilemma sharpened in the 1980s with the presidential campaigns of Jesse Jackson and the rise of Minister Louis Farrakhan in the eyes of white America. Since then black-Jewish relations have worsened. Jackson's "Hymietown" remark set off waves of Jewish rage. Farrakhan's response to Jewish threats against Jackson set off even more. And we all became locked into a spiral of accusations and demonizations. In the Jewish world, Jackson could not say enough to warrant forgiveness, and Farrakhan was dubbed the new Hitler. In the black world, Jackson and Farrakhan were viewed as heaven-sent for sustaining forms of Jewish identity and fund-raising predicated on anti-Semitism in America. The double standards for black and white anti-Semitic rhetoric were appalling. Both worlds grasped only snippets of the truth—namely, that progressive and liberal forces in general were collapsing in America while the two most progressive and liberal groups (blacks and Jews) were involved in a heartfelt yet cathartic sideshow. The media sensationalized it and projected a polarization more symbolic than real. Yet even symbols shape reality after much media interference.

With the white media discoveries of Leonard Jeffries and Khalid Abdul Muhammad, the obsession in the Jewish world with black anti-Jewish rhetoric increased. And given the growing influence of Howard Stern and other xenophobic loose-tongued Jewish talk-radio hosts, the concern in the black world with Jewish anti-black rhetoric increased. In short, the paranoia of two of the most paranoid groups in America was getting out of control—and clashing in ugly ways. Candid dialogue was badly needed.

Michael Lerner and I saw this need in 1989 and acted on it. We worked for five years on our book, *Jews and Blacks: Let the Healing Begin* (1995). We toured the country, lectured in over twenty cities—in black churches, Jewish synagogues, bookstores, community centers, colleges, high schools. The audiences were all multiracial. The responses were overwhelming. The spirit of honest conversation, collective struggle and racial healing was inspiring. Yet we received no financial support for our proposed black-Jewish conference and we were trashed by both visible neoliberal Jewish intellectuals and vociferous progressive black intellectuals. And with the advent of the O.J. verdict and Million Man March, our efforts for black-Jewish healing were in shambles. Lerner and I continued to agree to disagree, even as our agreements and disagreements grew deeper, but as a twosome we felt more and more isolated.

The sheer viciousness of the intellectual attacks on my work and life from the Jewish world caught me a bit by surprise. I've been on the battlefield for over two decades, so I am accustomed to principled criticisms and ad hominem ones. But the recent wave of venom and vitriol directed at me is new. Needless to say, I try to learn what I can from such contemptuous criticisms, keep my stride and do my work. And with all of us being the cracked vessels that we are, there will always be degrees of mendaciousness and tendentiousness, envy and jealousy, misunderstandings and misinterpretations in our human exchanges. Furthermore, the degraded state of public conversation in American culture leads us to lower our intellectual expectations in regard to a spirit of empathy, charity or generosity. But the virtual absence of fair-mindedness, the predominance of such intellectual obscenity and personal vulgarity bespeaks a gangsterization of the mind that behooves all of us to resist. Even among tormented and tortured journalists aspiring to serious intellectual work such as Leon Wieseltier, we expect more than third-rate hatchet jobs predicated on homework undone in the guise of lowbrow wit and middlebrow wordplay. Similarly, we look for more than paternalistic rankings (Ellen Willis), glib reputation assessments (Sean Wilentz), or weak efforts at mediation in leading liberal and progressive weeklies and quarterlies (Andrew Delbanco). In other works, the degeneration of black-Jewish relations is suffocating certain pockets of our intellectual life. How sad!

This degeneration can be seen in the responses of some of my old Jewish friends to the attacks. Silence. Avoidance. Evasion. Capitulation. Deference to power. Cowardly careerism. In other words, hardly any serious grappling with my texts or actions—just a shadow game with close colleagues and tribal loyalties. Many of my supportive Jewish friends reach these same conclusions. And most of my black friends simply say, we told you so.

For me, this painful situation raised a number of existential and vocational questions. What were the fundamental reasons I persisted in promoting black-Jewish coalitions? How would I define the sources of hope for such unpopular efforts? What is the most wise and moral response to such ugly disrespect and degradation? My fundamental commitments are to human decency, mutual respect and personal integrity. The common thread of these commitments is compassion or empathy. Needless to say, for a Christian, this thread flows from the love ethic of Jesus Christ; for a human being, it serves as the basis of a democratic mode of being in the world. Those great existential democrats—from Walt Whitman, Maurice Maeterlinck, John Dewey, Ida B. Wells-Barnett, Louis Armstrong, Abraham Joshua Heschel, Audre Lorde, and John Coltrane—all promoted forms of human connection mediated with compassion without dissolving diversity and differences. My own investment in black-Jewish alliances is not simply a political effort to buttress progressive forces in American society. It also is a moral endeavor that exemplifies ways in which the most hated group in European history and the most hated group in U.S. history can coalesce in the name of precious democratic ideals—ideals that serve as the sole countervailing force to hatred, fear and greed.

This political effort and moral endeavor will always cut against the grain. Jewish racism and black anti-Semitism are not only as American as cherry pie; they also are human responses to insecurities and anxieties. For a Christian and radical democrat like myself, the go-cart of compassion is dialogue based on a fundamental respect for the "other." This dialogue requires active listening and candid speaking. The aim is neither verbal conquest nor rational coercion; rather, it is to provide an occasion for openness so that a spirituality of genuine questioning can take root in one's mind, heart and soul. Such questioning is the vehicle for intellectual change and existential transformation. The openness that precedes such questioning requires that we be vulnerable enough—hence trusting enough—to be questioned in a transformative mode. This is why no one should be refused to enter such openness. Or to put it another way, no one is so far beyond the pale—so worthy of utter disrespect and contempt—that we give up on them in our dialogical efforts. Why so? Because of human fallibility and unpredictability. Dialogical dogmatism is a form of intellectual exclusion that chooses interlocutors with whom one is comfortable; it rests upon an unacknowledged ignorance of others and an undeniable arrogance toward others. Dialogical dogmatism is ideologically promiscuous—it lies with liberal and conservative, Left and Right, black and Jewish ideologues. The kind of dialogue I am calling for will always transgress the "respectable" bounds of dialogical dogmatists—yet it is the lifeblood of radical democracy and political breakthroughs. There is never any guarantee for success; yet the sheer existence of such dialogue is already a kind of success—for it means that decency, respect and integrity are still alive.

So in the midst of disrespect and degradation, I promote the practical wisdom of dialogue—that thin reed in the whirlwind of our times doomed to strong lip service and weak action that stakes a high moral ground in a cynical age. Like anyone's, my rage and anger flows and sometimes overflows—yet my commitment to dialogical action, alongside other forms of democratic action, is profound.

In regard to my defense of sustaining dialogue with black nationalists or my critical support of the Million Man March, my Jewish critics are eager to put forward loquacious utterances and engaged editorials highlighting my wrongheadedness. Again, I try to listen and learn from their criticisms, but I also recognize the double standards at work. I must denounce, isolate and make no contact with xenophobic black nationalists, but certain progressive Jewish intellectuals have no duty to identify and criticize the Negrophobic (or anti-Arab racist) sentiments of their neoliberal or progressive friends. No serious or substantive black-Jewish cooperation can emerge on such a one-way street.

Where then do we go from here? Black-Jewish relations—at the symbolic level—are in shambles. Yet there are significant black-Jewish efforts on the ground: in local communities between churches and synagogues, in the trade-union movement, between the Anti-Defamation League and black grassroots activists, among electoral coalitions and elected officiates. First, we have to change our ways. We must stop playing games with one another. We must be candid in our criticisms and respectful in our exchanges. Second, we must be more self-critical of ourselves, our positions and our vantage points. What powers and influences do we actually have? How do we use them? What are the major priorities in our agendas? Do we make them clear to others? How do we rationally defend them? Are they subject to rational scrutiny? What are the fundamental ideals we cherish? Are they the same ones we espouse publicly? Third, we must focus on principles and realities bigger than the immediate interests of the black and Jewish communities. Black-Jewish cooperation can never be based on a cold calculation of black and Jewish needs. Rather, it must be regulated by broad and universal ideals of democracy and decency, fairness and dignity, justice and freedom for all. But these ideals are empty if we continually treat those within and across our communities in a cold-hearted and mean-spirited manner. The best of the Jewish tradition puts a premium on mercy and justice: the best of the black heritage, on improvisation and experimentation. Both require bonds of trust and cords of empathy. Without them, black-Jewish cooperation is but sounding brass and tinkling cymbal.

SOURCE: "Walking the Tightrope: Some Personal Reflections on Blacks and Jews," by Cornel West, copyright © 1997 by Cornel West, from *Struggles in the Promised Land: Toward a History of Black-Jewish Relations in the United States,* edited by Jack Salzman and Cornel West, pp. 411–416. Used by permission of Oxford University Press, Inc.

Forty Eight

ON JACKIE ROBINSON

One of my highest honors in life was to be chosen by Rachel Robinson to write the fore-word for the new edition of Jackie Robinson's autobiography—alongside Hank Aaron's introduction. Rachel Robinson is one of the great first ladies of our time. And Jackie Robinson was one of the giants of our century.

THREE FUNDAMENTAL EVENTS BETWEEN March and June of 1947 in America changed the course of world history in the twentieth century. On March 12, 1947, President Harry Truman proclaimed in a historic speech before a special joint session of Congress the intention of the U.S. government "to support free peoples who are resisting subjugation by armed minorities or by outside pressures." This, the famous Truman Doctrine, was declared in response to both the beginning of the collapse of the most powerful empire the world has ever seen (the British empire) and the emergence of one of the most repressive, the Soviet empire. In short, Truman announced the aim of the American empire to police the world in the light of its democratic ideals and imperial interests.

On April 15, 1947, before 26,623 Americans (more than half of them black) at Ebbets Field in Brooklyn, Jackie Robinson became the first African American to play professional, major-league baseball. In this historic opening game against the Boston Braves, a dignified and heroic descendant of American slaves and sharecroppers who wore number 42 on his Dodger uniform played first base in one of the sacred spaces of American culture. More even than either Abraham Lincoln and the Civil War or Martin Luther King, Jr., and the civil rights movement, Jackie Robinson graphically symbolized and personified the challenge to the vicious legacy and ideology of white supremacy in American history.

Soon afterward, on June 5, 1947, Secretary of State George C. Marshall delivered an address at Harvard University's graduation ceremonies, in which he put forward an American plan for European economic recovery with huge U.S. assistance in order to combat Soviet domination. The basic requirements of the Marshall Plan were U.S. influence over the internal budgets of the European recipient states and the disproportionate purchase of American exports for European recovery.

These three events represent the most fundamental processes of this century—the end of the Age of Europe (and the preeminence of its last great empire), the acceleration of the challenge to white supremacy (a pillar of European imperialism and American history) and the move of the American empire to the center of the world-historical stage (in opposition to the Soviet empire). In this way, a historic presidential speech, an unforgettable baseball game and an influential commencement address take us to the very heart of the agony and anguish, the achievements and accomplishments of our time.

With the surprising collapse of the Soviet empire in 1989, the Truman Doctrine has run its course. And with the economic recovery of Europe—alongside the phenomenal growth of the U.S. economy—between 1947 and 1973, the Marshall Plan did what it set out to do. Despite the significant gains of the civil rights movement in the 1960s, the challenge to white supremacy in America remains incomplete, unfinished. That is why, today, the life and work, the achievements and suffering of Jackie Robinson continue to speak to us with such power and poignancy.

In 1947, Jackie Robinson not only symbolized all of black America on trial in the eyes of white America and the expansion of the ideals of democracy, he also represented the best of a traditional black quest for dignity, excellence and integrity. This quest was primarily a moral effort to preserve black sanity and spirituality in the face of white-supremacist barbarity and bestiality; it was a human attempt to hold on to dreams deferred and hopes dashed, owing mainly to slavery and Jim Crow in America. The deep and devastating effects of psychic scars, physical abuse and material deprivation could not suffocate the black tradition of moral struggle and political resistance. When Jackie Robinson states that he "never had it made," he means, in part, that he had to fight in a variety of ways and on a number of fronts to preserve both his sense of dignity and his integrity; and in part that he was able to fight primarily because of the love and support of those fighters who came before him and those who now stood by his side.

The most striking features of this marvelous book are its honesty, its courage and its wisdom. Here is a great American hero who refuses to be a mythical hero. Instead, he tells the painful truth about himself as a human being—someone who, like all of us, needs love, struggles with insecurity, makes mistakes, revels in achievements and weeps in sorrow. Here is a transracial figure beloved by blacks and whites who rails against the absurdities of white racism and the seductive security of black xenophobia. Here is a celebrity who takes us on a journey through the valleys and over the mountaintops of intimate relations with his family, friends and mentors. Here is one of the greatest athletes of our century disclosing his developing sense of political engagement and community empowerment as a liberal Republican in a right-wing Republican party. Here is a black man and father—with a strong sense of his masculinity—who talks about his maturity in terms of lessons painfully learned from his loving mother, his brilliant and self-confident wife, his adventurous children and his supportive father figures. I reveled in his exchanges—critical and respectful—with Malcolm X, Martin Luther King, Jr., Richard Nixon, William Buckley, Jr,. Black Panther leaders and Lewis Micheaux.

Jackie Robinson's life and book constitute an antiphonal "song of a great composite democratic individual." This grand phrase of Walt Whitman captures the *jazzlike* character of Jackie Robinson—his noble experiment in which restraint and performance, improvisation, and discipline under severe pressure are exercised with excellence; his openness to others; his generosity to others; and his relentless self-criticism without recourse to self-pity and self-indulgence. And yet, his disillusionment with America is real. Robinson cannot stand and sing the national anthem or salute the flag. His deep patriotism and his hatred of white supremacy will not allow him to engage in such empty gestures of country worship. He knows that "money is America's God" and that he is "a black man in a white world."

Jackie Robinson's historic challenge to white supremacy in America was not an attempt to "prove" himself and his humanity to white America. Rather, it was to *be* himself, to allow his God-given humanity to be seen, acknowledged and recognized by those who questioned it. He gained respect because he so deeply respected himself, because he respected black people and others. He willingly took on the awesome burden of symbolizing black humanity in the one arena of fairness in a country predicated, in part, on unfairness to black people. And he bore this burden with great dignity—not because he wanted to *be* somebody but, rather, because he was already a great *somebody* in a land where all black folk were nobody to most white people. This is why his grand example is, in the moving and wise words of George Will (with whom I rarely agree!), "One of the great achievements not only in the annals of sports, but of the human drama anywhere, anytime." This book reveals why and how Jackie Robinson's life was an exemplary testimony of the black and human "Love Supreme"—the same moral and spiritual ideal toward which Martin Luther King, Jr., Fannie Lou Hamer and John Coltrane asked us to aspire.

SOURCE: "Foreword," by Cornel West, from *I Never Had It Made* by Jackie Robinson. Copyright © 1995 by Rachel Robinson. Reprinted by permission of The Eco Press.

Forty Nine

ON JULIANNE MALVEAUX

Given all the chatter about public intellectuals in America, it is astonishing that the work and life of Julianne Malveaux do not receive more attention and admiration. She is an exemplary engaged intellectual who thinks and acts with great courage and boldness. I constantly look to her writings for insight and guidance. She is a national treasure.

JULIANNE MALVEAUX IS THE most provocative, progressive and iconoclastic public intellectual in the country. Her writings not only unsettle prevailing prejudices and undo conventional presuppositions; they also provoke passionate responses—positive or negative—precisely because she is so direct, honest and hard-hitting. Besides Noam Chomsky, Barbara Ehrenreich, Manning Marable and a few others, Julianne Malveaux is the most well-known progressive critic of contemporary American life. But she has yet to receive the serious attention she deserves. Needless to say, she has thousands of loyal fans who hang on her every transgressive word. Yet her powerful onslaught on economic inequality, white supremacy, male supremacy and just plain social meanness is gaining a larger audience in the 1990s. And rightly so. She is one of the last of a long line of American iconoclastic writers from Lydia Maria Child through H. L. Mencken to C. Wright Mills. Like them, she radically cuts against the grain of American culture and calls into question the reigning idols of American society.

Unlike most public intellectuals of our time, Julianne Malveaux possesses a Ph.D. in economics. And unlike nearly every academic economist, she speaks to a popular audience through the print and electronic media. She also is a powerful and poignant public speaker who is quite popular on the lecture circuit. In the tradition of Thorstein Veblen, John Kenneth Galbraith and Robert Lekachman, Julianne Malveaux writes in a clear and lucid prose that stays in touch with the complex realities of everyday people. This means that she cuts through the obscure jargon and remote dogma of neoclassical economists. She knows that perfect competition models downplay the actual operations of power in the economy and that individual consumers are not sovereign in markets often dominated by transnational corporations. She also realizes that economic analysis is inseparable from politics and culture. And, of course, it is impossible to understand the American

economy, politics and culture without grasping the subtle and not too subtle persistence of race and gender. Julianne Malveaux differs from most black and feminist critics in that she puts a premium on economic issues. She knows that white
and male supremacy are forms of social pathology—a kind of societal sickness—yet
she holds that much of it has to do with economic power and material privilege.
In other words, they are much more than individual prejudices and less than in-
born propensities. They are sustained by institutions and structures that hide and
conceal social misery and personal pain. And her courageous critiques of fellow
black and feminist intellectuals add much to the debate on race, gender and justice in our time.

Last, Julianne Malveaux is unique among prophetic public intellectuals owing
to her undeniable humor and fury. She is the only progressive thinker on the
scene with a profound sense of the comic. This sense is shunned by most radicals
primarily because genuine acknowledgment of one's own foibles seems to disempower an already weak Left. Yet Julianne Malveaux's grasp of the absurd character of the human condition and American life yields a humorous treatment of serious problems that produce both laughter and lament. To put it bluntly, I detect
a Chekhovian strand in her social and cultural criticism—a strand that fuels comedy and compassion. This deep comic sense is coupled with an existential fury—
a kind of spiritual indignation that remains on the surface. How rare it is to see
battling inside the soul of a progressive thinker an encounter of Chekhov's compassionate comedy with Billie Holiday's empathetic rage! This painful yet productive battle—which goes deeper than Du Bois's "double-consciousness" warring
in the souls of black folk—yields a distinctive form of an informed and inspiring
"madness" rarely seen in the annals of American letters. God bless the child that
got its own—even in ward 6! To be a black woman intellectual with personal integrity and prophetic commitment is to catch much hell—and raise some with a
smile on one's face!

SOURCE: "Foreword," *Sex, Lies and Stereotypes: Perspectives of a Mad Economist,* by Julianne Malveaux
(Pines One Publications, 1994), pp. xiii–xiv.

Fifty

CONVERSATION WITH BELL HOOKS

I first met bell hooks at a Socialist Scholars' conference in 1983. We were close colleagues and good friends at Yale for two years. We worked on our groundbreaking dialogical text, Breaking Bread *(1991), for another two years. Tanya McKinnon, our superb editor at South End Press, helped make it happen. bell hooks is the most prolific intellectual of her generation—a bold and courageous writer who probes the neglected dimensions and dark corners of our culture. It was a challenge and delight to work with her and travel the country to do joint dialogues with her. Our work together exemplifies black male and female solidarity—personal respect, critical scrutiny and common goals.*

bell hooks: Why do you think universities like Princeton, Duke, Harvard and any number of schools we could name, which were once completely uninterested in creating a diverse academic environment, are now engaged in promoting black studies? What's their agenda?

Cornel West: Well, we live in a very different world now. We saw the collapse of Europe in 1945. We are seeing the decline of the American empire in the 1990s. We've seen the dissolution of the Soviet empire in the latter part of the 1980s. It's a very different world—which means then that the struggles, the sufferings and the contributions of those who were once on the underside of these worlds: Third World people—Asia, Africa and Latin America—are emerging now, becoming tremendous powers, culturally, intellectually, artistically, even more so than politically and economically. And so these universities, which are in many ways repositories of the different kinds of shifts going on in the world as expressed intellectually, must indeed respond.

hooks: In some ways, that takes me back to comments we made about whether we can be oppositional in the academy. Certainly, one of the most exciting experiences I've had as a professor was teaching at Yale. And partially it was exciting because of the eagerness on the part of students of all ethnicities to engage in what Foucault has called "the insurrection of subjugated knowledges." To teach a course on black women writers and have hundreds of the students signing up, that lets you know that there has been a transformation in the academy.

West: That's exactly right. And I think this hunger and thirst that you talk about has much to do with not only the changing forces in the world, changing contexts in the world. We saw it in music in the 1960s, where there's been a kind of Afro-Americanization of white youth, and that's going on now internationally. And that in some ways prefigures what is farther down the road when it comes to intellectual focus on issues of race and "otherness."

hooks: Well, can you speak about that? I know one of the things that I'm confronting increasingly as a black academic is that often our black studies classes are peopled predominantly by white students and students of diverse ethnicities—more Asian students from all Asian ethnicities, more Chicanos, more Puerto Ricans and so on. What does this mean for the future of black studies? Does it mean that the nature of the discipline is changing? Or are we simply being more inclusive?

West: No, I think it's a good sign. Afro-American studies was never meant to be solely for Afro-Americans. It was meant to try to redefine what it means to be human, what it means to be modern, what it means to be American, because people of African descent in this country are profoundly human, profoundly modern, profoundly American. And so to the degree to which they can see the riches that we have to offer as well as see our shortcomings, is the degree to which they can more fully understand the modern and what modernity is all about, and more fully understand the American experience.

hooks: At a conference sponsored by Men Stopping Violence and the National Organization for Men Against Sexism, I tried to emphasize that all groups of men in the United States can understand masculinity better by understanding black masculinity, rather than constituting black masculinity as "other." Certainly, white men might learn more about the production of what it is to be men by studying about black men and how black men experience life in this society. It seems to me that in our liberatory pedagogies, we bring that kind of analysis of subjectivity to bear which says that studying "the other" is not the goal, the goal is learning about some aspect of who you are.

West: That's precisely right. Ralph Ellison used to make that point with great insight and profundity. And to the degree to which not just Americans, but modern persons accept that to understand themselves they must understand the Afro-American experience is the degree to which Afro-American studies is, in part, successful.

hooks: Cornel, you are unique in that you come to black studies from philosophy. Many of the traditional movers and shakers in black studies have been historians, literary critics, social scientists. Do you bring a different approach?

West: By being trained in philosophy?

hooks: Yes.

West: I think so. As a philosopher, I'm fundamentally concerned with how we confront death, dread, despair, disappointment and disease. These are existential issues. And sociologists, economists, social scientists, they are not primarily concerned with how individuals confront their inevitable doom, their inescapable extinction. So that there is a sensibility I, and other philosophers, bring to issues of meaning and value that other intellectuals may not have.

hooks: That focus on meaning and values is truly evident in your book *The American Evasion of Philosophy,* which explores the importance of American pragmatism.

Now this book is in many ways a difficult book to read, a rigorous book. And I think people should approach it with that understanding, because certainly the earlier works, *Prophesy Deliverance: Afro-American Revolutionary Christianity,* which came out in 1982, and then *Prophetic Fragments,* in 1988, are much more solidly rooted in a focus on black culture and black tradition. Many black readers would come to these books with some awareness of the fundamental ideas you are talking about—that might not be the case with the book on American pragmatism. What does prophetic pragmatism mean? What are its implications for black community?

West: It helps us to understand that we have to interpret both American civilization and the modern West from our vantage point. This is what *The American Evasion of Philosophy* actually is, an interpretation of the emergence, the sustenance and the decline of American civilization from the vantage point of an African American. It means then we have to have a cosmopolitan orientation, even though it is rooted in the fundamental concern with the plight and predicament of African Americans.

Now, what the text attempts to do is to argue that there are fundamental themes like experimentation and improvisation that can be found in the works of Ralph Waldo Emerson, for example, that are thoroughly continuous with the great art form that Afro-Americans have given the modern world, which is jazz. And therefore to talk about America is to talk about improvisation and experimentation, and therefore to talk about Emerson and Louis Armstrong in the same breath.

hooks: That is why I was very moved by our talking about prophetic pragmatism as "a form of third-wave left romanticism," which you said, "tempers its utopian impulse with the profound sense of the tragic character of life in history."

One of the things that seemed to me that you were trying to do in giving us this philosophical framework is to say that black people must theorize our experience in such a way that we come to understand our tragedies beyond solely the emotionally felt experience of that tragedy.

West: And the fact that when you look closely at jazz, or the blues, for example, we see a sense of the tragic, a profound sense of the tragic linked to human agency. So that it does not wallow in a cynicism or a paralyzing pessimism, but it also is realistic enough not to project excessive utopia. It's a matter of responding in an improvisational, undogmatic, creative way to circumstances in such a way that people still survive and thrive. This is a great tradition intellectually; in fact, it has had tremendous impact on the way in which Americans as a whole respond to the human condition, respond to their circumstances.

hooks: One unique aspect of your discussion with Bill Moyers was that you talked about "the vocation of the intellectual as trying to allow suffering to speak." How do we transform the meaninglessness that people feel into an effective form of struggle? It seems to me that right there, when black intellectuals start trying to answer that question, we begin the process of oppositionality in action, practice and theory.

West: That's right.

hooks: Could you say a little bit about the significance of theory?

West: Yes. Theory ought not to be a fetish. It does not have magical powers of its own. On the other hand, theory is inescapable because it is an indispensable weapon in struggle, and it is an indispensable weapon in struggle because it provides certain kinds of understanding, certain kinds of illumination, certain kinds of insights that are requisite if we are to act effectively.

For example, the Marxist tradition has always meant much to me because of its notion of commodification and the degree to which market forces have so fundamentally not only shaped our economy, but the way in which we understand value and use. And so to talk about multinational corporations, on the one hand, and talk about advertising, on the other, are indispensable ways of understanding the modern world and thereby indispensable ways of trying to locate and situate black people and give us some reasons for why we are catching so much hell.

hooks: Part of the contemporary project for the oppositional black intellectual is to address the significance of theory to our revisioning of black liberation struggle, in our attempts to address both the crisis of black people and the crisis that we're having in the culture as a whole.

That brings us to the critical issue of what place does the theorizing of white, Eurocentric intellectuals have for black people? I read Terry Eagleton's book, *The Significance of Theory,* and what I liked very much about his particular essay on theory was that he tried to talk about how everyone uses theory in their practical daily life, which is certainly what I've tried to stress in my work, particularly when speaking to black students who are questioning the significance of theory. What do you think about the fact that many of us are influenced these days by European theorists Michel Foucault, Julia Kristeva, Derrida, Lacan, and Third World, non-black theorists like Edward Said, Gayatri Spivak, Homi Bhaba? What do those intellectuals outside black experience have to teach us, say to us, that can in some way illuminate and enhance that struggle?

West: To be intellectual, no matter what color, means that one is going to be deeply influenced by other intellectuals of a variety of different colors. When it comes to black intellectuals, we have to, on the one hand, be very open to insights from wherever they come. On the other hand, we must filter it in such a way that we never lose sight of what some of the silences are in the work of white theorists, especially as those silences relate to issues of class, gender, race and empire. Why? Because class, gender, race and empire are fundamental categories black intellectuals must use in order to understand the predicament of black people. So there is, I would say, a selective significance of white intellectuals to the critical development of black intellectuals.

hooks: Concurrently, increasingly what we are seeing is that more and more white intellectuals are making black culture and black experience the subject of their intellectual and discursive practices. What do you think about that? Are these people our allies? Are we developing coalitions? Or are we being appropriated yet again?

West: There is something positive and something negative here. Look at the work of Eugene Genovese, a very important scholar on the subject of slavery. He is not always right, but often very illuminating. He has made a great contribution, yet at the same time, one recognizes that white scholars are bringing certain baggage with them when they look at black culture, no matter how subtle and sophisticated the formulations. Therefore, we must always be on guard to bring critique to bear on the baggage that they bring, even when that baggage provides certain insights.

hooks: Talk about it, Cornel.

West: So it's a positive and a negative thing. The thing we can't do is remain insular and think that we have a monopoly on how to understand our-selves. Because that is not the case at all. But we must be critical across the board.

hooks: As long as we, black academics and intellectuals, are doing work within the context of white supremacy, often what happens is that white theorists draw upon our work and our ideas and get forms of recognition that are denied black thinkers. The reality of appropriation has produced a real tension between many black academics and those white scholars and colleagues who want to talk with us. Often black scholars, especially feminist thinkers, tell me they fear ideas will be "ripped off" and "they" (white scholars) will get the credit. Black folks are willing to share ideas, but there is a feeling now that a white academic might take your idea, write about it, and you'll never be cited. This is upsetting many black scholars.

West: It is the Elvis Presley syndrome applied to the academic terrain. In-ternal dynamics of power make it very difficult for credits to be given where they are due, when that credit should be given to an individual who comes from a marginal, subordinated group within this country. It has to do with who has access to the legitimate and prestigious journals, who has access to the publishing houses and so on. We have seen this phenomenon historically, and the best that we can do to fight against it is to either establish our own institutional networks that would give our texts visibility, or simply continue to bring critique to bear on the ma-nipulation and the co-optation that goes on in the mainstream.

hooks: We also have to be willing to confront, in a positive way, those of our white colleagues who, in fact, see themselves as our allies. I once experi-enced a White woman scholar, whom I respect, give a talk where I felt that, in fact, she was laying out my own analytical and theoretical frame-work from *Ain't I a Woman* and getting credit. So I went to her and said I really felt that what I was hearing was my work without . . .

West: Acknowledgment.

hooks: Acknowledgment. And she, being a comrade in struggle, told me she would go back and read my work to see if she had, in fact, unwittingly taken ideas from me without citing them as mine. So I don't think we should always assume a negative intentionality. We all read things and pick up things and don't always remember the source it came from, and within a racist context, well, white people are accustomed to taking the labor of black people for granted. We have to see that the same thing can happen with intellectual labor, so that sometimes confronting that situa-tion in a positive way can make for a meaningful critical intervention.

West: I absolutely agree.

hooks: Another thing that makes you unusual as a head of black studies is being both a scholar in a highly traditional discipline like philosophy and your unique and profound engagement with popular culture. You write about music and art—can you speak about how you think cultural studies is linked to black studies?

West: That is a very difficult question. Let me say a few things about it. First, I focus on popular culture because I focus on those areas where black humanity is most powerfully expressed, where black people have been able to articulate their sense of the world in a profound manner. And I see this primarily in popular culture.

Why not in highbrow culture? Because the access has been so difficult. Why not in more academic forms? Because academic exclusion has been the rule for so long for large numbers of black people that black culture, for me, becomes a search for where black people have left their imprint and fundamentally made a difference in terms of how certain art forms are understood. This is currently in popular culture. And it has been primarily in music, religion, visual arts and fashion.

hooks: Don't you also think that those of us writing about popular culture are regarded with skepticism by traditional black academics who have been more engaged with "high culture"? Don't those black academics look at someone like you with skepticism, in the same way that more conservative white colleagues might look at you and say, you know, he's not really a philosopher, a real philosopher wouldn't be so interested in popular culture?

West: I think you are correct. What you have, on the one hand, is black scholars, who are deeply preoccupied with receiving respect from their white peers, trying to resist all black stereotypes. And, in many instances, running from some of the riches of black culture in order to convince their white peers that they are not a part, in any way, of what has been so very important to black people, black music, black speech, and black religion.

It is interesting that the history of black studies in the United States has been one in which black religion and music have played a very, very small role, even though black religion and music play a fundamental role in the history of black people. This has to do not only with the secular orientation of black intellectuals, but because so many black intellectuals believe that any association with black religion makes them look bad in light of the secular orientations of their white colleagues. So they run away from it. It seems to me that what we have to do is undermine all stereotypes while embracing what have been some of the very rich insights and contributions of the black folk, intellectually, politically and culturally.

hooks: The role of poetry in traditional black community is a prime example of that. So many of us came to performance art, to public speaking from both the black church and black high schools under segregation.

West: Right. Right.

hooks: We also forget that in the nineteenth century there was a tremendous emphasis on the oratory. And for a lot of black people that carried over and informed twentieth-century construction of black culture. I was raised in a working class black family where, when the lights went out and the candles were lit, my folks would say, get up and entertain us. Recite a poem.

West: I want to argue that music and rhetorical practices, especially black preaching practices, have been the two major traditions owing to the exclusion of black people in other spheres, even though many of us venture in those fields.

hooks: You often say that U.S. mass culture is disproportionately influenced by black culture. I think the critical question to ask is whether or not that influence is oppositional. Does black culture radicalize white American culture, Asian American culture, the culture of other ethnic groups?

West: It is oppositional, but there are different levels of oppositionality. There's what we call "thin" opposition, and then there's "thick" opposition. Thin opposition is a critique of American society that does not talk about the need for a redistribution of wealth, resources and power. Thick opposition is an attempt to call into question the prevailing maldistribution of wealth in this society. Thin opposition is important, but it is not sufficient. And black cultural influence has played a role in that thin opposition. Just affirming the humanity of black people in America is still, in many instances, a subversive act. Yet, "thick" opposition is rarely put forward openly in black culture.

SOURCE: "Cornel West Interviewed by bell hooks," *Breaking Bread: Insurgent Black Intellectual Life,* by bell hooks and Cornel West (Cambridge Mass.: South End Press, 1991), pp. 31–39.

PART NINE

This reader serves as a kind of fissure in my work. My turn to a more pronounced dramatic discourse requires a thorough grounding in the history of the arts—especially plays, poetry and music. So I plan to go underground and continue to immerse myself in Ernst Robert Curtius, Leo Spitzer, T. S. Eliot, Ralph Ellison, Erich Auerbach, Harry Levin, Edward Said, Helen Vendler, Harold Goddard, Harold Bloom, Sterling Brown, George Steiner, Robert Brustein, Eric Bentley, Walter Kerr and other towering critics who plunge into the depths of tragic and comic dimensions of dramatic literature. This kind of painstaking inquiry is requisite for any serious examination of the richness of modern black culture, especially the spirituals, blues, gospels and jazz. This inquiry should be comparative in character and historical in content—yet preserve the integrity of artistic judgment and the joy of aesthetic delight. My old projects of idiosyncratic treatments of David Hume and Josiah Royce are informed by this orientation. My exciting plan to write a major treatment of African American literature and modern Greek literature with the cre-

ative and wise cultural critic Eleni Mavromatidou will exemplify this new kind of inquiry. I also plan to finish a challenging book with Rev. Osagyefo Sekou—a brilliant young Black brother and thinker—on the Black generation gap and popular culture (Bridge over Troubled Waters).

My next long-term project is a meditation on Chekhov and Coltrane that delves into the distinctive conceptions of the tragic in American civilization and of the comic in Russian civilization—the two most influential and bewildering civilizations of modernity for the twenty-first century. My next published works will be Heart of American Darkness—*a Conradian narrative of the forms of social death, soul murder and violence (psychic and physical) in our past and present—and* I Ain't Noways Tired, *a bold venture in intellectual autobiography modeled on black musical forms. This interview with my dear brother and close friend Professor David Lionel Smith, Dean of the Faculty at Williams College, points me in my new direction. I tell my students it takes at least twenty-five years to lay an adequate foundation to do the kind of work one is called to do. I now think I am almost ready to begin to fulfill this calling.*

Fifty One

CHEKHOV, COLTRANE AND DEMOCRACY

David Lionel Smith: Thank you for agreeing to do this interview. Let's begin with the idea of the public intellectual. In some ways this is almost a misnomer. That is, it makes a distinction between intellectuals who operate within view of the public and other intellectuals. I wonder how good a distinction you think that is. There's certainly a history to the concept. One thinks of the "New York Intellectuals" and the left-liberal humanist agenda and commitments they espoused. But I wonder, since you are always on the list of "public intellectuals," how good a rubric you think this is and whether it makes distinctions that you consider valid.

Cornel West: First, let me say that it's always a pleasure to see and talk with you, David, and thank you for inviting me to engage in this conversation. The term "public intellectuals" can be misleading, because if we take seriously what it means to be an intellectual, and it goes back in many ways to the Russian intellectuals of the 1830s, to Vassarion Belinsky, dealing with the discrepancy between the social value and the social function of intellectual figures, who had been trained but felt that they had no place and therefore felt that they had a critical role in society. Or we might go back to the Dreyfus case in France, with Zola bringing his own critique to bear on the vicious anti-Semitism. To be an intellectual really means to speak a truth that allows suffering to speak. That is, it creates a vision of the world that puts into the limelight the social misery that is usually hidden or concealed by the dominant viewpoints of a society. "Intellectual" in that sense simply means those who are willing to reflect critically upon themselves as well as upon the larger society and to ascertain whether there is some possibility of amelioration and betterment.

On a deeper level, when we talk about intellectuals in the humanities, there is an even greater challenge, because I take quite seriously paragraph twelve of Vico's *The New Science,* where he says that "humanities" is derived from *humanitas.* That comes from the Latin *humando,* meaning "burying." Thus, to be in the humanities means to begin with the mass bodies, buried, that we have to come to terms with. We impose some intentional order on the world that connects the living to the dead, the quick to the gone. Therefore there's a historical dimension and an important role for traditions that try to consider the relation of those present to those past. That's an even deeper level of understanding the role of the intellectual than we find in Belinsky or Zola. It is the latter, Vico, to whom I feel closer. When you take the idea of the intellectual and add the adjective "public," it becomes misleading, because it gives the impression that the intellectual is someone who has a blueprint or is only functioning in a public sphere and is not concerned with the deeper issues of death, dread and despair and how those relate to issues of freedom and equality. Hence, I think it tends to misconstrue what one's fundamental calling is in the humanities. It is very different in natural sciences, where the issues of mass bodies is secondary, because you are fundamentally concerned with analyzing natural phenomena in light of past experience or trying to gain some control over nature. That's a very different kind of operation. I admire it, but it's not the kind of thing I do.

Smith: When this term is used by journalists or by activist intellectuals, it is often intended to distinguish between conventional academics who operate strictly within the academy and those who move beyond the walls of the academy. Must one operate beyond the academy to have public impact as an intellectual?

West: It's both dangerous and misleading to make this distinction. To operate beyond the academy can mean simply to be highly publicized or popular, that one attains notoriety, and that can be vacuous and hollow, yet one may still be viewed as a public intellectual. Similarly, there are those within the academy whose work has tremendous impact out in the broader world, though they personally remain within the academy. Such people, in conventional terms, may not be recognized as "public intellectuals," regardless of the impact of their work. I think of my friend and teacher John Rawls, for instance, whose *A Theory of Justice* has profound influence. It is work of great value. In my view, the exemplary intellectuals who move both within and outside the academy would include people like Edward Said and Garry Wills. These are people who have great influence in both worlds because of the integrity of their work. It is a matter of quality and substantive impact on the public issues of our day. These figures transcend the glib definitions of "public intellectual."

Smith: We are living in a culture that is increasingly a sound-bite culture, defined by short attention spans and inability to comprehend complex arguments. The way the media are managed leaves little space for having careful arguments or nuanced discourse. In such a culture, how much impact can an intellectual have?

West: That's a very good question. One challenge for intellectuals today is to try to channel wisdom, both intellectual and practical, into the televisual culture. By wisdom I mean eloquent insights that disquiet us, unsettle us and challenge us to think. This a difficult challenge, but it is possible. It requires one to speak in a language that is clear and palpable, yet nuanced and difficult enough that it requires people to rethink the categories and modes in which they understand the world. It is a critical orientation, but it also requires wisdom. Eloquence in a Ciceronian or Quintillian sense is still a way of unsettling people and forcing them to think differently. This can be done even in a televisual culture, and it is certainly what I aspire to do.

Smith: I think that anyone who has read your work or seen you lecture will recognize these themes as fundamental to what you've tried to accomplish. I wonder if you see a significant cadre of people who have that sense of calling for humanistic work in the terms that you are describing, or is it only a few lonely voices?

West: No, I think that more and more persons aspire to this calling. The problem is that in our market-driven culture, there are so many pitfalls and seductions. It is so easy to equate mere publicity and visibility with substantive public impact. Visibility and celebrity status can be confused with intellectual accomplishment, and these are delusions that all who aspire must be wary to avoid. It's very tough, but it can and must be done. Those in the past such as Reinhold Niebuhr, Hannah Arendt, James Baldwin and John Dewey managed to pull it off, but in our own time it is so easy to be superficial, because so much of the culture is superficial.

Smith: As a humanist intellectual observing public discourse at the moment, what is your assessment of the quality of discussions about politics and public life? For example, in the recent discussions of President Clinton's troubles, I've been shocked by the absence of cogent critical voices capable of helping us to understand the issues rather than just revel in the sensational details. How would you assess what you see happening now in the media?

West: It's really demoralizing and depressing to see such low-quality public conversation. On one hand, we have a lot of self-righteousness, reflected in the moralistic criticisms of the president. On the other hand, we have a kind of smug complacency, as if nothing is at stake, as if people can do anything and not be accountable for their actions. I make a strong distinction between the moralistic condemnation of individual acts and the moral outrage that deplores child poverty, the high incidence of AIDS, increasing inequality, the various kinds of backlash against immigrants and brown and black people. These, for me, are kinds of issues that justify a legitimate moral outrage within the democratic process that may spill over into political actions. That is nowhere near the center of the current public conversation, but we instead get moralism and smug complacency. These are the terms in which people are thinking about the activities in the White House and the Congress; and they are such truncated, impoverished ways of thinking. Maybe the downturn in the global markets will induce people to recognize that there are basic institutional and structural arrangements in place that need to be changed. It may take a major crisis, recession or depression on a global scale to make people focus on the fundamental problems. America has an unfortunate history of always waiting until our backs are against the wall to be begin facing our deeper problems.

Smith: It is depressing to note how deeply entrenched these forces are that distort and deflect the legitimate moral passions and make impossible the adequate discussion of serious issues. I wonder how you confront this reality without becoming depressed. I know that you are a deeply religious man and have often spoken of religious faith as an important sustaining force in the face of despair. As a humanist, do you find other resources of hope aside from religion?

West: Despair and hope are inseparable. One can never understand what hope is really about unless one wrestles with despair. The same is true with faith. There has to be some serious doubt, otherwise faith becomes merely a dogmatic formula, an orthodoxy, a way of evading the complexity of life, rather than a way of engaging honestly with life. Therefore, for me as Christian and humanist, I am reminded of Harold Goddard's splendid book on Shakespeare, which says that the greatest poetry tends to portray the human condition as a citadel of nobility threatened by an immense barbarism or a flickering candle in an infinite night. He doesn't say that in a self-righteous way. He just means that the possibility of sustaining hope is always difficult. If you are fundamentally committed to human dignity—this is true from Sophocles and Aeschylus to Chekhov, Toni Morrison and John Coltrane—you know that you are cutting radically against the historical grain. Any fundamental commitment to decency, dignity and democracy means that you are cutting even more fundamentally against the grain. You have to be aware of this. You have to be willing to look at the worst to push for the best. This is the old Thomas Hardy insight, stated in his "Tenebrae." I always resonated deeply with that. It means wrestling with despair and doubt but never allowing them to have the last word.

Smith: You mentioned Chekhov. One thing many people don't know about you is how deep a passion you have for Russian literature in general and for Chekhov in particular. What is it about Russian writers that you find so congenial to your own thinking and your own condition?

West: For one thing, the emergence of modern Russian civilization was predicated upon the quest for a national identity that remained fractured. It was fractured because of the Russian imperial demands that made it difficult for the Russian national identity to be expressed. The Russian writers—I mentioned Belinsky, but you also see it in Pushkin, Gogol, Dostoyevsky, Tolstoy, Chekhov, Turgenev, all the way up to Solzhenitsyn and Bitov—have understood that to come to terms with Russian identity and Russian soul, they had to explore the fundamental issues of what it means to be human: to wrestle with the problem of evil, to live an intense life in the face of death, to grapple with democratic possibilities and with social justice. To be an intellectual for them means to link the public and the existential issues. Those writers constituted the public sphere, the essential conversation from the informal circles that go back to Belinsky, all the way up to Pasternak and Solzhenitsyn, all under conditions of censorship, exploitation and oppression. They understand that something serious is at stake in intellectual work. They are meditating on death in its various forms: social death vis-à-vis the serfs, soul murder vis-à-vis the squashing of a potential that could never be realized owing to social constraints, premature physical death and so on.

I have been deeply attracted by these writers, because these are for me real soul mates: Chekhov most of all. Chekhov for me is the great writer of compassion. He understands the essence of the best of Russian orthodoxy: absolute condemnation of no one, forgiveness for all, compassion to all. For me as a Christian, those principles cut very deep. Chekhov was an agnostic, but he embodies in his writings—the great short stories, those four powerful plays, and especially *Three Sisters,* which for me is the greatest of twentieth-century plays, though it was first performed in January 1901, the first month of the century. Drama has been downhill ever since, though *Waiting for Godot* is a fascinating footnote. The waiting of the three sisters and the waiting of Didi and Gogo have some elective affinities, as critics have rightly noted. This at least is how it appears for me as a person and thinker, rooted in the blues sensibility, the tragicomic sensibility that you get from the great New World artists, blues musicians.

Smith: We have talked about a course you have planned to teach on Chekhov and John Coltrane. Can you tell our readers about the course and when you plan to teach it?

West: I'm building toward it. I've been teaching a course on the tragic, the comic and the political just to lay the foundation. I want to get a real handle on the tragic, the comic and the political. We read Sophocles' *Antigone* and Dante's *Inferno,* Shakespeare's *Hamlet,* Ibsen, Shaw, Chekhov, O'Neill, Tennessee Williams, Lorraine Hansberry, LeRoi Jones and others as a way of building toward Chekhov. I teach Chekhov a week in that course as a way of preparing myself for a course in which we will read Chekhov for seven or eight weeks. At the same time, I'm reading assiduously in the history of modern music in general and black music in particular so that I can begin to situate Coltrane. Maybe in two or three years I will be ready to teach a course featuring these two great artistic geniuses and spiritual figures. By "spiritual" I mean that they understand the connection between intellectual seeking and life-risking loving. You get this in the work of both. They are thus both not just great artists, they are spiritual figures of great cultures, who represent deep tendencies of those cultures. Their work signifies something profound in the cultures. Their work goes beyond technical virtuosity or their art and cuts very deep into the heart, mind and soul of any person who interacts with their work. For the twenty-first century this will be crucial. The worst scenario is the total triumph of market forces which leads to the gangsterization of everyday life with revitalized tribal mentalities and no effective countervailing forces against global capitalism. What Coltrane and Chekhov represent is the how indispensable nonmarket values of love, care, concern, service to others, intimacy and gentleness are to all of us who move from womb to tomb, pursuing any sense of meaning beyond money making and profit taking. That's a crucial message as we move into the next century. Can we avoid increasing forms of barbarism, or will the next century be as dark as the last?

Smith: Would you envision including other musicians in this course? I think of Charles Mingus, whose music represents more of the comic side. He is very inclusive, certainly. Compassion and religious feeling are present in his music, but the comic is more pronounced, just as in Coltrane's music the transcendent religious dimension is more pronounced. Would such work be part of the course?

West: Coltrane in so many ways is like the Hebrew Bible, which centers on *hesed,* loving-kindness at its best, and the New Testament, which deals with a love that is so rich and deep; but it doesn't really deal with an incongruity that sits at the center of the human predicament, which is the raw stuff of the comic. Thus, even the greatness of Coltrane would have to be examined in terms of what's missing. For me the sense of the comic is crucial, and there's no doubt that Mingus brings that. Actually, Chekhov is the great poet of the comic of incongruity, but it is very high comedy. He talks about failure and inadequacy of intelligence in the most sophisticated and intelligent way. To accent heroic action that is always self-critical and that therefore accents intellectual humility is tragic at its best. I understand tragic to refer to the freedom that humans have to explore the possibility of even greater freedom, but against constraints, usually constraints of which they are unaware. The comic is a way of acknowledging those limitations and the incongruity between those high aspirations and where one actually ends up. With Coltrane and Chekhov the tragic and the comic are in fascinating tension and hence they actually need one another. With Mingus, within the black musical tradition, you already have a wrestling with the most sophisticated forms of the comic, and of course I want to stress that the comic is in no way reducible to the humorous or even the satirical. It cuts much deeper, though it often embraces that.

Smith: As a teacher, when you present these concepts to young people, do they strike a resonant chord or not? Do they understand and see the importance of these paradoxes, or are they simply put off by them?

West: I think that they at first find this very alien. This kind of language cuts radically against the categories that they bring. Often the categories are rooted in the televisual culture or in what they expect academic life to be. Both are so predictable. Both are so flat that you have to awaken in young people the sense of awe, curiosity and wonder—the kind of Faustian restlessness and seeking. The language you use must become a part of that seeking. So we as teachers must ask ourselves, how do we tease out that sense of awe and accent the wrestling with the mystery of being? Once you do that and they are bitten by the bug of intellectual curiosity, it takes off in a number of different directions. That's the first challenge, especially for those of us in the humanities.

Smith: This points to another paradox in your work. On one hand you are a pragmatist, or at least your epistemology is pragmatic. On the other hand, you are a kind of idealist. Those two tendencies aren't usually linked, and a great deal of your work has been concerned with sorting through the linkages between these two contradictory tendencies. Would you comment on the response by critics to that aspect of your work? Do you feel that this aspect of your work has been accurately understood, and has your thinking changed any regarding the possibility of linking idealism to a pragmatic epistemology?

West: I appreciate that question because it involves so many fundamental issues. The first and foremost factor in my appreciation for the pragmatist tradition from Emerson, through Peirce, James and Dewey up through my friend, brother and mentor Richard Rorty, is its recognition that human existence is fundamentally historically conditioned. The radical contingency, the dynamism, the variability, these to me are indispensable ways of understanding who we are. On the other hand, I am also taken by the heroic actions radically against the odds, against the limits, which express courage, vision, the freedom to change ourselves and change the world. Pragmatism at its best tries to keep track of both. The Marxist tradition means much to me because it tells some fascinating stories about our historical conditionedess, the crucial role of how the dynamics of power at the workplace curtails potential, the crucial role that banking and corporate elites play, given their wealth and power, in making it difficult for working people actually to fulfill their potentiality. That's just one story among others. The same is true for narratives of white supremacy, male supremacy, homophobia. For me these are not categories of "PC-ness." They represent our historical conditions. The question is how can we attenuate and break out of these forms of conditionedness. There's a dialectical interplay between the structural, institutional and personal constraints in which we find ourselves and our agency. We are never totally suffocated by these. There's always some way of extending our courage and vision, manifesting our freedom in ways in which we can at least create some space to operate and expand the scope of possibility. Pragmatism at its best is able to do this.

My problem with pragmatism, given my Chekhovian Christian sensibility, is that it has no sense of the tragic, no sense of the comic, and therefore it is too narrow existentially. It is impoverished existentially. The one pragmatist who understood this tragic dimension is Josiah Royce. I've been working on Royce for a while and have taught some courses on Royce and Schopenhauer. I plan to write more on Royce. He didn't really have a sense of the comic, but his understanding of the tragic was quite profound. He remained a pragmatist, but with an idealist impulse. Personally, I'm less interested in being situated within the philosophical tradition and much more interested in making sense of the world, pulling from whatever intellectual tradition I can. I think that Montaigne makes more sense than all of them, even though I don't feel he has the truth. He comes much closer than others because he understands both our historical conditionedness, on the one hand, and the heroic agency we human beings have, on the other. But he has a much darker *Weltanschauung* than any of the pragmatists, including Josiah Royce, who has a profound sense of the tragic as a pragmatist, but also as a Christian.

Smith: In terms of your own work, the inquiry that you are describing begins in your doctoral dissertation, *The Ethical Dimensions of Marxist Thought* and it continues through your book on pragmatism, *The American Evasion* *of Philosophy.* Thus, this has been a central inquiry for you. It has many parts, but also clear continuity. Just to continue with this line of thinking, some of your recent work has been concerned with issues that are traditionally associated with the Right rather than the Left, such as family issues. For instance, you recently coauthored *The War Against Parents* with Sylvia Ann Hewlett. Some critics on the Left claim that you are becoming more and more conservative. Is this a fair response to your work?

West: No. I'd draw a very sharp distinction between conservative and preservative. For me the conservative has traditionally been much more concerned with order, hierarchy and privilege, whereas the preservative has been concerned with preserving certain kinds of values that can be used and deployed in the present in ways that expand democratic possibilities, the possibilities of freedom. I take tradition very seriously, and unfortunately, some of the more profound thinkers on tradition, like Edward Shils or Hans-Georg Gadamer or even T. S. Eliot—I've learned much from them, but the tradition that they are trying to conserve is very much different from the tradition that I am trying to preserve.

I am a radical democrat who believes that it is important to preserve those nonmarket values that convince ordinary people that it's worth taking a risk to fight for democratic principles. In *The War Against Parents* I am talking about those nonmarket values that need to be preserved. These values were very much at work in the lives of my parents and grandparents and many others of their generations. They weren't perfect. They were deeply shaped by patriarchal and homophobic ideas that need to be called into question. Still, there is no doubt that they had a depth of love and caring and service to something greater than themselves that needs to be preserved. Conservatives have no monopoly on such values. On the contrary, they promote unregulated markets that undermine such values. The book is in part about managerial greed and the market run amok that make it difficult for parenting, that ultimate nonmarket activity of nurturing and caring for young people, and render it more and more marginal. We've got to preserve nonmarket values, and yet that can be done without falling into any of the narrow conservative traps that end up promoting new forms of order, new forms of hierarchy, new forms of privilege. So I can understand many of my progressive friends and leftist comrades thinking that I have moved onto a terrain that conservatives have previously monopolized, yet I think that that is where progressives belong. We must get people to see that conservatives have no monopoly at all on values that are worth preserving.

Smith: Where do you see your work going? You mentioned the work on Chekhov and Coltrane, the cross-cultural inquiry into traditions of the oppressed—the "frog's eye perspective," to invoke Nietzsche and Benjamin. What other projects do you have in the near term and the longer term?

West: I've got a book coming out next year called *Heart of American Darkness,* and it's a book on the doings and sufferings of people of African descent. It is a very different take on Afro-American culture, its emergence and its development over time. It is much more centered around issues of different forms of death and ways in which this generates an intense sense of life and its relation to democracy. The issues of varieties of death and the possibilities of democracy loom large in the text. I am also working on an intellectual autobiography, going back to Sacramento, where I grew up, my struggles with the Black Panther Party—I was never a member, but I worked so closely with them—all the way up to where I am now. I've got a book that I've been working on about David Hume, which I think will be a very novel approach on the finest philosophical mind in the English language.

Smith: What aspects of Hume are you working on?

West: Well, it has much to do with Hume as the first exemplary modern European man of letters. I've got some background on Erasmus and others, but Hume, who emerges at a time when he was born a colonial subject in Scotland, before the Union Act of 1707, dealing with the metropole in London, unable to get excited about the academy and dropping out early. He was so precocious, writing the *Treatise Concerning Human Nature* in his twenties and then having a nervous breakdown when it was not received well. He was never able to teach in a university, so he became a diplomat and a tutor, but he wrote the most sophisticated works, philosophically and culturally, of the day. He was of course a white supremacist, who would play an important role in reinforcing some of the worst racist tendencies of Europeans, but on the other hand, there is the radical historicist, in some ways naturalist, not a solely but a thoroughgoing skeptic, which goes beyond skepticism. He lays bare the trajectories that would follow him, beginning with Kant, who could not read him well in English, to Hegel and Nietzsche. I am actually ending with Schopenhauer, the only great German philosopher of the nineteenth century who read English fluently. He actually translated Hume's work and wrote a long introduction to it. Schopenhauer thought that besides Kant and Plato Hume was the most important philosopher he had ever read. He never published any of this, which is fascinating. So even before you get to Nietzsche, that fascinating disciple of Schopenhauer, you really have to come to terms with Hume. Why is it that we don't understand the centrality of Hume in this broader sense and not just as an academic philosopher? He has been so domesticated. Livingstone and others are beginning to address this—scholars who have read Hume's *History of England*.

In addition, I have been writing a book on Royce, which I mentioned before. I want to write a book on how central Josiah Royce ought to be. It's very interesting that the first graduate course in philosophy in America was taught by Royce. It was a graduate seminar on Schopenhauer at Johns Hopkins University. Royce knew that this was a historic moment, and he probably couldn't do a more un-American thing than to teach a course on the great German pessimist philosopher. What is it about Royce that makes him so profoundly American, yet he believed that Schopenhauer was the greatest philosopher since Plato, as he said in his 1892 book, *The Spirit of Philosophy?*

Smith: I think a lot of readers will be astonished to discover your interest in the great skeptical philosopher David Hume and the great pessimist philosopher Arthur Schopenhauer.

West: They're crucial. I don't think that anyone should stop there, but they are brooks of fire that we must pass through if we hope to come up with anything that is substantive in terms of a discourse on faith or hope or possibility or democracy.

Smith: This brings to mind another question about your work, concerning your eclecticism. Some critics have suggested that your eclecticism reflects a kind of shallowness. Sometimes this is combined with comments on your charismatic speaking style, asserting that you are simply a skillful speaker who has borrowed bits of knowledge here and there, but not really thought them through carefully or mastered any discipline. This strikes me as an obtuse and grossly unfair response to your work, but let me ask you, how do you respond to this criticism?

West: One is that if what people are looking for is some kind of systematic, architectonic project, I can understand their criticism. My sensibilities are so Kierkegaardian, so Pascalian, so antisystem and anti-architectonic, that my work can look as if it is just a smattering of various sources. For me, figures like Emerson, Arnold, the early Du Bois are inspirations. They are all thoroughly eclectic, they are antisystem, they write wisdom literature. There is a sense in which I do aspire to wisdom. I think Sophocles is right. That's the best we can do. I think Isaiah Berlin is the finest European man of letters of our time; George Steiner is a close second. He has always been for me a tremendous source of inspiration. Like Emerson and Arnold, people said the same thing about him. I do not claim to be in the same class as Berlin, Emerson or Arnold and really don't care about that. I don't view intellectuals as race horses; I'm just trying to make sense of the world and love folks before I die. But there's no doubt that many of my inspirations are thoroughly eclectic. Berlin is totally essayistic, and I take very seriously the form that he chose to express his wonderful intelligence.

Smith: That response seems to me very consistent with your pragmatic streak: that way of thinking about the value of a work and the nature of a legacy. I wonder, if you were to speculate on yourself, looking from the outside at the body of your work, how would you like it to appear, and what would you like your legacy to be?

West: It's hard to say. I don't think of legacies so much, because it depends on the way the world is going. If the twenty-first century turns out to be as barbaric as the twentieth, then my voice could just be one voice in a wilderness, wedded to the discourses of democracy that just turned out to be marginal and impotent. If things turn out a bit better than that, then I would want to be part of the same intellectual chorus as Whitman, Du Bois, Dewey. Fundamental commitments to democracy, of course, but mine is a Christian voice with a Chekhovian tragicomic twist, representing the African Americans' attempt to come to terms with the dark side of modernity. It's very hard to say what the legacy will be. History is unpredictable, so I am not worried about legacies. I will say this, however. I hope that whatever legacy I leave, it will not be confined to the realm of ideas and texts. If I am anything, I am a thinker who is concerned with life in its most concrete forms. To be able to affect persons at a variety of levels of their lives, not simply academic intellectuals who will read texts and teach them, but to be able to reach out to touch people's lives and affect them, to feel that there is a certain energy, a certain concern, a certain love, a certain care that will be thoroughly anonymous, thoroughly invisible in the history of ideas but could live through the discussions in barbershops, in churches, in mosques, in nightclubs when people just remember someone who tried to do something with love and style, that to me would be just as important as to have a text taught at Harvard for the next hundred years. I have a very different idea of what consitutes a legacy than some of my fellow academics.

Smith: In the course of this interview, we have gone a very broad discussion of the public intellectual to a very personal assessment of your own work. Is there anything that you would like to add?

West: One is that in good Emersonian fashion, I've only just begun. After next year when these two texts are published, that will mark the end of a particular era in my work. When I take off with the Coltrane and Chekhov, I think that I will begin a whole new wave of work and texts and, I hope, insights. In that sense I am very excited. The foundation has been set now that will allow me a springboard, a launching pad. That's one of the things that I love about Harvard. It's so rich intellectually that I can see the next ten, twenty, thirty years taking me to so many different directions and, I hope, higher levels of work than what I've done in the past. So I feel that I'm just starting, and that's very exciting.

Smith: That prospect certainly is exciting. Thank you.

SOURCE: Interview by David Lionel Smith, Boston, October 12, 1998.

Notes

1. This claim is based on a particular periodization of the development of the Western world persuasively argued in Ernst Cassirer's *The Philosophy of the Enlightenment,* trans. Fritz C. A. Koelin and James P. Pettegrove (1932); Ernst Troeltsch's *The Social Teaching of the Christian Churches,* Vol. 1, trans. Olive Wyon (1931), pp. 23–34, and his *Protestantism and Progress: A Historical Study of the Relation of Protestantism to the Modern World,* trans. W. Montgomery (1912); and Peter Gay's magisterial work, *The Enlightenment: An Interpretation,* Vol. 1 (Knopf, 1966). For the classic Marxist treatment of the Enlightenment, see Max Horkheimer and Theodor Adorno, *Dialectic of Enlightenment,* trans. John Cumming (Herder & Herder, 1972), especially pp. 3–42.

2. For a classic treatment of this problematic of provinciality in the beginnings of the United States, see Merle Curti, *The Growth of American Thought,* 2d ed. (Harper & Brothers, 1951), pp. 3–126. Note also Max Lerner, *America as a Civilization* (Simon & Schuster, 1957), pp. 3–73. My own theory of the development of American provinciality is based in part on the seminal treatment of American culture by Geoffrey Thurley, *The American Moment: American Poetry in the Mid-Century* (St. Martin's Press, 1978), especially pp. 3–32.

3. Alexis de Tocqueville, *Democracy in America,* ed. Phillips Bradley (Knopf, 1944), Vols. 1 and 2; George Santayana, *The Genteel Tradition,* ed. Douglas L. Wilson (Harvard University Press, 1967); Van Wyck Brooks, *America's Coming-of-Age* (1915). The best secondary literature on de Tocqueville's unsurpassed analysis of American culture remains the superb extended essays by John Stuart Mill that accompany the de Tocqueville volumes. For insightful interpretations of Santayana's work, especially his classic 1911 essay "The Genteel Tradition in American Philosophy," originally given at the Philosophical Union of the University of California at Berkeley and first published in his *Winds of Doctrine* (1913), pp. 186–215, see Danforth Ross, "The Genteel Tradition: Its Characteristics and Its Origins," Ph.D. dissertation, University of Minnesota, 1954; Douglas L. Wilson, "Introductory," in *The Genteel Tradition,* pp. 1–25; and Morton White, *Science and Sentiment in America: Philosophical Thought from Jonathan Edwards to John Dewey* (Oxford University Press, 1972), pp. 241–246. The best recent books on the long and winding career of Van Wyck Brooks are James Hoopes, *Van Wyck Brooks: In Search of American Culture* (University of Massachusetts Press, 1977), and Raymond Nelson, *Van Wyck Brooks: A Writer's Life* (Dutton, 1980).

4. William James's notions were put forward in his address to the Anti-Imperialist League in 1903. See the Report of the Fifth Annual Meeting of the New England Anti-Imperialist League, November 28, 1903, with excerpts in Ralph Barton Perry, *The Thought and Character of William James,* Briefer Version (Harvard University Press, 1948), pp. 246–247. For a theory of American culture based directly on James's notions, see Thayer, *Meaning and Action: A Critical History of Pragmatism,* pp. 437–445. For a fine dramatic simplification of this theory, see Philip Rahv's well-known essay "Paleface and Redskin," in his *Image and Idea* (New Directions, 1957), pp. 1–6.

5. Herbert W. Schneider, *A History of American Philosophy,* 2d ed. (Columbia University Press, 1963), pp. 23–26; Joseph L. Blau, *Men and Movements in American Philosophy* (Prentice-Hall, 1952), pp. 27–35.

6. Garry Wills, *Inventing America: Jefferson's Declaration of Independence* (Doubleday, 1978), esp. pp. 167–319.

7. Schneider, *A History of American Philosophy,* pp. 55–61; Blau, *Men and Movements in American Philosophy,* p. 114. See also Andrew Delbanco, *William Ellery Channing: An Essay on the Liberal Spirit in America* (Harvard University Press, 1981).

8. Winthrop Jordan, *White Over Black: American Attitudes Toward the Negro, 1550–1812* (Norton, 1968), Pts. 1–3, esp. pp. 44–98, 179–265; Thomas F. Gossett, *Race: The History of an Idea in America* (Southern Methodist University Press, 1965), pp. 17–31.

9. W. E. B. Du Bois, *The Souls of Black Folk* (Fawcett Publications, 1961), pp. 16–17. The best secondary treatment of this classic text can be found in Arnold Rampersad, *The Art and Imagination of W. E. B. Du Bois* (Harvard University Press, 1976), pp. 68–90, and Robert B. Stepto, *From Behind the Veil: A Study of Afro-American Narrative* (University of Illinois Press, 1979), pp. 52–91.

10. The most important work on the retention of African practices among black people in the United States (and New World) remains Melville J. Herskovits's *The Myth of the Negro Past* (Beacon Press, 1958). For a superb recent treatment of this phenomenon, see Raboteau, *Slave Religion* (Oxford, 1978), pp. 4–92.

11. M. H. Abrams, *The Mirror and the Lamp: Romantic Theory and the Critical Tradition* (Oxford University Press, 1953), chap. 7, pp. 156–183, chap. 8, pp. 184–225. See also the influential essays by Harold Bloom, "The Internalization of Quest-Romance," in *Romanticism and Consciousness: Essays in Criticism,* ed. Harold Bloom (Norton, 1970), pp. 3–24, and "'To Reason with a Later Reason': Romanticism and the Rational," in his *The Ringers in the Tower: Studies in Romantic Tradition* (University of Chicago Press, 1971), pp. 323–337.

12. Jacques Barzun, *Classic, Romantic and Modern* (Little, Brown, 1961), pp. 1–17, 96–114.

13. Abrams, *Natural Supernaturalism* (Norton, 1971), pp. 11–140, 327–372, 411–462.

14. For the classic text on this subject, see F. O. Matthiessen, *The American Renaissance* (Oxford University Press, 1941). Other notable works include V. L. Parrington, *Main Currents in American Thought,* Vol. 2 (Harcourt, Brace, 1954), pp. 427–465; D. H. Lawrence, *Studies in Classic American Literature* (1923); R. W. B. Lewis, *The American Adam: Innocence, Tragedy, and Tradition in the Nineteenth Century* (University of Chicago Press, 1955), especially the Prologue, pp. 1–10; Richard Chase, *The American Novel and Its Tradition* (New York, 1957), esp. pp. 1–22; and Ihab Hassan, *Radical Innocence: Studies in the Contemporary American Novel* (Princeton University Press, 1961), pp. 34–60. This American search for newness is captured by the words of the two major literary figures of the period: Ralph Waldo Emerson and Herman Melville. In his renowned essay "Circles," Emerson states that "I am only an experimenter. . . . I simply experiment, an endless seeker, with no past at my back" (*Selected Writings of Ralph Waldo Emerson,* ed. William H. Gilman, [New American Library, 1965], p. 304). In his famous essay "Hawthorne and His Mosses," Melville writes, "Let us boldly contemn all imitation, though it comes to us grateful and fragrant as the morning, and foster all originality, though at first, it be crabbed and ugly as our own pine knots" (Herman Melville, *Moby-Dick,* ed. Harrison Hayford and Hershel Parker [Norton, 1967], pp. 546, 550).

15. Raboteau, *Slave Religion,* pp. 128–132. Note also Lawrence W. Levine, *Black Culture and Black Consciousness: Afro-American Folk Thought from Slavery to Freedom* (Oxford University Press, 1977), pp. 60–61.

16. Herskovits, *The Myth of the Negro Past,* pp. 232–235. The material conditions under which many Africans in the United States became Christians are worth noting: the structure of domination was that of a preindustrial form of slavery; a lower ratio of Africans to whites than that in Latin America facilitated more frequent and intense African-white interaction; and though only 4.5 percent of all Africans imported to the Western Hemisphere came to the United States and Canada, an incredibly high rate of natural increase soon quadrupled this percentage figure. Therefore most converts (though not all, such as the

poet Phyllis Wheatley) were American-born Africans struggling to make sense of and give meaning to life without an immediate relation of African customs and worldviews. For further elaboration on this matter, see Raboteau, *Slave Religion*, pp. 87–92.

17. Raboteau, *Slave Religion*, pp. 59–75.

18. This point is accented by E. Franklin Frazier, *The Negro Church in America* (Schocken Books, 1964), pp. 30–34. For a more dialectical treatment—which highlights the liberating and debilitating aspects of the black Christian churches—see Eugene D. Genovese, *Roll, Jordan, Roll: The World the Slaves Made* (Random House, 1974), pp. 159–284. See also the first-rate dissertation of James M. Washington, which is a pioneering study of the separate black Baptists, "The Origins and Emergence of Black Baptist Separatism, 1863–1897," Ph.D. dissertation, Yale University, 1979.

19. Lionel Trilling, *Beyond Culture: Essays in Literature and Learning* (Viking Press, 1965), p. 3. In a famous essay entitled "The Idea of the Modern," in *The Idea of the Modern in Literature and the Arts,* ed. Irving Howe (Horizon Press, 1967), Irving Howe writes, "Nihilism lies at the center of all we mean by modernist literature, both as subject and symptom, a demon overcome and a demon victorious" (p. 39). For a more affirmative view of modernism, see Peter Gay, *Freud, Jews and Other Germans: Masters and Victims in Modernist Culture* (Oxford University Press, 1978). The best general treatment of modernism is Malcolm Bradbury and James McFarlane, eds., *Modernism: 1890–1930* (Middlesex: Penguin Books, 1976), and the classic Marxist perspective is put forward by Georg Lukács in his influential essay "The Ideology of Modernism," in *Marxism and Human Liberation,* ed. E. San Juan, Jr. (Dell Press, 1973), pp. 277–307.

20. Virginia Woolf, "Mr. Bennett and Mrs. Brown," in *Collected Essays,* Vol. 1 (London: Hogarth Press, 1966), p. 321.

21. The major texts on the industrial provincial stage of American culture are Henry F. May, *The End of American Innocence: A Study of the First Years of Our Own Time, 1912–1917* (Knopf, 1957); Robert H. Wiebe, *The Search for Order, 1877–1920* (Hill & Wang, 1967); Samuel P. Hays, *The Response to Industrialism, 1885–1914* (University of Chicago Press, 1957); Chase, *The American Novel and Its Tradition*, pp. 117–236; Hassan, *Radical Innocence*, pp. 61–95; and the seminal essay by Herbert G. Gutman, "Work, Culture, and Society in Industrializing America, 1815–1919," in his *Work, Culture, and Society in Industrializing America: Essays in American Working-Class and Social History* (Vintage Books, 1977), pp. 3–78.

22. Alfred Kazin, *On Native Grounds: An Interpretation of Modern American Prose Literature* (Doubleday, 1956), p. ix.

23. This formulation follows Richard Rorty's brilliant contemporary remake of Santayana's essay, entitled "Professionalized Philosophy and Transcendentalist Culture," in *The Georgia Review,* 30th anniversary (Winter 1976), pp. 757–769. For a broader characterization of the pragmatist attack on idealism, see Morton White, *Social Thought in America: The Revolt Against Formalism* (Beacon Press, 1957). Note also Bruce Kuklick, *The Rise of American Philosophy: Cambridge, Massachusetts, 1860–1930* (Yale University Press, 1977), pp. 129–227, 233–401. Related treatments on the phenomenon of professionalism in American culture are Burton J. Bledstein, *The Culture of Professionalism: The Middle Class and the Development of Higher Education in America* (Norton, 1976), especially pp. 80–128, 287–334; and David F. Noble, *America by Design: Science, Technology, and the Rise of Corporate Capitalism* (Knopf, 1977).

24. August Meier, *Negro Thought in America, 1880–1915: Racial Ideologies in the Age of Booker T. Washington* (University of Michigan Press, 1963), pp. 161–278; S. P. Fullinwider, *The Mind and Mood of Black America: 20th Century Thought* (Dorsey Press, 1969), pp. 47–71; Abby Arthur Johnson and Ronald Maberry Johnson, *Propaganda and Aesthetics: The Literary Politics of Afro-American Magazines in the Twentieth Century* (University of Massachusetts Press, 1979),

pp. 1–63; and Julius Lester, "Du Bois and Washington," in his fine introduction to *The Seventh Son: The Thought and Writings of W. E. B. Du Bois,* ed. Julius Lester (Random House, 1971), Vol. 1, pp. 41–52.

25. This insight is but one of many in the superb essay by Harold Cruse, "Behind the Black Power Slogan," in his *Rebellion or Revolution?* (William Morrow, 1969), pp. 193–260.

26. For actual reprints of articles from *The Messenger,* see *Voices of a Black Nation: Political Journalism in the Harlem Renaissance,* ed. Theodore G. Vincent (Ramparts Press, 1973), pp. 43–51, 113–122. Reliable treatments of Owen and Randolph can be found in Philip Foner, *American Socialism and Black Americans: From the Age of Jackson to World War II* (Greenwood Press, 1977), pp. 265–287; Johnson and Johnson, *Propaganda and Aesthetics,* pp. 57–63; and Henry Williams, *Black Response to the American Left: 1917–1929* (Princeton University Press, 1973), pp. 80–93. For a fuller examination of Randolph, see Jervis Anderson, *A. Philip Randolph: A Biographical Portrait* (Harcourt Brace Jovanovich, 1972).

27. Similarly, reproductions of articles from *The Crusader,* the periodical of the African Blood Brotherhood, are in *Voices of a Black Nation,* pp. 123–136. Detailed treatments of this fascinating group are difficult to find. The best ones I know are Harry Haywood, *Black Bolshevik: Autobiography of an Afro-American Communist* (Liberator Press, 1978), pp. 122–131; Foner, *American Socialism and Black Americans,* pp. 309–311; Mark Solomon, "Red and Black: Negroes and Communism," Ph.D. dissertation, Harvard University, pp. 79–84; and Mark Naison, "The Communist Party in Harlem, 1928–1936," Ph.D. dissertation, Columbia University, 1975, chaps. 1–2.

28. N. R. Hanson, *Patterns of Discovery* (Cambridge University Press, 1958); Michael Polanyi, *Personal Knowledge: Towards a Post-Critical Philosophy* (University of Chicago Press, 1958); Thomas S. Kuhn, *The Structure of Scientific Revolutions,* 2d ed. (University of Chicago Press, 1970); and "Reflections on My Critics," in *Criticism and the Growth of Knowledge,* ed. Imre Lakatos and Alan Musgrave (Cambridge University Press, 1970), pp. 231–278. Imre Lakatos, "Falsification and the Methodology of Scientific Research Programmes," in *Criticism and the Growth of Knowledge,* pp. 91–196; Paul Feyerabend, *Against Method* (Schocken Books, 1975) and *Science in a Free Society* (Schocken Books, 1978). For serious critical responses to the demythologizing of science, see Israel Scheffler, *Science and Subjectivity* (Bobbs-Merrill, 1967) and "Vision and Revolution: A Postscript on Kuhn," in *Philosophy of Science,* Vol. 39, No. 3 (September 1972), pp. 366–374; Larry Laudan, *Progress and Its Problems: Towards a Theory of Scientific Growth* (University of California Press, 1977); and Clark Glymour, *Theory and Evidence* (Princeton University Press, 1980).

29. Ihab Hassan, *The Literature of Silence: Henry Miller and Samuel Beckett* (Knopf, 1968); *The Dismemberment of Orpheus: Toward a Postmodern Literature* (Oxford University Press, 1971); *Paracriticisms: Seven Speculations of the Times* (University of Illinois Press, 1975); *The Right Promethean Fire: Imagination, Science and Cultural Change* (University of Illinois Press, 1980); Raymond Olderman, *Beyond the Waste Land: A Study of the American Novel in the Nineteen-Sixties* (Yale University Press, 1972); Christopher Lasch, *The Culture of Narcissism* (Norton, 1978); Heinz Kohut, *The Analysis of the Self* (International Universities Press, 1971); *The Restoration of the Self* (International Universities Press, 1977); *The Search for the Self: Selected Writings of Heinz Kohut, 1950–1978,* 2 vols., ed. Paul H. Ornstein (International Universities Press, 1978); Jerome Klinkowitz, *Literary Disruptions: The Making of a Post-Contemporary American Fiction,* 2d ed. (University of Illinois Press, 1981). Relevant Marxist responses to and analyses of postmodernism include Fredric Jameson, *Marxism and Form: Twentieth-Century Dialectical Theories of Literature* (Princeton University Press, 1971); *Fables of Aggression: Wyndham Lewis, the Modernist as Fascist* (University of California Press, 1979); *The Political Unconscious: Narrative as a Socially Symbolic Act* (Cornell University Press, 1981); his insightful essay "Reification and Utopia in Mass Culture," *Social Text* (Winter 1979), pp. 130–148; Russell Jacoby,

Social Amnesia: A Critique of Conformist Psychology from Adler to Laing (Beacon Press, 1975); and Stuart Ewen, *Captains of Consciousness: Advertising and the Social Roots of the Consumer Culture* (McGraw-Hill, 1976). For a critical, even polemic, treatment of postmodernism, see Gerald Graff, "The Myth of the Postmodernist Breakthrough," *Tri-Quarterly*, No. 26 (Winter 1973), pp. 383–417, and his controversial book *Literature Against Itself: Literary Ideas in Modern Society* (University of Chicago Press, 1979). Of course, the basis of scholarship on postmodernism and mass culture was laid by the pioneering work of Max Horkheimer and Theodor Adorno with their classic essay "The Culture Industry: Enlightenment as Mass Deception," in *Dialectic of Enlightenment*, pp. 120–167, and the writings of David Riesman in his (along with Nathan Glazer and Reuel Denney) *The Lonely Crowd: A Study of the Changing American Character*, abr. ed. (Yale University Press, 1961); *Individualism Reconsidered* (Doubleday, 1955), esp. pp. 12–27, 126–163; and *Abundance for What? and Other Essays* (Doubleday, 1964), pp. 103–367.

30. This leadership fulfills the prophecy of Thomas Mann, the major German modernist writer, who writes in the last paragraph of his famous 1938 lecture given on his coast-to-coast tour, "I believe, in fact, that for the duration of the present European dark age, the centre of Western culture will shift to America" (*The Coming Victory of Democracy*, trans. Agnes E. Meyer [Knopf, 1938], pp. 66–67). Note also William Barrett's words regarding the situation of American intellectuals in 1945, "We were probably the last American generation to go through this old rite of looking toward Europe for our culture . . . that older exclusive filial relation to Europe—the sense of Europe as a unique treasure on which Americans must depend—was on the way out" (*The Truants: Adventures Among the Intellectuals* [Doubleday, 1982], p. 130).

31. Kuklick, *The Rise of American Philosophy*, pp. 565–572. See also Richard Rorty's "Introduction," in *The Linguistic Turn*, ed. Richard Rorty (University of Chicago Press, 1967), pp. 1–39. For a slightly different perspective, note my essay "Nietzsche's Prefiguration of Postmodern American Philosophy," *Boundary 2*, Vol. 9, No. 10 (Spring-Fall 1981), pp. 241–270.

32. This second theoretical moment of Afro-American philosophy constitutes its Foucaultian elements: the exploration of the complex relationship between knowledge and power, discourse and politics. For a similar yet more ambitious project, see Edward Said, *Orientalism* (Pantheon Books, 1978). Note that my aim is not to endorse the discursive idealism of Michel Foucault, but rather to incorporate some of his powerful insights into a more sophisticated Marxist analysis of the emergence of modern racism. I have just embarked on a huge project that deepens my concern in this chapter into a full-fledged volume.

33. Friedrich Nietzsche, *On the Genealogy of Morals*, trans. Walter Kaufmann and R. J. Hollingdale (Vintage Books, 1967); Michel Foucault, "Nietzsche, Genealogy, History," in *Language, Counter-Memory, Practice: Selected Essays and Interviews*, trans. Donald F. Bouchard and Sherry Simon (Cornell University Press, 1977), pp. 139–164.

34. Cf. Louis Althusser, "Marx's Relation to Hegel," in his *Politics and History* (Schocken Books, 1972), pp. 181–183. For trenchant criticisms of Althusser, see Stanley Aronowitz, *The Crisis in Historical Materialism: Class, Politics, and Culture in Marxist Theory* (Praeger Publications, 1981), pp. 68–69, 120–121, 325–327.

35. This insight bears the stamp of Foucault's long-drawn-out quarrel with vulgar Marxism. See Michel Foucault, *The History of Sexuality*, Vol. 1, trans. Robert Hurley (Random House, 1980), pp. 92–98; *Power/Knowledge: Selected Interviews and Other Writings, 1972–1977*, ed. Colin Gordon (Pantheon Books, 1980), pp. 109–145.

36. For the "classicism plus science" view of the Enlightenment, see Peter Gay, *The Enlightenment: An Interpretation*, Vol. 1, pp. 3–27, 313–321. For the importance of the Cartesian transformation of philosophy, see Richard Rorty's insightful metaphilosophical claims in *Philosophy and the Mirror of Nature*, esp. pp. 8–12, 45–51, 54–69, 136–140.

37. This understanding of the Renaissance derives from Aby Warburg's notion of *Ausgleichsformel* ("compromise formula"); and for Galileo's and Newton's protomodern worldviews, see Gay, *The Enlightenment,* pp. 269–277.

38. Benjamin Farrington, *Francis Bacon: Philosopher of Industrial Science* (Collier Books, 1961), pp. 78–106; Bertrand Russell, *A History of Western Philosophy* (Simon & Schuster, 1945), p. 544.

39. Martin Heidegger, "The Age of the World View," trans. Marjorie Grene, *Boundary 2,* Vol. 4, No. 2 (Winter 1976), pp. 348–349.

40. Gay, *The Enlightenment,* pp. 310–311.

41. Rorty, *Philosophy and the Mirror of Nature;* Abrams, *The Mirror and the Lamp.*

42. This claim, as well as my general argument, derives in part from the seminal study by George L. Mosse, *Toward the Final Solution: A History of European Racism* (Howard Fertig, 1978). This neglected work deserves much more attention than it has heretofore received.

43. Ibid., p. 10.

44. Jordan, *White Over Black: American Attitudes Toward the Negro, 1550–1812,* pp. 3–98; Gossett, *Race: The History of an Idea in America,* pp. 3–31.

45. Michel Foucault, *The Order of Things: An Archaeology of the Human Sciences* (Pantheon Books, 1970), pp. 132, 158.

46. Jordan, *White Over Black,* pp. 217–218; Gossett, *Race: The History of an Idea in America,* pp. 32–34; Ashley Montagu, "The Origin of the Concept of 'Race,'" in his *Man's Most Dangerous Myth: The Fallacy of Race,* 5th ed. (Oxford University Press, 1974), pp. 46ff.

47. Jordan, *White Over Black,* p. 220.

48. Ibid., pp. 220–221.

49. Gossett, *Race,* p. 36.

50. For their defenses of Blumenbach, see Jordan, *White Over Black,* pp. 223, 507; Gossett, *Race,* p. 39; and Montagu, *Man's Most Dangerous Myth,* pp. 41–45. Support for my viewpoint is found in Mosse, *Toward the Final Solution,* pp. 11, 21.

51. Most notably in the United States, Dr. John Augustine Smith, president of the College of William and Mary, and the famous naturalist Dr. Samuel George Morton of Philadelphia—both fervent proponents of black inferiority. Jordan, *White Over Black,* pp. 505–506; Gossett, *Race,* pp. 58–59.

52. Mosse, *Toward the Final Solution,* p. 22.

53. Ibid., p. 25.

54. Ibid.

55. Jordan, *White Over Black,* pp. 486ff., 514.

56. Ibid., p. 515.

57. Ibid.

58. Ibid., pp. 515–516.

59. Ibid., p. 520.

60. Ibid.

61. David Brion Davis, *The Problem of Slavery in Western Culture* (Cornell University Press, 1966), p. 403.

62. Gossett, *Race,* p. 45.

63. Richard H. Popkin, "Hume's Racism," *The Philosophical Forum,* Vol. 9, Nos. 2–3, p. 213.

64. Jordan, *White Over Black,* pp. 436–437.

65. Popkin, "Hume's Racism," p. 218.

66. Ibid.

67. Gay, *The Enlightenment,* p. 34.

68. Frank M. Snowden, Jr., *Blacks in Antiquity: Ethiopians in the Greco-Roman Experience* (Belknap Press, 1970), pp. 178–179.

69. Ibid., p. 179.

70. E. E. Sikes, *The Anthropology of the Greeks* (London, 1914); W. L. Westermann, *The Slave Systems of Greek and Roman Antiquity, Memoirs of the American Philosophical Society,* Vol. 50 (1955), pp. xi–180; Moses Hadas, *Hellenistic Culture: Fusion and Diffusion* (Columbia University Press, 1959); Adrian N. Sherwin-White, *Racial Prejudice in Imperial Rome* (Cambridge University Press, 1967).

CHAPTER 6

1. This phrase comes from the first line of Muriel Rukeyser's "Poem"–"I lived in the first century of world wars"–in her book *The Speed of Darkness* (1968), in *A Muriel Rukeyser Reader,* ed. Jan Heller Levi (New York: Norton, 1994), p. 211. In his magisterial treatment of this most violent of centuries, *The Age of Extremes: A History of the World, 1914–1991* (New York: Panthcon, 1994), Eric Hobsbawm suggests the numbers of this century's "Megadeath" toll to be 187 million (p. 12). Here he follows the estimate of Z. Brzezinski in *Out of Control: Global Turmoil on the Eve of the Twenty-First Century* (New York: Scribner, 1993). I think both scholars underestimate the death toll in this "most terrible century in Western history" (Isaiah Berlin's phrase).

2. In *Dusk of Dawn: An Essay Toward an Autobiography of a Race Concept* (1940), W. E. B. Du Bois writes, "Whatever of racial feeling gradually crept into my life, its effect upon me in these earlier days was rather one of exaltation and high disdain. . . . My African racial feeling was then purely a matter of my own later learning and reaction. . . ." In W. E. B. Du Bois, *Writings* (New York: Library of America, 1986), pp. 563, 638. See also Eric J. Sundquist, *To Wake the Nations: Race in the Making of American Literature* (Cambridge, Mass.: Harvard University Press, 1993), pp. 459–467; David Levering Lewis, *W. E. B. Du Bois: Biography of a Race, 1868–1919* (New York: Henry Holt, 1993), pp. 56–70; and Manning Marable, *W. E. B. Du Bois: Black Radical Democrat* (Boston: Twayne Publishers, 1986), pp. 5–15.

3. W. E. B. Du Bois, "The Talented Tenth," in *Writings,* p. 852. As Peter Gay rightly notes, "The question of the lower orders is the great unexamined political question of the Enlightenment. . . . [In the writings of the *philosophes* there is] snobbery . . . [there is] a certain failure of imagination . . . [and there is] a sense of despair at the general wretchedness, illiteracy, and brutishness of the poor." *The Enlightenment: An Interpretation* (New York: Norton Library, 1969), Vol. 2, *The Science of Freedom,* p. 517.

4. W. E. B. Du Bois, *The Souls of Black Folk* (New York: Fawcett Publications, 1961), pp. 48, 50, 75, 76, 83, 87, 101, 107, 109, 125, 126, 132, 139, 150, 170, 171, 182, 189. The last quote is from page 80.

5. Ibid., pp. 140–141.

6. In a brilliant essay, Shamoon Zamir makes a similar point about Du Bois. "As Du Bois details his curiosity and excitement at the novelty of the situation, his posture is very much that of an ethnographic participant-observer reporting from the field. . . . The feelings of the young Du Bois reproduce the same exoticism that led the white middle-class reading public at the turn of the century to seek out works that revealed how 'the other half' lived." Zamir grounds Du Bois's worldview in *The Souls of Black Folk* in Victorian moralism, Herderian romanticism and the historical realism of the Gospels (sorrow songs). Zamir suggests that Du Bois's sense of the tragic goes a bit deeper than I admit–but only a little bit deeper. See Shamoon Zamir, "'The Sorrow Songs'/'Song of Myself': Du Bois, The Crisis of Leadership, and Prophetic Imagination," in *The Black Columbiad: Defining Moments in African American Literature and Culture,* ed. Werner Sollors and Maria Diedrich (Cambridge,

Mass.: Harvard University Press, 1994), pp. 145–166, esp. 147–148. For Zamir's fascinating, yet ultimately unconvincing Hegelian treatment of Du Bois's early thought, see *Dark Voices: W. E. B. Du Bois and American Thought, 1888–1903* (Chicago: University of Chicago Press, 1995). For Du Bois on jazz, see Kathy J. Ogren, *The Jazz Revolution: Twenties America and the Meaning of Jazz* (New York: Oxford University Press, 1989), pp. 118–120.

7. For a provocative recent treatment of this age-old dichotomy created by intellectuals—the ultimate logic of which denies the full human status of the majority of people—see John Carey, *The Intellectuals and the Masses: Pride and Prejudice Among the Literary Intelligentsia, 1880–1939* (New York: St. Martin's Press, 1992). For direct references to black people—some of which resonate with Du Bois's—note pp. 52, 65, 121, 125, 148, 194f., 210. Needless to say, most of the figures Carey examines—such as José Ortega y Gasset, Knut Hamsun, T. S. Eliot, H. G. Wells, W. B. Yeats, Evelyn Waugh, Arthur Machen, George Bernard Shaw, Ezra Pound, Wyndham Lewis, D. H. Lawrence and Aldous Huxley—were either arch elitists or outright xenophobes. Du Bois's democratic sentiments tempered his elitism and xenophobia (e.g., his anti-Jewish stereotypes were toned down in later editions of *The Souls of Black Folk*). For example, note David Levering Lewis's analysis in *W. E. B. Du Bois*, p. 285.

8. Du Bois, *Dusk of Dawn*, in *Writings*, p. 596.

9. W. E. B. Du Bois, *The Autobiography of W. E. B. Du Bois: A Soliloquy on Viewing My Life from the Last Decade of Its First Century* (New York: International Publishers, 1968), pp. 221–222.

10. Lewis, *W. E. B. Du Bois*, p. 227.

11. This brief tilt toward the tragic in Du Bois's corpus may be contrasted with that most rare of despairing moments in Ralph Waldo Emerson's upbeat writings—namely, his often overlooked poem "Threnody," one of the great elegies in the English language, written in response to the death of his beloved five-year-old first son, Waldo. Note how Emerson wrestles with the overwhelming *irrevocability* of his son's death in its opening lines, with no reaching for reason or revelation: The South-wind brings "Life, sunshine and desire, / And on every mount and meadow / Breathes aromatic fire; / But over the dead he has no power, / The lost, the lost, he cannot restore; / And, looking over the hills, I mourn / The darling who shall not return."

12. Du Bois, *The Souls of Black Folk*, pp. 154–55. See also Keith E. Byerman, *Seizing the Word: History, Art, and Self in the Work of W. E. B. Du Bois* (Athens: University of Georgia Press, 1994), pp. 29–31.

13. Du Bois, *The Souls of Black Folk*, p. 153.

14. For a fascinating yet unpersuasive reading of this neglected moment in Du Bois that claims that "this suffering has no redemptive moment," see Paul Gilroy, *The Black Atlantic: Modernity and Double Consciousness* (Cambridge, Mass.: Harvard University Press, 1993), pp. 138–139. Gilroy rightly points out that Du Bois experiences "an awful gladness in my heart. . . . No bitter meanness now shall sicken his baby heart till it die a living death, no taunt shall madden his happy boyhood. Fool that I was to think or wish that this little soul should grow choked and deformed within the Veil! . . . Better far this nameless void that stops my life than a sea of sorrows for you" (Du Bois, *The Souls of Black Folk*, p. 156). Yet the first sentence of the chapter—"Unto you a child is born"—invokes Jesus of Nazareth (that most redemptive of figures). Du Bois also hears "in his baby voice the voice of the Prophet that was to rise within the Veil" while his son is alive. And he vows that his son's death "is not the end. Surely there shall yet dawn some mighty morning to lift the Veil and set the prisoned free. Not for me,—I shall die in my bonds,—but for fresh young souls who have not known the night and waken to the morning . . . some morning. . . ." (p. 156). This certainly is Du Bois in a tragic mood, yet his Enlightenment eschatology—with a small dose of Stoicism—gets the best of him. Like Candide in that marvelous Enlightenment novelette

Candide (1759) by the inimitable Voltaire, even in the midst of the deepest tragedies and absurdities, cultivation can still generate a harvest, rational control and moral action can still yield fruit down the road. In fact, Du Bois's salvific sentiments provide more hope for the future than Voltaire's witty and resilient Stoicism. Only Du Bois's incredible and torturous prayer in response to the Atlanta Riot—his classic "A Litany of Atlanta" (1906)—explores the tragic and absurd depths of the human condition. His desperate call for moral integrity and political action in the face of the "white terror" of human suffering and divine silence, as well as his embrace of the "dark sleep," is one instance in his corpus where he engages in the existential deep-sea diving of Tolstoy, Chekhov, Kafka, Coltrane and Morrison. For this sterling performance, see James Melvin Washington's canonical text, *Conversations with God: Two Centuries of Prayers by African Americans* (New York: HarperCollins, 1994), pp. 102–104. Washington's profound "Afterword: A Scholar's Benediction" captures my own Christian tragicomic sense of life—a sense grounded in the Christocentric humanism of Erasmus, Kierkegaard and Martin Luther King, Jr.; the tormented love ethic of Tennessee Williams, Leo Tolstoy and Toni Morrison; and the indefatigable compassion of Anton Chekhov, Muriel Rukeyser and John Coltrane. My own perennial wrestling with existential tension in history is deeply influenced by the profound corpus of Eric Voegelin.

15. For Du Bois's direct debt to the father of Victorian social criticism, Thomas Carlyle, see Lewis, *W. E. B. Du Bois,* pp. 74–75, 77, 78, 115–116, 120, 136, 148. The best general treatment of Carlyle's life and work is Fred Kaplan's *Thomas Carlyle: A Biography* (Berkeley: University of California Press, 1983).

16. Du Bois, "The Talented Tenth," in *Writings,* pp. 842, 861.

17. Du Bois's critique of patriarchy—black and white—grows and deepens in the course of his long career. For instance, see his 1920 classic essay "The Damnation of Women," from *Darkwater,* in *Writings,* pp. 952–68.

18. Matthew Arnold, *Culture and Anarchy,* ed. J. Dover Wilson (Cambridge: Cambridge University Press, 1960), p. 70.

19. Du Bois, "The Talented Tenth," in *Writings,* pp. 846, 847.

20. For superb synoptic treatments of two exemplary figures, see Thomas C. Holt, "The Lonely Warrior: Ida B. Wells-Barnett and the Struggle for Black Leadership," in *Black Leaders of the Twentieth Century,* ed. John Hope Franklin and August Meier (Urbana: University of Illinois Press, 1982), pp. 39–61; and Joseph P. Reidy, "Aaron A. Bradley: The Voice of Black Labor in the Georgia Lowcountry," in *Southern Black Leaders of the Reconstruction Era,* ed. Howard N. Rabinowitz (Urbana: University of Illinois Press, 1982), pp. 281–308.

21. Du Bois acknowledges this fact in *Dusk of Dawn* (in *Writings,* p. 690): "It still remains possible in the United States for a white American to be a gentleman and a scholar, a Christian and a man of integrity, and yet flatly and openly refuse to treat as a fellow human being any person who has Negro ancestry." As in Leo Tolstoy's magnificent short story "After the Ball" (1903), in which a genteel old colonel masks his hatred and cruelty toward a lower-class person, this paradox and hypocrisy undermines one of the crucial "truths" of the Enlightenment worldview and Victorian social criticism.

22. W. E. B. Du Bois, "The Talented Tenth: Memorial Address" (1948), in *A Reader,* ed. David Levering Lewis (New York: Henry Holt, 1995), p. 349.

23. Ibid., p. 350.

24. Two neglected gems in the rich Victorian tradition of social criticism especially pertinent in our precatastrophic postmodern times are L. T. Hobhouse, *Democracy and Reaction* (1904) and C. F. G. Masterman, *The Condition of England* (1909). In the former text, Hobhouse—a great anti-imperialist democrat of Edwardian England—echoes Du Bois's famous claim that "the problem of the twentieth century is the problem of the color-line." In the latter book, Masterman—the sagacious critic of English self-deception just prior to World War

I–writes: "Humanity–at best–appears but as a shipwrecked crew which has taken refuge on a narrow ledge of rock, beaten by wind and wave; which cannot tell how many, if any at all, will survive when the long night gives place to morning. The wise man will still go softly all his days; working always for greater economic equality on the one hand, for understanding between estranged peoples on the other; apprehending always how slight an effort of stupidity or violence could strike a death blow to twentieth-century civilization, and elevate the forces of destruction triumphant over the ruins of a world" (London: Methuen, 1909; p. 233).

25. George Steiner, "A Responsion," in *Reading George Steiner,* ed. Nathan A. Scott, Jr., and Ronald A. Sharp (Baltimore: Johns Hopkins University Press, 1994), p. 278. Steiner's critical attitude toward the academy echoes that of the grand old (Canadian-born) Harvard humanist Douglas Bush. His 1966 book on the greatest nineteenth-century English poet, John Keats, is one of the best we have, and his 1939 Alexander Lectures lament the loss of the "general reader." In the latter he states: "One may wonder, timidly, if a real revival of the humanities might not be inaugurated by a moratorium on productive scholarship . . . long enough to restore our perspective and sense of value. What a golden interlude we might have, with the learned journals temporarily withdrawn, with no scholarly lucubrations to read or write, no annual bibliographies to torment us with hundreds of things we must know if we are to be qualified to lead hopeful young men into the same labyrinth, with nothing to do, in short, but sit down in peace with the great books we ought to be soaking in! . . . In front of my desk are serried rows of card-indexes, bibliographies, and periodicals. Out of sight behind me are Holbein's portraits of Erasmus and More. 'Saint Socrates, pray for us.'" (quoted from Douglas Bush, *The Renaissance and English Humanism* [Toronto: University of Toronto Press, 1939], pp. 132–33). For one of the most powerful critiques of professionalized cultural studies in this century, see Geoffrey Scott's classic *The Architecture of Humanism: A Study in the History of Taste* (1914; reprint, New York: Norton, 1974).

26. For a brief examination of the slow demise of American exceptionalism in American historiography, see David W. Noble, *The End of American History* (Minneapolis: University of Minnesota, 1985). Note also Michael Kammen, "The Problem of American Exceptionalism: A Reconsideration," *American Quarterly* 45, No. 1 (1993), pp. 1–43.

27. Du Bois confronts this pessimism most strikingly in two of the most insightful and angry essays in his corpus–"The White World," in *Dusk of Dawn* (1940), and "The Souls of White Folk," in *Darkwater* (1920). These essays echo the themes in the work of the grand dean of Pan-African Studies in America, John Henrik Clarke. But in neither essay does Du Bois openly acknowledge that a long tradition of black cultural and revolutionary nationalists had already arrived where he seemed to be headed. Harold Cruse makes this persuasive argument in his classic work *The Crisis of the Negro Intellectual* (New York: William Morrow, 1967), pp. 330–336. For Du Bois's essays, see *Writings,* pp. 652–680, 923–938.

28. Henry Highland Garnet, "An Address to the Slaves of the United States of America of 1843," in *Black Nationalism in America,* ed. John Bracey, August Meier and Elliot Rudwick (Indianapolis: Bobbs-Merrill, 1970), p. 73.

29. It is no accident that these two groups serve as major preoccupations of the two towering European men of letters in our time–Isaiah Berlin and George Steiner. The recent revival around Berlin focuses on his pluralistic liberal political thought, but his greatness resides in his deep and empathetic interpretations of Russian intellectuals such as Turgenev, Belinsky, Bakunin and especially Herzen and Tolstoy. His powerful readings of Vico, Herder and de Maistre–though canonical–pale in the face of his self-invested and magisterial treatments of Tolstoy. In fact, his most famous essay, "The Hedgehog and the Fox" (originally entitled, in its shorter form, "Lev Tolstoy's Historical Scepticism"), is the best example of philosophic *phronesis* (practical wisdom) in this blood-drenched century. Section

6 of this magnificent essay—the pinnacle of his masterful corpus—represents the highest form of philosophic wisdom literature written in twentieth-century Europe—and Tolstoy is his major springboard. This essay, to be read and reread, is found in *Russian Thinkers,* ed. Henry Hardy and Aileen Kelly (New York: Viking Press, 1978), pp. 22–81, esp. 68–74. George Steiner's gallant attempt to focus our attention on early twentieth-century central European figures such as Hermann Broch, Paul Celan, Arnold Schoenberg, Robert Musil, Sigmund Freud, Rainer Maria Rilke and Franz Kafka is monumental and has yielded much fruit. For example, recent interest in Musil—due in part to the new edition of his novel *The Man Without Qualities* (1930), including previously unpublished sections, and of his timely essays, *Precision and Soul,* ed. Burton Pike and David S. Luft (Chicago: University of Chicago Press, 1990)—is growing. A Broch revival centered on his masterpiece, *The Death of Virgil* (1945), may be next. Yet Steiner's project began with the Russians—that is, with Tolstoy, Dostoyevsky and Shestov. His first book was *Tolstoy or Dostoevsky: An Essay in the Old Criticism* (New York: Knopf, 1959)—Tolstoy as Homeric bard vs. Dostoyevsky as tragic dramatist in response to the "dilemma of Realism" created by Dickens, Hugo, Stendhal, Zola and Flaubert. And the great work of Shestov (whose first book was on Shakespeare), *Athens and Jerusalem,* deeply influenced him. Steiner notes, "The nearing shadow of Hitler made me. . . . The dialectic of 'Athens/Jerusalem' has been perennial throughout my teaching and published work." And notwithstanding his marvelous readings of Kafka—a figure who shunned noise and music—Steiner states, "The question 'what in the world is music like?' has become for me the metaphysical inquiry incarnate. . . . It is, in Lévi-Strauss's arresting formulation, the invention of melody which remains the *mystère suprême des sciences de l'homme.*" See Steiner, "A Responsion," in *Reading George Steiner,* pp. 276, 280, 283, 284. Note the brilliant essays pertinent to my concerns in this superb volume by Robert Boyers, Guido Almansi, Ruth Padel, Edith Wyschogrod, John Bayley and especially Caryl Emerson. For a seminal effort to connect black arts to nineteenth-century Russian literature—in a call for "universalized particularity"—see Alain Locke, "Self-Criticism: The Third Dimension in Culture," *Phylon* 11 (1950), pp. 391–394. My attempt to link the situation in *fin-de-siècle* Russia, early twentieth-century central Europe and late twentieth-century black America rests in part on possible connections between Tolstoy, Kafka and black artists like John Coltrane and Toni Morrison. For a brief contrast of Tolstoy and Kafka, see Pietro Citati, *Tolstoy* (New York: Schocken Books, 1986), pp. 223–225. For fascinating and suggestive connections between Tolstoy, Chekhov and jazz, note Nabokov's pregnant remarks about the distinctive genius of Tolstoy—his "time-balance"; "his characters seem to move with the same swing as the people passing under our window"; "Tolstoy's prose keeps pace with our pulses"; or "the perfectly natural swing" in Chekhov's *The Seagull.* This characterization resonates with the formal improvisational freedom, "metrical adventurousness," verbal playfulness and syncopated responsiveness associated with black cultural expression—especially its most sophisticated artistic works, such as those of John Coltrane and Toni Morrison. Note Vladimir Nabokov, *Lectures on Russian Literature,* ed. Fredson Bowers (New York: Harcourt Brace, 1981), pp. 141–142, 282. An important historical treatment of the evolution of black culture is Roger D. Abrahams's *Singing the Master: The Emergence of African-American Culture in the Plantation South* (New York: Penguin Books, 1992). The best recent synoptic treatment of the origins of black culture is Sterling Stuckey's *Slave Culture: Nationalist Theory and the Foundations of Black America* (New York: Oxford University Press, 1987). A more interpretive examination of black music is LeRoi Jones's classic, *Blues People* (New York: William Morrow, 1963). The complex relation of the world-historical efforts of Tolstoy and Kafka to those of Armstrong, Ellington, Coltrane and Morrison to transfigure sadness and sorrow into great art based on meticulous explorations of the quotidian realities of degraded and devalued peoples requires serious inquiry

in the future. How do we account for these three incredible artistic peaks–Russian novel-
istic and theatrical preeminence, central European literary and epistolary achievements and
twentieth-century black musical and literary supremacy–in late modernity?

30. Du Bois's debt to Goethe's *Faust* was profound. And the word "striving" was–along
with "enjoyment"–the most Faustian of terms, rooted in Goethe's own idiosyncratic theory of entelechy in nature and man. "Striving" consists of a fundamental human urge to
embrace the world and takes the form of self-expression in thought and, above all, action.
The famous last words of Faust in Goethe's incomparable modern epic poem are worth
quoting here–they get at the heart and core of Du Bois's worldview: "Yes–this I hold to
with devout insistence, / Wisdom's last verdict goes to say: / He only earns both freedom
and existence / Who must reconquer them each day. / And so, ringed all about by perils,
here / Youth, manhood, age will spend their strenuous year. / Such teeming would I see
upon this land, / On acres free among free people stand. / I might entreat the fleeting
minute: / Oh tarry yet, thou art so fair! / My path on earth, the trace I leave within it /
Eons untold cannot impair. / Foretasting such high happiness to come, / I savor now my
striving's crown and sum." For Du Bois's special love for Goethe's work and his advice to
Fisk University students and graduates to immerse themselves in Goethe in order to ex-
pedite "the rise of the Negro people," see Lewis, *W. E. B. Du Bois*, p. 139. For a comprehensive and incisive reading of Du Bois's *The Souls of Black Folk* as itself a "striving" in the
form of a textual performance and narrative experiment in dramatic form, see Sundquist,
To Wake the Nations, pp. 457–539.

31. Du Bois, *The Souls of Black Folk*, p. 15. Du Bois's allusion to a European poet's powerful
metaphor of crying seems to echo the opening of Anna Julia Cooper's classic *A Voice from
the South* (1892)–the first major work of a black woman of letters in the United States,
which inspired the powerful writings of black women intellectuals like bell hooks, Patricia
Williams, Deborah McDowell, Kimberle Crenshaw, Alice Walker, Katie Cannon, Hazel
Carby, Michele Wallace, Paula Giddings, Wahneema Lubiano, Evelyn Brooks Higgam-
botham, Hortense Spillers, Angela Davis, Tricia Rose, Valerie Smith and Farah Griffin in
our day. In the preface, Cooper begins, "In the clash and clatter of our American Conflict,
it has been said that the South remains Silent. Like the Sphinx she inspires vociferous dis-
putation, but herself takes little part in the noisy controversy. One muffled strain in the
Silent South, a jarring chord and a vague and uncomprehended cadenza, has been and still
is the Negro. And of that muffled chord, the one mute and voiceless note has been the
sadly expectant Black woman, / An infant crying in the night, / An infant crying for the
light. / And with *no language–but a cry*." Cooper's explicit allusion to the self-description of
nineteenth-century Europe's great lyrical poet Alfred Tennyson–with his themes of the terror of loneliness and the preoccupation with death–resonates with the beginning of Du
Bois's text. W. H. Auden's famous characterization of Tennyson seems to apply to the existential starting points of both Cooper and Du Bois: "Two questions: Who am I? Why do
I exist? and the panic fear of their remaining unanswered–doubt is much too intellectual
and tame a term for such a vertigo of anxiety–seem to have obsessed him all his
life. . . . Tennyson became conscious in childhood of Hamlet's problem, the religious significance of his own experience." In short, the black predicament first emerged as Hamlet's
problem–the radical contingency of life, the sheer indifference of nature and human destructive thought and self-destructive action. Like the Russian intellectuals' obsession with
Hamlet–from Turgenev's torment in his influential essay on Hamlet (and Don Quixote) in
1860 to Tolstoy's scorn in his infamous renunciation of Shakespeare in 1906 and Kafka's
appreciation of Shakespeare (thanks to his Anglophilic friend Emil Weiss), despite his dis-
orientating experience of seeing Albert Bassermann perform Hamlet in Berlin in 1910–the
tragedies and absurdities bombarding black people in the New World made Hamlet's prob-

lem even more intense and urgent. In Tennyson's case, this intensity and urgency were due in part to an unhappy childhood at home and school (Louth Grammar School) and the early death of his best friend, Arthur Henry Hallam. For the quote in Anna Julia Cooper, see *A Voice from the South,* introduction by Mary Helen Washington, Schomburg Library of Nineteenth-Century Black Women Writers, Henry Louis Gates, Jr., gen. ed. (New York: Oxford University Press, 1988), p. i. For W. H. Auden's quotes, see "Tennyson," in *Forewords and Afterwords* (New York: Vintage Books, 1989), pp. 228, 229. For Kafka's brush with Shakespeare, see Ernst Pawel, *The Nightmare of Reason: A Life of Franz Kafka* (New York: Vintage Books, 1984), pp. 127, 217; and Frederick Karl, *Franz Kafka: Representative Man* (New York: Fromm International, 1991), pp. 252, 259. Hamlet's famous lines "The time is out of joint—O cursed spite, / That ever I was born to set it right!" and "To be, or not to be, that is the question" are fundamental themes in black strivings. This is why *flight* and *flow*—migration and emigration, experimentation and improvisation—are so basic to black history and life. And also why Hamlet's motifs of *mourning* and *revenge* are two dominant elements in the black cultural and political unconscious.

32. Du Bois, *The Souls of Black Folk,* p. 15.

33. Ibid.

34. This vicious white-supremacist reduction makes it difficult for black people to discuss and display their full humanity and variety among themselves—most clearly seen in the underdeveloped discourse on black sexuality in our era of AIDS. The formidable example of black gay intellectuals like the late Marlon Riggs and Kendall Thomas and black lesbian intellectuals such as the late Audre Lorde and Barbara Smith is indispensable in resisting this inhumane reduction.

35. Ralph Ellison, *Invisible Man* (New York: New American Library, 1952), p. 7.

36. Du Bois, *The Souls of Black Folk,* p. 148.

37. Ibid., p. 149.

38. Ibid., p. 150.

39. Ibid.

40. Ibid., pp. 16–17.

41. Toni Morrison, *Beloved* (New York: New American Library, 1987), p. 140.

42. Ibid., p. 251.

43. Ibid.

44. Du Bois, *The Souls of Black Folk,* p. 156.

45. James Baldwin, *Go Tell It on the Mountain* (New York: Dell, 1953), pp. 137–138.

46. Like Nina's precious words at the end of Chekhov's *The Seagull,* "Know how to bear your cross and have faith," or Irina's at the conclusion of *Three Sisters,* "I'll give my whole life to those who may need it."

47. Morrison, *Beloved,* pp. 87, 88–89.

48. Du Bois, *The Souls of Black Folk,* p. 157.

49. Ibid., p. 158.

50. Richard Wright, *Native Son* (New York: Harper & Row, 1940), pp. 20–21.

51. Ibid., pp. 285–286.

52. Ibid., p. 275.

53. Ibid., p. 277. Note Wright's allusion to "the last best hope of earth"—"America"—in Lincoln's famous message to Congress on December 1, 1862: "We shall nobly save, or meanly lose, the last best hope of earth." See Mark E. Neely, Jr., *The Last Best Hope of Earth: Abraham Lincoln and the Promise of America* (Cambridge, Mass.: Harvard University Press, 1993), p. v.

54. Wright, *Native Son,* p. 268.

55. Du Bois, *The Souls of Black Folk,* p. 159.

56. Needless to say, this theme of bondage applies above all to those obsessed not simply with oppression, but with the sheer concrete fact and potency of evil. Bigger's existential nihilism—his inability to run from himself (including the white supremacy in him)—echoes that of Ahab in Melville's classic *Moby-Dick* (1851), Attwater in Robert Louis Stevenson's late masterpiece *The Ebb-Tide* (1894) and Kurtz in Joseph Conrad's famous *Heart of Darkness* (1902).

57. Wright, *Native Son*, pp. 22–23.

58. Ibid., p. 388.

59. Du Bois, *The Souls of Black Folk*, p. 146.

60. Wright, *Native Son*, pp. 237, 238.

61. Ellison, *Invisible Man*, p. 11. For a fuller and richer elaboration of this Ellisonian insight, the classic works of Albert Murray, *Stomping the Blues* and *The Hero and the Blues*, are peerless.

62. Du Bois, *The Souls of Black Folk*, p. 161.

63. Wright, *Native Son*, pp. 109–110.

64. Du Bois, *The Souls of Black Folk*, p. 164.

65. Ibid.

66. Ibid., pp. 164–165.

67. Ibid., pp. 23, 41.

68. Richard J. Barnet and John Cavanagh, *Global Dreams: Imperial Corporations and the New World Order* (New York: Simon & Schuster, 1994). See also Benjamin R. Barber, *Jihad vs. McWorld* (New York: Random House, 1995).

69. For a powerful treatment of the negative impact of globalization on the most disadvantaged and vulnerable human beings on the globe, see Herb Addo (the major exponent of neoradical creative pessimism), "The Convulsive Historical Moment: Considerations from a Neoradical Third World Perspective," *Macalaster International* 1 (Spring 1995), pp. 115–148. Addo's sophisticated neo-Marxism leads him to conclude: "1) History is not just any old absurdity, but a patently silly absurdity; 2) global life is not only just a drama, but a dark drama; and 3) the Third World role in both is not just any old invigorating happy laughing farce, but a huge bad-humored farce" (p. 115). This apocalyptic—yet far from outlandish—prospect is also entertained in Giovanni Arrighi's magisterial *The Long Twentieth Century: Money, Power, and the Origins of Our Old Times* (New York: Verso, 1994), in which he concludes that humanity "may well burn up in the horrors (or glories) of the escalating violence that has accompanied the liquidation of the Cold War world order. In this case, capitalist history would also come to an end but by reverting permanently to the systemic chaos from which it began six hundred years ago and which has been reproduced on an ever-increasing scale with each transition. Whether this would mean the end just of capitalist history or of all human history, it is impossible to tell" (p. 356). Eric Hobsbawm reaches similar conclusions—but with a small dose of English reticence: "Our world risks both explosion and implosion. It must change. . . . If humanity is to have a recognizable future, it cannot be by prolonging the past or the present. If we try to build the third millennium on that basis, we shall fail. And the price of failure, that is to say, the alternative to a changed society, is darkness" (Hobsbawm, *The Age of Extremes,* p. 585). The most recent erudite world historian to look into the future and risk the curse of Cassandra is Felipe Fernandez-Armesto, who claims that "the day of democracy looks as if it has arrived, but it will prove to be a false dawn or a short spell of wintry light. . . . Recrudescent fascism is the great political menace of the near future. . . . Ethnic enmity is likely to continue to be a breaker of states. . . . It seems inevitable that in the next century the world will experience more rounds of ethnic cleansing . . . the massacres will be bloodier and the conflicts more prolonged. . . . The world, I feel tempted to conclude, will go on getting worse." *Millennium:*

A History of the Last Thousand Years (New York: Scribner, 1995), pp. 726, 727, 732, 736. Thomas M. Callaghy and John Ravenhill desperately attempt to temper such pessimism in "Vision, Politics, and Structure: Afro-Optimism, Afro-Pessimism or Realism?" and "How Hemmed In? Lessons and Prospects of Africa's Responses to Decline," in *Hemmed In: Responses to Africa's Economic Decline,* ed. Thomas M. Callaghy and John Ravenhill (New York: Columbia University Press, 1993), pp. 1–17, 520–563.

70. For the incredible empirical figures revealing the disparity between the wealthy and others, see Edward N. Wolff, *Top Heavy: A Study of the Increasing Inequality of Wealth in America* (New York: Twentieth Century Fund Press, 1995), pp. 7, 10, 11. For the two most important books on the decay of American democracy concealed by the political rule of liberal and especially right-wing elites, see the work of the progressive populist William Greider, *Who Will Tell the People? The Betrayal of American Democracy* (New York: Simon & Schuster, 1992); and that of the conservative populist Kevin Phillips, *Boiling Point: Republicans, Democrats, and the Decline of Middle-Class Prosperity* (New York: Random House, 1993).

71. Quoted from Gerald Horne, *Black and Red: W. E. B. Du Bois and the Afro-American Response to the Cold War* (Albany: State University of New York Press, 1986), p. 345.

72. A. N. Wilson, *Tolstoy* (New York: Fawcett Columbine, 1988), p. 257.

73. Pawel, *The Nightmare of Reason,* pp. 368, 427–430. Kafka writes, "I realized that if I somehow wanted to go on living, I had to do something quite radical, and so I decided to emigrate to Palestine. I probably would not have been able to do so; I am also quite unprepared in Hebrew and in other respects, but I simply had to have hope of some kind to latch on to." Although Kafka was not a Zionist, he might well have emigrated to Palestine if tuberculosis of the larynx had not ended his short life. Like John Coltrane, Franz Kafka died at forty.

CHAPTER 9

1. Benjamin Barber, *The Conquest of Politics: Liberal Philosophy in Democratic Times* (forthcoming), chap. 8.

2. Ibid.

3. Ibid. The best practical outline of the desirable economy I know is in Alec Nove's *The Economics of Feasible Socialism* (London: Allen and Unwin, 1983), pp. 197–230.

4. Roberto Unger, *Social Theory, Its Situation and Its Task: A Critical Introduction to Politics—A Work in Constructive Social Theory* (Cambridge: Cambridge University Press, 1987), p. 41.

5. Ibid.

6. Ibid., p. 14.

7. Ibid., pp. 18–22.

8. Ibid., p. 43.

9. Ibid., p. 214.

10. Ibid., pp. 214–215.

11. Ibid., pp. 223–224.

12. Ibid., p. 200.

13. Ibid., p. 216.

14. Ibid., p. 233.

15. Ibid., p. 219.

16. Ibid., pp. 165–169.

17. Ibid., p. 237.

18. Richard Rorty, "Solidarity or Objectivity?" in *Post-Analytic Philosophy,* ed. John Rajchman and Cornel West (New York: Columbia University Press, 1985), pp. 3–19.

19. For a preliminary effort in this regard pertaining to race, see Cornel West, "Race and Social Theory: Towards a Genealogical Materialist Analysis," in *American Left Yearbook* 2, ed. Michael Davis et al. (London: Verso, 1987), pp. 74–90.

20. See Foucault's influential essay "Nietzsche, Genealogy, History," in *Language, Counter-Memory, Practice,* trans. Donald F. Bouchard and Sherry Simon (Ithaca: Cornell University Press, 1977), pp. 139–164.

21. The best example of Foucault's powerful genealogical investigations is his work *Discipline and Punish: The Birth of the Prison,* trans. Alan Sheridan (New York: Vintage Books, 1979).

22. For a reading of Foucault that highlights this aspect of his work, see John Rajchman, *Michel Foucault: The Freedom of Philosophy* (New York: Columbia University Press, 1985), pp. 103–108.

23. Michel Foucault, "Truth and Power," in *Power/Knowledge: Selected Interviews and Other Writings, 1972–1977,* trans. Colin Gordon et al. (New York: Pantheon Books, 1980), p. 117.

24. Michel Foucault, "The Subject and Power," *Critical Inquiry,* 8, No. 1 (Summer 1982), pp. 777, 778.

25. Rajchman, *Michel Foucault,* p. 103.

26. Edward W. Said, *The World, the Text, and the Critic* (Cambridge, Mass.: Harvard University Press, 1983), pp. 221, 222.

27. In discussions with Professor Daniel Defert in Paris during the spring of 1987, he informed me that Foucault's letters contain evidence of deep familiarity with American pragmatism (Foucault's neighbor in Tunisia for two years was France's leading interpreter of American philosophy, Gérard Deledalle). Furthermore, Foucault's reading of materials produced by the Black Panther Party was instrumental in his turn toward the centrality of the strategic and tactical in genealogical work. My basic claim here is that certain Kantian residues still haunt Foucault's later work.

28. Raymond Williams, *Modern Tragedy* (Stanford, Calif.: Stanford University Press, 1966), pp. 48–49.

29. Hans-Georg Gadamer, *Truth and Method* (New York: Seabury Press, 1975), pp. 245–341. Edward Shils, *Tradition* (Chicago: University of Chicago Press, 1981).

30. Williams, *Modern Tragedy,* pp. 83–84.

31. Antonio Gramsci, *Selections from the Prison Notebooks,* ed. and trans. Quintin Hoare and Geoffrey Nowell Smith (New York: International Publishers, 1971), p. 348.

32. Ibid., pp. 348, 349.

33. Ibid., p. 417. For an elaboration of this Gramscian viewpoint, see Cornel West, "Religion and the Left," chap. 32 in this volume.

34. Said, *The World, the Text, and the Critic,* pp. 1–30.

35. For a prophetic pragmatist treatment of this matter, see Cornel West, "The Historicist Turn in Philosophy of Religion," chap. 25 in this volume. See also Cornel West, "On Leszek Kolakowski," chap. 28 in this volume.

CHAPTER 10

1. Alfred Kazin, *An American Procession* (New York: Knopf, 1984), p. 114.

2. Sidney Hook, *Pragmatism and the Tragic Sense of Life* (New York: Basic Books, 1974), pp. 1–25.

3. C. I. Lewis, *Collected Papers* (Palo Alto, Calif.: Stanford University Press, 1970), p. 108.

4. John Dewey, "The Need for a Recovery of Philosophy," *On Experience, Nature, and Freedom,* ed. Richard Bernstein (New York: Bobbs-Merrill, 1960), pp. 25, 26.

5. Josiah Royce, *Sources of Religious Insight* (New York: Octagon Books, 1977), pp. 144, 145–146.

6. William James, *Collected Essays and Reviews* (New York: Russell and Russell, 1969) p. 11.

7. John Dewey, "Philosophy and Democracy," *Characters and Events* (New York: Holt, Rinehart, and Winston, 1929), Vol. 2, p. 843.

8. Royce, *Sources of Religious Insight*, p. 159.

9. John Dewey, *Philosophy and Civilization* (New York: Peter Smith Edition, 1968), pp. 24–25.

10. Quoted from editor's introduction, Josiah Royce, *Fugitive Essays*, ed. Dr. J. Loewenberg (Cambridge, Mass.: Harvard University Press, 1920), p. 34.

11. Dewey, "The Need for a Recovery of Philosophy," p. 27.

12. Josiah Royce, *The Spirit of Modern Philosophy* (Dover Press, 1983), pp. 228, 229, 247.

13. Ibid., p. 266.

14. Royce, *Sources of Religious Insight*, pp. 153–54.

15. Royce, *The Spirit of Modern Philosophy*, pp. 469, 467.

16. Ibid., p. 469.

17. Josiah Royce, *The World and the Individual*, Second Series (Gloucester, Mass.: Peter Smith Edition, 1976), p. 387.

18. Ibid., p. 407.

19. Royce, *Sources of Religious Insight*, p. 157.

20. Royce, *The Spirit of Modern Philosophy*, pp. 461–462, 463, 465.

21. Ibid., p. 470, 471.

CHAPTER 12

1. The English translations I shall refer to throughout this essay are: *Twilight of the Idols*, trans. R. J. Hollingdale (Middlessex, U.K.: Penguin, 1968), and *The Will to Power*, trans. W. Kaufman and R. J. Hollingdale (New York: Vintage, 1968). References to these editions, designated *TI* and *WP*, respectively, will be incorporated in the text. The first work, written in 1888, was one of Nietzsche's last and best texts; the second is a selection from Nietzsche's notebooks, 1883–1888. Nietzsche's philosophical (and metaphilosophical) views have not been examined in relation to the latest developments in postmodern American philosophy primarily because of the distance between his work and Anglo-American philosophy. This distance exists owing to two basic reasons. First, Nietzsche and Anglo-American philosophers radically disagree on the appropriate mode of philosophizing, on how philosophy should be done, pursued and codified. For Nietzsche, philosophy is a consuming passion, a gay vocation—hence more adequately pursued in a literary mode for a intelligent general audience; for most Anglo-American philosophers, philosophy is a pedagogical activity, a serious profession—hence more adequately pursued in a technical mode for a highly specialized audience. Second, Anglo-American philosophers are noted (and notorious) for "their lack of historical sense." Therefore, their interest in and attention to philosophical figures preoccupied with history, for example, Hegel, Kierkegaard, Marx, Nietzsche, is minimal. It is not surprising that of the five major books on Nietzsche in English—Walter Kaufman's *Nietzsche: Philosopher, Psychologist, Antichrist* (Princeton: Princeton University Press, 1975), R. J. Hollingdale's *Nietzsche* (London: Routledge & Kegan, 1973), Arthur Donto's *Nietzsche as Philosopher* (New York: Macmillan, 1965), Crane Brinton's *Nietzsche* (Cambridge, Mass.: Harvard University Press, 1941), and J. P. Stern's *Friedrich Nietzsche* (New York: Penguin, 1979)—only one is written by an Anglo-American philosopher, namely, Arthur Danto. And Danto is an atypical Anglo-American (or analytic) philosopher, with diverse inter-

ests and publications ranging from Croce, philosophy of history and Sartre to Nietzsche and Schopenhauer.

2. It comes as no surprise that analytic philosophy, with its "lack of historical sense," has produced little historical reflection and interpretation of itself. Besides Richard Rorty's early introductory essay in *The Linguistic Turn* (Chicago: University of Chicago Press, 1967) and his recent book, *Philosophy and the Mirror of Nature* (Princeton: Princeton University Press, 1979), there is only John Passmore's *A Hundred Years of Philosophy* (Middlesex, U.K.: Penguin, 1970), that is pedantic reportage and straightforward exposition—neither historical reflection nor interpretation—of late nineteenth- and twentieth-century developments in European philosophy. The pertinent works of Frege, Meinong, Russell and Moore that I have in mind are Frege's classic "On Sense and Reference," in Peter Geach and Max Black, eds., *Translations from the Philosophical Writings of Gottlob Frege* (Oxford: Oxford University Press, 1952); Meinong's "The Theory of Objects," in Roderick Chisholm, ed., *Realism and the Background of Phenomenology* (California: Glencoe, 1960); Russell's "Meinong's Theory of Complexes and Assumptions," *Mind* 13 (1904), pp. 204–219, 336–354, 509–524; and Moore's "The Refutation of Idealism," in *Philosophical Studies* (London, 1922).

3. For noteworthy examples of naive (or commonsensical) realism, see G. E. Moore's "A Defense of Common Sense" and "Proof of an External World," in his *Philosophical Papers* (London, 1959); for Platonic realism, see Bertrand Russell's *Principles of Mathematics* (Cambridge, 1903) and to a lesser extent his *Problems of Philosophy* (New York, 1912); for critical realism, see Roy W. Sellars's *Critical Realism* (Chicago, 1916) and his "A Statement of Critical Realism," *Revue internationale de philosophie* 1 (1938–39): 472–498; and for internal realism, see Hilary Putnam's recent work, *Meaning and the Moral Sciences* (London: Routledge & Kegan Paul, 1978), Part 4, "Realism and Reason."

4. Nelson Goodman, *Problems and Projects* (New York: Bobbs-Merrill, 1972), pp. 29–30.

5. Ibid., pp. 279–280.

6. Ibid., p. 118.

7. Nelson Goodman, *Ways of Worldmaking* (Indianapolis, Ind.: Hackett, 1978), p. 138.

8. Willard Van Orman Quine, *From a Logical Point of View* (New York, 1963), pp. 40–41.

9. Ibid., p. 42.

10. Ibid., p. 43.

11. Wilfred Sellars, son of the aforementioned Roy Sellars, deserves a similar place, alongside Quine and Goodman. But his highly technical style of writing as well as his position at the University of Pittsburgh (slightly removed from the center of fashionable intellectual activity and notoriety) unfortunately has rendered his writings less accessible and influential.

12. Richard Rorty, "The World Well Lost," *Journal of Philosophy* 69, No. 19 (1972), p. 661.

13. Thomas S. Kuhn, *The Structure of Scientific Revolutions*, 2d ed. (Chicago: University of Chicago Press, 1970), p. 206.

14. Thomas S. Kuhn, "Reflections on My Critics," *Criticism and the Growth of Knowledge,* ed. Imre Lakatos and Alan Musgrave (Cambridge: Cambridge University Press, 1970), p. 266.

15. Goodman, *Ways of Worldmaking,* p. x.

16. Goodman, *Problems and Projects,* pp. 30–31.

17. Ibid., pp. 117, 118.

18. Quine, *From A Logical Point of View,* p. 44.

19. Ibid., p. 19.

20. Rorty, *Philosophy and the Mirror of Nature,* p. 367.

21. This phrase was popularized by Wilfred Sellars's influential University of London lectures originally entitled "The Myth of the Given: Three Lectures on Empiricism and the Philosophy of Mind" and now known simply as "Empiricism and the Philosophy of

Mind," *Minnesota Studies in the Philosophy of Science* 1, Herbert Feigl and Michael Scriven, eds. (University of Minnesota Press, 1956). For a brief, cogent and sympathetic elaboration on this myth, see Michael William's *Groundless Belief: An Essay on the Possibility of Epistemology* (New Haven: Yale University Press, 1977), chapter 2; and for the only treatment I know of how this myth functions in traditional philosophical hermeneutics, see my essay, "Schleiermacher's Hermeneutics and the Myth of the Given," Special Hermeneutics Issue, *Union Seminary Quarterly Review* 34, No. 2 (Winter 1979), pp. 71–84.

22. For C. I. Lewis's pertinent work, see his *Mind and the World Order* (New York: Dover, 1956) and "The Given Element in Empirical Knowledge," *The Philosophical Review* 61, No. 2 (April 1952), pp. 168–173. For H. H. Price's relevant work, see his classic *Perception* (London: Methuen, 1964). Lewis's book was first published in 1929, Price's in 1932. More recent defenders of the Myth of the Given include A. J. Ayer, *The Foundations of Empirical Knowledge* (London: Macmillan; New York: St. Martin's Press, 1958); R. M. Chisholm, *Theory of Knowledge*, 2d ed. (Englewood Cliffs, N.J.: Prentice-Hall, 1977); Jonathan Bennett, *Locke, Berkeley, Hume: Central Themes* (Oxford: Oxford University Press, 1971); and John L. Pollack, *Knowledge and Justification* (Princeton: Princeton University Press, 1975). For a survey of the variety of versions of the Myth of the Given, see J. J. Ross, *The Appeal to the Given* (London: Macmillan, 1970). Lastly, for a fascinating and original attempt to reject the myth and Quine's holism (at the same time!), see Clark Glymour's *Theory and Evidence* (Princeton: Princeton University Press, 1980).

23. Lewis, *Mind and the World Order*, p. 38.

24. Price, *Perception*, p. 4.

25. Lewis, *Mind and the World Order*, p. 39.

26. Price, *Perception*, p. 1.

27. Goodman, *Problems and Projects*, pp. 61–62.

28. Ibid., p. 9.

29. Goodman. *Ways of Worldmaking*, p. 7.

30. Sellars, "Empiricism and the Philosophy of Mind," p. 289.

31. Ibid., p. 293.

32. Price, *Perception*, p. 3.

33. Sellars, "Empiricism and the Philosophy of Mind," pp. 298–299.

34. Ibid., p. 300.

35. Rorty, *Philosophy and the Mirror of Nature*, p. 174.

36. Ibid., p. 181.

37. Ibid., p. 182.

38. Stanley Cavell, *The Claim of Reason* (Oxford, 1979), p. 226.

39. Quine, *From A Logical Point of View*, p. 46.

40. Goodman, *Ways of Worldmaking*, p. 22.

41. Rorty, *Philosophy and the Mirror of Nature*, p. 379.

42. Willard Van Orman Quine, *Word and Object* (Cambridge, 1960), p. 221.

43. Rorty, *Philosophy and the Mirror of Nature*, p. 122.

44. Sellars, "Empiricism and the Philosophy of Mind," p. 319.

45. Ibid., p. 316.

46. Maurice Blanchot, "The Limits of Experience: Nihilism," *The New Nietzsche: Contemporary Styles of Interpretation,* ed. and intro. David B. Allison (New York, 1977), pp. 122–123.

47. W. V. Quine, *Ontological Relativity and Other Essays* (New York, 1969), pp. 50ff.

48. Quine, *Ontological Relativity*, p. 87.

49. Goodman, *Ways of Worldmaking*, p. x.

50. Rorty, *Philosophy and the Mirror of Nature*, pp. 9, 10.

51. Kuhn, "Reflections on My Critics," p. 264.
52. Gilles Deleuze, "Nomad Thought," *The New Nietzsche,* p. 149.

CHAPTER 14

1. Fredric Jameson, *Marxism and Form: Twentieth-Century Dialectical Theories of Literature* (Princeton: Princeton University Press, 1971); further references to this work will be given parenthetically as *MF. The Prison-House of Language: A Critical Account of Structuralism and Russian Formalism* (Princeton: Princeton University Press, 1972); further references to this text will be given parenthetically as *PHL. The Political Unconscious: Narrative as a Socially Symbolic Act* (Ithaca: Cornell University Press, 1981); further references to this book will be given parenthetically as *PU.* I shall include in this "trilogy" *Fables of Aggression: Wyndham Lewis, the Modernist as Fascist* (Berkeley: University of California Press, 1979) since it was originally conceived to be a part of *The Political Unconscious* but was separated, enlarged and published as an independent work.
2. In the preface to *PU,* Jameson refers to the "flawed yet monumental achievements . . . of the greatest Marxist philosopher of modern times, Georg Lukács" (p. 13).
3. Fredric Jameson, *Sartre: The Origins of a Style* (New Haven: Yale University Press, 1961).
4. Jameson's treatment of Adorno in chapter 1 of *MF* is based on an earlier essay that appeared in *Salmagundi,* No. 5 (1967), pp. 3–43.
5. For Jameson's view of Adorno's negative dialectics as an aesthetic ideal, see *PU,* p. 52, n.29.
6. The major difference between Adorno and Derrida (or de Man), between a dialectical deconstructionist and a poststructural deconstructionist, is that the theoretical impasse the dialectician reaches is not viewed as an ontological, metaphysical or epistemological aporia, but rather as a historical limitation owing to a determinate contradiction as yet unlodged because of an impotent social praxis or an absence of an effective historical revolutionary agent. For interesting comments on this matter, see Stanley Aronowitz, *The Crisis in Historical Materialism: Class, Politics and Culture in Marxist Theory* (New York: Praeger, 1981), pp. 24–34.
7. See also *MF,* p. 373, where Jameson states that "we take a point of view not so much *philosophical* as *hermeneutic.*"
8. Herbert Marcuse, *Eros and Civilization* (New York: Random House, 1955), p. 29, quoted in *MF,* p. 113.
9. This traditional hermeneutic strategy is enunciated in the following passage in *MF:* "Thus the process of criticism is not so much an interpretation of content as it is a revealing of it, a laying bare, a restoration of the original message, the original experience, beneath the distortions of the various kinds of censorship that have been at work upon it; and this revelation takes the form of an explanation of why the content was so distorted and is thus inseparable from a description of the mechanisms of this censorship itself" (p. 404).
10. Note also his remark in *PU:* "That life is meaningless is not a proposition that need be inconsistent with Marxism, whose affirmation is the quite different one that History is meaningful, however absurd organic life may happen to be" (p. 261).
11. For Jameson's interesting remarks on religion, see *MF,* pp. 116–118 and *PU,* pp. 70, 292.
12. Jameson is one of the few Marxists who explicitly rejects a realist epistemological position. See *MF,* pp. 365–366. Note that he invokes the early work of the then American-style

Marxist Sidney Hook at this point. For a persuasive treatment of the "textual idealism" of poststructuralists, see Richard Rorty, "Nineteenth-Century Idealism and Twentieth-Century Textualism," in *Consequences of Pragmatism* (Minneapolis: University of Minnesota Press, 1982), pp. 139–159.

13. *PU,* pp. 139, 226.

14. *PU,* pp. 97, 141. Bloch puts forward this complex notion in "Nonsynchronism and Dialectics," *New German Critique,* No. 11 (1977), pp. 22–38. For Jameson's powerful critique of teleological and genetic forms of Marxism, see "Marxism and Historicism," *New Literary History* 11 (1979), pp. 41–73.

15. *MF,* p. 402.

16. Fredric Jameson, "Criticism in History," in *The Weapons of Criticism,* ed. Norman Rudich (Palo Alto, Calif.: Ramparts Press, 1976), pp. 31–50.

17. For the Lévi-Straussian language, see *PU,* p. 167 and for Frye's notion of literature, see *PU,* p. 70.

18. Yet I remain unconvinced that the cosmic body in Blake's anagogy is even roughly analogous to the individualistic bourgeois body. See Northrop Frye, *Anatomy of Criticism: Four Essays* (Princeton: Princeton University Press, 1957), pp. 119f.

19. Geoffrey H. Hartman, "Ghostlier Demarcations: The Sweet Science of Northrop Frye," in *Beyond Formalism: Literary Essays 1958–1970* (New Haven: Yale University Press, 1970), p. 40.

20. Hartman, "Ghostlier Demarcations," pp. 24–41; J. Hillis Miller, "Tradition and Difference." *Diacritics* 2 (Winter 1972), pp. 6–13.

21. Note Jameson's remarks in *MF:* "This formal character of the concept of freedom is precisely what lends itself to the work of political hermeneutics. It encourages analogy: assimilating the material prisons to the psychic ones, it serves as a means of unifying all these separate levels of existence, functioning, indeed, as a kind of transformational equation whereby the data characteristic of one may be converted into the terms of other" (p. 85).

22. Jameson explicitly states in *PU:* "I will argue that the critique [by poststructuralism] is misplaced" (p. 21).

23. For the classic reply to Nietzsche on this matter, though not a thoroughly satisfactory one, see Max Scheler, *Ressentiment,* trans. William Holdheim, ed. Lewis A. Coser (New York: Free Press, 1961), pp. 43–46, 79–89, 95–97, 103–111, 114.

24. Friedrich Nietzsche, *Beyond Good and Evil,* trans. Walter Kaufmann (New York: Vintage Books, 1966), p. 48.

25. Nietzsche remarks repeatedly that modern bourgeois European culture is an amalgam of various traditions, only one of which is the Judeo-Christian tradition. Yet what Nietzsche stresses, and Jameson ignores, is that Christian morality is a weapon of the oppressed against the oppressor, not simply a symptom of impotence. On this point, Jameson follows not Nietzsche, but Sartre. "The moral attitude appears when technical and social conditions render positive forms of conduct impossible. Ethics is a collection of idealistic tricks intended to enable us to live the life imposed on us by the poverty of our resources and the insufficiency of our techniques." This passage is an unpublished note of Sartre's quoted by Simone de Beauvoir, *Force of Circumstance,* trans. Richard Howard (New York: Putnam, 1965), p. 199.

26. This point is made most emphatically by Lucien Goldmann, *Immanuel Kant* (London: New Left Books, 1971), pp. 170–179. Hegel puts forward this critique in *Philosophy of Right,* trans. T. M. Knox (Oxford: Oxford University Press, 1967), pp. 89–103, and *Philosophy of Mind, Part Three of the Encyclopedia of the Philosophical Sciences* (Oxford: Clarendon Press, 1971), pp. 253–291. Jameson clearly grasps this point when he states, "As an ideological field,

conceptions of ethics depend on a shared class or group homogeneity, and strike a suspicious compromise between the private experience of the individual and those values or functional needs of the collectivity which ethics rewrites or recodes in terms of interpersonal relationships." Yet, unlike Hegel and Marx, Jameson clings to the notion that the historicizing of ethics results in a "going beyond" good and evil. In the same paragraph quoted he continues, "In our time, ethics, wherever it makes its reappearance, may be taken as the sign of an intent to mystify, and in particular to replace the more complex and ambivalent judgments of a more properly political and dialectical perspective with the more comfortable simplifications of a binary myth." The basic point here is that Hegel, Marx and Jameson agree that bourgeois ethics cannot do justice to the richness of moral experience without embarrassing equivocation. Yet Jameson believes that this has something to do with the binary oppositions of good and evil, whereas Hegel and Marx rightly hold that such poststructuralist itching does not require scratching, but rather getting rid of the source of the itch. The passage quoted is from Jameson, *Fables of Aggression,* p. 56.

27. David Couzens Hoy, "Hegel's Morals," *Dialogue* 20, no. 1 (1981), p. 99.

28. For a detailed examination of Marx's critique of Kant and Hegel on ethical approaches, see Cornel West, "Ethics, Historicism and the Marxist Tradition," Ph.D. diss., Princeton University, 1980, pp. 14–62.

29. As Richard Rorty notes, "The non-Kantian *is* a parasite—flowers could not sprout from the dialectical vine unless there were an edifice into whose chinks it could insert its tendrils. No constructors, no deconstructors. No norms, no perversions. Derrida (like Heidegger) would have no writing to do unless there were a 'metaphysics of presence' to overcome. Without the fun of stamping out parasites, on the other hand, no Kantian would bother to continue building." See "Philosophy as a Kind of Writing: An Essay on Derrida," *Consequences of Pragmatism,* p. 108. This is precisely the philosophical "game" Marx ignores, sidesteps and avoids. For Rorty's brilliant historical situating of this modern "game," see *Philosophy and the Mirror of Nature* (Princeton: Princeton University Press, 1979); for a leftist critique of this text, see Cornel West, "The Politics of American Neopragmatism," in *Post-Analytic Philosophy,* ed. John Rajchman and Cornel West (New York: Columbia University Press, 1985), pp. 259–275.

30. For his brief characterization of the French and American Left, see *PU,* pp. 54, 31.

31. Jameson does address the role of the Marxist intellectual in the academy in his essay "Marxism and Teaching," *New Political Science,* No. 2/3 (Fall/Winter 1979/1980), pp. 31–36.

CHAPTER 21

1. This figure describes the average expenditure on a child from birth to eighteen years, in a husband-wife household with an income in the $33,700–$56,700 range. See U.S. Department of Agriculture, Center for Nutrition Policy and Promotion, *Expenditures on Children by Families, 1995 Annual Report,* Publication No. 1528 (Washington, D.C.: GPO, 1995).

2. Viviana A. Zelizer, *Pricing the Priceless Child: The Changing Social Value of Children* (New York: Basic, 1985), p. 3.

3. Jane Addams, *Democracy and Social Ethics* (Cambridge Mass.: Harvard University Press, Belknap Press, 1964).

4. Carol Gilligan, *In a Different Voice: Psychological Theory and Women's Development* (Cambridge Mass.: Harvard University Press, 1982), pp. 149, 129.

5. Jean Bethke Elshtain, *Democracy on Trial* (New York: Basic, 1995), p. 129.

6. Gus A. Haggstrom, Linda J. Waite, David E. Kanouse and Thomas J. Blaschke, "Changes in the Life Styles of New Parents" (Santa Monica, Calif.: Rand Corporation, Dec. 1984), p. 61.

7. Diana DiNitto, *Social Welfare: Politics and Public Policy* (New York: Allyn & Bacon, 1995), pp. 169–170.

8. Stephanie Ventura, demographer, National Center for Health Statistics, telephone interview, December 10, 1997.

9. U.S. Bureau of the Census, *Child Support and Alimony: 1989,* Current Population Reports, series P60, No. 173 (Washington, D.C.: GPO, 1991).

10. Daniel R. Geyer and Steven Favasky, "Custodial Fathers: Myths, Realities, and Child Support Policy," *Journal of Marriage and the Family 55* (February 1993), pp. 73–89.

11. For an in-depth discussion, see Jack Kammer, "What Do We Really Know About Child Support?" *Crisis* (January 1994), p. 16.

12. Harry F. Harlow, "Love in Infant Monkeys," *Scientific American* (June 1959), pp. 68–74.

13. Willard Gaylin, "In the Beginning: Helpless and Dependent," in Willard Gaylin, Ira Glasser, Steven Marcus and David J. Rothman, eds., *Doing Good: The Limits of Benevolence* (New York: Pantheon, 1978), p. 10.

14. Urie Bronfenbrenner, "Discovering What Families Do," in *Rebuilding the Nest: A New Commitment to the American Family* (Milwaukee, Wis.: Family Service America, 1990), p. 31.

15. James Alan Fox, *Trends in Juvenile Violence: A Report to the United States Attorney General on Current and Future Rates of Juvenile Offending* (Washington, D.C.: Bureau of Justice Statistics, March 1996); Centers for Disease Control, "Rates of Homicide . . . Among Children," pp. 101–105; Select Committee on Children, Youth, and Families, *U.S. Children and Their Families,* p. 31, and National Law Center on Homelessness and Poverty, *Blocks to Their Future: A Report on the Barriers to Preschool Education for Homeless Children,* September 1997; Lloyd D. Johnson et al., *National Survey Results on Drug Use from the Monitoring the Future Study, 1975–1996* (Washington, D.C.: National Institute on Drug Abuse, 1997), Table 20-1; Karen W. Arenson, "Students Continue to Improve, College Board Says," *New York Times,* August 23, 1996, p. A16; Centers for Disease Control, *Morbidity and Mortality Weekly Report,* April 21, 1995, and *Suicide Deaths and Rates per 100,000, United States, 1989–1995,* unpublished data; National Center for Health Statistics, *Health United States 1996–97,* July 1997, Table 73, p. 193.

16. Carnegie Council on Adolescent Development, *Great Transitions: Preparing Adolescents for a New Century* (New York: Carnegie Corporation of New York, October 1995), p. 10.

17. Fox, *Trends in Juvenile Violence.*

18. Fox Butterfield, "Survey Finds That Crimes Cost $450 Billion a Year," *New York Times,* April 22, 1996, p. A8.

19. Barbara M. Jones, "Guns, Drugs, and Juvenile Justice: Three Aspects of the Crisis in Youth Violence," paper prepared for the Task Force on Parent Empowerment, April 17, 1996, p. 1.

20. Nancy Jo Sales, "Lost in the Park," *New York,* June 16, 1997, pp. 24–29; N. R. Kleinfield et al., "Lives Tangle in Park's Hidden World," *New York Times,* June 1, 1997, p. 1.

21. Centers for Disease Control, "Suicide Among Children, Adolescents, and Young Adults–United States, 1980–1992," vol. 44, no. 15, April 21, 1995, pp. 289–90; National Center for Health Statistics, Mortality Data Tapes, "Suicide Deaths and Rates per 100,000, United States, 1989–1995."

22. Sylvia Ann Hewlett, *Child Neglect in Rich Nations* (New York: UNICEF, 1993), p. 1.

23. U.S. Bureau of the Census, *1997 March Current Population Survey,* App. C, Table 20.

24. Joe Dalaker, statistician, Bureau of the Census, telephone interview, October 15, 1997.

25. *National Survey Results on Drug Use;* National Institute on Drug Abuse, "Facts About

Teenagers and Drug Abuse," NIDA Capsule Series (C–83–07), 1996; "Monitoring the Future Study: Trends in Prevalence of Various Drugs for 8th Graders, 10th Graders and High School Seniors," NIDA Capsule Series (C–94–01), 1996.

26. National Center for Education Statistics, *NAEP 1994 Trends in Academic Progress* (Washington, D.C.: GPO, Nov. 1996), p. iv.

27. National Center for Education Statistics, *Digest of Education Statistics, 1997,* Table 99, "High school graduates compared with population 17 years of age, by sex and control of school: 1869–70 to 1996–97," p. 108, December 31, 1997.

28. Carnegie Council, *Great Transitions,* p. 10.

CHAPTER 25

1. For intellectual explorations in the American grain for philosophy and theology, see John E. Smith, *The Spirit of American Philosophy* (New York: Oxford University Press, 1963); and Randolph Crump Miller, *The American Spirit in Theology* (Philadelphia: United Church Press, 1974). A more contemporary expression and examination can be found in John Rajchman and Cornel West, eds., *Post-Analytic Philosophy* (New York: Columbia University Press, 1985).

2. The major essays on the refinement and rejection of these philosophical distinctions are Carl G. Hempel, "Empiricist Criteria of Cognitive Significance: Problems and Changes" and "The Theoretician's Dilemma: A Study in the Logic of Theory Construction," in his *Aspects of Scientific Explanation and Other Essays in the Philosophy of Science* (New York: Free Press, 1965), pp. 101–122; 173–226.

3. For the persuasive arguments for Quine's epistemological holism and methodological monism, see his classic essay "The Dogmas of Empiricism," in his *From a Logical Point of View* (New York: Harper & Row, 1963), pp. 20–46; and his less rigorous personal reflections in "The Pragmatists' Place in Empiricism," in *Pragmatism: Its Sources and Prospects,* ed. Robert J. Mulvaney and Philip M. Zeltner, pp. 23–39.

4. Goodman's postempiricist antireductionism is best illustrated in his powerful essay "The Test of Simplicity" and his classic piece "The Way the World Is," in his *Problems and Projects* (New York: Bobbs-Merrill, 1972), pp. 279–294; 24–32. Goodman's full-fledged ontological pluralism is put forward in his *Ways of Worldmaking* (Indianapolis, Ind.: Hackett, 1978). For Quine's critique of Goodman, see *Theories and Things* (Cambridge, Mass: Harvard University Press, 1981), pp. 96–99.

5. Sellars's classic statement is "Empiricism and the Philosophy of Mind," in *Minnesota Studies in the Philosophy of Science,* vol. 1, ed. Herbert Feigl and Michael Scriven (Minneapolis: University of Minnesota Press, 1956), pp. 253–329.

6. For a more detailed account of this takeover, see Cornel West, "Nietzsche's Prefiguration of Postmodern American Philosophy," *Boundary 2: A Journal of Postmodern Literature,* Special Nietzsche Issue, Vol. 9, No. 10 (Spring-Fall 1981), pp. 241–270.

7. C. S. Peirce, *The Collected Papers of Charles Sanders Peirce,* 6 vols., ed. Charles Hartshorne, Paul Weiss and Arthur Burks (Cambridge, Mass.: Harvard University Press, 1933–1958), Vol. 1, p. 135.

8. The texts of liberation theology I have in mind are Gustavo Gutiérrez, *A Theology of Liberation,* trans. Sister Caridad Inda and John Eagleson (Maryknoll, N.Y.: Orbis Books, 1973); Mary Daly, *Beyond God the Father* (Boston: Beacon Press, 1973); and James H. Cone, *God of the Oppressed* (New York: Seabury Press, 1975).

9. Jeffrey Stout, *The Flight from Authority* (Notre Dame, Ind.: University of Notre Dame Press, 1981). This important book has yet to receive the attention it deserves.

CHAPTER 30

1. The term *democrat* (small *d*) refers to the political philosophy rather than the political party.
2. Michel Foucault credits Carl Westphal's 1870 article *"Archiv fur Neurlogie"* with presenting the first medical categorization of homosexuals as a "species" in *History of Sexuality: An Introduction* (New York: Vintage, 1978, 1990), p. 43.
3. Patrons of the gay and lesbian Stonewall bar in New York City revolted against ongoing police harassment in June of 1969. This rebellion is commonly used to mark the birth of the contemporary lesbian and gay liberation movement in the United States.
4. Robert Goss, *Jesus Acted Up: A Gay and Lesbian Manifesto* (San Francisco: HarperCollins, 1993).
5. The Rev. Peter Gomes is minister at Harvard Memorial Church and Plummer Professor of Christian Morals at Harvard Divinity School.

CHAPTER 35

1. Harold Rosenberg, "Criticism and Its Premises," in *Art on the Edge: Creators and Situations* (Chicago: The University of Chicago Press, 1983), p. 140.
2. Robert Storr, quoted in "The Global Issue: A Symposium," *Art in America* 77, No. 7 (July 1989), p. 88.

CHAPTER 36

1. John Dewey, *Art as Experience* (1934), *Later Works,* 10:278, ed. Jo Ann Boydston (Carbondale: Southern Illinois University Press).
2. Ralph Waldo Emerson, "The American Scholar," *Selected Writings of Ralph Waldo Emerson,* ed. William H. Gilman (New York: New American Library, 1965), p. 239.
3. Dewey, *Art as Experience,* 10:10–11.
4. Ralph Waldo Emerson, *Emerson in His Journals,* selected and edited by Joel Porte (Cambridge, Mass.: Harvard University Press, 1982), p. 136.
5. Richard J. Powell, *Homecoming: The Art and Life of William H. Johnson* (Washington, D.C.: Smithsonian Institution, 1991), p. 138.
6. Alain Locke, "Horace Pippin, 1888–1946," Horace Pippin Memorial Exhibition, exhibition catalogue (Philadelphia: The Art Alliance, 1947).
7. James Clifford, *The Predicament of Culture: Twentieth Century Ethnography, Literature and Art* (Cambridge, Mass.: Harvard University Press, 1988), p. 196.
8. Samella Lewis, *Art: African American* (New York: Harcourt Brace Jovanovich, 1978), pp. 105–106.
9. Michele Wallace, "Modernism, Postmodernism and the Problem of the Visual in Afro-American Culture," *Out There: Marginalization and Contemporary Cultures,* ed. Russell Ferguson, Martha Gever, Trinh T. Minh-ha and Cornel West (Cambridge, Mass.: MIT Press, 1990), pp. 47–48.
10. See "The New Cultural Politics of Difference," chap. 7 in this volume.
11. E. P. Richardson, *Painting in America: The Story of 450 Years* (New York: Thomas Y. Crowell, 1956), p. 389.
12. Martin Puryear, introduction to Powell, *Homecoming,* p. xix.
13. W. E. B. Du Bois, *The Souls of Black Folk* (1903; reprint New York: Penguin, 1989), introduction by Donald B. Gibson, p. 5.

14. Arnold Rampersad, introduction to *The New Negro,* ed. Alain Locke (New York: Atheneum, 1991), p. ix.

15. Alain Locke, ed., *The New Negro* (New York: Atheneum, 1991), foreword.

16. Ibid., pp. 223–224.

17. Ibid., pp. 222–223.

18. For Alain Locke's influence on the intellectual framework that shaped the practices of the William E. Harmon awards for distinguished achievement among Negroes and the 1928 to 1933 annual Harmon Foundation Exhibitions, see the fine essay by Beryl J. Wright, "The Harmon Foundation in Context: Early Exhibitions and Alain Locke's Concept of a Racial Idiom of Expression," *Against the Odds: African-American Artists and the Harmon Foundation,* ed. Gary A. Reynolds and Beryl J. Wright (Newark, N.J.: The Newark Museum, 1989), pp. 13–25. Leslie Bolling was the only "folk artist"—with no formal art training (though he did attend Hampton Institute and Virginia Union University)—who exhibited with the Harmon Foundation.

19. For Locke's complex development as an art critic—especially his modernist views of African and African American art—see his *Negro Art: Past and Present* (Associates in Negro Folk Education, Albany, N.Y.: The J. B. Lyon Press, 1936). See especially his discussion of the notion of the "primitive" in African and European art, pp. 93–116.

CHAPTER 37

1. John Summerson, *Heavenly Mansions* (New York: Norton, 1963), p. 111.

2. Charles Jencks, *Modern Movements in Architecture* (New York: Penguin, 1973), p. 51.

3. Aaron Betsky, "The End(s) of Architecture," unpublished essay; James Wines, *De-Architecture* (New York: Rizzoli, 1987), p. 38.

4. Roger Kimball, "The Death and Resurrection of Postmodern Architecture," *New Criterion,* June 1988, pp. 21–31, "Is Modernism the Enemy? The Case of Mies Van Der Rohe," *New Criterion* (May 1989), pp. 67–77.

5. Alan Colquhoun, *Essays in Architectural Criticism: Modern Architecture and Historical Change* (Cambridge, Mass.: MIT Press, 1981), p. 140.

6. Lewis Mumford, *The Myth of the Machine II: The Pentagon of Power* (New York: Harcourt Brace Jovanovich, 1970).

7. Colquhoun, *Essays in Architectural Criticism,* p. 13.

8. Quoted from Charles Jencks, *Le Corbusier and the Tragic View of Architecture* (Cambridge, Mass.: Harvard University Press, 1973), p. 67.

9. For assorted essays on Mies, see *Mies Reconsidered: His Career, Legacy, and Disciples* (New York: Rizzoli, 1986).

10. Robert Venturi, *Complexity and Contradiction in Architecture* (New York: Doubleday, 1966); Robert Venturi, Denise Scott Brown and Steven Izenour, *Learning from Las Vegas* (Cambridge, Mass.: MIT Press, 1972); Charles Jencks, *The Language of Post-modern Architecture* (New York: Rizzoli, 1977); *Post-modern Classicism* (New York, 1980); James Wines, *De-Architecture,* p. 38.

11. Mark Wrigley, "Deconstructivist Architecture," *Deconstructivist Architecture* (Boston: Little, Brown, 1988), p. 16.

12. Mark Jarzombek, "Post-Modernist Historicism: The Historian's Dilemma," *Threshold: Journal of the School of Architecture,* The University of Illinois at Chicago (New York: Rizzoli), Vol. 4, Spring 1988, p. 96.

13. Jencks, *Le Corbusier and the Tragic View of Architecture,* p. 102.

14. Quoted in ibid., p. 102.

15. Quoted in ibid., p. 109.

16. Quoted in ibid., p. 110.

17. Quoted in Stephen Gardiner, *Le Corbusier* (New York: Viking, 1974), p. 115.

18. The pioneering work of Darell Fields, Kevin Fuller and Milton Curry in their journal *Appendix* is of great significance to race and architecture.

Index